CW00336980

FIELDING'S
ITALY

Fielding Titles

Fielding's Alaska Cruises and the Inside Passage
Fielding's Asia's Top Dive Sites
Fielding's Amazon
Fielding's Australia
Fielding's Bahamas
Fielding's Baja
Fielding's Bermuda
Fielding's Birding Indonesia
Fielding's Borneo
Fielding's Budget Europe
Fielding's Caribbean
Fielding's Caribbean Cruises
Fielding's Disney World and Orlando
Fielding's Diving Indonesia
Fielding's Eastern Caribbean
Fielding's England
Fielding's Europe
Fielding's European Cruises
Fielding's Far East
Fielding's France
Fielding's Freewheelin' USA
Fielding's Kenya
Fielding's Hawaii
Fielding's Italy
Fielding's Las Vegas Agenda
Fielding's London Agenda
Fielding's Los Angeles
Fielding's Malaysia and Singapore
Fielding's Mexico
Fielding's New Orleans Agenda
Fielding's New York Agenda
Fielding's New Zealand
Fielding's Paradors, Pousadas and Charming Villages of Spain and Portugal
Fielding's Paris Agenda
Fielding's Portugal
Fielding's Rome Agenda
Fielding's San Diego Agenda
Fielding's Southeast Asia
Fielding's Southern Vietnam on Two Wheels
Fielding's Spain
Fielding's Surfing Indonesia
Fielding's Sydney Agenda
Fielding's Thailand, Cambodia, Laos & Myanmar
Fielding's Vietnam
Fielding's Western Caribbean
Fielding's The World's Most Dangerous Places
Fielding's Worldwide Cruises

FIELDING'S
ITALY

by
Lynn V. Foster
& Lawrence Foster

Fielding Worldwide, Inc.
308 South Catalina Avenue
Redondo Beach, California 90277 U.S.A.

Fielding's Italy

Published by Fielding Worldwide, Inc.

Text Copyright ©1997 Lynn V. Foster & Lawrence Foster

Icons, Illustrations Copyright ©1997 FWI

Photo Copyrights ©1997 to Individual Photographers

All rights reserved. No part of this book including the Fielding rating system may be reproduced, transmitted or utilized in any form or by any means, electronic or mechanical, including photocopying, recording, or by any information storage and retrieval system, without permission in writing from the publisher. Brief extracts for review purposes for inclusion in critical reviews or articles are permitted.

FIELDING WORLDWIDE INC.

PUBLISHER AND CEO	**Robert Young Pelton**
GENERAL MANAGER	**John Guillebeaux**
MARKETING DIRECTOR	**Paul T. Snapp**
OPERATIONS DIRECTOR	**George Posanke**
ELECTRONIC PUBLISHING DIRECTOR	**Larry E. Hart**
PUBLIC RELATIONS DIRECTOR	**Beverly Riess**
ACCOUNT SERVICES MANAGER	**Christy Harp**
PROJECT MANAGER	**Chris Snyder**

EDITORS

Kathy Knoles   **Linda Charlton**

Reed Parsell

PRODUCTION

Jebbie LaVoie   **Alfredo Mercado**
Martin Mancha   **Ramses Reynoso**

Craig South

COVER DESIGNED BY	**Digital Artists, Inc.**
COVER PHOTOGRAPHERS — Front Cover	**Marty Loken/Allstock**
Background Photo, Front Cover	**Robert Young Pelton/Westlight**
Back Cover	**Mike Yamashita/Westlight**
INSIDE PHOTOS	**Corel Professional Photos, Palermo APT, Italian Tourism Board, The Parker Company**

Although every effort has been made to ensure the correctness of the information in this book, the publisher and authors do not assume, and hereby disclaim, any liability to any party for any loss or damage caused by errors, omissions, misleading information or any potential travel problem caused by information in this guide, even if such errors or omission are a result of negligence, accident or any other cause.

Inquiries should be addressed to: Fielding Worldwide, Inc., 308 South Catalina Ave., Redondo Beach, California 90277 U.S.A., Telephone (310) 372-4474, Facsimile (310) 376-8064, 8:30 a.m.–5:30 p.m. Pacific Standard Time.

Website: http://www.fieldingtravel.com

e-mail: fielding@fieldingtravel.com

ISBN 1-56952-116-6

Printed in the United States of America

Letter from the Publisher

In 1946, Temple Fielding began the first of what would be a remarkable new series of well-written, highly personalized guidebooks for independent travelers. Temple's opinionated, witty, and oft-imitated books have now guided travelers for almost a half-century. More important to some was Fielding's humorous and direct method of steering travelers away from the dull and the insipid. Today, Fielding Travel Guides are still written by experienced travelers for experienced travelers. Our authors carry on Fielding's reputation for creating travel experiences that deliver insight with a sense of discovery and style.

Lynn and Larry Foster have created a guidebook that helps even the second-time traveler to Italy truly understand its people, their culture and their heritage. Whether it's by helping you select the best regional cuisine or choosing that perfect, little-known romantic hideaway, this is the guide that will make every trip to Italy as eye-opening as the one before.

Today the concept of independent travel has never been bigger. Our policy of *brutal honesty* and a highly personal point of view has never changed; it just seems the travel world has caught up with us.

Enjoy your Italy adventure with Lynn and Larry Foster, and Fielding.

R Y P

Robert Young Pelton
Publisher and C.E.O.
Fielding Worldwide, Inc.

DEDICATION

To the Vascos and Lentini of Gioia del Colle who, unlike the Montagues and Capulets of Verona, made everything possible.

ACKNOWLEDGMENTS

Thanks are most certainly due to the Italian Government Travel Office (ENIT) in New York as well as the many regional and local tourist offices throughout Italy. Our heartfelt thanks are also due to Grazia Festoso, for her insider's advice and delicious rabbit stew; and to Howard Foster, for his impeccable taste.

ABOUT THE AUTHORS

Lynn and Larry Foster

The Fosters have been so fortunate as to have traveled extensively in Italy and, more fortunate yet, to have lived in Siena as well as in Rome. They have joyfully explored the art treasures found in towns both small and large, and they have just as happily eaten their way through the various regional cuisines. Both their knowledge and pleasure in things Italian enhance this guide.

Lynn Vasco Foster, who is a freelance writer, has a Ph.D. in philosophy from Brandeis University and has studied at the Sorbonne and Harvard, where she was a researcher in art education.

Lawrence Foster, who has a Ph.D. in philosophy from the University of Pennsylvania, is the chairman of the Philosophy Department at the University of Massachusetts in Boston.

Fielding Rating Icons

The Fielding Rating Icons are highly personal and awarded to help the besieged traveler choose from among the dizzying array of activities, attractions, hotels, restaurants and sights. The awarding of an icon denotes unusual or exceptional qualities in the relevant category.

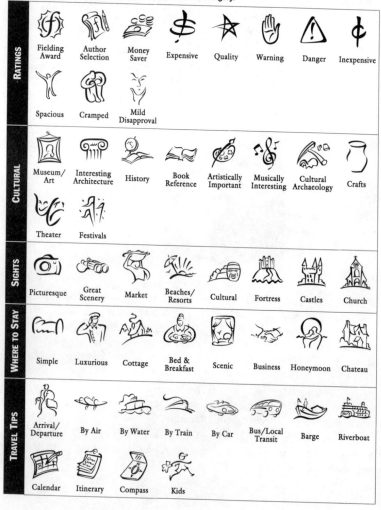

RATINGS

Fielding Award · Author Selection · Money Saver · Expensive · Quality · Warning · Danger · Inexpensive

Spacious · Cramped · Mild Disapproval

CULTURAL

Museum/ Art · Interesting Architecture · History · Book Reference · Artistically Important · Musically Interesting · Cultural Archaeology · Crafts

Theater · Festivals

SIGHTS

Picturesque · Great Scenery · Market · Beaches/ Resorts · Cultural · Fortress · Castles · Church

WHERE TO STAY

Simple · Luxurious · Cottage · Bed & Breakfast · Scenic · Business · Honeymoon · Chateau

TRAVEL TIPS

Arrival/ Departure · By Air · By Water · By Train · By Car · Bus/Local Transit · Barge · Riverboat

Calendar · Itinerary · Compass · Kids

ACTIVITIES

Downhill Skiing	X–country Skiing	Watersports	Sailing	Scuba Diving	Snorkeling/ Diving	Deep-sea Fishing	Freshwater Fishing
Swimming	Hiking	Walking	Relaxing	Golf	Tennis	Horseback Riding	General Sports
Cycling	Workout						

SPECIAL INTEREST

Nightlife	Singles	Romantic	Nude Beaches	Lecture	Spectacular Cuisine	Wine Tasting	Shopping
Cafe Stops	Gardening	Pro Sports	Mystery				

TABLE OF CONTENTS

LIST OF MAPS

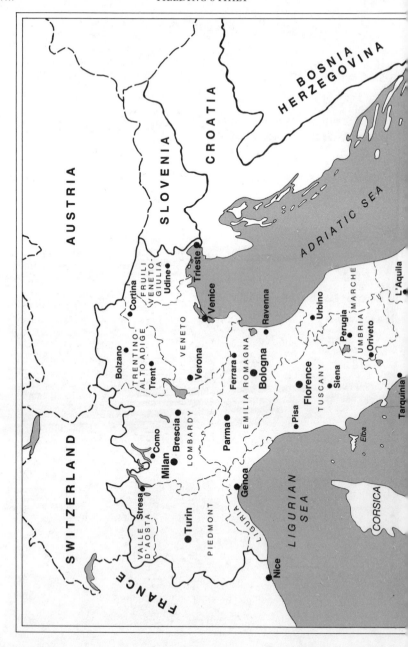

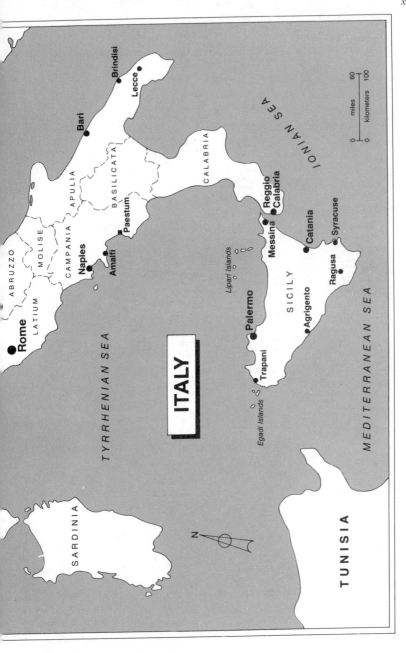

Legend

Essentials

H	HOTEL
†	YOUTH HOSTEL
✗	RESTAURANT
$	BANK
☎	TELEPHONE
❶	TOURIST INFO.
✚	HOSPITAL
☕	PUB/BAR
✉	POST OFFICE
P	PARKING
T	TAXI
S	SUBWAY
M	METRO
M	MARKET
S	SHOPPING
C	CINEMA
♥	THEATRE
✈	INT'L AIRPORT
✛	REGIONAL AIRPORT
✦	POLICE STATION
⚖	COURTHOUSE
🏛	GOV'T. BUILDING

■	ATTRACTION
✈	MILITARY AIRBASE
🕴	ARMY BASE
—	NAVAL BASE
⛴	FORT
🎓	UNIVERSITY
🏫	SCHOOL

Historical

∴	ARCHEOLOGICAL SITE
✂	BATTLEGROUND
♜	CASTLE
⛫	MONUMENT
🏛	MUSEUM
⚱	RUIN
🚢	SHIPWRECK

Religious

✝	CHURCH
⛩	BUDDHIST TEMPLE
🛕	HINDU TEMPLE
☪	MOSQUE
✿	PAGODA
✡	SYNAGOGUE

Activities

⛱	BEACH
▲	CAMPGROUND
🎪	PICNIC AREA
⛳	GOLF COURSE
🚤	BOAT LAUNCH
🤿	DIVING
🐟	FISHING
🏄	WATER SKIING
⛷	SNOW SKIING
🦅	BIRD SANCTUARY
🦌	WILDLIFE SANCTUARY
🌲	PARK
🏕	PARK HEADQUARTERS
⛏	MINE
🗼	LIGHTHOUSE
🌾	WINDMILL
⚓	CRUISE PORT
✈	VIEW
⬭	STADIUM
▬	BUILDING
🐘	ZOO
🌷	GARDEN

Physical

— — — ·	INTERNATIONAL BOUNDARY	🚶🚶	HIKING TRAIL
— — — —	COUNTY/REGIONAL BOUNDARY	▬▬▬	DIRT ROAD
PARIS ⊙	NATIONAL CAPITAL	++++++++	RAILROAD
Montego Bay •	STATE/PARISH CAPITAL	**RR**	RAILROAD STATION
Los Angeles ●	MAJOR CITY	— ⛴ —	FERRY ROUTE
Quy Nhon ○	TOWN/VILLAGE	▲	MOUNTAIN PEAK
—⑤—	MOTORWAY/FREEWAY	⬛	LAKE
—⑯③—	HIGHWAY	—	RIVER
————	PRIMARY ROAD	◖	CAVE
————	SECONDARY ROAD	🐚	CORAL REEF
— — —	SUBWAY	〰	WATERFALL
— 🚲 —	BIKING ROUTED	♨	HOT SPRING

©FWI 1995

INTRODUCTION

How to Use This Guide

No matter how many people hear that you're going to Italy, not one will ask why. The reasons are too obvious. They also are numerous, from ancient art to contemporary design, from Michelangelo and Leonardo to Barolo wine and truffles, from premier cities such as Rome to the scenic countryside of Tuscany, from elegant hotels on the Amalfi Coast to a simple trattoria in Verona. So many reasons, each providing a challenge to any guidebook. One reason no longer true, however, is that Italy is a bargain—and that in itself is another challenge.

Given what Italy has to offer, it might be enough for *Fielding's Italy* to guide you through cities and countryside, through art galleries and churches and ruins. Yet even this is insufficient. Today's traveler seldom has the time to take the requisite refresher courses for understanding 3000 years of Italian art (see "Art in Italy" chapter), or to absorb the variations that occur over regions (see the regional "History and Art" sections), much less to sort out all the paintings in the Uffizi or all the churches in Rome (see star-rated sights throughout *Fielding's Italy*). Art is so plentiful that psychiatrists in Florence have identified a hysterical syndrome caused by overexposure (when symptoms first become noticeable, limit yourself to 3-star sights).

While Italy's artistic wealth can create neuroses, its history is mindboggling. In a strict sense, there is no Italian history before 1860, when the present modern nation was created. All that preceded was fragmented into city states and small duchies, even into colonies of foreign powers such as France and Spain. This tangle of wars and shifting alliances is brought to bear only when it can enrich your travels—the development of the Renaissance in Tuscany, for example, or the Normans in Sicily (see the regional "History and Art" sections). And the most important historical trends are tied into the major artistic periods (see the "Art in Italy" chapter).

After guiding you through Italy's art and introducing you to its history, *Fielding's Italy* still is not complete. Vacationers do not live by art alone—and in Italy, they shouldn't. The food and wine is just as diversified as the country's history (see the regional "Cuisine" sections as well as "Eating Out" under city destinations), and part of the pleasure of vacationing here is sampling the offerings of each area (see "Eating Out" and "Restaurants" under the destinations), whatever your budget. In fact, the listings for both hotels and restaurants provide a wide range of choice in price and ambience, from the most elegant to the merely convenient, from the good bargains (the great ones are increasingly rare in prosperous Italy) to the most atmospheric country inns.

Then, too, the guide must help you plan your trip (see "Practical Travel Information" chapter, "Travel Tips" section for each region, as well as the "key" or city summary found at the beginning of each major destination). And, finally, the guide must help you cope with increased costs (see "Traveling on a Budget") not only by providing a wide choice of restaurants and hotels, but also by helping you to get around on your own, by bus not taxi, by train not car (see the keys and directories for the cities and towns as well as the "Travel Tips" for regions). Now if *Fielding's Italy* could only lower prices as well, you would be all set.

Star-Rated Sights

No single volume guidebook can cover all the sights of Italy. Thinned out and reduced to fit into *Fielding's Italy*, there still remain enough sights to sustain you through repeated visits. Although you certainly will organize any sightseeing around your own interests, the star-ratings can be useful aids. We have assigned from zero to three stars to sights and works of art based on a consensus as to which are the most important to see. There are two leading factors making up the consensus. If a work of art is always mentioned and, indeed, is even illustrated in art history texts, we took that to indicate a consensus about its importance. If a sight is considered a must-see by tourists, we have tried to incorporate it into the rating. In addition to scholarly mentions and tourist popularity, there is no doubt that at times our own tastes have influenced the ratings. Whatever flaws may have resulted, we hope the ratings enable you to have a more enjoyable trip.

★★★ Usually reserved for a collection of recognized important works and sights, such as found in a section of a city, a museum, or church. Single works rarely receive this rating, except when popularity raises them to icons, such as Leonardo's *Last Supper*, or the Pantheon.

★★ Among the most important works of an artistic style or period or of a famous artist. A collection (in a city piazza, a church, or museum) of numerous starred works.

★ A fine example of an artistic style or period, or of an artist's work. A good collection of such works, but perhaps of a minor period. Also, a special view or panorama.

No star • Worthwhile, but only if you have the time or interest.

Special Tips • Views never receive a higher ranking than one star. When tracking down the star-rated sights, note that the directions we give for churches follow the tradition that the high altar always is at the east end, even when it is not.

Hotel Ratings

We use a star (★), check (√), and flower (❀) system to rate hotels. This system is not the same as the official (and variable) star-rating of hotels by each regional government. The stars reflect numerous considerations, such as the size and furnishings of rooms, the quality of the view and lighting, the size and attractiveness of the bathrooms, and, of course, cleanliness. The amenities of a hotel are important too, such as whether it has restaurants, bars, swimming pool, tennis courts, or other sports facilities, and laundry or room service. The overall attractiveness and maintenance of a hotel also enter significantly into allotment of stars, as does the quality of its service. Finally, the stars reflect our subjective judgment on the hotels' overall quality and ambience. All of these factors, many intangible, enter into our final awarding of stars to guide your hotel selection.

★★★★★   Deluxe. An exceptional hotel that has the qualities of a four-star hotel plus some striking feature that makes it even more outstanding. The hotel excels in architecture, service, ambience or some other important characteristic that makes it one of the select few.

★★★★   Superior. A hotel with modern conveniences (a/c, TV, minibar, etc.) and quality service (concierge, porters, room service, etc.) as well as a pool, view or some such amenity. Or a smaller deluxe inn without some of the modern amenities, but with fine service and usually with superb ambience.

★★★   First Class. A very comfortable hotel, much like the four-star, but less well-decorated or without the pool, etc. Or a small inn without some of the amenities (like a minibar, or restaurant), but with tasteful decor and more often than not, ambience.

★★   A modern, commercial hotel, somewhat plain but with air conditioning and usually a restaurant. Or, an attractive pensione, perhaps without a/c but with ambience.

★   A simple hotel or pensione, often without air conditioning but clean and well-located.

No Star   If you are traveling on a tight budget and starred hotels are not available, you may find such a hotel acceptable, if only for a brief stay.

The check (√) reflects our judgment that the hotel is a particularly good buy in its category. The flower (❀) indicates the hotel has a special ambience—most often one evocative of some past epoch or one created with fine furnishings and art; occasionally, the ambience is created by a beautiful setting. The description of the hotel will elaborate on the symbols.

Hotels are grouped into price categories, starred, checked, beflowered and described. Within price categories, the order of the hotels reflects our judgment of relative quality. If you are traveling on a moderate budget, you can read the descriptions, check the star ratings, and if you are still undecided, you can just select the first hotel listed under the "moderate" category. Since preferences for hotels vary, read the descriptions to make sure you are selecting a hotel suitable to your tastes.

Restaurant Ratings

Restaurants are star-rated, price-listed and described. Icons in the margin can draw your attention to special places—especially those that are our personal favorites—and good buys. We use a five-star system of rating restaurants that takes into account the ambience and service as well as the cuisine. In addition to the recommendations of friends and restaurant critics, both Italian and American, our own dining experiences and personal preferences most certainly influence the rankings.

★★★★★   Sublime cuisine married to elegant or romantic ambience and polished service.

★★★★   Outstanding cuisine in a pleasant setting and with good service.

★★★   Very good cuisine and, in the case of trattoria specialties, perhaps the best in their category.

★★   Decent food and, in the case of pizza and bakery goods, perhaps the best in their category.

★   Acceptable food, included for the price, homey ambience, or convenient location.

Prices

Because the dollar-value of the lira is subject to considerable swings these days, we give all prices in lira. As this book is going to press the dollar, unfortunately falling in value, was equivalent to 1500 lira. It might be changed during your travels. Also, the lira price for restaurants and hotels fluctuates over the course of a year. There are regions, usually resorts, with high-season and low-season prices. There is inflation, usually 5-10 percent, that may be reflected in prices during the course of a year. Also, since 1992, hotel prices no longer are set by the government, making them all the more unpredictable. Prices are, however, the most accurate available as we go to press.

Restaurant Prices

The lower end of the price range given in this guide is based on a meal of either a pasta and entrée *(secondo)* or entrée and a salad or vegetable *(contorno)* without wine, but with tax and tip for one person. The upper end is based on a more elaborate feast of several courses. Those restaurants that serve à la carte meals are less costly, obviously, when a course is eliminated, an option usually available at all but the more expensive establishments. Prices rise remarkably with the addition of truffle dishes or seafood by the weight.

Restaurant Hours

Italians are extremely conventional in regard to when they dine. Most typically restaurants and trattorias open from 1 to 3 p.m. and 7:30-10 p.m. There are variations, of course. A good rule of thumb is that the better city restaurants usually don't open before 8 p.m. and many trattorias open by noon. In between times, look for a cafe (open throughout the day) or bakery (pizza comes out of the oven around 11:30 a.m.).

Hotel Prices

The prices included in this guide are based on high season rates for a room including tax, service and private bathroom. Reduced rates usually can be obtained in the off-season—or even the peak season if business is slow: in cities, expect weekend discounts; at beach resorts, expect the highest prices during July and August, Christmas and Easter holidays. "CP," or "Continental Plan" follows the price when a continental or buffet breakfast is included in the price. More elaborate meal plans are often required in resort areas during the peak season: the price is followed by "MAP," or "Modified American Plan," when breakfast plus lunch or dinner is included; "AP," or "American Plan," follows the price when all three meals are included.

Updates

We have made enormous efforts to provide the most up-to-date and accurate information, but between our visit and yours, hotels may change management, and restaurants, their chefs. While we cannot be responsible for the inaccuracies that must result from these constant changes in the tourism industry, we will make an ongoing effort to keep abreast of them. Your comments and suggestions would be most welcome and helpful. Write to us: Lynn and Lawrence Foster c/o Fielding Worldwide Inc., 308 South Catalina Avenue, Redondo Beach, California 90277.

PRACTICAL TRAVEL INFORMATION

Hotel reservations are recommended as far in advance as possible.

Tourism in Italy is well organized, with information offices to help you at airports and borders as well as in cities and the simplest *paese*, or village. As comfortable and easy as it is to get around Italy, foreign travel always requires some special adjustments and advance planning. Even if you're traveling deluxe with hotel concierge service available for arranging everything from city tours to opera tickets, you still might need to know how much to tip the concierge, or how to save on transatlantic phone calls. Budget travelers will have to rely more on themselves, from buying bus tickets to figuring out how to order a cup of "good old American coffee" in Italian. Although the practical information contained in this chapter should be useful to all travelers, much of the detail here and in the keys and directories to major cities will be most critical for those making their own arrangements.

Planning Your Trip

When to Travel

The best time to visit Italy is May and early June, and late September to November. The weather is generally pleasant and warm, from the Alps south to Sicily and the school-vacation crowds are busy at home. But even these seasons are very popular, enough so to require advance reservations. In fact, Italy is such a popular destination (and deservedly so) that it is hard to say when it might be safe to travel without reservations. The week before *Easter*, or *Holy Week*, and the *Christmas* season *(mid-December through Epiphany, January 6)* and any *balmy holiday weekend* are times the Italians themselves head for the smaller towns to sightsee, or to the beaches in the south, or to the ski resorts in the Apennines and Alps. You might, then, think you're safe in the larger cities, but certainly not in Vatican Rome, Florence or Venice. The only time you're guaranteed not to find the Italians in the cities is for *Ferragosto*, the last two weeks in August when everyone who can leaves for the mountain and beach resorts. In fact, this mass migration begins in July, intensifies in early August, and doesn't begin to let up until the schools reopen after the first weekend in September. The desertion of the cities makes them quieter, with less traffic, almost no cultural activities (during Ferragosto), and many closed restaurants. It does nothing to prevent foreigners from taking over the sidewalk cafes, filling the hotels, and forming long lines at museums. In the summer, no place is uncrowded in Italy. And if the crowds bother you, then maybe those few months not mentioned, especially November into early December and mid-January into February, are for you. The weather can be icy cold in the north (the Lake Region is closed), the sky can be cement gray for days in every region, and even in Rome and Sicily a raincoat with a lining is a good idea. Yet you can actually find a seat in the Sistine Chapel. And prices are at their lowest, for flights and hotels, and for tour packages.

Climate

Italy's climate is quite variable, so the local weather and resulting tourist seasons are described in more detail under each regional chapter. On the whole, people have a better impression of the Italian climate than it deserves. Hearing descriptions by German and British travelers who descend through the Alps for the more benign Mediterranean climate here, you might think Italy is the European equivalent of the Caribbean. In fact, winter can be harsh in the Po Valley and Rome can suffer long, cold, rainy spells from No-

PRACTICAL TRAVEL
INFORMATION

vember into February. Recent years have brought warmer weather—so much so that the ski season in the Alps has been a disaster and some Romans have stopped buying wool overcoats. Even if this trend continues, the winter is far from warm—bonfires roar in Rome's open-air markets to disperse the morning chill. The warmest areas, along the Amalfi drive south of Naples and in Sicily, produce oranges and lemons year-long, but again December to mid-February is not a time for bathing in the sea or even heated pools, not when the average high in both Naples and Palermo is under 60°F in January. Except in the mountains, summers bring occasional thunderstorms and intensely hot weather (in both Milan and Palermo the average high in July is 89° F), which can be particularly debilitating if you're not staying in air conditioned hotels in the cities. *You might be surprised at how many facilities lack either fans or air-conditioners—many Italian movie theaters simply close down rather than install such costly equipment.* But then again, this is the season of *al fresco* dining, one of the great pleasures of Italian travel. Whenever you go, as long as you are prepared for the conditions, you'll find Italy worth any inconvenience, whether it's the dampness and cold of December or the heat and crowds of August.

National Holidays

You may want to plan your trip around a special celebration, whether Spoleto's cultural festival, Siena's Palio, or Venice's many regattas. These local events are listed under the appropriate destination section in the guide. Although most legal holidays, or *feste*, aren't something to plan your itinerary around, they can affect whether the museums and restaurants, not just post offices and banks, are open. You can expect shops, banks, post offices and some restaurants to close on any of the following days, but museums and monuments are more difficult to predict. Monuments, such as ancient ruins or churches, rarely close, but they can. Museums often open, but for more limited hours—usually the same as their Sunday hours. Although you should always check locally, you might expect sights to be closed on those holidays with asterisks, then if they aren't, you'll be delighted. *Jan. 1, Jan. 6, *Easter, Easter Mon., Apr. 25, *May 1, *1st Sun. in June, *Aug. 15, Sept. 8, Nov. 1, Dec. 8, *Dec. 25, and *Dec. 26. Often, local feast days also result in closings, such as Apr. 25 in Venice, June 24 in Florence, Genoa, and Turin, July 15 in Palermo, Sept. 19 in Naples, Oct. 4 in Bologna, and Dec. 7 in Milan.

Language

Even if you can't speak Italian, you'll find it relatively easy to get around the country. At shops, Italians are expert at the simple gesture, the single word to prompt the right response out of the most tongue-tied customer. At tourist offices, at hotels and banks, usually someone can be found to speak English—now the required second language in schools. But *you'll feel better carrying a small traveler's phrase book.* When that doesn't help and the problem is over prices—of a taxi, a bill, a few slices of prosciutto—then having pencil and paper handy can resolve many problems. If you have time before your trip, you might enjoy taking a short adult education course—they usually focus on useful basic expressions to get you around.

Clothing

Seasonal requirements are not too different from the middle Atlantic of the U.S. or Britain. **Summers** are hot, though you will occasionally want a cotton sweater. Then, Italy is at its most informal—only at the most elegant hotel dining room or restaurant would men need a tie and jacket. But Italy is never so informal that shorts are acceptable anywhere but at resorts. *To satisfy dress codes for churches, you'll need to don full length slacks and cover up tank tops—women definitely need to bring a scarf to cover bare arms necessitated by the summer heat.* **Spring and fall** are variable, cool in the evening but warming up in the afternoon sunshine, so bring layers of dress that can be as easily peeled off as put on. Early spring and late fall, you'll want a light jacket, even a raincoat without a lining. Then too, men will more often find a sports jacket appropriate for dining out, and sweaters certainly will be appreciated. **Winter** dress depends on your destination. In the north, you'll feel happy to have a winter overcoat and even thermal socks for those marble cold and unheated country churches. Even in Sicily, a sweater will feel comfortable at night under a lined raincoat, though you might bring fall-weight clothes, not woolens. *Regardless of the season, bring comfortable walking shoes.* And don't pack more than you can carry yourself if you're traveling by train or bus. And remember, there are airline restrictions on how much baggage can be carried without charge (see "Plane" in the "Transportation" section).

Other Items to Take

You never know when you might need needle and thread, safety pins, tissues for wiping your hands, Band-Aids and an antiseptic cream, and, in the summer, insect repellent. All can be bought in Italy, but a store may not be nearby when you need them. If you are traveling budget class, bring an extra towel (especially if you're going to the beach) and a few hangers (useful, too, for drying wash).

Bring a necklace pouch or money belt to keep funds out of reach of pickpockets.

If you're a restless sleeper or particularly sensitive to noise, you may find earplugs your salvation during summer nights. Bring medicines, especially those with prescriptions, because you may not find an exact replacement, but plan on replenishing toiletries en route in order to keep your suitcase portable (profumeries carry fine shampoos; farmacie, toothpaste). And an extra pair of prescription glasses can save your trip from disaster. Sunglasses for anyone planning to drive are a must.

A Swiss Army knife can be useful, particularly for a picnic or snack while traveling. And binoculars or opera glasses can be essential for architectural details, carvings on monuments, or ceiling frescoes.

Your hair dryer or electric razor will burn out on the 115-volt and 220-volt alternating current used in Italy—the 220 is prevalent, but both types are found. A converter can help once you determine which voltage a hotel has. Even then you still need adapter plugs. And though the rounded two-pronged plug is common in Italy, so are a number of other configurations. Although you might try a converter and adapter kit found in many hardware stores, battery-operated appliances might be easier—or bring a safety razor.

Coin laundries are difficult to find. Even those *lavanderie* that claim to be "self-service" aren't, but at least they usually can do your clothes in a day. You may want to plan on washing some items yourself, so bring detergent, a flat disk stopper (it will work with any drain), and even a piece of rope for a clothesline.

Umbrellas and books in English are much cheaper in the U.S. than in Italy, as is camera film (hand check cameras and film at airport security points—the x-ray machines can blur film).

Planning Aids

The Italian government maintains tourist information offices abroad to dispense brochures, hotel lists, annual lists of special festivals, and the like for those planning a trip to their country. They also have a general information guide for travelers. Contact them with your questions.

Italian Government Travel Office (ENIT)

> *630 Fifth Avenue, Suite 1565*
> *New York, NY 10111*
> ☎ *(212) 245-4822*
> *12400 Wilshire Boulevard, Suite 550*
> *Los Angeles, CA 90025*
> ☎ *(310) 820-0098*

Office National Italian de Tourisme (ENIT)

> *1 Place Ville Marie, Suite 1914*
> *Montreal, Que HEB 3M9*
> ☎ *(514) 866-7667*

In addition, the Italian government subsidizes CIT (Campagna Italiana Turismo), a tour agency with modestly priced, individually designed tours as well as bus tours. These offices also sell **rail passes**. Offices can be found in Italian cities (see directories to destination cities below), in London, Toronto, Montreal, Los Angeles, and Chicago as well as:

CIT

> *342 Madison Avenue, #207*
> *New York, NY 10173*
> ☎ *(800) 223-7987, toll free in U.S.*
> *in NYC* ☎ *(212) 697-2100*
> *automated Italian Rail schedule* ☎ *(212) 697-2398*

If you plan to work in Italy, or to enroll in a university, you'll need a visa in addition to a passport. For these concerns and others in regard to documents and customs, contact the Italian consulate nearest you. Addresses can be obtained from:

Italian Consulate

> *1601 Fuller Street, N.W.*
> *Washington D.C., 20009*
> ☎ *(202) 328-5500, FAX 462-3605*

PRACTICAL TRAVEL
INFORMATION

Senior Citizens

There are many organizations that have discount travel options for senior citizens. The **American Association of Retired Persons** *(AARP, 1909 K Street N.W., Washington, D.C. 20049; toll free in U.S.* ☎ *[800] 227-7737)* is open to anyone 50 years and over willing to pay a small fee and the **National Council for Senior Citizens** *(925 15th Street N.W., Washington, D.C. 20005)* has travel information and tips on discounts. There are special tour operators, too; one with interesting educational and cultural tours is **Elderhostel** *(75 Federal Street, Boston, MA 02110)*, open to anyone 60 years old and over.

Students

The discounts and tours available to students are too numerous to overlook. A clearing house for this information is the **Council for International Education Exchange** *(CIEE, 205 E. 42nd Street, New York, NY 10017)* with information and services for youths under 26, students, and teachers. Write for their *Student Travel Catalog.*

Women Traveling Alone

Most women report that they have never experienced any special problems traveling through Italy, particularly in the north. Some report that restaurants fuss pleasantly over them when they are alone and that in the more elegant lounges they feel more at ease than when in the U.S. Even men in Rome and southern Italy aren't quite living up to their reputation for catcalls and bottom pinching, but are still active enough to be irritating. (Walking purposefully really helps to avoid some of these situations. Also, you might ask women for directions. And don't talk back or make eye contact with those pestering you.) The problems of traveling alone are the same worldwide for women and require some exercise of caution in Italy just as elsewhere. For example, *make sure your hotel is located in a good neighborhood* (avoid the areas around train stations especially), so that you feel comfortable dining out at night. *Carry money for emergency taxis* and walk on well-lighted, busy streets at night. And you might delay visiting remote villages, especially in the off-season, until you have some company or can arrange a tour. For example, the totally male-dominated cafes and piazzas of small-town Sicily will make you feel, at the very least, uncomfortable.

Disabled Travelers

Although there are no organizations providing travel discounts for the disabled, there are quite a number that facilitate travel. The **Travel Information Center** *(Moss Rehabilitation Hospital, Tabor & 12th, Philadelphia, PA 19141)* will send you travel tips and information for up to three cities for a small fee. **Mobility International** *(Box 3551, Eugene, OR 97403)* and **Whole Person Tours** *(Box 1084, Bayonne, NJ 07002)* are two organizations that publish regular newsletters and magazines for its members as well as organize special tours. The book, *Access to the World: A Travel Guide for the Handicapped* (published by Facts on File) is full of useful advice and hotel listings. And the **Information Center for Individuals with Disabilities** in Massachusetts *(ICID, Fort Point Place, 1st floor, 27-43 Wormwood St., Boston, MA 02210)* will send a list of specialized travel agencies, tour operators, and publications (small fee for out-of-state residents).

Tours

Although many people prefer to travel independently, making up their own itinerary and discovering their own hotels and restaurants, and most of all, making on-the-spot-changes to suit their tastes, there are tours to suit almost everyone. For those who don't want to travel with a group, an introductory city tour arranged locally (see city directories) might still be appealing, or a *package* might save money and allow enough independence to be enticing. Travel agencies and airlines purchase blocks of hotel rooms and airplane seats to create package deals that you as an individual can buy into at considerable savings, especially in the off-season. Comparison shop among the packages by checking the travel section in the Sunday paper of the city nearest you with an international airport, or consult a travel agent.

More organized travel can satisfy any number of interests. Maybe you don't like to travel alone or you don't like to make the myriad arrangements necessary for a trip. Or you wish to learn about Italian art or the ancient Greeks or Italian wines and cuisine. As any travel agent can advise you, there are tours for you with special itineraries and often even expert lecturers. The size of the tour can vary, from busload dimensions to mini-van capacity, and the price varies not just with size but with the quality of the accommodations, restaurants (if included) and whether there are lecturers and/or guides in addition to tour leaders.

Special Interest Travel

Whether you want to visit the great opera houses or bicycle on rural roads, you can usually find a way to plan such a trip on your own. Both the Italian Government Travel Office and CIT (see "Planning Aids" above) might be able to help you learn what is available, and a travel agent can facilitate making arrangements. But you should know that there is no Ticketron equivalent for making reservations at Italian opera houses or music festivals (**Dailey-Thorp**, ☎ *[212] 307-1555* in New York City, is the closest substitute). The Italian Government Travel Office can provide you with programs, dates and ticket prices, but making advance reservations on your own is extremely cumbersome. And although the Italian government is currently developing and promoting agritourism—or visits through the countryside, whether in the vineyards in Latium around Rome or in the Veneto hills, whether biking or by car—you may find such travel complicated if you don't speak Italian or if you never before have made a biking trip. Whatever your interest, if you are determined to do it on your own, search out information through associations, such as local opera societies or athletic groups and do some research in your public library (check the "Specialty Travel Index" and look for books on your subject, such as Random House's *Bicycle Touring in Europe*). Also, the following special interest tour groups might convince you that a prearranged trip is what you need after all.

Great Performance Tours ☎ *(212) 580-1400*
Ovations International ☎ *(800) 635-5576*
Walking Vacations ☎ *(800) 777-9255, toll free in U.S.*
International Bicycle Touring Society ☎ *(616) 459-8775*
Ciclismo Classico ☎ *(800) 866-7314, (617) 628-7314 for Italy by bike or hike*
Camping Tours of Europe ☎ *(516) 496-7400*
Academic Travel Abroad ☎ *(202) 333-3355*

Study in Italy

You may simply want to settle in a town for several weeks, learning about Italy by taking language, cooking, and culture courses designed for foreigners. Enrolling in such programs also is a good way of meeting people. Many language institutes can arrange housing too. These institutes have a tendency to cluster in Florence, Rome, and Siena (see town directories for a few listings) and other major destinations. In addition, the universities in Siena and Perugia have summer programs for foreigners and many American universities sponsor short-term study programs. To learn about what is available, check your library for a copy of Shaw's **Guide to Cooking Schools**, or contact CIEE *(205 E. 42nd St., NY, NY 10017; ☎ [212] 651-1450)* for the book *Work, Study, Travel Abroad: The Whole World Handbook* or the Institute of International Education *(809 United Nations Plaza, NY, NY 10017; ☎ [212] 984-5412)* for its book *Vacation Study Abroad*. The American In-

PRACTICAL TRAVEL INFORMATION

stitute of Foreign Study *(102 Greenwich Ave., Greenwich, CT 06830)* arranges for university study abroad.

Hotels

We have yet to find that convenient creation—the budget highway motel complete with ice machines, air conditioning (a/c) and pool. In fact, ice machines are not found much anywhere and air conditioning is rarely found in inexpensive accommodations. At beaches and mountain areas, it may not even be had in first-class facilities. Which brings us to warn you about Italian hotels: They can be very different from what you find in the U.S. Even the most deluxe establishments can have less than ample rooms for astronomical prices. What you do get is something rarely found in the U.S., but prized in Europe—service. You might also buy ambience: a 16th-century country villa or city palazzo, a medieval monastery furnished with antiques, or even a contemporary hotel with views of the Grand Canal in Venice. In many establishments, the towels can be no more than out-sized dish towels and the "showers" are the hand-held type, used for washing hair in the U.S. In modest establishments, the bathrooms can be spiffy with bright tiles, but so small that the shower simply rains down from the ceiling over everything below. There are marked changes occurring, but not everywhere or all at once. Terry cloth towels are increasingly visible and new hotels find shower stalls to be great space-savers over bathtubs. Air conditioning is becoming increasingly available, along with hairdryers and TVs—all items that have raised prices considerably.

The range of hotels, however, is greater than in the U.S. There are even a few single rooms in hotels, smaller (and often claustrophobically so) than the doubles but with fairer rates for the person traveling alone. The options in the lower price range are quite broad, although major cities rarely have budget level accommodations that include private baths and safe locations. This is no doubt due to the fact that the *pensioni* have been forced to upgrade into hotels by the government regulations that no longer separate hotel ratings from those for pensioni. Although some establishments still have the homey ambience of a pensione and still require meal plans (usually just breakfast), the required upgradings have increased their prices. The destination chapters in this book try to give a broad choice of hotels (see "Introduction" for explanation of star ratings and see "Hotel Quick-Reference Chart" for prices), not only for different pocketbooks but also for different tastes.

Beginning in 1992, hotel prices no longer were government controlled. Many hotels make it impossible not to take their continental breakfast (CP) so you should ask if its included in the price. (It's always worth a try to get out of it by asking how much the room will be without breakfast.) Resorts commonly require meal plans, breakfast and dinner or lunch (Modified American Plan, or MAP) but rarely all meals (American Plan or AP). If you're staying in budget-level or pensione-style accommodations, always make certain that you have both a toilet *(toelette)* *and* a bath *(bagno privato)* or shower *(doccia privata)* in your room, if that's what you want. Sometimes a request for "bagno privato" brings just one, and not the other. If you're at the hotel, you can simply ask to see the room ("Mi faccia vedere la camera?"), but when writing or calling, specify your choice. Heat is included in room prices, but not air conditioning in modest establishments, where there usually is a supplementary charge. In the off-season at resorts, there are official lower rates; everywhere that business is slow (July-August in many cities such as Venice and Florence or weekends in Milan and Rome) you might request a "sconto" because it's "bassa stagione."

Author's Observation:

In fact, there's never any harm in asking, or having your travel agent ask for a better price than the official "rack" rate. Many of the chain hotels, such as Intercontinental or Holiday Inn, routinely offer promotional or corporate discounts.

Advance reservations always are recommended, as far in advance as possible for April through October, Holy Week, and Christmas season. *And don't simply reserve a room, reserve a room with a view or one with twin beds or one with a shower, not a tub, or a quiet interior—whatever you prefer. You'll probably be disappointed if you try to negotiate these details upon arrival.* A travel agent can facilitate this process for you, but might charge you for long distance calls for modest hotels with no fax or representatives in the U.S. Hotels that don't accept credit cards usually require a one-night deposit to hold the room beyond 6 p.m. (Send an international money order if there's time—say three weeks.)

Apartments

If you wish to join the ebb and flow of Italian life—shopping at markets, sitting in the neighborhood cafe—or if you simply prefer to cook for yourself (and clean), then maybe you would like to rent a town apartment. Except for an officially designated *residenza* (minimum stay seven nights; contact local tourist office for a hotel list—*elenco d'alberghi*), you'll not find this an easy task on your own. Furnished apartments are rare due to high demand for housing in city centers. Rome, with its many visiting scholars and large foreign community, is something of an exception. There, the biweekly newspaper *Wanted in Rome*, found at newsstands, (or place an ad—V. dei Delfini 17, 00186 Roma; 679-0190) lists rentals, most by the month, but some just for the Christmas week. Some agencies list city apartments along with country villas—but expect to pay their commission. Among them are **Villas International** *(605 Market Street, San Francisco, CA 94105; toll free, in U.S.*

☎ *[800] 221-2260)* or **Families Abroad** *(194 Riverside Drive, New York, NY 10025;* ☎ *[212] 787-2434)*. Another option is to try to exchange your home for one in Italy. This process is facilitated by the listings of **International Home Exchange** *(Box 3975, San Francisco, CA 94119;* ☎ *[415] 382-0300)* with a membership fee for the catalog listing participants. Another option is to join a language program (see "Study in Italy" above). Many have their own housing arrangements, often rooms with families, but also apartments.

PRACTICAL TRAVEL INFORMATION

Villas

Renting a farmhouse or Renaissance villa, especially when the countryside is Tuscany, is a dream of many. Fortunately, there are many agencies making this possible, not just in Tuscany but from the Lombard Lakes to the Amalfi Coast. They charge a fee, of course, and many recommend that before renting a particular property you ask to speak to a previous tenant. Among these agencies are those listed above ("Apartments") as well as: **At Home Abroad** *(405 E. 56th Street, New York, NY 10022;* ☎ *[212] 421-9165);* **Posarelli Vacations** *(180 Kinderkamack Road, Park Ridge, NJ;* ☎ *[201] 573-9558);* **Rent-a-Vacation Everywhere** *(328 Main Street East, Suite 526, Rochester, NY 14604;* ☎ *[716] 454-6440)*. In Italy, there are several English-speaking organizations that are well regarded: **The Best in Italy** *(V. Ugo Foscolo 72, 50124 Florence;* ☎ *[55] 223-064, FAX [55] 229-8912)*, managed by a contessa and with some of the most luxuries properties in Tuscany; and **Solemar** *(V. Cavour 80, 50129 Florence;* ☎ *[55] 218-112, FAX [55] 287-157)*, with hundreds of diverse listings for Tuscany and Umbria.

Family Living

Staying with an Italian family is one way to enjoy a deeper cultural exchange when traveling, but it is not particularly easy to make arrangements. **Agriturismo**, staying at a farm or wine estate, is organized and regulated by the Italian government, but the accommodations vary enormously from fancy villas (that provide little people contact) to basic quarters on working farms where you may be expected to join in the daily labors. Each region has agriturism listings; write to them directly (see "Tourist Information" in the destination chapters) or contact Agriturismo (Corso V. Emanuele 101, 00186 Rome). There also are a few organizations, devoted to promoting world peace by bringing people together, that have listings (fee) of Italian families interested in receiving visitors for a few nights: contact **Great Expeditions Travelers Network** *(Box 18036, Raleigh NC 27619;* ☎ *[800]-743-3639)* or **Servas** *(11 John Street, Room 407, NY, NY 10038;* ☎ *[212] 267-0252)*. Language Programs in Italy also usually can make such living arrangements for the duration of your studies (see "Study in Italy" below).

Hostels

Hostels are not only cheap, they provide wonderful opportunities to meet travelers from around the world. For the single traveler, the camaraderie found at the hostels and the chance of finding travel companions make many of their inconveniences incidental. All these hostels, affiliated with the Hosteling International (check **American Youth Hostels**, *733 15th Street N.W., Suite 840, Washington, D.C. 20005;* ☎ *[202] 783-6161;* **Hosteling International-Canada, National Office**, *1600 James Naismith Drive, Suite 608, Gloucester, Ont K1B 5N4;* ☎ *[613] 748-5638;* or **Associazione Italiana Alberghi per la Gioventu**, *V. Cavour 44, piano 3, 00184 Rome;* ☎ *[06] 462-342*), no longer have any age limits for membership, some of the hotel rules can be particularly displeasing to the older married couples—such as the separation of sexes into different bunking areas. There also are curfews, daytime closings, restrictions of the length of stay in peak season and some total closings off-season. For more information, contact any of the above organizations.

Camping

If you like to camp and already have the equipment, you might enjoy traveling through Italy using the often scenically situated campgrounds that dot its seashores, lakes and countryside. The facilities vary from the very basic to the very elaborate, with bungalows, hotels, pools and other sports facilities. The Italian government rates them (for a list of sites write the Italian Government Travel Office under "Planning Aids"), and the Touring Club Italiano publishes a directory, *Campeggi e Villaggi Turistici in Italia*, available in bookstores throughout Italy. Of course, the savings on camping can be put toward the cost of renting a car. RV vehicles also can be rented, but reserve way in advance for July and August.

Documents

To travel in Italy and return home you need a valid passport, as does every member of your party. No other document is necessary for tourists remaining in Italy up to 90 days. Tourists can receive another 90 days by applying to the local *questura*, with proof of enough money to be self-supporting. This is necessary only if you have not been out of Italy—haven't even crossed the border into France—say during the first three months. *Hotels require that you leave your passport with them temporarily, because under law they must report your presence to the police.* If you are staying at a private home, then you are supposed to report your presence to the *questura*—this is part of Italy's antiterrorism program. In practice you will probably never encounter this situation unless you are studying at a language institute or staying in a rented villa. The only other document for tourists is an **international driver's license** (valid for one year), recommended for those who plan to rent a car but don't speak any Italian. The AAA issues the license and provides same day service to members and nonmembers. Appear with a valid U.S. license, two passport-size photos (they can make them on the spot, usually), and pay the current fee.

U.S. Passports

U.S. passports, whether new or renewed, are good for ten years and cost $55 (except for youths 18 years old and under, for whom a passport is good for five years only and costs $30); however, there is an additional $10 application fee if you apply in person. Children must have separate passports. To receive a passport, you need to obtain an application at a Passport Service office (in regional federal buildings or, barring their availability, a designated clerk of courts or post office listed under "Government Agencies" in the phone book). For your first passport, or if your current one is more than 12 years old, you need to apply in person (not children under 13) with the completed application, proof of U.S. citizenship (naturalization papers or certified copy of birth certificate) a signed photo I.D., and two recent identical passport photos, and you must pay the $55 plus an additional $10 in-person application fee (exact currency, check or money order). If you have a passport not more than 12 years old, then you can mail your application to the National Passport Center, *P.O. Box 371971, Pittsburgh PA 15250*, along with the old passport and a check or money order (made out to Passport Services). Although passports can be issued in emergencies within a day, it's best to apply as soon as possible, avoid the summer rush, and leave yourself a month to receive your passport. For further details, dial ☎ *(900) 225-5674* for automated information (35 cents per minute) or personal assistance ($1.05/ minute).

Canadian Passports

Obtain an application from a passport office, travel agency or post office. Then take the completed application to one of the regional passport offices or send it (Passport Office, Department of External Affairs, Ottawa, Ont. K1A 0G3) with proof of Canadian citizenship, two identical passport photos signed by you and cosigned by a professional who has known you for at least two years, and $35 Canadian. The passport is valid for five years. It's best to apply in winter.

British Passports

Apply in person at a local passport office with certified copies of birth, two recent identical passport photos signed and countersigned, and, if applicable, a copy of your marriage certificate, and £18. The passport is valid for 10 years except for those under 16 and takes about one month to receive.

Customs Restrictions

Italian Customs

Arriving by land in these days of European unity often requires no document or customs check. Airport arrival, however, always does, although customs checks are perfunctory. As a tourist, you probably aren't carrying anything to create problems—for example, you are permitted two still cameras a person plus 10 rolls of film and in addition a movie or video camera with ten cartridges of film. From outside Europe, you may bring in 400 cigarettes, two bottles of wine, one bottle of liquor.

U.S. Customs

All U.S. residents are exempted from paying duty on items with a combined retail value of $400 as long as they have not made other such claims within 30 days and as long as the articles are for personal use (not for resale). Families may pool their exemptions by filling out only one customs form. You may include within your exemption 200 cigarettes and 100 cigars. If you are over 21 and your home state has no more restrictive laws, you may include one liter of alcohol in your exemption. A flat rate of 10 percent duty is imposed on the first $1000 in excess of your exemption. If you have previously claimed your 30-day exemption, you may still bring in $25 worth of goods. Keep your sales slips available in case officials request them. You may avoid paying duty even on purchases in excess of $400 if you can prove they are antiques (more than 100 years old), or if they are drawings and paintings.

Many articles are restricted by the U.S. such as Cuban cigars or tobacco, as they are not permitted in the U.S. Lottery tickets and fireworks are prohibited. Products made with any part of an endangered species cannot be imported. Before losing a jaguar pelt wallet to customs, or whatever is the latest in designer leathers, call for a copy of the World Wildlife Fund's brochure "Buyer Beware" (☎ *[800] 634-4444* outside Washington D.C.) The U.S. also restricts the import of animals, meat (only specially cured prosciutto can be imported), plants and fruit. You can bring back dried mushrooms, however, and hard cheeses (aged 90 days or more), olive oil, vinegars and packaged goods, such as pastas. For more details write the U.S. Department of Agriculture, Washington, D.C. 20259, for their pamphlet. Prescription drugs should be accompanied with their prescriptions to avoid delays.

Try to bring all your purchases with you. Packages sent to your home are not covered by the $400 exemption, so you will have to pay duty. You may send unsolicited gifts to friends without duty being charged if the value is no more than $50. Only one package can be received at one address without duty being charged. Write on the package clearly: Unsolicited Gift of Value Less Than $50. Unless you are certain of exceeding your exemption with

PRACTICAL TRAVEL INFORMATION

these gifts, it is safer to carry them with you rather than take the chance of loss or damage through the mail.

Canadian Customs

Canadian citizens who remain out of Canada for at least seven days may receive an exemption on duty for personal goods with a value not exceeding $300. This exemption will be received upon written declaration, but only once each calendar year. In addition, an unlimited number of $100 exemptions can be claimed once each calendar quarter after absences of at least 48 hours and an unlimited number of $20 exemptions can be declared after absences of at least 24 hours. However, these exemptions categories cannot be combined after a single trip. You may bring in 50 cigars, 200 cigarettes and 1.1 liters of liquor or wine, or 8.5 liters of beer except under the $20 exemption. The first $300 in excess of your exemption will be taxed at only 20 percent of regular duty rates (alcohol and cigarettes not included). Families cannot pool their exemptions.

Carry your purchases with you, as any packages mailed will be subject to duty. Gifts to friends can be sent duty-free as long as they are marked as unsolicited gifts and have a value of no more than $40. For restricted or prohibited articles, check with Canadian customs. (All these amounts are quoted in Canadian dollars.)

Health Tips

Precautions

There are no special inoculations required for travel in Italy, but you should check with your physician for his or her recommendations. We recommend a tetanus shot if yours is no longer valid. If you have a hidden medical condition–such as allergies to common medications, epilepsy, a heart condition or diabetes—you might wish to wear an ID tag provided by **Medic Alert International** *(Box 1009, Turlock, CA 95381)*. Again, check with your doctor before paying the membership fee. In fact, if you have not been well, or have a chronic medical problem or disability, you should discuss health measures with your doctor.

Pollution

Although Italians always drink bottled mineral water with their meals, town *tap water is perfectly safe to drink.* On the highways, in rural areas or at city fountains, however, it is best not to drink the water—often there are even signs that it isn't potable. There may have been progress in the drinking water, but unfortunately this does not apply to the sea. *The Mediterranean has suffered from industrial and agricultural pollution everywhere,* including around Italy. When we know of problems or suspect them, we give warnings in the text. Generally speaking, most travelers find off-shore islands and the less-developed south the best for swimming but even there it's best to avoid urban areas. A 1993 report designated the following sea coasts the cleanest: Cinque Terre, Ischia, Gallipoli, around Lecce in Apulia, most of Tuscany and Lazio (but the sea at the Lido di Ostia near Rome just received a "bathable" designation in 1994, an honor that nearby Fregene, also in Lazio, has yet to achieve). And speaking of pollution, *the air* in Milan can become so smoggy that occasionally city officials call for car-free Sundays. Other major centers grapple with automobile pollution, Rome and Genoa among them. But the problem is not as persistent.

PRACTICAL TRAVEL INFORMATION

Emergencies

Medical emergencies come in a variety of forms. If you need medicine, you should know that each town designates a 24-hour pharmacy on a rotating basis. You can discover where it is by asking your hotel clerk or checking the schedule posted in the windows of all *farmacie*. First Aid, or *pronto soccorso* (also the expression for emergency rooms at hospitals, or *ospedali*) is available at major train stations, ports and airports, as well as at hospitals in towns. If you need a doctor, you might want to be prepared with information on English-speaking doctors in Italy by contacting the **International Association for Medical Assistance to Travelers** *(IAMAT, 417 Center St., Lewiston, NY 14092)* months before departure. American Express will try to locate a doctor for its members, and consulates can be of assistance. **In a medical emergency, dial the police at 113 or 112** and hope someone speaks English. Better yet, find someone to make the call for you at your hotel, if possible.

Insurance

Check your insurance policy for coverage abroad and special procedures to be followed for reimbursement. (Some Italian hospitals, particularly private ones, require cash payment at discharge.) Collect receipts and carry your insurance I.D. card with you. If your policy does not cover foreign travel, temporary ones are available through travel agents.

Money

At the time this book is going to press, 1500 Italian *lira* are equivalent to one U.S. dollar, but the exchange rate fluctuates, sometimes significantly, so check the financial page of a major city newspaper for the most current rate. (This rate will be a bit higher than the rate you'll actually get.) The lira comes in both coins and paper bills and in many denominations. Beware that Italians sometimes quote prices dropping the last three zeroes, so that instead of L10,000 you might just hear "L10."

Money Exchanges

You'll want to arrive in Italy with a small amount of lira on hand. The exchange rates at U.S. airports and banks are not the best, so limit the amount of your purchase there to just enough to get you through a day. *Usually the cheapest and easiest way to obtain money abroad is with your home town ATM bank card with Cirrus and/or Plus.* The fee per transaction (the maximum withdrawal permitted is the same as at your bank ATM) is minimal when compared to Cirrus and/or Plus on credit cards; it's usually less than fees at most money exchanges *(cambios)*; the exchange rate is better than any bank's. And you don't have to wait in long bank lines. Although many of the ATMs are inaccessible during non-banking hours, they remain our first choice for changing dollars into lira. To use your bank card, make sure you get a four-digit PIN access code before leaving on your trip. In Italy, look for bank ATMs marked *"Bancomat 3,"* or call Cirrus ATM locator in the U.S. ☎ *(800) 424-7787.*

Even if you do have Cirrus/Plus, you may want to carry **traveler's checks** as a backup. Certainly everyone will find **credit cards** useful and they often, though not always, provide you with the best exchange rates. If you are using traveler's checks, change them into lira only as you need them since the checks can be replaced if stolen. (Also, on departure you need receipts to exchange *more* than one million lira into dollars.) Usually the best rates are at banks, the worst at hotels, but everything is variable. While strolling around a town, you might note the various exchange rates in the banks (and at post offices, with special cambio windows in airports and other tourist areas), because they differ significantly. Recently, the best exchange for cash was at the post office; for traveler's checks, it often, but not always, was at the regional Risparmio banks. But if you're traveling with your ATM bank card with Cirrus and see an automatic machine with Bancomat 3, go for it. It's safest to change your money in the morning; some banks do have afternoon hours, but their cambio doesn't always function then, and those few banks in large cities that sponsor special cambios with extended hours for tourists often don't have the best rates. Banks are normally open weekdays 8:30 a.m.–1:30 p.m. and some reopen 2:30–3:30 p.m.

Emergency Money

If you are running short of money, American Express accepts personal checks from its cardholders toward the purchase of traveler's checks (but change them into lira elsewhere, the rates aren't the best at American Express). Its offices can be found in major cities and resorts (listed later under city directories). By applying for a PIN number from American Express as well as some Visa and Master Card accounts, you can withdraw money from their cash machines (usually in major cities only), but the Visa and Master Card service is comparable to floating a loan with interest and, as a result, is costlier than the American Express service. Although there are limits to the amount and frequency that you can use these conveniences, they permit more than enough for most travelers. If you're still in a bind, people can send moneygrams through American Express (☎ *[800] 543-4080)* within two days to Venice, Rome, or Milan, or to a travel agency or store (longer hours than a bank) through Western Union (2–9 days; ☎ *[800] 325-6000* in U.S. and ☎ *654-7678* in Rome). There are costs for all these services, but only the cabling of money is particularly expensive.

PRACTICAL TRAVEL INFORMATION

Author's Observation:

Not all hotels and restaurants accept credit cards. Sometimes you'll be surprised at the establishments—in protest over the fees they must pay credit card companies—that won't accept them. Plan to pay cash at hotels under three stars and at inexpensive and sometimes moderate restaurants. When you can charge, you'll just be appreciative rather than out-of-sorts for having to pay in lira.

The Most for Your Money

The cost of travel in Italy is at least as expensive as in the U.S.; in the cities, it is more so. And like travel in the U.S., you might want to budget your money to extend your trip or simply to enjoy some splurges. Some of the ways of cutting costs are the same—use buses not taxis, particularly from airports; travel off season; overnight in small towns rather than cities (Sorrento, not Naples for example; Siena, not Florence); fill up on daily specials called menu turistico occasionally (a steady diet of them is too monotonous).

Transport

Other cost-cutting measures are more peculiar to Italy. The country is small enough to avoid domestic flights—which are quite expensive—for most travel, and to instead substitute trains—only 4.5 hours between Rome and Venice, one of the longer trips unless you are heading to Sicily. Car rentals are expensive (see below), and gasoline and autostrada tolls are the highest in Europe. Check on the modestly-priced local tours of CIT or take regional buses to countryside sights (see appropriate destination section for information). If only a car will do, then at least check about conditions on the free secondary roads (see "Driving Tips" and SS routes listed under destinations). And check "Transportation" below for the best buys for any form of travel.

Eating

In Italy, *there can be a great difference in cafe prices between standing at the counter and sitting, sometimes three times the amount more for table service in a café* at a prime location. Of course, you'll sometimes want to sit on the finer piazzas over a drink, but most of the time you might stand. Take your breakfast at the counter (you get used to it after awhile). In the afternoon, have a stand-up sandwich or slice of bakery-fresh pizza or fruit from the market, and then sit down at a cafe to relax over coffee. Better yet, plan a picnic in a city park—a great way to save money, and also the best way to learn about Italian prosciuttos, salami, and cheeses (you need order only a little, an etto is 3 ounces).

Hotels

And in Italy, many hotels quote a room price that includes a continental breakfast. *Any hotel that doesn't require a breakfast, especially in peak season, is saving you some money,* since a cappuccino and cornetta at a cafe counter supplemented by a piece of fruit from the market usually will be better and less costly. How much you save depends on the hotel, but the pricier the room, the pricier the coffee and jams. You might book down a category occasionally, especially if you see an appealing hotel in our listings. And if you already are traveling inexpensively, you might occasionally try a room without private bath to save even more. If you're a group or family that makes a car rental price efficient, then maybe summer camping also is a good idea. Italian campgrounds can be quite lovely, and with swimming pools, sometimes even cabañas to avoid the necessity of bringing a tent.

More Tips

There are other hints: shop for the bank with the best exchange rates; call the U.S. with special access codes (see "Telephone" below); if you must choose among sights, between a church and a museum or a town walk and an ancient ruin, then decide by pocketing the too-often-hefty admission fees. You might even plan your itinerary to include a visit to less expensive regions, Umbria, say, rather than Tuscany; or Sicily, the best buy of them all. *But most importantly, plan in advance: The best car rental deals, rail passes, and package tours often can be purchased only outside Italy.*

Transportation

Plane

The two major **international** airports are in Milan and Rome, so you should expect to begin your trip at either of these cities if you're arriving by plane. Of course, you can bypass these cities by getting a connecting flight to Venice or Palermo, for example, and in the summer there are a few flights direct to the smaller cities, some transcontinental, but most originating within Europe. Or you might plan to pick up a rental car at the airport and head out for other parts (just remember you might have jet lag). Or maybe you'll just enter the cities to begin your rail travel. More specifics are given under the descriptions of these destinations. Major airline carriers from the U.S. are TWA, American, and Alitalia, with flights from New York, L.A., Chicago, Miami and Boston.

Price is important to most travelers, so we'll address our remarks to economy fares rather than the more comfortable business and first class. Fares are the highest in the summer (June–mid September), a bit lower during the "shoulders" of April–May and mid-September–October, and considerably lower in the off-season November–March (except for some dates around Christmas). Fares are less if you fly midweek, either in the late evening or at midday. But you will save the most if you reserve as far in advance as possible (except for special promotions) at least 21 or 30 days in advance at any time in order to get a good price. You'll find most reduced price tickets are based on round-trip purchase and have stiff penalties for any change after a specific date. Some also restrict the length you may stay. The cost savings of early-purchase, nonrefundable tickets is so great, that if you worry you might have to cancel due to an emergency, it is worth looking into special insurance that will cover the cost of your ticket (check with your travel agent). The best fares are offered in the off-season and often advertise in the Sunday travel section of metropolitan newspapers (in both Europe and North America). In addition, charters now can be not only inexpensive but reliable. Instead of fly-by-night airlines, charters often guarantee reserved seats on the major carriers, but some don't issue tickets with specific flight information until two weeks before departure, others serve only specific groups (CIEE, for students and teachers, toll free in U.S. ☎ *[800] 223-7402*). However, if Italy is only one of your destinations, a regular airline "excursion" flight might permit a stopover in London, say, or even Rome on a flight to Athens. To sort all this out, it helps to have a good travel agent. For summer travel, try to find one at least two months in advance.

Domestic flights are quite pricey. The only carrier is Alitalia, and its affiliate ATI. The lack of competition and resultant high prices are typical throughout Europe, an issue being debated by the European Community, but not yet resolved. Fortunately, you rarely will need plane travel for convenience. Yes, if you're heading for Sicily and landing in Milan or Rome, you'll want a flight. (In the peak season, direct, not the same as "nonstop," international flights can save you money.) But for the most part, *Italy is so small that you'll find land arrangements the most pleasant and convenient.* So much so that Alitalia books its international passengers to Naples and Florence on special trains from the Rome airport.

Luggage • On international flights you are permitted free of charge one carry-on (permissible only if it fits under the seat) along with a purse or camera bag, and two suitcases (combined together in length, height and width not more than 106 inches and no single bag more than 70 pounds). Extra

PRACTICAL TRAVEL INFORMATION

luggage is charged, and at a hefty rate. Check with your airline or travel agent as to their particular specifications. Domestic flights, except when they are continuations of international ones, permit only 44 pounds free of charge in economy class.

PRACTICAL TIPS

Luggage carts are available in Italian airports, found most often not where you arrive but near the entrance to the departures areas. They are coin-operated. Parking fees often must be paid within the airport, where a machine or clerk will validate your ticket before you insert it at the exit blockade.

PRACTICAL TRAVEL
INFORMATION

Italian train stations are always busy.

Train

European rail travel is only getting better. High speed "fast" trains are already chopping hours off of travel time between major cities and the Community of European Railways has great plans for the future. With the opening of the Channel Tunnel, the London to Paris fast train takes 3 hours and Paris to Milan journey is 5.5 hours. Already there is a special *rapido* train from Milan to Rome (under 4 hours), with a link to Naples. Regular trains involve ferry crossings of the Channel, so that the London to Milan train can take 20 hours; the daytime trips from Paris to Milan, about 8 hours. Not too surprisingly, urban train stations (*stazioni*, in Italian) are busy. And they are well equipped not only with car rental agencies, bus and subway connections, and shops and restaurants, but even with *alberghi diurni*—day hotels with showers, baths, barbers, sleeping rooms rented by the hour, and other such revivifying comforts. When you consider that Eurail passes (see below) permit first class travel through most of this network at discounted rates while avoiding the need to line up for tickets during peak season crowds, you might come to the conclusion that trains are the only way to travel through Europe. In addition, once the pass takes you nearly everywhere on the Italian peninsula, it then carries you on train ferries to Sicily, or even Greece. If you are traveling extensively through Europe by train, contact **Rail Europe** ☎ *(800) 438-7245;* or ☎ *(303) 443-5100*, the American office for European trains. Their automated information system is extremely helpful.

PRACTICAL TIPS

Arrivati you'll figure out but **partenze** *is "departure" and* **binario**, *"track."* • **Prenotazione obbligatoria** *is where you go in large stations for required reservations on IC trains; often you need to take a number and look for your turn on an electronic board.* • *Contact CIT (see "Planning Aids") for a summary of the train schedule, different in winter and summer, called* **Principali Treni**. *Or, anywhere within Italy, call* ☎ *1478-88088.* • *Without a pass, try to purchase your tickets at local CIT offices, or travel agencies where English explanations might be more likely.* • *If you're traveling first-class without a reservation, get a seat assignment from the platform official carrying blue tickets.* • *You can be fined for sitting in first-class with a second-class ticket and you will be fined if you fail to cancel your ticket in the yellow platform boxes.* • *Credit cards can be used for payment at ticket windows.* **BEWARE**: *Make sure your valuables are secure, especially on overnight trains.*

The **Italian State Railways** (*Ferrovie dello Stato*, or simply *FS*) is one of the cheapest in Europe. So much so that it does not pay to purchase a Eurail pass if you are traveling only in Italy. There are different kinds of trains to consider. The rapido trains are the fastest, and are the Italian contribution to the international service. These top-of-the-line trains, the so-called InterCity or IC, *usually* offer first-class as well as second-class service with reservations required, air conditioning, and dining cars (but more often meal trays at seat), as well as sleeping cars when appropriate. There are different types of rapido trains, including the fastest Pendolino trains (between Turin and Rome, Naples and Rome, Milan–Bologna–Florence–Rome, and Lecce–Bari–Rome), but all stop only at major cities and are more costly with a special reservation fee (not to pass holders). Then there are the expressi, and with more stops, the *diretti*, and last the *accelerati* or *locali*, mostly second class and recommended if they are the only way to reach your destination. While only IC trains may have dining cars, others may have minibars. Short runs may have nothing. Stops at major stations provide the opportunity to buy box lunches and bottles of both mineral water and wine from platform vendors. Trains can be crowded in the summer and holiday season, so you will want to reserve at those times (fee). But first-class cars often remain unfilled, so even if you have a second-class ticket, you can pay to upgrade.

Passes • There are special passes for the Italian State Railways alone in addition to the Eurail pass options. All offer unlimited mileage during a set period of time, and once you present your pass at the stazione for the first time to have it activated, you no longer need to stand in ticket lines. The Europass is good for Italy as well as for France, Germany, Spain and Switzerland for unlimited first-class travel for 5 to 15 days within a two-month period. The price varies with the number of countries visited and there are discounts for youths and two traveling together. Another Youth Pass permits unlimited travel on second-class trains for those under 26. The Flexipass covers 16 countries plus Italy and encourages more leisurely first-class travel, providing for 5, 10 or 15 days of train travel within a two month period. There are special rates for children, there are Youth Flexipasses (second-class only), and there are train-drive options. The most important requirement is that *they must all be purchased before your departure,* as these are incentive passes for foreign travel. Contact Rail Europe (in U.S., ☎ *[800] 438-7245*), CIT or any travel agent. For the Italian Railways alone, there are special reductions for anyone under 26 holding the *Cartaverde* (check with CIT or travel agents), there are reductions for children under 11, families with the *Carta Famiglia,* and for those over 60 with the *Carta d'Argento* (all must be purchased in Italy). In addition, there is the *Biglietto Chilometrico* pass, which permits up to 3000 kilometers (1875 miles) of travel in up to 20 trips within two months for up to five people (not necessarily related)—that is, if three of you are traveling together, you need travel only 1000 km each to make efficient use of the pass. *But* you need to validate each time, so you don't avoid ticket lines, and you must pay supplements on the rapido lines. It can be purchased in Italy or at any CIT office (see "Planning Aids").

Ferries

Ferries cross the Lombardy lakes. They link resort islands like Capri and Sardinia to the mainland, and they provide the only non-air route to Sicily. In addition, Adriatic ports provide service to Greece (Brindisi and Bari). More information is specified under the appropriate region and city. For domestic crossings, Tirrenia is the largest shipping line. If you wish to reserve a cabin for an overnight crossing, or plan to take a car, say from Genoa to Palermo, then you can reserve in advance in the U.S. Do so as far in advance as possible for the summer months by contacting a travel agent.

Bus

Within Europe most long-distance travel is by train. However, *Europabus* is a leisurely way to explore not just Italy, but also other countries. The price of a ticket really is for a tour that includes guides, hotels, and many meals. For information, check with CIT (see "Planning Aids"), the Italian representative. However, *pullman*, (Italian for intercity or long distance buses) is an invaluable means of travel within Italy. They supplement the areas where rail connections are non-existent (such as Florence to Siena) or a bit too *locali* (Siena to Rome) and they can be the most efficient means of travel in some *regioni*, such as Sicily where the highways are often better than the tracks. In fact, *pullman* is another reason not to purchase a Eurail pass if you are traveling only in Italy. Bus information is listed under the regional and city destination sections. Usually these local companies operate from the streets around the train station, rather than from terminals, and have nearby offices for the purchase of tickets, or you purchase on board.

Car Rentals

There is nothing more wonderful than ambling along country roads, pulling into villages as you wish, and stopping at wine estates or old farmhouses renovated into good restaurants. Such itineraries are given under the destination chapters along with an indication of how to get around by bus or train. In truth, a car offers the most spontaneity. It also can be one of the most expensive items of your trip. *Gasoline costs about $5 per gallon and autostrada tolls, particularly in the north, can be stunning* (the 50 miles between Lucca and Florence, for example, cost L6500). In addition, there are no "rent-a-wreck" or bargain deals as we know them in the U.S.

PRACTICAL TIPS

All cars with foreign plates qualify for emergency services (dial 116) by ACI, the AAA of Italy. Cars rented from the Milan and Rome airports also qualify for free towing service as long as you can produce an international plane ticket and rental agreement. The ACI map, "Italia No Problems," available at border tourism offices, is full of helpful tips and emergency numbers. For more information, call ACI ☎ (06) 44-77 and ask for their foreign assistance office.

You might appreciate some strategies for controlling the total cost. *First*, check whether your flight includes a fly/drive option that might bring you some savings. There are even Eurail pass options tied into discounted car rentals. **Whatever you do, reserve before departure**: rates are highest when arranged in Italy. *Second*, plan your itinerary to make the best use of a car. If you are beginning in Rome, say, don't pick up your car at the airport; wait until you are leaving the city. (Although you'll lose out on free towing service from ACI, you'll avoid a hefty airport surcharge on car rentals). Further, since drop-off charges are minimal in Italy, don't keep your car when staying for several days in a city–you'll save on parking as well as rental fees. *Third*, avoid paying collision damage insurance that can add from $5 to $10 per day to your rental cost. Many credit cards now have collision damage waiver policies (called "CDW") if you refuse the collision coverage and charge the rental to their card. If a rental agency refuses to allow you waive their collision damage, look for another agency. (**However, make sure your credit card covers Italy in its policy and make sure you understand the procedures.**) *Fourth*, look for a rental *with* unlimited mileage—costs per kilometer add up too quickly. *Fifth*, if you can, forego costly A/C, automatic shift, and large cars. *Sixth*, shop around. We've found Maiellano Tours (☎ *[212] 687-7725* in New York or through travel agents) to have some of the best rates. But if you are traveling for a long period of time (at least three weeks), consider leasing a Renault (☎ *[800] 221-1052* or *[212] 532-1221* in New York) or a Peugeot (☎ *[800] 678-0678, FAX [914] 835-5449*). Even if you have no desire to visit France, by flying to Nice you are only 25 miles from the Italian border and within easy driving distance of northern destinations (see *Land Routes into Italy*). Even though you can't charge it (and avoid the collision damage waiver) and even though you add mileage to your destination, the cost more than compensates. *Last*, when comparison shopping, make sure the price reflects the tax (18 percent), the mileage permitted, the total insurance fees and any drop-off surcharges, or airport pick-up fees, as well as the basic rate.

PRACTICAL TRAVEL INFORMATION

AUTHOR'S OBSERVATION

As if car rentals were not already too expensive, Italian rental agencies have made it more intimidating for motorists to exercise the CDW option (which may be why American Express and Diners Club have dropped coverage of Italy from their policies). Basically, Italian agencies put a hold on your credit card for sizeable sums–U.S. $900 was our recent experience; others have reported more–against future damages. Of course, none of this is charged to your card unless damage actually occurs and then your credit card policy should make payment. But many renters are deterred because, depending on their line of credit, the hold potentially ties up use of their card during the trip. If you have multiple credit cards, fight back: opt for the collision damage waiver.

Driving Tips

Although Italy has one of the highest accident rates in Europe, you'll be pleased to know that its death rate is one of the lowest and its accident rate has been declining. Its toll highways (*autostrade*, marked "A" on green road signs) are generally well-maintained. Difficulties of driving have more to do with truck congestion (especially bad on the GRA ring road around Rome, the road from Naples to Sorrento, and A-4, on the Milan to Venice run) and an adjustment to signs and different driving practices. The following tips might make your trip easier.

1. Buy a good road map.

2. Write the Italian Government Travel Office (see "Planning Aids") for information on traffic regulations and highway conditions.

3. Make sure you have an Italian phrase book, unless you already know how to say "fill it up" and can understand "*rallentare.*"

4. Road conditions—congestion, repairs, fog, ice, etc.—are flashed on *autostrada* signs with information on the towns between which the conditions are occurring. Since this information is often too late for making a detour, dial *autostrada* information in Rome (☎ *[06] 4363-2121*). In the winter, you should at least check the deadly fog conditions before setting out in northern Italy where 200-car pileups are not unheard of. Also beware of secondary roads along the coast during summer vacations—you'll find yourself at a standstill.

5. Speed limits on the *autostrade* are 110 kph (68 mph) for little cars; 130 kph (81 mph) for those with engines more powerful than 1100 cc. Fines for violations are hefty. On toll-free, limited access highways the speed limit for all cars is 110 kph; for secondary roads (SS roads), 90 kph (56 mph).

6. Italians drive with little space between vehicles, almost tailgating at 100 mph until they can pass! When you see one of those fast-moving Mercedes bearing down on you with flashing headlights in the passing lane, move over.

7. ACI, the Italian Automobile Club, maintains SOS phones every 2 km on the *autostrade*, here and there on some secondary roads. Otherwise, dial 116 to get service.

8. The best time to enter a town, and especially a city, is around 1:30 or 2 p.m. when everyone is at lunch. The congestion will have disappeared and you might even find parking easily. This is also a good time to travel on country roads that pass through towns. And Sunday is pretty good, too.

9. The *centro storico*, or historic center, of many towns has limited car access. In July and August, some places control crowd levels by not permitting cars into the center at all, only taxis. However, if you have a hotel reservation you are permitted to drive to your hotel to at least drop off luggage, and when possible, to park your car. Even during most of the year, there are traffic-free areas. In walled towns, you might find it simplest to park in the lots usually available on the perimeter. Or follow the blue "P" (parking) signs. If you are leaving belongings on the car seat, try to find a garage or guarded car park *(guardici)*—this is essential in large cities.

10. Gasoline, or *benzina*, stations usually open 7 a.m.–12:30 p.m., 3:30–6:30 p.m. or, in summer, 7:30 p.m. Many close Sunday and holidays but a few are self-service, operating automatically with a 5000 or 10,000 lira note. On the *autostrade* stations remain open 24-hours. *Benzina* is sold by the liter; per gallon cost is about $5.

11. During the winter, many major cities occasionally limit car access because of pollution caused by a combination of heating plants and gas fumes. These limitations apply temporarily, but often with no more warning than the morning's air quality index. Sometimes the restrictions, such as circulation for only odd-numbered (*dis-*

pari) license plates on odd-numbered days, even-numbered *(pari)* on others, exempt "out-of-state" license plate cars with catalytic converters. Check for more timely details about your destination with Autostrade Information (☎ *[06] 4363-2121* for English version), car rental agencies or tourist offices.

Danger

No entry

Closed to all vehicles in both directions

Yield

Oncoming traffic has priority

Tourist information

Parking prohibited or restricted

Standing and parking prohibited or restricted

Speed limit (in kilometers per hour)

End of speed limit

Uneven Road

End restriction

Road Signs

Although standardized for Europe, many of the signs aren't readily comprehensible to travelers from across the Atlantic. Note that red rimmed signs announce prohibitions and round signs are used to announce restrictions (or the end of them), green ones lead you to "A" roads, called *autostrade*, blue ones to secondary or "SS" roads.

Traveling in Italy

Sightseeing Tips

Opening hours have greatly expanded in recent years—some major *churches* remain open throughout the day (most still close, however, somewhere between noon and 4:30), as do major urban museums. It is not uncommon, however, to find museums holding firmly to the "9 a.m.–2 p.m., Sun 9 a.m.–1 p.m., closed Monday" schedule. So you might want to save church visits and outdoor sights for the afternoon. *Outdoor monuments,* such as ruins or country villas, gardens and the like, more often remain open throughout the day, from 9 a.m. until an hour before sunset. In fact, the hours for even indoor museums can vary with the season, longest in the peak season of summer, greatly curtailed in winter. Although specific hours are listed in the text of this guide, it's best to remain flexible. New hours might be posted suddenly, or a holiday (see above) might find a museum with too few workers to remain open. Off-season, also, is a time for repairs and rearrangements, so that you might find the gallery of a museum closed temporarily. A few strategies are in order: Try to arrive an hour before closing time to avoid finding the ticket office shut down. Before going out of your way to a site, try to check first that its hours haven't changed or renovations haven't closed it—especially in the off season. In reading schedules, know that Sundays are holidays, so that *festivi* refers to Sunday hours as well as those for holidays (see "National Holidays" above).

PRACTICAL TIPS

Churches and some palazzi have coin-operated light machines to illuminate works of art. It's easy to go through pounds of 100-, 200-, and 500-lira coins. Keep a supply handy. Sunday morning masses can cut off access to some chapels. In towns where you plan to visit several museums, check locally for one-price discounted passes–an increasingly popular option that is noted under our destination chapters.

Shopping

Although you might actually find better bargains on Italian clothing in U.S. discount stores, you certainly won't find the choice available in Italy. Also, the trendy housewares and the art galleries are fun to browse and shop in. In this increasingly hi-tech and industrial society, craft traditions that survive can produce quite costly items, and outdoor markets (bargain before purchasing) can be more interesting for the people than the wares. When a city or area has specialized wares, you'll find them described along with shops in which to buy them. Although large department stores remain open through the day, the majority of shops follow their traditional hours: *9 a.m. till 12:30 or 1 p.m., then 4 or 5 p.m. till 7:30–8 p.m.* Except during peak season at resorts or Christmas, all used to close on Sunday and an additional half day, usually Monday morning. *Local laws, however, in some of the larger cities now permit Sunday openings year-round and an increasing number of shops are doing just that in Rome, Milan, Venice and weekend resort areas.*

A Value Added Tax (VAT) is added to most items. You can claim a refund only for those purchases that add up to at least L520,000 at a single shop. They must be charged on major credit cards, and you must keep the *ricevuta fiscale,* or official receipt. To claim your refund (18 percent on clothing, 38 percent for jewelry) present the receipt and purchases to a customs officer when you are leaving Italy (difficult if your train is pulling out). The tax credit is applied to your credit card account.

Italian sizes are the same as the rest of the continent but distinct from British and American sizes. Salespeople can be helpful in suggesting the right size, but a conversion table might help, too. See **chart**.

| CLOTHING CONVERSION TABLE | | | | | |
Men	U.S.	It.	Women	U.S.	It.
Suits and Overcoats	36	46	Clothes	8	42
	38	48		10	44
	40	50		12	46
	42	52		14	48
Shirts	14	36	Shoes	5	35
	14.5	37		6	36
	15	38		7	37
	15.5	39		8	38
	16	41		9	39
	16.5	42			
	17	43			
			Children		
				4	125
Shoes	7	41		6	135
	8	42		8	150
	10	44		10	155
	11	45		12	160
	12	46		14	165

PRACTICAL TRAVEL INFORMATION

Crime

Everyone who goes to the movies knows about Italy's organized crime, based in Sicily, Naples, and Calabria. Even if the Italian government's all-out effort to end such crime doesn't succeed before your visit, it is really not organized crime, with its specific hit targets, that is the traveler's problem. Fortunately, crime in Italy is not routinely violent, so that travelers need concern themselves primarily with theft, especially pickpockets and purse snatchers, particularly in urban areas. A few precautions, such as the following, are recommended and you can call the U.S. State Department ☎ *(202) 647-5225* for the latest crime scams listed on a 24-hour, touch-tone-operated tape:

Be on the lookout for pickpockets (including the notorious gypsies who work in pairs or groups to distract you with a newspaper or baby) around train stations, in crowded buses and in flea markets.

Wear a money belt, or necklace pouch, or money clip tucked inside your waistband; put valuables in an unexpected spot—an inside jacket pocket, not the rear pants pocket.

Don't carry all your valuables with you. If you can, leave some of your money and even your passport (if you're not changing money) in the hotel's safe (*cassa di sicurezza*)—half of all thefts occur from hotel rooms.

Keep the numbers of traveler's checks listed separate from the checks themselves, along with your passport number and the place and date of issuance. And you might copy airline tickets and carry an expired passport to facilitate obtaining a new one.

If you find the streets around your hotel empty out at dark, check with reception about the safety of walking at night. In large cities, you might check about neighborhoods to be avoided (they rarely include the sightseeing area, especially in peak season—Italians love the historic centers of their towns so usually they are the most vibrant and safest part).

Don't leave valuables in a car, or if you do, put them in the trunk and the car in a guarded lot ("guardici"). In large southern port cities, pay for a garage.

Don't check baggage on trains.

Don't wear expensive jewelry, particularly south of Rome.

Police

There are many parallel police forces in Italy. Sorting them out can be confusing. The *Carabinieri* (part of the army) and the *Polizia Urbana* both deal with crime and each has emergency numbers to call (112 and 113) for prompt assistance; that for the Carabinieri (112) is more likely to reach someone English speaking. The more local *Vigili Urbani* deal with traffic matters, but also are often trained to give directions to tourists. The *Questura*, or foreign office, is where you register and receive permits for extended stays. In case of theft, you'll need a report from the Polizia or Carabinieri, for insurance reimbursement.

Tipping

Usually you tip in Italy when you would in the U.S. Despite the fact that service charges already are included in hotel and restaurant bills, these formal fees don't mean that tipping is inappropriate. They do mean that you normally shouldn't tip as much as at home. At a hotel, tip the doorman for calling a cab (L500), the bellhop for carrying your bags (L1,000–L1,500 each bag) or for room service (L1,000). Tip the concierge for a service rendered (maybe L5,000 or 10 to 15 percent of service, depending on quality of hotel and difficulty of service) and the chambermaid (L1,000 to L1,500 a day, less for long stays). When eating, a good rule of thumb is that even with the service already added to the bill, you should leave a little something extra. At a pizzeria or for a *prezzo fisso* meal it could be simply L500 to L1,000, the same for table service at a cafe, yet only a few hundred lira at the counter. At a good restaurant, plan on adding 5 percent to 10 percent, the lesser amount when the bill is high—some Italians tell us they don't think in terms of percentages, but simply tip between L5,000 and L10,000 depending on the quality of service, for two at a good restaurant.

Porters at terminals charge set fees, but you still might add L500 as a tip. Taxi drivers expect about 10 percent but you might consider a flat fee if the tab is high. Guides are tipped around L2,000–L2,500 per person, or 15 percent of the cost. Bathroom attendants expect L200–L300, maybe L500 in better establishments. Hairdressers in a neighborhood shop might receive a L2000 tip, but if you have more than a haircut, tip more.

Urban Transit

Whether you're riding a *city bus* or *subway*, or a *ferry* on a Venetian canal, you need to purchase your ticket in advance (at *tabacchi*, cigarette shops marked with "T" or newsstands in cities, at boat landings otherwise). Upon boarding a bus (usually the rear door is for boarding only; the center or, if nonexistent, the front door, for exiting), cancel your ticket in the machine. At subway platforms and ferry docks, do the same (sometimes boat officials cancel on board if there are no machines). The reason for this elaborate explanation, repeated often later on, is that you can be fined and embarrassed if you are found on board without a cancelled ticket. True, you won't see many Italians cancelling their tickets, but most operate with monthly passes. Special passes that may be useful to tourists are mentioned under specific destinations in the directory.

Official taxis are clearly marked; more often than not they are yellow or white and with meters. Even with the meter thrown, you have to consider that many meters have not been adjusted for price increases (there's a conversion chart the driver can show you). Also extra fees are common for airport trips, for night service (10 p.m.–7. a.m.), for luggage, holidays. You might ask for an estimated price before getting in for airport rides, and always when the meter isn't thrown.

Mail

The postal service can be completely unreliable. With luck, air mail letters to and from the U.S. take ten days, but three weeks is common, and longer not unheard of. For such service, you also pay more, about twice U.S. rates. Express mail service (C.A.I.) to North America, however, is available at competitive rates. To save money on air mail, you might purchase prepaid aerograms from the post office and send post cards with only a five-word greeting (more is the price of a letter). However, never send anything less than *via aerea* (air mail), except within Italy, when *raccomandata* (registered) and *espresso* (express) are better between cities without airports. You can buy stamps at face value at *tabacchi* (tobacco shops, marked with "T") or at the post office. Always mail your letters from the boxes just in front of the post office. Opening hours vary depending on whether they are the main office or not, but they at least are open 8:15 a.m.–2 p.m., till noon Saturday & last day of month, closed Sunday—they are the least busy during the Italian lunch that begins around 1 p.m.

To receive mail you can have a letter marked "Fermo Posta" sent to you at any town followed with the postal code (see appropriate destination chapters). Pick it up at the main post office. It might be safer to use the address of a hotel (where you have a reservation) or American Express offices (service available sometimes for cardholders only or at fee—check in advance with American Express).

Telegrams/Fax

Always sent through the post office, international telegrams are not cheap. Night letters are a little lower in price. If your message is lengthy, you might just phone instead, or look for shops or SIP and ASST telephone centers with public **fax machines**.

Telephone

Even if you plan to use your hotel phone (and pay surcharges), you sometimes will find yourself in need of a public phone. Phones accept *gettoni* (tokens worth L200), and/or 100-, 200- and 500-lira coins; some accept only credit cards or magnetic cards. They never hum or change tone while you dial, but do have a different tone for busy and ringing. **They may take over 30 seconds to connect, so wait for the ring**. To make a long distance call within Italy, add anywhere from six to ten coins (you can get them all back by pushing the return button at the end), and then dial the area code (listed in directory under appropriate destination chapter and hotel appendix) and the number. With each beep during your call, add another gettone.

There also are **magnetic phone cards** *(scheda telefonica)* purchased from machines (at SIP or Telcom telephone offices, *stazioni*) and over the counter (at *tabacchi*) and worth L5000, L10,000 or L15,000. Once you get the knack of using these cards, you'll wonder how you ever lived without them. Just follow these instructions:

- Break off the perforated corner of the card
- Lift the receiver of the special public phones
- Insert the card with the black T face-up—push it all the way into the machine until it disappears
- Dial the number
- When you hang up, the card reappears, but from a different, lower slot.

- If any money remains (how much is indicated on the phone), you can reuse the card for other calls.

International and intercontinental calls cannot be made from all public phones, but usually any phone accepting a magnetic card can connect you anywhere. Often, however, it's easiest to go to a phone office (SIP or ASST or Telcom, listed under city directories) where, even when fully automated, there are instructions and change machines and a choice of phones (including those accepting Visa and Master credit cards); at a few offices, found most often in train stations, there's a desk clerk who has you write down the desired number, points you to a booth, and meters your call *(telefone a scatti)*. Afterwards, you pay the clerk.

PRACTICAL TIPS

Italy's phone system is undergoing major upgrading. Most phone numbers will change in the next few years. You'll definitely want to know that dialing 12 reaches directory assistance for all of Italy (English sometimes spoken).

Peak rates to North America are charged weekdays 2–7 p.m., weekends 8 a.m.–2 p.m. International calls are taxed exorbitantly so that it is cheaper to call Italy from the U.S. than vice versa, although brief, off-peak calls have become more competitive. Make a quick collect call (dial ☎ *170* for international operator; dial 15 for Europe) and have someone call you back. Better yet, calling card holders for **AT&T** ☎ *(172-1011)*, **Sprint** ☎ *(172-1877)*, or **MCI** ☎ *(172-1022)* should use the indicated international access codes to charge calls from Italy at U.S. operator-assisted rates.

To directly dial Italy from the U.S. or Europe, mark your telephone company's international code, then add 39 for Italy plus the area code minus the first 0 (see appropriate destination chapters or hotel appendix), then add the phone number.

To call the U.S. without a calling card or operator, dial 001 (for U.S. and Canada), then the area code and number. Dialing 170 reaches an English-speaking operator.

Measurements

The metric system is in use in Italy so prices are not for miles but kilometers (0.62 mile), not for pounds but kilos (chilo; 2.2 pounds), not for quarts but liters (1.03 quarts), and not for feet but meters (3.3 feet).

Time Zones

Italy is six hours ahead of New York, nine hours more along in the day than Los Angeles. It changes to Daylight Savings Time the last Sunday in March, making it seven hours ahead of New York for one week, and then reverts to

Standard Time the last Sunday in October, making the time difference six hours again.

Miscellaneous

Remember there are dress codes for visiting churches. • Carry extra 100- and 200-lira coins for small fees, tips, and illuminating works of art. • *Public Bathrooms (WC, toelette* or *gabinetto)* can often be found in peak season near the cathedral or main piazza, and, in the north, can be surprisingly clean. Museums usually have facilities, and restaurants, of course, and cafes (choose a fancy one, if you can). On the road, cafes usually will do; facilities on the *autostrade* are excellent. • **Expressions to watch for**: *Piano Basso* (PB) is our first floor, so *piano 1* is the second floor. • H(ot) and C(old) on spigots are fortunately more often indicated by red and blue dots since "C" is for *caldo*, or hot. • Most recognize *senora* for woman and *senore* for man, but don't realize the pitfalls with the plurals, *senore*, for women, *senori*, for men. The Italians thoughtfully tend to avoid these words in marking their *gabinetti*. • *Chiuso*, or closed, is a word often encountered and *sciopero*, or strike, is often the reason. • Dates in museums use "a.C.," not "B.C." and "d.C.," not "A.D." • *Centro storico* is usually what you're looking for—the historic center of town.

Eating in Italy: Insiders' Tips

Although the prices of restaurants are explained in the introduction, and various cuisines and wines of Italy are described under each region, you might also want a few hints about dining practices.

Coffee and Brioche

The American breakfast is not only difficult to find, but when it is found, its price might ruin your appetite. Some first-class hotels offer cheeses and cold cuts, canned juice, and dry cereals in addition to the more traditional continental breakfast of *cappuccino* (expresso with steamed milk, and sometimes a dash of cinnamon) or *caffe latte* (expresso with heated milk) and some rolls, usually a sweetened *cornetta*, a brioche that can be filled with cream or jelly, or a *sfogliatelle*, flatter, like a ricotta-filled Danish. Italians eat this breakfast (*la colazione*) on the run, standing at the counter in a cafe. This is the cheapest way to breakfast. You might consider adding some fruit purchased at a store or market. If you don't like milk in your coffee, and you require a large cup or two every morning, then you might ask for a *caffe americano*. If this elicits only a blank expression, ask for a *caffe lungo* (they add a bit more water to the expresso) or see what *caffe largo* brings forth. The responses will definitely vary with the region and familiarity in serving tourists. Or perhaps you like expresso (*espresso* in Italian, but really simply *caffe*) but not first thing in the morning—you can cut it with just a drop or two of steamed milk (*caffe macchiato*—there's also *latte macchiato*, or warm milk with a drop of coffee). And decaf, when available, is *caffe Hag*.

Caffe Manners

Having adjusted to the Italian breakfast, you need to know a bit about the cafe routine. First and foremost, cafes are called *caffe* sometimes, usually when they are a bit elegant with a pastry shop, and *bar* almost always. Secondly, they have two prices, both posted near the cash register—one for counter service (*al banco*) and the other for table service (*al tavola*), the latter commonly costing twice as much for drinks and desserts, but not usually meals. For counter service, you need to go to the cash register and pay in advance and then present your receipt (or *scontrino*) to the counterperson. Some people seem daunted by all the Italian involved in this, but really it's no different from ordering for table service and more often than not you can simply point to what you want, and the counterperson will relay the information to the cashier. (Just try it, you'll see it's easy.)

Main Meals

Whether there is a difference between lunch *(pranzo)* and dinner *(cena)*, depends on where you eat. Restaurants have the same menu, whether it's served from *12:30–2:30 p.m. or 7–10 p.m.* (hours in cities often are a bit later, and on the whole, northerners eat earlier than Romans and southerners). But some offer a *menu turistico* at lunch, a set price *(prezzo fisso)* meal that includes cover (*coperto*, a nonnegotiable fee for place settings and bread) and service as well as several courses. Sometimes mineral water and wine also are included. These meals can be tedious except when they become *menu degustazione* at the finer establishments, where the chef has arranged a sampling of his or her specialities for the day. A *menu turistico* can save you money, a *degustazione* may not (also it is just as often available in the evenings).

Since you probably don't want to eat two full meals a day every day, this raises the issue of how to eat one meal lightly. And you may not want to order even one Italian meal on a daily basis, since it ordinarily includes more courses than we're used to—at least an antipasto (appetizer) or pasta, if not both, and at least an entree of meat or fish and a *contorno*, or vegetable (normally everything is a la carte, even the *contorni*, from spinach to a tossed salad). Dessert is optional. Although the finest, most expensive *ristorante* expects you to indulge in a full meal, **most restaurants let you be more selective—you might have only half a pasta course (mezza porcione) or even eliminate the entree**. Even more flexible are the trattorias where you might treat yourself at the antipasto table, if there is one, and follow up with a bowl of soup. Still, this might be either too much or too costly, especially twice a day.

PRACTICAL TRAVEL INFORMATION

Pizzerias

In the evening, a *pizzeria* might be just what you want. Most open only at night, and some serve more than just pizza. The custom is a pizza a person, as they are smaller and lighter (less cheese) than in the U.S. Italians eat them with knives and forks. (Beware: a *peperone* pizza is with roasted sweet peppers. For that other stuff, ask for *salsiccia calabrese* or *salsiccia piccante*.)

Snacks and Picnics

PRACTICAL TRAVEL INFORMATION

But what to do when you really want a mere snack or salad? Many cafes have *panini* (Italian sandwiches with a slice of cheese or prosciutto), *toast* (grilled cheese sandwich), or *tramezzini*, an array of white bread sandwiches, and sometimes they serve local specialties, too. *Alimentari*, small groceries, and *salumerie*, cheese and cold-cut stores, often will make you a *panino* for *portare via* (take out) and almost any *forno*, or bakery, sells thick pizza by the slice (really by the kilo) just before the lunch closing. *Rosticcerie*, with a few tables or stools for quickly eating what is often mediocre food, do have roasted chickens for takeout. Which brings us to the picnic, an especially great way of sampling the wines and foods of Italy, whether in a city park or along a country road. Again, if you don't speak Italian, you'll find that pointing and Italian courtesy will get you through at the shops. Expect to say how much you want (remember prices are in kilos, and 100 grams, over 3 ounces and called an *etto*, is quite a lot of prosciutto for two Italian-style sandwiches) and to pay before receiving your package. Special places to shop for picnics and snacks are listed under the destination chapters in the directories and the restaurant sections.

Soup and Salad

Just a salad or soup and salad? That's difficult, although in some sophisticated cities, such as Bologna and Milan, *sala da te* and one-course restaurants offering lighter food and salads (*insalatone*, or "large" salads) are becoming stylish. Some gourmet *alimentari* offer marinated vegetables, but generally, it's easier to settle for some fruit from a shop or market. You might just select vegetables and salad at a full service *enoteca* or *viniero* (tavern), or even at the much despised *tavola calda* (cafeteria), but look the food over first—it can be some of the worst in Italy. When we know of good places to eat lightly or to have a salad, we list them under the appropriate destination chapter.

Desserts

Desserts, such as cookies and even fruit pies (crostata), can be found in the *forni* but more sumptuous desserts, such as *canoli*, shells filled with sweetened ricotta, or *tiramisu*, a chocolate-and-cream delight, are found at *pasticcerie*, or pastry shops most often attached to a cafe. *Gelato*, Italian ice cream renowned for the intensity of its flavors, from *gianduia* (hazelnut milk chocolate) to *lampone* (raspberry), can be found at cafes (best to look for the *produzione propia* sign for "house made") and *gelaterie* that seldom sell any-thing else. If you're in doubt about a flavor you might ask for *un assaggio* ("a taste").

Wines

Wines are described later under the appropriate region and major cities. There are few areas that don't produce wines in Italy, but certainly those from Piedmont, the Veneto, and Tuscany are the most respected. In recent decades there has been an upgrading in Italian wines, brought about by new standards for labeling. "Chianti," for example, no longer can simply be ap-plied to any wine a producer wishes, but now, when "DOC" or "DOCG" appear on the label you are guaranteed that it is from the traditional district of Tuscany and that its grape contents satisfy the new standards. DOCG sometimes is reserved by a vineyard for its better DOC wines. *But don't limit yourself to these classifications alone. Some of the most prestigious wines aren't yet included under these standards, because they include nontraditional grapes—like cabernet in the Chianti region; some of the most delightful table wines, young and fruity whites, freshly pressed novella reds come without such guarantees.* In 1992 a new classification, "IGT," was introduced in an at-tempt to include many of these wines. Usually simple trattorias have only the local wine or *vino di casa*, most often served unmarked in a carafe. The best restaurants seldom have carafe wine, but their markup is not usually as great as in the U.S. Yet you might still want to visit a good wine shop, or enoteca, to purchase wine. These sometimes are straightforward shops, but many times they also are wine bars that provide the more affordable opportunity to taste the great wines, such as Barolo and Amarone, by the glass.

Miscellaneous Tips

A few other items: Whole fish and some meats, such as steak Florentino, are priced by the *etto*, or 100 grams, on menus. To get a rough estimate of an order, triple that price or, when you are shown the fish or steak, ask how much the one you select will cost. • **Reservations:** You can't go wrong mak-ing reservations—even if the place is empty, you haven't lost anything. • **Or-dering:** Italians no more than sit down and they order their mineral water (*con gas*, for carbonated) and wine, and sometimes even an appetizer. So when your waiter appears too quickly, you can order these items too. If you aren't given enough time to decide, just say *un attimo* (one moment). • **Shop Hours:** 8 or 9 a.m.–1 p.m., 4:30 or 5–7:30 or 8 p.m., closed Sunday and one other afternoon that varies with the city and the season, but usually it's Wednesday or Thursday, except July and August when it is Saturday instead. • **Ferragosto:** Not only are the food shops closed from Saturday at lunch until Monday morning, but many restaurants close up for vacation during these last two weeks of August. It can be frustrating, especially on weekends. If you find yourself caught without a restaurant or picnic cache, look for a bar/

cafe—usually you can buy a bottle of milk or a snack—or seek out a hotel restaurant. • **Food Glossary:** For menu reading, check the Italian vocabulary in the appendices.

Emergencies

• If you are in danger or require immediate medical assistance, dial ☎ *112* or ☎ *113*, for the police.

• If your car breaks down, dial ☎ *116* for towing by the Automobile Club of Italy; on autostrade, ACI has emergency phones every few kilometers.

• Consulates provide invaluable services in case of emergencies. They can replace lost passports, advise you on doctors and medical facilities in case of injury and serious illness, explain Italian law, but not circumvent it, and refer you to a lawyer in case of arrest. They also can contact your family in case of such emergencies. The embassies in Rome all have 24-hour emergency numbers (U.S., ☎ *[06] 46-741;* Canada, ☎ *[06] 440-2991;* Great Britain, ☎ *[06] 482-5551*), as do the consulates in cities like Milan, Florence, and Naples. Honorary consuls often are located in other towns. For phone numbers and listings, contact the embassy or check the directories in the destination chapters.

ART IN ITALY

Gold mosaics gleam in the light of Sant' Appolinare Nuovo, Ravenna.

Italy is so rich in art that **UNESCO** estimates it holds within its borders 80 percent of Europe's artistic heritage, and 40 percent of the world's. In a country that is merely the size of California, art more than fills countless museums and churches. It spills over hillsides with Greek temples and Roman amphitheaters and burrows into them with Etruscan tombs. It graces piazzas and bridges, and embraces entire towns. It can be found just about everywhere with such stupefying density as to strain the Italian treasury for its preservation.

Italy has so dominated Western art history that it has even created the terminology—the "Gothic" period referring to the "barbarian" style created beyond its side of the Alps, the "Middle Ages" being that less glorious peri-

45

od between *its* ancient Roman heritage and its revival in the Renaissance. In truth, Italy's classical roots have inspired much of its art, not just the Renaissance. The fascination with the human form, appropriate for those naked gods of the Greeks and Romans, would constantly recur in Italian art, from the simple figures on northern Romanesque portals through 19th-century Neoclassicism. It would even lead to the permanent schism between Rome and the Eastern Church in the 8th century. The Roman arch, the ancient basilica and rotunda would constantly inspire, even when the Gothic cathedral did not. The sheer monumentality of ancient Roman art would transform the Early Renaissance into the High and create a Baroque style to proclaim to the Protestants victory over the reformed Catholic Church.

Yet to speak of Italian art is somewhat misleading. *There rarely was an Italy to create "its" art.* Only the south was part of Magna Graecia, not Rome or the north. Ravenna and Venice belonged to Byzantium, not Florence. Palermo was conquered by the Normans, Milan by the Lombards. Naples was alternately ruled by Spain and France. Rome, and only Rome, was the capital of the Catholic Church. Throughout the shifting alliances and formations of independent states, Italy was unified only under ancient Rome and not again until 1870, when it became a modern nation. Such political fragmentation produced an extraordinary diversity of styles in any given period, from the Lombard Romanesque to the Norman, from the Florentine Renaissance style to the Venetian and Roman.

The following description of artistic periods can only introduce the major artists and trends, and by no means can exhaust every stylistic variation or even mention every worthy artist. Local schools are more thoroughly explored under the regional "History and Art" sections.

Classical (c. 750 B.C.–A.D. 330)

Greek (8th-3rd century B.C.)

The coasts of Sicily and southern Italy formed the limits of the known world for the Greeks. Here, their myths had Ulysses undergo his trials with the wind god and Cyclops, and here, too, he would find the entrance to Hades as well as the Elysian Fields. By the 8th century, the Greeks had established cities in this region; Syracuse in Sicily and Cumae near Naples were among the earliest. The cities would multiply and expand, becoming some of the most powerful in the Greek world. The Etruscans prevented settlements along the north Tyrrhenian coast, and eventually Rome would conquer all these cities of Magna Graecia. But from the 6th through the 5th centuries magnificent Doric temples would be built in both Sicily (at Selinunte, Agrigento, and Segesta) and southern Italy, at places such as Paestum. These temples still stand today as some of the finest examples of Greek architecture, their fluted columns with unadorned Doric capitals stoutly rising to support the entablature and pediment above. Although only a few temples were sculpted with reliefs (museums at Paestum and Palermo), Greek sculpture was nonetheless imported and included copies of the great sculptors Pheidias, Myron, and Praxiteles, of the Classical period (490-320 B.C.) as well as the less idealized and more vigorous works by Lyssipus and other Hellenistic artists (320 B.C. into the Roman period). Painting flourished, first in the black-figured vases imported from Corinth and Athens, and later in the more naturalistic red-figured ones that were at first imported from Athens, or Attica, but that by the 5th century B.C. were being produced within Sicily itself. Few Greek wall paintings have survived, but Paestum boasts a rare example in its museum. The art continued through the centuries, but Magna Graecia never took up the later architectural styles of the graceful Ionic order with scrolled capital, or the more ornate Corinthian with its acanthus leaves. However, it did construct some magnificent open-air theaters down into the 3rd century B.C., those at Syracuse and Segesta among them.

While Magna Graecia endowed Italy with its own Greek ruins, the legacy of Greece would be far greater. Its gods would be the Etruscan and Roman gods. Its paintings and sculptures would influence theirs. After Rome conquered Greece, Greek art became its symbol of civilization and culture. Not only were Greek sculptures carried off to the new capital city to be publicly displayed, but Romans commissioned vast numbers of personal copies. Today, Italy is one of the greatest repositories for Greek art, and most that is known about its sculpture has been learned through the marble copies commissioned by the ancients (see museums in Rome, Naples, and Syracuse).

Etruscan (7th–3rd century B.C.)

Around 700 B.C., Etruscan cities emerged throughout most of central Italy—cities like Tarquinia in Latium, Volterra in Tuscany, Perugia in Umbria. Eventually they would bequeath their city plans, their temple architecture, their chariots and their gladiatorial contests to the Romans. Although it's known that the Etruscans simply merged with the Romans, their city walls and arched gates becoming the foundations for Roman ones, their beginnings have been far more baffling. Most scholars now believe that the Etruscans began as the prehistoric peoples of central Italy, called the Villanovans. Great metallurgists with a plentiful supply of iron and other ores, they soon engaged in maritime trade with Greece and the Orient and were stimulated to a higher civilization, now called Etruscan. Their cities have mostly disappeared. Their wooden temples decorated with terracotta ornaments and lifesize figures, like that of the Veii Apollo *(in Villa Giulia, Rome)*, no longer stand. Yet they left archaeologists with tombs filled with most of their belongings—beautifully engraved mirrors, fine bronze figurines, exquisite gold granulated jewelry *(Vatican Museum, Villa Giulia, both in Rome)*, and imported Greek vases, some of the exceptional quality of the Francois krater painted in Athens in the 6th century B.C. *(Museo Archeologico, Florence)*. They also frequently painted their tomb walls, such as the hundreds at *Tarquinia*, with scenes of the afterlife. And their sarcophagi and cremation urns were carved with elaborate scenes from Greek mythology, running the gamut of style from the Greek Classical through the Hellenistic. But the Etruscans' own style infuses their art, often lending it a domesticity not found in Greek art. To the bewilderment of the Greeks, Etruscan women joined their men at banquets, enjoying the music, dancing and food. And they are seen in just these banquet poses atop their sarcophagi and urns, husband and wife reclining in very homey comfort *(Villa Giulia, Rome; Museo Guarnacci, Volterra)*. This Italic realism also informs their magnificent lifesize bronze sculptures and portrait busts, such as that of Brutus and the Capitoline wolf *(Palazzo Conservatori, Rome)*. Their taste for realism and portraiture of both women and men would continue through Roman art, whether funerary or Imperial.

The well-organized Etruscans banded into a league of 12 cities. They flourished well into the 4th century B.C., and to the north they continued longer. At times they expanded to the south near Naples and they pushed north to the foothills of the Alps. But by 90 B.C. they all became citizens of Rome and were forgotten. Now only art in museums and their city walls and tombs speak of their centuries of domination.

Roman (200 B.C.–A.D. 330)

Until the Late Republic (200-27 B.C.), Roman art really didn't distinguish itself from its Greek and Etruscan predecessors. Some say that it never separated itself from Hellenism and, in fact, represents a long and slow decline of Greek art. Yet most scholars today dispute such a simplistic view. Although Roman art embraced the humanistic values of the classical world (at least until the Late Empire) and extolled the artistry of both Etruscan and, especially, Greek artists—it created its own forms in art and put them toward purposes never dreamed of by their predecessors.

As early as the Republican period, Roman borrowing in city planning fused into a new form. In the many colonia, or military camps, built through the growing empire, but especially on the Italian peninsula at this time, the city becomes a Greek grid, but one with Etruscan improvements—two broad main streets organize the town, the decumanus from east to west, the cardo from north to south, and arched gateways define the entrances to the city. Such plans can be seen today in Ostia near Rome and Pompeii and Herculaneum outside of Naples. The arched gates still stand on what was the frontier town of Rimini on the Adriatic, and throughout the Italian peninsula. Such planning would evolve through the later Imperial periods, until the axiality of Roman towns would push into the central square, or forum, and bring you to the raised platform and single front of a temple. Unlike the individualized and independent temples of Greece, Roman buildings related to each other. This is best seen in the capital itself where the construction of enclosed colonnades, or basilicas, and the completion of the Tabularium or archives (78 B.C.) gave a completely Roman definition to the Forum.

And in the private sphere at this time, the Romans created the country villa, a successful fusion of architecture and art with nature. The sculptures that surrounded an atrium pond or fountain were Greek or copies of Greek works, but the purpose was new. The paintings on the villa walls may have followed Greek ones in their impressionistic brush strokes, their use of chiaroscuro. But as the paintings explored greater depth and illusion (60-30 B.C.), they soon turned villa walls into the new genre of idyllic landscapes—bringing the outside into the home. And in both mosaics and paintings the Romans also created still lifes such as never had been seen. The villa form, best preserved at Pompeii and Herculaneum, spread throughout Italy and continued into the Imperial age when Hadrian built his sublime villa at Tivoli (A.D. 138) and Maximian lavished his with exquisite mosaics in Sicily at Piazza Armerina (A.D. 300).

Also emerging in the Late Republic was a wealth of portraiture. Although funerary art always demanded private portraits, the flamboyant and powerful leaders of this period, such as Julius Caesar, Sulla and Pompey, required public monuments as well. The styles would borrow from the realism of both the Etruscans and the heroic idealism of the Greeks, but the most penetrating portrayals would be Roman.

But it is not until the early Imperial period, when Augustus was granted power of emperor in 27 B.C., that Roman art takes on its most public and enduring role—that of propaganda. Greek artists may have carved the reliefs on Augustus' Ara Pacis, or "peace altar" in Rome, but not only is the elegant Classical style wedded with Roman concreteness, it also proclaims Augustus' slogan of peace through power. Such official state art became the medium of communication across the empire, and required a clearly recognizable emperor for its effectiveness. This form of artistic propaganda on the glory of Rome and its emperors soon spread through the empire from Spain to Mesopotamia with countless statues of the armored emperor-as-warrior, or the toga-clad emperor-as-pious-ruler, and eventually even the naked emperor-as-god. The need for propaganda created new forms—the triumphal arch, erected from Augustus' time till Constantine's (A.D. 330) and its variant, the colossal column preferred by Trajan (A.D. 113) and Marcus Aurelius (A.D. 193). Whether as panels on the triumphal arch, or as epic narratives (the first of their kind) spiralling around a column, the propaganda campaign generated some magnificent bas reliefs. The increasingly monumental scale of sculpture and architecture declared the greatness of the empire.

Having chosen to unite its empire through art, the emperors also proved their beneficence by building aqueducts, public baths and theaters (such as the two exceptional ones still seen at Verona to the north and Taormina in Sicily). Such massive undertakings led to the development of the most distinctive contribution of Roman art: its architecture. Since Republican times, the Romans had preferred the vault and arcade to the Greek column and lintel. With their development of concrete, the strength of Roman walls and arches and domes permitted them to envelope space and create monumental interiors. But even this unique accomplishment was given a respectful Greek veneer, with each story defined and adorned by the Greek orders—the first Doric, the second only sometimes Ionic and often Corinthian, and the third Corinthian or a combination of Ionic and Corinthian. These decorations formed a relief on the arcaded facades of buildings like the Colosseum (A.D. 80), and sometimes became a freestanding screen, as on Septimus Severus' triumphal arch (A.D. 203; Roman Forum). By the 4th century, the Romans dropped the classical veneer entirely and built vast and continuous surfaces of brick, such as the walls of Constantine's Basilica (A.D. 313). But whether building a palazzo, temple or law court basilica, the Romans created interiors. Even their theaters and amphitheaters grew side walls to enclose them.

Roman emperors built and adorned cities spread over several continents. And Roman citizens were avid collectors of art, whether for their country villas, home altars, or funerary monuments. The exact style varied over the centuries—that for public art depended on the reigning emperor's tastes, and personal art often followed suit. Under the egomaniac Nero (A.D. 54–68), an ornate Hellenistic style dominated, while under the Stoic Hadrian (A.D. 117–138), the idealized forms of the Classical would be revived. But with Marcus Aurelius (A.D. 161–180), the self-confident and classical ideals displayed in his equestrian statue would begin to fade. Marcus was the last of the great emperors, and with him ended the golden age of Roman art. Then, beginning with Septimus Severus' triumphal arch, classical human proportions were ignored in what is considered a more popular or provincial style, rather than an Imperial one. In the disintegrating phase of the Late Empire (A.D. 283-393) art becomes even less classical, turning instead to Eastern stylization and introspection, such as in Constantine's faraway portrait gaze (colossal head, Palazzo Conservatori, Rome) or the blocklike, almost inhuman forms of the porphyry sculpture "The Tetrarchs," now stuck on the side facade of San Marco in Venice. Whatever the style, the Romans produced an astounding amount of art, leaving for future generations thousands upon thousands of carved monuments, mosaic floors, and painted walls.

When Roman art ends is somewhat of a controversy—even determining when the Empire ends is difficult. Many date the end of the art to the collapse of the Western Empire (A.D. 476), while others see it continuing through the Early Christian phase and into the Byzantine era of Ravenna (6th century), until finally even this lingering of the Eastern Empire disappears, too. For the sake of exploring Early Christian art separately, we shall choose A.D. 330 as our closing date, the year in which the first Christian emperor, Constantine, moved his capital from Rome to Byzantium.

Early Christian & Byzantine (c. 330–800)

Although the first visual images of Christianity appear after A.D. 200 in catacombs from Milan to Syracuse, they initially are more ciphers than art. At times, they are simply indistinguishable from Roman art—reworked pagan sarcophagi or idyllic paintings. After Constantine's edict of A.D. 313 legitimizing Christianity, the forms of Christian art become more elaborate as they move out of the catacombs. Decorated instead are churches—the tribunal of the Roman basilica now the apse for the Christian altar (*Santa Sabina in Rome*, 5th century), the Roman house atrium with fountains now a narthex, or entrance courtyard to the church (*Sant'Ambrogio, Milan*, 4th century), the Roman rotunda now mausoleum churches or freestanding baptisteries (*St. John Lateran in Rome*, 4th century).

Whether church mosaics and frescoes or funerary sarcophagi, the style closely followed that of the Late Empire. What becomes distinctive is the changing symbolism—the sacrificial lamb of the ancients becomes the symbol for Christ; the lyre-playing shepherd Orpheus becomes Christ leading his flock of symbolic sheep out of limbo; the vines and peacocks of Dionysian renewal rites become symbols of Christian resurrection—never more magnificently than in the 4th-century mosaics of *Santa Costanza in Rome*. With time, some of the more blatantly pagan themes would be replaced, and symbols of triumphant emperors would become Christ's triumph over death. By the 5th century, classically executed mosaics depicting scenes from the life of Christ would cover the triumphal arch over the altar of *Santa Maria Maggiore in Rome*, and a crucifixion scene would be carved on the door of *Santa Sabina* (also in Rome), while Christ's immersion in water would be seen in the mosaics of the Neonani Baptistery in Ravenna.

While the classical poses and themes were redefined in Early Christian art, the Late Empire style itself became increasingly appropriate to the new spirituality of the message. With the capital of the Empire in Constantinople, Eastern influences changed the course of the art—the head became frontal, the eyes disproportionately large and abstracted, and the three-dimensionality of naturalism gave way to rhythmic surface patterns. Art no longer concerned itself with the beauty of the classical human form. Sculptors drilled away the individualized portrait; mosaicists assembled mask-like faces that looked inward to the soul; architects stripped facades of columns and arcades, the bricks emphasized the spiritual interior of light and space. The style evolved, becoming increasingly abstract. It became Byzantine (c. A.D. 550) when isolated, almost weightless figures were silhouetted against plain gold backgrounds of the apse mosaic or painted icon.

This other-worldly trend was certainly aided by political events in the West. Not only was Rome sacked by the Goths in A.D. 410, but the entire peninsula was a battleground for centuries—among various northern barbarian groups and between them and the Eastern Empire trying to reestablish itself in the West. Although Byzantium was able to hold on to Sicily and parts of the Adriatic coast around Ravenna and the south, eventually most of Italy was conquered by the Lombards (6th century) and Sicily was lost to the Moslems. Such upheavals hardly supported the self-confidence of classical art.

Amid these turbulent times, the cities of Rome, Milan and Ravenna, seats of the earliest bishoprics, witnessed the greatest evolution of Early Christian art. But it was only in 6th-century Ravenna that Byzantine art flowered so magnificently in the church of San Vitale, an enduring legacy of Justinian's attempt to revive the Western Empire. Justinian's tradition would continue in the "revived Empire" until the 8th century, and Byzantine mosaics and paintings would continue in Italy until the 13th-century fall of Constantinople to the Turks. But classical art was not lost. Even Justinian's Byzantine mosaics are a glorious fusion of Eastern, Christian, and above all, classical chiaroscuro and foreshortening. And if the purely classical was banished from religious art, it flourished in minor arts like ivory carving and appeared on mosaic floors if not mosaic walls. The figural tradition was never abandoned; not in the most rigid Byzantine expression and not in A.D. 726 during the Iconoclastic ban. In Italy, classicism survived not only Christian transformation, but the Dark Ages as well.

Romanesque (1000–1250)

The early Middle Ages is most notable for the monastic movement and the crusades, both of which contributed to Romanesque art. The monastic movement architecturally evolved in northern Europe into French-style abbeys. These monumental and harmoniously proportioned churches had round Roman arches and massively constructed rib vaults. A proliferation of chapels was added to the Early Christian basilica to accommodate so many monks praying a set number of hours each day. Both sculpture and painting were subordinate to this architecture, mere adornments to the altars or Biblical story decorations that happened to be added to the portals. But more Eastern ornamentation was introduced through the crusades—fearsome demons carved on capitals or around portals as warnings against earthly temptations. Painting, where the tradition persisted, remained primarily Byzantine. The Romanesque church was a spiritual space, both serene and austere, where humans were small creatures seeking salvation in God's universe.

Although the French Romanesque abbey occasionally appears in rural Italy, such as Sant'Antimo in Tuscany, more regional styles developed. It can be said that Venice was so Eastern that it skipped the Romanesque entirely, and Rome had so many Early Christian churches, it too participated less significantly in the new style. But everywhere in Italy where the commerce of the crusades reawakened former Roman towns—in the north, where Milan, Piacenza and Modena are stimulated by the trade of Venice; in central Italy, where Pisa is an active maritime power; and in the south, where the Normans established themselves in Apulia and Sicily—new cathedrals are built. The sculpture is more figural than in the rest of Europe, proving the peninsula's deep classical roots. And continuing Early Christian preferences, the Italian church is frequently divided into a freestanding campanile and separate baptistery. But apart from these shared features, regional diversity requires separate consideration of at least three Italian Romanesque styles.

Lombard Romanesque

Some have thought Lombardy the location of the "First Romanesque," where experimentation with vaulting to replace the open-timbered roof of the Early Christian basilica led to the chapel bays, the piers, and the galleries of the Romanesque style. Though the ribbed vaults of Sant'Ambrogio in Milan are no longer believed to be the forerunners of the new style, there is little doubt that Lombardy and Emilia built cathedrals that influenced others—south to Apulia, north to Germany, and west to Barcelona. The flat brick facade of the pure Lombard church was unadorned except for pilasters running the height of the building. At the top, blind arcades or recessed arches joined the pilasters in a design called "Lombard bands." A few reliefs of interlacing designs or demons completed the Lombard cathedral, such as San Michele at Pavia. The Emilian architect Lanfranco added a porch with flanking lions to the central portal at Modena (1099), and the sculptor Wiligelmo added Roman style friezes, narrating Old Testament stories (1100s). Soon the lion porches and the more elaborate sculpture would be found on other northern duomos, at Piacenza, at Verona's San Zeno where Niccolo carved the jambs, and at Parma, where the great sculptor Benedetto Antelami decorated the baptistery with Italy's first Last Judgment scene (late 12th century). The northern style remained austere at the same time that its sculptural style and narratives advanced.

Tuscan Romanesque

Tuscany created a more sumptuous Romanesque style, particularly in architecture. Columns, often reused ones from antiquity, replaced the piers so common in the north and locally quarried marble substituted for Lombard bricks. Although Florence preferred inlaid geometric designs on the marble facades of San Miniato al Monte and its duomo baptistery, *sculpture* was an important element in the rest of Tuscany. At far more influential Pisa, where contrasting marble formed stripes over the duomo facade, and tiers of arcades decorated the upper half, sculpture appeared above the door, on the columns of the arcades, on the pulpits and interior, and even on the bronze doors of Bonnano da Pisa. The Pisan style spread to nearby Lucca, which charmingly enlivened the facade sculpture, to Pistoia, where Gruamonte carved the tympanums, and even as far as Sicily, where Bonnano carved the doors for the Monreale Cathedral. Although painting was not as important as sculpture, Tuscany and Umbria created the 12th-century painted crucifixes that would continue into the Gothic period with the work of Coppo di Marcovaldo and the great Cimabue.

Norman Romanesque

The most lavish and most distinctive form of Romanesque architecture was limited to southern Italy, where the Normans conquered and remained during the 11th and 12th centuries. By utilizing the arts and skills of the diverse peoples they ruled, the Normans created a new style, especially in Sicily. The three masterpieces of the style are found around Palermo: the Cappella Palatina, and the Monreale and Cefalu duomos, each a fusion of Byzantine, Arabic and Roman architecture. From the Arabs came the mosque-like domes, the crenellations and graceful arabesques, the elaborately carved wooden ceilings. From the Greeks came the mosaic tradition resulting in some of the most extensively gold-covered walls in existence. From the Latins to the north came the columns and their carved capitals, interlaced round arches and chevron-designed facades. Together, these elements created solid and powerful churches with elegant interiors in a style that was as Eastern as Romanesque. In Apulia, the style took a purer Latin form, such as at San Nicola in Bari where even the Lombard lion porch is found.

Gothic (1250–1400)

While north of the Alps the Romanesque style evolved into the soaring and light-filled spaces of Gothic churches, in Italy the Gothic was resisted. The style never arrived in Rome, which had been vacated by the popes for Avignon. Where it did arrive, in Naples where the French ruled, and in the north, it arrived late. More comfortable exploring its own classical traditions,

Italy nonetheless incorporated elements of the Gothic into the diverse art styles of its city states. Naples' Santa Chiara and Milan's cathedral most closely approximate the true Gothic style; elsewhere, pointed arches and ribbed vaulting adorned cathedrals, but seldom resulted in Gothic airiness and height. Gothic asymmetry and window tracery also characterized secular buildings, among them the Doge's Palace in Venice and the Palazzo Vecchio in Florence, but these buildings remained uniquely Italian. Though Italian architecture was more squared than soaring, more Romanesque than Gothic, it achieved pleasing results—the brilliant facades of the Siena and Orvieto cathedrals, the lacy arcading of Venetian palaces, the warm-hued marbles of the Florence cathedral, and the spacious preaching nave of the San Francisco in Assisi.

Sculpture shows the same local development as architecture, with Nicola Pisano's work influenced by the realism of ancient Rome (Pulpit in Pisa baptistery), not just the expressiveness of the French Gothic (pulpit in Siena cathedral). And Pisano's son, Giovanni, created the very Tuscan facade on the Siena duomo, complete with Roman columns and capitals, despite his studies in France. For his masterpiece, however, he too borrowed from the Gothic narrative style, dramatically depicting religious scenes in his animated facade sculptures and stirring pulpits in Pisa and Pistoia.

Nowhere does Italy distinguish itself more in this period than in the medium of *painting*. Gothic walls supported painting only in the form of stained glass, while Italian walls continued to be covered with frescoes and mosaics. In France and Germany, painting was confined to illuminated manuscripts; in Italy, paneled altar paintings and mosaics in the Byzantine style continued through much of the 13th century. Perhaps it was this attachment of Italy to painting that permitted it to revolutionize art. Perhaps its knowledge of foreshortening as well as the modeling effects of light and shade—techniques preserved in Byzantine art since ancient times—provided the skills for painting realistically. For whatever reasons, it was in Italy that art was revolutionized at the end of the 13th century, through the genius of the Florentine painter Giotto (1277–1337).

The trend toward realism was already apparent in the pantheistic delight in nature found in Gothic art and in the religious movement of St. Francis of Assisi. It was found, too, in the materialism of the emerging middle class in the Italian city states. Realism was already found in the classical forms of the Pisani, yet it was one thing to create three-dimensional sculpture and quite another to recreate the illusion of spatial depth on the flat surface of a chapel wall or altar panel. This Giotto accomplished. In Padua, in Florence, and perhaps in Assisi, too, Giotto created a space in which humans walked and gestured, talked and wept. He told the same Biblical stories and he narrated the same lives of the saints, but he did it naturalistically.

Giotto may have been the most recognized artist of his time, but he was not alone. He may have been influenced by Pietro Cavallini (c. 1240–1330) whose light-filled work and voluminous figures adorned Roman churches. In Siena, an entire school of painting developed from the more Byzantine style of Duccio (active 1278–1318). There, Simone Martini (active 1315–44) retained the graceful patterns of the Gothic and Byzantine; he painted elegant and slender bodies rather than the monumental forms of Giotto, but his style was nonetheless realistic. And he may very well have produced the first totally secular portrait since ancient Rome. The Lorenzetti brothers further established the Sienese school—Ambrogio Lorenzetti painted the first true landscape since ancient times in his elaborate fresco *Allegory and Effects of Good and Bad Government* (Palazzo Pubblico, Siena).

Through the Roman, Sienese and Giotto schools, painting would take a new course, one that would dominate Western art until the advent of cubism. The course was interrupted in 1348 by the Black Death, a devastating plague that killed both the Lorenzetti brothers and turned art back to Byzantine conservatism. Not too far away, in Burgundy, the delicate realism of Simone Martini would be revived in the *International Gothic* style, a style that returned to Italy around 1400 in the works of Gentile de Fabriano (1360-1427) and inspired early paintings of the Renaissance.

Early Renaissance (1400s)

Although the traditions of antiquity had already influenced Italian art, it is not until the *quattrocento* (1400s) that a new art is consciously founded on their revival. Italy, a country covered with Roman ruins, could never forget its past as the center of an empire. But that past, pagan as it was, hardly found glorification during the church-dominated middle ages. It required the individualism of the increasingly wealthy bourgeoisie to identify with the humanistic ideals of antiquity. It took the unbounded material success of the Florentine republic to identify itself with ancient Rome, and even Athens. Not until then could there be a renaissance, or rebirth, of classical ideals.

It is in Florence, ironically a city with few ancient ruins, that Renaissance art is created. In this businesslike city-state where the world's finances could be controlled by the newly invented double-entry balance sheet, it seemed that human effort and reason could accomplish anything worth accomplishing. Not surprisingly, it is in Florence that Donatello's (1386–1466) statues come to depict saints as confident citizens, their feet planted firmly on this earth and their gaze totally worldly. It is here that Masaccio's (1401–28) frescoes show the life of Christ unfolding in the familiar streets of Florence. And it is here that Brunelleschi (1377–1446) created an architecture scaled to human proportions.

ART IN ITALY

The Florentine revival of classical forms resulted in a deep break with the middle ages. For the first time since antiquity, sculpture stood free of church portals and again expressed civil pride, not just Christian virtues, as in Donatello's heroic equestrian sculpture in Padua, *El Gattemelata*. Naturalism banished icon-like paintings of the madonna for the freer compositions of Fra Angelico (1387–1455), and it replaced cluttered medieval panels with single scenes unified by a central perspective. Realism infused art, even to Masaccio showing the very earthly suffering of the poor in his Brancacci murals and to Piero della Francesca (1416–92) painting Federigo da Montefeltro with wrinkles and imperfect nose. The human form itself became worthy of admiration and was celebrated in sculptures such as the young and very nude *David* by Donatello and, later, by Michelangelo.

Nowhere was the break with Gothic art more complete than in architecture. And in no other realm did one artist do so much to contribute to the new forms. Filippo Brunelleschi not only designed the ribbed dome that would dominate architecture for centuries, he created the basic geometric vocabulary of Early Renaissance architecture. Then, too, he was the first to formulate mathematical perspective for creating impressions of space and depth. Under Brunelleschi's hand, the classical rounded arch supported by columns appeared where heavy compound piers had formerly held pointed ones. The ribbed dome of the Florence cathedral forever eliminated the flat roofs of the Italian Gothic. Symmetry replaced the picturesque; geometry, not whim, dictated the proportion of part to whole. Awesome religious heights were reduced to human scale, colorful frescoes to the architectural purity of white walls and *pietra serena* (gray stone). With Brunelleschi's *Spedale degli Innocenti*, a new age of architecture began.

Renaissance art reclaimed the Roman dome and revived portraiture and freestanding sculpture. Yet the Renaissance in no way simply copied the past. The forms of antiquity were reinterpreted, often totally transformed, or even rejected, for newer and lighter elements. Pagan forms were converted to Christian symbols—the dome represented the heavens, the perfect proportions of the church reflected celestial harmony, naturalism depicted not only civic leaders but the sufferings of Christ. And Renaissance rationalism led to the systematic use of vanishing point perspective, codified by Leonbattista Alberti (1404–72) and resulting in a realism unlike anything that had preceded it. Scientific inquiry made human nudity not just a matter of aesthetics, but also a subject for serious study that was reflected in the art of Antonio del Pollaiuolo (1432–98) and Luca Signorelli (1450–1523). Early Renaissance art was more than antiquarianism. It was a perfect reflection of quattrocentro Florence—self-confident and bold, worldly, yet profoundly religious.

Along with Masaccio, Donatello and Brunelleschi, the three founders of the Early Renaissance, Florence nurtured an incredible number of exceptional quattrocento artists. These Florentine artists spread the Renaissance through northern and central Italy, and south to the Kingdom of Naples, through commissions from wealthy city-states and guilds—and even through occasional exile during politically intense times. Paolo Uccello (1397–1475), Filippo Lippi (1404–69), and Donatello worked in the Veneto. The sculptor Lorenzo Ghiberti (c. 1381–1455) in Siena. Alberti in Mantua and Ferrara. Fra Angelico in Perugia and Rome. Piero della Francesca in Urbino and San Sepolcro. The city itself did much to spread the new style by attracting artists from many regions to its workshops, such as Jacopo Bellini (active c. 1423–70) who would beget an artistic dynasty in Venice.

The Renaissance soon saw considerable diversity. Siena was reluctant to relinquish its Gothic grace, so instead infused painting with its own elegance while also producing one of the fine sculptors of the Early Renaissance in Jacopo della Quercia (1374–1437). Umbria incorporated the serenity of its forested slopes into the style of Perugino (1445–1523) while mountainless Ferrara created fantastic and gnarled hills for the Po basin. In Padua, Andrea Mantegna (1431–1506) put Donatello's sculptural realism into his paintings and created a precise, almost illusionistic style that spread through northern Italy. Nowhere was the Renaissance more richly transformed in the quattrocento, however, than in Venice, where the great painter Giovanni Bellini (c. 1430–1516) produced the brilliant colorism that would make Venetian art influential for centuries to come. Not all great artists were tied to schools or regions; the singular Antonello da Messina's (1430–79) many travels outside his native Sicily led to a wondrous fusion of the Italian style with Flemish light. And not all contact with Renaissance artists stimulated local creativity—Naples produced no important school, nor did Milan despite (or because of) the presence of Leonardo; Rome would await the next century.

Despite such diversity, the end of the quattrocento witnessed a most distinctive trend toward courtly art. Gone were the guilds and unpretentious bourgeoisie who commissioned the frank republican works of the early Donatello. In their stead was the new aristocracy, living off the wealth of their merchant forbearers while studying Plato and writing poetry in urban palazzi and country villas. Lorenzo de Medici had no title, but he lived as sumptuously as the dukes of Milan. The condottieri of Mantua, Ferrara and Urbino had fought their mercenary way into duchies and titles like count and marquis. As the courts replaced the guilds in commissioning artists, murals of family exploits and pleasures, such as Mantegna's of the Gonzaga in Mantua, covered walls instead of religious and civic subjects; palaces like Luciano Laurana's (died 1479) in Urbino and Medici and villas such as Giuliamo da Sangallo's (c. 1443–1516) demanded a style not suitable for churches.

Paintings became more luminous and richly colored, from Bellini in Venice to Benozzo Gozzoli (1420–97) in Florence, and they became elegant and full of the pageantry of the International Gothic from nearly a century before. Sculpture became polished and refined, whether in the work of Andrea Verrocchio (1435–88) in Florence or Francesco Laurana (1420–1503) in Urbino. At times architecture became outrageously lavish, such as G.A. Amadeo's (1447–1522) marble facade commissioned by Milanese dukes for the Certosa di Pavia. Appropriately, courtly taste is exemplified best by the Florentine artist working for a Medici: from the humble realism of Masaccio, the quattrocento ends with the graceful allegorical paintings of Sandro Botticelli (1445-1510), who thought nothing of sacrificing anatomical accuracy for the beauty of his reborn Venus.

High Renaissance and Mannerism (1500s)

The greatest period of Italian painting is the High Renaissance (1494-1527), a period actually defined by the devastating Italian Wars, beginning with the first French invasion and ending with Spain's Sack of Rome. These troubled times precipitated a crisis in Renaissance confidence, sending Signorelli to Orvieto to paint his anguished apocalypse and causing others to create a more perfect world in their art than could be found on this earth. By mid-century the conquest by Spain intensified the emotionalism of Late Renaissance art and produced the disharmonies of Mannerism. Despite these signs of distress, the *cinquecento* (1500s) found enough political stability to produce Leonardo da Vinci (1452–1519), Michelangelo (1475–1564), Raffaello Santi, or Raphael (1483–1576), and Tiziano Vecellio, or Titian (c. 1485–1576). These artists created the High Renaissance style notable for its harmony and balance as well as for its virtuosity.

The quattrocento experimented constantly to achieve realism in art. It often struggled to fuse the accuracy of its newfound realism with beautiful design. By contrast, the naturalism of the *cinquecento* is effortless. Leonardo's *sfumato*, or blurred edges technique breathed life as well as beauty into the *Mona Lisa*. Michelangelo's chisel liberated the human form from blocks of marble, abandoning the awkward musculature ("sacks of nuts," said Leonardo) of his predecessors for perfection not seen since ancient Greece. There was nothing that couldn't be accomplished by the genius of these artists, whether the light captured by Titian's brush or the spatial depth controlled by Raphael's exquisite compositions like the *School of Athens*.

Rome would be the patron of the High Renaissance style, although once again the beginnings were in Florence, however briefly. For the first few years of the 16th century, Florence witnessed its citizen Michelangelo produce his heroic marble statue of David, and saw the return of Leonardo from

Milan after his completion of the *Last Supper*. And while the two resided in that city, Raphael arrived to study their work and to produce a series of Leonardo-inspired madonnas.

But it was in Rome that the new classicism was created. Under the increasingly ambitious Renaissance popes, Rome again was to become a great artistic center rivaling the grandeur of its ancient past. The popes commissioned the period's finest artists, and under Julius II (1503–1513) the awesome project of rebuilding St. Peter's and the Vatican was begun, a project that would inspire the monumentality of the High Renaissance style. The architect Donato Bramante (1444–1514) came from Milan, and with him arrived ideas gleaned from Leonardo's drawings of organic, centrally planned buildings. Soon the flat walls of the Early Renaissance would become fields of light and shadow pierced by deep niches and projecting sculpture. Soon the light-filled space of the Roman Pantheon would be mirrored in Bramante's plan for a dome-covered St. Peter's. On the ceiling of the Sistine Chapel, Michelangelo would perfect his heroic human figures. And in the *stanze*, or rooms of the papal apartments, Raphael would foreshadow the Baroque in his use of color and the spiral movement of his greatest compositions.

The High Renaissance style was often copied and followed, but it failed to spawn the variety of schools and quality of artists of the quattrocentro. Correggio (1494-1534), working in Parma, was one of the few to inspire it with his own emotion and vision. Only one region vied with Rome, and that was Venice. Its lagoon location provided natural defenses against French, Spanish, and papal armies alike. Amidst such stability, Venice created a High Renaissance style uniquely its own. In place of Roman monumentality were the atmospheric landscapes of Giorgione (1477–1510). In place of human anatomy were the fleshy nudes of Titian, the sensuous tones and warm colors of Venice itself. And instead of the malleable, yet sturdy walls of Bramante, were the airy double arcades of the San Marco library by Jacopo Sansovino (1486–1570).

With the Sack of Rome in 1527, Italy was transformed. Except for Venice, the Italian city states that produced the Renaissance disappeared under the crown of Spain. Bramante, Leonardo and Raphael already were dead. Michelangelo lived on, much as Titian in Venice, to experiment with forms that influenced artists in the centuries to come. Michelangelo created the Medici chapel and Laurentian library in Florence, brilliant works whose fluidity and dynamism can no longer be called classical. Even the *Last Judgment* in the Sistine Chapel left behind the serenity of the High Renaissance. Titian's brush found the freedom to cast light over surfaces that foreshadowed Turner in the 19th century; his portraits became emotionally charged and tormented. He was joined in Venice by other great artists: Tintoretto (1518–94) with his mystical paintings, Paolo Veronese (1528–88) with his splendid and luminous surfaces and vestiges of Mantegnesque illusionism, and Andrea Palladio (1508–80) whose many villas and magnificent churches remained strongly classical. Even if these artists no longer emphasized the harmonious relationships of High Renaissance art, their work was honestly passionate, clear in purpose, and brilliantly probing.

Yet the Late Renaissance witnessed, too, more artificial and preening styles. If the change in political conditions left little room for Renaissance confidence, the masters of the High Renaissance seemingly left little to achieve in art. Inheriting the virtuosity and technique, many artists of the Late Renaissance seem to have nothing to communicate. Their surfaces are beautiful and titillating, their colors and human figures a bit eccentric and distorted, their nudes quasierotic even in religious contexts. Although this lack of classicism could be seen earlier, with Pontormo (1490–1557) in Florence and Parmigianino (1503–40) in Parma, by the 1540s it became so prevalent, yet deviant from the naturalism of Renaissance art, that it has achieved the label of "Mannerism." Unlike the Venetian school of the late 16th century (which many call "Mannerist," too), the style of architects Giulo Romano (c. 1499–1546) in Mantua and Sanmicheli (1484–1559) in Verona is capricious—some say neurotic—compared to the restraint of Palladio. In Florence, the artists pandering to the ducal court of the Medici more often than not produced decorative and vapid works compared to the passionate results of Tintoretto. The painter Bronzino (1507–72) and the sculptor Giambologna (1529–1608), and occasionally the work of Benvenuto Cellini (1500–71), leave Florence artistically richer. But the stylized repetitions of Giorgio Vasari (1511–74) emphasize the end of the visual experimentation and study of nature epitomized by Leonardo and the Renaissance. As the Counter Reformation takes root, Mannerism is finished, too.

Baroque (1600s & 1700s)

The Italian Baroque evolved through several phases during the nearly two centuries of its existence. The transitional phase from Mannerism is called the Early Baroque, while the later and most glorious period of the style is known as the High Baroque. Throughout the period, there are more conservative classical trends, especially in the Late and Rococo periods, but even then the bold vivaciousness of the style can be found flourishing in numerous regions of Italy.

Early Baroque

The Early Baroque actually began in the late 16th century, when it banished the artificiality of Mannerism for a clearer, more tangible realism. It also rejected the paganism of the High Renaissance nude and the calmness of its symmetry for more dramatic portrayals of humble, but martyred saints. Early Baroque art grew out of the Counter Reformation, a period when the Catholic Church tried to prove its moral authority against Martin Luther's charges of corruption. During this somber period in which the very existence of the church was threatened by the spread of Protestantism, artists painted the holy stories of the Church under the watchful eyes of priests and received commissions only when they inspired reverence for its dogmas.

By the end of the century, Protestantism was on the wane. The church, re-generated by the reforms of Charles Borromeo and Philip Neri and rejuve-nated by the spirituality of mystics like Theresa of Avila, had new doctrines to proclaim and new churches to build. Under Sixtus V (1585–90), Rome would be revived and artists would flock to the capital. In a monumental ef-fort at city planning, the pope opened new streets to the pilgrimage church-es, like St. John Lateran and St. Peter's, and graced them with new piazzas crowned by fountains and ancient obelisks (technically not pagan once topped with their Christian crosses). Large new churches were erected with high cupolas spreading light through their wide congregational spaces. A fa-vorite architect for these was Giacomo della Porta (1539–1602), who de-signed the facade for the first Jesuit church, Il Gesu, and who completed Michelangelo's dome for St. Peter's. But most of the architecture was more conservative than good, even though the innovative Carlo Maderno (1556–1629) would later add a facade to St. Peter's that in its central masses and projecting columns previewed the lively movement of the High Baroque. All the churches, true to Counter Reformation orthodoxy, shunned the central plan or rotunda so favored by the High Renaissance. Even Bramante's plans for St. Peter's were radically altered by the addition of a nave to create a thor-oughly Christian Latin cross.

It is in painting that the Early Baroque excelled in Rome, when around the 1590s, Michelangelo Merisi, known as Caravaggio (1573–1610) arrived from Lombardy and Annibale Carracci (1560–1609) came from Bologna. In Rome they both absorbed the lessons of the High Renaissance, the bulky figures of Michelangelo's Sistine Chapel and the compositions of the classi-cal painting style. But each did so differently. In his religious works, Carav-aggio was one of the greatest interpreters of the Counter Reformation. His paintings had a realistic clarity to them, down to the dirty feet of his peasant-like saints. Yet by placing them against an almost abstract background and bathing them in *tenebroso*, or his technique of contrasting light and dark, he elevated them into the realm of the intensely religious.

Although Caravaggio's paintings with their spiritual light and charged emotion seemed perfect expressions for his age, he in fact found little official favor and often had paintings rejected for their "irreverent" realism. Anni-bale Carracci achieved far greater success. Combining the monumental forms of the Roman High Renaissance with the colorism of Venice, Annibale produced paintings that were more classical. He, too, depicted peasants and grandly gesturing saints, but in a more idealized manner that proved pleasing to Rome and produced many generations of followers. His most important work was ceiling frescoes for the Farnese Palace, celebrating a forthcoming wedding. Secular—in fact based on classical mythologies about love and eros, and illusionistic as well—the frescoes showed a Rome quite willing to leave the Counter Reformation behind.

The Early Baroque created an unusual variety of styles. In its emphasis on realism, many artists returned to drawing from nature and developed an interest in genre paintings—Caravaggio's *Basket of Fruit*, for example, or Annibale's *The Butcher Shop*. Despite the later development of the romantic landscape by the Neapolitan Salvatore Rosa (1615–1673), Italian artists considered such secular art to be secondary. But the foreigners in Italy during the 17th century, such as the landscape artists Nicholas Poussin and Claude Lorraine, devoted themselves to the development of these genre paintings. More in the Italian tradition were the many Bolognese painters inspired by Annibale as well as by the art academy he established with his artist brother Agostino (1557–1642), but there were many others who continued painting in the grand style, like Guercino (1591–1666). A few provincial artists, like Federico Barocci (1526–1612) of Urbino, produced the increasingly dramatic art of the period, but, in fact, the Baroque was a Roman style.

High Baroque (1622–1680)

Although the Italian states had made their peace with Spain, mostly through neutrality and tribute payments, their economic fortunes continued to decline through the 17th-century. Nonetheless Italy was about to embark on one of its most joyful and creative periods of art. Or, rather, Rome was, because the lavish patronage of the pontiffs had little to do with textile manufacturing and sea trade. The Church was feeling triumphant. No longer did Protestant outcries against the idolatry and sinful opulence of Roman Catholicism intimidate it. By 1622, when its major reformers were canonized, becoming St. Theresa, St. Ignatius and the like, the Church was more than ready to glorify them and itself—through art.

The High Baroque was fortunate to have culturally progressive popes like Urban VIII (1623–44) and geniuses such as the multitalented Gianlorenzo Bernini (1598–1680), the architect Francesco Borromini (1599–1667), and the painter and architect Pietro da Cortona (1596–1669). Their chemistry produced an artistic explosion. They would design organic, centrally planned churches and dedicate them to the austere reformer St. Charles Borromeo; they would create richly textured and undulating edifices for the simple rituals of St. Philip's Oratorians. Although the architectural rhythms of their own churches didn't permit frescoes, they would turn the chaste whiteness of Early Baroque churches into heavenly spheres and transform their flat ceilings into illusionistic domes on which were painted the infinitudes of heaven and the apotheosis of the new saints.

But the bold inventiveness of the High Baroque was in no way a break with the religious zeal of the earlier movement. Other epochs had used art to instruct, the middle ages almost to catechize, the Early Baroque to inspire. The High Baroque wanted nothing less than to create a religious experience. Caravaggio may have isolated St. Paul's vision of mystical light, but Bernini's marble *St. Theresa* draws you into her moment with Christ, lifting you on the emotional cloud of her fluttering skirt. Maderno may have suggested movement with the light and shade created by his flat walls and projecting columns, but Borromini's San Carlo church moves ceaselessly, stirring you in an upward movement toward the celestial light of the cupola. Correggio had painted Parma's domes open to the sky, but Cortona's ceiling for the Palazzo Barberini pulls you up into the vortex of its glorious heavens.

The High Baroque may have been most inspired in its religious art, but it was also prodigious and wondrous in the secular realm. Just as Bernini's religious sculptures capture a single climatic moment, so his magnificent portrait busts and papal tombs arrest a flickering glance, reveal a telling expression or gesture. While the brilliance of Borromini's and Cortona's churches are never matched by the more restrained palazzi of this period, Borromini's trompe l'oeil colonnade for the Palazzo Spada is at least witty. However classical their facades, palazzi interiors often include those extraordinary allegorical ceiling frescoes—none grander than Cortona's for the Palazzo Pitti in Florence, where stucco ornamentation was added as well. And Rome itself was beautified by the creation of perfectly harmonized piazzas, made ebullient by Bernini's sculptures of water and stone.

The High Baroque carried many other artists through the 17th century, such as the architect Carlo Rainaldi (1611–91) and the painter Giovanni Lanfranco (1582–1647), both of whom worked in Rome, but Lanfranco spent most of his time frescoing the ceilings of Naple's churches. Naples, in fact, would attract a number of Roman artists as it continued to evolve its own version of the Baroque into the 18th century. Although the curving surfaces, the elaborate domes of High Baroque architecture, never penetrated to Naples, flat walls were transformed instead by the dazzling polychrome marble inlays and stucco ornaments of Cosimo Fanzago (1591–1678). In the north, Tuscany preferred a kind of antiquarianism to the restlessness of the new style, but Venice joined in with the architecture of Baldassare Longhena (1598–1682), whose Santa Maria della Salute church showed the same organic, central plan of Roman ones, if on a more subdued note. But it was only in Turin, where the dukes of Savoy were building their new capital, that another Baroque architectural genius was spawned, Guarino Guarini (1624–83) whose great conical dome for the Cappella della Sindone (Chapel of the Holy Shroud) equaled anything created in Rome.

Baroque influence did not end in Italy. Europe's Catholic monarchs were as interested in glorifying themselves as the Church. Louis XIV found that only the lively facades of the Baroque could organize his massive palace at Versailles. But like many monarchs, he preferred a more stately compromise than Roman artists offered, and the plans both Cortona and Bernini submitted for the Louvre were rejected. Yet Cortona's stucco and fresco techniques would have their French following in a style identified with the monarch, and Bernini's sculptural style would be imitated, but not invigorated, for even longer.

Late Baroque/Rococo (1700s)

By the 18th century, Rome no longer was the art capital of Europe. Even before Bernini's death, the patronage of kings and dukes was drawing artists away from Rome. New international styles had their origins elsewhere, most often in Paris. When the Turin architect Filippo Juvarra (1685–1736) designed the Frenchified Palazzo Madama for the Duke of Savoy, he was the first to introduce a foreign style into Italy. Even the greatest Italian painter of the period, Giam Battista Tiepolo (1696–1770), created his grandest ceiling frescoes for the Kaiser in Germany. Although Tiepolo's Venice would produce the only important Italian school of painting in this period, the smaller genre paintings of Canaletto (1697–1768) and the two Guardis, Francesco (1712–93) and Giovanni (1698–1760) were produced for an international, not Italian, market.

The Rococo style may have had its origins in the classicism preferred by monarchs as well as the delicate creations of France. Yet Italy did in fact produce its own, more monumental version that was an extension of the Roman Baroque. In Rome itself, there was a flurry of activity in the second quarter of the century that produced the Trevi Fountain, along with other monuments. There was even more activity in the extreme north and south, two areas where there were foreign courts to pay the bills—in the south, Spanish Aragonese and Bourbons ruled; in Piedmont in the north, the Austrian Hapsburgs. In Naples, in Catania, in Turin, even in tiny towns like Noto in Sicily and Lecce in Apulia robust regional styles extended the Italian Baroque well into the 18th century. But late in the century Tiepolo would die in Madrid, out of fashion. And Luigi Vanvitelli's (1700–73) Versailles-like palace and gardens at Caserta, near Naples, stated most eloquently that Italy no longer set the fashion.

Modern (1800s & 1900s)

Throughout the 19th century, Italy was either staving off the foreign domination of the French or Austrians, or fighting for its own unification, or Risorgimento, as a modern nation. Not too surprisingly, it no longer led Europe into new artistic ventures. Yet it was the art archive of Europe, inspiring others as it had so long inspired itself. Never bereft of talent, it contributed individual artists to the new, if foreign, movements. When Napoleon swept through Italy (1797–1815), he brought with him the neoclassicism so befitting a new emperor. Italy would be swept along with the style so welldefined by the French painter Jacques Louis David. Of course, Italy could quite easily identify with its classicism and even produced the greatest sculptor of the period, Antonio Canova (1757–1822), who wedded Bernini's silky surfaces with the static poses then fashionable. Later, when Titian's flickering brush and Venetian light inspired the Impressionists, Florence's Macchiaioli painters, such as Giovanni Fattori (1825–1908), created their regional variation out of the *macchia*, or patch.

Twentieth-century art witnessed an increasing internationalism. Again Italian artists have participated, including such renowned painters as Amedeo Modigliani (1884–1920) and Giorgio de Chirico (1888–1978), such recognizable sculptors as Marino Marini (1901–80). Recognition, too, has fallen on its many architects, such as Carlo Scarpa (1902–78) for his Mondrian-inspired detailing, Pier Luigi Nervi (1891–1979) for his sleek buildings of reinforced concrete, and the contemporary Gae Aulenti, who now designs Europe's most exciting museums, including the Museo d'Orsay in Paris. At times there have been entire movements, originating in Italy, such as the kinetic aesthetic of Futurism that flourished however briefly (1909–15) in the works of painter-sculptor Umberto Boccioni, the painter Gino Severini, and others, before settling into the Fascist style preferred by Mussolini.

Italian art history is far from over. New art movements, such as Arte Povera, or art made of plain materials, enliven the galleries of the cities. International awards rarely fail to find a worthy Italian, from the filmmakers Giuseppe Tornatore and Gabriele Salvatore (winners, respectively, of the Academy Award for *Cinema Paradiso* in 1990 and *Mediterraneo* in 1992) to the architect Aldo Rossi (1990 Pristzker Prize) for the Hopperesque geometry of his creations. And design permeates all elements of society, from fashion to Memphis furnishings, from hi-tech light fixtures to garlic presses.

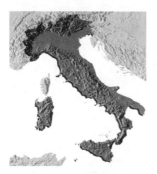

LAND ROUTES
INTO ITALY

Outdoor cafes rim the harbor of fashionable Portofino.

Much like the Gauls and the Goths before you, the allure of the riches to the south may speed you through the frontier regions of Italy. In case you do have the time to explore or find yourself needing accommodations along the way, we offer these introductions to parts of Italy not often visited thoroughly. Far from an exhaustive listing of each road into Italy—most routes from Switzerland, for example, simply drop you to the Lake Region which is covered in a separate destination chapter—the section emphasizes the Italian regions themselves.

The Italian Riviera

**From Nice, France into Italy
Route: Ventimiglia to Genoa & the
Riviera di Levante, then Pisa**

Mountains lock in Italy's northwest coast, protecting it from winter winds and landlocked invaders alike. From the western border with France, curving around the Ligurian Sea at Genoa and dipping south to Tuscany, the Alps confine fishing villages to craggy coves and force city streets up mountain sides. This *regione* of Liguria has always faced the sea. Its history has been the history of its port capital, Genoa, one of the great seafaring city states, along with Pisa and Venice, during the Middle Ages. After defeating its rival Pisa (1290), Genoa created a trading empire that extended from Sardinia into North Africa and on to the Crimea and Syria. The sea made Genoa one of the wealthiest cities in Europe—its customs duties in 1293 were seven times the entire revenues of the king of France. But a century later, Genoa would be defeated at sea by its rival Venice. Greatly weakened, but always desired as a port, Genoa was subjugated by outsiders for centuries—the Milanese Visconti, French and Spanish emperors, and Piedmontese Savoys.

Today the region is known more for its small beach resorts and its pesto sauce than for its history. Although its days of glory are well behind it, the region still lives off the sea, from the commercial port of Genoa to fishing villages and beach towns known best as the Italian Riviera. Once the Via Aurelia (SS 1) from France to Tuscany forced you around the mountains, taking you up and down their slopes to the beach towns and even through the center of Genoa. Now the autostradas (A-10 Ventimiglia to Genoa 165 km, 102 mi.; A-12 Genoa to Pisa 190 km, 118 mi.) ride high above the coast, tunneling their way through mountains and offering only glimpses of the sea below while speeding you along to other parts of Italy—even Rome (700 km, 434 mi.) can be driven in less than a day from Nice (only 40 km, 25 mi. from the border) and Pisa is just about half that distance.

Whether to stop in the area may very well depend on the time of year and your means of travel. By car, the massive sprawl of modern Genoa is almost too intimidating to think of a visit, yet car ferries to Sardinia and Sicily depart from here. By train, you can get off right in the center and enjoy the sights, even for a few hours. In July and August, the resorts are nightmarishly congested so that stopping casually, by car or train, without a reservation would be a mistake. Then, the traffic off the autostrada is so bad it isn't even recommended that you make a luncheon stop unless you have lots of time and reason not to worry about parking your car. And if you plan a leisurely visit in advance, you should know that—with the exception of Cinque Terre—this coast is an especially polluted part of the Mediterranean. Development, too, has marred the romance of many resorts, such as Rapallo on the Riviera di Levante (between Genoa and Pisa), and age has tarnished turn-of-the-century stars, such as San Remo on the Riviera di Ponente (between France and Genoa). *But if you are traveling when it is the right moment to dawdle, we introduce you to the sights of Genoa, and give you a few special places along the more scenic Riviera di Levante to explore.*

Genoa

Italy's greatest seaport is Genoa (*Genova* in Italian). Its 700,000 citizens crowd into the small harbor area and spill up the mountainsides in search of housing. No matter how high on the hill they go, the focus is always the sea. Appropriately, two of its most famous citizens were sailors—Christopher Columbus and Andrea Doria (1499–1560), who managed to strike a deal with Charles V for Genoa's relative independence in exchange for financing the Spanish empire's mercenary fleets.

What to See and Do

While Columbus' glory was found elsewhere, the presence of the wealthy Doria family in Genoa is hard to miss, especially along palace lined avenues above the old town that speak to the wealth Doria's arrangement brought to the city in the 16th century. The most famous avenue is ★ **Via Garibaldi**, laid out in 1555 by Renaissance architect Galeazzo Alessi and easily reached on a walk between the Stazione Principe (with a pause at the nearby 17th-century **Palazzo Reale** at *V. Balbi 10; upstairs is a gallery with Venetian and Dutch art, open daily 9 a.m.–1:30 p.m., Wed.–Sat. till 6:30 p.m., L8000*) and the 19th-century main square Piazza de Ferrari. Not only are the mansions on Via Garibaldi themselves worthy of note *(Palazzo Doria is at #6)*, but a stroll of the traffic-free street reveals frescoes *(at #5)*, a grotto *(at #7)*, and gardens in the Municipio *(at #9)*. Two mansions contain art museums whose collections of Flemish and Dutch paintings (both Rubens and Van Dyck visited the city) prove that the patrician families still had money to spend well beyond the 16th century. The two share guards and alternate morning and afternoon openings (Tues.–Sat. 9 a.m.–6 p.m., Sun. till noon; L6000). The first is ★ **Palazzo Bianco** *(at #11)*, where on the third floor you can see Flemish paintings by Van der Goes, Van Dyck and Rubens, as well as Italian and Genovese paintings. Across the street is the ★ **Palazzo Rosso** *(#18*; built 1670s), decorated with 18th-century frescoes, its 3rd-floor *salas* are furnished with four ★ Van Dyck portraits, the stars in the two-floor *pinacoteca* that also includes Veronese, Titian and Rubens.

Older sights are in the *centro storico*, located between the grand avenues of Garibaldi and XXV Aprile and spilling down to the harbor below. Although street crime should deter you from aimlessly exploring the tangle of narrow streets here, during the daytime bustle you'll want to visit: the ★ **Piazza San Matteo** *(just off P. Ferrari on Salite S. Matteo)* with early mansions of the Doria family and their family church, the black and white striped ★ **San Matteo**, its Gothic facade emblazoned with inscriptions about the Dorias themselves. The Romanesque ★ **San Lorenzo Cathedral** *(just below P. Ferraro on V. San Lorenzo)*, was founded in 1118 but exhibits French Gothic influence in its unusual fa-

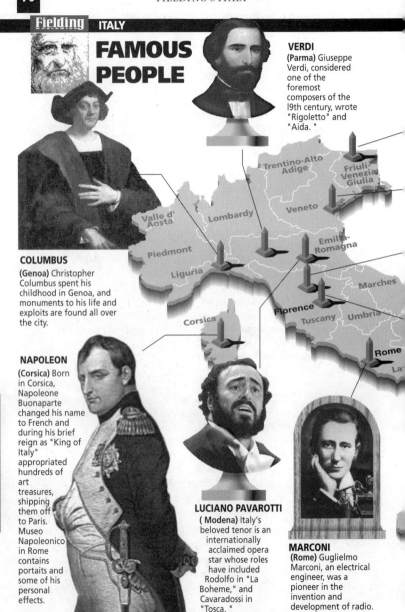

Fielding ITALY

FAMOUS PEOPLE

VERDI
(Parma) Giuseppe Verdi, considered one of the foremost composers of the l9th century, wrote "Rigoletto" and "Aida."

COLUMBUS
(Genoa) Christopher Columbus spent his childhood in Genoa, and monuments to his life and exploits are found all over the city.

NAPOLEON
(Corsica) Born in Corsica, Napoleone Buonaparte changed his name to French and during his brief reign as "King of Italy" appropriated hundreds of art treasures, shipping them off to Paris. Museo Napoleonico in Rome contains portaits and some of his personal effects.

LUCIANO PAVAROTTI
(Modena) Italy's beloved tenor is an internationally acclaimed opera star whose roles have included Rodolfo in "La Boheme," and Cavaradossi in "Tosca."

MARCONI
(Rome) Guglielmo Marconi, an electrical engineer, was a pioneer in the invention and development of radio. He won the Nobel Prize for physics in 1909.

Trentino-Alto Adige

Friuli-Venezia Giulia

Veneto

Valle d' Aosta

Lombardy

Piedmont

Emilia-Romagna

Liguria

Marches

Corsica

Florence

Tuscany

Umbria

Rome

La

Genoa

GALILEO

(Friuli) Best known for his work as an astronomer, Galileo developed the telescope and was the first to see sunspots, mountains and craters on the moon.

ANTONIO VIVALDI

(Venice) Vivaldi ((1678-1741) wrote more than 400 concertos, 23 symphonies and 75 sonatas.

MARCO POLO

(Venice) Born in Venice in 1254, Marco Polo was captured while fighting for Venice against Genoa and wrote accounts of his travels to China while in prison from 1296-1298.

LEONARDO DA VINCI

(Tuscany) One of the most prominent men of the Italian Renaissance, he is most famous for his "Last Supper" mural and "Mona Lisa" painting.

MICHELANGELO

(Florence) Best known for painting the ceiling of the Sistine Chapel in the Vatican. Prior to embarking on the Sistine project, he was a sculptor.

SOPHIA LOREN

(Naples) Born Sofia Sciolone, she is famous for films such as *Aida, The Key* and *Judith*. She won the Best Actress Oscar in 1961 for her role in *Two Women*.

ARCHIMEDES

(Sicily) Born in Syracuse, Sicily, then a Greek colony, mathematician Archimedes is credited with discovering specific gravity.

Abruzzi
Molise
ium Cam ania
Naples
Apulia
Basilicata
Calabria
Sicily

Genoa

cade and fine rosette window; inside, there's the notable Renaissance Chapel of St. John the Baptist (left aisle), along with a British bomb that miraculously failed to explode and destroy the church in World War II. Dropping down to the harbor on V. San Lorenzo you'll find the arcaded **Piazza Caricamento** that was the heart of the medieval port. Here is the **Palazzo San Giorgio** (1260 with a 16th C. addition), once the seat of government, later of the powerful St. George bank of Genoa. Via P. Reale leads off the piazza back into old town and in a block intersects with Via San Luca, the former main street of Genoa. Following San Luca left for several blocks, you come near ★**Palazzo Spinola** *(on P. Pellicceria to the right)*, the 16th-century mansion still handsomely decorated and home to the Galleria Nazionale d'Arte *(Tues.–Sat. 10 a.m.–7 p.m., Mon. 9 a.m.–1 p.m., Sun. 2–7 p.m.; L8000)* with Italian and Flemish art, including Antonella da Messina's ★ *Ecce Homo*, Van Cleve's ★ *Adoration of the Magi*, and Van Dyck's ★ four Evangelists. From here, you continue straight across V. Maddalena and climb a few blocks to Via Garibaldi.

Where to Stay

Many hotels, convenient to the sights, lie in the more modern, safer area above the centro storico and between the two train stations.

Jolly Plaza   L290–365,000 CP   ★★★★

V. Martin Piaggio 11, 16122; ☎ *839-3641, FAX 839-1850.*
Single L290,000 CP. Double L365,000 CP.

The Jolly has an excellent location on the Villeta di Negro park, just above the central Piazza Corvetto. A tasteful renovation in 1992 of two Neoclassical buildings has made this Jolly an unusually elegant branch of the chain and its 120 well-appointed rooms couldn't be more convenient. Restaurant. Bar. Parking.

Savoia Majestic   L230–330,000 CP   ★★★

V. Arsenale di Terra 5, 16126; ☎ *261-641, FAX 261-883.*
Single L230,000 CP. Double L330,000 CP.

This is a 19th-century hotel retaining some of its former splendor in the high-ceiling lobby with mirrored walls and formal dining room. Its 120 rooms vary from old-fashioned to commercial modern, depending on the year of renovation; solarium, American bar, garage and location across from Stazione Principe.

Europa   L150–200,000 CP   ★★

V. delle Monachette 8, 16126; ☎ *246-3537, FAX 261-047.*
Single L150,000 CP. Double L200,000 CP.

Hidden down an alley off Via Balbi, a block from Stazione Principe, is this sleekly modern hotel with 80 flawlessly maintained, small rooms. Breakfast room. Bar. Roof terrace. Parking (fee).

Agnello d'Oro   L115–150,000 CP   ★

V. delle Monachette 6, 16126; ☎ *246-2084, FAX 246-2327*
Single L115,000 CP. Double L150,000 CP.

A hotel in the same alley as the Europa that offers a hodgepodge of 38 rooms (no a/c) in different styles, none stylish, but many surprisingly large with good modern tiled baths. A good buy, especially when you negotiate breakfast and parking in the room price.

Where to Eat

Genoa's versions of pesto have made it famous, for parmesan cheese enriches the usual sauce of basil, oil and pine nuts. Here you find it most frequently on *trenette*, the local fettuccine. *Pansotti* is also richly Ligurian, a delicious cheese-filled ravioli with walnut cream sauce. Fish, of course, is emphasized in the Ligurian cuisine, from *branzino*, or sea-bass, in white wine, tomato and garlic, to the local bouillabaisse known as *burrida*.

Gran Grotto $$$ ★★★★

V. Fiume 11r; reserve at ☎ *564-344.*
Meals L60–100,000; closed Sat. lunch, Sun., late Aug.
To sample refined Genovese cuisine, come here. Located on the park in front of the Stazione Brignole, and serving pesto on a seabass gnocchi, vegetables in delicate pastries for appetizers.

St. Cyr $$$ ★★★

P. Marsala 8r, located north of P. Ferrari on P. Corvetto; reserve at ☎ *886-897.*
Meals L55–90,000, closed Sat. lunch, Sun., Christmas, & late Aug.
Borrowing dishes from throughout Genovese history, this lovely restaurant offers *trenette al pesto* as well as French *soupe a l'oignon*, shrimp salad along with Pied-montese *filetto al Barolo.*

Trattoria Rina $–$$ ★★

V. Mura delle Grazie 3r; near the port, ☎ *207-990.*
Meals about L50,000; closed Mon., Aug.
For lots of old-fashioned ambience and Ligurian homecooking, follow V. Ravecca south of P. Dante almost to the docks; the pesto and the seafood are very good.

Mario Rivaro $ ★

V. Portello 16r; reserve at 277-0054.
Meals L30–50,000; closed Sun., Aug.
Simpler trattorie abound on the edges of old town, but the popular Rivaro, down a lane next to Corso Garibaldi 3, comes highly touted. Yet we found the *pansotti* inedible. Traditional focaccia is served with the meal, however, and the *trenette al pesto* is okay.

Snacks

Around the corner from Rivaro is **City Bar** *(Corso Garibaldi; 11:30 a.m.-4 p.m.; L5–10,000 per item; no credit cards)*, where you may find the salads and pasta offerings pleasing when good weather permits al fresco dining. The 19th-century elegance of **Caffè Mangina** *(V. Roma 91 at P. Corvetto; closed Mon.)* is a fine place to relax over pastries.

Directory

Telephone Code 010 **Postal Code 16100**

Tourist Information

APT *(*☎ *246-2633)* at train stations and airport; British Consulate, *V. XII Ottobre 2 (*☎ *564-833);* U.S. Consul, *V. Dante 2 (*☎ *584-492).*

Arriving

Airport 7 km from town, with bus connections to center; domestic flights.

Genoa

Ferries

Tirrenia Navigazione, Stazione Marittima, *Pontile Colombo 16126 (☎ 258-041)* with service to Sardinia (about 20 hours) and Sicily (24 hrs.).

Trains

Stazione Principe, west side of city, and Stazione Brignole, northeast side, connected by bus #33, have excellent service to the Riviera di Levante on the Milan (under 2 hours) to La Spezia (1 hour) IC trains, as well as to the French border (1 hour), Pisa (2 hours), and Rome (5 hours).

Driving

Exit Genova Oeste from A-10 for area near Stazione Principe. Autostrada connections to Ventimiglia-Menton at French border and to Nice (190 km, 118 mi.), to Florence (485 km, 292 mi.) and other major cities.

Caution

There must be a reason police patrol the centro storico and harbor in groups of six! Be alert here. After dark and on holidays, when streets are deserted, avoid this area or take taxis.

Riviera di Levante

The spring and fall are wonderful times to visit this region, and though many facilities close during the winter, even then the weather is often balmy enough to make a brief visit enjoyable. The Genoa to La Spezia train stays close to the coast, but tunnels mar most sightseeing efforts. A-12, with its many tunnels, provides the most efficient means of car travel; off-season you might try SS 1, Via Aurelia. In season (Holy Week, July-Aug.), many hotels require meal plans.

Practical Tip.

One of the easiest and most scenic ways to get around this coast during the high season is by boat. A car can almost be a hindrance given the traffic congestion and mountains. All the ports have boat tours to other coastal towns—for example, Portovenere and Portofino to Cinque Terre, Genoa to the entire Riviera.

Portofino

One of the most picturesque inlets along the coast has become its most fashionable resort. There's a castle a half-hour walk with sea views out to the *faro* (or lighthouse), and a nature preserve (Portofino Vetta) for serious hiking to the abbey and village of San Fruttoso (1.5 hours) that can be reached by boat as well, but not by road. But the primary action takes place in the piazza on the tiny harbor, where you sit in a cafe wondering who owns all those luxurious yachts.

Where to Stay and Eat

The range of hotels is great in Portofino, but the number of hotels is limited. So limited are the number of rooms, that most visitors are here only for a stroll and, perhaps, a meal of Ligurian seafood in one of the very pricey restaurants around the harbor. The nearby resort city of Santa Margarita Ligure has more facilities and even a beach, and just south is the Ca' Peo.

Hotel Splendido   **L560–915,000 MAP**   ❀★★★★★

16034 Portofino; ☎ *(0185) 269-551, FAX 269-614; closed Jan. 3–Easter.*
Single L560,000. Double L720–915,000 with two meals.
A magnificent villa-style hotel favored by movie stars and royalty for its stunning park setting overlooking town and sea, and its 65 individually decorated rooms, fine restaurant, heated pool, tennis.

Hotel Eden   **L180–260,000 CP**   ★

16034 Portofino; ☎ *(0185) 269-091, FAX 269-047; closed early Dec.*
Single L180,000 CP. Double L260,000 CP.
Right in the village of Portofino, this hotel has 9 small rooms around a garden and a veranda.

Da Puny   **$$$**   ★★★

Portofino harbor; reserve at ☎ *(0185) 269-037.*
Meals L70–120,000; closed Thurs., mid-Dec.–mid-Feb.
This restaurant has long maintained a reputation as one of the best seafood restaurants with an enchanting setting. Credit cards: none.

Paninoteca L'Isolotto   **$**   ★

steps from the harbor; ll:30 a.m.–6 p.m.; L5–12,000 per item
A half-block from the beautiful harbor, this informal snack bar has the virtue of modest prices for decent pasta and stuffed focaccia served at their outdoor tables. Credit cards: none.

Ca' Peo   **$$–$$$**   ★★★★

Strada Panoramica, at 16040 Leivi a village above Chiavai; reservations required
☎ *(0185) 319-696.*
Meals L60–100,000; closed Tues. lunch, Mon., Nov.
A short drive south (20 km) of Portofino is one of Italy's fine country inns, this one with great sea views and Ligurian cuisine as well as 5 bungalows (L165,000).

Practical Tips

Tourist Information: *V. Roma 35 (*☎ *[0185] 269-024)* • **Arriving**: Portofino is reached by turning off A-12 at Rapallo (30 km, 18.5 mi. south of Genoa) for Santa Margarita Ligure (3 km), then Portofino (another 5 km). By train, change to the Portofino Mare bus at Santa Margerita Ligure. **Beware:** Cars are turned away from Portofino when the one public parking lot is full. In the high season, if you don't have a hotel reservation, consider arriving by bus or boat.

Cinque Terre

Named for the five fishing villages found along this rugged coast, the Cinque Terre are the least developed on the Italian Riviera. Until recently, the only way to visit was by train or boat, but now the most northern village

(Monterosso al Mare) and the most southern two (Riomaggiore and Manarola) can be reached easily by car. There are few facilities here except for Monterosso, which has the ambience of a working-class beach town (laundry hangs from windows, women push baby strollers while their husbands sip expresso at the Bar Centrale, trains clamor through—Portofino, it is not). Monterosso has many virtues, one being that it's the easiest entry to the Cinque Terre National Park that preserves the wildness of nature here— rough sea and cliffs that form the dramatic settings for the villages with their colorfully painted houses. Most people—and there can be many of them, from busloads of Italian school children to German backpackers—come to visit all five villages from Monterosso, the only one with a sandy beach, to Vernazza, the most *caratteristica;* they visit by local train (a disappointing subway-like ride tunneling through the mountains) or boat, but most satisfyingly by hiking the winding, and sometimes demanding, *Sentiero Azzuro* ("blue path") that climbs the hills (often in steep steps) between the villages and crosses the cliffs high above the sea (path sometimes narrow and without guard rail). The 10-mile path takes a day to negotiate, including the return train to your starting point. The path is no more than a 30-minute promenade above the sea between Riomaggiore and Manarola where it is known as the "*Via dell'Amore*"; the difficult climb from Monterosso to Vernazza (under two hours) is more satisfying. Hiking across vineyards, olive and lemon groves, and fields of wildflowers, leaves lasting memories—it is why people rave about Cinque Terre. If you don't hike, you might still enjoy the simple life of this region; just pick one of the smaller villages to stay overnight (Vernaccia or Manarola, say), bathe in the delightfully clean, tempting, blue Mediterranean and dine on mussels prepared with freshly picked lemons and the local white wine.

Where to Stay

Monterosso has numerous facilities and is the best place to look first in the off-season or if you're without a reservation. If none of the following hotels seem right for you, consider Portovenere.

Porto Roca	**L210-295,000 CP**	

19016 Monterosso; ☎ *(0187) 817-502, FAX 817-692; open Easter to Nov. Single L210,000 CP. Double 295,000 CP.*

Both first-class hotels in the Cinque Terre are in Monterosso and this one is the best. Located on a hill at the far edge of the village (reachable by foot or taxi; hotel van pick up from train station) and with sunning terraces, restaurant, and 42 pleasant rooms, most with furnished balconies and the priciest ones with sea views.

Colonnina	**L105,000**	★

19016 Monterosso; ☎ *(0187) 817-439, FAX 817-439; Easter to Nov. Single/double L105,000.*

A modern, airy hotel located in the winding medieval streets off the lower marina with twenty simple rooms (no a/c) and a garden.

Arch of Constantine, Rome

Trentino castle

Adige Valley

Ca' d'Andrean
L75–95,000 ★

in Manarola; ☎ *(0187) 920-040, FAX 920-452; closed late Nov.*
Single L75,000. Double L95,000.
The garden and ten rooms here (no a/c) are the most comfortable in Manarola.
Credit cards: None.

Marina Piccola
L75–95,000

in Manarola; ☎ *(0187) 920-103, FAX 920-966; closed Jan.*
Single L75,000. Double L95,000.
For a sea view, reserve one of the rooms (no a/c) at this simple hotel.

Barbara
L45–70,000

in Vernazza; ☎ *(0187) 812-201.*
Single L45,000. Double L70,000.
In Vernazza, the best bet, even without a private bath, is the Barbara's fourth-floor
location overlooking the tiny marina. Credit cards: None.

Where to Eat

Moretto
S–SS ★★★

in Monterosso; P. Colombo 13, near the lower marina; ☎ *(0187) 817-483.*
Meals L45–65,000.
The best of the local Ligurian cuisine can be enjoyed al fresco here, where delicious
pesto is served on freshly made trofiette (squiggles of gnocchi-like potato dough),
the mussels and clams are redolent of lemon, and the porcini mushrooms are picked
fresh (early summer and fall) from nearby forests and grilled with herbs. The local
white wine made by the Coopertiva is the perfect accompaniment. There are more
striking settings, if not better seafood.

Marina Piccola
SS ★

in Manarola; ☎ *(0187) 920-103.*
Meals L50–75,000; closed Thurs., Jan.
A good choice for its terrace by the harbor and seafood specialties.

Al Castello
S–SS ★

in Vernazza; ☎ *(0187) 812-296.*
Meals: L45–65,000; closed Wed. except July–Aug., Nov.–May 1.
At the top of the village on a terrace with panoramic views and local seafood for din-
ing.

Picnics

For picnics, you can shop in the centro storico (near the lower harbor) of Monterosso
at the wine and food shops; or along the main street of Vernazza, where there are alimentari with fresh fruit and a forno with foccacia farci or a spinach tart. Both villages have
benches along the waterfront, or you can carry your prizes into the hills where there is an
occasional picnic table.

Directory

Tourist Information
In Monterosso, on seafront walk near stazione (☎ 817-506; open Easter–Nov.),
with information on all five villages.

Cinque Terre

Getting Around

The information office in Monterosso provides hiking maps and train schedules •
Local trains between Levanto and La Spezia run frequently, passing through all five
villages —Monterosso, Vernazza, Corniglia (reached by a steep climb), Manarola,
and Riomaggiore —in just 20 minutes. If you're visiting several villages, buy the
Cinque Terre day-pass. • Other, *rapido*, trains use these stazioni: be sure of the
track *(binario)* for the local train, sometimes reached by an underpass *(sottopassag-
gio)*. • Boats offer a scenic way to tour for those without the time to hike.

Arriving

The Cinque Terre are just north of the busy naval port of La Spezia (105 km, 65
mi. south of Genoa) and reached quickly by train (from Genoa or La Spezia); less
quickly by road (Monterosso is 32 km, 20 mi. on a winding, forested road from the
Brugnato exit from A-12; Riomaggiore is 14 km, 7 mi. on a road from La Spezia/
Portovenere). Arriving by car, you must park your car at the lots on the edge of the
towns; in Monterosso there are taxis to take you and your baggage to hotels in the
centro storico. (The new part of town, where you can park your car, is too sterile to
consider except for its good beach.)

Portovenere

Portovenere sits on a promontory beyond La Spezia, dominated by a hilltop castle and the omnipresent sea. Terrace restaurants nestle in its harbor,
narrow alleys lead through the old town, a fine park offers strolls. There's
windsurfing and water-skiing, though the sea here doesn't always tempt
swimmers and the beach is a narrow pebble strip. The great advantage of
Portovenere for many is that it has the fine characteristic setting of the Italian
Riviera, yet at surprisingly reasonable prices: here it is easy to find a hotel
room with a sea view; enjoy a meal harborside. And the frequent boats to
Cinque Terre make it a convenient base for hikes and visits to those villages.

Where to Stay and Eat

Royal Sporting   **L160–290,000 CP**   ★★★

19025 Portovenere; ☎ *(0187) 790-326; FAX 529-060; closed mid Oct.–Easter.*
Single L160,000 CP. Double L290,000 CP.
The best hotel is this tasteful and modern resort just a 5-minute walk from the center and with its own beach club, large pool, and tennis court. Most of the 60 rooms
(a/c) are ample and with balconies and sea views. Restaurant, bar, garage.

Grand Hotel Portovenere   **L165–225,000 CP**   ★★★

V. Garibaldi 5, 19025; ☎ *(0187) 792-610, FAX 790-661.*
Single L165,000 CP. Double L225,000 CP.
The Grand has undergone (and is undergoing) various stages of renovation, but for
the moment the lobby of the central hotel is "Italianate Modern" and there's a gym
with hydromassage, a restaurant and bars. Although the 50 rooms vary in decor,
many have sea views, some terraces.

Taverna del Corsaro   **$$–$$$**   ★★★

Lungomare Doria 102; ☎ *(0187) 790-622.*
Meals L65-95,000; closed Tues., Jan. & June.

Dining around the marina, you can find inexpensive fixed-price meals or dine modestly à la carte at the Trattoria Iseo; but for the best prepared seafood in town head for the Taverna.

Practical Tips

Portovenere is reached through the city of La Spezia by a 14 km, 9 mi. well-marked spur road. From La Spezia train station (for the Genoa [115 km, 71 m] and Rome [418 km, 260 m] line), there are buses and taxis. It is only a few hours by car from Lucca and Pisa.

Piedmont and Valle d'Aosta

Valle d'Aosta is rimmed by the tallest peaks in Europe.

From France and Geneva into Italy
Route: Mont Blanc to Aosta and Turin

The Alps, with their glaciers and evergreen forests, their raw cliffs and pastures, dominate these two regions of Italy. Valle d'Aoste is rimmed by the tallest peaks in Europe—the Matterhorn (*Il Cervino*, in Italian, 14,777 feet) and Monte Rosa (15,306 feet) on the north, Mont Blanc (*Monte Bianco* in Italian; 15,873 feet) on the west, and Gran Paradiso (13,401 feet) to the south. Here, feudal lords built castles to protect themselves from each other as well as from thieves marauding the ancient route to Gaul. And here St. Bernard dogs were first trained (17th C.) to aid lost travelers. Piedmont (*Piemonte* in Italian), or foot of the mountains, has a more benign terrain as its name indicates, even though it is hemmed in by the Alps on three sides, it opens on the west to Lake Maggiore and the fertile Po valley. While Valle d'Aosta is the land of skiers and mountains climbers, more diversified Piedmont also is known for its lakes (see Lombardy "Lake Region") as well as its Barolo and Asti Spumanti wines, its white truffles, and its Fiats produced at industrial Turin.

Although these regions were first united by Augustus, the princes of the House of Savoy accomplished the same feat in the 11th century, and repeatedly fended off intruders like the Visconti of Milan and the neighboring French. But the French influence in the area, from the Valdostani *patois* spoken in many villages to the haute cuisine of Turin, results not simply from proximity. The French conquered the area repeatedly, first during the Renaissance Italian Wars when Charles III permitted the Savoys to rule, while maintaining control of the Alpine passes and finally, under Napoleon in 1796. Again and again, the Savoys reasserted their control, often with the aid of Austria, and never more magnificently than in the 17th and 18th centuries when they built Turin into a worthy and very Baroque capital. The most enduring legacy of the Savoys, however, was during the Risorgimento, or the struggle for the unification of modern Italy. It was Vittorio Emanuele II of Savoy, along with his advisor Camillo Cavour, who sparked the northern Italian independence movement against Austria in 1859 that eventually, with Giuseppi Garibaldi's leadership on the battlefield, created the new Kingdom of Italy. The Savoy duke became the first king of modern Italy.

In the past, the Gauls and Romans, Frederick Barbarossa and Napoleon used the northern St. Bernard Pass that now links Aosta to Switzerland by tunnel. But the Mont Blanc tunnel, since its opening in 1965, has been the major car route from the west into Italy. At the foot of the Mont Blanc is one of Italy's most chic ski resorts, **Courmayeur**, where you can travel over the mountain by cable car to Chamonix, its sister resort in France. But if you stick to the tunnel, by car or international bus, the route first arrives at the former Roman town of Aosta (35 km, 22 mi.) before dropping south through the Dora Baltea valley flanked with its medieval castles to the large city of Turin (an additional 115 km, 71 mi.). There are variations on the route, of course. You can easily use the St. Bernard tunnel, only 35 km, 22 mi. north of Aosta, or you can avoid Turin by heading east to Milan instead (220 km, 136 mi. from Mont Blanc). But Turin is a natural destination since it is well-connected to most of Italy, not just Milan, but also Genoa to the south and Emilia Romagna and Tuscany. Aosta provides a convenient stopover for exploring scenic neighboring valleys with their castles, or even ascending Mont Blanc by cable car. Turin is not only a convenient metropolitan transportation center, it also should be explored for its Baroque architecture and museums. And from there, you can arrange trips into the wine areas around Alba and Asti.

Note: Traffic through the Mont Blanc and St. Bernard tunnels (or *trafori*, in Italian) can be very congested in the summer; truck traffic is almost always heavy. Some prefer the route of Pepin the Short to the south, now made through the Mont Cenis tunnel (Traforo del Frejus, in Italian) found midway between Chambery, France and Turin. • November-June check on road conditions before setting out on any of these routes.

Aosta

Although some industrial development and modern growth mars the perfection of its Alpine setting, Aosta is completely medieval and traffic-free within its ancient Roman walls. Today's main street **Via Sant'Anselmo** quickly links the **Arco di Augusto** (25 B.C.) with the original main gate of **Porta Pretoria**, then continues as Via Pretoriane to the main piazza, **Place Chenoux**, and the town hall. It is an easy town to stroll and casually sightsee. Midway between the two ancient arches, up Via Priorato, is the Romanesque **Sant'Orso** with its Gothic facade, interior with venerable frescoes (11th C.), and ★**cloister** (12th C.) with French Romanesque capitals carved into Biblical scenes and fantastic monsters. Nearby are the excavations of the 5th-century church of **San Lorenzo** and a small *museo*. Then, clustered just north of the Porta Pretoria, are the ruins of the Roman Theater and the lesser ones beyond, of the amphitheater. And behind the town hall is the **cathedral**, with medieval floor mosaics (choir).

Nearby Sights

As capital of the Valle d'Aosta, the small town is the crossroads of the area. From here you can take quick bus rides or drives to the enchanting castles of **Sarre** and **St. Pierre** just a few miles west (8 km on SS 26 towards Courmayeur, around the intersection with SS 507 for Cogne). Maybe you'll continue to Cogne (30 km, 19 mi.), entrance to the **Gran Paradiso National Park** (open year-round; overnight facilities in Cogne), the former hunting grounds of Vittorio Emanuele II, now the largest Alpine nature preserve in Europe. (Hiking in summer, cross-country skiing in winter; wildflowers in profusion May/June). Two of Piedmont's finest castles, however, lie to the south. The best, ★**Fenis** (*9 a.m.–7 p.m., but winter 10 a.m.–5 p.m.; closed Tues.; L4000; about 20 km, 12 mi. on A-5*) was rebuilt in the 14th century and in addition to the turrets and crenellations, it contains a fine chapel and frescoes in its courtyard. Near Verres is the **Castle of Issogne** (*closed Mon.; winter 10 a.m.–5 p.m., summer 9 a.m.–7 p.m.; L4000*), rebuilt in the 15th century and with frescoes too. Both can be reached by bus from Aosta, and Issogne is just 1 km southwest of the Verres *stazione* on the Aosta-Turin line.

Where to Stay

Europe   L180–255,000   ★★

P. Narbonne 8; ☎ *236-363; FAX 40-566.*
Single L 180,000. Double L255,000.
Near the main piazza, this hotel offers 71 rooms, a restaurant, access to parking.

Aosta

Turin   **L85–120,000**   ★

> V. Torino 14; ☎ 44-593, FAX 361-377; closed mid-Nov. to mid-Dec.
> Single L85,000. Double L120,000.
> A simpler hotel that has 50 decent rooms (no a/c), restaurant, and access to parking
> at the nearby stadium.

Where to Eat

Vecchia Aosta   **$–$$**   ★★

> V. Porta Pretoriane 4; ☎ 361-186.
> Fixed-price meal L35,000 A la carte L30-55,000; closed Wed., early June, late Oct.
> In town, enjoy the summer garden and polished service while dining on regional
> specialties as well as seasonal dishes such as *zuppetta di porcini.*

Trattoria Piemonte   **$**   ★

> V. Porta Pretoriane 13; ☎ 40-111.
> Fixed-price meal L30,000; closed Fri., Nov.
> Although you might have trouble sampling the regional *morcetta* (dried reindeer
> meat), *fonduta*, or fondue, is popular and found at this pleasant family-run "brasse-
> ria."

Directory

Telephone Code 0165   **Postal Code 11100**

Tourist Information

> APT, P. Chanoux 8 (☎ 236-627; FAX 34-657)

Transportation

> Bus & train stations, P. Manzetti, several blocks south of main piazza with 2-hour
> diretto train service to Turin, more cumbersome routes to Milan (change at
> Chivasso). • Buses are most efficient in this region, including international ones. •
> At Aosta, A-5 begins its path to Turin (115 km) and SS 26 to Mont Blanc (35 km).

Seasons

> The high season in Aosta is Christmas, Holy Week, and July- Sept.; for neighboring
> ski resorts the winter ski season is from Dec.– Mar.

Turin

The capital of Piedmont, while the industrial capital of Italy with its Fiat
plant, is also the elegant and cultured city created by the Savoys. Although a
city of one and a half million, the center of Turin (or *Torino* in Italian) is
quite manageable for visiting the palazzi and churches of its great Baroque
architects, the inventive Guarino Guarini and the more classical Filippo Juvarra. Turin's Via Roma is not only its Fifth Avenue but also the main avenue
linking its major parks and piazzas as well as the sights clustered about them.

What to See and Do

Around Piazza Castello

> Beginning at its northern end is the large Piazza di Castello with the **Palazzo Mad-
> ama** in its center. The Palazzo encapsulates the city's history, incorporating a medi-
> eval fortress and ancient Roman gate behind the French-influenced facade designed

by Juvarra (1718). Inside, the **Museo Civico** in the fortress is reached by Juvarra's double staircase and light-filled vestibule; among the many artifacts and paintings collected from the *regione* is a particularly fine Antonella da Messina ★ *Portrait of a Man* (15th C.). On the northwest corner of the square is the ★ **Church of San Lorenzo**, its interior sumptuously dressed in marble and dominated by Guarini's weblike perforated dome (1680). Just north is the Savoy's **Palazzo Reale**; walk through the courtyard and turn left at the end; then to the right is the **Cathedral** (P. San Giovanni; 15th C.) with its famous ★★**Cappella della Sindone** *(behind the apse, entrance in the left aisle; 9:30 a.m.–noon, 3–5:30 p.m., but Sun. closed for mass 10:30–11:30 a.m.)*, or Chapel of the Holy Shroud. While carbon dating in 1988 proved that the cloth mysteriously imprinted with the image of Christ could not have been his burial cloth (it dates to the 14th C.), the chapel itself (late 17th C.) is Guarini's masterpiece—reason enough for a visit. The soaring intricate dome, almost Moorish with its skeletal intersecting ribs, fills the chapel with the sun's rays once believed to have imprinted the shroud.

Turin offers a plethora of architectural sights.

Around Piazza San Carlo

South of the Piazza Castello, along Via Roma, you come to the social center of Turin, the **Piazza San Carlo.** Its south end is flanked by two churches by Juvarra. But just before reaching this popular meeting place, turn left one block for the Accademia di Scienze that houses Turin's two most respected museums: on the first two floors, the **Egyptian Museum** (*Museo Egizio, 9 a.m.–7 p.m. Tues.–Fri., till 2 p.m. Sat.–Sun.; L12,000*) exhibiting the Savoy collection that is unrivaled in Europe; upstairs, the ★**Galleria Sabauda** (*Tues.–Sun. 9 a.m.–2 p.m.; L8000*), its first rooms devoted to paintings of the Italian Renaissance (Fra Angelico, a notable Pollaioli and Mantegna, and others), and the more famous Flemish and Dutch Room with Van Eyck's ★ *St. Frances Receiving Stigmata*, Memling's ★ *Scenes of the Passion*, Van Dyck portraits, a Rembrandt. Just north of the Accademia is the piazza with Guarini's richly ornamented ★**Palazzo Carignano** (1679), that housed Piedmont's first parliament (mid 19th C.) during the Risorgimento.

Parks and Views

When you tire of the austere arcades of Turin's grand avenues, explore its softer, more beautiful side along the River Po and in the lovely hills across the river. Simply following the 17th-century arcades of Via Po east out of the Piazza Castello, and crossing the river to the **Church of Gran Madre di Dios**, you arrive at a more intimate neighborhood of shops and homes around **Via Monferrato** at the base of the verdant hills. Looking back at the center, you see Turin against its backdrop of snow-peaked Alps. The **riverfront parks** of Turin make for wonderful strolls. The finest is **Parco del Valentino** (bounded by Corso Vittorio Emanuele and Via Dante), with its fake 19th-century castle ("Borgo Medievale"), botanical gardens, lake and paddle boats, and caffè and restaurants, and lovely promenade ("Viale Virgilio"). For those with time, however, the most extraordinary views of Turin's beautiful setting can be enjoyed on a brief country excursion to Juvarra's ★**Basilica di Superga** (*10 a.m.–12 p.m., 3–5 p.m.*), built by the Savoys in thanksgiving for the end of a French siege. About 15 miles away on a hilltop with fine views, the visit is enjoyably made by tram (*#15 from V. XX Settembre near P. Castello to Sassi, then transfer for a 20-minute cable car ride*).

Industrial Turin

For those interested in the Fiat side of Turin, **Lingotto** (*V. Nizza 262, south of the center;* ☎ *664-4111*), the original Fiat factory (1920) that so impressed Le Corbusier, has been converted by the famed architect Renzo Piano into an immense convention center with a public annex of shops and concert hall. And speaking of cars, the **Museo Carlo Biscaretti di Ruffia** (*Corso Unita d' Italia 40, south of Parco Valentino; 10 a.m.–6:30 p.m., closed Mon., L8000*), among the largest auto museums in the world, has one of the first Fiats (1899).

Where to Stay

Jolly Principi di Piemonte   **L365–440,000 CP**   ★★★★

V. Gobetti 15; 10123; ☎ *562-9693, FAX 562-0270.*
Single L365,000 CP. Double L400-440,000 CP.

On its own piazzetta off V. Roma near the fashionable P. San Carlo, the Jolly offers a grand lobby, good service, 108 fine rooms, restaurant and lounge.

Victoria   **L180–250,000 CP**   √★★★

V. Costa 4, 10123; ☎ *561-1909, FAX 561-1806.*
Single L 180,000 CP. Double L220-250,000 CP.

In the center, but in a quiet cul de sac off Via Pomba, this hotel is our favorite for the country-style comfort of its lobby, filled with fresh flowers and fine prints, antiques mixed with wicker furnishings, and with windows overlooking a garden. The comfort doesn't disappear in any of the 90 ample and thickly carpeted rooms with attractive baths. Sunny breakfast room; bar. Prices vary with size of room, but all are good buys.

Astoria **L120–155,000 CP** ★

V. XX Settembre 4, 10121; ☎ *562-0653, FAX 562-5866.*
Single L120,000 CP. Double L155,000 CP.
A block from the Stazione Porta Nuova in the center, this old-fashioned hotel has recently had a major overhaul; its 62 rooms remain beige basic, yet highly functional (a/c, good baths). Quieter interior rooms overlook flowered courtyard. Garage.

Where to Eat

Piedmontese food follows the northern taste for butter rather than oil, *polenta* often instead of pasta (stuffed moon-shaped *agnolotti* are Piedmontese, however). But there are really two traditions, one quite French with wine sauces (and why not, given the superb regional reds—Barolo, Barbaresco, and the lighter Dolcetta di Barbera and Dolcetta di Alba—as well as Asti and Gavi whites), and the local melted *fontina* made into fondue. But there is the Italian country tradition too—the game of the mountains, the white truffles and porcini mushrooms of the foothills, the vegetables of the plains made into thick soup or a *bagna caoda* (raw vegetables dipped into a sizzling anchovy oil). Both traditions can be sampled in Turin, along with its famous *grissini*, or breadsticks.

Vecchia Lanterna **$$$** ★★★★★

Corso Re Umberto 21; reserve at ☎ *537-047.*
Fixed-price meal about L60,000. À la carte L60–100,000. Closed Sat. lunch, Sun., part of Aug.
One of Turin's (and Italy's) finest restaurants is in the French tradition. You might begin with a pate de fois gras or grilled snails, before continuing on with a sea bass in Barolo sauce.

Del Cambio **$$$** ★★★★

P. Carignano 2;reserve ☎ *546-690.*
Fixed-price business lunch L60,000. À la carte L75–100,000. Closed Sun. & Aug.
Opened in 1757, this historic restaurant shares the piazza with Guarini's palazzo of the same name. Here Cavour dined on the same classic Piedmontese cuisine served today in the ornate dining room of mirrors, chandeliers and gilded walls—bagna caoda, agnolotti and *finanziera*, a beef and chicken stew cooked with wine.

Birichin **$–$$** ★★★

V. Monti 16; ☎ *657-457.*
Meals L35–50,000; closed Sun., a week in Aug.
If stewed brains and big prices aren't appealing, then catch a taxi to this family-run trattoria south of the Stazione Porta Nuova. An unpretentious neighborhood dining spot with prices to match, the Birichin's seafood is anything but ordinary. The appetizer of *scaloppa di cernia* (seabass) would be a winning choice anywhere as would the buttery, homemade tortelli stuffed with sea nettles ("ostriche"), walnuts

and basil. Everything is quite wonderful. The service is pleasant; some English is spoken.

Brek $ ★ ★

P. Carlo Felice 22; 549-611.
Hours open: Mon.–Sat., ll:30 a.m.–3p.m.; 6–10:30 p.m. Meals L15,000–25,000
This upscale cafeteria with a garden patio is a good choice for a light meal.

Snacks

Turin is known for its historic cafes, hazelnut chocolates called "gianduotti," and pastries. Whether you opt for tea sandwiches or pastry, the local Cinzano or Martini vermouth or espresso, look for the ornate **San Carlo** and **Torino** around the Piazza San Carlo, and the 100-year-old **Mulassano** on the Piazza Castello. Just below Piazza San Carlo, **Paradice** *(V. Roma 305)* is a local favorite for ice cream; across the street, the Caffè Zucca is famous for its chocolates. For picnics, check out the food shops on Via Monferrato, near the Church of Gran Madre; for wine buying and tasting, we suggest visiting the **Antica Enoteca del Borgo** *(Monferrato 4)*.

Directory

Telephone Code 011   **Postal Code 10100**

Tourist Information

APT, Stazione Porta Nuova and V. Roma 226 near P. San Carlo (☎ 535-901)

Getting Around

Bus #4 runs from Stazione Porta Nuova to P. Castello on XX Settembre, just west of V. Roma.

Arriving

Airport (16 km, 10 mi. by bus to Porta Nuova stazione) with daily domestic flights to major cities; there's also a Turin bus from Milan's Malpensa airport. • **Stazione Porta Nuova**, at south end of V. Roma, with frequent train service to Milan (under 2 hours), Venice (4-1/2 hours), Aosta (2 hours). **Bus terminal**, west edge of town, connected to stazione by bus #9 or #15, with service to Aosta, Courmayer and other nearby towns, as well as Geneva and other international destinations. • Turin lies 150 km, 93 mi. from Milan, 715 km, 443 mi. from Rome; 335 km, 208 mi. from Bologna.

Nearby Vineyards

Although the wine country of Tuscany is better-known, **Piedmont** produces more quality controlled wines than any region in Italy. From the Langhe region come two of Italy's most prestigious red wines, the venerable Barolo and the Barbaresco; from the Monferrato region, its most famous bubbly white, Asti Spumante (Moscato d'Asti). These wine regions, clustered in the hills near **Alba** (60 km, 37 mi. south on A-6 to SS 231) and **Asti** (55 km east on A-21 or by train), just an hour from Turin, are becoming popular destinations for tourists. The stunning landscape, pleasant country inns, and plentiful enoteca for wine tastings, make a car tour through these regions satisfying even for the non-oenophile. The area around Alba and south into the Langhe hills, the heart of Barolo and white truffle country, is quite special. In the fall, from September to late October, the wine harvest joins the truffle season to make for a culinary epiphany.

You might simply consider a drive through the Langhe, but an overnight trip can encompass some of both regions in a leisurely manner. One such trip might begin in the southern Monferrato region near Asti. Here the country-side opens to castle-topped hills and Alpine views as you wind through **Canel-li** and **Santo Stefano** where the best moscato vines grow, then climb the sinuous mountain road to tiny **Mango**, with its castle home for the regional enoteca *(closed Tues.)*. From Mango you can head into the Langhe region on the scenic mountain road between **Neive** and lovely **Barbaresco**, with several *cantine* (wine shops) offering tastings clustered near its church. On the way to the medieval city of **Alba**, where there's a truffle market in the fall (daily for much of Oct.; weekends only till Dec.), the dramatic scenery of the Langhe introduces itself: steep, picturesque hills and Nebbiola vines maniacally planted wherever the oak forests and land permit; snow-capped Alps suddenly appear, rimming the horizon, then vanish with mountain turns. From Alba, you can visit the heart of the Dolcetta d'Alba wine country around the beautiful old village of **Diano Alba**, or try to find **Barolo**, a tiny village little more than a castle with an enoteca inside and several *cantine*, or explore more of the beautiful Barolo country in the hilltowns to the north, like **La Morra** or **Verduno**. There's more, of course, much more.

Where to Stay

The hotels and small inns of the region are never sumptuous, but they are usually comfortable and often scenically situated.

Real Castello   **L115–170,000 CP**   ✖★★★

12060 Verduno, Cuneo; ☎ *(0172) 470-125, FAX 470-298; closed Nov.–Feb.*
Single/double L115–170,000 CP.
Just 15 km southwest of Alba, you can fully imbibe the Langhe ambience at a walled 18th-century castle located in a hilltop village where walks provide stupendous views of the Langhe valley. The two Burlotto sisters manage this wonderful inn, one rules the kitchen and gracious ★★ **dining room** (open to the public by reservation; meals L45–75,000); the other, the estate vineyards. Many of the 15 rooms have brocaded bedspreads, antique bedboards, fresco-covered walls; all the corner rooms in the oldest part have views of the Alps and the lovely garden. Rooms in a 19th-century annex have larger baths. Prices, unusually modest, vary with size and ambience.

Hotel Barolo   **L110,000**   ★★

V. Lomondo 2 in Barolo; ☎ *(0173) 56-354, FAX 56-354; closed early Feb.*
Single/double L110,000.
The grapevines come almost to the doorstep of this relatively new, but tranquilly situated inn overlooking the town castle and surrounding verdant hills. There's a

wrap-around terrace for dining and reading; 30 fresh rooms, simple but quite ample. A good restaurant (the ★ ★ **Brezza**; meals L30–50,000) and cantina.

Savona
L95–135,000 ★★

P. Savona 2, in Alba 012051; ☎ (0173) 440-440, FAX 364-312.
Single L95,000. Double L135,000.

This rambling hotel would be absolutely first-class with a little renovation; for the moment it has 100 a/c rooms, an outdoor cafe, sala da te, restaurant and garage.

Where to Eat

Vecchio Tre Stelle
$–$$ ★★★

Strada per Alba, Localita Trestelle in Barbaresco; closed Tues., ☎ (0173) 638-192.
Meals L30–50,000

We were just ambling along, leaving Barbaresco towards Alba, when we decided to stop for a bite to eat at what appeared to be a simple roadside restaurant. We proceeded to savor a meal worthy of a planned stop; the antipasto alone included rabbit salad, carpaccio with fresh porcini, asparagus with creme fraiche, a flan of squash. If you overeat, there are some inexpensive rooms here, too, with views of the Alps.
Credit cards: None.

Gener Neuv
$$–$$$ ★★★★

Lungo Tanaro 4 in Asti, Aug.; reserve at ☎ (0141) 557-270, FAX 436-723.
Fixed-price lunch L55–90,000 Fixed-priced dinner L75–100,000. À la carte L60–100,000. Closed Sun. dinner, Mon.

One of the finest country inns is situated along the beautiful Tanaro river (turn left at river, as exiting Asti to the south). If you're fortunate the daily degustazione menus will include a choice of its duck agnolotti and its sweetbreads stew *(finanziera)*. Finish with the zabaione al Moscato.

Belvedere
$$ ★★★

P. Castello 5 in La Morra; ☎ (0173) 50-190, FAX 50-190.
Meals L45–70,000; closed Sun. night, Mon., Jan.–Feb.

On its panoramic terrace enjoy a wonderful array of vegetable antipasti along with delicious *tajarin* with tartufi and ambrosial agnolotti.

Locanda Antico Borgo
$–$$ ★★★

P. Municipio 2 in Barolo; reserve at ☎ (0173) 56-355, FAX 56-355.
Fixed-price meal L40–55,000. À la carte meal L40–60,000; open noon–2:15 p.m., 8–10:30 p.m. except lunch Wed. & Thurs., late Feb., Aug.

With only 10 tables, a few on a terrace, this restaurant is as small as the village where it's found. Each day there's a special menu with a few choices for each course, all finely presented and prepared —a superb tajarin with zucchini, quail with fresh porcini, a hazelnut brownie straight out of the oven with Moscato sauce. Appropriately, there's an eight-page wine listed devoted to Barolos; another of regional wines.

Snacks

Enoteca Peccati di Gola *(V. Cavour 9 in Alba)*, just over a block from the main piazza, sells regional wine, cheeses, porcini and the like; **Io, Tu, e I Dolci** *(P. Savona in Alba)* makes irresistible chocolates from the local hazelnuts.

Nearby Vineyards

Directory

Tourist Information

In Alba, *Corso V. Emanuele 19* (☎ *[0173] 35-833; FAX 363-878);* In Asti, *P. Alfieri 34* (☎ *[0141] 530-357; FAX 538-200);* both have useful materials for visiting vineyards.

Getting Around

Only a car will do: Reserve a rental in Turin, Milan or Genoa.

Arriving

Both Asti and Alba are easily reachable by autostrada from Turin (1 hour), Milan (2 hours) and Genoa (2 hours) • Asti has train service from Turin and Milan.

Practical Tips

During the fall, reserve well in advance at hotels and restaurants • Get a good road map of Piedmont • Distances are short, but winding around narrow mountain roads requires time and patience • By arranging your tour to begin in Alba or Asti, you can pick up useful materials for exploring Le Langhe or Monferrato.

The Dolomites

The Brenner Pass into Italy from Austria
Two Routes: Innsbruck to Cortina, then Venice and Innsbruck to Bolzano & Trent, then Verona

The Dolomite mountains offer some of the most spectacular Alpine scenery in Europe. These rugged sandstone formations rise between the Adige and Piave rivers, their wind-carved peaks formed into primordial shapes while green forests and lush meadows soften their slopes. In 13 B.C. Augustus followed the Adige River north and crossed the Brenner Pass (*Passo di Brennero*) into what today is Austria. Many have followed—most often in the reverse direction. Whether Attila or Charlemagne, these invaders have found the route an excellent one through the Alps into Verona. Throughout its history, the region, now called Trentino-Alto Adige, has had great ties with either Germany or Austria, becoming part of Italy only in 1918. The most northern province of Alto Adige is the South Tyrol and more German is spoken than Italian, although signs are bilingual. Against the snow-covered peaks rise church steeples, not campaniles, and Tyrolean architecture and customs predominate.

You can use the Brennero Pass to drop quickly to Verona (275 km, 171 mi.) by train or A-22. Beyond the border, Munich is 135 km, 84 m; Salzburg 160 km, 99 mi. But there are variations on this route that are more picturesque. If Lake Garda is your destination, consider leaving A-22 at Trent and following lovely SS 45 bis south to Riva di Garda (42 km, 26 mi.).

TRENTINO CASTLES

VALLE DELL'ADIGE

Trentino is famous for its castle landscape. Along Valle dell'Adige, runs the historical road linking Italy to the center of Europe, and along this road are some of the area's most fascinating architectural wonders.

SABBIONARA D'AVIO

Traveling from Verona, the first castle you encounter is an example of 14th century architecture influenced by the Veneto style. It belonged to the Castelbarco family at the height of their power between the 13th and 14th centuries.Beyond the entrance tower are a sequence of buildings and vineyards. Inside are impressive frescoes.

CASTELLO DI ROVERTO

Most of Roverto's history is documented in this castle from the time of the Castelbarco family to World War I. At the end of the 18th century it was occupied by Napoleon's French soldiers, then by Austrians who maintained its fortresslike appearance by maintaining the moats, wallwalks, secret passages, gunloops and bastions.

CASTEL BESENO

This majestic castle looks like a fortified town spread across the hill. Towers, battlemented glacis, huge bastions and blunted barbicans alternate in the elongated outline of the stronghold's profile. Two walls surround the fortress.

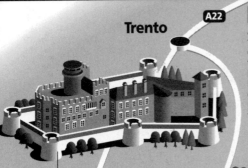

Trento A22

CASTELLO DI PERGINE

An example of a medieval alpine fortress cum residence with a system of walls and towers surrounding the top of Tegazzo hill, above the town. It is dominated by the Gothic style lord's residence. Historians believe it dates from Longobard times. Highlights are the hall of arms and the frightening dungeon.

CASTELLO DEL BUONCONSIGLIO

This castle consists of two main units, the medieval Castelvecchio built in Romanesque-Gothic style and the Renaissance Magno Palazzo. The older section has a medieval tower and drawbridge, while the newer section features masterpieces by famous artists on the vaults, ceilings and walls of the palace.

CASTEL PIETRA

Built on enormous rocks, this castle stands at the foot of Castel Beseno hill, beyond the Rio Cavallo. Many important field battles were waged around it in the 15th and 16th centuries. Inside are frescoes of mysterious medieval figures, interesting staircases and a gloomy cellar where prisoners were kept.

VALSUGANA AND PRIMIERO

Valsugana, linking Trento to Veneto, was one of the two imperial Roman roads (Claudia Augusta Altinate) that ran through Trentino to Rhaetia.

CASTEL IVANO

Ivano's high, bare walls leave no doubt as to its medieval origin and military function. Famous European artists, Wagner and Eleonaora Duse, stayed here in the 18th and 19th centuries. The tower rooms and dungeons are awe-inspiring, while the gardens still give the impression of a busy village.

The Dolomites

Fielding | TRENTINO CASTLES

(For castle tour information, contact Trentino Tourism, ☎ 0461-914-444)

CASTEL ROMANO

Standing atop Sant'Antonio hill, this castle was used to "spy" on all the surrounding villages. Built in the 12th century, it suffered much damage over the years during military action. Its most distinctive features are its granite stonework, arrow slits, loop-holes and thick walls. Only six windows remain.

CASTEL STENICO

This castle is significant for its mixture of styles from the 13th and 14th centuries. The assorted buildings and wards are incorporated in the southern curtain wall and enclosed by a strong external curtain wall toward the north. Many interesting frescoes decorate the interior.

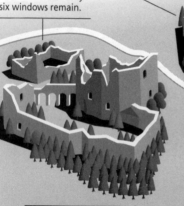

PIANA DEL SARCA AND GIUDICARIE

A number of castles and manor houses are also found along the plain of the lower Sarca River.

ROCA DI RIVA DEL GARDA

This lakeside castle was built in the 12th century as an external defense to the walled town. It has four corner towers and a drawbridge as well as the largest square keep of any of the Trentino castles.

The Dolomites

CASTEL CALDES

Built in the first half of the 1 3th century, this castle overshadows the houses around it at Caldes village. The top floor of the square tower is decorated with Baroque paintings. On the side by the chapel courtyard an ashlar doorway leads into a large hall. An elegant newel staircase made of red stone leads to the top floors.

CASTEL THUN

This baronial residence features three Gothic turrets, a Spanish doorway, five towers, a drawbridge and a moat. A curtain wall encloses a tournament field, Basilian tower and library tower. The library has a baroque stucco ceiling and houses more than 10,000 books.

43

VALLI DEL NOCE

The Noce Valleys northeast of Trento feature a number of castles and manors among the celebrated orchards of Valle di Non.

Trento

45

CASTEL TOBLINO

This castle evokes romantic images from its surroundings as well as its architecture. Set on the water, surrounded by mountains, marsh vegetation and vines, it is an appealing blend of alpine rustic and Renaissance design. A restaurant in the castle is open from March to November.

CASTEL CAMPO

A22

Set at the end of a winding road through the woods, this turreted castle is anchored to a rugged hill between the Duina and the Rezola streams. It was founded in the 11th century and used as a hillfort refuge. The inside of the castle was painted by Carlo Donati with late-Gothic revival and post art nouveau decorations.

The Dolomites

And if you have time, you definitely (season permitting) should explore the beauty of the Dolomites by taking the Dolomite Road (SS 241 & 48) from Bolzano to Cortina d'Ampezzo (110 km, 68 mi.), one of Europe's most majestically scenic routes. And if you drop to Venice from Cortina (163 km, 101 mi.) on SS 51 through the Piave valley and then on A-27, you will be following the Renaissance route to the Brenner used by Venetian traders. Whether you're just driving through and enjoying the scenery, or whether you are joining the bicyclists, backpackers, the mountain climbers and the skiers (there are almost 8700 miles of ski runs in the Dolomites) in taking advantage of the various seasons, the following brief guide to the major towns and sights should be useful.

Bolzano

If arriving from the south, Bolzano seems strikingly "un-Italian," from its lacy Gothic spires and tidy flower boxes to the thick pretzels sold in the picturesque Piazza delle Erbe market. The Tyrolean capital of Alto Adige province, Bolzano offers a pleasant *centro storico*, despite some surrounding industry. Although you can walk the few historic blocks, such as Via dei Portici, quite quickly, you probably are here for convenience, not sightseeing. Bolzano's center is compact and easy to maneuver for a quick stopover, with parking lots, bus and train terminals just a few blocks from the main square of Piazza Walther. From here you can arrange transportation east into the Dolomites and, in summer, along the Dolomite Road to Cortina.

Where to Stay

Park Hotel Laurin   **L250–315,000**   ★★★★

    V. Laurin 4; ☎ *311-000, FAX 311-148.*
    Single L250,000. Double L300–315,000.
    This recently renovated belle epoque hotel overlooks a park, just behind the main square, Piazza Walther. The 90 a/c rooms have period style furnishings and some, balconies and park views. A highly respected restaurant. A fine garden and heated pool.

Asterix   **L120,000**   ★★

    P. Mazzini 35; ☎ *273-301, FAX 260-021.*
    Single/double L 120,000.
    A reasonably convenient hotel, even if it is across the river and several blocks down Corso Liberta. And the price is right for its 24 rooms (no a/c), breakfast bar and garage.

Where to Eat

Zur Kaiserkron   **$$**   ★★

    P. della Mostra 1; ☎ *970-770.*
    Meals L55–70,000; closed Sat. night, Sun.
    This restored old inn serves some very traditional, yet inspired Tyrolean cuisine: venison with juniper berry sauce, blinis with zucchini and creme fraiche.

Da Abramo $$ ★★

P. Gries 16; ☎ 280-141.
Meals L45-65,000; closed Sun., part of Aug.
Located not too far from the center, but across the river. In the summer the outdoor terrace here is as fine as the Italian food of fish and risotto, quail and polenta.

Directory

Telephone Code 0471 **Postal Code 39100**

Tourist Information

AAST, *P. Walther 8* (☎ *970-660; FAX 980-128);* APT, *P. Parrocchia 11,* just off main square (☎ *993-808),* for information on nearby Alpine sights.

Transportation

The Bologna-Brennero train provides local service and continues north to Munich.

SAD buses *(V. Perathoner 4, behind P. Walther;* ☎ *450-111)* link Bolzano with nearby ski resorts and peaks, including the Passo di Sella Apr.–Sept., as well as with Cortina (3.5 hours) along the famous Dolomite Road, but in summer July–Sept. only.

Bolzano lies just off A-22, 120 km, 74 mi. south of Innsbruck and 155 km, 96 mi. north of Verona.

Trent

A bit austere in the northern fashion, Trent (*Trento* in Italian) is nonetheless Italian—in its language, in the Venetian frescoes that cover many palazzi in its *centro storico*, and in its customs and cuisines. The capital of the semi-autonomous region of Trentino-Alto Adige, Trent is historically most famous for the church reforms promulgated in the Council of Trent (1545-63) in response to the Protestant movement sweeping Europe. But much of the town architecture dates from earlier medieval times, from the handsome **★Piazza del Duomo** with its predominantly Romanesque church, complete with a very Italian lion porch, to the **★Castello del Buon Consiglio** *(winter 9 a.m.–noon, 2–5:30 p.m., summer 10 a.m.–7 p.m., closed Mon.; L6000).* This richly frescoed residence of the ruling bishops has a number of parts, from the 13th-century Castelvecchio, with its Venetian cortile, to the 16th-century Palazzo Magno. Apart from the enjoyable walk between these two sights (up the Via Belenzani from the duomo, right along Via Roma and its continuations—Manci and S. Marco) and the surrounding streets, you'll find the city a convenient stopover. Its location at the foot of Monte Bondone where the Trent and Adige rivers meet is attractive and the old section is right next to the train and bus terminals. Facilities, especially the food, are good.

Where to Stay

Accademia L185–255,000 CP ★★★

V. Colico 4 at Cavour; ☎ *233-600, FAX 230-174.*
Single L185,000 CP. Double L255,000 CP.

Just a block away from the duomo, the 40 well-appointed rooms (no a/c) of this handsome inn are in a modernized medieval mansion; parking.

America   **L115–160,000**   ★★

V. Torre Verde 50; ☎ 983-010, FAX 230-603.
Single L115,000. Double L160,000.

This commercial hotel is on a traffic-ridden main street near the Castle, but most of its 43 carpeted rooms are quiet. The hotel is comfortable with a restaurant, bar, parking.

Where to Eat

If dining indulgences aren't in your plans, shop around the streets near the duomo to make a picnic at the Giardini Pubblici only a few blocks away in Piazza Dante. For regional wines such as a Spumante Trentino Classico, or reds such as Santa Maddelena or Teroldego Rotaliano, visit the well-stocked enoteca **Lunelli** *(Largo Carducci 12, several blocks north of the duomo).*

Chiesa   **$–$$**   ★★★

V. San Marco 64; ☎ 238-766.
Meals L45–65,000; closed Wed. night, Sun. part of Aug.

A good reason to stop in Trent is to eat, especially here. Near the castle and in an old palazzo itself, you find Chiesa through a gate, set back in a walled garden. Its ambience is as contemporary as its food is nouvelle—salmon-filled ravioli in a sauce of orange zest and little shrimp, duck with onion relish, veal braised in apple. The service is attentive, the prices not bad, especially the moderate-priced presso fisso meal, but even à la carte the main dish includes the service, cover and even some vegetable accompaniment.

Directory

Telephone Code 0461   **Postal Code 38100**

Tourist Information

AAST, *V. Alfieri 4, on P. Dante (☎ 983-880; FAX 984-508).*

Transportation

Train and bus terminals near P. Dante.

Bologna to Innsbruck trains stop here and continue on to Munich in north, Rome in south.

Trent is just off A-22, 50 km, 31 mi. south of Bolzano, 100 km, 62 mi. north of Verona.

The Dolomite Road

The drama of the scenery along the ★★★ **Dolomite Road** between Bolzano and Cortina d'Ampezzo is comparable to the American Southwest. Here the mesas and buttes, the pinnacles and turrets often are iced with snow or cloaked in Alpine forest, but they also have their surreal badlands, their naked white sandstone cliffs, and sudden ominous cloud-cast shadows. In good weather (the only time to make this trip), following the often spiraling road requires patience (expect to stop for the many tourist buses maneuvering the turns), but not much hardship. Facilities are excellent throughout, at the Tyrolean ski villages and at the refuges atop peaks. You might take a chair lift for views, especially around the most breathtaking area of the Passo di Sella, or you might arrange a biking or hiking trip through the region, exploring it more intimately. Even by car you can follow alternate routes, tracking down the highest peak Marmolada (11,000 feet, south of Canazei on SS 48) or Ladin villages (SS 242, north of Passo di Sella) in the Val Gardena around Ortisei, where managers of modern Tyrolean ski lodges still speak ancient Ladin, a combination of Celtic and Latin.

Route

Just north of Bolzano, turn east at Cardano onto SS 241 and travel through the narrow gorge of Val d'Ega, past castles and Lake Carezza before arriving at the village of Canazei. Continuing north from Canazei, pick up the fabulous Passo di Sella (SS 242). After exploring the summit of the Sella, backtrack and climb the Passo di Pordoi, for its exceptional views of the various ranges. Then continue east on SS 48 through glorious mountainscapes, all the way through the Falzarego Pass where you drop to Cortina. *Distance* 110 km, 68 mi. *Time* At least a half day.

Where to Stay and Eat

There are **ski lodges** and **inns** not only in villages like Arabba (near Passo di Pordoi), Canazei and the Val Gardena, but along the road, too. Restaurants can be found in the same places, but you'll be sorry if you don't plan a picnic along the road—pulling off where there are tables for enjoying the shade of the forest and a running creek, or sitting atop one of the passes enjoying a great panoramic view. If you've forgotten to pack a lunch, then look for one of the scenic refuges, such as **Refugio Monte Pallido** (SS 242 Passo di Sella) where the views are good, the food hearty polenta and sausage.

Practical Tips

Tourist Information

Check with the Bolzano or Cortina tourist offices for maps and weather conditions.

Beware

The passes often are closed by snowfalls from Nov. to June. Check weather conditions and alternate routes before setting out.

Cortina d'Ampezzo

This elegant international ski resort couldn't be more beautifully situated in a hollow ringed by towering snow-capped mountains. The village itself is in modern make-believe Tyrolean. A rushing stream cuts through the center, marking the beginning of the pedestrian-only main street, Corso Italia, with its designer boutiques. The 1956 winter Olympics brought Cortina considerable fame and extensive facilities—not only bobsled runs, but public saunas and indoor olympic pools and the like. In the summer, Cortina is busy with hikers and other visitors to the Dolomites, in the winter, ski chalets and elegant hotels are filled to capacity.

Where to Stay

High season (Christmas, Holy Week, March, Aug.) prices indicated here are considerably higher than the rest of the year. Except for the Panda, hotels require meal plans. Note that hotels operate only seasonally.

Miramonti Majestic   L500–900,000 MAP

Pezzie 103; ☎ *42-01, FAX 867-019; open Christmas–Apr., July–Sept.*
Single L500,000. Double L900,000. Price includes two meals.
On a mountain slope just about 1 mi. south of the village this hotel has its own extensive grounds that include golf, tennis, an indoor pool and spa. The chalets and 121 rooms have fine views and timber ceilings, but are in no way rustic in their comforts and appointments. Restaurant, lounges. Parking.

Menardi   L229–400,000 MAP

V. Majon 110; ☎ *24-00, FAX 862-183; open Christmas–Apr., mid-June–mid-Sept.*
Single L120,000. Double L400,000. Price includes two meals
Just north of town, the Menardi's 48 cozy rooms (some with views) are in a farmhouse now turned into a comfortable chalet on very attractive grounds.

Panda   L115–190,000   ★

V. Roma 64; ☎ *860-344, FAX 860-345; closed May–June, Nov.*
Single L115,000. Double L190,000.
In the village, but many of the 18 immaculate rooms in this modern ski chalet have balconies and mountain views.

Da Beppe Sello   L125–200,000 CP   ★

V. Ronco 67; ☎ *32-36, FAX 32-37.*
Single L125,000 CP. Double L200,000 CP.
Here there are 13 rooms in a beautiful location just above the town.

Where to Eat

The favorites all cluster in the mountains just east of the village, where they look over Cortina below.

Da Beppe Sello $$–$$$ ★★★

V. Ronco 67; ☎ *32-36, FAX 32-37.*
Meals L45–70,000; closed Tues.; mid-Apr.–mid May, late Sept.–Nov. 1.
Exit town in the direction of Falzarego and you'll come first to this rustic restaurant with grand views and traditional foods for this part of the Veneto region—polenta dishes and grilled meats as well as trout.

Tivoli $$–$$$ ★★★★

V. Lacedel 34, 2 km from center; reserve at ☎ *866-400, FAX 34-13.*
Meals L45–70,000; closed May–June, Oct.–Nov., & Mon. in Jan., July, Sept.
Up the road after Beppe Sello is the more refined Tivoli with stupendous food to match the views from the summer terrace. This probably is Cortina's best restaurant. Everyone agrees the ravioli here, with smoked ricotta and poppy seeds *(semi di papavero)*, should not be missed, but try the polenta-stuffed pigeon, too.

Meloncino   **$$–$$$**   ★ ★ ★

in Gilardon; reserve at ☎ 861-043.
Meals L40–75,000; closed Tues., June & Nov.
On the roady beyond Tivoli, about 3.5 km from the center, is another restaurant
with great views from both its log cabin-style restaurant and summer terrace.
There's particularly fine food, too—risotto with mushrooms, roasted kid or rabbit.

Snacks

The pasticcerias along the Corso Italia are inviting and **Febar** *(at #17; closed Tues.)*
has sandwiches along with a good selection of wines by the glass, beer by the mug. **Pizzeria Pandino** *(V. Roma 68)*, on the south edge of town, has very good pizza. For an
aperitivo, **Bar della Poste** in the hotel of that name *(P. Roma 14)* has been a favorite since
Hemingway made it famous, and **Enoteca Cortina** *(V. del Mercato 5; shop hours with
later closing in-season; closed Sun.)* offers many fine wines by the glass.

Directory

Telephone Code 0436   **Postal Code 32043**

Tourist Information
   P. San Francesco 8 (☎ 32-31; FAX 32-35)

Transportation
   In summer local buses run on the Dolomite Road to Bolzano (July–Sept.) and on
   other day excursions. ATVO buses run daily to Venice (about 2.5 hours).

   Cortina is 163 km, 101 mi. north of Venice and 110 km, 62 mi. east of Bolzano on
   the Dolomite Road.

   Venice trains to Calazodi Cadore, 30 km or 19 mi. south, connect with Cortina by
   bus.

Seasons
   Most everything is open Christmas till April and June–mid Sept., but the better
   hotels seldom stay open longer.

The Friuli

From Central Europe into Italy
Two Routes: Austria to Udine & Aquilea, then Venice
Croatia to Trieste & Aquilea, then Venice

Bounded on the north by the Alps shared with Austria, and on the east by
the Dinaric Alps of Slovenia, the Friuli softens to a rich agricultural valley
around Udine before flattening out to the miles of beaches surrounding the
Adriatic on the south. The full name of this region, the Friuli-Venezia
Giulia, is as complex as its history. Not too surprisingly, cultural influences
from both Austria to the north, Croatia and Slovenia to the east are apparent, and near Udine, the indigenous Friuli dialect includes traces of both
Serbo-Croate and German. Although the Austrians ruled the Trieste area for
over 500 years (1382-1918), the Venetian Republic had a much broader in-

The Friuli

fluence and conquered most of the area by the Early Renaissance (c. 1420), controlling it until the end of the 18th century when Napoleon and the Austrians took over. Even in the Trieste area the lions of San Marco are found on town gates and the Venetian dialect is sometimes spoken. This predominantly Italian identity of the region led to Italy's costly struggle for it during World War I—a struggle commemorated in Ernest Hemingway's *A Farewell to Arms*. Trieste itself, despite centuries of Austrian rule, opted for unity with Italy in 1918. Perhaps the foundation for this Italian identity in such a diversified area began two millennia ago when the Romans positioned themselves here, later granting its consulship to no less a luminary than Julius Caesar.

The Friuli is not much visited for itself. Those enamored of the air-cured *prosciutto* di **San Daniele**, so delicate that white wine is an appropriate accompaniment, might explore the countryside 20 km (12 mi.) west of Udine. In the village of San Daniele, sample the thinly cut slices wrapped around breadsticks at the cafe **Casa del Prosciutto** *(V. Ciconi 24, downhill from main square; closed Tues.)*, where they cure the hams themselves. Those seeking a few hours on the beach might combine a visit to lovely **Grado** with the sights of nearby Aquilea (see below), but should be warned that pollution along the Trieste Riviera marred sea bathers enjoyment in 1989 (official warnings were only for those with open cuts). Most likely travelers are making their way to Venice from Vienna. From Vienna, the train and highway both cross the Alps at Tarviso (about 530 km, 329 mi.), then drop to Udine (A-23) before continuing to Venice (on A-23 south, then A-4 west; 230 km, 143 mi. from Tarviso). Travel from Croatia is tragically limited, but begins in Trieste, and then continues on the Trieste-Venice train or A-4 west into Venice (160 km, 100 mi.). Detours on either route can be made to Aquilea, from Udine on the northern route and from the Cervignano stop on the Trieste train. Udine and Trieste are both pleasant and have facilities convenient for travelers.

Special Tip

For those with a car, the best way to enjoy the Fruili is by spending a bucolic afternoon in the rolling hills of the Collio wine region above **Cormons** *(26 km east of Udine, near Gorizia)*. A visit is greatly enhanced by a meal at the following inn:

La Subida   **$$**   ★★★★

2 km north of Cormons; reserve at ☎ [0481] 60-531, FAX 60-531.
Meals L45-70,000;closed Tues., Wed., early Feb., early July.

You can dine very well at this charming country inn, also known as "Al Cacciatore." Much of the wonderful food comes from the inn's farm and vineyards. If you're lucky, the changing menu will include fagottini with porcini, stinco (braised veal shank), or braised duck breast. Credit cards: None.

Hotel Felcaro L70–120,000 ★ ★

V. San Giovanni 45; ☎ *[0481] 60-214, FAX 630-255.*
Single L70,000. Double 120,000.

If too mellow to travel, you can overnight in this tranquil 400-year-old farmhouse
on the edge of Cormons with a pool and restaurant.

Udine

Udine is the historical center of the western Friuli province and sits at the
base of the Alpine foothills amid fertile fields. Like most towns of the area, it
has Roman foundations overlaid with medieval ones from the period of rule
by the feudal bishops called the Patriarchs of Aquilea. The later Venetian period is proclaimed in the central **Piazza della Liberta**, complete with its *loggia*
of ogive arches and a column with St. Mark's lion on top. But for the tourist,
Udine is an attraction for the light-filled frescoes by the great Rococo artist,
G. B. Tiepolo. Just a block along Via Veneto from the Piazza della Liberta,
you have your choice of paintings by the young Tiepolo (c.1726): A few
steps to the right are those in the **Piazza del Duomo** (in the right aisle of the
cathedral, chapels 1, perhaps 2, and 4; and his ★ *"Assumption,"* in the Oratorio della Purita to right of duomo—*ask duomo sacristan for entry*). And
two blocks to the left of Via Veneto, through the park, are his finest works in
Udine at the **Palazzo Archivescovile** where they ★ surround the stairs and
adorn the gallery and the Sala Rossa *(ring at curia Mon.–Fri. 9 a.m.–noon)*.
Other streets can be explored, some with canals filled with rushing streams
from the River Torre. A climb to the hilltop **castle** on a clear day brings views
of the nearby Alps.

Where to Stay and Eat

Astoria Hotel Italia L190–255,000 ★ ★ ★

P. XX Settembre 18; ☎ *505-091, FAX 509-070.*
Single L190,000. Double L255,000.

This is the best hotel in the centro storico. The grand spaces of its 19th-century
building make for fine public rooms, and good management provides 74 comfortable rooms along with one of the better ★ ★ ★ restaurants in town (L50–65,000).
Fee for garage.

Quo Vadis L60–90,000 ★

Piazzale Cella 28; ☎ *21-091, FAX 21-092.*
Single L60,000 Double L90,000

On the edge of the centro storico, but just a 10-minute walk to the sights, this hotel
has 25 small rooms in linoleum modern, with very functional baths—get an interior
for quiet. Breakfast bar.

Alla Buona Vite $–$$ ★ ★

V. Treppo 10; ☎ *21-053.*
Meals L45-65,000; closed Sun. dinner, Mon., Aug.

Centrally located and with a menu that emphasizes Venetian-style seafood, this restaurant gives you a chance to sample the regional white wines such as the Sauvignon or Tocai from Collio Goriziano.

Directory

Telephone Code 0432   Postal Code 33100

Tourist Information

AAST, *P. 1 di Maggio 7* (☎ *295-972; FAX 504-743*).

Transportation

Trains from both Venice and Trieste run frequently; stazione south edge of town, 15-minute walk or bus #1.

Buses to Aquilea (under 1 hour) and rest of region, station near stazione.

Udine lies 90 km, 56 mi. south of the Austrian border, 140 km, 87 mi. northeast of Venice; and 75 km, 47 mi. northwest of Trieste. For center, take "Udine Sud" exit from A-23.

Aquilea

Founded in 181 B.C. by the Romans, Aquilea not only served briefly as Julius Caesar's camp, but also as Augustus' for his five years of war against Germanic tribes. For centuries, it was the market city for northern Europe, and soon after Constantine issued his edict protecting Christianity in A.D. 313, a basilica was founded here along with an important archbishopric. In A.D. 452, Attila repeatedly sacked the town and in the 6th century, the Lombards replaced him, sending its citizens to the safety of the offshore island of Grado, where another basilica was founded. Aquilea was practically abandoned until the 11th century, when Patriarch Poppo united the various bishops of the Friuli with their capital at Aquilea.

What to See and Do

Today, Aquilea is a small farming town graced by its remarkable Early Christian ★★**Basilica** *(P. Capitolo; closed 12:30–3 p.m. in winter)*. Patriarch Poppa built the Romanesque basilica over the 4th-century one, retaining the original ★mosaic pavement with its scenes of a rooster and turtle fight, of Jonah and the whale, and portraits of the donors. In the crypt under the choir are *frescoes* (12th Century; *fee*) and in the ★**cripta degli scavi** *(entrance off left aisle; 9 a.m.–3 p.m., Sun. till 1 p.m.; L3000)* are several levels of ★mosaics dating from an Augustan-period house up to the late 4th century. Behind the basilica the lovely cypress-lined **Via Sacra** takes you along what little remains of the ancient Roman port to the Porto Fluviale Romano where you can glimpse the unrestored forum and other **Roman ruins** through a chainlink fence. A 10-minute walk from the Basilica, on the main road towards Grado, gains your entrance to the **Museo Archeologico** *(V. Roma; 9 a.m.–6:30 p.m., Sun. closed 1–2 p.m.; 9 a.m.–2 p.m. in winter, Sun. till 1 p.m., closed Mon.; free)* with Roman portrait busts, gems, and mosaics. Once you've toured Aquilea, you might visit **Grado** (10 km, 6 mi. south) its beautiful basilica (6th Century), medieval streets, and beach now joined to the mainland by a causeway.

Where to Eat

A picnic would give you the greatest flexibility in planning your day, but there is a restaurant/bar near the basilica and Grado has a selection of simple hotels and trattoria. You might try:

All'Androna   **$–$$**   ★★
Calle Porta Piccola 4, Grado; ☎ *(0431) 80-950.*
Meals L45–65,000; closed Tues. except in summer, Christmas–Mar. 1.
Right behind the basilica in Grado you can dine on good homemade pastas and seafood.

Directory

Telephone Code 0431

Tourist Information
    Pro Loco, *P. Capitolo 1 (*☎ *91-087)*, across from basilica; open Apr.–Oct. 31.

Transportation
    Buses stop 1/2 block from the basilica, from Udine (38 km, 23.5 mi. north on SS 352), and the Venice-Trieste train stop at Cervignano (9 km, 5.5 mi. north) as well as from Grado (10 km south).

Trieste

Although under Roman and Austrian domination for much of its history, and only occasionally Venetian, Trieste did not flourish until the 18th century when Venice was well in decline. Then, under the Hapsburgs of Austro-Hungary, Trieste flourished as a great port for central Europe as well as a cultural center, famed for the performances in its Teatro Verdi opera house, for the intellectual life of its Viennese cafes, and for the broad avenues lined with 18th- and 19th-century neoclassical buildings.

What to See and Do

Today, Trieste no longer flourishes. At the extreme eastern frontier of Italy, it is somewhat disconnected from the rest of the country while having been separated from its traditional neighbors in Slovenia and Croatia since WW II. Yet the city retains some of the intriguing cultural ambience that attracted turn-of-the-century travelers on the Orient Express and writers like James Joyce, who wrote *Portrait of the Artist as a Young Man* while he was a teacher here. The port area is quite striking, for amid old warehouses and facing anchored ships are elegant 19th-century neoclassical squares—none more important than the **Piazza dell'Unita d'Italia**, with its ornate town hall and cafes, that opens to the harbor. There are no great sights here—a Roman theater, a Venetian castle atop the ancient Capitoline Hill (bus #24). In good weather the grandiose architecture is made more welcoming by the outdoor terraces of restaurants and you'll want to stroll along the esplanade overlooking the harbor. And you should walk through the beautiful park of **Miramare** (7 km north of stazione on Strada Miramare; 9 a.m.–5 p.m.) where the ill-fated Maximilian and his wife Carlotta, who later faced their sad destiny in Mexico, built their castle (1855) on a rocky promontory overlooking the sea. Then again, you might just want to spend your hours in Trieste in one of the grand cafes.

Where to Stay

Duchi d'Aosta   **L250–330,000 CP**   ★★★

P. Unita d'Italia 2, 34121; ☎ *73-51, FAX 366-092.*
Single L250,000 CP. Double L330,000 CP.

There's no better location in Trieste. The hotel's handsome 19th-century architecture and sitting rooms with Venetian chandeliers provide Old World charm, despite the modernization of the 50 smallish rooms, some with harbor views, into more comfortable ones. Fine restaurant, popular bar. Limited parking.

Al Teatro   **L95–115,000**   ★

Capo di Piazza G. Bartoli, 34100; ☎ *366-220, FAX: 366-560.*
Single/double L95–115,000.

Just a few steps off P. dell'Unita, this hotel has long been favored by performers at the nearby Teatro Verdi. The 45 bright and ample rooms (no a/c) have parquet floors, simple furnishings and modernized baths (though some are without private baths).

Where to Eat

The specialties here are as often Hungarian as Venetian, as likely to be *gulasch* or *jota* (bean soup with sauerkraut and potatoes) as seafood or *risotto*. Fortunately, the desserts most often are Viennese.

Antica Trattoria Suban   **$$–$$$**   ★★★★

V. Comici 2; reserve at ☎ *54-368*
Meals L50–75,000; closed Mon., Tues., most Aug.

Here is where you can enjoy the most refined "Old World" cuisine. The *palacindhe* (crepes filled with basil and vegetables) and *jota* are offered next to duck with almonds and chicken Kiev. Located on the eastern outskirts (follow V. Giulia) with dining under an arbor in summer.

Ai Fiori   **$$**   ★★★

P. Hortis 7; ☎ *300-633.*
Meals L45–65,000; closed Sun., Mon., Christmas, Aug.

For Venetian seafood, this is an attractive choice found just 4 blocks or so from P. dell'Unita, off V. Cadorna. If you're hungry and speak no Italian, the easiest way to enjoy the wonderfully fresh food here is to order the more than ample degustazione menu. A little knowledge of Italian can bring an assortment of the warm antipasto di pesce, the homemade pasta, usually served with shellfish, and well-grilled fish. Everything is fresh and prices are reasonable.

Buffet Benedetto   **$–$$**   ★★

V. XXX Ottobre 19, near P. Oberdan; ☎ *631-655.*
L35–50,000 for a light meal; closed Mon., Aug.

Comparable to Venice's tiny wine osterias, where you stand or sit to enjoy the display of dishes for the day, are Trieste's buffets. This is one of the more sophisticated with an array of antipasti and pasta and modestly-priced when eaten informally at the counter.

Trieste

Caffè

There are not as many Viennese coffeehouses as there used to be, but the enduring favorites should keep you busy. Two in particular preserve their 19th-century ambience. Founded in 1830, the elegant **Caffè Tommaseo** *(on esplanade, 2 blocks north of P. dell' Unite at V. San Nicolo; closed Mon.)* has been gloriously refurbished and even those short of lira can enjoy the live piano waltzes (evenings) from the stand-up bar in the rear. In the more commercial part of the city above Via Caduta, the **Caffè San Marco** *(V. Battisti 18; closed Wed.)* is the perfect traditional spot to sip your coffee over a newspaper in the afternoon, or to enjoy *sacher torte* and waltzes in the evening.

Directory

Telephone Code 040   **Postal Code 34100**

Tourist Information

APT, *Stazione Centrale (☎ 420-182);* U.S. Consul: ☎ *660-177;* British Consulate: ☎ *302-884.*

Special Events

In the summer, plays and concerts are performed at the Castle San Giulio and Miramare as well as in the Roman theater.

Transportation

For Castello Miramare take bus #6 from stazione to Barcola, then switch to #36 (about 1/2 hr.).

From the stazione north of center, but within walking distance, trains depart for Venice, Udine, and Rijeka (*Fiume* in Italian), in Croatia.

Trieste is 160 km, 100 mi. to Venice by A-4; 50 km, 31 mi. to the SS 351 turnoff from A-4 to Cervignano and then Aquilea; and 70 km, 43 mi. from Rijeka.

Ronchi airport, 32 km, 20 mi. northwest, with domestic flights is connected by bus with the *stazione.*

Trieste

Trieste

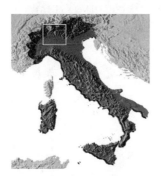

MILAN AND LOMBARDY

Milan's Gothic Cathedral boasts 2245 statues and a forest of spires.

History and Art

Two contrasting regions compose Lombardy: the majestic Alps with the glacier-formed lakes of Como, Maggiore and Garda—their beauty extolled since Roman times; and the fertile basin of the Po river, as flat and monotonous as a plain can be—gratefully veiled in fog the winter-long and revealed in summer with patterns of windbreaking poplars, the crisscross of rivers and canals. Both geographies have played their parts in Lombard history. The

107

SWITZERLAND

E9

Lake Maggiore

Lake Como

Tremezzo

Varenna

Lugano

Bellagio

Lake Lugano

Stresa

Cernobbio

Como

Orta San Giulio

Lake Orta

S-36

A9

A8

A4

PIEDMONT

Milan

A4

Ticino River

A7

S35

Certosa di Pavia

A26

Pavia

Po River

LOMBARDY AND THE LAKES

TRENTINO

a River

N

| 0 | miles | 24 |
| 0 | kilometers | 40 |

Riva del
Garda

S45

Lake
Iseo

Gardone
Riviera

VENETO

rgamo

Brescia

A4

Lake
Garda

Oglio River

Sirmione

A4

S236

A21

Mincio River

Adda River

Mantua

Cremona

Po River

Sabbioneta

A21

EMILIA

ROMAGNA

A1

safe riverine trade routes across the plain from Venice made the cities flourish, and the Alpine passes permitted trade to the rest of Europe, but also invasion.

On the frontier, Lombardy has experienced almost as many invasions as Sicily to the south—Milan alone was conquered 40 times and razed to the ground twice. But its Alpine location made it susceptible not to the Greeks but rather the Celts, not to Arab splendor but instead the Goths, the Lombards or Longobards (so-called for their beards), and the Franks. These northern contacts left their imprint, not only in the name of the region, but in its non-Mediterranean character, in its cuisine, and certainly in its artistic preference for the linear and expressionistic, for decorative spirals and arabesques.

One invader did come from the south, of course. And when Rome conquered this region of Celtic tribes (around 225 B.C.), the Italian peninsula was unified for the first time. Unification hardly made the Celts happy. In fact, they fought alongside Hannibal when he arrived in the Po Valley after his extraordinary journey through the Alps with 90,000 troops, cavalry, and war elephants. But by the time of Julius Caesar, this region, called Cisalpine Gaul, was peaceful enough for him to make his military reputation by launching attacks across the Alps from here. The Roman cities at Brescia, Pavia, Mantua, Como and Milan would assimilate so well that they could boast as native sons the great Roman poets Catullus (b. 84 B.C.), Virgil (b. 70 B.C.) and the natural historian Pliny the Elder (A.D. 23) and his nephew. By the time of Constantine, Milan was briefly the capital of the Western Empire and the site of that emperor's famous edict declaring tolerance for Christianity (A.D. 313).

But when the Western Empire ended, it ended quickly in Cisalpine Gaul. The northern tribes poured through the Alpine passes. In the 6th century, the Lombards conquered and remained for two centuries, with their capital at Pavia. They ruled south to Siena and Pisa, east through most of the Veneto, as well as in scattered duchies at Spoleto and Benevento. By the time they were defeated by Charlemagne (A.D. 774), they had intermarried so long with the Romans that they, too, spoke Latin. They became so identified with northern Italy that when Holy Roman Emperors wished to assert their traditional rights in Italy, they were crowned not just by the Pope in Rome but also with the Iron Crown of the Lombards.

During the early Middle Ages, the ancient Roman cities of Lombardy were revived by Venice's precocious sea trade. Commerce meant wealth, and wealth meant a renewal of church construction that led to the Lombard Romanesque style (see Art History), with its northern abstract arabesques and blind arcading. And once the thriving towns united in the Lombard League against Frederick Barbarossa's meddling, and defeated his German knights at

Legano (1176), they also won the right to self government. Conflicts continued, however, for control of the fledgling republics, during a period of so-called Guelf (papal sympathizers) and Ghibelline (German emperor sympathizers) turbulence. As noble fought noble, and as feudal serfs fought town guilds, the towns still managed to build their proud symbol of the commune, the brick Gothic *broletto*, or town hall.

Republicanism breathed only too briefly. The feuds were so continuous, the noble estates with the armies of serfs so disruptive, that an entire new class of leader was born, the *condottiere*, or mercenary war captain. In each town, peace was brought by condottieri or by an alliance with a neighboring town powerful enough to provide such protection. In the end, the middle-class *comune* was lost, its broletto replaced by a ruling lord's castle. Gian Galeazzo Visconti epitomizes this 14th-century period. From the time he murdered his uncle Barnabo of Milan and joined that estate with his own in Pavia, he was unstoppable. He conquered not only Lombardy, but most cities from Piedmont to Padua, and from Pisa to Parma. He almost starved Florence into submission, but that fortunate city instead saw him die of plague outside their gates in 1402. Florence and Venice would hire their own condottieri to successfully diminish this Lombard empire. But the cunning Gian Galeazzo had founded the great duchy of Milan that would continue to trouble them for a century to come.

During the *quattrocento*, when republican values catapulted Florence into the Renaissance, Lombardy lay under ducal tyranny. It would remain so throughout the Renaissance as the last Visconti married his daughter, Bianca, to Francesco Sforza, a condottiere from a landless family, who willingly fought the citizens of Milan for three years in order to place the ducal crown on his head. Even those cities not controlled by the Visconti-Sforza dukes were ruled by Venice or by lords such as the Gonzaga of Mantua, who also converted their skills as condottieri into noble titles.

Although the northern courts lacked republican values, everything else they could purchase. At Milan, Ludovico Sforza and his wife Beatrice d'Este created the most brilliant court in Italy, one that for nearly 20 years could boast the residence of two geniuses of the Renaissance, Leonardo da Vinci and the architect Donato Bramante. At Mantua, where Beatrice's more famous sister Isabella reigned—sometimes alone, more often with her Gonzaga husband and son—Mantegna was in residence and Alberti's most important churches graced the town. Later, the Mannerist Giulio Romano would be at his most creative as the Gonzaga court artist. Northern preference for the Gothic, with its love of color and decorativeness, never exactly vanished, but Lombardy did produce its own Renaissance artists. In Milan, they tended to be overwhelmingly influenced by Leonardo, like the accomplished Bernardino Luini (c. 1480–1532), though Vicenzo Foppa of Brescia

History and Art

(1428–1515) and Bartolommeo Suardi of Milan, called "Bramantino," (c. 1465–1530) brought their own originality to the Lombard school. The Pavian sculptor and architect Giovanni Antonio Amadeo (1447–1522) and his masterpiece facade at the Certosa di Pavia were quintessentially Lombard.

Ludovico Sforza may have created the most sumptuous court; he also is said to have been the ruin of Italy. In 1494, thinking that Naples and the Borgia pope, Alexander VI, were scheming against him, Ludovico began the Italian Wars by inviting the king of France to conquer Naples. Italy became the battleground of foreign nations. Eventually, in the Battle of Pavia (1525), the emperor Charles V would capture Francis I on the country estate of the Sforza, and Spain would rule the formerly independent city states of Milan and Mantua, and others like Brescia and Pavia would be sacked. Throughout the conflicts, the courtly life endured, becoming even more ostentatious as the surrounding world fell apart. Guilio Romano's summer Palazzo del Te was built for the Mantovan visit of Charles V. Later, the Italian Baroque flourished in the courts. Poets, musicians and storytellers all received their patronage, and artists sculpted ducal busts as well as designed sets for lavish festivals. It was in the palaces of both Milan and Mantua that the 16th-century monk Matteo Bandello told his stories, ones that later inspired Shakespeare's *Romeo and Juliet* and *Much Ado About Nothing*. The first true opera, *Orfeo*, by the Lombard Monteverdi, was performed for the Gonzaga in 1607. Theater was a passion, resulting in specially designed buildings such as the Olympic Theater (late 16th century) at the tiny court of Sabbioneta. And the evening's music and dance might be accompanied by violins crafted by the Stradivari and Guarneri families of Cremona.

While the Italian genius could survive the initial period of foreign rule, it eventually wilted. Spain permitted the local nobility to rule with little intervention, as long as the taxes were paid. The Sforza lasted only briefly in Milan; the Gonzaga endured until the 17th century. When, in 1700, the last of the Spanish Hapsburgs died, most of Lombardy passed to the Austrian branch of that imperial family. Until Italian unification under the Risorgimento (1848), the Austrians ruled with quite a firm hand, only the revolutionary Napoleon disrupting their control (1796–1814). By then, the neoclassical mansions, the art and tastes of the elite, were mostly borrowed from foreign soil.

Modern Lombardy

Lombardy, or *Lombardia* in Italian, is still the land of Monteverdi with its renowned opera house, La Scala. It's still the land of the decorative, with the colorful geometrics of contemporary Memphis design. The fashion industry, though, has now replaced medieval armour. It remains the bridge between northern Europe and the rest of Italy, with Milan the center of communications and finance for all of the peninsula.

Lombardy is the heart of the industrialized north. Where canals once formed a system of commerce to the sea, now multilane autostradas, congested with trucks, speed past the steel works, the cotton and silk mills, between Milan and Verona. More to the south, from Mantua to Cremona and Pavia, Lombardy is gentler, more agrarian, but unmistakably involved in agribusiness at its most sophisticated. Lombardy is also the most populous region of Italy and one of the most prosperous.

Despite the jarring modern aspects of some parts of Lombardy, the region preserves the beauty of the lake district and the history and art of the valley towns. A turn off the highway at Brescia shows the best ruins of ancient Cisalpine Gaul, while Pavia, Como and Milan offer outstanding Romanesque churches and Cremona and Bergamo, perfect medieval piazzas. The Sforza castle in Milan and the ducal palace in Mantua, Leonardo's *Last Supper* and the Certosa di Pavia are only a few of the Renaissance treasures that deservedly attract tourists year after year.

Cuisine

Everyone knows the essentials of Italian cuisine are olive oil and pasta. Everyone, that is, except the Italians of Lombardy. Here, butter replaces olive oil in cooking and we have even witnessed a Milanese spreading it on bread. Although both rice and wheat are grown in the Po basin, it's the rice that inspires numerous dishes and thickens the regional minestrone, not pasta. In the countryside, pasta doesn't even rank with *polenta*, the cornmeal gruel (sometimes made into a tastier quiche-like form) that in ancient times fed Roman soldiers and the Etruscans before them. In the Alps, where pasta is traditional, it's made with buckwheat and mixed with potatoes into an oddity called *pizzoccheri*.

Like all Italian cooking, however, Lombard cuisine results from its geography and the produce yielded by the land. The flat Po Valley is easily flooded into rice patties and Lombardy has superb grazing land—especially for dairy cows. As Italy's greatest producer of milk, Lombardy, not surprisingly, has a cuisine rich in butter and cream. Its cheeses include the blue-veined Gorgonzola (when *dolce*, rather than aged, it's deliciously creamy and not too sharp), the dull Bel Paese, the soft *stracchino*, the Parmesan-like *grana padana* from Lodi, and *mascarpone*, a fresh cream cheese used to layer cheeses into a sinfully rich torta, or mixed with sweets to make desserts. And here, much like its neighbors across the Alps, are desserts topped with *latte-miele*, or whipped cream.

Cuisine

And speaking of its not too distant neighbors, Lombardy's invaders have come from the north. The Germanic Goths and Lombards and especially the 19th-century Austrians may have brought a taste for the heavy and rich to this region that shares their severe winters. Unlike the more Mediterranean-oriented regions of Italy, Lombardy likes its meats stewed, or *stufato*. Instead of the Tuscan meats grilled over an open hearth, here you have braised veal shank *(ossobuco)* and the boiled version of a mixed grill *(lesso misto)*. Instead of bistecca alla fiorentina, Lombardy offers *cotoletta alla milanese*, or breaded veal chop. There's even *bresaola* instead of proscuitto, the cured beef so dry it must be served with drops of olive oil. And there's the Spanish-introduced *cassoeula* (pork and cabbage stew) so popular in Milan. Although the French did briefly occupy Lombardy, the region's preference for paté and saying "bon jour" comes from admiration, not conquest. But whether the preference for frogs and snails results from such adulation or rather the plentiful supply from Pavia's river, is unclear.

The Alpine valleys, foothills and riverine plain of the Po produce more than dairy, meat and rice, of course. There are the peaches from the Po Valley, the walnuts and mushrooms from the north, the game from the mountains, and eels and trout from the lakes. And, of course, there are the vineyards. Here, once again, Lombardy is unusual. Its **wines** are seldom exported and are little known compared to the Milan-brewed Campari aperitivo. Yet the vineyards often border those of more famous wine-producing regions without equalling Piedmont's great Barola and Barberesco reds, or the Veneto's Soaves and Valpolicella. Nonetheless, Lombardy offers some fine wines. Even the Oltrepo of Pavia, said to be the most disappointing of the three wine regions, grows the venerable Barbera grape and makes such reputable DOC reds as Barbacola. And the Casteggio whites of the region are pleasingly light and, under the Clastidium label, superb. Certainly the Nebbiola vines of Alpine Valtellina can't match the complexities of Barolo, yet the region produces the DOC Valtellina Superior with its good, ruby red Sassella and Grumello wines. The district of Brescia produces the DOC whites of Lugano that vie with neighboring Soaves, and the Riviera del Garda competes with the nearby Bardolino reds. Other wines from the Brescia region are definitely worth sampling, especially Franciacorta's reds, chardonnay and bubbly spumante.

Travel Tips

Climate and Seasons

Lombardy really has at least two climates, that of the lakes and Alpine region and that of the Po basin. In the winter, when the mountain resorts boast clear sunny skies and snowy slopes for skiing, the Po basin is warmer (the average high in January for Milan is 39° F, the low is 36°), rainier, and often covered with dense fog. Although the cold is not really a deterrent to travel for the historic cities in the low-lying Po valley, **the fog can obscure the landscape and make driving dangerous as well as ground planes at both of Milan's airports**. In the Alps, some of the passes are blocked by winter snowfalls, and the lake region hotels are closed. In the summer, the mountain lakes throb with vacationers seeking their cooler air while Milan and the valley are soggy with heat and humidity (July, the hottest month in Milan, has an average high of 84° F, and a low of 73° F). But for all of Lombardy, the late spring and the fall are wonderful times to travel.

Arriving

Milan is the hub of transportation in northern Italy, which makes getting into Lombardy quite easy. The two airports of Malpensa (transcontinental flights mostly) and Linate (domestic and European) are not just convenient to Milan, but are within easy striking distance of Lakes Maggiore and Como, as well as the town of Bergamo. By renting a car at the airport, you can avoid Milan altogether if you want. Two lake towns, **Stresa** and **Como**, are about an hour by car from Malpensa if you want to overnight somewhat near the airport. (*The Busto Arsizio exit from the A-8/9 is best for Malpensa.*) Otherwise, the faster trains and buses will take you into the center of Milan, where you can make arrangements to other parts of Lombardy—but note that the city has numerous train stations (all linked by subway) and you might have to switch, depending on your itinerary. For details, check the Milan directory and key as well as "Practical Tips" under your other destinations. Milan is linked to Italy (and Europe) through an elaborate autostrada system: A-1, or the Autostrada del Sole, is the main highway linking northern and southern Italy, and runs via Bologna (210 km, 130 mi.), Florence (300 km, 186 mi.), to Rome (575 km, 357 mi.); A-4 stretches west to Turin (140 km, 87 mi.) and east to Trieste (420 km, 260 mi.) with a stop at Venice (270 km, 167 mi.) along the way; A-7 heads west to Genoa (145 km, 90 mi.) before linking with A-10 to the French Riviera, and yet others link up with the Swiss border.

Getting Around

As always, car rentals give you the most flexibility and enable you to stop off at more places; they are readily available in Milan or at the airports. The train connections between towns are good, especially from Milan to the provincial, or country, capitals such as Bergamo, Brescia, Cremona, Mantua, Como and Pavia. Buses fill in the gaps and increase your options, and ferries and boats cross the lakes. The distances seldom are great; from Mantua to Milan it is only 158 km, 98 mi.; from Milan to Como 48 km, 30 mi. Beware that the autostradas around Milan can be horribly congested during rush hours.

Milan

Key to Milan

Sights

This world-famous capital of Italian fashion and design counts shopping as one of its major tourist attractions. The historic center contains more than Leonardo's *Last Supper*; it also includes superb museums like the Brera and Poldi Pezzoli, the famous Sforza castle, and numerous exceptional churches.

Excursions

The Certosa di Pavia (25 km, 15-1/2 mi.) and Bergamo (48 km, 30 mi.) are half-day trips from the city. Other towns and the lakes are easily reached from Milan, too, but just as easy to stay in since they are less expensive, less congested, and with less summer heat than Milan.

Nearby Waters

The Lake Region around Como is as beautiful as it is reviving in the summer heat.

Festivals and Events

La Scala, the world's most famous opera house, begins its season Dec. 7, and performances continue through July. Trade fairs, fashion and design shows fill up the Milanese calendar except during July and August.

Shopping

Haute couture along with the latest in ready-made fashions and avant-garde home furnishings are stylishly displayed in the boutiques around Manzoni, Montenapoleone and Brera streets.

Accommodations

Commerce puts a high demand on Milanese hotels, which means they are not only pricey, but also that you usually get less for your money than elsewhere.

Eating Out

Milan is a wonderful city to dine in, with restaurants specializing in the local cuisine as well as the most sophisticated nuova cucina. Even the *panini*, or sandwiches, here take on a certain daring combination of ingredients.

Getting Around

Although not all streets are closed to traffic, it's best to walk through the historic center, where the sights and shops cluster. Public transportation is excellent, radiating out from P. Duca d'Aosta (stazione centrale) and P. del Duomo and connecting the hotels and train stations with the sights. There is a subway or *metro* ("MM") in addition to buses and trolleys (called "trams"). All operate 6:15 a.m.–midnight.

Arriving

Two airports, Malpensa for most trans-Atlantic flights and Linate for many domestic and European flights, are connected to the stazione centrale by bus (note: taxis cost more than most would want to pay); rapid trains to European as well as Italian cities (under 3 hours to Venice, and 4 hours to Rome on the Pendolino); and an

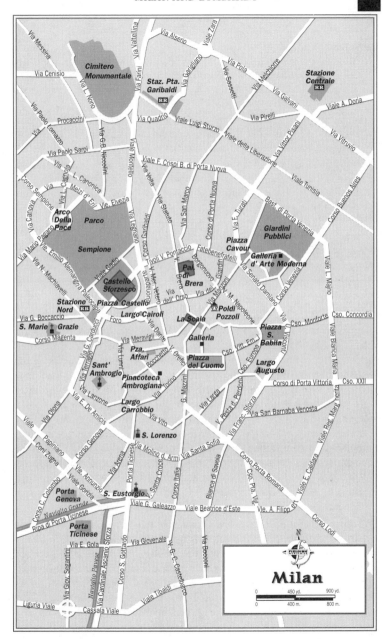

Milan

0   450 yd.   900 yd.

0   400 m.   800 m.

elaborate autostrada system befitting this industrial city, make Milan easily accessible.

Special Tips

Milan is counted among the most expensive cities in the world; its prices are 20 percent higher than the national average. The metro instead of taxis, early reservations at the more "moderately" priced hotels, and light eating at the many (and superb) "fastfood" spots can enable you to splurge at other times.

A one-price pass, the **Museo-Card**, to all the museums, from small church collections to the Poldi-Pezzoli, is well-worth the price if you plan to visit at least five museums. Buy it at the tourist office or museums. It's good for six months

The traditional clothing shop hours (closed Sun., Mon. morning, and 1-4 p.m.) are rapidly changing; shops in the centro storico can be found open on Sundays (not department stores) and an increasing number don't close at lunch (particularly department stores).

Corriere della Sera, the daily newspaper, carries the latest museum schedules and listings of cultural events.

Milan really closes down on holidays, especially Aug. and the Christmas season through Jan. 6, when many restaurants and small hotels close, too.

Good reading: Stendhal's novel, The *Charterhouse of Parma*, is set, in part, in Milan.

Milan, or in Italian, *Milano*, is a vibrant city and, with a population approaching two million, is second only to Rome in size. In most respects, the Milanese believe their city to be second to no city, especially not to Rome. Such confidence may be rooted in a long history of dominance in the north. As the seat of the Western Empire under Constantine, ancient Milan competed with Rome and, in the fourth century, its bishop—Saint Ambrose being the most famous—was the equal of Rome's pope. Milan, of course, was one of the great city-states of the Renaissance, when it often was anxious to annex Florence, outwit Venice, or subdue Rome. But for all the cunning diplomacy and endless battles of the Visconti and Sforza dukes, Milan became even more subjugated to foreign rule than its southern rival Rome. It's said that this proud city received its due, however briefly, when Napoleon liberated it from Austria and named Milan capital of the Italian Republic (1802) and then a few years later, of the Kingdom of Italy.

Whether Milan today is the "true" capital of Italy, as many Milanese claim and just as many Romans complacently ignore, is an issue that will continue to rage. This modern city is, however, the undisputed capital of finance and industry. Its newspaper, *Corriere della Sera*, is one of Italy's most quoted, its Feltrinelli publishers one of Italy's most prestigious, and its own Giorgio Armani and Gianni Versace are among its many great fashion designers. With just 2.5 percent of Italy's population, Milan generates 10 percent of its gross national product and enjoys 28 percent of the national income. The Milanese lords of today, unlike the courtly Sforzas and Renaissance nobility who scoffed at commerce, are Italy's most successful merchants.

Many travelers despair of Milan's modernity. Since repeated bombings in World War II destroyed parts of the city, high-rises and sprawling suburbs are more characteristic than Renaissance palazzi. Industrialization and rapid growth have left their mark, too, with traffic jams and smog. But these irritations are worth suffering: the historic center contains treasures from a past when Christian devotion built fine Romanesque and Gothic churches and courtly good taste patronized Leonardo and Bramante. Far from being preserved as ghostly monuments, the historic center is full of contemporary vitality. The rooftop of the duomo is where the chicly attired take their late afternoon passeggiata. The handsomely restored mansions of Via Solferino house the trendiest restaurants, those of Montenapoleone the most established designer boutiques. The basement of Sforza castle may house an exhibit of that endangered art form, the record jacket. The restoration work on an 18th-century facade may be hidden behind a witty trompe l'oeil canvas. The historic sights are not in Italy's most picturesque or romantic setting, but they are wrapped in Milanese flair.

What to See and Do

Piazza del Duomo ★

This large rectangular piazza is the heart of Milan. Although closed to traffic, it is hardly a quiet spot. As the social center of the city, Milanese gather here to chat and to be seen, to walk atop the duomo and to sit in the cafes of the *Galleria*. As the city center, people arrive here in buses, trams, and subway trains on their way to other parts of the city. To the north through the Galleria is La Scala and the Via Manzoni; west along Via Dante is the Castello Sforesco; south is Sant' Eustorgio and the Porta Ticinese; and east, the pedestrian shopping avenue of the *Corso V. Emanuele*.

The piazza is the historic center of Milan too. Under its geometric pavement lay the excavated remains of ancient Roman baths as well as the 4th-century baptistery where it's said that the saintly Bishop Ambrose baptized the future Saint Augustine. Just northwest of the piazza, around **Piazza Mercanti**, remains part of the medieval city where the Visconti first exerted their control and where their coats of arms still adorn the gray and white marble of the Loggia degli Osii. The cathedral itself was built, on the 1386 order of the great Gian Galeazzo Visconti, over part of the first ducal palace. The order to finish it was given in 1805 by another great, Napoleon.

Duomo   ★ ★

This famous Milan landmark is the best example in Italy of the French Gothic style. Even though its forest of spires and vaults are soaring and even though Parisian architects were consulted on its plans, the duomo retains the broad and static proportions of an Italian church. The 14th-century plans called for an elaborately carved church, but it's hard to believe that medieval masons could have envisioned the facade that accumulated over the next five centuries. Now draped with a total of

2245 statues, the marble facade includes 16th- and 17th-century elements, an 18th-century spire culminating in the gilded "Madonnina," and innumerable 19th-century, neo-Gothic gables and pinnacles. The main bronze doors are of this century, the last installed as recently as 1965. All this finery is best viewed from the south and around the apse. But better yet are the ★★**rooftop walkways** where you can admire the details of the gargoyles and the exterior of the dome (1490) designed by the northern Renaissance architect Amadeus *(7 a.m.–5 p.m., winter till 4 p.m.; elevator entrance outside north transept; fee for stairs cheaper)*.

Entering the ★**interior**, you'll readily believe that this is one of the largest churches in the world, second in Italy only to St. Peter's. The original Gothic conception of the duomo is overpowering here, as the great height of the vaults and the light diffused by stained glass create an awesomely vast and complex space. The 52 immense piers that divide the church into a nave and four aisles have exceptional 14th-century ★*capitals*. The verticality of the nave draws you to the apse, where you are surrounded by stunning 15th-century ★*stained glass window*s. A door to the right of the main altar leads to the crypt, or scurolo, containing Milan's 16th-century bishop, St. Charles Borromeo.

The Duomo is open *7 a.m.–7 p.m. June to Oct.; otherwise 9 a.m.–4:30 p.m.* MM1 and MM3 stop at Duomo. Near the main entrance, there is access to the 4th-century baptistery excavations *(10 a.m.–noon, 3–5 p.m., closed Mon.)*. The development of the different styles of the cathedral can be best seen at the **Museo del Duomo** *(Tues.-Sun. 9:30 a.m.–12:30 p.m., 3-6 p.m.; L7000)*, housed in a wing of the neoclassical Palazzo Real (opposite south transept).

Galleria Vittorio Emanuele II

Even under winter skies, light pours through the elegant glass roof of this late 19th-century "mall." Lined with cafes and shops, the Galleria is a busy passageway between the piazza and La Scala.

Nearby

In the warren of busy streets just southeast of the Piazza del Duomo are two worthwhile sights for those who have a little extra time. ★**Pinacoteca Ambrosiana** *(P. Pio XI 2, down C. Cantu from Orefici/Dante; closed for restoration; otherwise 9 a.m.–5 p.m., closed Sat.; L8000)* may not contain the greatest work of any painter, but who cares when Botticelli (Room I), Leonardo (Room IX), Raphael (Room X), Caravaggio—a beautiful ★*Basket of Fruit* (Room XI), and Veronese (Room XIII), and the Milanese Luini (Room IX) and Bramantino (Room VII), are among the artists. The galleries are on the second floor of this library, which contains an edition of Petrarch illustrated by Simone Martini and a Leonardo codex (copies displayed in Room XIII). Follow Via Spadari to Torino, then turn right for the tiny church of ★**San Satiro** *(closed noon–3:30 p.m.)*, reconstructed in the 1470s by Bramante, his first architectural work. The original 9th-century San Satiro now stands to the rear as a chapel, its exterior encased in a Bramante design. Next to it is a very Lombard Romanesque campanile. In the handsomely coffered interior, Bramante ingeniously created a false apse to make a nearly flat wall look like the fourth arm in his

Milan

ideal plan of a cross (side views are best for detecting the illusion.) *Metro stops on MM1 at Cordusio, MM1 & MM3 at Duomo.*

Around Via Manzoni ★★

The fashionable and elegant Via Manzoni stretches from the Piazza della Scala to the 12th-century double archway, or arco, built as part of the city walls against Frederick Barbarossa. From the Piazza della Scala, the Galleria links the area with the duomo. Through the arco are the Piazza Cavour and Giardini Pubblici, pleasant beginnings to the more modern city. In and around the avenue are some of the city's most important art collections as well as shopping districts.

La Scala Theater   ★

Via Manzoni at P. della Scala.

Centuries ago the Visconti family founded the church of Santa Maria alla Scala. Today the church is gone, but the name continues in its more famous replacement, the Teatro alla Scala. This most renowned opera theater in the world has introduced many an Italian opera, including Verdi's Otello as well as his Falstaff. Every aspiring opera singer dreams of performing here; the established fear their downfall. Built in 1776, the exterior of La Scala is unprepossessing, the interior intensely red and opulently neoclassical and with superb acoustics. Entrance is through the **Museo Teatrale** *(in portals to left; 9 a.m.–noon; 2–6 p.m., Oct.–Apr., closed Sun. Nov.–Apr. 30; L5000),* which contains memorabilia pleasing to any opera buff including a cast of Chopin's hand. *Metro stops on MM1 and MM3 at Duomo.*

Pinacoteca di Brera   ★★★

V. Brera 28.

The Brera district is approached on Via Verdi (next to La Scala), which turns into Via Brera, then to Solferino. This handsome quarter has undergone considerable renovation in recent years and includes galleries of art and avant-garde design as well as numerous popular restaurants. Two institutions give the neighborhood its special character, the offices of the newspaper Corriere della Sera and the Brera Art Gallery.

The Brera contains masterpieces of some of the greatest Italian artists: Giovanni Bellini's ★★ *La Pieta* (c. 1468), extraordinary in the grief expressed by the interlocking faces of Mary and her dead son, as well as a pensive ★ *Madonna with Child;* Mantegna's startlingly foreshortened ★★ *Dead Christ* (after 1466); Piero della Francesca's perfectly still ★★ *Madonna and Child with Saints* (c. 1472), with the kneeling Duke of Montefeltro; Raphael's early ★★ *Marriage of the Virgin* (1504), its spatial unity on the brink of his later High Renaissance style; the second of Caravaggio's ★ *Supper at Emmaus* (post 1606), more subdued than the famous first one, yet still bathed in spiritual light; and Tintoretto's ★ *Discovery of St. Mark's Body.* But the Brera's importance extends beyond these paintings. It contains the greatest collection of Northern Italian art with representations from the various schools that flourished from the 14th through the 18th centuries. From Venice there are Veroneses, Titians, and Tintorettos as well as Carpaccios, Vivarinis, and fine portraits by Lorenzo Lotto. In the Paduan style there is the ★ *Madonna della Candelleta* (1490s) by the Venetian Carlo Crivelli, in the Emilian-Romangna style are works by Correggio, the Carracci—including a self-portrait by Annibale—and

Guido Reni. And Lombardy itself is represented by fine works, among them those of Foppa, Bramantino and Luini. There are Flemish works, too, and a collection of modern Italian art.

The museum has been undergoing reorganization for a number of years and it's possible to find some of the galleries closed. Open Tues.–Sat. 9 a.m.–5:30 p.m., Sun. till 12:45 p.m.; L8000. Subway stations at Manzoni (MM3), Lanza (MM2), and Cairoli (MM1) are convenient.

Museo Poldi Pezzoli   ★★

V. Manzoni 12.

Before Via Manzoni intersects Montenapoleone and Milan's most fashionable shopping district, it passes this elegant mansion, donated in 1879 to the city along with the outstanding private art collection of the aristocrat Gian Giacomo Poldi Pezzoli. Inside, at the top of a spiral staircase, you find the superb paintings of the collection. To the left are the Lombard rooms, containing Vicenzo Foppa's 15th-century ★ *Portrait of G.F. Brivio*, and the Leonardo-influenced works of B. Luino and Andrea Solario. Straight ahead is a room with Flemish works, including several by Cranach. From there, a room to the right contains the museum's early Renaissance masterpieces: Antonio del Pollaiolo's ★★ *Portrait of a Young Woman* (1460s), whose face is full of character and whose pearly gauze hairdress is delicately drawn; Botticelli's delicate ★ *Madonna with Child*, with Mary's neck exaggerated to create a graceful tilt of her head, and even Christ's crown of thorns rendered wispy rather than threatening as contrasted with the later, disturbing *Lament over Dead Christ*; Mantegna's very tender ★ *Madonna with Sleeping Child*; Piero della Francesca's *Saint Nicholas*; and Giovanni Bellini's *Christ Resurrected*. Continuing to the left, rear corner of this floor, you come to rooms with later Venetian works as well as some fine 14th-century panel paintings, including one by Pietro Lorenzetti.

The museum is open 9:30 a.m.–12:30 p.m., 2:30–6 p.m. except Sat. until 7 p.m.; closed Mon., no Sun. afternoon hours Apr. 1–Sept. 30. L10,000. MM3 Montenapoleone stop is nearby.

Around Sforza Castle ★★

From the Piazza del Duomo, Via Dante leads west to the broad 19th-century boulevards of the Largo Cairoli area. Here is the great castle of the Sforzas. In ancient times, the area was the site of a gate in the Roman wall. In medieval times, the Visconti built their fortified palace here, and throughout Milan's history the site has been occupied by anyone seeking power—from republican upstarts in the 15th century to the Austrians in the 19th. As the city flourished under a united Italy and grew to where the Romans had built their walls, the castle was preserved as a museum and surrounded by the great Parco Sempione. Not too far away is Santa Maria delle Grazie with Leonardo's *Last Supper*. From there it is an easy enough walk to the magnificent Romanesque church of Sant'Ambrogio, perhaps with a stop along the way for the Leonardo exhibits in the Museum of Science.

Castello Sforzesco takes visitors back to the Renaissance.

Castello Sforzesco ★★

Piazza Castello near Largo Cairoli.

This castle is not to be missed—even if you never wish to see another medieval tomb or Renaissance painting. Standing in front of its battlement towers, marked with the coiling serpents of the ducal coat-of-arms, you can easily understand why Napoleon called it a symbol of tyranny and ordered its dismantling. Crossing the moat, you are drawn into what was the richest and most powerful court of the Renaissance. Here Leonardo da Vinci and Bramante lived for many years under the patronage of Ludovico Sforza and his wife, Beatrice d'Este. Across a vast courtyard (where summer concerts are performed) and through a door to the right, you come to the 2-story complex of Musei Civici (again, to the right), housed in the ★ **Ducal Court**. A walk through the handsome displays of the museums here (particularly those of the Lombard sculpture on the ground floor), is a walk through the Renaissance apartments that still include fragments of Leonardo's arbor design for the ceiling frescoes in the Sala delle Asse (Room 8) and the glorious gilded ceiling of the ducal chapel, just a few steps farther on. Along the way you might admire two fine sculptures:

Bonino da Campione's once silver and gilded ★ *Monument to Bernabo Visconti* (c. 1363), with the severely proud Bernabo rigidly astride his horse (Room II) as well as Michelangelo's last, and unfinished, work, the touching ★ *Rondanini Pieta* (Room XV). Upstairs are furnishings from the castle as well as the ★ **Pinacoteca** (reached through stairs in entrance hall), with its ★ *Madonna and Child*, by a youthful Giovanni Bellini, and works by Andrea Mantegna, Filippo Lippi (Room XX), and Correggio (Room XXI) as well as a roomful of wonderful portraits that include works by Bellini, Correggio, Titian, Tintoretto, and Lotto (Room XXV). If you still have time, the fortified residence of the castle (**La Rochetta**) contains collections of Egyptian and ancient art, and musical instruments.

The castle is open 9:30 a.m.–5:30 p.m.; closed Mon.; free. It can be walked from the duomo, but also is near the Cairoli subway exit of MM1, Cadorna or Lanza of MM2 as well as on many tram and bus lines.

Santa Maria delle Grazie

Corso Magenta at Caradosso.

Although the brick and terra cotta exterior of this 15th-century church by Guiniforte Solari is itself pleasing to the eye, it is the commissions of Ludovico Sforza that have made it a tourist mecca. Under his sponsorship, Leonardo painted the *Last Supper*, one of the most famous works in Western art, and Bramante built a church addition that was seminal to High Renaissance art. Inspired by Leonardo's architectural drawings, Bramante designed a centrally planned church that was added to the original nave of delle Grazie. This new domed crossing and apse, really four arches supporting the central drum, not only predicts later radial plans of the High Renaissance, but also encloses the spatial volumes so indicative of that style. Both the interior and exterior (best seen from V. Caradosso, where you look at the dome across Bramante's small, delicate cloister) are richly decorated in Lombard taste, with an intriguing interplay of circular, wheel-like motifs.

Facing the main church portal, the *cenacolo* ("refectory") containing the ★★★ *Last Supper* (1495) is to the left. Most refectories contain a mural of the last supper, but Leonardo's was the first to portray the dramatic moment in which Christ said to the apostles, "One of you will betray me." Captured here are the psychological reactions of each individual, including Judas (4th from left), whose guilt is suggested by the shadows on his face rather than his traditional isolation on the opposite side of the table. Not only is each figure carefully studied by Leonardo, but all are united into a harmonious composition of four groups with three apostles. Christ is placed in the very center, the focus of both psychological and linear perspective. Only recently have some of the delicacy of details and luminous colors over which Leonardo labored been returned to the mural. Restoration continues, but no amount of work can eliminate the dreadful deterioration that started within a few years of its completion because Leonardo chose not to use true fresco technique (it didn't give him enough time to achieve his subtle sfumato effect). Subsequent repaintings and "restorations" as well as wars (Napoleon's troops used the refectory for stables) and Milanese humidity have taken their toll. A door was even cut through it. Despite all this damage, the painting is miraculously still spellbinding.

The church closes noon–3 p.m. The cenacolo is open Tues.–Sun. 8:15 a.m.–1:45 p.m.; L12,000. To protect the Last Supper *from pollution, you enter and exit through multiple filtration chambers; only 25 visitors are permitted at one time and only 10 minutes are allowed in front of the painting (binoculars useful). Expect at least a half hour wait.* From the castle, walk SW to P. Cadorna (also a MM2 stop), then follow Boccaccio to Caradosso. From the duomo, take the #24 tram. If you're walking to Sant'Ambrogio, conside*r a stop on the way at the* **Museo Nazionale della Scienza e Tecnica** *(V. San Vittore 21; 9:30 a.m.–4:50 p.m., closed Mon.; L10,000),* most famous for its Galleria Leonardo with models of the great artist's inventions. (From delle Grazie, follow Via Zenale south, then turn left onto San Vittore, which passes the museum before crossing V. Carducci and arriving at Sant'Ambrogio.)

Sant'Ambrogio Church   ★ ★
P. Sant'Ambrogio near V. Carducci and Lanzone.
Founded in A.D. 386 by St. Ambrose, this early church retains in its crypt the saintly remains of Ambrose as well as two Christian martyrs. After an earthquake in 1117, the church was rebuilt and became the archetype for the Lombard Romanesque style. Retaining ancient Roman aspects of the early church, the basilica has no transept and is entered through an atrium (fine arabesques and grotesques carved on capitals of main portals). Its sturdy brick facade with arcades is flanked by a Romanesque tower on the left (with full length pilasters, called Lombard lines) and a 9th-century tower on the right. The atmospheric, rib vaulted interior contains an exceptional Romanesque ★ *pulpit* (left side of nave) set atop a fine Early Christian sarcophagus (4th century). In the main apse above the crypt is a *tabernacle* with 4th-century columns (and 9th-century capitals) enclosing a ★ *gold and silver altar* (A.D. 835). At the end of the left aisle is the 4th-century martyrdom chapel of San Vittore with lovely ★ *5th-century mosaics.*

Sharing the piazza with the church is the Universita Cattolica, housed in the former Ambrosian monastery with its two Renaissance **cloisters by Bramante**: the Doric one, with its subtle rhythm of forms, is said to be his most mature work in Milan. *Since the main church facade is blocked by the atrium, little of the exterior architecture can be appreciated during closing hours (noon–3 p.m.).* The church is near public transportation, if you need it: MM2 Sant'Ambrogio; bus #50 from Duomo.

Other Sights
If you have more time to explore Milan with its many museums and churches, then you might consider a total change of pace by going to the **Galleria d'Arte Moderna** *(V. Palestro 16, near the Giardini Pubblici; Tues.–Sun., 9:30 a.m.–5:30 p.m.; free).* Housed in the splendid, 18th-century neoclassical villa where Napoleon resided briefly, the museum contains works by the French Impressionists *(piano 1)* as well as Lombard artists. (Take MM3 Cavour; MM1 Palestro.) In the area south of the duomo, following Via Tocino to Corso Porta Ticinese (or take tram #15), you can visit two fine churches in this area that ends with the Porta Ticinese and the nearby *navigli,* the few remaining canals of what once was a vast network crisscrossing Lombardy and linking Milan with cities as far away as the port of Genoa. Here Beatrice d'Este arrived for her wedding on a gilded

barge from Ferrara. Today the **Navigli district** (tram 15 to Porta Ticinese, then walk 2 blocks right; or MM2 Stazione Garibaldi) is the focus of redevelopment, with outdoor markets and shops, restaurants and nightclubs. More significant are the churches: **San Lorenzo Maggiore** *(Corso Porta Ticinese; closed noon–3 p.m.)* may be Milan's earliest church, founded after Constantine's edict of A.D. 313. Although renovated over the years, the church retains its classical central plan as well as the 16 fluted columns in front, now separated by trolley tracks. The most significant Early Christian art is found in the Chapel of Sant'Aquilino (off south side) with its very early (4th-century) ★ *mosaics of Christ and the apostles.* Further along the Corso, near the Porta Ticinese, is the church of ★ **Sant'Eustorgio** *(closed noon–3 p.m.)*, founded in the 11th century, enlarged in the Renaissance (note the three chapels on the south side). Not to be missed is the ★ *Cappella Portinari* (1462; *entrance down to chapel at rear of apse; fee)*, based on a Brunellschian design by the Florentine Michelozzo, but executed with Lombard decorative touches such as minarets (exterior). The interior is exquisite with stucco angels on the base of the dome and Vicenzo Foppa's frescoes, *Life of St. Peter Martyr.* The medieval ★ **tomb** (1339) again shows the Portinari family's Tuscan preferences (they were Florentines, themselves) as it was designed and partially carved by the Pisan Giovanni di Balducci (note "Temperance," the caryatid, second from left, and the figures in the tabernacle.)

Festivals and Events

Milan is a city of trade shows rather than religious pilgrimages. Its spring and fall fashion shows and its spring general trade show are international events. Yet the feast of patron St. Ambrose is one religious day that marks an event uniquely important to Milan—the opening of the **opera season at La Scala**. From December 7 (eve of the feast) through early summer, there are performances. Gallery seats, good enough to hear if not to see, often can be obtained at the last minute, but seats go on sale 10 days before and most require advance reservations not easily made from abroad. To reserve tickets (up to two per performance; 15 percent surcharge), fax **La Scala** (☎ *[392] 877-996)*; confirmation is by phone or fax. For schedule information, you can browse the Web at http://lascala.milano.it. Or make plans in advance with your hotel concierge, if you have one. And if you're in Milan early enough, check the computer next to the ticket window for seat availability and program details. *(Ticket office open Tues.–Sun. 10 a.m.–12:30 p.m.; 3:30–5:30 p.m. and for performance night until 9:30 p.m.; information ☎ 7200-3744; noon–7p.m. except Sun.).* There are many concerts, movies (the **Angelicum**, *P. Sant'Angelo 2, off Moscova*, has some in English), and theaters (the **Piccolo Theater**, *V. Rovello 2*, is highly respected). Performances can be checked in tourist publications such as *Milano Mese.*

Shopping

The names in Italian fashion, as well as such foreign ones as Chanel and Ungaro, are found on the boutiques in the area anchored by **Via Montenapoleone** *(MM3 Montenapoleone)*. The polished elegance of the shoppers and shops hint at the prices to be paid here. Delimited by Via Manzoni and Corso Venezio and the traffic-free Via Spiga (parallel to Montenapoleone), the district is crisscrossed by smaller streets and distinguished by the renovated 19th-century palazzi that form its setting. Whether you take a stroll for people watching (Milanese men must be the most stylish in the world) or just window shopping, the area is an essential part of seeing the sights of Milan. To get a taste of what's offered here, consider that Montenapoleone boasts **Gucci** leather accessories, **Ferragamo** shoes, **Valentino** and **Gianni Versace** clothing. It also has the exquisite fitting shoes of **Tanino Crisci**, the precious jewels of **Faraone** (affiliated with Settepassi of Florence) and **Mario Buccellati**, as well as the Italian antiques of **Geri Antichita**. But the smaller streets are not to be missed because they offer the designs of many famous Milanese. On *Via Spiga* there's the avante garde **Krizia** and popular **Gianfranco Ferri** as well as the trendy costume jewelry of **Sharra Pagano** sharing the street with the famous Roman jeweler, **Bulgari**. *Via Sant'Andrea* also is important and includes **Missoni** knits along with the witty fashions of **Moschino**. Here, too, are the Italian objects d'arte and antiques of **Domenico Piva**. To find the showroom of **Giorgio Armani**, however, you need to cross Manzoni for Via Borgonuovo.

Nearby, you might find the relief of slightly lower prices. South of Piazza Babila, the **Emporio Armani** *(Durini 22)* anchors several shops of that designer's less expensive line. The pedestrian Corso V. Emanuele leads to the duomo where you find **La Rinascente** *(P. Duomo north side)*, Italy's largest department store, and **Galtrucco** *(P. Duomo 2)*, famous for its yard goods, including silks from Como. For the best buys, check-out the second-hand designer clothes at **Michela** *(Corso Venezia 8)* or take a quick bus ride (#60) or taxi to **Il Salvagente** *(V. Bronzetti near Corso XXII Marzo)* for discounted designer clothes.

For those interested in Milanese design, not fashion, there's no one place for feasting your eyes—although the decor of the **Hotel Spadari al Duomo** (see hotels below) comes close, even if nothing is for sale. The most sumptuous of Italian leather furniture can be seen at **Poltrano Frau** *(Manzoni 20 at Montenapoleone)*. A number of design shops cluster south of Piazza Babila, anchored by the furniture of **Cassina** *(Durini 16)* and **Arflex** *(Borgogna 2)*, around the corner. Nearby is **Morongomma** *(Corso Matteotti 14)*, where you might find some stylish odds-and-ends for office or car in the latest trendy materials of rubber and vinyl. **High Tech** *(P. XXV Aprile 12, north side)* looks like a Pier 1 spin-off, but tucked away upstairs and in the backrooms are Italian-designed housewares and furnishings, including Alessi teapots; Aldo Cibic's new "standard" (read functional, rather than his formerly voluptuous Memphis style) chairs. While here, you might visit **L'Archivolto** *(V. Marsala 2 at Solferino)* a bookstore and gallery (check the display window across the street) with items designed by both Italian (Maurizio Duranti's wooden candlesticks; an aluminum lamp by Aldo Rossi) and international (a letter cutter by Richard Meier) architects.

There are two other shopping districts, both best when their open air markets are on. In the **Brera district**, there is an *antiques fair* along with a flea market the third Saturday of the month *(V. Fiori Chiari at Madonnino)*, but any shopping day you can find interesting items here, among them antique furniture and jewelry shops on Via Fiori Chiari, and boutiques on Brera-Solferino. The **Navigli district** is especially famous for *street markets*, full of clothing and curios at lower prices than you'll find elsewhere: On Via Calatafimi (behind Sant'Eustorgio) the market takes place each Saturday; on Viale Papiniano (between MM2, S. Agostino and Darsena canal), it's every Tuesday morning and Saturday. An *antiques and flea market* sprawls near the Naviglio Grande on Via Ripa Ticinese the last Saturday of the month except July and August. (MM2 Stazione Genovese or tram 15 from duomo.) Shops are blossoming near here, too, such as the funky used clothing boutiques on lower Via Porta Ticinese and the galleries and nearly-antique shops along the Naviglio Grande.

<h2 style="text-align:center">Where to Stay</h2>

Trade fairs and commerce keep hotels full and, unfortunately, prices up. You will find yourself paying more than usual for your hotel and receiving far less in exchange. Acceptable inexpensive accommodations with private baths are rarities and the few "value for your money" hotels are often booked. To make matters worse, many of the smaller hotels close in August and over the Christmas holidays. If you are set on staying in a certain hotel, make your arrangements as early as possible.

Most of Milan's deluxe hotels are outside, but not far from, the historic center and cluster around the broad boulevard of the Piazza della Repubblica and the nearby Piazza Duca d'Aosta, anchored by the central train station. Although these hotels are accessible to the sights, and in some instances are within walking distance to them, we think Milan is more pleasant when experienced from the center where there is less traffic and more charm. Whatever your preferences, you'll find that all the following hotels are near enough to the sights to be just a few subway stops away from the castello or duomo, or within walking distance.

Unless stated otherwise, all rooms are air-conditioned (a necessity for the heat sensitive during Milan's humid summer months).

<h2 style="text-align:center">Very Expensive</h2>

Principe di Savoia   **L615–700,000 CP**   ★★★★★

Piazza della Repubblica 17, 20124; ☎ *62-30, FAX 659-5838.*
Single/double L615–700,000 CP.
From the gloved hands of the bellhops to the chandeliers of the elegant lobby, from the frescoed rooms and stained glass ceiling of the lounge, you know you have arrived at one of Milan's most fashionable hotels. The 235 units are spacious, decorated with rich fabrics and interesting architectural details. Fine service. Restaurant. Indoor pool. Garage. A Ciga hotel. MM3 Repubblica.

Excelsior Gallia   **L485,000**   ★★★★★

Piazza Duca d'Aosta 9, 20124; ☎ *67-85, FAX 6671-3239.*
Single/double L485,000.
Built in the grand style of the 1920s, the ornate and refurbished Excelsior sits proudly on the immense and busy square of the stazione centrale. The 266 rooms vary in style; some are modern, others are more traditional, and those overlooking the piazza have high ceilings and old world charm (as well as whispers of the traffic below). Gracious service. Restaurant, handsome lounge. Gym, sauna, steam bath. Garage. MM 2&3 Stazione Centrale.

Four Seasons Milano   **L610–725,000**   ★★★★★

Via Gesu 8, 20121; ☎ *77-088, FAX 7708-5000.*
Single/double L610–725,000.

Having opened only in 1993, the upstart Four Seasons already is challenging the venerable Ciga hotels listed above. And for good reasons. Its location in the heart of the Montenapoleone shopping district is ideal; its conversion of a 16th-century monastery couldn't be more tasteful with traces of original frescoes decorating the vestibule, Renaissance cloisters covered with glass roofs, and a baronial fireplace set into the lounge; but the overall ambience is contemporary. Most of the 95 rooms overlook a quiet, sun-filled courtyard; the bathrooms are sumptuous with heated floors, no less. Service could use some European polish, but shoeshines are free. Two restaurants, piano lounge. Garage. MM3 Montenapoleone, MM1 S. Babila.

Grand Hotel et de Milan L550–700,000 ❀★★★★

Via Manzoni 29, 20121; ☎ *723-141, FAX 8646-0861.*
Single/double L550–700,000.

With a superb location in the Montenapoleone district, this recently refurbished hotel once was the residence of Verdi. The lobby retains its Victorian decor, the Art Deco lounge is covered with a leaded glass ceiling; a mahogany elevator used by Verdi has been restored and the parlor where he composed *"Falstaff,"* now a suite, contains his furnishings. The 100 units are not luxuriously appointed but rather have an old-fashioned ambience created with antiques, hardwood floors, and marble baths; those on the lower floors have high ceilings; those facing the street are noisy. Sophisticated service. Two restaurants. Lounge. MM3 Montenapoleone.

Duomo L370–550,000 ★★★★

Via San Raffaele 1, 20121; ☎ *88-33, FAX 864-2027.*
Single L370,000 CP. Double L550,000 CP.

On the Piazza del Duomo, a traffic-free street, this hotel has an ideal location. Unfortunately it is edging up towards a higher price category. Oriental rugs and shining marble floors bring a sophistication to the contemporary decor of the lobby. The 160 units are highly variable; some split-level suites have views of the duomo spires. Roof garden. Restaurant. Access to garage. Bar. MM1 & 3 Duomo.

Expensive

Spadari al Duomo L390–425,000 CP ❀★★★

V. Spadari 11, 20123; ☎ *7200-2371, FAX 861-184.*
Single/double L390–425,000 CP.

Near the Duomo, this boutique hotel is a must for anyone with an interest in modern Milanese design, even if it's just for a drink in the lobby bar painted with a Memphis-style fresco by Valentino Vago or for a glance at the entrance furnishings by famous architect Ugo La Pietra and the lobby sculptures by Fontana and Gio Pomodoro. You have to stay overnight, however, to see La Pietra's furnishings for the 40 rooms (all sunny and attractive with good bathrooms; some with great city views), hung with interesting paintings by some of Milan's most promising artists. It's all the project of architect Urbano Pierini. MM 1 Cordusio, MM 3 Duomo.

Bonaparte L370–445,000 CP ★★★

V. Cusani 13, 20121; ☎ *85-60, FAX 869-3601.*
Single L370,000 CP. Double L390–445,000 CP.

Textured wallcoverings, thick carpeting and windows over the trees of the Piazza Cairoli create a smart, contemporary ambience for this hotel, located near the Castle. Service is efficient. The solidly furnished 40 rooms are ample, with sitting areas and baths with good towels and robes. There's some traffic noise; you might want an interior. American bar with pleasant breakfast room. Garage. MM1 Cairoli; MM2 Cadorna or Lanza.

Manin   **L250–315,000**   ★★★

Via Manin 7, 20121; ☎ *659-6511, FAX 655-2160; Closed Christmas season & Aug.*
Single L250,000. Double L295–315,000.

A block from the Piazza Cavour and across from the Giardini Pubblici, the Manin is another modern hotel with a decent location. The 110 modern and carpeted rooms (with safes) vary considerably, a few have garden views. Garden. Restaurant. Bar. Parking. MM3 Turati.

Moderate

Manzoni   **L160–210,000**   √★★

Via Santo Spirito 20, 20121; ☎ *7600-5700, FAX 784-212.*
Single L160,000. Double L210,000.

In the middle of the Montenapoleone shopping district and on a traffic-free street as well, this hotel occupies a pleasant 19th-century mansion. Although not a full-service hotel, the tastefulness of the decor, the quiet of the 52 carpeted and ample rooms with modern baths, make this a surprisingly good buy. Breakfast room. Bar. Garage. MM3 Manzoni or MM1 S. Babila. Credit cards: None.

Ritter   **L170–220,000 CP**   ★★

Corso Garibaldi 68, 20121; ☎ *2900-6860, FAX 657-1512.*
Single L170,000 CP. Double L220,000 CP.

On the edge of the fashionable Brera district near the Moscova subway stop, this hotel's reasonable prices must come from its location just outside the thick of the tourist area. Disguised as an apartment building, it offers carpeted and comfortable sitting rooms and 90 well-furnished, modern units. Bar and buffet breakfast. MM2 Moscova.

Europeo   **L200–245,000 CP**   ★★

Via Canonica 38, 20154; ☎ *331-4751, FAX 331-0541; Closed Aug.*
Single L200,000 CP. Double L245,000 CP.

Not far from the arena of Sempione Park, this attractive hotel may not be quite as convenient as some, but then it boasts a nice garden with a pool along with its 45 unusually well-furnished rooms for this category. Bar and breakfast room. Garage. Just 10 minutes from P. Cairoli on #57 bus that stops almost in from of the hotel.

Casa Suissera   **L200–240,000 CP**   ★

Via San Raffaele 3, 20121; ☎ *869-2246, FAX 7200-4690; Closed Aug.*
Single L200,000 CP. Double L240,000 CP.

A few steps from the duomo, this modern hotel offers 45 clean and quite decent rooms. Bar and breakfast room. MM1&2 Duomo.

Almost Inexpensive

Grand Duca di York   **L140–185,000**   ★

Via Moneta 1a, 20123; ☎ *874-863, FAX 869-0344.*
Single L140,000. Double L185,000.
Tucked away behind the Pinacoteca Ambrosiana, this hotel is no longer reminiscent of the country villa its facade promises. The modernized interior, too spartan and beige, includes a large lobby and bar and 33 good-size rooms with ample baths; those with terraces are most pleasant. Roof terrace. Parking. A decent buy. MM1 Cordusio.

Star   **L130–190,000**   ★

Via dei Bossi 5, 20121; ☎ *801-501, FAX 861-787; Closed Aug.*
Single L130,000. Double L175–190,000.
On one of the medieval streets running between Via Dante and La Scala, the Star offers a homey lobby along with its central location. The 30 rooms are small and plain, but adequate. Bar with breakfast room. MM1&2 Duomo.

Antica Locanda Solferino   **L165,000**   √★

Via Castelfidardo 2, 20121; ☎ *657-0129, FAX 657-1361; Closed late Dec.*
Single/double L165,000.
In the old Brera district at Via Solferino, this pensione is a picturesque 15-minute walk to La Scala. Sharing a 19th-century building with the popular Solferino trattoria (in the basement; odors may invade interior rooms during summer), the 11 rooms (no a/c) here are not just clean and sunny, but attractively decorated with chintz curtains and lace, 19th-century prints, and armoires. Nothing fancy, but pleasant and in very high demand. Reserve months in advance. MM2 Moscova.

London   **L115–165,000**   ★

Via Rovello 3, 20121; ☎ *7202-0166, FAX 805-7037; Closed Christmas season and August.*
Single L115,000. Double L165,000.
On one of the narrow, medieval streets just north of Via Dante this immaculate hotel has helpful desk service, 29 carpeted rooms (all small and a bit plastic, but functional and with a/c and central location). Bar. MM1 Cordusio.

Where to Eat

Milanese Cuisine

Milan has lent its name to many dishes, but none is better known than *cotoletta alla milanese*, the breaded veal chop that led to Vienna's more famous weiner schnitzel. *Risotto alla milanese*, subtly flavored with saffron and wet enough with butter to be spoon eaten, may be only locally favored as a first course, but can be enjoyed by all as the traditional accompaniment to ossobuco. Watching the Milanese savor such hearty, bland fare reminds us of our own favored childhood meals, although ours would invariably include mashed potatoes—and sometimes so do those of the Milanese. Such homecooking can become inspired in the hands of Milanese chefs and reinterpreted into countless kinds of risotti and scaloppine dishes. Nuova cucina adds its variants, a touch of Gorgonzola for a tanginess otherwise too often absent, along with countless styles of raw fish or beef *carpaccio*. But dining in Milan has always transcended the purely regional to include

French-influenced pates and souffles, as well as the Spanish *cassoeula* of pork and cabbage. Today it encompasses Tuscan *papparadelle* with porcini and Venetian *frutti di mare*. Its wine lists are as likely to include a Dolcetta d'Alba from Piedmont as a ruby Sassella from Valtellina, and may offer champagne instead of Lugano spumante. Milanese dining is great—and it's cosmopolitan.

The Great Restaurants

Proof of Milanese wealth and good taste is the number of highly respected (and expense-account expensive) restaurants. Just recently it could be said that two of those rare restaurants receiving celestial ranking by both Michelin and Guida d'Italia were in this city or its environs. Although the renowned Gualtiero Marchesi has moved 70 km east to provincial Erbusco in the Franciacorta district of Brescia (see "Lake Iseo"; ☎ *(030) 770-3129*) it leaves other extraordinary choices behind.

Antica Osteria del Ponte $$$

> *P. Negri 9 in Casinetta di Lugagnono, 20081 Abbiategrasso;* ☎ *(02) 942-0034, FAX 942-0610; reservations required.*
>
> *Fixed-price lunch: L75,000. Fixed-price dinner: L150,000. À la carte: L100–150,000. Closed Sun., Mon., Christmas season, Aug.*
>
> One of the great restaurants in Italy, this highly esteemed eatery may not be in center city, but many would travel more than the necessary 20 km beyond the Porta Ticinese to reach it. And the journey along the Naviglio Grande is a pleasant way to approach a fine country inn with elegant service and appointments, as well as a summer garden. As one would expect of a restaurant of this caliber, the wine cellar is excellent and the cuisine is inventive, yet strictly Italian—raviolo of foie gras or truffles in broth and fagottino of shellfish, and rabbit with eggplant caponata. The degustazione menu is recommended (and, at lunch, it's a bargain in the expensive category).

Scaletta $$$

> *P. Stazione Genova 3;* ☎ *5810-0290.*
>
> *Meals L70–115,000. Closed Sun., Mon., and Aug.; reservations a must.*
>
> If not in the star-studded heaven of Del Ponte, then this restaurant is at least in the stratosphere. Intimate and decorated with contemporary paintings and sculpture, Scaletta is the most sought after restaurant in central Milan (reserve as early as possible). Here the preparations change often and always are memorable, from the sea-bass gnocchi in shellfish sauce to the lamb in garlic cream and the ginger ice cream.
>
> Credit cards: not accepted.

Aimo e Nadia $$$

> *V. Montecuccoli 6;* ☎ *416-886, FAX 4830-2005.*
>
> *Fixed-price lunch: L55,000 & 95,000. Fixed-price dinner: L95,000. À la carte: L90–135,000. Closed Sun., lunch Sat., early Jan. and Aug.; reservations recommended.*
>
> This exceptional, small restaurant receives stars and high rankings and a steady flow of people willing to arrive at its location far from the center. The quality of chef Aimo Moroni's creations, which vary with the seasons, certainly merit them—from the uncooked fresh tomato soup and risotti with mushrooms to the shrimp-stuffed squash blossoms and lemon mousse.

Milan

Alfredo Gran San Bernardo $$$ ★★★★

V. Borghese 14; ☎ *331-9000, FAX 655-5413.*
Closed Sun., Sat. (only in June–July), Aug., & Christmas season; reservations recommended. Meals L75–100,000.

This is the traditional place to dine on authentic Milanese cuisine. Just out of the center near the Cimitero Monumentale, Alfredo's creates the sublime in risotto milanese (either plain "all'onda" or pancake-like "al salto"), cassoeula, ossobuco with polenta, of course, and that very Milanese tripe stew, busecca.

The More Affordable

Fortunately, so much exquisite cuisine seems to spill over; unfortunately, so do the prices. You can dine well, however, without breaking the bank. While strolling through the city, you might want to browse for restaurants in the Brera district (V. Fiori Chiari, closed to traffic, is always pleasant) or along the canals of the Navigli area. The following are worth a detour.

Osteria del Binari $$ ★★★

V. Tortona 1, just behind Stazione Genova; ☎ *8940-6753, FAX 8940-7470.*
Fixed-price dinner L55–75,000. Dinner only, closed Sun, mid Aug.; reservations recommended.

On the edge of the trendy Navigli district (cross over the foot bridge at the Stazione; it's one door to the left), the Osteria serves a fixed-price dinner that is almost too generous. Whether dining in the charming wood paneled rooms in winter or under the grape arbor in the huge summer garden, Italians fill every table, bringing their families to celebrate the countrylike ambience and bounty of very good, if not great, food. The meal begins with a wonderful assortment of breads, crepe-like foccacio, pate, and stuffed vegetables; there's some choice for the other courses, though they change daily: maybe a gnocchi with speck and porcini or risotto with seafood; steak with balsamic or stuffed swordfish. Then a pause for cheese before deciding among the delicious house-made desserts. Arrive hungry.

Bistrot di Gualtiero Marchesi $$ ★★★

Rinascente, 7th floor, V. San Raffaele 2; ☎ *877-159.*
Fixed-price meals L50–70,000. Closed Mon. at lunch, Sun., Aug.

Right in the heart of Milan and set atop the Rinascente department store (there's a side door for the restaurant), Bistrot offers stunning views of the duomo spires along with a menu designed by the great Gualtieri Marchesi. Although not the signature restaurant of the master chef, the contemporary setting is as pleasing and fresh as the food, be it risotto milanese or a tuna steak in sesame with a puree of eggplant. In the evening there's a piano bar. The degustazione menus are sensibly priced.

Quattro Muri $$ ★★★

V. San Giovanni Muri 2 at Buonoparte; ☎ *878-483.*
Meals L50–70,000. Closed Sun., lunch Sat., most of Aug., and Christmas season; reservation recommended.

Near the Sforza Castle, here there's a wonderful romantic garden in which to dine in summer and excellent food that includes homemade pastas (gnochetti nero with salmon; fettuccine alle vongole veraci), a fine array of seafood choices (swordfish with rughetta; arugula salad with crabmeat) as well as Florentine steaks.

Buriassi da Lino   **$$**   ★★★

V. Lecco 15 at Casati; ☎ *2952-3227.*
Meals L45–75,000. Closed Sun., Sat. lunch, Aug.; reservation required.
Several blocks north of the Giardini Pubblici is this polished restaurant where you should begin with crostini of mushrooms and gamberetti and choose whatever pasta is recommended (the tagliatelle with pesto and funghi is a specialty), before continuing on to the fine meat and fish available.

Antica Trattoria di Domenico e Maria   **$$**   ★★

V. Montevideo 4, near MM2 S. Agostino; ☎ *837-2849.*
Meals L45–65,000. Closed Sun., Aug.
Located just west of the Navigli, the trattoria is much admired for its old-fashioned ambience and traditional Milanese cuisine, from the antipasti to the duck and cabbage variation on cassoeula and veal milanese. Some think its risotti are the absolute best in Milan, and that's saying something.

Good Buys

Snack Bar Peck   **$**   ★★

V. Victor Hugo 4, ☎ *861-040.*
Meals L20–40,000. 7:30 a.m.–midnight; closed Sun.

To eat well inexpensively you might want to forego traditional table service and try to sit at one of the counters at this classy cafeteria owned by the famous Milan food shops. The sandwiches are good and the same price as elsewhere, but you also have a wide choice of delicious items, from seafood salad to a savory *stufato*, or stew. You even have your choice of liqueurs to be sprinkled on your macedonia of fruit. Pick and choose to keep the price down, and try to avoid the peak lunch hours.

Brunch   **$**   ★

Rooftop at Rinascente Department Store, P. Duomo.
Meals L10–25,000. Noon–11 p.m., closed Sun.
A more relaxing option is the table service and great duomo views at Brunch, Gualtieri Marchesi's effort at fast food and it is what ready-made is to coutiere. You can pick from any number of modest fixed-price meals or just enjoy a piatto unico (one-plate meal) of very fresh buffalo mozzarella with red peppers and eggplant.

Insalatone, Panini & Pizza

Unusual panini (such as vegetarian sandwiches of eggplant and artichoke) can be found in caffe and paninotecas all over the city, from the strategically located **Paninoteca** *(Fiori Oscuri & Brera)* across from the **Pinacoteca Brera** and **I Panini di Befi** *(V. Cesare Beccaria, south of Corso Emanuele)* near the duomo, to the night time *birreria* hangouts in the Navigli. For even lighter eating, many caffe have a mini tavola calda at lunch, such as **Bar Castello** *(V. Beltramo)*, with a shady terrace across from the castle for melon and prosciutto or macedonia of fruit; **Pattini e Moroni** *(Solferino 5 at Arcona)* is a good bakery with lots to snack on and a tea room and tavola calda around the corner. The most current Milanese rage, however, is for *insalatone* ("big salads," which are not so big as simply larger than a dinner salad) and other single platter meals called, *piatti unici*, enjoyed in a restaurant setting. Here are a few examples to add to the "Good Buys" above:

Ristorante Victoria $ ★★

V. Clerici 1.
L10–15,000 per dish. Closed Sun.
A good choice for lighter eating, just two blocks west of La Scala and with brocaded curtains and art deco details. Although the Victoria Caffe on the corner serves panini, for an insalatona of shrimp, celery and radicchio or scamorza cheese with arugula, walnuts and mushrooms, you must walk farther down the street for the restaurant door; there're pastas and pizza, too.

Grand'Italia ★★

V. Palermo 5.
L6–12,000 per dish. Closed Tues., lunch Sat., Aug.
Another good choice, this place has a beer hall ambience and shared tables when crowded, but bargain prices on a very satisfying insalatona Manzoni (baby shrimp. slices of Parmesan, tender greens). There's stuffed focaccia, carpaccio, daily pastas and thick-crusted pizza —all good. A popular place, especially after the theater; in the evening, arrive by 8 p.m.

Calafuria ★

V. dell'Unione 8.
Pizza L6–10,000. Closed lunch Sun., Sat.
Convenient to the duomo, this trattoria serves decent wood-oven pizza lunch and dinner.

Gourmet Shops and Caffe

Peck's is a Milanese institution. We've already mentioned its cafeteria on Victor Hugo, but in the same area (just south of Piazza Cordusio) are its extraordinary food shops. At *Via Spadari 9* you find the salumeria, and across the street, the gastronomia with cheese and wine, fresh pasta and the finest prosciutto, along with cooked pheasants, their heads so delicately tucked, and quails with sausage wings. Around the corner on Cesare Cantu is their roticceria *(closed 2-4 p.m. and Sun. afternoon and Mon.)* with all manner of prepared foods for take out (or for a very hassled stand-up lunch).

A caffè visit is a must, whether to sip an espresso or a Campari, that very Milanese aperitivo. **Cova** *(V. Montenapoleone 8; 8 a.m.-8 p.m. except Sun.)* has been serving its elegant high teas since 1817, long enough to claim to be the inventors of panetonne, the dome-shaped breakfast bread sprinkled with candied fruits and raisins. The setting is superb whether at the bar or in the sala da te. Another refined cafe and sala da te is **Sant'Ambroes** *(Corso Matteotti 7; 8a.m.-8p.m. except Mon. mornings, Sun.)*, known for its sweets, from miniature fruit tarts to chocolate truffles (morning cappuccino comes with a chocolate). To enjoy your aperitivo in the trendiest of Milanese bars, try **Coquetel** *(V. Vetere 14, near San Lorenzo)* with a vast wine list and a decor devoted to works of contemporary Italian artists. A great summer choice for ice cream is **Gelateria Tiffany** *(V. Ascanio Sforza 29; closed Tues.)*, located on a canal barge in the Navigli district.

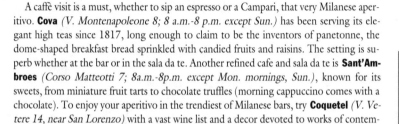

Directory

Telephone Code 02   **Postal Code 20100**

Airlines

Alitalia, *V. Albricci 5 (☎ 62-81-817).*

Airports

Malpensa, 48 km. 30 mi. north near Varese on A9 then A8, for intercontinental flights; **Linate** (7 km, 4 mi. east) for many domestic and European flights. **Flight Information** *(☎ 7485-2200).* **Airport Buses** depart east side of stazione centrale; purchase tickets inside at Doria Agency. At the airport, purchase tickets inside at hotel reservations office. For timetables: Malpensa bus, *(☎ 868-008);* Linate, *(☎ 669-0836).*

Albergo Diurno

For public bathrooms and showers go under P. Duca d'Aosta, down subway elevator in front of stazione centrale (7 a.m.–8 p.m.).

American Express

Via Brera at Monte di Pieta (☎ 855-7277).

Books in English

American Bookshop, *V. Camperio at P. Cairoli;* **Feltrinelli**, *V. Manzoni 12.*

Buses

ATM, office in Duomo subway stop *(☎ 875-494)* and day passes sold here and stazione centrale stop. Purchase tickets in advance at newsstands and tabacs. See also "metro." **Intercity** buses for most destinations in northern Italy leave from P. Castello (MM2 Cairoli) or nearby P. Cadorna for Pavia.

Car Rentals

Major agencies at airport and town, including **Europcar**, *V. Galvani near Hilton* *(☎ 607-1051)* and **Hertz**, *P. Duca d'Aosta 9 (☎ 659-8151).* **Mose Bellina** *(☎ 308-0180)* rents chauffeur driven cars.

Consulates

Hours are Mon.-Fri., usually 9 a.m.–4:30 p.m. or so with a midafternoon closing: **United States**, *V. Principe Amadeo 2/10, near MM3 Turati (☎ 290-351);* **Canada**, *V. Pisani 19 (☎ 669-7451, emergencies ☎ 6698-0600);* **Great Britain**, *V. San Paolo 7 (☎ 869-3442).*

Emergencies

Police *(☎ 112-113),* ambulance *(☎ 7733)* or first aid *(☎ 3883).*

Groceries

Olivieri, a salumeria on *V. Spiga near Manzoni* or **Peck's Roticerria**, *V. Cesare Cantu near Pinacoteca Ambrosiana,* for prepared gourmet foods. Fruit shops and bakeries line V. Solferino (continuation of V. Brera) and Corso Garibaldi; there's a morning vegetable market on V. Marcello, 4 blocks north of Giardini Pubblici on V. Lecco. A respected enoteca is **Cotti** *(Solferino 42 at Castelfidardo).*

Metro

Metropolitana Milanese, or MM as the subway signs say, has 3 lines with maps in each station. Purchase tickets at tabacs, newsstands or machines in station. Service, like buses, 6:15 a.m.–midnight.

Post Office

Central office at V. Cordusio 4, near P. del Duomo. Mon.–Fri. 8 a.m.–8 p.m., Sat. till 1 p.m.; and, on a trial basis, Sun. 8:30 a.m.–7 p.m. **Telegrams**, 24-hour service.

Sports

Swimming: The indoor pool **Cozzi**, *V. Tunisia 35 (☎ 659-9703)*, is centrally located. **American Health Fitness Center**, *V. Montenapoleone (☎ 7600-5290)* has day passes for its facilities. There's golf, squash, tennis too—check with APT tourist office.

Taxis

Yellow or white metered taxis with stands at P. del Duomo, P. Scala, P. Cairoli, and the train stations. Or dial ☎ *67-67.*

Telephones

ASST, in Stazione Centrale, 7 a.m.–8 p.m. Telecom/SIP, Galleria V. Emanuele, 8:10 a.m.–9 p.m.

Tourist Office

APT, P. del Duomo, south side at Marconi *(☎ 7252-4300; FAX 7202-2999)*, open 8:30 a.m.–8 p.m. except Sat.–Sun. 9 a.m.–1 p.m., 2–5 p.m. in summer. Branches at stazione centrale and airports. *Municipal Information* on cultural events, the Galleria at P. Scala *(☎ 870-545)*, in Italian only.

Tours

3-hour city tours, Tues.–Sun., and a 75-minute tourist tram tour, are sponsored by APT *(☎ 7252-4300; fee)*. **CIT**, *Galleria V. Emanuele (☎ 866-611)* and others offer excursions.

Train

Stazione Centrale, P. Duca d'Aosta is most frequented one information *(☎ 67-500)*; Stazione Porta Garibaldi (with car transport) and Stazione Lambrate also have trains to Pavia, Bergamo, Como and Stresa.

Tip: Tickets can be reserved and delivered to your city hotel for a very reasonable fee; call ☎ *6698-1013.*

On the Road

The Lake Region

The Italian lakes have inspired Catullus and Virgil, Goethe and Wordsworth, Shelly and Keats, D.H. Lawrence and Hemingway, Rossini and Donizetti. The shores have been sought after by tourists since the time of Julius Caesar to the Scaligeri of Verona and the Visconti of Milan, from Goethe and Gabriele d'Annunzio, to the thousands upon thousands of Italians, English, and Germans who have followed them. They all have left their mark—in Roman ruins, castles and medieval towers, villas and botanical gardens, hotels and lakefront cafes.

The scenery is breathtaking, from the sheer sandstone cliffs of the Dolomites that crowd the blue waters of Lake Garda to the snow-covered Alps that dominate the north of lakes Como and Maggiore. From spring through the fall, the gentler and verdant hills surround the lakes with stately cypresses and spreading chestnut trees, and gardens wash the hillsides with the colors of April rhododendrons, May azaleas, summer roses and hydrangea, and the fall harvest of lemons and grapes and brilliant dahlias.

Although the centuries of enjoyment have often increased the beauty of the lakes with their terraced gardens and tiled-roof villas, they have also tarnished it. The lakes suffer varying degrees of pollution—many Italians no longer swim in Como and Maggiore and some stay by their hotel pool even at Garda.

Some towns, once reachable only by boat, are now inundated with busloads of tourists and the rambling of constant traffic along their *lungolago*, or lakefront drive. While officials build plants to clean the lakes and some towns divert traffic from the center, the level of tourism seems to increase and can, in July and August, and even in September around Lake Garda, be overwhelming, especially if you are visiting the lakes for an escape from it all. But at any time of the year, some towns remain less disturbed than others; some hotels wrap themselves in quiet bliss. You still can leave city sightseeing behind you and breathe in the mountain air, only bestirring yourself for an occasional ferry ride on the lake, a visit to the garden of a grand villa.

If you are without a car, you probably plan a visit to one lake, touring it by ferry. Lakes Como and Maggiore are less than an hour from Milan, Lake Garda the same from Brescia and Verona. With a car from Milan or Milan airport, some travelers explore a number of the lakes, perhaps beginning with Lake Maggiore, crossing it by car-ferry and continuing north around Lake Lugano into Switzerland and over to Lake Como. From Como they head down to Bergamo before continuing on the autostrada to Lake Garda. From Garda they go on to Verona and Venice. The less restless might simply visit lovely Lake Orta from nearby Maggiore, or explore the vineyards near small Lake Iseo above Brescia.

Lake Tips

Seasons

The lake season is from spring through fall, with most facilities closing during the winter. The spring (March to mid-June) is the favorite with those visiting for the formal gardens around lakes Maggiore and Como; the fall (September-October) is usually the time of the clearest skies and the most dramatic scenic views. In any season, though, the lakes can be misty or hazy, the mountains invisible. July and August are the busiest months and the best for watersports. March, April and October are the quietest (apart from Easter), a time when some hotels drop their prices or even close, and a time when the ferries run less frequently.

Touring the Lakes

The three major lakes can be toured by car along their shores, or partially toured by a combination of road and car ferry *(traghetto auto)*. They may also be toured by ferries *(batteli*, or the larger *traghetti)* getting off at villages where you wish to explore a church or castle, and then boarding the next ferry for another stop. Whether you combine both forms of travel or stick with just one, there are a few fact to keep in mind. The lake roads often have obstructed views—villas, tunnels, vineyards—and, on weekends and during the summer, can be jammed with traffic. The ferries are the most relaxing way to tour; the only way to feel embraced by the lake. But they can be time-consuming and complicated to coordinate if you try to do too much, like make a complete lake tour in one day. If you do have just one day, consider an organized boat tour or select just a few places to visit. You can save time, too, by eating on the ferries or by taking the *aliscafi*, or faster hydrofoils, in one direction. (**Note:** Hydrofoils don't stop at as many towns and they are not open-air. They cost about 50 percent more than the ferry, but are proportionately even faster.)

Watersports

It's hard for us to say when a lake has become too polluted, but we can report that many Italians swim at Garda and Orta, but not in Como and Maggiore, where we have been told by locals not to swim. At the latter two lakes, most towns have public pools. And of course so do many of the hotels, even the more modest ones. The lakes often have paddle boats, water-skiing, sailing and windsurfing facilities. If watersports are the reason for your summer visit, Garda's facilities are the most developed.

Map

If you are making a grand tour of the Lake Region, ask the APT tourism offices in Milan or any Lombard city (Stresa on Maggiore and Riva del Garda are not in Lombardy) for their excellent map of Lombardia and the lakes.

Lake Maggiore

Lake Maggiore begins beneath the frosty Alpine peaks of Switzerland, then its greenish waters quickly turn Italian and gradually change to blue as the mountains subside into the verdant hills and lush vegetation of the south. Only near Stresa does the lake widen to wash the shores of the picturesque Borromean Islands and set them in mountain frames. It is a beautiful lake and one made famous by 19th-century vacationing monarchs as well as visits by Wagner and Toscanini, Flaubert and Stendhal. Visited by many foreigners, especially the Swiss, the southern part of the lake is nonetheless the domain of the Milanese, whose taste bless it with the best restaurants of the lake region. If only the second largest lake in Italy, *Lago di Maggiore* is grand enough to be divided not just between Switzerland and Italy, but in Italy between Lombardy (west coast) and Piedmont (east). Yet its history has been primarily tied to that of Milan, and its contemporary fame rests more on its world-class music festival, Stresa's Le Settimane Musicali, than on size.

Lake Maggiore was a favorite of 19th century monarchs.

Most travelers find themselves settling into the same remarkable spots as Czarina Alexandra and Queen Victoria. Stresa is at the center of such **a typical visit**, which always includes the villas and gardens of the Borromean islands, just off-shore, as well as the extraordinary flower beds at the Villa Taranto in Verbania-Pallanza. Those who wish to see the northern reaches of the lake take the **ferry tour to Locarno, Switzerland**. Others do an historical exploration of the Borromeo family that still owns two of the islands, just as they have since they were feudal lords in the 12th-century. These travelers climb to the castle at **Angara** *(end Mar. to end Oct., 9:30 a.m.–12:30 p.m., 2–6 p.m. except Jul./Aug. 3–7 p.m.; L4000)* on the southeast coast and pay homage at **Arona**, birthplace of St. Charles Borromeo, and enjoy the views of Angera on the opposite side of the lake. Others might visit the ruined castles on the islands across from the pretty resort of **Cannero Riviera** or the Renaissance church at **Cannobio** (both north and on the west shore). And along the east shore, **Laveno** has good views of the Borromean islands from its embarcadero, and great panoramic ones from atop Poggio Sant'Elena (funicolare). To the north of Laveno is **Luino** (17 km, 10.5 mi.) birthplace to Leonardo's follower, Bernardino Luini, and a lakeside town with a nice lungolago to stroll. All pleasant enough for ferry stops or short drives, but only if you are lingering. Nearby Lake Orta (see below) is a more interesting day excursion.

The **accommodations and restaurants** around the lake attest to the demand over the centuries. The most extensive facilities are in Stresa, which has convention capacity, as well as modernized and modern hotels with saunas, whirlpools, and the like. Other resorts are smaller, usually quieter, and without the same level of facilities. On the whole, the restaurants are quite good, and sometimes exceptional. The cuisine is varied, usually including the lake fish, but sometimes prepared Lombard style, occasionally Emilian, and often Piedmontese, with its delicious use of various *funghi* from nearby mountains and its superb wines, which include not just the noble Barola but the more affordable Ghemme reds and Gavi di Gavi whites.

ARRIVING AT THE LAKE • Stresa is 80 km, 50 mi. northwest of Milan on A-8 autostrada to Castelleto. On the same route it is just 30 km, 19 mi. from Malpensa airport. There also are bus and train (Simplon line) connections that reach Stresa within an hour. The most scenic route from the east is around Lake Lugano (see that section below).

GETTING AROUND THE LAKE • Lake Maggiore is almost 40 miles long and three miles at its widest. Its roads have fewer views than you might expect, that on the east side being more like a pleasant country road, and that on the west often surrounded by villas. The drive from Stresa to Locarno, Switzerland is 55 km, 34 mi., and faster than the ferry tour, but not as delightful (the tour includes ferry one-way for 3 to 3.5 hours and return on aliscafo in 1.5 hours; passport necessary). The ferries for the Borromean islands leave frequently from Stresa, Baveno and Pallanza (where there is a special stop for the Villa Taranto). The lake time alone is 50 minutes in one direction between Stresa and Pallanza, and you may find the Stresa-Pallanza day pass the easiest and most economical way to make the full tour. **Note:** *Special night-time ferry service twice weekly in the summer.* Car ferries cross the lake frequently from Intra on the west (20 km, 12 mi. north of Stresa and just above Pallanza) to Laveno on the east coast (20 minutes).

Practical Tips

The entrance fees for the villas on the islands are pricey, and that for the Villa Taranto is not much less. You might want to save a few pennies by cutting your ferry costs by coordinated visits, maybe even seeing all of them on a day pass (ferry: L15,000), with lunch in Stresa or Pallanza.

Stresa

This elegant resort of the Victorian age commands picturesque views of the Borromean islands from the broad and open sweep of its lungolago. The village bustles with shops and restaurants. There is golf nearby and a cable car (from Stresa Lido, north of town), that goes up Mt. Mottrone for grand panoramic views. And the **Villa Pallavicino** *(just south of town; 9 a.m.–6 p.m. mid Mar. through Oct.; L8000)* with gardens and a zoo (exotic animals roam free in the park) deserves more attention than it gets, given the competition from the islands. But Stresa also is a modern convention center, not a quietly retiring resort. Its own **Settimane Musicali** (with exquisite chamber music and international soloists, performing both in town and in the island villas) fills the hotels for performances (usually first three weeks of Sept.). *Any time the lungolago—though locally called Corso Umberto and Corso Italia, really it is SS 33, or the lakeside road for the Simplon pass—is just too busy with traffic.* But Stresa remains *the* resort of the lake, offering too many conveniences for the tours and brief sojourners to pass up.

Where to Stay

If traffic noise bothers you, you might prefer rooms with garden, rather than lake, views.

Des Iles Borromees   **L345–580,000 CP**   ❀★★★★★

Corso Umberto 67; ☎ *30-431, FAX 32-405.*
Single L345–375,000 CP. Double L510–580,000 CP.
Set back from the lakeshore in a park, this stately hotel still offers stunning views. Opened in the 1860s and used by Hemingway as a setting for *A Farewell to Arms*, the hotel has more recently been updated. Although its lobby, and much of the room decor, remain in the Belle Epoque style, the comforts of the 182 rooms are guaranteed. Lakeside exercise park and beach, two pools, fitness center with massage, sauna and steam, grass tennis court, access to golf and restaurants and lounges.

La Palma   **L230–260,000**   ★★★

Corso Umberto 33; ☎ *933-906, FAX 933-930; closed Dec.–Mar.;*
Single L230,000. Double L260,000.
This hotel is more modern and modest than those from the grander days of travel, but it's situation across the road from the lake provides the views that have made Stresa famous. There are gardens, a restaurant, a lakeside pool and heated sunning terrace and 128 comfortable rooms, most with balconies and views. Parking.

La Fontana   **L90–110,000**   √★★

V. Sempione nord; ☎ *32-707, FAX 32-708; closed Nov.*
Single L90,000. Double L110,000.
Just beyond the north end of the Corso, this villa is set back in a garden and has 19 large rooms (no a/c), some overlooking the lake, others the mountains and garden. Breakfast bar. Kindly service. No elevator. Parking. A bargain.

Where to Eat

Emiliano   **$$–$$$**   ★★★★

Corso Italia 52; reserve at ☎ *31-396; FAX 33-475.*
Fixed-price meal L55,000. À la carte L60–120,000. Closed Wed. lunch, Tues., mid Jan.–Feb.
If you can, dine here. Superbly prepared and innovative cuisine is served in an ambience that is quietly elegant. The luncheon menu offers two set-priced meals (mod-

erately expensive) that give you an opportunity to sample the exquisite range of dishes without breaking the bank—one such meal began with a terrine of lake salmon, continued through a sublime tortelli with walnut sauce, then a quail casserole, and on to wonderful sweets. The à la carte menu is very expensive, available lunch and dinner, and may include an inspired gazpacho-like *passata di pomodoro*, or a papparadelle with pine nuts, shrimp and pesto.

Al Rustico $–$$ ★ ★ ★
> *V. Selvalungo in Someraro, 4 km above Stresa; reserve at ☎ 32-172.*
> *Meals L30–50,000. Closed Wed.*
> For Piedomontese cuisine, leave the lake road and climb the winding country lane up the hills behind Stresa. Here a wing of the family house has been panelled with logs, furnished with a fireplace and ample wooden tables, set with glistening tableware. While the chef prepares your meal, enjoy the traditional *bagna caoda*, or bubbling anchovy-flavored oil for dipping raw vegetables. Then proceed with the season's offerings, definitely sampling the *baci del chef*, a kind of ravioli, or a tender steak in black peppercorns, scallopini in wild mushrooms. Although there are a number of pleasant trattoria in the center of Stresa, most differ little in price from these two unusually fine restaurants.

Taverna del Pappagallo $ ★
> *V. Principessa Margherita 46; ☎ 30-411.*
> *Closed Tues., Wed.; L20–35,000.*
> Cozy dining rooms and a garden for enjoying a plate of gnocchi or, in the evening, pizza.

La Botte Birreria $ ★
> *V. Mazzini 6, off P. Cavour.*
> *Closed Wed. Meals L12–20,000.*
> Sooner or later everyone finds the nearby La Botte Birreria, which is open lunch and dinner for just a snack, maybe soup and salad, a sandwich, or a simple hearty meal.

In the lakefront park and free of traffic noise, the

Caffè La Verbanella di Willy
> *Corso Italia across from Regina Palace; 8 a.m.–midnight.*
> Offers sandwiches and snacks from a terrace with panoramic views, and the shops behind the Piazza Cavour have plenty of supplies for your picnic.

Directory

Telephone Code 0323 **Postal Code 28049**

Tourist Information
> **APT**, *V. Principe Tomaso 70 (☎ 30-150; FAX 32-561)*

Festival
> Le Settimane Musicali *(Via R. Bonghi 4)*, check with them or tourism information for the schedule and exact dates in August/September.

Lake Maggiore

Arriving

Stresa is the best-connected town on the lake, with buses, trains, tours, ferries and aliscafo, all converging here on the southwestern side of the lake. From A-8, follow the Sasteletto exit.

Borromean Islands

The three Borromean islands create a most picturesque setting in the bay formed by Stresa and Pallanza. Travelers to Lake Maggiore spend most of their time visiting two of them: Isola Bella and Isola Madre. Between them is the Isola Superiore, better known as **Isola dei Pescatori** promoted for its typical fishing village. In fact, you can see much of this island while at dock or sailing past, so you may just want to cruise by.

Isola Bella   ★

10-minute ferry ride from Stresa; 40 minute ride from Pallanza. Open end-Mar. to end-Oct., 9 a.m.–noon, 1:30–5:30 p.m.; L12,000.

Much of the charm of the Borromean islands derives from the outrageousness of this one. Begun in 1670 by one of the Borromean counts, the entire island, with its palace and gardens, was made into the shape of a ship. The entrance fee into the palace takes you through rooms with 18th-century Venetian chandeliers and mirrors, with gilt and tapestries, with paintings by notables and copiers of notables, with beds slept in by Napoleon, with family theaters and the wonderful old puppets that performed in them. The tour continues to the bizarre grottoes, designed for cooling off on hot summer days, and reaches its climax on the "prow," with the sculpture garden. It is truly amazing, whatever your taste.

Isola Madre   ★

10-minute ferry ride from Pallanza; 40 minutes from Stresa; end-Mar. to end-Oct., 9 a.m.–noon, 1:30–5:30 p.m.; L12,000.

So different from the mind-boggling Bella, this island doesn't seem to belong to the same family. The truth is that it doesn't belong to the same century. This villa, with its 19th-century collections of dolls and puppets, dates to the 16th. The gardens here are magnificently tranquil and strolled by all manner of exotic and colorful birds, from peacocks to partridges. Birds hide in the ancient fullness of the trees, parrots squawk on their flight between them. And in the spring, the azaleas and rhododendrons are in bloom.

Practical Tips

There are cafes on all the islands, and restaurants on Isola Bella, but you probably will do better lunching on the mainland. These islands are easily combined into a half-day trip, but they usually are added to a visit to the gardens at Pallanza (see below) on a one-day ferry pass.

Pallanza (Verbania)

Pallanza is a small resort that had the sense to divert SS 33 away from its tranquil waterfront and attractive town. Bypassed by most traffic, it offers a good lakeside retreat. And it offers one of the main attractions of the lake, the botanical gardens of the ★**Villa Taranto** *(Apr. through Oct., 8:30 a.m.–*

dusk; L9000; entrance located across from lake, 2 km north of town center). Although the park grounds have no lake views and offer no visit to the 20th-century villa of the Scottish captain Neil McEacharn, they are the largest of all the gardens and offer the most colorful and scintillating flower displays all season long. Certainly the camellias, rhododendrons, and tulips of April, combined with the azaleas of May, make the spring the most popular time for a visit. But even October has its color with special exhibits of hundreds of types of dahlias, with asters, and more exotic Amazonian water lilies.

Where to Stay

The only flaw in this relaxing resort is that most of its hotels encourage meal plans. But usually they aren't required with a brief stay.

Majestic   **L170–285,000 CP**   ★★★

V. Vittorio Veneto 32; ☎ *504-305, FAX 556-379; closed mid Oct.–Easter.*
Single L170,000 CP. Double L285,000 CP.
Just outside of town, to the north, is this hotel with a fine veranda and garden at the side of the lake. The decor could be improved; it's a bit dull and worn, but the setting makes up for it. There are 119 rooms, many with views, restaurant and bar, covered pool and tennis.

Where to Eat

Milano   **$$**   ★★★

Corso Zannitello 2; reserve at ☎ *556-613.*
Closed Tues., late Jan.–early Feb., part of July. Meals L50–75,000.
There is no doubt where to eat. You'll head straight for the only restaurant right on the lake in town, the lovely Milano has food that lives up to its location. Try the variety of the fish *piatto misto*; each offering, whether smoked, marinated, or sauced, is delicious, as is the lasagne *pasticcio* of eggplant and zucchini.

Caffè Bolongaro

P. Imbarcadero.
Closed Mon.
This spot has a nice outdoor terrace and modestly priced offerings, including wood-oven pizza. Up Via Ruga, at the side of town hall, you'll find the forno, alimentari and wine shop.

Directory

Telephone Code 0323   **Postal Code 28048**

Tourist Information:
Corso Zanitello 8 (☎ *503-249; FAX 503-249)*

Name
Pallanza has joined other towns in forming a larger governing unit called "Verbania," a name that often appears in place of "Pallanza."

Arriving
Pallanza requires a turn off SS 33 at about 15 km (9 mi.) north of Stresa. There are two ferry stops at Pallanza; one is closer to Villa Taranto but with less frequent ser-

vice. Aliscafo service is infrequent but Pallanza is part of the regular ferry schedule to the Borromean islands and Stresa.

Lake Orta

It is easy to be enchanted by the small *Lago d'Orta*, tucked away in Piedmont to the west of Lago Maggiore. Just beginning to experience development, the lake road is not yet inundated by traffic (except summer weekends), and the lake itself is still popular for swimming as well as waterskiing, windsurfing, and sailing. Not so large as to demand much effort at sightseeing among its green rolling hills, you can sit at a cafe, especially in the evening when stone churches and medieval towers are illuminated around the lake, and simply take it all in. (The lake is 1/2 mile across, 8 miles long). This is most enjoyable in the picturesque town of Orta San Giulio and the captivating Isla San Giulio in front of it.

Orta San Giulio

The town of Orta ranks as the San Gimignano of the lakes, not for its medieval towers, which it doesn't have, but for its charm. Its seemingly ancient stone cottages with distinctive slate roofs climb the hillside next to the lake, forming cobblestone lanes for wandering. A pilgrimage path continues the climb all the way to **Sacro Monte** (20 minutes), a wooded nature preserve with fabulous views that also is a religious center with 20 chapels (1591-1770) dedicated to St. Francis Assisi and adorned with almost 400 rather unsettling life-size terra cotta scenes of his life. (The Monte can be reached by car, too, from the entrance road at the top of town.) Back down on the lake, the 16th-century town hall, its loggia still painted with traces of coats-of-arms, grace the main piazza. Here, too, arcades shelter cafes that look out onto the lake with its Isla San Guilio. The entire town has an artsy-craftsy tone, with shops selling imported wooden toys and handknitted sweaters, as well as Piedmont wines, local salami, cheeses, and honey. In June it sponsors the Festival Cusiano of antique music; in September, a series of fine pianists. Many of the performances take place on the island. In fact, a visit to the ★ **Isla San Giulio** is a must. The ferry leaves frequently from the main piazza for its brief journey to the tiny but beautiful island that was basically abandoned in the Renaissance, thereby preserving the purity of its architecture—from the doll-like town hall to the massive Romanesque campanile of the church of ★ **San Giulio** *(open 9:30 a.m.–11 a.m. and 2–6 p.m.)*. Founded in the fourth century by the saint, who is said to have made the island habitable by ridding it of dragons and serpents, the church underwent numerous rebuilding during the 10th and 12th centuries. Its interior has some charming 14th-century pier frescoes and a remarkable 11th-century black marble pulpit. After seeing the church, a stroll around the village takes too little time. You'll want to return here, or simply not leave.

Where to Stay

San Rocco   **L225–350,000 CP**   ★★★★

V. Gippini 11; ☎ *911-977, FAX 911-964.*
Single L225,000 CP. Double L350,000 CP.

Indicative of some of the development occurring around the lake is this totally contemporary and chic hotel. It's well designed, too, so that it blends in with the centro storico on its south end with rock walls and slate roof. Stretched out along the lakefront, the hotel offers 74 comfortable rooms, restaurant and piano bar, pool, sauna, gym, many water sports and its own boat for excursions. The several other hotels are more old-fashioned.

La Bussola   **L160–250,000**   ★★

28106 Orta San Giulio; ☎ *911-913, FAX 911-934; closed Nov.*
Single L160,000 with 2 meals. Double L250,000 with 2 meals.

Just outside the centro storico, on a hill overlooking the lake. The 16 rooms here are smallish, but those with views more than compensate for the size. Pool in garden. Sunning terraces. The only drawback is the required meal plan in season.

Orta   **L95–145,000**   ★

P. Motta 1; ☎ *90-253, FAX 905-646; closed Nov. to Apr.*
Single L95,000. Double L145,000.

If you want to avoid the meal plan, try one of the rooms with lake view at the Orta. Right on the main square and lake, with 35 plain rooms (no a/c), but homey common areas. Sunning terrace, restaurant. Parking.

Where to Eat

There are lots of places on the main square to have a snack, a one-course meal with salad, or pizza. Perhaps the most strategically placed of these is **Caffè Venus** with one side of tables along the old town hall, the other on the lake, and yet a third straddling both.

Ristoro Olina   **$–$$**   ★★

V. Olina 40; closed Tues.; ☎ *905-656.*
Meals L40–60,000.

The food at this very pleasing trattoria serves seasonal specialties, such as the 10 different preparations of porcini mushrooms in the fall. You'll find it just off the main piazza and on the street where numerous shops sell all manner of tempting picnic foods.

Villa Crespi   **$$$**   ★★★★

☎ *911-902; FAX 911-919.*
Fixed-price meal L85–100,000. À la carte L670–90,000.

For serious dining, travel one mile east around the lake to this 19th-century, and outrageously Moorish, inn. Dine on appetizers like rabbit and prune terrine and an unusual tortelloni of eggplant and fish ragu, followed by excellent fish or lamb with herbs.

Directory

Telephone Code 0322   **Postal Code 28016**

Tourist Information:
    APT, *V. Olina 9 (* ☎ *911-937; FAX 905-678).*

Getting Around

Orta San Giulio is small and easily walkable, with cars banned from the centro storico. Ferries leave from the main square for frequent excursions to Isla San Giulio (10 minutes) as well as an occasional trip to other towns on the lake.

Arriving

82 km, 51 mi. northwest of Milan by A-8 (Sasteletto exit), then SS 33 from Novara, Orta is reached by car or bus. Trains reach to Novara. From Stresa, it is just over one-half hour, by the Gravellona/Omegna Road. A more scenic tour, and longer one, is over Monte Mottarone, down to Omegna where the narrow road joins that of the lake.

Lake Lugano

Most of Lake Lugano lies in Switzerland. The three sections overlapping into separate corners of Italy are quite small. In Italy, the lake is called by the relatively unknown name of "Lago Ceresio." Although the lake under any name is not properly part of our tour, some of its best scenery can be enjoyed on a drive between lakes Maggiore and Como. The waters of the lake itself are the most polluted of any, but still popular for water-skiing. The waters are safely below as you skirt the dramatic northern rim where the Swiss Alps crowd into the lake. In a half hour from either Menaggio (30 km, 18 mi.) at Lake Como (the most scenic stretch) or Luino (25 km) at Lake Maggiore, you enter the Swiss city of Lugano and pass along its lake front.

ROUTE BETWEEN LAKE MAGGIORE AND LAKE COMO • Although the southern parts of Maggiore and Como are most rapidly linked by autostrada A-8 and A-9, the more scenic route is around Lake Lugano. From Stresa on Lake Maggiore, you want to cross the car ferry from Intra to Liveno, then drive up the west lake shore (SS 394) to Luino. From Luino head west toward Ponte Tresa (either on the quiet Swiss road that runs along the Tresa river from Fornasette, or the Italian). From Ponte Tresa head north along the lake, passing briefly yet another lake, the tiny Swiss Muzzano, before entering the city of Lugano. From Lugano the road climbs west toward Porlezza, then begins its descent to Menaggio on the center of Como's west shore, 35 km, 22 mi. north of the town of Como. The trip, with border crossings, is 70 km, 43 mi. from Laveno to Menaggio, and under 2 hours. To Stresa, add the 20-minute ferry crossing and another 20 km, 12 mi. **Tip:** There are two border crossings. Remember your passport.

Lake Como

The most romantic lake is Como *(Lago di Como)*. Moody in its misty evenings, narrower and more intimate than other lakes, Como deserves its considerable fame. Tawny cliffs form dramatic settings against the blue lake, while Alpine peaks wait for the clearest days to suddenly reveal themselves, sparkling in the sun. Here the grandest hotels set themselves apart, wrapped in their gardens. The villas boast a Canova sculpture or two, as well as azaleas and palm trees, hydrangea and oleander, lemon and olive groves. If reading in the morning sun becomes tiresome, you can plan a ferry ride to an abbey, try to track down the spring where Pliny had his villa, or stroll through one of the formal gardens open to the public. In the evening, you might join the many English vacationers dancing to some oom-pah-pah hotel orchestra. But then again, you may not. In fact, it is only the city of Como, with its notable duomo and centro storico, that can arouse you to sightsee. And therein lies the magnificence of the lake—that there is really nothing to do but to enjoy it.

Part of Como's narrowness comes from its upside-down Y shape. Beautiful Bellagio sits on the end of a promontory that divides the southern lake in two, forming the arms of the Y. It is the west arm, anchored by the city of Como, that is most visited and most developed. A **typical visit** usually begins with an arrival at the city of Como, where the tourist office provides information on the entire lake and where the full-day organized ferry tour begins its journey. Instead, you can take a regular ferry or drive SS 340 to Cernobbio (the view of the Villa d'Este is best from the lake) on your way to the twin resort towns of Tremezzo (1 hour 50 minutes by ferry; 40 minutes by hydrofoil; 28 km, 17 mi. by road) and Cadenabbia, which have the gardens of the Villa Carlotta between them. Here at lake center, you (and your car) can cross the full lake from Cadenabbia on the west to Varenna on the east shore with stops at Bellagio in the middle in under one-half hour. A visit to one of the two gardens at Bellagio and, if there's time, to the Villa Monasterio at Varenna, and then most people return to Como (by ferry 2 hours; by hydrofoil 40 minutes; by car 31 km, 19 mi. on scenic, narrow SS 583). But your visit can include more, of course. The northern, more mountain-dominated part of the lake has its pleasures too. Along the west side is the resort of Menaggio (8 km north of Tremezzo) and above it is the town of **Dongo** (3-hour ferry ride from Como; 17 km, 10.5 mi. on SS 340 above Menaggio), filled with the memories of Mussolini's capture while he was trying to escape to Switzerland with his mistress. And here they were both shot. Across the lake, the 11th-century church and cloister of **Abbazia di Piona** offers Romanesque peace (14 km, 9 mi. north on SS 36 above Varenna; or by ferry). And if you are driving the northeastern shore, you might take an excursion to **Sondrio** (38 km, 24 mi. east of Colico) the heart of the wine region that produces Lombardy's Valtellina Superiore reds. And then there's the eastern arm of the Y, where the lake dips to the industrial town of **Lecco**, but whose shores are the least developed. Here you can explore by ferry from Bellagio (1 hour 15 minutes one way) or drive the coast from Varenna (SS 36, 26 km to Lecco), but note that the most scenic part of this corniche like route is just south of Varenna itself.

Lake Como

The **accommodations and restaurants** are strung out along the west side of the lake, though Bellagio on its promontory is a major tourist destination and Varenna on the east shore does have a few facilities. Although the setting is wonderful and the accommodations more often than not excellent (including one of Italy's finest, the **Villa d'Este**), the food is decent but not worthy of a pilgrimage. Like most of the lake region, it includes fish from the lake—the trout, often smoked for an appetizer, the laverello and tasty salmoncello cooked in lemon and capers, and the very local *misoltitt* (sun-dried fish appetizer) and *mataloc* (a breakfast bread made with figs, raisins, and nuts).

ARRIVING AT THE LAKE • The city of Como is 45 km, 27 mi. north of Milan and reachable by train, bus, and the A-9 autostrada. Although there are small roads leading from Bergamo to Como (SS 342; 32 km, 20 mi.) and to the car ferry at Varenna via Lecco (SS 342 and SS 36 for 75 km, 47 mi.), these routes can be time-consuming if you're caught in small-town traffic jams. Perhaps the most scenic route is from Lake Maggiore via Lugano in Switzerland (see "Lake Lugano" above).

GETTING AROUND THE LAKE • Lake Como is 30 miles long and, at its widest, 2.5 miles across. You can traverse it by traghetto (4 hours one way), aliscafo (1.5 hour one way), or you can cross it at its mid-point by traghetto or traghetto auto (10 minutes from Cardenabbio to Bellagio and another 15 minutes from Bellagio to Varenna). There are specially priced one-day ferry passes (no aliscafi rides included) that are a good deal if you are planning a full day on the lake. There are restaurant facilities on some of the ferries. Roads from Como encircle the lake and outline the Bellagio promontory. (**Note:** *Use your horn at blind curves.*) Buses from Como connect with the main lake towns.

Como

At the foot of several Alpine passes into Italy, Como thrived in Roman times and continued to be a valued city during the middle ages, when the Visconti of Milan and Frederick Barbarossa fought over it. In the 16th century it was a textile center for silk, which even today brings great prosperity to Como. Though no longer a cultivator of the raw fiber, Como produces two-thirds of Italy's finished silk and one-third of the world's. It is to Como that fashion designers come to plan the silk patterns for their next season's line. So much activity may make Como a bad choice for a retreat to the lake, but it is a convenient and pleasant base for the daytripper and provides a change of pace for those staying at the lake resorts.

What to See and Do

Despite its modern industry, Como has a beautiful location along the lake. Its centro storico, still partially enclosed by 12th-century walls, offers a few medieval churches and piazzas to enliven the brief stroll through its streets. From the spacious Piazza Cavour on the Lungo Lario and lake, head into the town on Via Plinia and you'll quickly arrive at the ★ **duomo** *(closed noon-2:30 p.m.)*, a splendid marble church that began in the Gothic style but was finished in the Early Renaissance style of the local Comacini sculptural school, responsible for the richly ornamented facade. Flanking the central portal are two native sons, Pliny the Elder and Pliny the Younger, both proudly enthroned there despite their paganism. To the side of the church is the striped marble loggia of the 13th-century *broletto*, or town hall. In the duomo is a lovely altar painting of the *Enthroned Madonna*, by another Lombard, Bernardino Luini (south aisle, next to transept). After the duomo, the street changes its name to Vittorio Emanuele before reaching the picturesque square of **San Fidele** with its Lombard Romanesque basilica. A block to the right, you'll find Via Carducci leads you left out to the **old walls** and the traffic of the modern city. You can continue walking, armed with the tourism office map, to the church of ★ **Sant'Abbondio** (A.D. 1093), 15 minutes away. Hideously hemmed in by industry and traffic, you may want to forego this Romanesque church. If not, the silence of its strong stone interior will be your reward. For **silk shopping** one of the most prestigious producers is **Mantero** *(V. Volta 68; Mon.–Fri. only, closed 12:30–2 p.m.)*; its old city office (walk in #68 and ring bell) sells designer ties and scarves. For factory discounts, drive less than one km along the western lake shore *(V. Cernobbio, on left; closed 12:30–2 p.m.)* to the designer outlet of **Ratti**.

Where to Stay

If you need to overnight, the facilities in Como are good.

Metropole & Suisse   **L170–230,000**   ★★★

P. Cavour 19; ☎ *269-444, FAX 300-808; closed Christmas season.*
Single L170,000. Double L230,000.
Across from the lake, this renovated and quite chic hotel has 70 rooms, many with lake views; bar, terrace restaurant, garage.

Barchetta Excelsior   **L235–255,000**   ★★★

P. Cavour 1; ☎ *32-21, FAX 302-622.*
Single/double L235–255,000.
Efficiently modern with 80 rooms, those in front with lake views; restaurant and bar.

Tre Re   **L75–125,000**   ★

V. Baldoni 20; ☎ *265-374, FAX 241-349; closed Christmas season.*
Single L75,000. Double L125,000.
Just two blocks from the Piazza Cavour, you find 30 rooms, no a/c, restaurant and parking. Convenient for an overnight.

Where to Eat

Raimondi   **$$–$$$**   ★★★

In the Villa Fiorita hotel, V. Cernobbio 12; ☎ *573-105; FAX 570-379.*
Closed Mon., Christmas season, half of Aug. Meals L55–80,000.
On the lake, about one km west of the old city, this establishment serves fine Lombard dishes (risotti, lakefish with rosemary) to accompany its beautiful setting and views.

Lake Como

Pasticceria Belli   ★★

V. Emanuele 7; closed Mon.
Meals L25–40,000.
In the old city try the luncheon antipasto table in the sala da te or simply treat yourself to the tiny cream puffs and chocolates, the little prosciutto and croissant sandwiches in the handsome shop.

For a **picnic**, look at the fine *"gastronomie"* shops near Piazza Volta (just off P.
Cavour), to right of Barchetta hotel; here, too, is a vegetable market (V. Baldoni).

Directory

Telephone Code 031   **Postal Code 22100**

Tourist Information

APT, *P. Cavour 16 (☎ 274-064; 301-051)* with information on the entire lake as
well as Lombardy.

Jazz Festival

One week in July in P. San Federale. Contact APT.

Transportation

The main ticket office for ferries and hydrofoils is right in front of the P. Cavour.
Here day passes and one-day tours can be arranged. • The stazione is a 15-minute
walk from P. Cavour, on west side of town; bus available. • Buses to lake towns
leave from east end of Lungo Lario.

Cernobbio

Not so much a place to sightsee, Cernobbio is instead a resort made famous by its grand hotel, the Villa d'Este. But the village on the western
shore is pleasant, the lakefront is tranquil (the shoreline road is diverted away
from the water, and forms the main street, or Corso, of the town), and there
are a number of less luxurious accommodations and decent restaurants to
make for a good vacation even if your budget can't manage the Villa d'Este.

Where to Stay

Villa d'Este   **L570–750,000 CP**

22010 Cernobbio; ☎ 34-81, FAX 348-844; closed Nov.–Mar.
Single L570,000 CP. Double L655–750,000 CP.
It began as a cardinal's villa in the 16th century and became the possession of semi-
exiled czarinas and queens thereafter. Since 1873 it has been a hotel, renowned for
its luxury and beauty and still the haunt of princes and dukes. Set in an immense
lakeside park, the villa retains its regal decor with marble columns and frescoed ceilings and offers 180 magnificently appointed rooms. There are swimming pools, a
beach, tennis, sailing, an 18-hole golf course nearby, Turkish baths, a health club
and whatnot. The restaurants are elegantly situated for the views and there are bars
conveniently located. The service is impeccable.

Miralago   **L115–160,000 CP**   ★★

22012 Cernobbio; ☎ 510-125, FAX 248-126; closed Nov.–Feb.
Single L115,000 CP. Double L160,000 CP.

If the opulence of the Villa d'Este is not for you, try this waterfront hotel. It's bright and cheerful with 30 simple rooms, no a/c, but many with views of the lake. Restaurant and terrace and just a short walk to the public olympic-size pool.

Where to Eat

Along the Corso are tea rooms and a fine **Gastronomia** *(Corso 49)* for picnic shopping.

Hosteria **$$** ★★

V. Garibaldi 3, closed Sun.; reserve at ☎ 510-151.
Meals L50–75,000.

A pleasant place to dine, with considerable attention to the daily offerings. Located just a half-block from the lake, this tiny inn specializes in lake fish, such as smoked trout or lavarello with sage, as well as fine pasta.

Directory

Telephone Code 031 **Tourist Information**

V. Regina 33b (☎ 510-198)

Arriving

A 12-minute ferry ride from Como (no aliscafo service) and just 5 km by car or bus on SS 340.

Tremezzo/Cadenabbia

These two resorts on the western shore offer many facilities, but we prefer other towns for an overnight. *There is just too much traffic along the lakefront,* caused by the cars and tour buses zipping through on SS 340. But you should visit one or the other village just to see the ★**Villa Carlotta** *(open daily 9 a.m.–6 p.m., Apr.–Sept.; 9:30 a.m.–11:30 p.m., and 2–4:30 p.m. Mar. & Oct.; L8000),* just a brief walk from the embarcadero of either Tremezzo or Cadenabbia. The villa, its magnificent staircase, and gardens were constructed in the 18th century, but later revamped in a rather glorious Empire style for Princess Carlotta. Although the springtime azaleas and rhododendrons attract throngs of visitors, the art collection inside the villa and the views of the lake are pleasing all season long. The plaster frieze inside the villa was begun for Napoleon just before his downfall, and it encircles a room with a number of Canova sculptures—the most famous, Cupid and Psyche, is only a copy.

Practical Tips

Arriving

Tremezzo/Cadenabbia are at the center of the lake, just across from Bellagio. The regular ferries and aliscafi take you to Tremezzo and from Tremezzo to Bellagio, then to Como. Cadenabbia, less frequented by the regular ferry, is nonetheless the location of the car ferry to Bellagio and Varenna. In the summer, twice a week there're special night crossings (till midnight) between Cadenabbia and Bellagio. Buses from Como link the resorts by road.

Bellagio

At the center of the lake on the tip of the promontory, Bellagio's location couldn't be more beautiful. It is surrounded by the lake on three sides, with views of the picturesque hills and villas of the west shore as well as the wilder rugged cliffs of the eastern shore. Despite the narrow roads down the promontory that tie Bellagio to the rest of Lombardy, it feels quite pleasantly like a self-contained island with lots of gardens and paths to explore—down to the little church and houses at San Giovanni, up the stepped streets to the tiny duomo, and across the island to the miniature port of Pescallo with its sailboats. Most day-visitors come for the grander sights of Bellagio, enjoying the gardens and lake promenade at the neoclassical ★**Villa Melzi** *(9 a.m.–6:00 p.m., Mar.–Oct.; L5000; a 5-minute walk to the right upon landing at the P. Mazzini)*, or the Rockefeller Foundation's formal gardens and fabulous views of the lake, especially the Lecco branch, at the ★**Villa Serbelloni** *(gardens open to public by 2-hour tour at 10:30 a.m. and 4 p.m. from mid-Apr. through mid-Oct.; closed Mon.; L5000; located up hill beyond duomo).* And then there are the boutiques for shopping on Piazza Mazzini, across from the ferry landing, and the lakeside cafes for resting. Even when the hotels are full, Bellagio is restful. And when the ferries depart with the last visitors, the tranquility is sublime.

Where to Stay

Grand Hotel Villa Serbelloni   **L320–650,000 CP**   ❀★★★★

V. Roma 1; ☎ *950-216, FAX 951-529; closed mid-Oct.–Apr.*
Single L320,000 CP. Double L450–650,000 CP.

On the tip of Bellagio amid formal garden terraces surrounded by the lake, this grand old hotel should not be confused with the villa of the same name. The hotel retains its graceful veranda, its sitting rooms with overstuffed chairs and high ceilings, chandeliers and pianos and 78 rooms with gilded decor and views of lake or town (avoid rear rooms). In the gardens are the heated pool, the tennis court, as well as a terrace restaurant and bar. There's a fitness and beauty center. Evening entertainment. Boats. Garage.

Belvedere   **L135–215,000 CP**   √★★★

V. Valassina 33; ☎ *950-410, FAX 950-102; closed Nov.–Mar.*
Single L135,000 CP. Double L215,000 CP.

On the far side of Bellagio, this hotel, set on terraces above picturesque Pescallo, commands breathtaking views of the dramatic, Lecco branch of the lake. The Belvedere is within walking distance of the duomo, yet apart from it all. The 50 rooms (no a/c) vary, some garden units have terraces, a few in the hotel have balconies; all are comfortable, if not fancy. Just reserve one with a view. Ample buffet breakfast. Restaurant and bar with views. Gardens and sunning terraces. A good swimming pool. Parking. A good buy.

Lake Como

Where to Eat

Probably because the British tourists, who have long frequented Bellagio, most often take meal plans at their hotels, there are few restaurants in Bellagio. Some competition would be helpful. But we have no complaints about **Gelateria del Borgo** *(Garibaldi 44);* don't leave without trying their *nocciola* (hazelnut chocolate) ice cream. Nearby on Garibaldi are food and wine shops if you want to picnic.

La Grotta $ ★★

Sallita Cernaia 14, up from P Mazzini; ☎ *951-152.*
Meals L20–40,000.
Unlike other restaurants, La Grotta has no beautiful terrace, but it serves the best food for the money. The stone vaulted back room is air-conditioned, the pizza is excellent, the pasta, pretty good.

Barchetta $$–$$$ ★★

Salita Mella 13, up from P. Mazzini; reserve at ☎ *951-389.*
Closed Tues. except July–Sept. Meals L50–80,000.
The lovely Barchetta is good, but overpriced. It takes the lake fish and smokes it, or slices it thin for carpaccio, skewers and serves it with capers, or dries it for missoltot accompanied by polenta.

Bilacus $–$$

Salita Serbelloni 9; up from P. Mazzini; ☎ *950-480.*
Closed Oct.–Mar. 15. L35–55,000.
And then there's Bilacus. Yes, celebrities do seem to eat here (we saw Vanessa Redgrave). There's a nice terrace, but it also serves the only bad pasta in Italy.

Entertainment

Another British influence is in the evening entertainment. Most nights you can put on your dinner jacket and waltz with the Rolls Royce crowd at the **Grand Hotel**, or roll up your sleeves and do the fox trot lakeside, with the **Hotel Excelsior Splendide's** *(Lungolago Manzoni)* orchestra of two accordions and drums.

Directory

Telephone Code 031   **Postal Code 22021**

Tourist Information

Near duomo *(*☎ *950-204; closed Tues., Sun.),* but maps posted on P. Mazzini and Lungolago, near ferry docks.

Arriving

Ferries and autoscafi, as well as car ferries, make Bellagio easy to reach from the lake; and buses along SS 583 reach the town within 45 minutes from Como. **Beware:** *The Varenna car ferries leave from the Lungolago Manzoni, not the ticket office on the Piazza Mazzini.*

Varenna

A lovely fishing village on the eastern shore, Varenna visitors usually head straight for the car ferry dock that bridges the central lake. But the village itself is worth some quiet exploration. From the dock, a picturesque promenade (the "passerella lago;" about 1 km) skirts the lake and winds through medieval ramparts; it passes restaurants and outdoor cafes on a tiny marina and continues by the Hotel du Lac before climbing steps to the upper village. At the end, the town is to the left; just to the right is the **Villa Monastero**, a 16th-century monastery now a center of scientific studies, but with romantic lakeside gardens open to the public *(Apr.–Oct., 10 a.m.–12:30 p.m., 2:30–6 p.m.; L3000).*

Where to Stay and Eat

Du Lac   **L140–230,000 CP**   ★★
V. del Prestino 4, ☎ *830-102, FAX 831-081; closed Jan.–Feb.*
Single L140,000 CP. Double L230,000 CP.
There are a number of modest hotels here, but none is more scenic then this small hotel, blessed with a lakefront location on the passerella; the 18 rooms include suites and vary in price; not all have views. You might want to spring for one with a terrace over the lake. Restaurant and dining terrace with views. Garage. Dining or snacking along the passerella is highly recommended, even if the food is just decent, you'll be too relaxed to be dissatisfied.

Vecchia Varenna   **$$**   ★★
5-minutes from dock on passerella; ☎ *830-793.*
Closed Mon., also Tues. in Feb.–mid-Mar., & Jan. Meals L45–60,000.
It is tucked under a medieval stone arch on a ledge by the lake and serves an inventive assortment of lake fish and traditional pastas; such as gnocchi with rabbit ragout.

Bar Molo
10-minutes from dock on passerella
Overlooking the small marina, this cafe has interesting sandwiches and some salads.

Directory

Telephone Code 0341   **Postal Code 22050**
Arriving
The location of the car ferry, with frequent trips to Bellagio (15 minutes) and Cernobbio and a few to Menaggio. Reachable by road via Lecco (26 km on SS 36).

Menaggio

One of the most popular resorts on the west side, Menaggio has a fine setting looking back over the drama of the central lake area. Although the main street can get tied up with traffic, there are quieter parts, too, as well as a golf course (4 km, 2 1/2 mi.) in the hills behind.

Where to Stay and Eat

Grand Hotel Victoria   **L190–265,000 CP**   ★★★★
V. Castelli 11; ☎ *32-003, FAX 32-992.*
Single L190,000 CP. Double L265,000 CP
Commanding a lakeside spot with good views, this renovated 1806 hotel still has some fine architectural flourishes. There are 53 modern rooms *(no a/c)*, a garden

pool, a beach front with windsurfing. Terrace bar and decent restaurant, ★★**Le Tout Paris** (☎ *31-166)* that serves saltimbocca along with the crepes suzette *(meals L60–90,000).*

Menaggio offers a panoramic lake view.

Directory

Telephone Code 0344   **Postal Code 22017**

Tourist Information

 P. Garibaldi 8 (☎ 32-924)

Arriving

 Menaggio is 36 km north of Como on SS 340 and is connected by bus with both Como and Porlezza on Lake Lugano (12 km, 7 mi. on SS 340 west). There are ferry and aliscafo connections as well as an occasional car ferry to Bellagio and Varenna.

Lake Iseo

 The fourth-largest of the Lombard lakes, Lake Iseo *(Lago d'Iseo)* is scarcely known. Mountains crowd its shores, and an occasional castle makes a romantic statement here and there. You can drive around the lake, but better yet, you might take the ferry from Sulzano on the east coast for the 10-minute ride to the tranquil island of **Monte Isola** where you can climb up (40 minutes) to the sanctuary of the Madonna della Ceriola for a panorama of the lake. Or visit medieval **Iseo**, a gracious resort village on the south shore of the lake, its piazzas and dock area on the lakefront passeggiata (Lungolago Marconi) made pleasant for lingering by numerous outdoor cafes. South of Iseo are the **Franciacorta wine estates** (follow "Rovato" not "Brescia" signs), where you can sample Lombardy's more prestigious whites (DOC Pino Bianco di Franciacorta and a vintage champenoise) and DOC reds in the towns near Cortefranca. Although the Franciacorte landscape can't compare with the Tuscan or Piedmont wine regions, it soon will become better known as people flock to here to visit Gualtiero Marchesi's new inn located near the esteemed Ca' del Bosco vineyards.

Where to Stay and Eat

Gualtiero Marchesi L'Albereta   L240–350,000 CP   ✿★★★★

V. Emanuele 11, 25030 Erbusco in Brescia; closed Jan.; ☎ (030) 776-0550, FAX 776-0573.
Single L240,000 CP, double L300–350,000 CP.
Speeding on the autostrada, it's hard to believe that only a few minutes away is a bucolic countryside. Less than an hour from Milan and Verona and just 5 km from the A-4 Rovato exit, you climb the vine covered and rolling hills of Erbusco to the summit location of this inn where Italy's great chef has created his stunning retreat from Milan. The inn and restaurant (see below) are set in an evergreen park, amid gardens and with views of Lago Iseo in the distance. The inn, when completed, will have 12 rooms and 27 suites, some with Jacuzzi, all richly decorated and each unique. Sliding glass panels create an indoor/outdoor setting for the pool; there's a gym, Jacuzzi, and a tennis court; library and billiard room.

Gualtiero Marchesi $$$ ★★★★★

Closed Mon., Sun. dinner, most of Jan.; reserve at ☎ (030) 776-0562.
Fixed-price lunch L65,000, fixed-price dinner L100 & 150,000, à la carte L85–140,000.
The primary attraction of the inn (see above), however, is the restaurant even though Michelin demoted it from three stars to two in 1997. It always is bustling with business meetings and diners just about as soon as it opened in 1993. Among the four dining rooms and alcoves is a porticoed and glass-enclosed veranda with frescoed walls and views. The menu changes daily, but the chef is known for his creative, often somewhat French inspired dishes, such as *quenelles* (here called "*tortino di luccio*") an aromatic consomme of mushrooms as well as the traditional, *costoletta di vitello alla milanese.*

Ambra   L90–120,000   ★

Lungolago Marconi near dock; ☎ 980-130, FAX 982-1361; closed Nov.
Single L90,000. Double L120,000.
If you've come to visit the lake, however, Iseo has a few simple hotels, including this fifties-modern locale with 30 (no a/c) rooms, some with balconies and lake views.

Trattoria Leon d'Oro $ ★

Largo Dante 2.
Closed Jan., early Nov., and Mon. Meals L20–45,000.
Near the Ambra are the lakeside outdoor tables of this relaxing spot for a salad and simple platter of lake fish.

Il Volto $$ ★★★

V. Mirolti 33.
Closed Thurs. lunch, Wed., and July. L45–65,000.

The food is more important than the view, try this one on the main traffic-free street of town. A fine osteria, with lake fish, of course, but quail and other dishes are served too, to go along with a fine degustazione of Franciacorte wines.

Directory

Telephone Code 030   **Postal Code 25049**

Tourist Information

In Iseo, *Lungolago Marconi 2* (☎ *980-209; FAX 981-361)*, with useful maps of the region.

Arriving

Iseo lies just 25 km, 15.5 mi. northwest of Brescia, to which there are bus connections along SS 510. It is near Bergamo, (40 km west), and can be visited on your way to Lake Garda by a short detour (10 km, 6 mi. north) off A-4. • Erbusco is reached directly from the A-4 Rovato exit.

Getting Around

The lake is 15 miles long, 3 miles wide. Ferries from Iseo go to most points on the lake; those from Sulzano go directly to the island. • Erbusco is about 15 km, 9 mi. from Iseo by car

Practical Tip

Pollution results in "divieto di balneazione" signs in many part of the lake.

Lake Garda

Lake Garda *(Lago di Garda)* has some of the most dramatic lake scenery, especially on its northern shores, around Riva del Garda, where sandstone massifs vie with villages for waterfront footage. Every hill seems capped by medieval towers and roccas, or forts, and each town boasts a Renaissance fresco, a Gothic church. The hills flatten in the south and the lake spreads like a great sea. Its benign climate encourages many vineyards, as well as apple orchards and lemon groves. Although Garda is often claimed to be one of the most beautiful lakes (and it is), it leaves an indelible impression not of romantic landscapes but rather of summer fun and family vacationers. Here more than any other lake, activities are water oriented with windsurfing and swimming, paddle boating and water-skiing. Beautiful and lively, the lake is also large—the largest in Italy—and divided up among Lombardy on the east, the Veneto on the west, and Trentino to the north.

Lake Garda's two most important towns are **Desenzano** (a pleasant starting point for a tour rather than a resort), found on the southern, flat plain of the lake, and Riva del Garda on the north. Ferries and aliscafi begin and end their navigation of the lake at these towns. The most important resort is Sirmione, on the peninsula in the south, guarded by a commanding Scaligeri castle. A visit to the many lakeside towns is facilitated by an **encircling road** that is famous for its tunneled stretch through the rocky cliffs between Gargnano and Riva del Garda on the west coast (SS 45 bis). The road brings with

Lake Garda

it, and to many of the towns, too much traffic. Garda is so popular with Italian families in the summer and with German bus tours all season, that the traffic can mar your enjoyment of the lake—especially in villages hemmed in by the cliffs, like Limone sul Garda, where there often is barely room to walk. The ferries and alsicafi offer a quieter approach to the towns, if not necessarily tranquil streets upon your arrival. Whether you drive or float, the most **typical tour** includes Sirmione for its castle and Roman ruins, Gardone Riviera for its lavish Villa Il Vittoriale, and Riva del Garda for its magnificent location and fortified centro storico. There are other attractions, if you have time—the large resort **Malcesine**, on the east coast, houses its town hall in a 16th-century Venetian guards' palace and its small museum in a Scaligeri castle. And it promises great views atop its funicolare. South of Malcesine is the highly regarded view from lovely **Punta San Vigilio**. By car you can head into the mountains west of Gargnano for the panoramic views from the **Madonna of Monte Castello** at Gardola. And you can explore the **wine estates** with their venditta diretta ("direct sale") signs for Lombard reds called Riviera del Gara (on the road west of Desenzano) and the white Lugana (on the road east of Sirmione); or the famous red Bardolino of the Veneto (on east coast, near town of same name).

The **accommodations and restaurants** are more plentiful than at any of the lakes, but you should still make reservations from mid-June through September and for any weekend stay. The cuisine includes lake trout and eel as well as the bounty from the nearby Adriatic. The Lugana white wine is light and pleasing.

ARRIVING AT THE LAKE • The southern part of the lake is near both Brescia (A-4 to Desenzano exit, 25 km, 15.5 mi.) and Verona (A-4 to Sirmione or Desenzano exit, 40 km, 24 mi.) and both are connected to Desenzano by train and bus. Brescia has buses to west-coast towns, too, like Gardone, and Verona to Malcesine. Trent is most beautifully connected to Riva del Garda by SS 45 bis (42 km, 26 mi.), but the Brennero autostrada A-22 also has two lake exits; the one for Rovereto is 15 km east of Riva. There's bus service between Trento and Riva and the Brennero train at Rovereto is linked by bus with Riva.

GETTING AROUND THE LAKE • Lake Garda is 32 miles long and 10 miles at its widest point in the south. It is crossed by car ferry from Maderno on the west to Torri di Benaco (30 minutes) about once an hour. Its length is criss-crossed by ferry (4 hours Desenzano to Riva) and aliscafi (1.5–2 hours) several times a day, with shorter crossings more frequent. There are ferries with restaurants for efficient use of your sightseeing time. The road, of course, is usually the fastest route between towns on the same coast. Buses connect the larger towns, leaving Desenzano for the west and east coasts.

Sirmione

There are several Sirmioni. One is the modern roadside town on the flat of the lake's south shore. Another is the two-mile spit of road with modest hotels lining each side, as it juts out onto the lake. The third is the headland of the peninsula where the famous resort can be found, surrounded by water and announced by the crenellated majesty of the ★ **Scaligeri castle**. Here you must park your car (or have a hotel reservation) before crossing the moat into the old town. And it is this last Sirmione that deserves the fame. Its picturesque centro storico is small, but full of shops and with outdoor cafes in the main Piazza Carducci, where you catch the ferry. You can visit the 13th-century Scaligeri castle of the famous Veronese family, admiring its imposing ramparts as well as the views from its keep *(open 9 a.m.–6 p.m. summer; 9 a.m.–4 p.m. winter; closed Mon.; L8000).* You can follow Via V. Emanuele out of the village to the promontory covered with gardens and verdant with parks. Here the encircling road leads to a few lucky hotels as well as the public lido and Roman "grottoes" on the northern tip of Sirmione (half-mile walk, bicycle ride or, in season, pneumatic trolley ride). But first you might stop at the lakeside spa with its warm sulfur springs used since the time of Catullus, who had a villa in Sirmione. In fact, the ★ **Grotto di Catullo** *(9 a.m.– 6 p.m. in summer, till 4 p.m. winter; closed Mon.; L8000)* on the northern point are claimed to be the ruins of his villa. Although there is no decisive evidence that these romantically situated ruins belonged to the poet Catullus, they are ancient, Roman, and of a villa that offers views and walks that are lovely.

Where to Stay

Note: All these hotels are in the traffic-free zone of Sirmione. If you have a reservation, stop at the tourism office for a permit to take your car into the centro storico and to your hotel. Taxis available.

Villa Cortine Palace L300–500,000 ✿★★★★

V. Grotte 12; ☎ *990-5890, FAX 916-390; closed end-Oct. to Easter.*
Single L300,000. Double L460–500,000.
The most relaxing hotels are those lucky ones in the gardens of the promontory. This extraordinary one is near the grottoes, but totally set apart in its own large park behind locked gates. There is a 100-year-old villa with exquisite common areas and 59 very comfortable rooms in a more modern wing. Terrace restaurant and bar (meal plans required in season), private beach, heated pool, tennis.

Olivi L115–165,000 ★★★

V. San Pietro: ☎ *990-5365, FAX 916-472; closed Jan.*
Single L115,000. Double L165,000.
Set in a quiet garden enclave off the lake, this well designed hotel has tasteful decor. Many of its larger front rooms with balconies (a little costlier, but worth it) have views; all have smart bathrooms. Restaurant, bar. Good pool in garden. Parking.

Lake Garda

Eden   L100–155,000

P. Carducci 17; ☎ 916-481, FAX 916-483; closed Nov. to Mar. 1.
Single L100,000. Double L155,000.

Right on the main square of the old town. Picturesque, if not as quiet as the promontory, the Eden's location might appeal to those on a short visit. The hotel is refurbished in a surprisingly grand style; its 33 rooms with lake views are recommended. Restaurant, cafe on square, sunning terrace by lake.

Ideal   L85–150,000

V. Catullo 31; ☎ 990-4243, FAX 990-4245; closed Nov. to Apr.
Single L85,000. Double L150,000.

Back on the lovely promontory, you find these 25 quiet rooms (no a/c) and a garden terrace restaurant.

Where to Eat

Probably because so many hotels require meal plans, Sirmione is far from being a culinary capital. But there are some acceptable choices, including some with attractive settings.

La Rucola $$–$$$

V. Strentelle 7; reserve at ☎ 916-326; FAX 916-326.
Closed Thurs., mid-Jan.–mid-Feb. Meals L65–80,000.

Tucked away in the old town near the castle is this elegant dining spot. Along with the lake specialties, there are such treats as Chateaubriand and duck with pine nuts.

Grifone $$

V. Bisse 5; ☎ 916-097; FAX 916-548.
Closed off-season. Meals L45–65,000.

The best feature here is the dramatic setting: an outdoor terrace with views of the rugged castle ramparts as well as the lake. Although the location is tempting (you're sure to succumb), we found the fish specialties disappointingly mediocre.

Piccolo Castello $$

V. Dante 9; closed Tues.; ☎ 916-138; meals L45–65,000.

Try this eatery next door to Grifone, where you can dine on the quaint balconies and enjoy salmon or scampi.

There are plenty of shops for gathering together a picnic. And there are plenty of gelaterias, but try **Cioccomenta** *(V. Emanuele 11).*

Directory

Telephone Code 030   **Postal Code 25019**

Tourist Information

   APT, *V. Marconi*, just outside moat *(☎ 916-245).*

Bike Rentals

   Green Walk, *V. Verona 47 (☎ 990-4034).*

Arriving

   Sirmione is just 5 km from the A-4 exit, 8 km (5 mi.) from Desanzano. Ferries and aliscafi make lake connections with the old town.

Lake Garda

Gardone Riviera

The lakeshore road separates Gardone's village from its hillside gardens. Fortunately the village and its older lakefront hotels have been preserved in a quiet nook below the road and other hotels hide away in the hillside above it. Atop the hill is ★ **Il Vittoriale** (*gardens open 8:30 a.m.–8 p.m. in summer; 8:30 a.m.–12:30 p.m. & 2:30–5 p.m. in winter. House visited by tour only 10 a.m.– 12:30 p.m., 2:30–6 p.m. in summer, till 5 p.m. in winter. Admission L15,000 both villa and gardens; L7000 gardens only*), the lavish and somewhat outrageous villa of the poet and playwright Gabriele d'Annunzio (d. 1938). Like the Roman villas that preceded his, d'Annunzio's includes an amphitheater where his plays as well as music and dances are performed during July and August (☎ *20-130 for information*). Apart from the pleasures of the lake and villa, Gardone is favored for hillside walks.

Where to Stay

Grand Hotel   **L170–290,000**   ★★★★

25083 Gardone Riviera; ☎ *20-261, FAX 22-695; closed Nov. to Apr. 1.*
Single L170,000. Double L290,000.
Located on the lake where it has entertained princely visitors for a century. Although it has lost a bit of its glamour, it is still a lovely hotel with 180 stately rooms, almost all with lake views. The road runs by the rear of the hotel with little damage to its ambience of lakeside gardens and quiet. (Make sure your room faces the lake.) Terrace restaurant and bar (meal plans encouraged); pool and golf course 10 minutes away.

Montefiori   **L80–125,000**   ★★

V. dei Lauri 8; ☎ *290-235, FAX 21-488; closed Nov.*
Single L80,000. Double L125,000.
Set off in a park above the lake, this hotel offers 36 quiet rooms (no a/c), a restaurant, bar, tennis and pool. Parking.

Where to Eat

Villa Fiodorliso   **$$$**   ★★★★

V. Zanadelli 132; ☎ *20-158; FAX 290-011.*
Closed Tues. lunch, Mon., mid-Jan.–mid-Feb., Nov.–mid Dec. Meals L70–100,000.
Just north of the Grand Hotel, the road passes on its right the unmistakable Venetian pink of this restaurant. With a shady terrace overlooking the lake for lunch and an elegant dining room, you can enjoy expertly prepared dishes that transcend the usual menu limits of grilled lake fish and include rabbit and kid, all spiced deliciously.

Casino   **$$–$$$**   ★★★

V. Zanadelli 14; ☎ *20-387.*
Closed Mon., Jan., Feb. 50–75,000.
Just a bit farther along is another good, if more casual restaurant. This lakeside villa has handsome interior dining rooms with high stucco ceilings, as well as terraces right over the water. At lunch you pick and choose as you want, the pasta is good, the salads wonderfully fresh, and the service pleasant.

Lake Garda

Directory

Telephone Code 0365   **Postal Code 25083**

Tourist Information

Small office (☎ *20-347; FAX 20-347)* near embarcadero and town map at bus stop.

Arriving

Gardone is 24 km, 15 mi. north of Desanzano, and 42 km, 26 mi. south of Riva, on the west coast. It is connected to both towns by bus, ferry and aliscafo (the embarcadero is next to the Grand Hotel).

Riva del Garda

Riva's location is one of the most dramatic. From the land side, you enter its medieval streets through the gates of the old town walls and meander to the lakefront where craggy cliffs, rising steeply from the lake, form the west side of the port. The passeggiata around the lakefront takes you from the embarcadero, past some of the hotels, over to the moated 12th-century **rocca**, now a local museum displaying some ancient Roman artifacts among other items. Continuing around the rocca and along a park you come to the **Punta Lido**, where a long pebbly beach and calm swimming waters can be found. For views from the eagle's vantage point, take the funicolare, on the west of town, up to the Venetian **bastion** (1506).

Where to Stay

Hotel du Lac et du Parc   **L160–390,000**

V. Rovereto 44; ☎ *551-500, FAX 555-200; closed late Oct.–late Mar.*
Single L160,000. Double L320–390,000.

Most of Riva's hotels are found in the rather congested modern section to the east of the centro storico. This is an elegant exception. Surrounded by a park and manicured lawns next to the lake, the modern hotel offers 230 of Garda's most comfortable rooms, several restaurants and bars (MAP required in season), an outdoor heated pool, indoor pool, tennis, a private beach. Parking.

Bellavista   **L135–175,000**

P. Cesare Battisti 4; ☎ *554-271, FAX 555-754; closed Nov.–Easter.*
Single L135,000. Double L175,000.

Next to the embarcadero in the centro storico are a few older, favored hotels. The Bellavista with its 32 rooms, many with views (no a/c), is a decent choice here and the lack of restaurant avoids the too-often required meal plan.

Where to Eat

Vecchia Riva   **$$**

V. Bastione 3; ☎ *555-061.*
Closed Tues. in off season only. Meals L45–65,000.

Just outside the Porta San Marco, you find the Vecchia Riva. With smoked fish appetizers and interesting preparations of seafood as well as lake fish and veal.

Al Volt   **$–$$**

V. Fiume 73; closed Mon. and Feb.; ☎ *552-570; FAX 552-570. Meals L40–55,000.*

Lake Garda

Just inside the Porta San Marco is this handsome spot with decent home cooking—especially the pastas.

The morning market and shops in the centro storico have all you need for a snack on one of the beaches by the lungolago. And the **Caffe Pellini** has not just ice cream but prime views of the lake.

Directory

Telephone Code 0464   **Postal Code 38066**

Tourist Information

   APT, *Giardini Porta Orientale 8*, east of Rocca (☎ *554-444; FAX 520-308*).

Arriving

   Riva is the major town in the north, linked to the rest of the lake by ferry, aliscafo, and bus.

On the Road

Lombard Historic Towns

The convenience the Celts found in the location of ancient Bergamo or the Etruscans discovered at Mantua, the Romans at Brescia, and the Lombards at Pavia, has yet to disappear. These ancient towns continue to prosper from the foot of the trans-alpine trade routes and the vast valley of the Po. Far from being empty shells of their former splendid selves, these towns and, in the instance of Brescia and Bergamo, cities, have expanded considerably beyond their medieval and Renaissance walls. While they all seem to share in the success of Lombardy's industrialization, their historical diversity couldn't be greater. Brescia and Bergamo were ruled by Venice for four centuries. Pavia and Cremona were dominated by the dukes of Milan, and Mantua (and its satellite, Sabbioneta) managed independence by playing off Venice against Milan. The results are highly distinctive cities.

It is the rare traveler who plans to "do Lombardy." More than likely, you plan to visit Lake Garda and will stop at Brescia, too, or you will stop at Bergamo and Milan while at Lake Como. Or you've been to Venice or Bologna and want to stop on your way to Malpensa airport at an historic town such as Mantua or Pavia. The interesting churches at Pavia, the art treasures of the Gonzaga court at Mantua, the charm of medieval Cremona, or the views and art museum at Bergamo will reward you for your detour, but need not detain you long.

Bergamo

There can be no doubt about Bergamo's charms. Scenically situated at the base of the Alps, the fortified hill town of old Bergamo captivates you with its perfectly preserved medieval streets, the fine Romanesque porches of its duomo, and its tiny squares in which to enjoy a meal or sip a coffee. Only 30 miles along the autostrada from Milan, Bergamo attracts the city dwellers and their business companions for an amiable lunch alfresco or even for a weekend retreat at hillside villas.

Where the Milanesi now join the Bergamashci in their strolls through gardens and hillside paths, the Venetians had constructed fortifications against these very Milanesi. As the most western outpost of the Republic of Venice (1428-1797), Bergamo's walls were thick and defensively effective until Napoleon conquered all of northern Italy. Now the massive 16th-century walls have been converted into peaceful spots for viewing the countryside and enjoying passeggiati, even though Venice still proclaims its power at the Porta Sant'Agostino with the winged lion of San Marco.

What to See and Do

As you will immediately realize upon arriving in Bergamo, there are two towns: **Bergamo Alta**, the historic hill town, and **Bergamo Bassa**, the modern city 400 feet below it and connected to its predecessor by both road and *funicolare*. You arrive—by car, train, or bus—in Bergamo Bassa, a bustling city of over 100,000 that manufactures textiles (silk and cotton) and processes agricultural products. Although the sections around Via Pinga and the exceptional Accademia Carrara (see below) retain some of their historic character as former suburbs of the hill town, the rest of lower Bergamo was built at the beginning of this century and has a certain monumental sterility to it that reflects the Mussolini era. Its most appealing sections are right through the Porta Nuova with its Doric temples, to the Piazza Matteotti flanked by park-like walks, and then to the adjacent Piazza Vittorio Vento with its arcaded buildings. The grand avenue of Vittorio Emanuele marches straight through these squares to the base of Bergamo Alta, where you can pick up the tunneled cable car or drive up to the edge of the old city (**Note:** in summer, especially weekends, cars may be banned.)

Citta Alta   ★

A brief ride in the cable car and you arrive in the *citta alta* at the Piazza Mercato delle Scarpe. From here the traffic-free Via Gombito takes you to the ★**Piazza Vecchia**, a favorite place to dine while savoring the stagelike perfection of the small square. Even the 17th century elegance of the library (on the Via Gombito side) fails to mar the medieval ambience. Across from the library is the **Palazzo della Ragione** (1199), stunning with its Venetian lion and diagonal staircase and, despite 15th-century remodeling, very medieval with its loggia linking the two main squares of the town. Next to it stands the **12th-century tower** that still tolls the curfew each evening even though no one heeds its call *(steps for view at top; 10 a.m.– 12:30 p.m., 2:30–6 p.m.)*.

Walking through the loggia of the palazzo you come to the ★**Piazza del Duomo**, an even tinier and older square. To your right is the gemlike octagonal baptistery (1340) by the Lombard master Giovanni da Campione. To the left is the duomo, too often rebuilt, and now with a 19th-century facade. In front of you is the north side of the Romanesque **Santa Maria Maggiore** church with its ★Gothic porch (note the playful figures next to the lions) and surmounted by sculpture of the Virgin enthroned—all work by Campione. Wedged next to this is the ★**Cappella Colleoni** *(closed noon–2:30 winter, till 3 summer),* the 15th-century chapel designed by Amadeo, whose Lombard taste for the ornamental makes it hard to believe he was a Renaissance architect. But the exuberant facade is fascinating, even if fussy. The chapel was built for the tomb of Venice's most famous condottiere, Bartolomeo Colleoni, who was born in Bergamo and commemorated by Verrocchio's famous equestrian statue that still commands attention in Venice. Based on Amadeo's lavish tombs (Colleoni's daughter Medea is buried here too), you can guess that Colleoni was paid well for his services. Not completed until the 18th century, the interior contains later works, too, such as Tiepolo's ceiling frescoes. You can enter Santa Maria Maggiore through the lion porch on the opposite, south side and discover a Baroque interior that seems wild after the calm of the medieval facade. On the west wall is a large tomb with wings embracing a medallion and hovering over piano keys, an appropriate enough monument to another native son, the musician Gaetano Donizetti.

San Vigilio

If you're still in a wandering mood, follow the extension of Via Gombito west to the cittadella, and continue to the Porta Sant'Allesandro. Here you can pick up a bus (or funiculare, when functioning) further up the mountain (about 10 minutes) to San Vigilio and its castle and views. Or you might take a very **scenic walk** back to lower Bergamo (about 20 minutes): off the Piazza Mercato delle Scarpe, follow Via Dipinta, a quiet street lined with Renaissance palazzi and overlooking the verdant terraces of the old Venetian walls. At the Porta Sant'Agostino, walk through the gateway, then turn left and amble through the orchards of the pedestrian lane of Via Noca to arrive in the citta bassa right next to the Accademia Carrara.

Accademia Carrara ★★

Founded as an art school in 1780 by Count Giacomo Carrara, the Accademia Carrara *(9:30 a.m.–12:30 p.m., 2:30–5:30 p.m., closed Tues., L3000, but free Sun.)* also houses on its second floor his exquisite painting collection, expanded with works from other collectors. The paintings often are small, seldom retouched, and stunning for their patina and color. There are minor (17th century) Flemish works by the masters (Room XIII) and representatives of the northern Renaissance schools (Luini of Milan, Tura of Ferrara, and rooms full of thoughtful portraits by the 16th-century Bergamese G.B. Moroni). Given the history of this city, it's not surprising to find the Venetian school represented best of all, from the Vivarini and Bellini through Titian (Room VI), Guardi and Tiepolo (both Room XV). Some of the finest of these are Giovanni Bellini's ★*Portrait of a Young Man,* and ★*Madonna in Blue with Child,* Carpaccio's (attrib.) *Portrait of Doge,* and the Paduan Mantegna's ★*Madonna with Child*—all in Room III. In Room II are other fine works, mostly Tuscan, such as Botticelli's portrait of the arrogant ★*Giuliano de'Medici,* and the softer, more Gothic ★*Portrait of Lionello d'Este,* by Pisanello as well as Lorenzo Monaco's ★*Christ in Sarcophagus,* and Signorelli's small *Madonna col Bambino.* And we still need to mention Raphael's ★*Saint Sebastian* (Room VII).

Bergamo

Where to Stay

Although the restaurants here tend to be a little pricey, the hotels are more reasonable—probably reflecting the relative demand of each. The **citta alta** has only a few rooms for visitors and they are more often than not booked:

Il Gourmet   **L90–135,000**   ★★

V. San Vigilio 1; ☎ 437-3004, FAX 437-3004; closed Christmas season.
Single L90,000. Double L135,000.
Just outside the Porta San Alessandro of the citta alta, this country inn has great views over the countryside; the 10 rooms (no a/c) are nothing fancy, but the setting and relaxing ambience are worth the advance planning required to reserve a room. Well-respected terrace restaurant (see below) Parking.

San Vigilio   **L145,000**   ★★

V. San Vigilio 15; ☎ 253-179, FAX 402-081; closed early Jan.
Single/double L145,000.
Farther up the hill (take the funiculare/bus San Vigilio from Porta S. Allesandro) than Il Gourmet, the inn has just 7 (no a/c) rooms in this park like section of town. Lovely terrace restaurant "I Musicanti."

When you find these rooms booked, your best bets are two modern hotels in the **citta bassa**:

Excelsior San Marco   **L210–290,000**   ★★★

P. della Repubblica 6; ☎ 366-111, FAX 223-201.
Single L210,000. Double L290,000.
A first-class hotel along V. Emanuele with some views of the citta alta, and 175 comfortable rooms, restaurant, lounge and parking.

Arli   **L95–145,000**   ★★

Largo Porta Nuova 12; ☎ 222-014, FAX 239-732.
Single L95,000. Double L145,000.
Just a few steps from the main intersection of lower Bergamo and with 48 well-appointed, and comfortable rooms (no a/c), but make sure you reserve an interior. Bar. Limited parking.

Where to Eat

In all likelihood you'll want to dine in the **citta alta**.

Taverna del Colleoni   **$$$**   ★★★

☎ 232-596; FAX 232-596.
Closed Mon., most of Aug. Meals L70–110,000.
Right on the Piazza Vecchia is this excellent restaurant for *nouva cucina* and proof that the Bergamashci can prepare their ravioli (here, with sweetbreads and porcini) as exquisitely as the Emiliani.

Gourmet   **$$–$$$**   ★★

V. San Vigilio 1; ☎ 437-3004.
Closed Tues., Christmas season. Meals L60–80,000.
The food is fine, the summer setting, stunning—under a grape arbor with panoramic views—at this establishment just outside the S. Alessandro gate of the citta

alta. The pastas can be unusual, the fish is always fresh, whether in saffron or basil, and the veal in ginger and black pepper quite fine.

Da Ornella $-$$ ★

#15; ☎ 232-736.
Closed Fri. lunch, Thurs., Christmas, and July. Meals L35–55,000.
Lower-priced fare can be enjoyed in the citta alta along Via Gombito, such as at Da Ornella where you can enjoy the smoked trout from nearby lakes and the traditional quail with polenta.

Perhaps the best dining is your own picnic atop the gardens of the Venetian walls. The shops along Gombito have all you need, as well as something you don't—the local sweet called *polenti e uccelli*, sugary cornmeal with a bit of chocolate in the middle. Or simply enjoy a panino in the **Caffe del Tasso** on the Piazza Vecchia or the more elegant **Caffe del Colleoni** on the Piazza Vittorio Veneto, in the town below. If you're caught below, **I Carati** *(XX Settembre 43; closed Tues.; ☎ 244-279. Meals L45–65,000)* offers good dining at sensible prices.

Directory

Telephone Code 035 **Postal Code 24100**

Tourist Information

APT, *Papa Giovanni XXIII 106 (☎ 242-226; FAX 242-994)*, one block north of stazione.

Getting Around

From the train station and along Vittorio Emanuele, the #1 and #3 buses go to the funicolare for the citta alta (same ticket for both bus and funicolare); and, when the funiculare is not working or cars prohibited, the #1 continues up to the citta alta. (**Note:** Cars are banned on weekend nights after 9:30 p.m., and 10 a.m.–12 p.m, 2 p.m.–dusk on Sundays and holidays.)

Arriving

Milan is 50 km, 31 mi. on A4 west; Brescia about 60 km on A4 east; both can be reached quickly by train.

Pullman buses leave P. Marconi to Brecia, Como, and Lecco.

Local airport has limited service, but Linate is this side of Milan and Malpensa is 85 km, 53 mi.

Brescia

Despite its prime location between Lake Garda and Lake Iseo at the foot of the Alps, Brescia attracts fewer travelers than most historic cities. A convenient stopover on the route between Milan and Venice, this city of more than 200,000 is perhaps just a bit too modern to be a tourist favorite. Yet its location has given it a rich history, attracting settlers even before the Celts and flourishing under the Romans as Brixia and under the Lombards as a duchy. In medieval times it was a great manufacturer of silk and wool, as well as arms—something the Beretta company continues to do today. With so much going for it, Brescia was envied by stronger city states, and fought over by the Visconti of Milan, the Scaligeri of Verona, and the Malatesti of Rimini, until finally, in 1496, it was subjugated by Venice. More recently it fought off Austrian rule (1849) and joined Italy as part of industrial Lombardy.

What to See and Do

All this history has left its mark on the historic center, where you will find intriguing remains of the Roman city and traces of the Lombards. Then, too, there is Venice's style in the paintings of the pinacoteca and architecture of the magnificent Piazza della Loggia. Much of the *centro storico* is comprised of pleasant Austrian-built boulevards, such as the arcaded Corso Zanardelli, bordered by neoclassical buildings. But you'd be wise to concentrate on the older sections they surround.

Duomo Area

By beginning in the massive Piazza Vittoria, dating from the Mussolini era, you can work your way back through history. Passing through the portal at the piazza's north end you leave behind the chill of modern fascism and enter a time when Venice was supreme. Its power resulted in the elegant Renaissance ★**Piazza della Loggia**, surrounded by lovely portals and the handsome Torre dell'Orologia, with two statues striking the hours, just like the clock at San Marco in Venice. The loggia itself stands on the west side, a beautiful 16th-century building by many Venetian artists, including Sansovino and Palladio. (The fine carving of the friezes and pediments warrants a close look.) The dome of the new cathedral and tower of the medieval town hall cast their shadows from the square found through the portal under the clock tower. The **Piazza del Duomo** is the heart of medieval Brescia, despite the addition of the new 17th-century duomo and renovations to the *broletto*, or town hall. This large open square still hears the 11th-century tower ring in meetings of the city council and remains graced by its wonderfully round Romanesque "old" duomo.

Forum Area   ★

At the north end of the duomo piazza, exit to the right and cross over to the Via dei Musei, one of the main streets in Roman Brixia. A little farther along you come to the **Piazza Foro**, which retains the shape of the ancient forum as well as considerable ruins. Most interesting is the ★**Capitoline Temple** *(Tues.–Sun. 9 a.m.–12:30 p.m., 3–5 p.m., Oct.–May; Tues.–Fri. 10 a.m.–12:30 p.m., 3–6 p.m., Sat.–Sun. till 7 p.m. June–Sept.; L5000)*. The complex had been covered in a landslide, not to be rediscovered until the last century. Finding the temple (A.D. 73) exposed in the midst of the medieval city makes it all the more fascinating. Inside the temple is a ★ *museum* (through door to left of middle cella and up stairs) that contains ancient artifacts found throughout the city—jewelry, glass, Egyptian pieces, as well as a fine 5th-century B.C. Greek relief and a ★ *Winged Victory*, once part of the charioteer sculpture that stood atop the temple roof. If you wish to explore a bit more, walk another block on Via Musei to Piamarta for the **Basilica of San Salvatore** and **Monastery of Santa Giulia** (same hours as Capitoline Temple; L5000), founded in 753 by the Lombard king Desiderius and granted land endowments so vast they included not just nearby Cremona but also Benevento far to the south. One of the largest monasteries in Italy at the time, the basilica was further enlarged by the Carolingians in the 9th century and the monastery continued to expand through the Renaissance. Today the church is a museum of Early Christian art where you can still find the crypt from the original Lombard church and the Roman columns used by the Carolingians in the nave, but ongoing excavations through the church floor into more ancient times may limit access. The monastery has been renovated into a civic museum for special exhibitions.

Pinacoteca

Near the forum, quaint medieval streets, such as Via Gambera, wind their way to Via Carlo Cattaneo where you can turn right and find your way back to the duomo. Or you can follow Via Gallo off Musei and continue on Via Crispi to reach the **Pinacoteca Tosio Marinengo** *(Piazza Moretto; Tues.–Sun. 9 a.m.–12:30 p.m., 3–5 p.m. Oct.–May; Tues.–Fri. 10 a.m.–12:30 p.m., 3–6 p.m.; Sat.–Sun. till 7 p.m. June–Sept.; L5000).* Housed in a 16th-century palazzo is an extensive collection of Brescian art. As you might expect, the paintings show both the influence of Leonardo in Milan and Giorgione and Bellini in Venice, but the sober realism is purely local and best seen in the work of the 15th-century artist Vicenzo Foppa, and the 16th-century Girolamo Saroldo and more famous Moretto. Also exhibited here are paintings by Raphael, Tintoretto and Lotto.

Where to Stay and Eat

Hotel Vittoria L290–395,000 ★★★★
Viale X Giornate #20; ☎ *280-061, FAX 280-065.*
Single L290,000, double L355–395,000.
Elegant and centrally located with 65 rooms. Restaurants and a/c.

Master L125–185,000 ★★★
V. Apollonio 72; ☎ *399-037, FAX 370-1331.*
Single L125,000. Double L185,000.
Located out near the castle: its 76 rooms are comfortable and with garden views. Restaurants and a/c.

Antica Trattoria Pergolina $$ ★
V. Musei 65; ☎ *46-350.*
Closed Mon., Sun. night, Aug. L45–65,000.
A convenient and charming restaurant is the Antica Trattoria Pergolina with an open hearth for grilling the local *capretto*, or kid.

La Sosta $$–$$$ ★★
V. San Martino della Battaglia 20; ☎ *295-603.*
Closed Mon. and Aug. Meals L60–80,000.
Near the Pinacoteca, enjoy the handsome 17th-century setting for somewhat pricey, international-style cuisine.

Along **Via Carlo Cattaneo** are good shops for making your own lunch or simply picking up a slice of bakery-fresh pizza.

Brescia

Directory

Telephone Code 030   **Postal Code 25100**

Tourist Information

> **APT**, *Corso Zanardelli 34*, just a half-block east of P. Vittoria (☎ *43-418; FAX 293-284*).

Getting Around

> Limited car access in centro storico, but there's underground parking at P. Vittoria. Bus D from stazione and nearby bus terminal drops you at P. Vittoria.

Arriving

> Venice lies 180 km, 112 mi. east on A-4, Milan less than 100 km, 62 mi. west.
>
> Bergamo and Verona are within an hour's reach by train or pullman bus.

Mantua

Mantua, in Italian *Mantova*, was the only small city state in Lombardy to keep its independence throughout the Renaissance. Here the Gonzaga ruled, not Milan or Venice. Surrounded by the lakes of the Mancio river, the city was easily defended. Crossed by six rivers, including the Po, the ducal lands were extremely fertile and capable of sustaining the population. It was the cunning of the Gonzaga, however, not just the location of their territory, that enabled them to survive. From Ludovico, to Francesco and his son Federico "Il Bello," the Gonazaga played off the great powers of the Renaissance against each other, strategically intermarrying among them and selling them their services as *condottieri*—or simply their promises not to fight. Of course, the Gonzaga didn't always succeed, but even when Francesco found himself imprisoned by the Venetians, the Mantovans were fortunate to be ruled competently by his famous wife, Isabella d'Este. (So competently that Francesco wrote her "we are ashamed to have as a wife a woman who is so ruled by her head.") Mantua maintained its freedom for four centuries of Machiavellian scheming, and it grew wealthy in the process.

Perhaps because Mantua was not a large state, the Gonzaga had to display their wealth more lavishly to keep up with the other dukes. For whatever reason, the Gonzaga court was one of the most elegant in Europe. Here popes and emperors were entertained and here the greatest artists of the time were commissioned. Although Leonardo never made his sketch of Isabella d'Este into a painting and though Michelangelo failed to heed princely invitations, Mantua did benefit from the work of Alberti, Pisanello, Correggio, Titian, and others, but most importantly from two court artists responsible for all manner of projects—Andrea Mantegna and Giulio Romano.

With some of the most fertile farmlands in Italy, Mantua today is a prosperous community. Its growth has resulted in one lake becoming landfill, but three sides of the small and somber town remain surrounded by water. Changes in Mantua's artistic heritage, however, began in the 16th century

Santi Cosma e Damiano, Forum ruins

Colosseum, Rome

Rome view from St. Peter's

Vatican City, aerial view

when Charles I of England bought many of the finest Gonzaga paintings. Others followed suit as the Gonzaga faced hard financial times; works from their collection now appear in museums throughout the world. No one, however, could take the churches and palaces, the statuary and frescoes. As you approach Mantua through the Gate of San Giorgio, you see the ducal palace reflected in the lake (or, in the winter, enshrouded in mist) and then enter the town that conserves the legacy of the Gonzaga.

What to See and Do

Around the Ducal Palace   ★★

The vast and cobbled **Piazza Sordello** is the place to begin your tour. Here the ducal palace (east side), confronts the medieval palazzi of the Bonacolsi (west side), whom the Gonzaga defeated in their 1328 bid for power. Rising at the south end is the former Romanesque **cathedral**, its tower still intact, but the facade now ornamented with some rather silly 18th-century Baroque statues. The ★ interior, with its stucco vaults and frolicking putti, is the Manneristic work of Giulio Romano who renovated the church (1545) in the grand manner he brought from Rome. A corridor off the left aisle leads to an Alberti-style chapel, perfectly symmetrical and with a trompe l'oeil coffered ceiling.

It's the ★★**Ducal Palace** that makes a visit to the piazza a must. A world unto itself, this "small" Renaissance court contains parks (now public, like the one right of the main entrance), gardens and courtyards, a castle connected by drawbridges, and 500 rooms. Not all the palace is open to the public and the guided tour (required for visits) takes you to only some of the highlights. The neoclassic appartamenti are extraordinarily ornate and sometimes even sumptuous (such as the Gallery of Mirrors) or in bad taste (such as the "Hanging Gardens"), but they usually have an eye to comfort as well, such as wall tapestries for warmth that just happen to be artistic treasures, based on cartoons by Raphael. Throughout your visit you'll see some fine antiquities, paintings by Tintoretto and Rubens (just after the Gallery of Mirrors) and others. At the beginning of your visit is the ★**Sala di Pisanello** with rare fragments of a Pisanello fresco, recovered in 1966 from under layers of later decorative schemes. The knightly battle scene (c. 1446) and the recovered sinopie, or underdrawings, in an adjoining room, show the verve with which Pisanello handled nature, and especially, horses. Near the end of the tour, and worth every second just to see it, is Mantegna's ★★★**Camera degli Sposi** (1465- 74), with his nearly life-size portrait of Ludovico Gonzaga and his family accompanied by their dog, dwarf and other courtly attendants. In contrast to the picturesque quality of Pisanello's International Gothic style, Mantegna's frescoes are full of Renaissance classicism and sculptural solidity. Instead of Arthurian tales, Mantegna presents us with the intimate details of life in this palace during the quattrocento. Always illusionistic, Mantegna incorporates the real fireplace mantel as the floor in the fresco, his ceiling, with its expanding sky and teetering flowerpot, transcends Renaissance realism and anticipates the Baroque. Mantegna decorated all of this castle room, including the other delightful frescoes on the Gonzaga family history.

Accompanied visits only; groups leave on half hour. Mon.–Sat. 9 a.m.–1 p.m., 2:30–6 p.m.; Oct.& Mar. till 4 p.m. only; Nov.–Feb. till 3:30 p.m. only; Sun. 9 a.m.–1 p.m. and also, except July-Aug., 3-6 p.m. If making a special detour around holidays, check tourist office or palace (☎ 320-283) for schedule changes. L12,000.

Around Sant'Andrea ★

The walk to the church of ★ **Sant'Andrea** is brief yet full of Medieval ambience. A block outside the south archway of the **Piazza Sordello**, you pass on your left the small Piazza Broletto with its 13th-century statue of Virgil (born in a nearby village), then the adjoining Piazza delle Erbe with its crenellated buildings and round, 11th-century church. From here you have the best view of the impressive dome of Sant'Andrea, although that church fronts the Piazza Andrea Mantegna, a few steps further along and on your right. Alberti's design for this Renaissance basilica (1470) was one of his most influential. The facade is inspired by a triumphal arch with pilasters recalling classical temple facades. The monumental barrelvaulted interior shuns aisles and replaces them with the rhythmic alternation of chapel openings and piers, a device later used by Bramante in Rome and by the Jesuits in their 17th-century churches. *Mantegna's tomb* (first chapel, left) was built from his own design and includes his *Holy Family*, and a bronze bust that may be a self-portrait.

Palazzo del Te ★

The Palazzo del Te (1527–34), near the Piazzale Veneto and a 20-minute walk from the older section (basically on a straight from in front of Sant'Andrea to the palazzo), was built elegantly enough to entertain Emperor Charles V. Once an island retreat for Federico in the summer, the modern city has encompassed it. It is considered a masterpiece of Mannerism by some and "neurotic fantasy" by others, like the scholar James Ackerman. Wherever you are in this debate, there is no doubt Guilio Romano in building this villa moved far away from the classical values of his teacher, Raphael. The architecture is often intensely rusticated with oversized, disturbing forms. There are asymmetrical motifs, off-center windows, and, in the courtyard, even blanks where forms should repeat. Whether you find all of this unsettling or a witty comment on Renaissance architecture, you can't help but be overwhelmed by the murals inside, be they the voluptuous ★ *Cupid and Psyche* in the Sala di Psiche, with its wedding feast panorama; or those in the ★ Sala di Gigante, a 16th-century apocalyptic painting that in its frenzy covers every door, vault, and wall. *Open 9 a.m.–6 p.m., closed Mon.; L12,000.*

Where to Stay

San Lorenzo	L230–265,000 CP	✿ ★ ★

P. Concordia 14; ☎ 220-500, FAX 327-194.

Single L230,000 CP. Double L265,000 CP.

The best place to stay in town is located just behind the Piazza dell'Erbe. The handsome old-fashioned common areas are red carpeted and with chandeliers; the 45 rooms have modern comforts. Breakfast bar. Pay garage.

Mantegna   **L95–145,000**   ★ ★

V. Fabio Filzi 10/b; ☎ 328-019, FAX 368-564.
Single L95,000. Double 145,000.
Well-positioned between the Palazzo del Te and Ducal Palace just off V. Principe
Amadeo, this neat commercial hotel has 40 large rooms and conveniences such as a
hair dryers and off-street parking included in the price. Bar.

Broletto   **L95–140,000**   ★

V. Accademia 1; ☎ 326-784, FAX 221-297; closed Christmas.
Single L95,000. Double L140,000.
The rooms, some overlooking the piazza Broletto, are efficient and surprisingly
well-appointed for the price.

Where to Eat

Aquila Nigra   **$$**   ★ ★ ★ ★

Vicolo Bonacolisi 4; ☎ 327-180, FAX 324-180.
closed Sun. night, Mon. (only in Apr./May and Sept./Oct.) and early Jan., Aug. Meals
L50–70,000.
In a palazzo just off the Piazza Sordello. Not only convenient but serving some of
Mantua's finest cuisine, from calamari stuffed with ricotta, basil and tomato and the
local tortelli di zucca to other regional dishes that, in their richness, often prove the
proximity of Emilia Romagna.

L'Ochina Bianca   **$**   ★ ★ ★

V. Finzi 2; ☎ 323-700.
Closed Tues. at lunch, Mon., early Jan. & Aug. Meals L30–45,000.
On the west side of the centro storico near the end of V. Cavour, this country-like
trattoria is decorated with rustic wooden beams, tile floors and both contemporary
paintings and folk art. It's a soothing spot to enjoy a zucchini flower salad, roast
pork with red peppers and black olives, and other delightful items at reasonable
prices.

Al Garibaldini   **$$**   ★ ★

V. Longino 7; ☎ 328-263.
Closed Wed. Meals L45–60,000.
Near Sant'Andre, this refined restaurant, set in a lovely cortile during the summer,
serves pastas such as linguine with green and black olives and tomatoes, grilled vegetables and carpaccio and heartier fare such as roasted pork.

Snacks

The Piazza dell'Erbe not only has a decent pasticceria (the **Caravatti**; closed Wed.),
but it also has a morning market for your picnic shopping. Around the corner is the **Caffe
Miro**, a perfect spot in the summer when you can enjoy the facade of Sant'Andrea while
munching on panini or pizza at an outdoor table.

Directory

Telephone Code 0376   **Postal Code 46100**

Tourist Information
   APT, *P. Mantegna 6 (☎ 328-253, FAX 363-292)*

Reading

Kate Simon's *A Renaissance Tapestry: The Gonzaga of Mantua*

Arriving

Linked to the Veneto (Verona is 40 km, 25 mi. north) and Emilia Romagna (Modena is 65 km, 40 mi. south) by A22 (exit Mantova nord is best) and by train, Mantua also is just 160 km, 100 mi. from Milan, to which it has direct train connections. The stazione is a 10-minute walk on V. Emanuele to the *centro storico*. There are regional buses, too, leaving from P. Belfiore.

Special Tip

All museums close Jan. 1–5.

Sabbioneta

Sabbioneta can be quickly reached from either Mantua or Cremona, or visited while traveling between the two. But Sabbioneta makes sense, if it can make sense at all, only from the perspective of Mantua. Sabbioneta was the provincial estate of one of the minor branches of the Gonzaga family. But Vespasiano Gonzaga (1532–91) in no way found himself a minor figure. He built his own Renaissance town to surround his own personal court, complete with a press for fine books, a museum for his collection of antiquities, a theater for performances, and even an academy for those he dreamed of patronizing. The few streets form tidy blocks, the entrances to town are marked by a Porta Imperial and a Porta Vittoria, and the Piazza Ducale is flanked not just by the palazzo but also by the requisite churches—that of Santa Maria Assunta being quite sweet. Sabbioneta is like a stage set, but one that leaves you a little troubled that the only act ever played was Vespasiano's.

Today the village, long abandoned, is being restored. You can walk around by yourself, noting that the synagogue and many of the palazzi are in sad states of disrepair. But the frescoes and numerous equestrian statues of Vespasiano in those buildings that have been restored (such as the handsome theater based on a Palladio design, the ducal palace as well as the summer palace, and others) can be toured only with a guide. (*Tours depart from the ufficio turistico 9 a.m.–noon, 2:30–5 p.m., till 6 p.m. in summer; closed Mon. except holidays; L12,000.*)

Where to Stay and Eat

In town, there's a tiny albergo on the main street of Vespasiano Gonzaga as well as a few restaurants and the **Santa Cecilia Cafe** right on the Piazza Ducale. If you've driven, you'll have noticed a number of inns and restaurants near the road outside the centro storico. But just a bit farther by car is one of Italy's great restaurants:

Del Pescatore   **$$$**   ★★★★★

in Canneto sull'Oglio, 25 km, 15.5 mi. northwest of Sabbioneta; reserve at ☎ (0376) 723-001, FAX 70-304.

Fixed-price meal L120,000. À la carte L90–135.000. Closed Mon., Tues., Christmas, early Jan., late Aug.

3 km north of ss 10 at Piadena, midway between Cremona and Mantua. Ranked among the top restaurants in Italy and one of only two with Michelin's highly coveted three stars, the small and beautiful Pescatore is worthy of a detour whether for the memorable tortelli or the duck in balsamic or something so unusual, yet simple, as grilled eel. In warm weather there's garden dining.

Directory

Tourist Information

Ufficio Turistico, *V. Gonzaga* (☎ *[0375] 52039*), in front of parking area. Tours of the buildings (the only way to visit) leave from here (Tues.–Fri. 9 a.m.–noon, 2:30–5 p.m. in winter; Apr.–Sept. 9 a.m.–noon daily, 2:30–6 p.m., but Sat.–Sun. 1:30–7 p.m.).

Special Events

Antique Fair, mid-Mar.–mid Apr.; Music and Dance Festival, summer.

Arriving

Sabbioneta is about midway on the Mantua/Parma road and is slightly more complicated to reach from Cremona (55 km, 34 mi. along SS 10 toward Mantua, then south at Piadena to Casalmaggiore where you turn left to Sabbioneta). Daily buses make the 35 km, 22 mi. trip from Mantua.

Cremona

It's hard not to think of violins when hearing about Cremona, but once you've seen its picturesque Piazza del Comune, you'll remember it for more than Stradivarius. In fact, the modern and prosperous town of Cremona preserves two periods of its history: the medieval, when it flourished as a free republic before being subjugated by the Visconti; and the Baroque, when rococo palazzi were built to the melodies of native-born Monteverdi and the genius of the Stradavari and Guarneri violin makers. Cremona today exploits its position in the center of the Po Valley by engaging in some very sophisticated agribusiness. But the art of violin-making continues.

What to See and Do

Piazza del Comune   ★★

The Piazza del Comune contains no single masterpiece, and sets no major trends. It is simply and romantically medieval. By day, it's warmed by the deep hues of Gothic brick, the sienna stucco of the houses; by night, when shrouded in mist, its arcades are full of shadow and intrigue. The separate buildings of this harmonious ensemble are worthy of note too. The freestanding and octagonal **baptistery** (1167) is pure Romanesque. To its right is the **Palazzo del Comune** (1206, and heavily modified); the interior **museo** holds a few precious violins crafted by the masters *(open June–mid Aug. Tues.–Sat. 8:30 a.m.–6 p.m.; Sept.–May and Sun. closed noon–3 p.m.; L5000 includes admission to Affaitati Palace)*. Next door is the fine Gothic ★ **Loggia dei Militi** (1292), its three upper windows richly decorated in terra-cotta, a very

Cremonese trait. Across from these civic buildings rise the splendid bell tower, the ★**Torrazzo** (1250–67), another example of Gothic architecture, and the delightful Romanesque ★**duomo** (founded 1107), with accretions from many centuries. The Romanesque austerity of the interior is hidden under acres of frescoes, the most startling and illusionistic ones by the Mannerist Il Pordenone (1521; hard to see). The side chapels contain 16th-century paintings in luminous colors (note the Pordenone in the first chapel, right). The Lombard Renaissance artist Amadeo carved the panel ★ *S. Imario Giving Alms* in the left transept.

Other Sights

To explore the rest of Cremona a bit, you might follow Via Solferino out of the square to the shady Piazza Roma. Diagonally across you pick up the Via Palestro bordered by Renaissance and Baroque palazzi, many with Cremonese terra-cotta details. The **Affaitati Palace** *(at #17)* was begun in 1561 and has a notable cornice *(along Via Dati)*. Inside are two museums, one on violin-making (the **Museo Stradivarius**) and the other with collections from all periods of Cremona history, including the Roman (the Museo Civico). *Both open June–Aug. Tues.–Sun. 8:30 a.m.–6 p.m.; Sept.–May Tues.–Sat. 9:30 a.m.–noon, 3–5:45 p.m.; Sun. a.m. only; joint fee of L5000 includes admission to Palazzo del Comune Museum.* A few more steps up Via Palestro is the rococo and remarkable **Palazzo Stanga**. At Via Bertesi, turn left to the Corso Garibaldi and you begin a loop back to the Piazza Roma. First, notice the Renaissance **Palazzo Raimondi** *(#179)*, which now houses the International School of Violin-Making. Further along the Corso you pass the **Sant'Agata piazza** with its interesting assortment of buildings from the Gothic to the neo-classical. And then, if you have time, consider a right turn at Milazzo for a detour to the fine church of **Sant'Agostino** *(Via Guido Grandi)*, very Lombard Romanesque in design despite its 14th-century construction, and with Perugino's *Madonna and Saints* in the 5th chapel, right.

Where to Stay

Continental　　　　　　　　　**L100–160,000**　　　　　　　　★ ★

P. Liberta 27 ☎ *434-141, FAX 434-141.*
Single L100,000. Double L160,000.
Modern, dull, and much like a motel, but the 57 ample rooms have a/c and the location just outside the historic center is still walkable to the sights. Parking.

Astoria　　　　　　　　　　　**L75–110,000**　　　　　　　　　★

V. Bordigallo 19; ☎ *461-616, FAX 461-810.*
Single L75,000. Double L110,000.
A few steps off Solferino in the centro storico, this pensione-style hotel has welcoming service and 32 plain, clean rooms (no a/c) and a comfortable breakfast bar. Limited street parking.

Albergo Duomo　　　　　　　　**L55–130,000**　　　　　　　　★

V. Gonfalonieri 13; ☎ *352-242, FAX 458-392.*
Single L55,000. Double L130,000.
This small inn offers 23 rooms (no a/c) and a restaurant just a few steps behind the Palazzo del Comune.

Where to Eat

Ceresole $$–$$$ ★★★★

V. Ceresole; reserve at ☎ 30-990.
Closed Mon., Sun. dinner, and Aug. Meals L55–80,000.
For exquisite dining, Ceresole comes highly recommended. In this stylish and quite elegant restaurant located behind the duomo, you can enjoy traditional risotto with pumpkin as well as delicately prepared turbot with tomato and eggplant.

Porta Mosa $–$$ ★★

V. Maria in Betlem 11; reserve at ☎ (0372) 411-803.
Closed Sun. Meals L35–55,000.
Located near the old wall southeast of the centro storico is a plain yet good osteria with lots of wines to sample by the glass and hearty pasta and traditional dishes to accompany them.

Snacks

You might want to make your own meal from the fine cheeses and house-made salami sold at **Formaggio d'Italia** *(P. del Comune)*, or try the Cremonese torrone, nougat candy produced here, along with the pastries at the handsome **Lanfranchi** *(Solferino, 1/2 block from duomo)*. Across the street you can purchase another local product, *mostarda di frutta*, a kind of relish for the braised meats preferred in Lombardy.

Directory

Telephone Code 0372 **Postal Code 26100**

Tourist Information
  APT, *P. Comune 5* ☎ *(21-722; FAX 21-722)*

Arriving
  In the center of the province, Cremona is not far from most other spots in Lombardy (just 50 km from Brescia on A-21 and 60 km on SS 10 from Mantua), or even Emilia Romagna (Piazcenza is 35 km, 22 mi.). There are a few routes for covering the 85 km, 53 mi. from Milan. Trains from Pavia to Mantua stop at the stazione at the end of V. Palestro (bus #1 to center, or walk), as does the diretto Milan train.

Pavia

Just an hour south of Milan's Porta Ticinese, along the canal built by the Visconti, you arrive at Pavia. Along the way you pass the extraordinary Certosa di Pavia, also built by the Milanese dukes. But it is not until you pass through modern Pavia into the centro storico that you come to an era in which the Visconti did not rule.

The center of Pavia today remains medieval; its churches are superb examples of Lombard Romanesque and numerous towers speak of that period when its many feuding nobles made it known as the city of 100 towers. And Pavia's history stretches back to the Dark Ages when the Lombards, or Longobards, established their capital here. Before then, as early as the third century B.C., the Romans had built this town on the Ticino river, critically near where it flows into the Po.

What to See and Do

Today you must wind your way through a considerable modern city (population about 90,000) that not only is involved in agribusiness, but also in the production of Necchi sewing machines. But once you find the street, **Strada Nuova**, bounded on the north by the Castello Visconteo and on the south by a reconstructed covered bridge, you will have found the traffic-free old city that still follows its Roman grid plan. In and along this street, you stroll past the palazzi and take brief detours to churches and piazzas.

San Michele Church   ★

From the south, turn right onto Corso Garibaldi until you find the tiny Vicolo San Michele (on the right) for San Michele Church. Founded in the 7th century by the Lombards, it is here that Charlemagne celebrated his defeat of those people by assuming the Iron Crown of Pavia in 774, an act that many would repeat as Holy Roman Emperor. When Frederick Barbarossa followed suit in 1155, the church had assumed its present Lombard Romanesque perfection, with roofline arcading, superb reliefs around the three portals, and friezes of mythological animals (now sadly eroded). The interior contains more interesting friezes and finely carved capitals.

Piazza Leonardo Da Vinci

Straddling the center of the Strada Nuova, just a few blocks north of Corso Garibalai, are other pleasant buildings. Left off the strada you come to the Piazza Vittoria. Although the large piazza hides its market underneath, its medieval civic buildings and Renaissance **duomo** (some additions by Leonardo and Bramante, closed till 1999) are presented on a smaller piazza off the south end. At the strada and Via Mentana, on your right, are the 16th-18th century buildings of the much older **university**, where Christopher Columbus was a distinguished visitor and where Volta laid the foundations for the modern light bulb. Behind the university is the fine **Piazza Leonardo da Vinci**, which held three medieval towers until one collapsed in 1989.

San Pietro   ★

At the Piazza Castello on the north end of the strada, turn left on Matteotti, then right on Grizotti for the church of ★ **San Pietro in Ciel d'Oro** (1132) with its impressive Romanesque interior. The altarpiece, ★ *Arca di Sant'Agostino* (1132), is a masterpiece of northern sculpture, ornate yet with fine caryatids at the base. The shrine is said to contain the relics of St. Augustine while its carvings depict his life. In the crypt are the remains of the Roman philosopher Boethius (☎ *476-524)*, who was imprisoned and executed here under orders of the Goth, Theodoric.

Castello Visconteo

The Castello Visconteo (*open 9 a.m.–1:30 p.m.; closed Sun. except June–Nov. and Mon. year-round; L5000)*, built by the Visconti around 1360, was called "most notable" by Petrarch, and indeed the interior shows considerable care for the comfort of its inhabitants. Here the Museo Civico, with its many components, presents artifacts from the Roman and Lombard periods, as well as a painting gallery that contains a Giovanni Bellini and a Correggio, among others.

Nearby

Certosa di Pavia is a marvel of architectural detail inside and out.

★ ★ **Certosa di Pavia** *(SS 35 8 km, 5 mi. north of Pavia and 25 km, 15.5 mi. south of Milan by bus, train, or car).* Once a great park stretched from the Castello Visconteo to this Carthusian monastery. As you cover this distance today it's odd to reflect that right here, where Beatrice d'Este enjoyed her country rides, the kingly Francis I was taken prisoner by Charles V in the Battle of Pavia. Before these empire builders used Italy as their battlefield, the dukes of Milan had built the lavish certosa to hold their tombs. Founded in 1396 by Gian Galeazzo Visconti, the monastery and church are fundamentally Italian Gothic. But Ludovico Sforza commissioned Amadeo in 1492 to create an appropriately splendid new facade for the church that is considered the apogee of northern Renaissance architecture.

At the end of a stately, tree-lined road, you enter the monastery through a vestibule frescoed by Luini, but it's hard to focus on anything except the amazing church facade seen across the courtyard. The profusion of sculpture of the facade, the wealth of detail and color, can make you lightheaded—and yet it's unfinished. Closer up you can begin to see the classic details of Amadeo's Renaissance forms and the exceptional carvings around the portal (by Briosco). And while many of the buildings bordering this courtyard relied on trompe l'oeil effects rather than sculpture (except for the Palazzo Ducale), there was no skimping on the church interior, which is a symphony of patterned marble. Most seasons, your visit will be by group tour that will definitely include the ★ **tomb** (1497) of

Ludovico Gonzaga and Beatrice d'Este (left transept). Then, through a door to the right of the inlaid choir stalls, you will find the lavabo, with its marble fountain and well (attributed to Amadeo) and a Madonna painted by Luini. In the right transept is the austere tomb of Gian Galeazzo Visconti and through a door here you enter the ★ **small cloister**, with its graceful arcades, and exceptional Cremonese terracotta decorations. (Look back over the door for Amadeo's delicate relief *Madonna Enthroned*.) The **large cloister** (south through the small one), with its lavish monks quarters are still in use, but by the Cisterian order rather than the original Carthusians.

The certosa is closed Mon., open 9:30–11:30 a.m., 2:30–6 p.m. May–Aug., till 4:30 p.m. Nov.–Mar., till 5 p.m. otherwise. Free. Your visit is by tour, accompanied by a monk, during the busier part of the year. Tours begin on the half hour inside the church. Trains and buses (more frequent) from either Pavia or Milan leave you within walking distance of the certosa.

Where to Stay and Eat

There are small inns at both the certosa and in Pavia, but given your proximity to Milan it is most likely lunch you're seeking.

Chalet della Certosa $ ★

☎ *934-935.*
Closed Mon. Meals L30–50,000.
At the certosa, the terrace restaurant and cafe of the Chalet della Certosa couldn't be more conveniently located across the street.

Locanda Vecchia Pavia $$–$$$ ★★★

V. Cardinale Riboldi 2; reserve at ☎ *304-132; FAX 304-132.*
Closed Mon., Wed. lunch; early Jan., Aug. Fixed-price lunch L55 & 100,000. Fixed-price dinner L75 & 110,000. À la carte L65–110,000.
In Pavia, you might find a delicate presentation of the locally favored frog's legs here, but the menu varies with the day's purchases at the market. The quality is consistently good. Located near the apse of the duomo.

Pizzeria Marechiaro $ ★★

P. Vittoria 9; ☎ *23-739.*
Closed Mon. Pizza L8–20,000.
Right on the market square in Pavia; you can select a light meal of antipasti, if you like.

Directory

Telephone Code 0382   **Postal Code 27100**

Tourist Information
    APT, *V. Fabio Filzi 2 (*☎ *22-156; FAX 32-221)*

Arriving
    About 20 miles south of Milan on the Genoa autostrada or SS 35, Pavia also lies just an hour west of Piacenza, 1.5 hours of Cremona. Both Pavia and the Certosa di Pavia are most often visited as excursions from Milan, and the bus (terminal near Piazza Castello in both Milan and Pavia) and train (stazione western edge of centro storico in Pavia) service is excellent.

Pavia

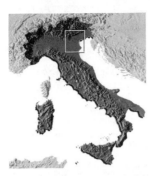

VENICE AND
THE VENETO

San Giorgio Maggiore seems to float over Venice's canals.

History and Art

When Venice comes to mind, it is hard to concentrate on fertile valleys and volcanic hills, like the Berici near Vicenza and the Colli Euganei near Padua, that enliven the Veneto plain. Canaletto images of light reflecting off water make the southern Po river border seem irrelevant, though its presence determined much of the history of neighboring regions—Lombardy to the west, Emilia Romagna to the south. No matter that the dramatic Dolomites

History and Art

and their foothills form the northern border; it is the Adriatic coast, nibbled away by lagoons and flooded by marshes, that has given the Veneto its distinctive history. The Veneto's borders echo those of Venice's mainland expansion: its hills and towns, embellished with Palladian villas and Bellini altarpieces, shared in the great city's artistic bounty. Here, it is Venice that matters.

Yet in ancient times, Venice didn't exist. It was at Verona the Romans built their roads into an ever-expanding empire, and it was from Verona they launched so many battles into the land of the Goths. It was on the mainland at Padua, not the lagoon, that Livy was born and at Verona, the poet Catullus and the architect Vetruvius. It was south at Ravenna, not here, that Augustus built the great Adriatic port. Not until the fifth century, when the empire battled Alaric the Goth outside the gates of Verona and suffered the destruction of Veneto towns by Attila the Hun, that refugees fled to the safety of the lagoon islets. Even then, the fishing hamlets were merely temporary havens until the Empire restored order. Then, the Lombards invaded, burning Padua, sacking most of Italy, and worse, remaining. Then, and only then, did the lagoon villages grow into towns.

While the mainland lived under Lombard rule and then suffered through the Franks' reconquest for the pope, the islet sanctuaries knew only Byzantium. While most of Europe stagnated, these islands did quite well by trading salt and provisions with Constantinople, by then somewhat isolated in the increasingly Islamic Mediterranean. So when Charlemagne tried to expand the reconquest to the lagoon, these communities had little interest. Turning their backs on terra firma, they united to protect their trade with the East and founded a common government away from the easy reach of pope and Frankish emperor alike. The government was located on some islets around one of the least accessible canals, the Rio Alto, later the "Rialto" of the Grand Canal. And if that wasn't enough to guarantee the peace, they expanded their navy. Thus Venice was born, a free and maritime republic, in A.D. 811.

Venice may have arrived late in history, but took little time to surpass her neighbors. By the time the crusaders needed transport to the east, the maritime republic was ready with ships. In the enthusiasm of so much war against the infidel, somehow Christian Constantinople was conquered (1204), much to Venice's advantage. By the time Treviso and Padua and Bassano were struggling free of the tyrant Ezzelino da Romano, Venice had already monopolized the spice trade, introducing Europe to sugar and controlling the distribution of pepper. Its most adventurous merchant, Marco Polo, made his way to the cinnamon and ginger of China by 1275. In the early 14th-century when Padua, Treviso and Verona enjoyed some independence under the protection of ruling families, Venice controlled the Dalmatian

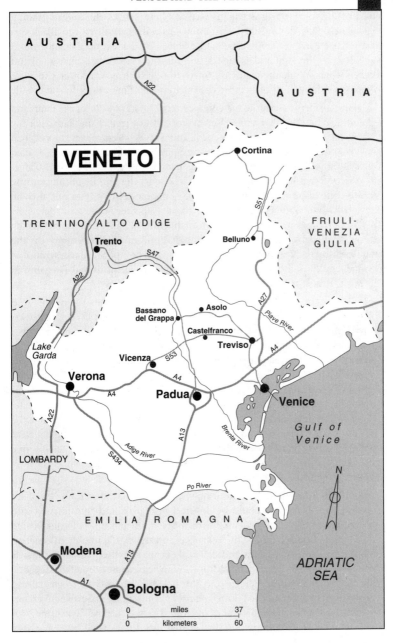

coast of the former Yugoslavia, as well as Crete and Corfu, and its trading rights included Alexandria, Constantinople and beyond, to the Black Sea and farther east. Its ships carried the spices of the exotic Orient around Gibraltar, to England and Flanders, and returned laden with furs, wool and French wines. While the mainland towns fought their way through the feuds of medieval Italy, Venice became the greatest maritime power in the world.

Making its fortunes on the seas, Venice tactfully stayed out of the mainland struggles. When the Scaligeri of Verona took over Vicenza and Padua, or the Carraresi of Padua fought with Verona and Treviso, Venice was busy. When the Visconti expanded their Milanese empire to Verona and Padua, it paid more attention. And when opportunity arose with the death of Gian Galeazzo Visconti in 1402, Venice was quick to act. By the middle of the century, Venice controlled not only what comprises the modern Veneto, but also the Fruili to Udine. Spurred on by threats to its sea power in the East, especially the fall of Constantinople to the Ottoman Turks (1257), and the new trade routes opened by the Portuguese, Venice concentrated its energy on the mainland. By the end of the century, the winged lion of St. Mark, symbol of Venice, could be found all the way to Rimini in the south and Bergamo in the west, almost to Milan.

Straddling the East and West, Venice rose from mud flats to empire. And from these two worlds it created a unique state. Its doge lived in quarters sumptuous enough for an eastern pasha and was paraded through the town on special occasions. In fact, the doge, or duke, was a symbol appropriate to the wealthy and aristocratic republic. But with Italian cynicism worthy of the later Machiavelli, the checks on his power reduced him to a mere figurehead. For the Venetians, the enduring health of their commerce couldn't be entrusted to a personality cult. Venice was in the hands of the anonymous state, so much so that barely a doge's name leaves its imprint on history, unlike the Medici of Florence, or even the Scaligeri of Verona. The resultant wealth spread beyond the doge, it spilled over into low taxes and greater internal peace than enjoyed by any Renaissance state. Soon it was known as La Serenissima, the most serene republic.

Just as the state could dress itself up with a doge, so the warehouses of sea captains and merchants could be covered in marble and transformed into palazzi. Eastern styles intertwined with western, the glimmer of gold frosted facades and church cupolas, the sensuous and the exotic breathed Venetian air into the Roman basilica and classical forms. On the mainland the arts flourished, but in the Italian tradition, with the magnificent Romanesque church of San Zeno at Verona and the rich brick beauty of town halls in Padua and Treviso, and the Giotto frescoes in the Arena, or Scrovegni chapel of Padua. But Venice's San Marco created a style called Byzantine Romanesque that really may be simply Venetian. Its ducal palace may have been inspired by Padua's arcades, but its lacy ogival arches and its opulence belong to the East. Or, then again, they are simply Venetian. Straddling two worlds, Venice's focus was commerce, but its style was far from pedestrian.

The taste for the exotic and the silky, the preference for Byzantine richness, may have blinded Venice to the new beauty of the Early Renaissance. Not until its expansion on the mainland did Venice begin to relinquish the Gothic for the classical forms and realism already spreading through the Veneto. Even then it embraced the Gothic elegance of Verona's Antonio Pisanello (c. 1395–1455) rather than the harder realism of Florence's Uccello. And though the Veneto was transformed by the visit of Donatello, who sparked the genius of Andrea Mantegna (1431–1506) in Padua, Venice continued to savor the Byzantine conservatism of Antonio Vivarini (1420–c.1480) and his family. It took Giovanni Bellini (1430–1516) to create a Renaissance style out of the local love of nature and rich detail. But not until his workshop learned the oil-painting techniques of Antonello da Messina did even Giovanni produce the light and vibrant color that would be the hallmark of the Venetian school.

Once again a latecomer, Venice soon replaced Florence as a center of art. Its style spawned local schools, not just in nearby Padua, but in Brescia, Bergamo, and little Bassano. In Venice itself, the school was so fertile as to encompass the diverse styles of Vittore Carpaccio (c. 1460–1525), whose anecdotal scenes are elevated by the infusion of limpid Venetian light, and Carlo Crivelli (1435–c. 1495), whose hard, bony figures are nonetheless draped in dense Venetian color and detail. The school is so talented as to make it easy to overlook an artist of the caliber of Cima da Conigliano (1460–1518) while impossible to forget Giorgione (c. 1475–1510), who turned the Venetian landscape into poetry.

Venice was not done. Even after the rest of Italy was trying to recuperate from the Italian Wars that ended the High Renaissance in Rome, La Serenissima was exploding with the brilliance of Titian's (c. 1485–1576) color, the glowing surfaces of Veronese (1528–88), and the flickering light and shadow of Tintoretto (1518–96). These artists continued to evolve, foreseeing the Baroque with their dynamic compositions and high emotion, liberating their brushes to cast light and movement in a manner that would inspire artists from Velasquez and Turner through the Impressionists and into the 20th century.

The Renaissance lasted in Venice almost through the entire *cinquecento*, a period when Venetian nobles enjoyed the money they had so impressively amassed. The Ottoman Turks might restrict them in trade, but the wealth was already in hand and there were artists to render it into the enduring legacy of the Venetian republic. They spent, not just on paintings, but on palazzi, too—perhaps one by Mauro Coducci (c.1440–1504) from Bergamo, or Michele Sanmicheli (1484–1554) from Verona. They proved their piety with donations to their scuole, or charitable confraternities, and helped build churches designed by the local Lombardi family as well as the mainland's Andrea Palladio (1508–80). And they filled their churches not just with paintings, but also with glorious music—over 100 masses by Palestrino (1525–94), and choral music by the Gabrielli (till 1612). The state was hardly forgotten as its sea battles and glory were commemorated in monumental paintings for the ducal palace.

Venice's decline was caressingly slow. Even when money ceased to come in from treaties with the Turks, and even when the modern nation states of Portugal and Spain proved too formidable on the sea, Venice continued. It even found the energy to battle and defeat the Turks at Lepanto in 1571, and again in 1669, but simply couldn't hold on. It could still delight the eye with Baldassare Longhena's (1598–1682) Baroque church Santa Maria della Salute, and provide the senses with the first public opera, by Monteverdi. Its great painting tradition soared to the ceiling frescoes of G. B. Tiepolo (1696–1770), who exceeded the Baroque illusionism of even Pietro da Cortona and Bernini. And it simply dazzled all of Europe with Giorgio Massari's (d. 1753) stately palazzi, with Vivaldi's choir, with Carlo Goldoni's (1707–93) 260 comedies, and with Carnival celebrations and spellbinding fireworks and doge-led processions. In the end, only foreigners could afford the paintings of Canaletto (1697–1768) and the Guardi (till 1793), and the neoclassicism of Antonio Canova (1757–1822) was more international than Venetian. Venice's vitality, finally, was spent.

Venice endured as an independent state for 1000 years. It was centuries after Florence had succumbed to Spain and centuries after Rome had been sacked that Venice abdicated to Napoleon (1797). Empires have come and gone, but few have put on such a splendid show.

Modern Veneto

The beauty of La Serenissima remains, despite the threats of floods and high tides. But the entrance to the once great city is rarely from the sea. Instead, industrial Mestre, with its oil and chemical refineries, provides a disconcerting portal to the old republic. All of the Veneto, however, is thriving. There's agribusiness, like Verona's efficient viniculture, Vicenzia's soybeans, and the sugarbeet crops of the south. And there's considerable industry—Verona also manufactures shoes and clothes, Vicenza is a tanning and leather center, Bassano produces all those familiar Italian ceramics of fruit and roosters. Venice, in addition to its primary industry of tourism, produces glass on Murano island, just as it did in the Renaissance. And the services industry is appearing, in Padua's financial houses and in electronics at Vicenza, where they proudly remind you that Federico Faggin, inventor of the silicon chip, was born. Except for the Asolan hills to the north and the Euganean to the south, the land is not especially scenic. But through the congestion and bustle of the modern towns lie their historic centers, still rewarding.

Cuisine

The cuisine of the Veneto, more than any of its northern neighbors, is heavily oriented toward the Mediterranean. Though not completely wedded to olive oil, it is primarily so, even though Padua likes its pasta in the buttery Emilian style and butter finds its way into certain preparations. More than oil, it is the seafood of the Adriatic that dominates, even in the mainland cities like Verona. The spiky scampi, the tiniest clams, tender *seppioline*, or squid, and *polipetti*, or octopus, are combined into delicate salads, cooked into a risotto or soup, served on spaghetti, and simply grilled or fried. The fish seem endless—*triglie*, or red mullet, *coda di rospo* (toadfish tail), *San Pietro*, or John Dory fish, turbot, sole and more. Of course, there's baccala, sauteed lightly *alla veneta*, or stewed away *alla vicentine*, and, in Venice, mashed into a pate *al mantecato* then spread on polenta. The regional bounty still has freshwater trout and salmon from Lake Garda to add, as well as a salty accent of caviar from the Po delta.

On land, the Veneto is equally blessed. With the fertile mainland valley complemented by the Dolomites and their foothills to the north, and the Euganean hills to the south, the region also is diversified. Wheat and corn flourish in the valley. Apples and pears as well as beans come from mountainous Belluno, figs from a precious strip of Lake Garda, and peas from along the lagoon. Peaches are plentiful, along with blueberries and cherries, and grow in the Berici hills near Vicenza, as well as in the Euganean hills. White asparagus comes from Bassano del Grappa, romaine-shaped radicchio gets its name from Treviso, chestnuts, walnuts and all manner of mushrooms are found in the hills, but none are so valued as porcini. Then you add the game from the hills and count the ducks from the Venetian lagoon, and the cuisine begins to assume some heartiness. Once you consider the pepper and saffron, the nutmeg and tarragon so long monopolized by La Serenissima, the spice trader, there's also a cuisine of great variety.

This Veneto cornucopia transforms into both simple country dishes as well as refined ones. No dish is more traditional than *pasta e fagioli*, a soup of pasta and beans so thick that a drop of golden oil is added to thin it before eating. Then, too, there's *risi e bisi*, or spring fresh peas cooked with rice as they can do well only in Venice. In fact, it is rice along with seafood that is so characteristic of the region, from a *risotto nero* with squid and its ink, or one with asparagus, or radicchio, or even duck. Pasta crops up of course, often as the handcut *bigoli*, a thick spaghetti served *all'anatra*, or in duck ragu. It can just as easily be an elegant fettucine with scampi or a tagliatelle with the local porcini and walnuts. But any mention of the basic rice and beans must be completed with a note about *polenta*, which forms part of the local triad. Polenta can be found fluffily layered with baccala or its corn flavor a counterpoint for roasted game well-seasoned with tarragon. Wherever beans or rice aren't, usually there's a spot for a slice of polenta.

After enjoying an antipasti di pesce with octopus spiked with caviar, or *granzeole*, crab, served with just lemon and oil, and sampling fish grilled with those peppercorns from the Orient or cooked in paper with saffron, you can understand why seafood is the choice of the region. In addition you can choose game, or wonderful salads of seasonal greens with shavings of porcini or an antipasto of smoked Garda trout. The Veneto does serve meat dishes, too. As an antipasto, there's speck, a smoked ham that is the equivalent of other regions' prosciutto. And among the secondi, there's the omnipresent *fegato all veneziana*, or calves liver with onions, and the even richer *perverada* sauce for game—a brew of sausage, anchovies, liver and herbs.

A discussion of the Veneto's bounty must include its **wines**, some of the best known to Americans. The Veneto is first in Italy in the number of controlled content, or DOC, wines. And the *provincia* of Verona, with its dry, simple white Soave, its pleasant ruby Bardolino, and its deeper Valpolicello, is Italy's greatest exporter. These good wines achieve greatness with Valpolicello's Amarone, a complex wine that should be matured for at least four years. This being the Veneto, there is more, of course. The Piave valley above Belluno produces the mellow red Rabaso. Farther north you find the white Prosecco di Conegliano in its *frizzante*, or bubbly form, that has become a popular aperitivo throughout Italy. If you are traveling in the foothills around Asolo, the DOC Montello e Colli Asolani has not only a light red but its own fruity Prosecco frizzante. And south, near Padua, the Colli Euganei labels include a wide range of wines, the rosso and the blush considered the best. Not to be forgotten is the strong liquor, *grappa*, so important to Bassano that it's part of the town name.

Travel Tips

Climate and Seasons

The official off-season in Venice is November into March, when, like the rest of the north, the weather is foggy and cold (Jan. average high 42° F, low 34° F) and when, unique to Venice, rains most often create *aqua alta*, high tides that splash quays. But snow is rare, and although fogs make for airport delays and some difficult driving, travel certainly is feasible. In fact, Venice has started promoting winter travel with a revival of carnival celebrations, and some travelers are finding the off-season special, with its lack of crowds.

Summer is, of course, the most crowded, and the weather can be sultry hot (average July high in Venice 87° F, low 67° F) sending the Veneziani to the Lido, Lake Garda, or the Asolo hills. For the entire region, the fall and spring offer the best conditions, with the average highs in the 60s, lows in the 50s.

Arriving

The Marco Polo airport in Mestre, just outside of Venice, is the major airport of the region, with some European flights. Train service to historic Venice (Santa Lucia station) is good, with the fastest train from Milan arriving in 3 hours, from Rome in 4.5, Bologna 1.5. International trains include the sumptuous Orient Express to London (contact your travel agent), and the IC train to Yugoslavia (8.5 hours), and a connector to Trent for the Austrian border at Brenner (5.5 hours). Autostrade connect Venice with the Dolomites to the north (A-27); Bologna to the south (A-13; 150 km, 93 mi.), from there A-1 for Florence (275 km, 170 mi.) and Rome (530 km, 329 mi.); and on A-4 west for Milan (265 km, 164 mi.), east to Trieste (146 km, 90.5 mi.). But if you are arriving from Milan or the north, it's more likely that your first destination in the Veneto will be Verona. Although there's a small airport at Verona, primarily for domestic flights, your arrival probably will be by the Brennero train (4 hours) or A-22 (260 km, 161 mi.); or the Milano train (2 hours), or A-4 (135 km, 84 mi.).

Getting Around

The distances are not great in the Veneto. It is only 105 km, 65 mi. between Venice and Verona by autostrada; and 40 km, 24 mi. from Padua north to Bassano del Grappa. Probably you just plan a stopover in Padua after visiting Venice, perhaps adding a night or two in Verona, on your way to Lombardy. For this, trains and buses will serve you well. If you are interested in Palladio's architecture, adding Vicenza to this list is easy, too. But if you want to see more towns, or country villas or the scenery of the foothills of the Dolomites, then you need either a fair amount of time or a rental car. Rental arrangements can be made in the airports as well as the stazioni in Padua and Verona. Try to arrange your rental so you don't pick it up until you're leaving Venice.

Venice

Key to Venice

Sights

The singular beauty of Venice, the uniqueness of a canal city without cars, is enough to warrant a trip. Then add the splendor of San Marco, the Gothic richness of the Ducal Palace, the Palladian churches, the museums and scuolas with their Bellinis, Carpaccios, Titians, Tintorettos and Tiepolos, and you'll find there is never enough time to see it all.

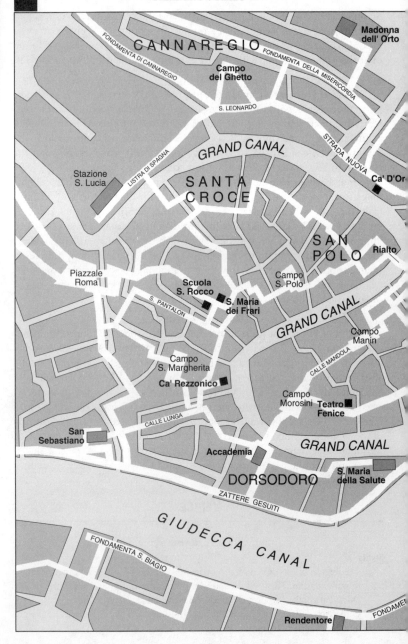

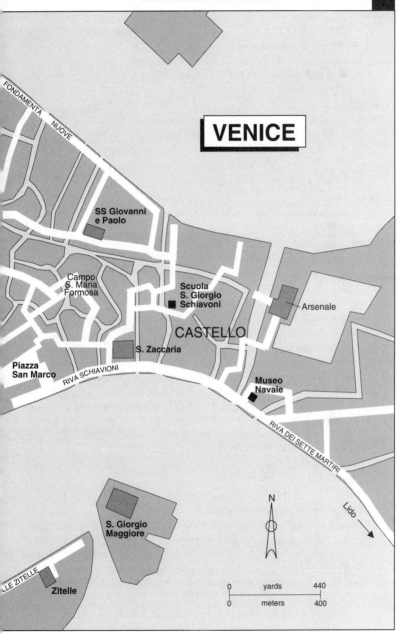

VENICE

FONDAMENTA NUOVE

SS Giovanni
e Paolo

Campo
S. Maria
Formosa

Scuola
S. Giorgio
Schiavoni

Arsenale

CASTELLO

Piazza
San Marco

S. Zaccaria

RIVA SCHIAVONI

Museo
Navale

RIVA DEI SETTE MARTIRI

Lido →

N

S. Giorgio
Maggiore

LLE ZITELLE

Zitelle

| 0 | yards | 440 |
| 0 | meters | 400 |

Excursions

The lagoon islands, especially Torcello, and a leisurely boat trip past the villas on the Brenta Riviera.

Nearby Beaches

The famous Lido is a short *vaporetto* ride away, though you may want to save your swimming for the highest (and cleansing) tide.

Festivals and Events

Carnival, 10 days before Lent; *Vogalonga*, late May; *Festa del Redendore*, 3rd Sun. in July; *Festa della Salute*, Nov. 21; *Regata Storica*, 1st Sun. in Sept.; *International Film Festival*, in Sept. at the Lido; *Biennale d'Arte*, odd-numbered years June-Oct.

Shopping

Traditional lace and glass, carnival masks.

Accommodations

In all categories, pricier than in most of Italy, but reservations a must for most of the year.

Eating Out

Good Venetian seafood and risotto can be enjoyed in a variety of settings.

Getting Around

You can wander through Venice on foot, on both sides of the Grand Canal. Except for the most traveled and well-signed routes (S. Marco to Accademia, S. Marco to Rialto bridge), you need a map. **TIP:** Buy one with a street index.

Canal travel can not only save time and energy, it can be both necessary (to arrive and depart, for example) and picturesque. The main ferry, the #1 *vaporetto*, runs from the Tronchetto parking lot, to the P. Roma and Ferrovia, along the Grand Canal to San Marco—from P. Roma to San Marco takes about 45 minutes—then on to the Lido. The #1 makes all stops, the #34 varies the route a bit and also has fewer stops. There is a much faster, pricier #82, with fewer stops and a shortcut route to the P. Roma. All run every 10 minutes, except late at night. (There is a *biglietto turistico* for unlimited rides on the #1 and #34; the 24-hour one hardly is economical, the 3-day pass might be.)

There are other lines that you will find useful, so pick up a free route map from the ACTV office (P. Roma) or tourist office.

Buy tickets at landings and cancel them in the machines before boarding. If there is no ticket office, buy once you're aboard.

There are other boat services, private *taxi acquei* that can be called or found at many landings, and the more expensive *gondola*, which is best on the quieter back canals. There also are *gondola-traghetti* (at signs marked with a small gondola), a shuttle service across the Grand Canal when bridges are none too near. Usually you stand during the crossing, but the price is low and the ride is in a gondola.

Addresses

Venice lists addresses according to its six *sestieri*, or districts (San Marco, Dorso-duro, San Polo, Castello, Cannaregio and Santa Croce), not according to streets. In fact, street names often repeat themselves in the different districts. To make matters worse, the numbering system doesn't give you a clue as to where a building is in the district. Usually we give the nearest campo or actual street, in addition to the address (when we don't mention the *sestiere*, it's San Marco) so that you might have a chance of finding what you're looking for.

Arriving

Marco Polo *airport*, with international and domestic flights, is in Mestre, and connected to the P. Roma by bus (one half hour) and taxi, and more dramatically to San Marco by *motoscafi* (45-minute express boat) and water taxi. *Train* service (Santa Lucia stazione, not Mestre-Venezia, is the place you want) and *bus* service right up to the Grand Canal entrance at P. Roma to the historic city. By *car*, you skim through the ugly industry of Mestre on a 2.5-mile causeway that links the interesting islands of Venice with the mainland at P. Roma (Rome 530 km, 329 mi.; Milan 265 km, 164 mi.). Then you worry about parking.

There is nothing ordinary about an arrival in Venice. At some point you leave terra firma and step into your gondola, water taxi, or water bus vaporetto. If you're traveling deluxe, then a private water taxi can whisk you from the airport to the canal closest to your hotel, and if it happens to be the Grand Canal, you'll pull into the front door. But most people arrive at P. Roma or the nearby Ferrovia, places of great confusion. Here are a few hints for survival.

Bring luggage you can carry or be ready to hire an official *portabagaglio*, or porter. Porters receive a fee for the baggage plus their vaporetto fare if they accompany you. (Porters are available at major landings as well, if you just need assistance in getting to your hotel). You also pay a charge for carrying more than one suitcase on the *vaporetto*.

In the summers, be prepared for the parking lots at the P. Roma to be full, especially if you arrive late in the day. Check at the Marghera tourist office (Mestre road) before bypassing outlying lots, like Tronchetto, which is the most convenient one. Better yet, try to arrive by train or bus, not car.

Try not to arrive on a weekend.

Pick up a free "mappa" of water bus routes at the ACTV office and get oriented.

Special Tips

Venice is so packed with tourists in the summer that there were rumors the number permitted on weekends would be restricted. Although this turned out to be false, you should try to visit other than July/August and avoid weekends for the high season, mid-Mar. to Nov. 1.

The cost of paying for your rental car while it's parked for days in some farflung lot, may give you adequate reason to pay the fee for non-roundtrip use, and drop it off at the rental agency (make sure you have a second contract for a car on departure). Many suggest parking your car in Padua or Treviso, then taking the frequent trains (half-hour rides) into Venice, but you'll find this a costly—or even impossible— option as the lots at the stazioni are full day and night. Instead, check to see if your Venice hotel offers discounted parking—many do.

Once you realize that you can visit only on an August weekend in your rental car, here's what you do: Reserve a hotel with quiet garden or canal view two months in advance, if possible. If crowds bother you, select a hotel away from San Marco—say in Dorsoduro. • Plot your sightseeing so you visit St. Mark's very early or late, when day-trippers are less likely to be swelling the crowds. • Arrive early in the day and head straight for the Tronchetto parking lots.

Weather

Minor flooding still occurs in Venice, especially during the rainier winter season (Nov.–Mar.). Usually the *aqua alta* recedes within a few hours and affects only the lowest areas. But you might want to check conditions in advance, at any season, if there has been an inordinate amount of rain in Italy.

Costs

Venice is pricey, but not outrageously so compared to Milan or Rome. But here even the pizzerias add service charges to the bills and most art churches charge small entrance fees.

Good reading

Henry James' *Italian Hours* and Mary McCarthy's *Venice Observed*.

Even before marble palazzi lined the Grand Canal, Venice (or *Venezia*, in Italian) had its visitors. Before the light-filled paintings of Canaletto and Guardi spread dazzling images of the floating city around the world, Venice embraced tourists. During the crusades, soldiers marched here for ships to the land of the infidel, and Venice thrived. In 1299, it signed a treaty with the Turks to guarantee a monopoly on pilgrimages to Jerusalem, and Venice grew. When it became the greatest maritime power of the Renaissance, Venice housed merchants from Bohemia as well as the Levant, elegant Greeks and hearty Slavs. And when the Arsenal no longer produced a new galley each day, when the Venetian fleets were no more, the world still came to Venice to see the gleaming gold mosaics under St. Mark's domes, the Byzantine splendor of its palaces, the Bellini, Titian and Tintoretto altarpieces of its churches. Now, long after Venice bowed to Napoleon and ceased to be an independent state, its palazzi are emptying, as its citizens find the comforts of *terra firma* too compelling. Yet Venice is far from deserted. The grand city flourishes, as it has for centuries, from its tourism.

Venice is surely one of the world's most exotic cities. A gondola ride through its moonlit canals is everyone's dream. Walks along narrow *calli* (or paths), across the 400 bridges that span the 114 canals, are enchanting. Mornings awakening to fog horns, not car horns, to the hum of ferries, the slap of waves against the quays, are delightful. Instead of streets, there is the *rio*, or canal; the *fondamenta*, or quay. A small expanse of land, large enough to be a piazza, is called "campo," or field. Everywhere there are reminders of Venice's uniqueness, down to the garbage barges and gondola traffic jams.

Venice

But the reality of Venetian living can be less than romantic. The *aqua alta*, or high tide, washes the campi at least 40 times a year and sometimes floods them alarmingly, as in 1966. The canal odors can be less than pleasing in the summer. The maintenance difficulties caused by too few plumbers and laborers and increasing numbers of seasonal, wealthy occupants has rendered many homes uninhabitable. The result has been a decline in population to 80,000—less than half that of 40 years ago and considerably less than the 200,000 of its heyday.

Engineers are experimenting with a high-tech dike called "Moses" to control the flooding, and many palazzi are undergoing government facelifts. Venice, fortunately for us all, will survive awhile longer—but as a tourist city. Although we all can laugh with the Venetians at the exaggerated gondola tour, complete with accordionist and aging tenor performing "O Solo Mio," few are prepared for the crowds, especially in the summer. Some flee Venice, despising it. Others retreat to the quiet back canals and smaller churches, where often, even in summer, there is no one else. It is some consolation that Venice has been like this for a long time, and that Henry James, a century ago, described it as a living museum. And though the crowds today are larger, the ambience at times Disneyesque, it is well to remember that we're just part of the tradition that began with the crusaders in Venice, a city that must always have seemed unreal.

What to See and Do

Grand Canal ★★★

From the Piazzale Roma, the chaotic terminus of the mainland road, you step onto a vaporetto and begin a ferry ride down Venice's breathtaking main street. From the Piazzale to the Ducal Palace, the Grand Canal flows by Gothic palaces with their ogival (pointed) windows, elegantly traced, and continues by others richly ornamented but with the classical balance of the Renaissance, the heavy rustication of Mannerism, the animation of the Baroque and the exuberance of the Rococo. It passes under the 16th-century **Rialto bridge**, packed with shops and shoppers, and continues under the bridge at the Accademia to arrive at the Ducal Palace. Here the intersection of canals, called the "Bacino," is marked by the fabulous palace and its accompanying Piazzetta San Marco, while across the water are the magnificent churches of Santa Maria della Salute and San Giorgio Maggiore, standing like sentinels on each side of the Guidecca Canal, marking the original entrance from the sea.

No amount of repeated travel on the canal can diminish the pleasure of this architectural parade. With the lagoons serving as Venice's defense works, the palazzi could be free of fortifications, open and gay. Their large windows drink in the Adriatic light; their arcaded first floors gladly receive boats that once filled these bottom-floor warehouses of the aristocratic merchants. Each trip across the canal on a traghetto, or up and down on a vaporetto, reveals new details of the more than 100 palazzi built during Venice's centuries of glory. If you are so lucky to get a seat at the front of a **#1 vaporetto**, you'll find it difficult to disembark at your stop.

Some of the finest palaces have been converted into museums so that you can explore them more thoroughly, enjoying the frescoed ceilings, the views of the Grand Canal from their balconies, as well as the collections. Chief among them is the ★ **Ca d'Oro** *(#1 vaporetto at Ca d'Oro, east bank above the Rialto bridge; open 9 a.m.–2 p.m.; Sun. till 1 p.m.; L4000)*, the most exquisite example of a Gothic palazzo, and one much inspired by the doge's. Originally, in the 15th-century, its facade was completely gilded. Inside, the Moorish courtyard and Mudejar balustrade emphasize just how Eastern Venetian architecture could be. Here the Galleria Franchetti exhibits Venetian and Flemish art, the most notable work being Andrea Mantegna's ★ *St. Sebastian*. On the west bank a bit father

north is Longhena's Baroque ★ **Ca Pesaro** *(#1 vaporetto at S. Stae; 10 a.m.–4 p.m., Sun. till 12:30 p.m.; closed Mon., hours often extended Apr.–Oct.; L5000)* with its lavishly decorated 18th-century rooms housing the Galleria d'Arte Moderna. Back toward the Accademia bridge is Longhena's most remarkable Baroque palace, the ★ **Ca Rezzonico** *(#1 vaporetto at Ca Rezzonico 10 a.m.–4 p.m., Sun. 9 a.m.–12:30 p.m.; closed Fri.; Apr.–Oct. Sat.–Thurs. 10 a.m.–5 p.m.; L5000)*. Though begun in 1660 by Longhena, the palace and its decorations weren't completed until the 18th-century by Giorgio Massari. Now the Museum of 18th-century Venice, the piano nobile has been furnished with two G.B. Tiepolo ★ ceiling frescoes to create a "home" of the period, if a rather outrageously ornate one. Across the canal is Massari's more classical **Palazzo Grassi** *(1749; #82 or #34 vaporetto at S. Samuele)* with its stairwell frescoes and important, but temporary, exhibits of modern art.

Piazza San Marco ★★★

The history of Venice is reflected everywhere in this extraordinary set of squares, the immense Piazza San Marco in front of the basilica and the smaller Piazzetta leading to the lagoon. Initially, the area was a vegetable patch bisected by a canal. Then, when the remains of St. Mark were stolen in the 9th-century from Alexandria, the first church was built to hold the relics. Later victories and lootings proclaim the magnificence of La Serenissima, from the bronze horse (stolen in the sack of Constantinople, 1204) atop the basilica to the winged lion that is the symbol of Venice and its saint (a golden chimera brought back from Persia in the 12th-century) standing on one of the marble columns of the piazzetta. Amid the Byzantine opulence of the basilica domes, the intricacy of the Gothic ducal palace, the richly textured Renaissance facade of the library and governmental arcades, there is little doubt that this was the political and religious center of the Venetian republic.

Today tourist, Venetian, and pigeon alike jostle for space in the square: The Venetian to enjoy a passeggiata greeting friends and watching tourists; the pigeons to be fed, twice a day at government expense (legend has them involved in the founding and fate of the republic); and the tourists just to gape. The most leisurely gaping is from one of the cafes, the *Florian* (founded 1720) and *Quadri* (1775) being the most traditional, especially when their orchestras perform in the evening. But Wagner preferred the most recent *Lavena*. As you try to focus on the components that make up the fabulous scene here, you'll notice the **campanile** (reconstructed after 1902 collapse; 9 a.m.–7 p.m. in season,

10 a.m.–4:30 p.m. Nov.– Apr.; L5000) originally a lighthouse, then the bell tower calling nobles to the palace, guild workers to their jobs, and announcing executions between the columns of the piazzetta. At its base is a beautiful ★**loggetta** by Sansovino (c 1550). Harder to sort out until you're near is the charming ★**clock tower** (15th-century) decorated with signs of the zodiac and leading to the Mercerie, a series of shopping streets that end at the Rialto. On the top of the tower, two bronze statues, so tarnished they are called "the Moors," strike the hour. At night, the crowds have thinned, the cafe bands are in full swing and the monuments are beautifully illuminated.

There are two vaporetto stops convenient to the piazza. "San Marco" is near the park, just west of the piazzetta and served by lines 1, 34 and 82. "San Zaccheria" is east, along the Riva degli Schiavoni, and is served by the number 1 and 52 (to the islands).

Piazza San Marco was the political and religious center of the Venetian Republic.

San Marco ★ ★ ★

The present church, a late flowering of the Byzantine style, was begun in 1063, and expanded and more lavishly ornamented through later centuries. Its facade mosaics (only the left one is original to 1260) describe the founding of the church with the stolen relics of St. Mark. Many of its reliefs and columns come from older, even 5th-century, churches and Roman ruins. The central bronze doors are 6th-century Byzantine, the ★ ★ **portal** itself—note the intricate carvings—is magnificently Romanesque. Although the Greek cross plan of the church and its five Eastern domes were directly inspired by Constantinople, St. Mark's is actually a triumphal statement of Venice's independence from Byzantium. In a form true to ancient

Rome, four galloping horses (copies, originals in museum) dominate the church facade. In pure classical, rather than contemporary Romanesque style, ancient and full columns adorn it. And everywhere the facade is covered with "borrowed" trophies, especially the south facade, where one enters the Ducal Palace. It is here the sculpture of the fearfully clutching ★ *tetrarchs* (A.D. 300), stolen from Constantinople, and the porphyry column from Syria, once a symbol of Genoa's rule, speak of Venice's total domination of the Adriatic. Such politics on a church facade are a good reminder that this awesome church was the chapel of the doges, used for public ceremonies. Not until 1807 did it become a cathedral.

As magnificent and political as is the exterior, the interior is profoundly religious and affecting. The 13th-century mosaics in the **atrium** are the finest in the church; all depict scenes from the Old Testament, none better than that of the ★★ *Creation*, found to the extreme right. Stepping into the **interior** couldn't be more overwhelming. The flickering light, the ★★ glittering mosaics (most from the 12th- and 13th-centuries), the ★ patterned marble floors and ★ marble columns (there are 500 of them, ranging from classical to Romanesque), the exotic galleries for women—all create a density of space that is dazzling, an opulence that can only be Venetian. If you find yourself capable of more than breathing, you might visit the apse. Here the high altar contains the urn with St. Mark's remains and behind it is the ★★ **Pala d'oro** *(open 9 a.m.-4:30 p.m.; Sun 2-5 p.m.; in winter 10 a.m.-4 p.m. and Sun. 2-4 p.m.; L3000)* made in Constantinople in A.D. 976 and later embellished by the Venetians—a brilliantly bejeweled gold altarpiece that must be seen illuminated. Here, too, is Sansovino's ★ sacristy door with graceful Renaissance reliefs (note the *Entombment* and *Resurrection*). With the ticket you purchased to see the pala, you also visit the **tesoro**, or treasury (same hours; right transept) containing precious objects from the sack of Constantinople—Byzantine gold, chalices, and reliquaries.

The **Loggia dei Cavalli**, the balcony over the church facade shared with the bronze horses, and the Museo Marciano, containing the original bronzes, can be reached by the stairs leading off the atrium near the central interior door. The ★★ original horses now are believed to date from the time of Hadrian (A.D. 2nd-century) and were later taken from Rome to Constantinople. Even after the Venetians brought them here, they once again were taken as booty—this time by Napoleon. They were returned to Venice in 1815 and are now preserved in the museum along with mosaics and tapestries. Also here are entrances to the **galleries** where you can better view the mosaics and domes. *(The area is open 9:30 a.m.-5 p.m. Apr.-Oct. 10 a.m.-6:30 p.m.; L3000.)*

San Marco is open to tourists 9:30 a.m.-5 p.m., Sun. 2-5 p.m., although its hours for religious services are longer. Concerts often take place here in the evening, and are worth seeking out. Sacristan-led group tours are available most days.

Ducal Palace

Next to San Marco, and a perfect foil to its sumptuous decorations, is this official residence of the doges. While the simple upper screen of the facade, lightened with delicate patterns of pink and white marble, allows your eyes to rest after seeing the basilica, you soon discover its two lower stories of colonnades. Far from simple, the Palazzo Ducale is in fact the most resplendent example of the Venetian Gothic style. Its famous facade, begun in 1340, enriches the piazzetta and canal with its Gothic arches topped by a second, more elaborate arcade with quatrefoil roundees and lacy detailing. As remarkable for their engineering as their beauty, these colonnades were constructed when much of the top floor (surviving from a devastating fire) was already in place.

Passing through the flamboyant ★ **Porta della Carta**, next to the south trophy wall of St. Mark's, you enter a palace where its doges lived well, but almost as prisoners of the state. Restricted in travel, business, and even choice of marriage partners and friends, the doge was ruled by the Senate and the secret proceedings of the Council of Ten. Not too surprisingly, he also shared his opulent palace with these more powerful offices of the Venetian republic.

Everything here is to impress the visitor with La Serenissima, from the **Scala dei Giganti** (1484), designed by Antonio Rizzo and named for Sansovino's immense ★ statues of Mars and Neptune at the top of its steps, to the following ★ **Golden Stairway** (begun 1538), based on a Sansovino design and named for its gilded grill-work that accompanies you to the second-floor with the Doge's apartments and on to the third floor Council of Ten. Lavishly painted by Venetian artists of the 16th- and 17th-centuries (to replace those destroyed in earlier fires), the great rooms would read like an art history as well as political science, if only so many of the Tintorettos, Veroneses, and too few Titians, had not been overly restored into drabness.

A visit is a must. Although the path through the palace is variable, changed for temporary exhibits and special events, you will probably want to make an effort to seek out the more impressive paintings, using the following selective tour as a guide. For a more thorough visit, check the map of paintings found in each room. If the second-floor **doge's apartments** (reconstructed after 1483 fire) are open, the antechamber contains globes and maps with routes of Venetian merchant-explorers, like Marco Polo. More often you start on the third floor, where the **Sala delle Quattro Porte** (Room of Four Doors) has a remarkable ★ stucco ceiling with Tintoretto paintings and an easel painting, *Neptune and Venus*, by G. B. Tiepolo as well as a Titian. Next to it is the **Anti Collegio** with four Tintorettos, including his ★ *Bacchus and Ariadne* as well as Veronese's ★ *Rape of Europa*. This is followed by the Collegio, with Veronese's ★ *Battle of Lepanto* behind the throne and a fabulous ★★ ceiling with his paintings. Through a door on the opposite side of the Room of Four Doors, you find the **Sala Bocca di Leone**, adjoining the chambers of the Council of Ten and containing the notorious mail slot (the lion's mouth) for accusations submitted to the council. Back down on the second floor is the chamber of **Maggior Consiglio**, or the Great Council, where nobles met to elect the various officers, including the committee members who chose the doge. Surrounding the room are portraits of the doges, that of Doge Falier, beheaded for treason in 1355, represented by an empty frame. The views of the Palladian churches from the balcony are more pleasant and Tintoretto's ★ *Paradise*, or *Coronation of the Virgin*, and Veronese's ceiling, ★ *Triumph of the Virgin*, more glorious. From here you might follow the signs to the prison, descending to the **Bridge of Sighs** (1603) and the dungeons made famous by Casanova, who escaped from them.

The palace is open 9 a.m.–7 p.m. in season, 9 a.m.–4 p.m. Oct.–Apr.; tickets sold till 1 hour before closing; L16,000 includes entrance to Museo Corner. Visits often in groups, accompanied by custodian Facilities include bookstores and a cafeteria.

AUTHOR'S TIP

Don't miss the Itinerari Segreti, *a one-hour tour (in Italian) of locked and "secret" sections of the palace. After the tour, you can visit the rest of the palace. You must reserve in advance at the ticket office or call ☎ 2-49-51.* **Times**: *Thurs.–Tues. at 10 a.m. & noon.* **Price**: *L10,000.*

Library   ★★

Standing opposite the palace on the piazzetta is Sansovino's 16th-century masterpiece. Charged with the difficult task of designing a Renaissance building amid the splendor of the ducal palace, Sansovino nonetheless succeeded. He established the classical orders and balance of Renaissance forms, but with repetitions and deep, shadowy windows that echoed and balanced the richness of the palace. He also wrapped the building around to front the canal and extended its forms by adding the loggetta to the campanile. The end result complements the palace, but just as importantly, doesn't compete with it. His accomplishment didn't prevent Sansovino from being imprisoned, when a nasty storm caused some stucco to fall off the ceiling. Only the intervention of influential friends, such as Titian, gained his release.

Museo Correr

In the arcaded palace, closing the west end of the Piazza San Marco, the museo is the city museum with a rather specialized collection of robes worn by the doges and other Venetian memorabilia. The upstairs **pinacoteca** contains a ★ *Pieta* by Antonello da Messina (Room 11), a roomful of works by the Bellini family, including Gentile's *Il Doge Mocenego* (Room 13), and some noteworthy Carpaccio's, including his famous genre piece ★ *Le Cortigiane* (Room 15). Large temporary exhibitions are shown here, too. *Open 10 a.m.–4 p.m., Sun. 9 a.m.–12:30 p.m.; closed Tues.; Apr.–Oct. Wed.–Mon. 10 a.m.–5 p.m.; L16,000 combined ticket with Ducal Palace.*

Accademia and Dorsoduro ★★★

Dominating the south side of the Grand Canal at the Guidecca is the magnificent church of Sant Maria della Salute. Nearby are the smaller canals and calli of the district of Dorsoduro. Walks through this area, especially between the Salute church and Venice's finest painting galleries at the Accademia, take you through a charming neighborhood that was favored by the English-speaking community at the turn of the century. Here John Ruskin stayed in a pensione and Ezra Pound resided. Though the foreign community no longer is so large, or illustrious, its presence is felt in the old Anglican church (Campo San Lio), and especially in Peggy Guggenheim's palazzo, now a museum. Though certainly rewarding for those who visit, Dorsoduro has not yet been inundated by the crowds at San Marco.

Gallerie dell'Accademia ★★★

Just across the Grand Canal on the Accademia bridge, you come to this superb museum of Venetian painting. The museum takes you from the richly detailed patterns of the Gothic through rooms brimming over with Early Renaissance masters like Giovanni Bellini and Carpaccio and the High Renaissance brilliance of Veronese and Tintoretto, to the 17th-century Baroque of G. B. Tiepolo. If there are too few Titians, perhaps those rare works by Giorgione make up for it.

On a first visit you'll probably want to be selective. In the **first hall** of medieval art, there's an entrancing Paolo Veneziano ★ polyptych (1350s) and an exquisite ★ reliquary. Among the many paintings of the Early Renaissance, including the large altarpieces of Bellini (★ *Giobbe Altarpiece*, 1480s) and Cimi di Conigliano (★ *Doubting Thomas*) in Room II, you should definitely reserve time for the smaller paintings in Rooms IV and V. Room IV contains Mantegna's ★★ *St. George*, so influential on the early work of his brother-in-law Giovanni Bellini, who here has numerous fine paintings, including his ★★ *Madonna and Child with Saints Paul and George*. Also note two non-Venetians, Piero della Francesca's ★ *St. Jerome with Donor*, and Hans Memlings' ★★ *Portrait of a Man*. Room V presents a chance to study Giovanni Bellini's genius, with his four brilliant variations of ★★ *Madonna and Child*. Here, too, is his emotionally compelling ★★ *Pieta*, as well as two works by Giorgione, the haunting and enigmatic ★★ *La Tempesta*, (1505) and the portrait of an old woman, angry with age in ★★ *Col Tempo* (attrib.) **Room X** is rich in 16th-century work and includes a Veronese masterpiece ★★ *Supper at the House of Levi*, (1573). Glowing with Venetian color and filled with exotic jesters, midgets and turbaned slaves, Veronese originally intended this work as a Last Supper—which explains the odd presence of Christ at the table. When the Inquisition insisted the painting be changed, Veronese complied by changing the title. Here, too, is Veronese's ★ *Madonna Enthroned*, and Titian's last work, the ★ *Pieta*, (1576), meant for his tomb, but never finished. Deeply spiritual and painted with bold, broken strokes, the Pieta includes the artist's self-portrait in the kneeling figure of St. Jerome. The many Tintorettos here (★ *St. Mark Frees the Slave* (1548) and ★ *Transporting St. Mark*) and in **Room XI** are characteristic in their shocking foreshortening and drama. And in case you thought Veronese had introduced you to the Baroque, Room XI proves otherwise with his ★ *Annunciation* so near G. B. Tiepolo's ceiling fresco, ★ *Exalting the Cross*. Down a corridor, a number of small rooms continue the exhibits with a variety of later paintings, including more Tiepolos, Canalettos and Guardis. But you aren't yet finished. Nearly at the end of the next corridor, turn to **Room XX** for the enormous paintings of the ★ *Procession of the Relic of the True Cross*, (1496) by Gentile Bellini, et al., for a taste of 15th-century Venice, from its wooden bridges to dandy gondoliers. Farther down this corridor is **Room XXI**, with Carpaccio's ★ *Scenes from the Life of*

St. Ursula (1495). And the **last room** before exiting, taken whole from a religious confraternity, or *scuola*, retains Titian's ★ *Presentation of the Virgin* (1530s). *Open 9 a.m.–2 p.m. except July-Sept. 30 till 7 p.m. and Sun. till 1 p.m.; tickets (L12,000) sold till 1/2 hour before closing.*

Peggy Guggenheim Collection   ★★

Stroll from the Accademia toward the Salute church, and after the Campo S. Vio, cross the Rio San Vio and continue through picturesque alleys, for the entrance to the gardens and art collections of Peggy Guggenheim. Though the works by Brancusi, Ernst, Rothko, Motherwell and others may not belong to the Venetian tradition, they can enrich your stay. *Open 11 a.m.–6 p.m.; closed Tues.; L10,000.*

Santa Maria della Salute   ★★★

By the time you visit this imposing Baroque church (begun 1631), it will already seem like an old friend. But no matter how many times you view its beautiful silhouette from Piazzetta San Marco, no matter the times you've noted its tall dome, immense spiraling volutes, and its triumphal arch over the main portal, you'll be pleased by a visit. The church was built as an offering of thanks for the deliverance of Venice from the 1630 plague. Its highly centralized and octagonal shape can be enjoyed best from inside. Here Palladian grey stone on white stucco softens the Baroque, while the design of the pavement and the Gothic altarpiece infuse the church with their warmth. In the **sacristy** (left of high altar; donation), you discover Titian's daringly foreshortened ★★ ceiling frescoes (1542) of Old Testament scenes (note *Cain Killing Abel*) as well as his altarpiece ★★ *San Marco Enthroned*, with the luminous colors of his early work surrounded by roundels of nearly impressionistic portraits of the apostles. On another wall is Tintoretto's dynamic ★ *Marriage at Cana*. *The church is closed noon-3 p.m. Reached by #1 Vaporetto, Salute stop.*

Other Sights

Running along the Guidecca Canal, behind the Salute church, is the Fondamenta Zattere. A walk here is open and breezy with a sense of the sea. Past the gelaterias you find Massari's **Gesuati church** (1726) with an altarpiece (1st chapel, right) and ceiling frescoes (★ *St. Domenic Instituting the Rosary*, 1737) by G. B. Tiepolo *(Vaporetto #2 or #5 Zattere stop).* More off the beaten track and with paintings that can also be difficult to see, is the small church of ★ **San Sebastiano** *(closed Sun. morn. and noon-3 p.m.).* Veronese lived nearby and is buried here. He painted the sacristy ceilings and even the organ cover, but the best of his works are on the ★ high altar and church ceiling (★ *Triumph of Mordecai*, a sumptuous trompe l'oeil). *Reached from San Basilio stop on Vaporeto #82 at the end of the Zattere, or from Ca'Rezzonico via Campo S. Barnabo to Calle Longa.*

Campo San Rocco in San Polo ★★

From the vegetable and fish **markets** at the south side of the Rialto bridge, through a tangle of paths and piazzas running towards Dorsoduro, is the San Polo district. In its middle is the large campo of the **San Polo church** (hidden in the back are the young G. D. Tiepolo's ★ *Stations of the Cross*, 1747). Deeper into the district is the Campo San

Rocco with Tintoretto's best paintings in the Scuola di San Rocco and exquisite Titians in its Frari church. *These sights are most directly reached by the S. Toma vaporetto stop on line #1.*

Basilica Santa Maria Gloriosa dei Frari   ★★

More simply known as the Basilica dei Frari (founded 1250), this great hulking church contains splendid art. The first altarpiece, left of the entrance, is Titian's ★★*Pesaro Madonna* (1519), with its fleshy Christ child and careful portraits of the Pesaro family. But the focus is all on the Madonna despite Titian's revolutionary placement of her off-center. On the high altar is another Titian masterpiece, the ★★*Assumption*, (1518) with pulsating color and rapturous movement that seems to lift the Virgin into heaven. In a chapel to the right is Donatello's compelling polychrome wooden statue of ★ *St. John the Baptist*, a work which did much to bring Renaissance realism to Venice. Farther right, through the sacristy gate, is Bellini's light-filled triptych, ★★*Enthroned Madonna and Child*, (1488), in which the actual frame, used as the Madonna's throne, creates illusionistic depth. *The church is open to tourists 9:30 a.m.–noon except Sun., and 2:30–6 p.m. every day; L1000.*

Scuola di San Rocco   ★★

Nearby on the campo, next to the church of San Rocco, is the *scuola*, or religious fraternity, dedicated to charitable works. In Venice these scuole vied with each other in commissioning artistic works to decorate their halls. San Rocco contains ★★**Tintoretto's masterpieces**, three grand rooms covered with his ghostly forms and flickering light for a total of more than 50 paintings. Standing in these rooms that are everywhere painted by an artist of such religious intensity can be as exhausting as it is enthralling. Perhaps the two most important rooms are up the grand staircase, where you enter the **Sala Grande** (1575-81), painted for the overall impact of the many scenes from both the New and Old Testaments (note the ceiling painting of ★★*Moses Striking Water from the Rock*). On an easel, there is a Titian ★*Annunciation*. Through this sala is the **Sala dell'Albergo** (1564-67) with its 40-foot long *Crucifixion*, filled with tumultuous crowds, a cross that towers so high it's off canvas, while at its base a touching ensemble huddles around Mary. Also in this room are easel paintings by Giorgione (sometimes attributed to Titian): ★ *Christ with Thorns* and ★ *Christ with Cross*. The **ground floor** paintings, if you have the stamina to look, are the latest (1583-87), and the most ethereal. *The scuola is open 9 a.m.–5:30 p.m. Apr. through Oct.; otherwise 10 a.m.–1 p.m. daily, weekends till 4 p.m. L6000.*

East of San Marco ★★

This route quickly loses the crowds of the main piazza and takes you to a Bellini masterpiece and delightful Carpaccios. You can connect the scuola to the church of S. S. Giovannia and Paoli in "North of San Marco," if you have a good map. And if you approach San Zaccheria from the Riva degli Schiavoni, you may want to look at G. B. Tiepolo's ceiling fresco, ★ *Triumph of Faith*, (1754) in **Santa Maria della Pieta**, where Vivaldi was choirmaster from 1703-45.

San Zaccheria   ★ ★

The large campo, so near the Riva degli Schiavoni and St. Mark's, is surprisingly tranquil. The church greets you warmly during tourist hours with taped classical music, and Bellini's altarpiece ★ ★ *Madonna and Saints*, (1505; 2nd altar, left; light machine) completes the serene setting. Despite the subtlety of the painting, it can hold your attention from across the church, especially when the afternoon sun plays across its surface. Closer, its stillness and extraordinary light are mesmerizing. The carved pilasters of the frame, echoed in the painting, draw you closer yet, but just enough to gaze more intently at the scene before you. Understandably, this is considered one of the great works of the Early Renaissance. On the opposite side of the church is the entrance (fee) for the ★ **Chapel San Tarasio** (right apse). Here, the Renaissance vault paintings of saints and ★ fleshy putti (1442) by the Florentine Andrea Castagna contrast with the contemporary, but Gothic, altars by Venetians. *The church is open for "visita artista" 10 a.m.–noon, 4–6 p.m.*

Scuola San Giovanni degli Schiavoni   ★

The walk here from the Zaccheria is picturesque, up the alley of San Provolo to the canal and bridge leading to the 16th-century church of **San Georgio dei Greci**. Without crossing the bridge into what was the Greek community of merchants, follow Rio San Lorenzo to the second bridge. Then cross, and walk to this Slavic scuola, a confraternity of Dalmatians. Inside the headquarters is Carpaccio's cycle of ★ frescoes on their patron saints (1508). As usual, this artist captures the Venice of his time in an almost anecdotal style, notable for the uniquely Venetian light that infuses each scene. *Open 10 a.m.–12:30 p.m.; 3–6 p.m.; in winter Sun. till 12:30 only; closed Mon.; L5000.*

Museo Storico Navale

Castello 700276.
At the end of the Riva degli Schiavoni, you come to the Campo San Biagio and this museum with its models of old Venetian ceremonial barges and galleys and an exhibit of gondolas. Just up the Arsenal Canal is a branch of the museum, a warehouse with ships from the 19th and 20th centuries, sitting under the watchful eye of the impressive Renaissance gate of the original Arsenal. *Open 9 a.m.–1 p.m.; Thurs. 2:30–5 p.m.; L2000.*

North of San Marco ★

A longer walk than that to the east, but one that nearly everyone makes, at least partially, on their way to the Rialto bridge. Passing through the clock tower of the piazza, you follow the series of congested, shop-lined streets known as the Mercerie. This is the shortest route to the Rialto. But most of the sights are farther along, where the walking becomes more pleasant, and forms a loop back to San Marco.

San Salvatore   ★

Just before the Rialto, the Mercerie opens to this campo and church. The Renaissance interior of the church was finished by Sansovino and contains a late painting by Titian, the "Turneresque" ★ *Annunciation* (1560s; on right, before high altar; light machine). To its right is Sansovino's ★ *Tomb of Doge Venier*. To the left of the apse is *Supper at Emmaus*, by a Bellini follower. *Closed noon-3 p.m.*

Santa Maria dei Miracoli ★

Ignoring the Rialto bridge, and continuing north, turn off the Salizada Canciano for the Piazza Santa Maria Nova. Here, off to the side, is Pietro Lombardi's 1481 Renaissance jewel box, wrapped in gray, white, and coral marble. The exceptionally rich ceiling contrasts with the marble geometric panels of the interior walls, but harmoniously so. Everything here is finely executed, from the balustrade and sculpture to the carved altar screen. *Open 9:30 a.m.–noon daily; in summer 2:30–6 p.m. and winter 3–5 p.m., except Sun.*

SS Giovanni e Paolo ★★

Just a short walk on Gallina, over a few bridges and you enter this large campo, the stage for Verrocchio's commanding ★★ *Equestrian Monument to Bartolommeo Colleoni* (1481). High on a pedestal is Venice's famous condottiere, charging his horse into battle. The vitality of the composition is as stunning today as it was influential in the Renaissance. Sharing the surrounding space is one of Venice's largest churches, the Gothic SS Giovanni e Paoli. The interior contains numerous paintings, a too-early Bellini triptych (2nd chapel, right) and a Lorenzo Lotto *Almsgiving*, (end chapel, right transept). But the most momentous works here are the carved tombs of 25 doges.

Santa Maria Formosa

Looping back towards San Marco, leave Colleoni behind you and head south on Bressano, then turn right into this campo. In this section many of the house entrances are by individual bridges and around the quiet piazza are some fine palazzi. The church, rebuilt by Coducci in 1492, contains a lovely Bartolomeo Vivarini *Madonna della Misericordia*, (1473; 1st chapel, right). Just south of the piazza is the atmospheric 16th-century ★**Palazzo Querini Stampalia**, its piano nobile furnished to the last century and containing a collection of Venetian paintings *(open 10 a.m.–12:30 p.m. and, in summer, also 3:30–6 p.m.; closed Mon.; L5000)* that includes ★ *Presentation in the Temple* by Giovanni Bellini. The Calle Bande out of the Formosa campo leads back into the Mercerie.

Other Sights

The **Cannaregio** section is even farther north, wedged between the Ca d'Oro and the lagoon. But if you have time, you can meander its streets to the **Ghetto**, a *getto*, or foundry until the 14th-century, then the area where Jews were confined, and valued for their medical skills and ability to pay taxes, until Napoleon's arrival. It is this ghetto that has given all the others their name. One of the old synagogues, the Scola Grande Tedesca (1528), is now also a **museum** *(P. Ghetto Novo; 9 a.m.–6 p.m. except Sat.; off-season 10 a.m.–3:30 p.m.; L4000)*. Near the lagoon is the ★**Madonna dell'Orto** (reached by vaporetto #5 from the Fondamenta Nuove near SS Giovanni and Paolo). *Closed noon–4.* Considered the finest Gothic church in Venice, this one is notable for the paintings it contains. Tintoretto lived in the parish and is buried here. Among his paintings for the church are ★★ *Presentation of the Virgin*, (1552; end, right aisle, over sacristy door; light machine) and a Michelangelesque ★ *Last Judgment*, (1561; right wall, high altar). Also here is a beautiful *St. John the Baptist and Saints*, (1493; 1st chapel, right aisle) by Cima de Conegliano.

Just east on Fondamento Contarini are a few relief panels, one of a man leading his camel, decorating merchants' houses.

On the Lagoon ★

There is a point during any visit to Venice when you need to escape it. That's the best time to cruise its canals and lagoon. The most relaxing trip is to the island of Torcello. The easiest is right out from the Piazzetta San Marco to one or more of the three Palladian churches on the west side of the Guidecca canal. The most disconcerting, because of the sudden rediscovery of car traffic, is to the **Lido**. If you want to sun yourself at the beaches of the Lido (swimming is not particularly recommended because of pollution), take the #1 or more direct #6 vaporetto from Riva degli Schiavoni to Piazzale Elisabetta (15–20 minutes), where bus A runs on the lungamare to the beaches and casino (5 minutes).

Giudecca Canal   ★

A tour on the Guidecca Canal can bring you to the classical doors of the three Palladian churches that, along with the Salute, compose such a magnificent scene from the ducal palace, especially at night when they are illuminated. The most popular is the nearest, **★San Giorgio Maggiore** *(closed 12:30–2:30 p.m.; San Giorgio stop)*. Sitting on its own little island, the church offers fine views back over the doge's palace and San Marco. The views get better from the top of the campanile (9:30 a.m.–12:30 p.m., 2–6 p.m., L2000; elevator in left transept; L2000). Begun in 1566, the white church interior exemplifies Palladio's lightness and clarity. In the chancel are two Tintorettos, including a ★ *Last Supper* almost dissolving in broad brush strokes. Continuing up the canal with Guidecca Island on your left, you pass the second Palladian church, the tiny **Zitelle**, its facade just as well enjoyed from the ferry. Father along the island, you come to third and best of Palladio's churches, the **★Redentore** (San Giacomo stop). Begun in 1577, the facade of the church harmoniously weaves together four classical temple facades. The interior has a purity of forms not seen since Brunelleschi, though these have the fullness of the High Renaissance. This church, built in thanks for the end of the 1575 plague, was the site of an annual visit by the doge. The event is still commemorated in the Festa del Redentore.

The #52 & 82 vaporetti connect the churches with the San Zaccheria stop as well as the Zattere.

Islands

The most popular islands are strung out in the lagoon to the north of Venice, off the Fondamenta Nuove. **★Torcello** is the farthest away (about 40 minutes), and this tiny flat land mass, isolated amid flocks of sea birds in the lagoon, gives a memorable impression of what Venice originally was. Torcello itself was once a dependency of Ravenna and a bustling island of 20,000, but malaria (and Venice) ended its importance by the 15th-century. Today the island offers a 10-minute tranquil walk along a canal to its ★ Cathedral *(L1500; 10 a.m.–12:30 p.m., 2–4 p.m.)*, founded in A.D. 639 and rebuilt in 1008. Inside this simple, but moving church is one of the finest mosaics in Venice, covering the apse with gold and presenting a beautifully elongated ★ ★ *Virgin and Child*, dating no later than the 12th-century. In the right apse chapel is a 9th-century mosaic, while on the rear wall is an early 13th-century ★ *Last Judgment*, much restored, but with scenes of considerable charm. In front of the church is the museum of Torcello and the church of Santa Fosca (11th-century). After sightseeing, you can bargain with some vendors from Burano for lace or just choose your restaurant for a leisurely lunch. There is a restaurant for each price category, it seems, plus a cafe. For the two finer ones see "Where to Eat."

Not far from Torcello is **Burano** (35 minutes from Fondamenta Nuove, but sometimes reached on the return from Torcello), famous for centuries for its lace that evolved from making fish nets. Still a fishing village, and one with brightly painted houses and little canals, Burano continues to produce lace. The *Scuola Merletto* (main piazza), both a museum but, sadly, no longer a lace-making school, is the best place to acquaint yourself with the technique *(9 a.m.–6 p.m., except Sun. 10 a.m.–4 p.m., Mon. closed; L3000)*. You can also buy lace here, as well as from the vendors and shops in the village. **Murano** (just five minutes from Fondamenta Nuove) has been the glassmaking center of Venice since the 13th-century and was a source of Venetian wealth through the 16th-century, when it finally lost the monopoly on the process for making mirrors as well as colorful crystal. Murano is actually a tiny Venice, of five islands connected along a large canal. Glass factories, where you can see the glass being blown, are open to visitors as is the *Glass Museum (Museo Vetrario; on main canal; 9 a.m.–7 p.m., but Nov.–Mar. Thurs.–Tues. till 3 p.m.; fee)*. But if you want to escape the heavy pressure to buy glass and the tour boats, there is only the 12th-century *SS Maria e Donato* (across from museo) and its mosaic walls and floor for a retreat.

Murano has been the glassmaking center of Venice since the 13th century.

Special island tours leave from the Riva degli Schiavoni, but you can make arrange-ments by yourself on the Fondamenta Nuove for the #12 ferry that leaves about once an hour. Also Murano is a stop on the #52 vaporetto (take circolare sinistra) from S. Zaccheria.

Brenta Riviera   ★

Along the Brenta canal between Padua and Venice, wealthy Venetians built their summer villas in the 16th-century and *Il Burchiello*, a deluxe, horse-pulled barge, transported them. Today Siamic Express *(in Padua:* ☎ *[49] 660-994, FAX 662-830)* can book a comfortable boat tour of the villas, with stops at the most famous, such as Palladio's **Villa Malcontenta** (also known as Villa Foscari), and the **Palazzo Pisani** at Stra, with its ballroom brilliantly frescoed by G. B. Tiepolo. Lunch can be purchased on the full-day tour that may return from Padua (or vice versa) by bus or train. Tours depart Apr.–Nov. The Brenta tour can be made by ACTV bus or car, too, following the towns of Oriaga, Mira, Dolo and Stra on SS 11 between Mestre and Padua. Check tourist office for opening days of the villas, especially that at Stra.

Festivals and Events

Venice's **carnival**, those ten licentious days before Lent (usually in February), declined after the 18th-century and ceased altogether during Mussolini's rule. In 1980 carnival celebrations were renewed, if more tamely, complete with the traditional masks of the commedia dell' arte. Although not everyone now wears black cape and white mask, the revival has been judged a tourist success with concerts and staged events. The week after Ascension day (usually end of May) is the **Vogalunga**, a rowing event that is enthusiasti-cally embraced by locals despite its relative newness. Perhaps its popularity taps on the tra-dition of the **Festa dell' Ascensione**, when for centuries the doge celebrated Venice's marriage to the sea. Two other festivals reenact the old ceremonies, when the doge crossed the canals on a bridge of boats in thanksgiving for the deliverance of Venice from the plague. The Guidecca Canal is crossed in the **Festa del Redentore** (3rd Sun. in July) and the Grand Canal in the **Festa della Salute** (Nov. 21), both accompanied by colorful processions and preceded by fireworks the night before. The Regata Storica (1st Sun. in Sept.) also revives colorful traditions, with a costumed procession and reenactment of a 16th-century regatta on the Grand Canal.

Although the September **International Film Festival** at the Lido (most events in Cin-ema Palazzo near hotel Excelsior) has a certain glamour to it, many of the movies may seem old-hat, given earlier releases in the U.S. But the international exhibit of modern art held June–Oct. every odd year as part of the Venice **Biennale d'Arte** (in Giardini Pubblici, "Giardini" stop on #1 vaporetto, and the Palazzo Grassi) is highly respected by all.

Until the 1996 fire, operas and plays were performed at the opulent **Teatro La Fenice** (1790, but rebuilt; San Fantin 2549, a few blocks north of Largo Marzo XXII), the oldest theater in Venice and one of the most important opera houses in Italy. Rossini and Bellini wrote works especially for La Fenice and some of Verdi's most famous operas (*La Travi-ata*, for example) had their premiere here. Until 1999 La Fenice's orchestra and chorus will be performing in Tronchetto—it isn't expected that the reconstruction of La Fenice will be completed even by then, however. A concert in **San Marco** can't miss for ambience, while chamber music at Vivaldi's **Santa Maria della Pieta** (Riva degli Schiavoni; Mon. & Thurs.) couldn't be more traditional, especially when followed by a dessert at the Florian on P. San Marco. Also, check with APT for special concerts in other beautiful settings.

Then, too, there's gambling at the **Casino Municipale** for those who have passports to establish they aren't Italian nationals and are willing to pay an admission (L18,000). In the high season the Casino is at the Lido *(Lungomare Marconi 4; reached by special motorboat from the piazzetta);* during the winter it is at the Palazzo Vendramin Calergi on the Grand Canal *(Strada Nuova in Cannaregio 2040).*

Shopping

Shop hours are typically Italian in that many close for the pranza (1–3 or 4 p.m.). But in the high season many not only remain open all day, but also on Sunday—the big day for Italian families to visit.

There are more than enough shops selling antiques and finely crafted goods around San Marco. Right on the Piazza is the jeweler **Nardi**, with original designs and antiques, as well as the most respected lace shop, **Jesurum** *(behind San Marco church at Ponte Canonica 4310).* Also on Piazza San Marco are the more famous glass manufacturers, the inventive **Venini**, **Pauly**, and **Salviati** whose main showroom, with its modern mosaic, has probably already grabbed your eye from the Grand Canal. (The San Marco shops will take you there by boat). Through the west arcade you come to the Larga XXII Marzo with antiques (**Cassini**), fine silk scarves (**Delphos**) and the exquisite Fortuny silks of **Venetia Studium**. Continuing west, the lanes take you past designer boutiques with names like **Missoni** and **Krizia**, art and antique galleries (look for **Trois** near Campo Maurizo), until you exit in the Campo Morosini with the witty display windows and clothing of **Fiorella**.

On the opposite side of the canal, art galleries cluster around the Guggenhein museum in Dorsodoro—here, too, are the interesting glass designs of **Cenedese** (near the Salute church). Past the Accademia, the contemporary furniture of Scarpa catches your eye. Between Campo San Barnaba and the Frari church, there are intriguing shops filled with buttons, old door knobs and brass fittings on Botteghe and Cappeller streets. Also, this is where you should be for **Venetian masks**. With the revival of carnival, artisans once again make the traditional white masks called "bauta." You can find Harlequin faces and sun gods and moon goddesses all year. They can be made of leather, gilded wood and *carta pesta*, a kind of papier-mâché. Once we even saw them made of dough in a pizzeria. But the best are said to be at **Mondonovo** (*Rio Terra dei Pugnia*, near Campo S. Margherita), worth a visit just to browse.

You can buy **lace** and **glass** on the islands, too. Any visit to the island Murano will convince you of the quantity of glass still produced. The museum will also tell you how little of it is of grand quality. You can buy your souvenirs at Murano, if you can bear the hard sell. And just as true, any visit to the island of Burano will convince you how little handstitched lace is now made and the reason for its expense. But the lace sold in some of the island shops and, especially, at the Merletto museum (also available at Jesurum) is good quality. Most lace available in Venice is imported from Asia; most is machine made. At least there is a large selection.

Where to Stay

Hotels tend to cluster primarily into two groups—the very expensive and the moderate. All tend to be pricier than their equivalents elsewhere, especially when you add the price of breakfast that is invariably included. The very expensive category can outstrip even Milan in its prices, though there are some hotels that fill out the lower spectrum of this category—hotels that would be only expensive in other cities. The moderate category includes many palazzi that have been renovated into intimate inns, many with peaceful gardens. You would be wise to reserve at least two months in advance, especially at the smaller hotels, during the high season (April-mid Nov., Christmas, and carnival). Surprisingly, you can be lucky mid-July-Aug. when the inundation of daytrippers chases out the overnight tourist—many hotels officially lower their rates then as well as in the off-season.

Unless indicated, the following high-season prices don't include breakfast (CP). Rooms with canal views can be not only pricier, but noisier. All room prices include air conditioning unless stated otherwise.

Very Expensive

Cipriani   **L995–1,200,000 CP**   ★ ★ ★ ★ ★

Isola Giudecca 10, 30133; ☎ *520-7744, FAX 520-3930.*
Single/double L995–1,200,000 CP. Closed mid-Jan.–Feb.
There is no quaint Venetian ambience about the very contemporary Cipriani. Set off on one of the small islands of the Guidecca, the tranquil hotel is surrounded by gardens and a lagoon. Each of its 98 superbly appointed rooms looks over the water; some have glimpses of Palladio's churches. Excellent restaurant, numerous lounges and bars. Shops. Large heated pool, tennis, sauna. A private boat with 24-hour service to San Marco (five minutes) approaches the doge's palace by its traditional glorious entrance from the Bacio and returns you poolside when you're ready to retreat.

Gritti Palace   **L570–900,000 CP**   ★ ★ ★ ★ ★

Campo Santa Maria del Giglio 2467, 30124; ☎ *794-611, FAX 520-0942.*
Single 570,000 CP. Double 750–900,000 CP.
A 15th-century palace of a doge, this modernized hotel sits by the Grand Canal not far from San Marco. Today, its 88 rooms vary in size and view, but all are appointed as exquisitely as the many formal sitting rooms (and writing rooms, too, of course) with antiques, oriental rugs and chandeliers. Known for its excellent service. Terrace cafe on Grand Canal and respected restaurant. A Ciga hotel with boat service to those on the Lido.

Danieli   **L400–765,000**

Riva degli Schiavoni 4196, 30122; ☎ *522-6480, FAX 520-0208.*
Single L400,000. Double L620–765,000.
The 15th-century palace of Doge Dandolo is the centerpiece of this complex of buildings that now includes 230 rooms of varying vintage, decor and view, but all definitely of the deluxe class offered by the Ciga chain. The Danieli, next to the official doge's palace and on the Grand Canal, has a romantic pedigree that lists George Sand, Dickens and Wagner among its guests. The marble court and ogee arches, the immense fireplace, ornate ceiling and Venetian glass chandelier of the Gothic

palazzo compose an unforgettable hotel lobby. There's a roof terrace restaurant, and Ciga boat service to the Lido.

Bauer Grunwald   **L360–650,000 CP**   ★ ★ ★ ★ ★

Campo San Moise 1459, 30124; ☎ *520-7022, FAX 520-7550.*
Single L360–400,000 CP. Double L500–650,000 CP.

A few steps from San Marco and looking over the Grand Canal, the Bauer shows two distinct faces—its Gothic palace next to the canal and its ultra modern facade on the campo. The interior between them harmonizes their differences with porphyry marble floors and traditional decor. The 200 rooms vary according to the wing they're in, but all are comfortable. Terrace restaurant on canal and lounge with rooftop views. Efficient service.

Excelsior Lido   **L375–685,000**   ★ ★ ★ ★ ★

Lungomare Marconi 41, 30126 Venezia Lido; ☎ *526-0201, FAX 526-7276. Closed Nov.–Apr. 1.*
Single L375,000. Double L600–685,000.

Near the casino and right on the beach is the rambling neo-Byzantine style Ciga hotel. Completely modernized, the hotel offers the most luxury at this resort and, in fact, did much to make the Lido world famous. A terrace of gardens and swimming pool leads down to the beach, lined with its unending rows of cabanas. The 230 rooms are large, most with sea views. Restaurants, lounges with music. Tennis. Boat service to Ciga hotels in Venice. For those who want the beach emphasized rather than Venetian sightseeing.

Des Bains   **L420–500,000 CP**   ❀ ★ ★ ★ ★

Lungamare Marconi 17, 30126 Venezia Lido; ☎ *526-5921, FAX 526-0113. Closed Nov.–Apr. 1.*
Single L420,000 CP. Double L500,000 CP.

This turn-of-the-century hotel inspired Thomas Mann's *Death in Venice* and became the setting for Visconti's film of the novel. With its own private park set across the road from its beach, the hotel still offers the art deco style that enchanted its first guests, but its 204 rooms have modernized comforts. Terrace restaurant, lounge. Large pool, sauna, tennis. Boat service to Venice, but clearly this relaxing location is not the most ideal for those with limited sightseeing time. A Ciga hotel.

Expensive

Londra Palace   **L350–425,000 CP**   ★ ★ ★ ★

Riva degli Schiavoni 4171, 30122; ☎ *520-0533, FAX 522-5032.*
Single L350,000 CP. Double L425,000 CP.

This handsome hotel overlooking the Grand Canal has considerable charm and good service for its rates (only high season weekends are above the expensive category). Although the non-"superior" rooms can be smallish, all 69 are elaborately decorated with antiques—a few overly so—some with Turkish balloon-style canopies, others with Rococo headboards, one even with a wood panelled bath. About half the rooms have balconies overlooking the canal, the others have enchanting views over roof tops. For a greater splurge, consider the rooftop suite with windows on three sides. Respected restaurant, handsome bar.

Saturnia International | **L385–520,000 CP** |

Largo Marzo XXII 2398, 30124; ☎ *520-8377, FAX 520-7131.*
Single L385,000 CP. Double L450–520,000 CP.

Just outside P. San Marco, but not on the canal, is this intensely Gothic hotel, a large part of which belonged to a doge in the 14th-century. Today the lobby has an ornamented ceiling, the bar is panelled, and there are many architectural details adding to the period ambience. The 95 pleasant rooms can be quite ample, especially the "superiors." Well-known restaurant with summer garden.

Gabrielli Sandwirth | **L350–430,000 CP** |

Riva degli Schiavoni 4110, 30122; ☎ *523-1580, FAX 520-9455.*
Single L350,000 CP. Double L400–450,000 CP.

Another complex built around an original Gothic palazzo. Some of the 110 traditional, somewhat small rooms have canal views and there is a lovely roof garden. The older buildings are full of old fashioned ambience, from beamed ceilings to chandeliers. Restaurant. Bar. Closed mid-Nov.-Feb.

Metropole | **L410–525,000 CP** |

Riva degli Schiavoni 4149, 30122; ☎ *520-5044, FAX 522-3679.*
Single/double L410–525,000 CP.

Right on the Grand Canal, this smart first-class hotel has pleasant service and 64 comfortable rooms, most with canal views (especially over the small *rii*). Restaurant, panelled bar with views of quay.

Moderate

La Fenice et des Artistes | **L195–310,000 CP** |

Campiello della Fenice 1936, 30124; ☎ *523-2333, FAX 520-3721.*
Single L195,000 CP. Double L270–310,000 CP.

This intriguing hotel is on a favorite square behind the Teatro Fenice. Famous for the many performers who stay here, the hotel adds its own attractive touches to the 67 ample rooms (fee for a/c) eclectically decorated with antiques and ranging in style from the rustic (viga ceilings) and Victorian to art deco. There are a favored few with terraces and views of courtyards or *rii*. Old-fashioned sitting rooms and garden. Breakfast bar. Famous restaurant. The San Marco vaporetto stop is closest.

Pensione Accademia | **L150–235,000 CP** |

Fondamenta Maravegie 1058 in Dorsoduro, 30123; ☎ *523-7846, FAX 523-9152.*
Single L150,000 CP. Double L215–235,000 CP.

Most of the 29 large, bright rooms have been renovated recently and upgraded with classy bathrooms (pricier); others are plain, but the ambience more than makes up for it. Formerly the 16th-century Villa Marvegie, the Accademia sits on a tiny promontory where the Rio San Trovaso approaches the Grand Canal. Passing through its iron gates is like entering a private world of lovely gardens and grand salons decorated with 19th-century furnishings. The drawback is its deserved popularity as a *pensione* (only breakfast required, though). Reserve months in advance. Located on the first canal west of the Galleria Accademia, not far from the vaporetto stop.

Flora | **L195–250,000** |

Larga XXII Marzo 2283a, 30124; ☎ *520-5844, FAX 522-8217.*
Single L195,000. Double L250,000.

Overlooking a garden and surrounding one of its own, this hotel offers some chance for tranquility just a few steps from P. San Marco. There's a tiny red velvet sitting room and 44 units (fee for a/c), some too small and the quietest with garden views. Breakfast bar.

Do Pozzi L185–235,000 CP ❀★★

Larga XXII Marzo 2373, 30124; ☎ 520-7855, FAX 522-9413.
Single L185,000 CP. Double L235,000 CP.

Near San Marco, but tucked away from its crowds, this quaint hotel surrounds a pleasant cortile, filled with plants and chairs for relaxing. The 29 rooms are smartly maintained, if small (fee for a/c). Those overlooking cortile preferred. Decent restaurant.

Pausania L190–275,000 CP ❀★★

Dorsoduro 2824, 30123; ☎ 522-2083.
Single/double L190–275,000 CP.

Just down the canal of Campo San Barnabo (near Ca'Rezzonico), this 14th-century palazzo has been handsomely modernized. The old stone courtyard remains, as do the facade columns now seen, quite strikingly, through the plate glass window of the sitting room. The 24 rooms are ample, comfortable and quiet. Breakfast bar. Garden.

San Stefano L170–230,000 CP ★★

Campo Morosini 2957, 30124; ☎ 520-0166, FAX 522-4460.
Single L170,000 CP. Double L230,000 CP.

This completely modernized hotel offers breakfast overlooking one of Venice's favorite piazzas as well as 11 small, brocade-decorated rooms (the quietest are on the rear courtyard; fee for a/c). Near the Accademia bridge, on the San Marco side, the location couldn't be more convenient.

Inexpensive

Agli Alboretti L135–200,000 CP √★

Rio Terra Marco Foscarini 884 in Dorsoduro, 30123; ☎ 523-0058, FAX 521-0158.
Single L135,000 CP. Double L200,000 CP.

This cozy inn has 19 rooms (fee for a/c) that can be quite small, with bathrooms so compact that A.J.P. Taylor wrote he could wash only one side, but his right side was the cleanest ever. Yet Taylor stayed here a long time, and with reason. Despite all, the rooms are comfortable and carpeted, the location near the Accademia couldn't be better, and there's a fine garden. Restaurant.

La Calcina L110–165,000 CP ★

Zattere 780 in Dorsoduro, 30123; ☎ 520-6466, FAX 522-7045.
Single L110,000 CP. Double L165,000 CP.

La Calcina is fine if you get a room with the view, once enjoyed by John Ruskin, over the Guidecca Canal. The 37 rooms are relatively spacious (no a/c; some w/o private bath). From P. Roma, the Zattere stop of the #82 vaporetto is most convenient.

Da Cici   **L85–115,000**   √

Fondamenta Ca' Bala 222 in Dorsoduro, 30123; ☎ *523-5404, FAX 522-2271. Closed Nov.–Feb. 1.*

Single L85,000. Double L95–115,000.

In a tranquil section near the Salute church, this plain but clean pensione offers you a tiny garden, views over a small rio and 50 rooms (no a/c; some w/o private bath). When Ezra Pound lived around the corner, the famous stayed here when they came to visit. Breakfast room. A good buy.

Where to Eat

It's often said that you can't eat well in touristy Venice. This is simply untrue—never have we had such tender clams, delicious *zuppa di pesce*, or such arrays of seafood in the *antipasti di pesce*. Such food is never inexpensive and in Venice, at its most famous restaurants, it is very expensive indeed. But there are trattoria with good calamari fritti, *risotto nero alle seppie* (with cuttlefish and its ink), and *fegato alla Veneziano* (if you want liver with onions). And the tiny osterie and wine bars have decent food at modest prices.

The Famous

The best known restaurants of Venice are loved as much for their ambience as for their food, which tends toward the international.

Harry's Bar   **$$$**   ★★★★

Calle Vallaresso 1323; ☎ *528-5777, FAX 520-8823.*

Closed Mon.; reservation recommended; L135–200,000.

No place could be more famous than this, the original Harry's Bar. Made famous by Ernest Hemingway, it now seems popular with everyone despite its extraordinary prices. (There are set-priced menus, however, that are merely expensive). While you can just visit the bustling bar (see below) the food has a reputation, too, from the carpaccio (said to be invented here) and risotto nero (L53,000) to the unforgettable fegato veneziana (L74,000) and desserts. The service is impeccable. Portions are as large as the prices. Near the San Marco vaporetto stop.

Do Leoni   **$$$**   ★★★

Londra Hotel; ☎ *520-0533.*

Closed Tues. dinner in winter; reservation recommended. Meals L85–125,000.

Dining here is on a terrace overlooking the Grand Canal. The former Les Deux Lions, has changed its chef, its name and cuisine (now less French, instead more traditional Venetian seafood), but not its quality and elegant ambience.

Locanda Cipriani   **$$$**   ★★★★

Torcello island; ☎ *730-150, FAX 735-433.*

Closed Tues. and Nov.–mid-Mar.; reservation recommended. Fixed-price L70,000. À la carte L85–135,000.

Harry's also owns this country inn with its lovely garden dining and fine risotto and gnocchi, delicate veal and fresh crayfish. A boat from in front of Hotel Danieli takes you to the Locanda at noon and brings you back around 3 p.m., enough time to dine leisurely and to see the church mosaics, too, but the Torcello ferry not only gives you more time, it's much cheaper.

Antico Martini $$$ ★★★

Campo San Fantin 1983; ☎ *522-4121, FAX 528-9857.*
Closed for lunch Nov.–Mar.; reservations advised. Meals L75–140,000.
The classic service here and the elegance of the chandeliered dining room are perfect complements to the crayfish sautée appetizer and Chateaubriand and more traditional risotto and involtini of salmon. Located on the attractive piazza to the side of the Teatro Fenice, Martini has less formal terrace tables in the summer.

Venetian Seafood

Al Covo $$–$$$ ★★★

Campiello delle Pescaria 3968 Castello; ☎ *522-3812.*
Closed Wed., Thurs., Christmas season, part of Aug. Fixed-price lunch L45,000. À la carte L85–135,000.
You eat extremely well at this restaurant, found just off the Riva di Schiavoni, where Texan Diane Rankin and her Italian chef husband, Cesare Beneli, have wedded their considerable talents. The ambience is relaxed, the service, simpatico, and the seafood is as fresh as any in Venice. The menu depends on what the market provides for the day, but includes the traditional chef's tour de force, the antipasto di pesce, as well as pasta with scampi and grilled fish. Desserts (carrot cake) are clearly in American hands here.

Corte Sconta $$–$$$ ★★★

Calle Pestrin 3886 in Castello; ☎ *522-7024.*
Closed Sun., Mon., Jan., mid July–mid Aug. Fixed-price meal L70,000. A la carte L45–85,000.
The best way to enjoy the better restaurants specializing in Venetian seafood is to let them serve you the antipasto di pesce (always expensive) followed by just a pasta or grilled fish. This informal restaurant, located on a tiny street just off the Riva degli Schiavoni, and northeast of Campo Baniera e Moro, is a favorite spot for such a meal. If the weather is good, take a table under the arbor in the courtyard and let the enthusiasm of the owner (English spoken) help you plan your meal, for here there's no written menu, only the catch of the day. The antipasto di pesce always includes some of the house delicacies, like the traditional baccala mantecato (incredibly good), as well as the tiniest and sweetest clams in lemon and oil, a morsel of delicate spider crab or other crustacean, a variety of marinated dishes, from shrimp with herbs to octopus with roe. You can follow this feast with the fish for the day, maybe the *triglie*, or red mullet, in lemon sauce and whole peppercorns, the tenderest calamari fritti, or just about the best spaghetti alle vongole you can imagine.

Osteria da Fiore $$$ ★★★★

Calle del Scaleter 2202A in San Polo; ☎ *721-308, FAX 721-343.*
Closed Sun., Mon., Aug. & Christmas season; reservation recommended. Meals L70–110,000.
Difficult to find (on an extension of Calle Bernardo that leads off of the n.e. corner of Campo San Polo), but since one critic proclaimed Da Fiore one of the best restaurants in the world, travelers have been tracking it down. The seafood is fresh and outstanding, like all the restaurants in this section; the delicacies may include sea-

Venice

Venice

food salad and mussel soup, soft shell crabs and baked turbot wrapped in a radicchio leaf. Desserts are excellent, service a bit disorganized.

Hosteria Da Franz   **$$–$$$**   ★★★

Fondamenta San Giuseppe, also called San Isepo, 754 in Castello; ☎ *522-0861.*
Closed Tues. and Jan. Meals L60–90,000.

Yet another wonderful seafood restaurant, this one is located just a five-minute walk from the Giardini stop on vaporetto #1. Again, there's no menu, but English is spoken, and the fish and crustacea are very fresh. The antipasto may bring marinated gamberoni with polenta along with an assortment that often includes some crayfish. The pasta can be unusual and good—spaghetti with shrimp, peperoncino flakes and bits of tomato or a pasticcio of fish. In good weather, you dine outdoors next to a tiny canal (bring insect repellant).

Less Costly Seafood

Madonna   **$–$$**   ★★

Calle Madonna 594 in San Polo; ☎ *522-3824, FAX 521-0167.*
Closed Wed., end Dec.-Feb. 1; and early Aug. Meals L35–60,000.

One of the best buys in Venice. Located near the Rialto bridge market, this trattoria has a lively ambience and a simple meal of mussels or zuppa di pesce with salad is completely satisfying; the addition of a filet of poached salmon or some fried shrimp will raise the price but still within moderate range. But if you're tempted by the display of spider crabs…

Da Remegio   **$$**   ★★

Salizzada dei Greci 3416, Castello; reserve at ☎ *523-0089.*
Closed Mon. dinner, Tues., Jan., mid July-mid Aug. Meals L40–60,000.

Near the Scuola San Giorgio, this small trattoria has a lot of local ambience and all-round good seafood.

A Meat Fix

Ai Gondolieri   **$$–$$$**   ★★★

San Vio 366, Dorsoduro; ☎ *528-6396.*
Closed Tues.& late July–early Aug. L50–80,000.

Set off to the right just past Campo San Lio, as you walk towards the Guggenheim museum is this small, handsome restaurant where seafood is shunned for soups of mushrooms and vegetables and cuts of beef, veal, rabbit and lamb—and, of course, fegato alla veneziana. The kitchen and service are both a bit slow.

Trattorias

The trattorias offer both Venetian seafood as well as meat dishes.

Osterial al Milion   **$–$$**   ★★

Corte al Milion 5841; ☎ *522-9302.*
Closed Wed. L40–55,000.

This cozy trattoria is tucked away in a piazzetta just off S. Giovanni Crisostomo, the first right above the Rialto bridge on your way to Ca d'Oro. At the entrance is an old wine bar with snacks (like crab legs); the trattoria serves good Venetian food, especially recommended is the ample portion of coda di rospa in black peppercorn sauce.

Al Bacareto $ ★ ★

Calle delle Boteghe, San Samuele 3447; 528-9336.
Closed Sat. dinner, Sun. Meals L30–45,000.
A local favorite and not far from the Accademia bridge, this lace-curtained trattoria
with a few tables spilling over the sidewalk near Salizzada San Samuel serves terrific
risotto (order the daily special) and pastas (try the tagliarini in fish sauce). Add an
insalata verde (better than the mixta) and the good, but inexpensive house wine and
you, too, will become a devotee.

Antica Locanda Montin $–$$ ★

Fondamenta di Borgo 1147, Dorsodoro, ☎ 522-7151.
Closed Tues. night and Wed. Meals L40–60,000.
A romantic approach through the covered alley of Calle Eremite, off the main drag
of Toletta, between the Accademia and Campo San Barnaba, brings you to the
Locanda. In the summer you sit under the arbor of its large courtyard and choose
from acceptable entrees of grilled meat and fish, and start with a tasty peporanata (a
caponata of red pepper) or good spaghetti Adriatic, with seafood.

Taverna San Trovaso. $ ★

Fondamenta Priuli 1018 in Dorsoduro; ☎ 520-3703
Closed Mon. Meals L25–45,000.
Closer to the Accademia and next to the Rio San Trovaso is this neighborhood trattoria with its cozy first-floor dining room of wood panelling and brick vaults. The
very decent food ranges from *cotoletta* and *spezzatina* (stew), to seafood and pizza,
and the prices couldn't be more modest.

Et cetera

There are lots of ways to eat just one course, or to dine more lightly. The usual pizza
options are here, of course, including the Taverna San Trovaso above and the more expensive al fresco dining by the Giudecca Canal provided by **Alle Zattere** *(Zattere 795,
next to the Gesuati church; closed Tues.)*. The fashionable **Al Teatro** *(Campo San Fantin
1917; closed Mon.)* serves pizza as well as tasty soups and pasta at its favored location
near the Teatro Fenice. And Harry's Bar has a more modest (but still pricey) alternative
in **Harry's Dolci** *(Fondamenta San Biagio, Giudecca Island; ☎ 522-4844; closed Tues.,
except July–Sept., and Nov.–Apr.)*, just off the vaporetto at Sant'Eufemia. While you can
come just for dessert, there are Harry's gnocchi and carpaccio, too, as well as a fixed-price
meal (L70,000). And, then, there are the vini.

Vini

Venice has its own way of eating simply and cheaply. Throughout the city, you'll find
pubs tucked away behind "*vini*" signs. These rustic wine bars, locally called *bacari*, have
no menus, but the food is usually displayed on the counter. Just point to the plate of
grilled eggplant or sandwiches, or ask for the day's pasta or *risotto*. Everything will be
served at the table you choose (if you don't stand) along with your glass of wine. Once
you've found a few, you'll keep spotting them as you walk around; just follow the crowds
for an early lunch or snack before dinner *(around 12:30 there's still plenty of food; many
bacari close 1–5 p.m. and again at 8 p.m.)*. The most traditional *bacari* are like Spanish
tapa bars and serve only appetizers (called *cicchetti*) and sandwiches, like the well-known

Cantina Do Spade *(in the Do Spade arcade, off Ruga Rialto, south of the market; closed Sun.; Aug.).* Others have more ample luncheon fare, such as the respected **Ca d'Oro** *(also called "La Vedova"; Calle del Pistor 3910 near Ca d'Oro stop; closed Sun. morning, Thurs.),* found by turning right at Strada Nuova 3946. Convenient to San Marco is **Vino Vino** *(Ponte della Veste 2007; food served noon–2:30 p.m., 7–11 p.m., closed Tues.);* just off Larga XXII Marza on the way to the Teatro Fenice, has a good selection of wines by the glass, lots of *cicchetti*, and very good pasta and one-course meals.

Picnics and Gelati

If you shop at the market near the Rialto, or take out food from **Pastificio & Fino** *(Campo S. Barnaba near Ca Rezzonica),* or a *panino* from a caffè, you can enjoy it along a quiet quay like the Zattere, or sitting on a bench of the Giardinetti Reali *(San Marco vaporetto stop)* or the Giardini Pubblici (Giardini stop, *vaporetto* 1). If you're going to the Lido, the shops on the Grand Via can supply you before you take a bus or taxi to the beach. Two comfortable spots to sit and enjoy an ice cream are the **Paolin**, with elaborate concoctions to work your way through while sitting on the Campo Morosini and **Nico** *(Zattere 922; closed Tues.)* right on the quay and famous for its chocolate hazelnut *(gianduia)* ice cream.

Caffè/Bars

The three famous caffès of the Piazza San Marco have already been mentioned. At least once during your visit, you should splurge on a ring side seat to sip your coffee. In the evening you can savor the orchestral accompaniment to a *Venetian aperitivo* by ordering a Prosecco frizzante (a pleasant bubbly white wine) or a *sprintz*, the Campari and soda combination dating from Austrian rule. **Harry's Bar** *(Calle Vallaresso 1323)* has been inventing its own drinks and exporting them around the world, but they say that no combination of peach juice and champagne is as good as the *Bellini* prepared right here—nor more expensive, perhaps. For a quieter, yet beautifully Venetian spot, try the formal lobby bar at the **Daneli**.

Directory

Telephone Code 041   **Postal Code 30124**

Airport

Marco Polo airport *(☎ 260-9260),* 9 km, 5-1/2 mi. north. The way to reach S. Marco is on a Cooperativa S. Marco motoscafo, or express boat (buy ticket inside terminal), or costlier water taxi. Cheaper is the ATVO bus to P. Roma.

Albergo Diurno

Near San Marco, behind Ascensione post office.

American Express

S. Moise 1471, west of P. San Marco *(☎ 520-0844).*

Books in English

Il Libraio, off San Barnabo on *Fondamenta Gheradini 2835 A* (Dorsoduro).

Bus

P. Roma, ACTV terminal to Brenta villas, Padua, Treviso; ATVO for airport.

Car Rentals

P. Roma and airport, for terra firma travel: **Avis** (☎ *523-7377*), **International** (☎ *520-6565*), and others.

Consuls

U.S., and Canada, none; Britain, near Accademia, *Dorsodoro 1051* (☎ *522-7207*).

Emergencies

Dial 113 (police), ☎ *523-0000* (medical).

Ferries/Vaporetti

ACTV (☎ *528-7886*), main office P. Roma with free route map of *vaporetti* and *motoscafi* (also available at tourist office). Buy tickets at landings. Major *vaporetti* lines have 24-hour service, but run only hourly midnight to dawn.

Gondolas

Stations at San Marco (Vallaresso), Riva degli Schiavoni, etc.; base charge for up to five riders for 50-minute ride, official rates are seldom honored. Set price first.

Groceries

Market, south bank of Rialto bridge; and in the neighborhoods, like Dorsoduro between Accademia and Guggenheim Collection, or Strada Nova, near Ca d'Oro.

Parking

In season, the *P. Roma* outdoor public lot is always full. Next to it is an indoor garage (twice the day rate) often with available space in early morning. Cheaper and with more space are outlying lots like *Tronchetto* (off Mestre-Venice road), with vaporetto service into Venice.

Police

Questura, ☎ *520-3222*.

Porters

Portabagagli stands at train station, P. Roma, major squares of city, etc. Official rate includes two bags, not vaporetto fare, but establish fee in advance.

Post Office

Ascensione, just through west arcade P. San Marco, with telegraph service.

Shopping

North and west of P. San Marco for antiques and Italian designer boutiques. Traditional lace and glass (see islands), found here, too, as well as in Dorsoduro.

Taxi

Taxi acquei, or motorboat taxis found at landings along quays, like Ferrovia, P. Roma, San Marco, Rialto, etc., or call ☎ *523-2326*. **Car taxis** at P. Roma. For both, establish fare in advance.

Telephone

Telcom, P. Roma (8 a.m.–9:30 p.m.); in train station. (open 24 hours); and next to post office near San Marco (Mon.–Sat. 8 a.m.–8 p.m.).

Tourist Office

APT, *Palazetto Selva*, near P. San Marco vaporetto stop. (☎ *522-6356;* Tues.–Sun. 9:30 a.m.–12:30 p.m., 2–5 p.m.). Kiosks at ferrovia and bus station (mostly hotel reservations; fee), and on Mestre road at Marghera (seasonal).

Tours

CIT Viaggi, *San Marco 48/50* (☎ *528-5480);* **Official Guides** *(☎ 709-038).*

Train

Ferrovia Santa Lucia (☎ 715-555), one stop from P. Roma on Grand Canal; vaporetti and water taxi service. **Note:** There are two Venice stazioni: you want "Santa Lucia," not industrial "Mestre-Venezia."

Padua

Key to Padua

Sights

Giotto's greatest frescoes at the Scrovegni Chapel, the Basilica of S. Anthony, and works by Donatello and Mantegna.

Excursions

Euganean Hills, 15 km, 9 mi. southwest, with their old monasteries, villas, and mud bath spas set amid the dramatic hills; *Brent Riviera*, from Padua to Venice by boat (see "Venice"; contact CIT).

Accommodations

Nothing deluxe, but comfortable first class hotels and more modest ones available.

Eating Out

The local cuisine is inspired by nearby Venice and Bologna and served in pleasant variety of restaurants.

Getting Around

Except for bicycles, the centro storico is delightfully free of traffic. Buses run the periphery, connecting the major piazzas, but the center is small enough to be walked.

Arriving

Venice is only 35 km, 22 mi. to the east and is connected by trains and buses every half-hour, as well as by the Venice/Mestre airport bus. Verona (80 km, 50 mi.) and other Veneto towns are connected by frequent (nearly every hour) departures of buses and trains. Padua is on the Milan-Venice and Bologna-Venice train lines, and the A-4 and A-15 autostrade.

Special Tips

Many use Padua as a base for visiting Venice. Without a car, this is quite feasible since trains take about half-hour. But Paduan hotels book up, too, especially on weekends, and if you have a car, you may find the long-term garages (at bus and train stations) not only as costly as those in Venice, but just as full.

 Museum Pass A one-for-all pass can be bought at any of the sights requiring fees.

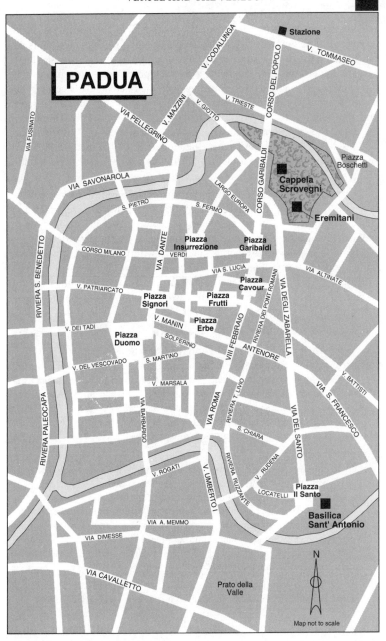

Livy, born in the nearby Euganean Hills, might be the most famous Paduan, but the city's history hardly ended with the fall of ancient Rome. Padua prospered in medieval and Renaissance times, when wealthy merchants and bankers paid for chapels adorned by Giotto and his followers, like Altichiero, by native son Mantegna, and by the genius sculptor Donatello. The busy city attracted the mendicant priest Anthony, who died here and whose supposed miraculous interventions on behalf of the populace led to his sanctification and the building of his wondrous basilica. Padua's university, founded in 1222 and the second oldest in Italy, not only boasted Petrarch, Copernicus, and Galileo as lecturers, it invented the modern scientific method of experimentation and inspired its student, William Harvey, to postulate his theories about the heart and blood circulation.

Today, Padua again prospers from the north's agribusiness. Much of Padua was destroyed in WW II, including Mantegna's chapel in the Eremitani, considered by some the greatest artistic loss of the war. Though much of the rebuilt city of 230,000 is industrial or simply drab, the historic center is pleasant, if not Italy's most picturesque. Even without cars, the streets bustle with students on their bicycles and the cafes around Piazza Cavour and Piazza delle Erbe buzz with conversation. An occasional canal adds its charm as you walk between the major sights, from the Eremitani complex in the north with Giotto's Scrovegni frescoes to the church of "Il Santo," south.

What to See and Do
Piazza Eremitani ★★★

Tucked into the northern wall of old Padua, just east of the main street, Corso Garibaldi, is this complex of important buildings, built around the ancient Roman **Arena** (A.D. 6) now a public garden, and the 13th-century church of the Eremitani. *Except for the Eremitani church, all the following sights are entered through the complex of the Museo Civico Eremitani (Tues.–Sun. 9 a.m.–7 p.m., till 5:30 Oct.–Mar. 31) where one fee (L10,000) is paid for the museum and the Scrovegni Chapel.*

Cappella Scrovegni   ★★

In 1300 Enrico Scrovegni purchased the land around the ancient amphitheater for the construction of his palazzo. A few years later he built a family chapel here, known now as the **Arena Chapel**, in atonement for his father's usury, which of course resulted in the family fortune. Giotto was commissioned to do the ★★★-frescoes which would become so seminal in the development of Renaissance painting. Beginning with the Annunciation above the altar, scenes from the *Life of the Virgin* continue to the right, on the upper wall and wrap around the chapel. Below them are scenes from the *Life of Christ*. Interrupting them, above the door, is the *Last Judgment*.

These Biblical stories rendered into human narratives are considered Giotto's masterpieces of early realism, from the emotion captured in *Joaquin Expelled from the Temple*, (#1, upper right) and the anguish of the Deposition, (#3, lower left), to the monumental forms in *Joaquin Dreams*, (#5, upper right) that fill real space. Binoculars help to see the intensity of Christ's gaze in *Kiss of Judas*, (#3, lower right), the tenderness of *Joaquin and Anna's Embrace*, (#6, upper right). In the apse are frescoes by Giotto's followers and ★ statues of the Virgin and two saints by that other Tuscan genius, G. Pisano. **Note**: During peak tourism, visits to the chapel may be limited to 20 minutes. In summer, check before buying your ticket.

Museo Eremitani

Quite a number of collections are housed here in the modernized convent of the Eremitani. Among them is the **Museo Archeologico**, with its extensive collection of antiquities; another is the **Collezione Emo Capodilista**, with Venetian and Flemish paintings, mostly from the schools rather than the brushes of the famous, with the notable exception of some Tintoretto portraits; and yet a third, the **Museo Civico**, its paintings for years housed next to the Basilica Sant'Antonio, but now transferred here. The ★ 14th-century collection, includes Giotto's ★ crucifix designed for the Scrovegni sacristy, and later Paduan and Venetian Renaissance works that count among them Giovanni Bellini's ★ *Portrait of a Young Senator*, and two small paintings attributed to Giorgione. Closed noon–3:30 p.m.

Church of Eremitani   ★

Even if much was lost in the WW II bombing, the rebuilt church *(closed noon-3:30)* definitely is worth a visit. Enough remains of Mantegna's fresco cycle in the ★ Ovetari Chapel (last chapel, right transept; 1448) to make you mourn the loss of the rest. On the left wall, are fragments of *Martiro San Giacomo;* behind the altar, the *Assumption*; and best preserved on the right, the ★ *Martyrdom of S. Cristofo*, with its bold composition, illusionistic space, and beautiful classical architectural details. A machine (well worth the small fee) pictures the frescoes before their destruction. In the apse are Giottoesque frescoes.

University and Central Piazzas ★

In the center of the old city, Corso Garibaldi becomes Via Febbraio VIII, intersected by Via Manin from the west, Via San Francesco from the east. Just above the intersection is the Piazza Cavour with its cafes and, across the street, the neo-classical **Caffe Pedrocchi** (1831). This unbelievably elegant, 19th-century gathering spot for scholars was the setting for a student uprising against the Austrians, an important event in the Risorgimento. Still nearby is the headquarters of the University, the **Palazzo Bo** (Febbraio VIII 2), where you can visit the 16th-century courtyards frescoed with the old coats-of-arms of the student body. If renovations are completed, visit the ★ Theater of Anatomy (1594), the first in Europe where students, like William Harvey in 1602, observed autopsies. Up Via Manin you come to the **Palazzo della Ragione** *(1219)*, its hipped-roof making it look most like a train station. While formerly the law courts, the palazzo stands amid the markets of the **Piazza delle Erbe** and **Piazza deile Frutti**, with stalls flowing between them in its ground floor loggia. Farther west (off P. Frutti) are the quaint **Piazza Signori** with Italy's oldest astronomical clock tower (1344), then the small **Piazza Capitano**, and still west, the **Piazza Duomo**.

Piazza del Santo ★★

Continuing south, but shifting east of the main street where it picks up traffic and following the more picturesque Riviera Ruzzante, you arrive at the busy square holding the ★★**Basilica Sant'Antonio** *(6:30 a.m.–7:45 p.m., in winter only till 7 p.m.)*, known best as "Il Santo." Construction began in 1231 over the tomb of this most beloved of saints, and the church that grew is a fantastic blend of Romanesque and Byzantine, with a considerable dash of Venetian opulence. From the exterior, with its many domes and minarets, to the beautiful interior with the saint's lavish ★tomb (left aisle, center), the church is flocked by masses of pilgrims. As you walk among this intensely religious scene, note, if you can, the ★high altar (1445), sculpted by Donatello, the rococo treasury (rear of apse), and the ★Chapel of S. Felix (right aisle, center), with its frescoes, especially the magnificent ★*Crucifixion* (1372), by Giotto's most inspired follower, Altichiero.

Sharing the piazza with the church are two notable sights: Donatello's ★★*Gattemelata* (1447), his masterful sculpture of one of Venice's condottiere, the first bronze equestrian statue since antiquity. And the ★**Oratorio di San Giorgio** *(right of church entrance; 9 a.m.–12:30 p.m., 2:30–7 p.m. summer, 4:30 p.m. winter; L3000)*, frescoed in the gloriously warm colors of Altichiero (note the ★*Crucifixion*, and ★*Coronation*), and other Giotto followers (begun 1377). The same ticket gains entrance upstairs at the **Scuola del Santo**, where a young Titian contributed three scenes (#1, #12, #13) to the frescoes on the *Life of St. Anthony* (1511), his only works in this medium.

Where to Stay

Even off season, the few hotels in Padua's centro storico can be booked on weekends, when many combine a trip to the Saturday market in the Prato della Valle (just south of St. Anthony's) with a pilgrimage to Il Santo. Unless otherwise specified, hotels are air-conditioned.

Moderate

Majestic Toscanella   **L170–260,000 CP**   √★★★

P. dell'Arco 2, 35122; ☎ *663-244, FAX 876-0025.*
Single L170,000 CP. Double L195–260,000 CP.
In the best location on a traffic-free piazzetta just below the Piazza delle Erbe, this small, charming hotel offers 38 quiet and well-decorated rooms. Good service and ample breakfast. Restaurant and lounge. Garage parking (fee). A good buy.

Plaza   **L175–255,000 CP**   ★★★

Corso Milano 40, 35139; ☎ *656-822, FAX 661-117.*
Single L175,000 CP. Double L240–255,000 CP.
Just a few blocks from the centro storico, but unfortunately in the dreary modern section. The Plaza is a business hotel, efficient but tasteful, and all the services you would expect to go with its 140 modern rooms. Restaurant. Bar. Garage.

Donatello   **L135–210,000**   ★★

Piazza del Santo, 35123; ☎ *875-0634, FAX 875-0829. Closed mid-Dec.–mid-Jan.*
Single L135,000. Double L210,000.
Overlooking the busy piazza, this small commercial hotel just bustles with its terrace restaurant and bar. 42 decent rooms; some with views of Il Santo. Garage (fee).

Inexpensive

Leon Bianco   **L125–155,000**   ★★

P. Pedrocchi 12, 35122; ☎ *875-0814, FAX 865-6184.*
Single L125,000. Double L155,000.

Owned by the same family as the Majestic, this small, smartly modern hotel is
located in the traffic-free area just behind the famous Caffè Pedrocchi. The 22 comfortable rooms have been renovated. Rooftop breakfast room in good weather.

Albergo San Antonio di Padua   **L80–100,000**   ★

San Fermo 118, 34137; ☎ *875-1393, FAX 875-2508.*
Single L80,000. Double L100,000.

Just inside the old wall on the north side of town near V. Dante, this nicely maintained hotel offers 34 plain (no a/c) rooms, most with private baths. Breakfast
room. Closed early Jan.

Where to Eat

Whether you prefer the Adriatic specialties and the risotti from Venice or the buttery
density of Emilian pastas, Paduan restaurants will satisfy you with both. And if you want
to experiment a bit with wines, those from the nearby Colli Euganei, especially the rosso,
are pleasant.

Antico Brolo   **$$–$$$**   ★★★★

Corso Milano 22; 656-088, FAX 656-088.
Closed Mon. and Aug. Fixed-price lunch L40–60,000. A la carte L50–85,000.

Varied and innovative cuisine may be found at this comfortable restaurant near the
Teatro Verdi. You can enjoy the homemade pastas and desserts here along with a
changing assortment of dishes such as risotto with melon and squash flowers,
stuffed endive, and sweet and sour pork, as well as some seafood. At lunch, fixed-
price options are surprisingly moderate in price.

Enoteca Angelo Rasi   **$–$$**   ★★★

Riviera Paleocapa 7; 871-9797.
Meals L40–55,000; closed Sun., Aug.

Along the canal on the western edge of the old city, this respected wine shop also
has a fine reputation for the food to accompany it. The menu changes almost daily
with both traditional and innovative offerings. In good weather there's a terrace to
further enhance the pleasure of dining here.

Il Dotto   **$–$$**   ★★

V. Squarcione 23; ☎ *875-1490.*
*Closed Sun. night, Mon., part of Aug. Fixed-price lunch L35,000. A la carte L40–
55,000.*

Conveniently located in the medieval center is this pleasingly old-fashioned restaurant, found just south of Piazza Erbe. You can enjoy the rather Emilian style cuisine
of ravioli with pumpkin and walnuts, and deliciously sweet scampi in curried apple
vinegar. The service is attentive, and there is a prezzo fisso meal that is quite a bargain considering the elegant selections offered.

Padua

Snacks

Snacking is an art form in Padua. Starting at 5:30 you can join the Paduans in the passeggiato around the center or pick your spot at one of the cafes—certainly the neoclassical splendor of **Il Pedrocchio** *(closed Mon.)* for a cappuccino, the **Cavour** across from it for pastries, or the earthier cafes on the Piazza dei Frutti, where you can buy your pistachios at a market stand and eat them with an aperitivo at the cafe of your choice. In the **Piazza delle Erbe** shellfish stands suddenly spring up, selling oysters, crab claws, and other delicacies to their stand-up customers. And if all that simply won't do, try a salad or simple pasta at **Brek** *(just off P. VIII Febbraio near Caffe Pedrocchi; closed Sun.)* or shop in the market for a picnic in the gardens of the Arena.

Directory

Telephone Code 049   **Postal Code 35100**

Airport

Allegri airport, V. Soria to the southwest connected by ACAP bus (#6 & #18), with limited domestic and charter flights; Marco Polo airport at Venice, ATP bus to Padua train station.

American Express

V. Risorgimento 20 (☎ 666-135).

Books in English

Feltrinelli, V. San Francesco 14.

Bus

ATP and others, V. Trieste on P. Boschetti just north of P. Eremitani, for Veneto and other cities. Reservations required *(☎ 820-6811);* **ACAP**, ticket offices at stazione and P. Signori; *(☎ 662-055)* for local buses and Euganean Hills.

Car Rentals

At train station, **Avis** *(☎ 664-198)*, **Europcar** *(☎ 36-094)*, and others.

Groceries

Market in piazzas Erbe and Frutti.

Parking

Near major piazzas like Eremitani, Duomo, Prato della Valle.

Police

Questura, foreigners' office, *Riviera Ruzzante 13.*

Post Office

Corso Garibaldi 25.

Shopping

Along the arcaded streets between Largo Europa and P. dell'Erbe, and, for antiques and old prints, V. Cesare Battista.

Swimming Pool

Comunale di Nuoto, south of Prato della Valle, with outdoor pool.

Taxis

Major squares—Stazione, Frutti, etc.

Telephone

> **Telcom**, alley behind Caffe Pedrocchio *(9 a.m.–7 p.m.)*; also, *Corso Garibaldi 31 (8 a.m.–9 p.m.)*.

Tourist Office

> **APT**, at stazione *(☎ 875-2077)*, open 9 a.m.–7:30 p.m. except Sun. 8 a.m.–noon, in summer; and Museo Eremitani *(☎ 875-1153)* closed Mon.

Tours

> *APT*, 3-hour tours of city, check Eremitani office; CIT, for Brenta Riviera, V. Matteotti 12.

Train

> P. Stazione 10-minute walk north of centro storico *(☎ 875-1800)*; ACAP local bus to Corso Garibaldi and P. Santo (#3).

Verona

Key to Verona

Sights

> The ancient Arena, the Scaligeri tombs, the Castelvecchio museum, and the churches with their Titian, Pisanello and Mantegna altarpieces, highlight the charms of this historic city.

Nearby Waters

> Lake Garda is only 40 km, 24 mi. west on A-4.

Festivals and Events

> Summer brings opera in the Arena, Shakespeare in the Roman Theater.

Accommodations

> Good selection, from most deluxe to inexpensive; those in the center book up quickly.

Eating Out

> Most famous for its wines, Verona offers earthy osterias for wine tastings in addition to its highly respected restaurants.

Getting Around

> Though taxis, buses to modern sections, and car rentals are available, the historic center is mostly closed to traffic. Fortunately, it is easily walked.

Arriving

> The ancient crossroads for Milan to Venice and Trieste, and for Germany and Austria south into Italy, Verona lies today at the intersection of those train lines (Milan and Venice in 1.5 hours on fastest train) and autostrade (A-4, 105 km, 65 mi. to Venice). The local airport has domestic and a few European flights.

Verona is a popular destination. Julius Caesar, Theodoric the Goth, and Pepin the Great are only a few of the earliest visitors who favored it. The Veronesi fought over it in prolonged family feuds, so typical of the Middle

Ages as recreated in Shakespeare's *Romeo and Juliet*. Out of the feuding came the della Scala family, or the Scaligeri, who brought about the golden age of Verona under Cangrande I (1308–1329). The beautiful city next to the looping Adige river continued to attract interlopers, Milan's Gian Galeazzo Visconti among them, so it finally asked for protection from La Serenissima and became a Venetian possession for 400 years.

Verona wears its history well. With enough Roman ruins standing to be a fitting treatment to native son Vetruvius (who may have been the town's original planner), Verona is nonetheless an important and lively modern city of almost 300,000. Surrounded by the walls of the Romans, the Visconti, and Venetians, the city gates are simply delightful architecture rather than weighty reminders of battles past. And as if it didn't have a rich enough history, Verona has created some in celebration of Shakespeare's play—Juliet's tomb here, Romeo's house there. But even the Scaligeri smile from their Gothic tombs, and there's a sunniness to the town that emanates from the pink glow of the marble covering everything from palazzi to sidewalks.

What to See and Do

Castelvecchio was built by Scaligeri in 1354.

Except for the Castelvecchio, few of Verona's sights take much time to see, so they are best strung together on walking tours. The only sights not easily walked are the Renaissance fortifications by the architect Sanmicheli, responsible for the impressive gates, such as Porta Nuova (c.1523), that you see when approaching the centro storico.

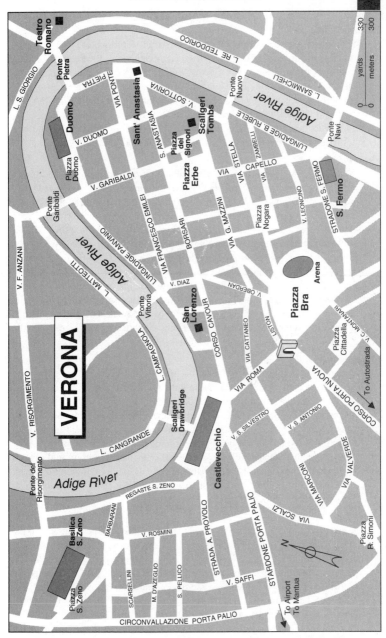

VERONA

Teatro Romano
Ponte Pietra
Duomo
Piazza Duomo
Sant'Anastasia
Scaligeri Tombs
Piazza dei Signori
Piazza Erbe
Ponte Garibaldi
S. Fermo
Piazza Nogara
Arena
Piazza Bra
San Lorenzo
Piazza Cittadella
Scaligeri Drawbridge
Castlevecchio
Basilica S. Zeno
Piazza S. Zeno
Piazza R. Simoni

Adige River

L. RE TEODORICO
Ponte Nuovo
L. SAMMICHELI
Ponte Navi
LUNGADIGE B. RUBELE
VIA PONTE
V. SOTTORIVA
S. ANASTASIA
VIA DUOMO
L.S. GIORGIO
V. DUOMO
V. GARIBALDI
VIA FRANCESCO EMILEI
LUNGADIGE PANVINIO
BORSARI
VIA STELLA
VIA CAPELLO
VIA ZAMBELLI
VIA G. MAZZINI
V. LEONCINO
STRADONE S. FERMO
V. DIAZ
V. OBERDAN
CORSO CAVOUR
VIA CATTANEO
LISTON
VIA ROMA
V.C. MONTANARI
CORSO PORTA NUOVA
To Autostrada
V. F. ANZANI
V. RISORGIMENTO
L. MATTEOTTI
L. CAMPAGNOLA
Ponte Vittoria
L. CANGRANDE
Ponte del Risorgimento
REGASTE S. ZENO
BARBARANI
V. ROSMINI
SCARSELLINI
M. D'AZEGLIO
S. PELLICO
V. SAFFI
STRADA A. PROVOLO
STARDONE PORTA PALIO
V.S. SILVESTRO
V.S. ANTONIO
VIA MARCONI
VIA VALVERDE
VIA SCALZI
To Airport
To Mantua
CIRCONVALLAZIONE PORTA PALIO

yards   330
meters 300
0   0

Walk to Major Sights

Piazza delle Erbe ★

This picturesque market square is shaped by the ancient forum of the city. A great variety of architecture surrounds it, from the much revamped merchant's building (1301) on the south and the frescoed palace on the north (both built by the Scaligeri) to the Baroque Palazzo Maffei (1668) on the west. In the center, amid the umbrella covered vegetable stands, is the Venetian column of the lion of St. Mark and the Madonna of Verona fountain, made from a Roman statue. On the north side, next to the Torre dei Lamberti (begun 1172) walk through the arch "della costa," with its hanging whale's rib, to enter the Piazza dei Signori.

Piazza dei Signori ★★

While just on the opposite side of the buildings of the market square, this piazza couldn't be more tranquil and dignified. In the center stands a statue of Dante. During his exile from Florence, he first found refuge here with the Scaligeri, whose crenellated palazzo fronts the north end of the piazza. In appreciation, Dante extolled Cangrande I in the 17th canto of his *Paradiso*. To the left of the palazzo is the beautiful Renaissance ★**Loggia del Consiglio**, its Venetian influence best seen in the delicate pilasters borrowed from a Bellini painting. Along the right, or west side of the Piazza, two buildings lead into interesting courtyards. The first, near Piazza delle Erbe, is the **Cortile del Mercato Vecchio** inside the Romanesque Palazzo Ragione. Here you discover a fine Gothic staircase under the shadow of the Torre dei Lamberti (elevator access for view). Next, **Sanmicheli's portal** (1530) in the law courts of the Palazzo del Capitano leads to another cortile, this one with the eccentric Porta Bombardiera (1687) and its cannons.

Scaligeri Tombs ★★

Walk out the north end of the Piazza dei Signori, and on the right you'll see the Scaligeri's private chapel, **Santa Maria Antica**. Over the door is the remarkable Gothic *arche*, or ★★tomb of Cangrande I (died 1329), with dogs holding the ladder, or *scale*, that is the family coat of arms, just as their chosen title was "can" or "dog." Atop the tomb is the enchanting equestrian statue (original in Castelvecchio museum) of the first "great dog," smiling somewhat madly at the world. In the cemetery enclosed by fine grillwork are the richer and later tombs of ★Mastino II (or, "Mastiff the second," c. 1351) and, in the rear corner, Cansignorio (begun 1375 by Bonino da Campione). The Romanesque interior of the chapel is touching in its simplicity.

Piazza Bra ★

A short walk along pedestrian Via Mazzini from the Piazza Erbe brings you to the major social center of Verona, the Piazza Bra. Cafes line the wide marble pavement called "Il Liston," and evenings bring the Veronesi enjoying their passeggiata. The piazza is often the first seen by travelers if they enter the centro storico through the old walls at the Corso Porta Nuova and the **Portoni della Bra** (1389), built by the Visconti. The vast open space of this piazza is dominated by the magnificent first-century Roman ★★**Arena** *(8 a.m.–6:30 p.m., till 1 p.m. on performance days; closed Mon.; L6000)*, one of the largest in existence and with a seating capacity of

22,000. The interior is in perfect shape and its top rows provide good views over the city.

Castelvecchio ★★

A five-minute walk west of Piazza Bra on Via Roma brings you to this stronghold of the city, used by every conqueror since it was built by the Scaligeri in 1354 along with its magnificent drawbridge (pedestrian use only; reconstructed after WW II) spanning the Adige river. In 1958 the great Italian architect Carlo Scarpa renovated and adapted the castle for use as a museum for Veronese art from the middle ages to Italian unification. The Mondrian-like details of Scarpa's work, the beauty of the castle and its exhibitions shouldn't be missed, from the 14th-century sculpture on the ground floor to the Venetian paintings of Jacopo and Giovanni Bellini (Room XIX), Veronese and Tintoretto (Room XXIII). *Open 8 a.m.–6:30 p.m.; closed Mon. L5000. Only guide to museum sold at newsstands.*

San Zeno Maggiore ★★

A 10-minute walk from the Castelvecchio, along the river and with fine views of the bridge and castle, this church is one of the few sights that some might want to reach by bus *(#7 from Castelvecchio)* or taxi. This magnificent basilica (not to be confused with S. Zeno's oratorio) is one of Italy's great Romanesque churches. Its ★★ **main facade** includes a fabulous lion porch in the Lombard Emilian style and allegorical scenes on the portal jambs, all notably carved by Niccolo in the 12th century. Just as precocious are the Biblical reliefs on the doors (expanded 1120) that represent the first use of bronze casting in northern Italy since antiquity. Along with these wonders are a lovely wheel of fortune rosette window (12th C.) and a campanile begun in 1045. On the left side of the church is a quaint **cloister** with some Scaligeri tombs. The church **interior** is impressive, even majestic, and full of frescoes from different periods. On the high altar is Mantegna's ★★ *Enthroned Madonna and Child with Saints* (1456), his first important altarpiece and a work that bequeathed illusionism to northern Italian art. The columnettes of the original frame are echoed in the painting, and between them, Mantegna painted a sublime garland of fruit that creates space deep enough to walk into. The predella panels are copies. (Light machine on right.) *The church is closed noon–3 p.m.*

Other Sights

To complete the loop of your tour, note the ancient **Arco di Gavi** next to the Castelvecchio and then follow Corso Cavour back to the Piazza delle Erbe. Along the way pause to enjoy the rich second-story facade of Sanmicheli's Manneristic ★ **Palazzo Bevilacqua** (1532) and the sturdy Romanesque church of **San Lorenzo** found across from it. Then you come to yet another ancient Roman gate, the **Porta dei Borsari**.

North Section Walk

From the Piazza delle Erbe, follow the Corso Anastasia to the largest church in Verona, ★ **Sant'Anastasia** (begun 1290; *closed noon–3 p.m.*) with a well-carved wooden door framed with bas reliefs. To the left of the facade, there is another Veronese Gothic tomb above the convent gate (1320). Just inside the church are two holy water *fonts*, startling for the realism of the hunchback statues supporting them. In the last chapel on the left is Lorenzo Veneziano's *Madonna of the Rosary*, (14th C.), and in the left transept chapel, above the sacristy door, is the reason for your visit—the fairy-tale beauty of Pisanello's ★ ★ *St. George and the Princess*, (circa 1433). Following Via Duomo to the west, if traffic permits, you quickly arrive at the ★ **Duomo** (also known as "Sant'Elena"; *closed noon–3 p.m.*), a combination of Romanesque and Gothic elements. The two Romanesque ★ portals have interesting sculptures, that on the side has a capital of Jonah and the whale; around the lion porch (1139) on the front are knightly scenes with figures that seem like Oriental ivories. The interior holds a Titian, full of color and diagonal movement, in the first chapel left (★ *Assumption*, light machine). Behind the duomo, circle back toward Sant'Anastasia along the river. Across the river you can see **Castel San Pietro** (Austrian, 19th C.), atop the hill where the Romans before them had a fort, too. Below is the **Roman Theater**, founded by Augustus. You can continue along the river on Via Sottoriva or cross the river on the **Ponte Pietra**, the Roman bridge rebuilt after WW II, and visit the theater *(8 a.m. till 1:30 p.m.; closed Mon.; L5000)* with its fine views from the upper tier.

Romeo and Juliet

The feuding Capulets and Montagues epitomize the conflicts that afflicted so many medieval Italian cities. The compelling story was recounted long before Matteo Bandello, the 16th-century official storyteller for the Mantuan court, wrote it down and long before Shakespeare borrowed the plot, setting it in Verona. For those romantics who like to mix their fiction with reality, Verona has obliged with the following tour: The Gothic facade at *Via Arche Scaligeri 2* (behind the P. Signori) has been designated as **Romeo's House** while the quaint 13th-century courtyard at *Via Cappello 23* is now **Juliet's**. (You can see the cortile and balcony without paying to see the interior, empty unless there's a special art exhibit). A 14-century tomb in the Cappuchine convent is now **Juliet's Tomb** *(8 a.m.– 6:30p.m.; closed Mon.; L5000)*. A bit inconvenient to reach, you might glimpse the 1st century Roman **Lion's Gate** (extension of Via Cappello at V. Leoni) before heading south to Via Pallone, and turning through the walls to Via Pontiere, where you'll find the Tomba di Giulietta.

Festivals and Special Events

Summer brings delightful settings for performances in Verona. In July and August, the ancient Arena is the fabulous setting for operas. To get the program in advance, write to the *Ente Lirico Arena, Piazza Bra 28, 37121 Verona*, or call ☎ *590-109 or 800-5151 or, on the Web, http://www.cosi.it/verona/eng./verona_home.html*. For tickets write the Ente or go to Arcovolo 8 of the Arena. The same months feature the Shakespeare Festival, with performances in the Roman Theater. For program information, call ☎ *807-7111*; tickets go on sale early June at Arcovolo 18 of the Arena ☎ *(590-089)*.

Where to Stay

Verona has a substantial number of hotels, but many lie outside the historic center. Whatever their location, they can be completely booked during conventions, such as the wine fair in the fall. During the summer, those in the center are booked early. It's best to

reserve in season. Those listed below are all in the historic center and have air conditioning unless stated otherwise. For exact prices, see the "Hotel Quick-Reference" chart.

Very Expensive

Due Torri Baglioni   L485–580,000 CP   ❀★★★★

P. Sant'Anastasia 4; ☎ *595-044, FAX 800-4130.*
Single L485,000 CP. Double L580,000 CP.
From the moment you enter the blank, modern facade of Due Torri and pass into
the plush Gothic cortile that serves as its lobby, you know that you have found one
of the exceptional hotels of Italy. Said to preserve the tradition of hospitality that
stretches back to the 14th-century when this palazzo was the Scaligeri guest house,
the hotel offers 100 rooms furnished in a variety of moods and styles with antiques
from the 18th and 19th centuries. Fine service. Restaurant and lounge. Parking.

Expensive

Victoria   L220–350,000 CP   ★★★★

V. Adua 6; ☎ *590-566, FAX 590-155.*
Single L220,000 CP. Double L280–350,000 CP.
Set back in a series of courtyards behind the Porta Borsari, the Victoria has created
a smart, contemporary hotel around the exposed stone walls and wooden beams of
the ancient Roman ruins and medieval convent that formerly stood here. The 78
rooms are tastefully appointed and comfortable. Restaurant. Piano bar. Sauna, gym
and solarium. Garage. A good buy.

Colombo d'Oro   L195–300,000   ★★★

V. Cattaneo 10; ☎ *595-300, FAX 594-974.*
Single L195,000. Double L250–300,000.
In a tiny piazza near the Piazza Bra, this comfortable and quiet hotel has 51 decent
rooms with large windows and recently renovated baths. Breakfast room.

Accademia   L220–370,000 CP   ★★★

V. Scala 12; ☎ *596-222, FAX 596-222.*
Single L220,000 CP. Double L285–370,000 CP.
In a substantial 18th-century palazzo just off Via Mazzini, this hotel has a modern
decor and the appointments of a full-service, first class hotel, including 106 well-
appointed and ample rooms, restaurant, bar, and garage.

Moderate

Antica Porta Leona   L150–170,000   ★★

Corticella Leoni 3; ☎ *595-499, FAX 595-499.*
Single L150,000. Double L170,000.
A few blocks east of the Piazza delle Erbe, this Renaissance palazzo shares its charming piazzetta with the ancient Porta Leone. The building has been thoroughly but
tastefully renovated with the stone fireplace left in place in the lobby and interesting
architectural details in the 36 rooms. Breakfast bar. Parking. Fee for a/c.

Bologna   L150–175,000   ★★

Rubiani 3; ☎ *800-6990, FAX 801-0602.*
Single L150,000. Double L175,000.

Just off Piazza Bra, this hotel offers 33 small but decently appointed rooms with carpeting and even minibars, and modern baths. Restaurant. Fee for a/c.

Inexpensive

Giulietta e Romeo   **L100–145,000**   ★ ★

V. Tre Marchetti 3; ☎ *800-3554, FAX 801-0862.*
Single L100,000. Double L145,000.

On a quiet street just one-half block from the Arena, this hotel deserves two stars for the friendliness of its desk staff; its 29 rooms, recently renovated, are carpeted and with modern baths. Nice touches, like good towels, make for a comfortable stay. Breakfast bar.

Aurora   **L75–100,000**   ★

V. Pellicia 12; ☎ *594-717, FAX 801-0860.*
Single L75,000. Double L100,000.

The 22 rooms are tiny and many of the showers rain from the ceiling onto everything, but the views of the Piazza delle Erbe from the terrace and most rooms and the nice service make it appealing. No a/c.

Where to Eat

A surprising number of fine restaurants can be found in the heart of Verona, and quite a number of them emphasize the Adriatic seafood that characterizes Venetian cooking, adding some fresh fish from nearby Lake Garda as well as potato gnocchi along with the traditional polenta. The wines of the province include the well known Soaves, Valpolicellos and Bardolinos.

The Finest

Il Desco   **$$$**   ★ ★ ★ ★

V. Dietro San Sebastiano; ☎ *595-358, reservations required.*
Closed Sun., first week Jan., late June. Meals L85–135,000.

In a handsome old palazzo east of the Piazza Signori, this may very well be the best of the best restaurants. The cuisine transcends the purely local with offerings such as gnocchi in fondue, artichoke tarts, stuffed pigeon with lentils and sea bass wrapped in lettuce.

Arche   **$$$**   ★ ★ ★ ★

V. Arche Scaligeri 6; ☎ *800-7415.*
Closed Mon. lunch, Sun., Jan. Fixed-price meal L80–100,000. A la carte L70–120,000.
Just north of the P. Signori, this fine restaurant, a close second to Il Desco, has a pleasing old-fashioned ambience. Only seafood is served—try the ravioli stuffed with bass, or fish prepared anyway they offer.

Dodici Apostoli   **$$$**   ★ ★ ★

Corticella San Marco 3; ☎ *596-999.*
Closed Sun. dinner, Mon., late June-early July. Meals L75–120,000.

In a 14th-century building, just south of Piazza delle Erbe, is the oldest and most famous restaurant in the city. Although dining under its frescoed ceiling and enjoying the lovely presentation of the food may be ample reason to come here, many say the food has slipped and the pigeon with mushrooms, and salmon en croute, no longer are quite so grand.

Gondolas, Venice

Grand Canal, Venice

Italian fish vendor

Rialto Market, Venice

Trattorias

Tre Marchetti $$ ★★

Vicolo Tre Marchetti 19/b; ☎ *803-5756.*
Closed early Sept. & Sun., except July–Aug. Meals L45–65,000.
Near the Arena, this trattoria has understandably been discovered by opera stars and opera buffs alike. There are lots of traditional Veronese dishes to choose from, including *bigoli* (fresh spaghetti) and *ossobuco*.

La Torretta $$ ★★

P. Broilo #1; ☎ *592-752.*
Closed Sat. lunch, Sun. Meals L50–75,000.
Found by turning toward the duomo, just before the Ponte Pietra, this small restaurant in an ancient building with wooden beams is rightly popular for its enthusiastic service and decent food—an antipasto table (smoked trout, marinated eggplant, etc.) that is generous, a tortelli with pumpkin that's delicious, a carpaccio made with arugula, and rabbit served with polenta nera.

Al Bersagliere d'Armando $$ ★★

Vicolo Pallone 1; ☎ *34-932.*
Closed Sun. (except July-Aug.) and June. Meals L45–70,000.
A five-minute walk east of the Arena, a block north of Via Pallone, this bright and lively family-run trattoria serves only seafood, and it's very fresh. Try the antipasto di pesce, really enough for a meal, with plates of seasoned clams and oysters, stuffed crab and other delights. Less pricey is the savory zuppa di cozze, the light calamari fritti, and the simply prepared, but perfectly cooked salmon.

Brek $ ★

Piazza Bra.
Closed Sun. Meals L12–25,000.
For a one-course meal or a full-course one, for salads and whatnot, try this good self-service cafeteria on the Piazza Bra where you can take your tray outside and eat looking over the Arena.

Osterie

Bottega del Vino $$ ★★

Scudo di Francia 3a, off Mazzini; ☎ *800-4535.*
Closed Tues. Meals L40–60,000.
Verona has very old wine bars, called *osterie*. Some are quite earthy, serving their sandwiches and *spontini* (snacks) and, of course, glasses of Veronese wines, in nameless enclaves like the **osteria** at *Via Pellicciai 32*. Others are more elaborate, with wine offerings extensive enough to sometimes include the regal Amarone and menus befitting a trattoria, such as this one. This charming tavern with glasses of wine and antipasti served at the bar in front, and traditional cuisine (lots of polenta dishes) served in the modest restaurant in the back.

Inexpensive Pizza

Pizzeria Impero $ ★

P. Signori; ☎ *803-0160.*
Closed Wed. Pizza L6–15,000.

Verona also has lots of pizzerias, but none has a better view than the Impero, right on the Piazza Signori and with a flavorful vegetarian pizza to make you even happier.

Pizzeria Liston   **$**   ★

Dietro Liston 19; ☎ *803-4003.*

Closed Wed.; reservation recommended. Pizza L6500–15,000.

Behind Piazza Bra, the Liston has a few outdoor tables in a quiet lane and very good pizza.

Picnics

One of the most beautiful meals you can enjoy is your own picnic on the San Pietro hill across the Ponte Pietra, or in the nearby and lovely **Giardini Giusto** *(open 9 a.m.–dusk; L5000).* The fruits in the Piazza delle Erbe can be supplemented by the fine cheeses and cold cuts down the street at **Maculan** *(V. Cappello 18a)* where there's a good bakery around the corner on Via Stella.

Directory

Telephone Code 045   **Postal Code 37121**

Airport

Catullo airport in Villafranca, 9 km, 6 mi. southwest; **APT** bus and taxi to Verona; flight information ☎ *809-5666.*

American Express

Viaggi Fabretto, *Corso Porta Nuova 11,* ☎ *800-9040.*

Bus

APT, P. XXV Aprile, across from train station, for Lake Garda and airport.

Car Rentals

Hertz ☎ *800-0832,* and others.

Emergencies

Police, dial ☎ *112* or *113.*

Groceries

P. Erbe market and nearby shops; for wines, **La Bottega di Nonno Francesco**, *V. Leoni 4.*

Parking

P. Cittadella and others near town gates.

Police

Questura, foreign office, ☎ *596-777.*

Post Office

P. Viviani, 1 block east P. Signori.

Shopping

Via Mazzini for clothing; Corso Anastasia and V. Sottoriva for antiques.

Swimming Pool

Piscina Comunale, V. Galliano, ☎ *567-622* beyond San Zeno Maggiore, with outdoor and covered pool.

Taxi

    P. Erbe, P. Bra, train station, etc.; or dial ☎ *532-666* (6 a.m.–midnight).

Telephone

    Telcom, *V. Leoncino 53;* 9 a.m.–1 p.m., 3:30–7:30 p.m.

Tourist Office

    APT, *V. Leoncino 61*, ☎ *592-828*, FAX *800-3638*, on P. Bra, 8 a.m.–8 p.m., Sun. 9 a.m.–2 p.m.; and *P. Erbe 42*, ☎ *803-0086*, (closed Sun. and holidays).

Tours

    Cangrande, *V. della Casa 5*, ☎ *591-788*, for city tours CIT, *P. Bra 2* ☎ *591-788;* authorized guides, ☎ *918-514*.

Train

    Stazione Porta Nuova, south of centro storico; #2 AMT bus to P. Bra and P. Erbe; information ☎ *590-688*.

Train station

    Albergo Diurni, to right as exit.

On the Road

Small Towns of the Veneto

Between Verona and Venice are a surprising variety of towns and landscapes. In the valley are cities, like Vicenza and Treviso as well as moated villages, like Castelfranco. In the beautiful foothills of the Dolomites, there's thriving Bassano del Grappa, birthplace to that Italian firewater called *grappa*, and the poetic retreat of Asolo, and its even gentler wines. From the valleys to the peak of Monte Grappa, thick walls and castles proclaim the medieval feuding of the large towns—Verona, Padua and Treviso, too—at the expense of the smaller ones between them. But along with the crenellated roofs and narrow cobblestone lanes of these towns are the sunny palazzi of Venice's mainland expansion.

While the presence of La Serenissima can be detected in church altars painted by Bellini and Veronese (Vicenza) as well as Giorgione (Castelfranco), and in town halls planned by Baroque architect Giorgio Massari (Asolo), it is everywhere proclaimed by the architecture of Palladio. From Vicenza, almost completely overhauled by this architect's projects, to Bassano where its famous bridge resulted from his design, the classical forms and airy interiors of this High Renaissance artist can be found. Most influential are his country villas, crowning nearly every hilltop. Built for the Venetian aristocracy that no longer found sea trade profitable, these 16th-century villas were often working farms, but grandiose ones, like the Villa Barbaro/Maser near Asolo that was frescoed by Veronese. Their design was so satisfactory, so practical yet noble, that they can be found recreated in the work of his followers, such as the gifted Scamozzi, and as far afield as Virginia where Thomas Jefferson's Monticello stands.

You can enjoy a visit through this area by car, picking and choosing among the Palladian villas that cluster most intensely around Vicenza, and making your way between Verona and Venice by swinging to the north through the Venetian foothills that are especially refreshing in the summer, but with fewer visitors in the spring and fall. Without a car, you may find the trip too cumbersome, even though there are buses to Asolo and some of the villas

can be visited by public transport from Vicenza. *The finest hotel is found in little Asolo, and one of the most satisfying meals at Barbesin, on the road outside tiny Castelfranco.*

Villas

Along many of the smaller roads of the Veneto, around Venice, in the Dolomite foothills, and especially near Vicenza, you will see a great number of regal Palladian and Palladian-style villas. Visits to some are described under Vicenza, Venetian Foothills, and Venice (see "Brenta Riviera"). But if these have only whetted your appetite, then check with the tourism office in Vicenza for their brochure *Ville Vicentine.* Although their brochure is overwhelming, you can plot a sensible driving tour to those clustering to the north of Vicenza around Thiene, and to the south, near Longare. You may require a computer to chart a course through the disparate visiting hours of the villas, most still privately owned, but you can simply look through the gates at those without sculpture or frescoes, regardless of the hours.

Festival Tip

The village of Marostica (27 km, 17 mi. north of Vicenza on the way to Bassano) reenacts a 500-year old legend in its medieval town square with a colorful, fully costumed *Living Chess Game,* in which most of the inhabitants participate. Celebrated every even year, usually for several days in September. *Check for details with the Vicenza tourist office.*

Vicenza

In some ways Vicenza confounds one's expectations. So often called "the beautiful city of Palladio," you come to imagine its streets lined with mini-Monticellos and glistening white churches like San Giorgio Maggiore in Venice. The fact is that in Vicenza we are dealing with urban palazzi and municipal buildings rather than isolated country villas or island churches. The familiar Palladian silhouette rarely exists amid the surrounding centuries of other buildings. Too often the buildings seem overscaled for their setting, more satisfactory expressions of their owner's egos than of good town planning. The modern city numbers more than 100,000 residents, and though cars are banned from the center, their fumes have prevented anything from being glistening white. Once one adjusts expectations to reality, Vicenza offers some satisfying strolls and sightseeing. And two villas, guaranteed not to disappoint, are just a few minutes away. If you're staying the night, you'll see Vicenza at its loveliest when illumination highlights the architectural beauty of the Corso and Basilica, while obscuring some of the decay.

What to See and Do

The major sights of the city lie in and around the Corso Palladio that runs east to west through the easily walkable centro storico.

Around Piazza dei Signori ★

The ★**Palazzo del Comune** (at #98), looking monumental and very bank-like, is the former Palazzo Trissimo, home of Palladio's patron and begun by that architect's assistant and successor, Scamozzi, in 1592. Here, turn south a block to enter the ★★**Piazza dei Signori**, dominated by one of Palladio's most monumental works, the ★**Basilica** (1549), with its elegant, and very Venetian, two levels of arcades anchored by a 12th-century tower. Not a church at all, but rather the palace of justice, the Basilica represents Palladio's skill in masterfully hiding the difficult-to-hide and irregular arches of the original Gothic building behind his symmetrical classical arcade. His solution was the "Palladian arch," or double columnettes on each side of the openings. Opposite is another Palladian work, the ★**Loggia del Capitano** (1570), never finished but impressive with its oversized pilasters. On the back side of the Basilica is the Piazza delle Erbe, and to its left, beyond the columns of Venetian domination, is the small Piazza Blade with its Gothic church. From here return to the Corso and go right. You'll pass the notable Venetian Gothic palace called the **Ca d'Oro** *(#147)*, then the simple **house of Palladio** *(#163)*.

Around Piazza Matteotti ★

At the end near Piazza Matteotti, set back on the left in a garden courtyard, is the ★★**Teatro Olimpico** *(9:30 a.m.–12:30 p.m. every day; and 3–5:30 p.m. & Sun. 2–7 p.m. in high season, 2–4:30 p.m. except Sun., mid-Oct.–mid-Mar.; L5000)*. This was Palladio's last building (1580), but the first covered theater in Europe. The ★ trompe l'oeil stage set, perfectly convincing for the classical plays and concerts still performed here (*323-781* for information), is in fact only 14 yards deep. It was designed by Scamozzi. The entrance ticket also gains admission to the **Museo Civico** *(9 a.m.–noon, 2:30–5 p.m., Sun. 9:30 a.m.–12:30 p.m., 2–7 p.m.; L3000 but free Sun.)*, around the corner on Piazza Matteotti. Even if you don't visit the museum with its second floor pinacoteca of Venetian paintings, you should note the splendid building that houses it, Palladio's ★**Palazzo Chiericati** (1550).

Town Walks

There are other brief and pleasant walks through town—from the Piazza delle Erbe west to the Piazza Duomo, or south of Piazza Blade to the picturesque San Michele bridge and north on Cesare Battista to the Gothic church of San Lorenzo. But the best is near the Teatro Olimpico, where just off the Corso is the church of **Santa Corona** *(closed noon–3 p.m.)* sheltering within Giovanni Bellini's ★ *Baptism of Christ*, (last chapel left) and Veronese's ★*Adoration of the Magi*, (use light machine; 3rd chapel right). From here continue west on Santo Stefano until you come to the rear side of the stately ★**Palazzo Thiene**, its rusticated facade and courtyard designed by Palladio. The front of this palazzo *(Contra da Porti 12)*, painted with frescoes, was designed by Lorenzo da Bologna (1498). Then, you can stroll to the right on the **Contra da Porti**, the most handsome street in Vicenza, lined with palazzi in both the Venetian Gothic *(#19 and #14)* and Palladian *(#11 and #2)* styles.

Nearby Sights   ★★

A 15-minute bus ride (#8 from stazione) takes you to Vicenza's two famous villas. Although the city is beginning to encroach on these summer retreats, the villas and their country settings are worth glimpsing through locked gates on closing days. The most famous is ★★**La Rotonda** *(Mar. 15–Oct. 15, grounds open Tues.– Thurs., 10 a.m.–noon, 3–6 p.m.; Wed. only for visits to residence or by appointment ☎ 321-793; L5000 for interior, L3000 for grounds only)*, also known as the Villa Capra-Valmarana after the various owners. The model for the Jefferson Memorial in Washington, D.C., Chiswick House near London, and for so many other buildings in both countries, La Rotonda is already familiar, but still resplendent in its geometrical simplicity. Perfectly symmetrical, its four classical temple-like facades seem designed just to frame countryside views for the owners. Only the statue-lined entrance drive breaks the symmetry. It is a five-minute park-lined walk to the second villa, ★★**Villa Valmarana "ai Nani"** *(Mar. 15–Nov. 15 Thurs., Sat., Sun. and festivi 10 a.m.–noon, and, except Sun., 3–6 p.m. May–Sept., otherwise 2:30-till 5 or 5:30 p.m., or call ☎ 321-803; L5000)*. This villa, though not by Palladio, has a beautiful park, a garden wall topped with sculptures of dwarfs (hence, the "ai nani"), and a villa designed in the 17th century by the Muttoni. But the reason to visit on opening days is the interior, covered with exuberant ★frescoes by G.B. Tiepolo (1757). Even the guest house is frescoed, but in the less heroic style of G.D. Tiepolo.

Just south of town rises ★**Monte Berico** with its fine views and pilgrimage church Basilica of Monte Berico (rebuilt 17th century), approached by a portico of 150 arches and 17 chapels lining Via X Guigno. Inside the church, to the right of the high altar is a Belliniesque Pieta, (1500) by Bartolommeo Montagna, and down the steps to the left of the altar (in a room to the left) is Veronese's ★ *Supper of St. Gregory*, (1572). Although the two famous villas above are just at the foot of Monte Berico (there is a good view of the Villa Rotonda from behind the church), the idyllic, if long walk between them, has been closed off.

<h2 style="text-align:center">Where to Stay</h2>

The choice is limited.

Campo Marzio   **L185–220,000**   ★★★

V. Roma 21; ☎ *545-700, FAX 320-495.*
Single L185,000. Double L220,000.
The best choice, on the west end of town just outside the old wall, is this modern and first-class hotel, with 35 well-appointed rooms, restaurant, bar and parking.

Cristina **L120–145,000** ★★

Corso S. Felice 32; ☎ *323-751, FAX 543-656.*
Single L120,000. Double L145,000.
Also convenient, but on a busy street a few blocks east of town is this hotel with'50s
architecture on the outside and a bit more warmth for the 30 rooms in the interior.
Breakfast bar. Sauna (fee). Garage.

San Raffaele **L95,000** √★

V. X Guigno 10; ☎ *323-663, FAX 545-767.*
Single/double L95,000.
Just below the Basilico Monte Berico, this monastically simple pensione has a lovely
garden setting and 24 bright rooms with linoleum floors. Breakfast bar. Parking.
Buses do run here, but obviously this is not the most convenient location.

Where to Eat

Cinzia & Valerio **$$–$$$** ★★★

Piazzetta Porta Padova 65; reserve at ☎ *505-213, FAX 512-796.*
Closed Mon., 1 week in Jan., Aug. Meals L60–90,000.
A short ride from the Piazza Matteotti is what many consider Vicenza's best restaurant. In a relaxing setting, you can choose among the seafood specialties that range
from shellfish antipasti and risotto nero to pasta with lobster sauce and a casserole
of John Dory fish.

Scudo di Francia **$$** ★★★

Contra Piancoli 4; ☎ *323-322.*
Closed Sun. night, Mon., and Aug. Meals L45–60,000.
Our favorite restaurant in town is located near the Piazza Signori. You can enjoy
your meal under the vaulted ceiling of a 15th-century Venetian palace where
Goethe once stayed. At one end, large windows overlook a garden and throughout
the dining rooms, an old-fashioned graciousness prevails. The food is very good,
whether a simple antipasto of gamberetti, or the heady flavors of pasta stuffed with
truffle and prosciutto or guinea hen in porcini.

Vecchia Guardia **$** ★

Contra Pescherie Vecchie.
Closed Thurs. L35–50,000.
Just west of the Piazza delle Erbe is this very popular trattoria. Try getting a table
outside to enjoy your simple meal, from the *tipico* thick spaghetti called "bigoli"
and seafood to the good pizza.

Gran Caffè Garibaldi

P. Signoria 5, closed Tues. night, Wed.
The perfect spot to enjoy your morning cappuccino, midday sandwich and, most
certainly, your evening aperitivo, is from the terrace of this handsome restaurant.
Overlooking the Basilica. There's also a modest restaurant upstairs, where some
tables have views of the piazza, too.

Picnics

Picnicking is a great idea in Vicenza, whether you find a bench in the enchanting gar-
den of the Teatro Olimpico or the Giardino Salvi (west end of town), or climb up to the

grounds of La Rotonda or the slopes of Monte Berico. A wonderful shop is **Il Ceppo Gastronomica** *(Corso Palladio 196, near the Teatro)*, with grilled chicken breasts, marinated vegetables, in addition to the usual cold cuts.

Directory

Telephone Code 0444   **Postal Code 36100**

Tourist Information

APT, P. Matteotti ☎ *320-854, FAX 325-001.*

Getting Around

Buses, taxis, rental cars, and tours to villas and Monte Berico (mid-Apr.–Nov. 30, Sat. morning; reservations required at Siamic Express, *IV Novembre 19;* ☎ *514-511).*

Arriving

Stazione and FTV bus terminal just southwest of centro storico; walk Viale Roma, or take bus, to Corso Palladio.

Parking near stazione or P. Matteotti, opposite side of centro storico.

A-4 runs 50 km, 31 mi. west to Verona, 30 km east to Padua and 65 km, 42 mi. to Venice. SS 53 takes you 40 km northeast to Treviso via Castelfranco.

Castelfranco Veneto

Really no more than a castle surrounded by a few modern streets, this village has a surprising number of good reasons for a visit. The castle, built by Treviso in 1199 as protection against Padua, is still moated and with many of its walls intact. Not only is it picturesque, but Castelfranco holds a masterpiece by its native son, Giorgione. In the center of the castle, where the short main street of Via Preti meets Garibaldi, is the **duomo** *(closed noon–3 p.m.)* and in the chapel right of the apse is Giorgione's ★★ *Enthroned Madonna with Saints,* (c. 1502), his only altarpiece and an absolutely riveting one, from the gleaming armour of St. Liberalis to the poetic landscapes that emerge from the background. Yet another reason to visit is the restaurant Barbesin.

Where to Stay and Eat

There are a few modern hotels near the castle if you're in need of one, as well as restaurants. But if you can, head to the northern outskirts of town for:

Barbesin   **$–$$**   **★★★**

V. Montebelluna 41 in suburb Salvarosa di Castelfranco; ☎ *490-446; closed Wed. night, Thurs., early Jan., and Aug.; L35–55,000.*

Actually on the Vicenza/Treviso road, locally called Via Circonvallazione Est, you reach Barbesin by turning right off Via S. Pio X from the center, looking for it on the left side of the road. Driving from Treviso, it's on the right at the first intersection (Cristoforo Colombo) into the center of Castelfranco. All these directions are worth it, if it helps you enjoy a meal here. Although an unpretentious, modernized inn, the food is very good, indeed. We've had a *pasticcio ai funghi,* that was the quintessence of wild mushrooms and thinly sliced hare with a sublime sauce of green peppercorns and wild blueberry vinegar. Whatever the season, your meal is bound to be wonderful, full of spring asparagus, winter artichokes, or the wild mushrooms of late summer.

Directory

Telephone Code 0423   **Postal Code 31033**

Arriving

Castelfranco is along SS 53, 30 km, 19 mi. from Vicenza, 26 km, 16 mi. from Treviso. A pleasant country road north arrives in 18 km, 11 mi. at Asolo. There are buses from Vicenza and Treviso.

The Venetian Foothills

Maybe the flatlands of the Veneto have become too much. Or you simply can't take the heat. Or maybe you're looking for a retreat from the larger towns. Here in the foothills of the Dolomites, running from the striking Monte Grappa on the west through the gentler hills of Asolo to Montebelluno (32 km, 20 mi.), you may find just what you need. The air is fresher, the vegetation is lush, and views from the peak of Monte Grappa above Bassano can be spectacular. There are lots of villas dotting the landscape—Longhena's **Ca'Rezzonica** with its Canova sculpture garden (just south of Bassano del Grappa), Palladio's **Villa Emo** with its frescoes by G.B. Zelotti *(south of Montebelluna in Franzolo di Vedelago; ☎ [0423] 487-040; open weekend afternoons except mid-Dec.–Feb. 1)*—but none are so famous as the Villa Barbaro at Maser (see below). There are even stunning memorials—**Canova's tomb**, designed by himself in Possagno, where he was born (north of Bassano) and the **Tomba de Brion** in the San Vito cemetery (off Castelfranco road south of Asolo), designed by the modern architect, Carlo Scarpa. All make for pleasant drives in the countryside, while hunting them down. But if you've come to rest, then you may find the little town of Asolo too beautiful to leave.

Bassano del Grappa

Although prettily situated next to the Brenta river, Bassano del Grappa shouldn't be your destination if it is tranquility you're seeking in these hills. The town is part of a thriving ceramics industry that spills over onto the surrounding roads, making for some congestion. But if you're more in a mind to explore than to get away from it all, Bassano can be a convenient base since it has the most facilities. A pleasant, if brief glimpse of the town can be enjoyed by the river where the Palladio-designed bridge, the ★**Ponte degli Alpini** crosses into the old town. At the town end of the bridge is the Nardini grappa distillery, in operation since the 18th century when Bassano first invented the liquor. Up the hill, you wind your way through arcades and a series of medieval and Renaissance piazzas that are most notable for the artistic

works of the Bassano family that adorn the facades on the Piazza Liberta as
well as the walls of the **Museo Civico** *(Tues.–Sat. 9 a.m.–12:30 p.m., 3:30–6:30
p.m., Sun. 3:30–6:30 p.m. only; L5000)* in the Piazza Garibaldi. Following Via
Barbieri left out of the last piazza, you come to the valley views from the
Viale dei Martiri that leads right to the top of the town, marked by the Porta
Grazie and Giardini Pubblici.

Where to Stay

Next to each other and just outside the Porta Grazie are two hotels:

Belvedere   **L150–200,000 CP**   ★★★

> *P. Giardino 14;* ☎ *529-845, FAX 529-849.*
> *Single L150,000 CP. Double L200,000 CP.*
> A tasteful, modern hotel with good service and 98 comfortable rooms (those off the
> main street quieter). Restaurant. Bar. Garage.

Brennero   **L70–100,000**   ★★

> *V. Tarino 7;* ☎ *228-544, FAX 227-021.*
> *Single L70,000. Double L100,000.*
> A small, modern hotel with 22 rooms (no a/c). Closed Christmas season.

Where to Eat

San Bassiano   **$$–$$$**   ★★★

> *V. Martiri 36; reserve at* ☎ *521-453, FAX 525-111.*
> *Closed Sun. and Aug. Meals L55–85,000.*
> Just two blocks away from the Porta Grazie dine on the best of the regional harvest,
> from spring asparagus to late summer porcini, combined with both seafood and
> game.

Da Renzo   **$–$$**   ★★

> *V. Volpato 60;* ☎ *503-055.*
> *Closed Mon. night, Tues., and Jan. Meals L40–65,000.*
> With a summer terrace overlooking the river, Da Renzo is a good spot to enjoy sea-
> food. It's just to the left of Palladio's bridge as you approach town.

Cafes abound but none are so traditional as the **Taverna Nadini** *(closed Mon.)* where
you can buy a shot or bottle of its famous grappa. A good *salumeria* for a picnic is just up
the hill at *Via Matteoti 4.*

Directory

Telephone Code 0424   **Postal Code 36061**

Tourist Information

> Largo Corona d'Italia, near Viale delle Fosse *(*☎ *524-351, FAX 525-301).*

Getting Around

> The centro storico is best walked. Parking is near the Porta Grazie, north side of
> town.

Arriving

> Bus service is best, from Vicenza (34 km, 21 mi. northeast on SS 248), Treviso (47
> km, 29 mi. via SS 53 then north) and there's local service to Monte Grappa (sum-

mer season only) and Asolo. Bus terminal within walking distance of tourism office. For trains, the Venice-Trento stops here once daily.

Asolo

Robert Browning lived here for years. Eleanor Duse asked to be buried here. There's a reason—Asolo is beautiful. Picturesque streets. Hillsides covered with flowers and trees. Wonderful vistas. You can just come and sit in the cafe on the main piazza. Maybe you'll climb the Via Collegio to the old town gate and views beyond or to the ancient rocca. Perhaps you'll look for the Lorenzo Lotto in the duomo, or shop for the local Colli Asolani wines. Certainly you'll breathe in the clear air, and relax.

Where to Stay

There are only two hotels in this small town.

Villa Cipriani   **L325–450,000**   ★★★★

V. Canova 298; ☎ *952-166, FAX 952-095.*
Single L325,000. Double L400–450,000.
A romantic retreat in a 16th-century villa, with extensive gardens and wonderful views. A Ciga hotel with a Relais & Chateau restaurant.

Duse   **L200–250,000 CP**   ★★

V. Browning 190; ☎ *55-241, FAX 950-404.*
Single L200,000 CP. Double L250,000 CP.
Right on the main square and with 12 tastefully designed rooms, some with bird's-eye views of campaniles and rooftops. Breakfast room.

Where to Eat

Alla Torre   **$–$$**   ★★

SS 248 in San Zenone degli Ezzelini; ☎ *567-086, FAX 567-086.*
Closed Wed. lunch, Tues., early Nov. Meals L30–50,000.
There are restaurants in town, but you might consider a short drive toward Bassano to enjoy the fine outdoor setting of Alla Torre with good food in the local tradition.

Another restaurant that knows what to do with the seasonal produce of these hills is **Barbesin** (see Castelfranco), only a 20-minute drive south. For outdoor snacks, the **Caffè Centrale** is perfectly located next to the main square and the market, and the shops along Via Browning, especially the **Gastronomiche Ennio** at #151, have what you need for a picnic.

Directory

Telephone Code 0423   **Postal Code 31011**

Tourist Information

On main piazza (☎ *529-046, FAX 524-137*), next to Museo Civico; useful information for excursions.

Arriving

Buses connect village with Montebelluna and Bassano, with Treviso and, once a day, Venice. Just north of SS 248, Asolo lies 14.5 km, 9 mi. east of Bassano, 17 km, 10.5 mi. west of Montebelluno, and 38 km, 23.5 mi. from Treviso via SS 53 to Castelfranco, then north on a country road.

Treviso

Villa Barbero at Maser

This most famous of Palladio's villas, known more simply as the ★★**Villa Maser**, was built in 1559 for a family that counted a doge of Venice among them. It is still a working farm, complete with horses and dogs and corn-fields. Simply driving by, you can enjoy the **family ★ chapel** sitting astride the road and the handsomely proportioned villa, its roof adorned with chimneys rather than urban statuary. But if you time your visit right, you can also enter the villa, covering your shoes with the provided slippers, and enjoying the delightful ★★**frescoes by Veronese** (1560) that decorate Palladio's rooms. Amid the allegorical paintings and country scenes, are the light and playfully illusionistic ones of the family at home—the mistress Barbaro leaning over a balcony, dogs chewing contentedly on bones, a hunter entering a trompe l'oeil door (believed to be a Veronese self-portrait). And in the rear garden there's an elaborate grotto by Alessandro Vittorio.

Directory

The **villa** (☎ *[0423] 565-002*) is open Tues., Sat., Sun. 3–6 p.m., except 2–5 p.m. Oct.–May; L5000.

Arriving

Located on SS 248, 9 km east of Asolo, 7 km west of Montebelluna, where you join SS 348 south to Treviso (25 km, 15.5 mi.).

Treviso

Even within the 15th-century Venetian walls and encircling moat of rivers and canals, Treviso is primarily a modern, well-planned city of 100,000. It shelters a pleasant, if much diminished old town, despite the fact that half of Treviso was tragically destroyed overnight in a WW II bombardment. In the very center, painted facades recall centuries of Venetian domination, while thick medieval walls speak of the difficulty of independence, achieved by Treviso only briefly at the end of the 13th century. Picturesque canals and blocks of arcades add to the ambience. In the ★**Piazza dei Signori** everyone congregates—under massive arches of the Romanesque **Loggia dei Cavalari** and around the adjacent **Palazzo dei Trecento** (1217; restored). From this pi-azza you can lose yourself in narrow streets or follow arcaded ones, until, eventually, you emerge into the more modern town. Then, if you want, you can seek out the frescoes, most in unfortunate shape, by the post-Giotto art-ist Tommaso da Modena at the **San Francesco** church (first chapel right), its vast spaces a transition to the Gothic, and the **San Nicolo** (1303) and its chap-ter house (best preserved). On a rainy day, other Tommaso frescoes can be seen in the **Museo Civico Bailo** (*Borgo Cavour 22; open 9 a.m.– noon, 2–5 p.m.; Sun. a.m. only; Mon. closed; L3000*) along with a Giovanni Bellini *Madonna and Child*, (Sala 8), and in the next sala, a Lorenzo Lotto and Titian portrait.

Where to Stay and Eat

Continental   **L170–220,000**   ★★

V. Roma 16; ☎ *411-216, FAX 55-054.*
Single L170,000. Double L220,000.
If you find it convenient to overnight here before heading early to Venice, there are
several hotels on the perimeter. The Continental is the most central hotel, being the
on the south edge of town near the stazione and with 82 rooms.

Albergo Beccherie   **L85–100,000**   ★★

P. Ancilloto 10; ☎ *540-871, FAX 540-871.*
Single L85,000. Double L100,000.
Also known as the Campeol, this small hotel is tucked behind the Piazza Signori and
offers 16 ample rooms, modernized and with good baths, some with canal views (no
a/c) that belong to the restaurant of the same name, across the street. Some parking
(enter centro storico off V. Matteotti at Indipendenza).

Beccherie   **$–$$**   ★★★

See above for address; ☎ *56-601, FAX 540-871.*
Closed Sun. night, Mon. late July. Meals L40–60,000.
For traditional cuisine, this is the place to go. Its medieval building has been made
into a bright and attractive trattoria; in the summer there's al fresco dining. The
sopa coada (a stew of wine, pigeon, and bread) and heavily sauced *faraona* (guinea
hen) with polenta are very *trevigiana*. More familiar are the risotti, perhaps made
with the Romaine-shaped radicchio from Treviso; or truffled veal.

Snacking is easy around the Piazza dei Signori with its cafes.

Directory

Telephone Code ☎ **0422**   **Postal Code 3110**

Tourist Information

   APT, *V. Toniolo 41* ☎ *547-632, FAX 541-397*, southeast side of town, just off the
main drag of the Corso del Popolo.

Getting Around

   The P. Signori area is closed to traffic (except for hotel access), as are a few of the
streets that lie just outside it.

Arriving

   Trains (half-hour) and buses to Venice are frequent and convenient, while trains to
Vicenza (1 to 2 hours) and buses to other Veneto towns are adequate. From terminals (south edge of town), take bus to center (5 minutes). • Verona is 80 km, 50
mi. west via Vicenza (40 km) on SS 53 and A-4 • Venice is 30 km, 19 mi. south on
SS 13.

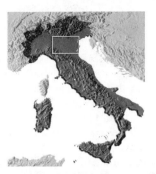

BOLOGNA AND EMILIA ROMAGNA

Twilight descends on Bologna, famed for its gastronomy.

History and Art

Although the Apennines form a border to the south, the most striking characteristic of Emilia Romagna is its flatness. Flat where the Po flows, flatter and bog-like at the delta where that river joins the Adriatic. So flat that towns as early as Etruscan Marzabotta outside Bologna had street grids even before the Romans. So unprincely flat that court artists, like Francesco del Cossa, created landscapes of craggy mountains for the dukes of Ferrara. So

251

monotonous, in fact, that Duke Borso d'Este ordered his Ferrarese subjects to build him a mountain in 1471.

Across this Po basin, canals and waterways would form a vast network for trade and communication. But the most significant link would be the 150-mile road engineered by the Roman M. Aemilius Lepidus in 187 B.C. from Rimini on the Adriatic to Piacenza on the Po. On the Adriatic was Rimini, such a stronghold of Rome that to this day the region, now with Ravenna, is known as Romagna. But the Via Emilia stretched from this security into the barbarian frontier defined by the Rubicon, for it was built to tame and maintain the newly conquered Celtic territory of Cisalpine Gaul. Eventually, its reach would extend across the Alps and into France. And it would become the route over which Christianity would spread, the Eastern church in Ravenna bring the word to Milan, and from there into northern Europe. Over the centuries, the direction would reverse and the Emilian Way would carry pilgrims to Rome. For millennia it would link Italy's great farming communities where the Po and its many channels didn't reach. Even today the Via Emilia remains one of the main byways of the region.

Emilia Romagna is a modern political *regione*. Only since Italian unification in the 19th century have the sandy beaches of Romagna been administratively united with the cultivated valley of Emilia. Since there never was an Emilia, or even a unified Romagna, the simple name of the region belies its historical complexity. There were many independent cities, and like most of Italy these cities had their powerful families—the Este of Ferrara, the Malatesta of Rimini, the Pepoli and Bentivoglio of Bologna. They fought the wars of the Guelphs and Ghibellines (and incidently, forced Frederick Barbarossa into signing a truce in Parma), as well as more local ones to establish their control. In their success, the free cities, or communes, built their town halls and the wealthy families commissioned altarpieces and chapels that give each city its artistic richness. Unlike most regions, no one city emerged from the constant battles of the Middle Ages strong enough to dominate.

The fragmentation of the area gave an opening to stronger powers. The Visconti made many efforts to control the region from Milan, and did succeed in taking over Parma and Piacenza for various periods. Ferrara, always more likely to be sympathetic with Venice, was able to maneuver its independence through the wiles of the Este family. Ravenna was under papal authority, but Venice established itself there briefly. And someone was always trying to overtake Bologna; more often than not, the pope.

In fact, it is the church more than any power or institution that gives some historical unity to the artificial state of Emilia Romagna. From the 8th century on, it nominally controlled Romagna as part of the Papal States. But not until the 16th century, when Pope Alexander VI sent his son Cesare Borgia to take direct control, was the area threatened. The Malatesta were evicted

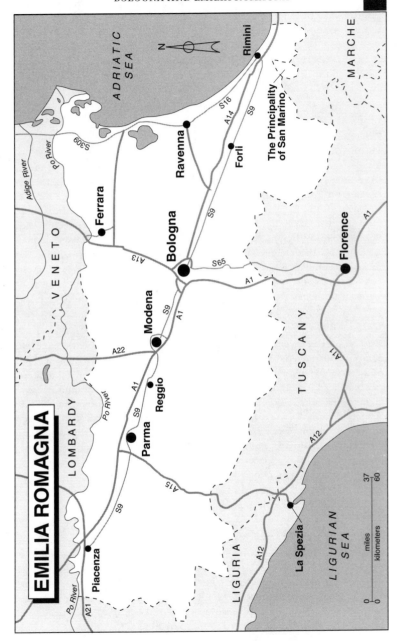

from Rimini (good riddance, said its citizens). The Este bided their time by marrying Alfonso d'Este to the pope's already twice-married daughter, Lucrezia Borgia, but eventually they would be outmaneuvered and sent packing to Modena in 1598, after 350 years of opulent rule. Julius II subdued Bologna. Pope Paul II secured Parma and Piacenza as a duchy for his Farnese family. Not until Napoleon's invasion did papal authority end in Emilia. Romagna, though, remained part of the Papal States until Italian unification in 1859.

Not only did the church politically exploit Emilia Romagna, it inspired some of the greatest art in the region. The glittering 6th-century mosaics in Ravenna result from an extraordinary flowering of the Byzantine church. The Romanesque churches along the Via Emilia rose in response to the 11th-century commerce of medieval pilgrims and the French tastes brought with them. Local inspiration added the distinctive lion porch of the serene Lombard Emilian church, and local sculptors added the very human, and sometimes almost freestanding, figures to the facades at Modena and Parma. Certainly, the strong church presence during the Counter-Reformation contributed to Emilia's importance in Early Baroque art. While the greatest works of native son Annibale Carracci are in Rome, the region is renowned for the art of the late 16th-century, including the work of Ludovico and Agostino Carracci in Bologna, as well as that of Bartolommeo Schedone (best seen in Parma).

 But the Renaissance art of Emilia Romagna fits into no simple theme. The Carracci, and indeed, the later Baroque painters like Guido Reni (1575–1642) and Guercino, also of Bologna, derived much of their swooning gestures and fleshy tomes from that High Renaissance genius Antonio Allegri, known as Correggio (c.1490–1534). Working in Parma, Correggio was the sole provincial artist to create paintings that are equal in genius to Raphael and Titian. Monumental and often complex, his work nonetheless has an emotional energy that is unique. The illusionism of his frescoed ceilings are his masterpieces and influenced not just the Carracci, but later Baroque artists like Bernini. As influential as Correggio was to become, in his own day he shared the artistic stage with Parmigianino (1503–40), known for the sophisticated but emotionally sterile style of Mannerism that the Carracci so rebelled against.

Before Correggio, it was Ferrara rather than Parma that produced a school of Early Renaissance art. The Este were great patrons of the arts. Early in the quattrocento they bought Pisanello, Jacopo Bellini, Alberti, Piero della Francesca and Mantegna to their court. Such a persistent presence of great artists and patronage produced a minor but polished school of late quattrocento painting. Artists such as Cosimo Tura (1430–95), Francesco del Cossa (1435–78) and Ercole de'Roberti (1456–96) were among those who contributed their own northern emotional intensity, and chalky, gnarled forms to create a distinctive, and somewhat eccentric, Renaissance art style. Although Ferrara continued to produce artists into the next century, such as the Giorgionesque Dosso Dossi (b. 1490), it failed to sustain the quality of the earlier school.

For all that might be said about the artificiality of this *regione*, it contains within its modern borders numerous art cities. And, given that it never was a natural cultural region, it has actually produced two Emilian schools of art, that of a very distinctive form of the Romanesque church, and that of the rapturous painting school that Correggio began and the Bolognesi developed.

Modern Emilia Romagna

In a region that has for centuries produced scientists of the caliber of anatomist and physicist Luigi Galvani and the inventor Guglielmo Marconi, it is not surprising to find a center of modern high technology. And in the case of a region that has so long been the breadbasket of Italy and as early as the 18th century was packaging its sausages for export, it seems right that much of this technology is applied to the processing and transport of food. With Italy's largest modern freight depot and one of its finest universities, Bologna is at the center of regional trade. But the trade is not just in canned fruits and vegetables of the region, or only its cheeses, mortadella and prosciutto. It also is in the machines that process the food and package them. In fact, Emilia Romagna is the second largest exporter of food technology, behind West Germany but ahead of the United States.

Along the Adriatic, Rimini and the independent principality of San Marino continue to function largely as busy beach towns despite increasing pollution of the sea. Although the central Adriatic has not suffered as much as the area around Venice, the summer of 1989 found many bathers alarmed by yellowish algae flourishing on the fertilizers deposited by the Po river. Ravenna, now surrounded by chemical refineries rather than the sea, contributes its own contaminants to the region.

Needless to say, a region with so much industrialization and diversification in its economy is typical of the prosperous north. Bologna is said to have the highest per capita income in the country and all the cities seem to be thriving. Although the countryside is not Italy's most scenic, the cities contain an inner core of artistic treasures that warrant their high levels of tourism.

Cuisine

Of course, you already know about parmesan cheese and prosciutto. Now all you need to add is that they are hallmarks of Emilian cuisine. Then consider that homemade pasta, such as fresh *tagliatelle*, or noodles with eggs, or deliciously stuffed rings of *tortelli* and their larger version *tortelloni*, or even spinach *lasagne*, all had their beginnings here in Bologna. What could be more Italian than parmesan, prosciutto and pasta?

The cuisine benefits from the richness of this land of the Po valley, Italy's greatest producer of cereal. Emilia Romagna grows wheat, especially durum wheat that makes its pasta so flavorful and makes Romagna's flat *piadini* bread so delicious. Its livestock number among the greatest, too, and yield the butter and cheese, the veal, the pork and the ham so essential for the cuisine. But it's not just the land that can take credit, for the prosciutto di Parma, miraculously *dolce*, requires little salt in its curing because, it's said, of the quality of the air. Then, too, the human hand for centuries has pounded the skin to make it smooth and shiny and unrivaled—except by prosciutto di San Daniele. And though the air has little to do with Parma's cheese, maybe seven centuries have resulted in the perfection of parmigiano reggiano, justly touted as the best, from the delectably and just sliceable *stagionato* to the grating age of a *sardo*.

The ingredients are already at hand for some of the most typical dishes of Emilia Romagna. There's the meat-laden *bollito misto*, boiled odd parts—ribs, tongue and the like—along with hunks of beef, pork and chicken served with broth and spiced with relishes. And there's the odd *zampone* of Modena, or pig's feet stuffed with sausage. More familiar is *ragu*, or that meat sauce created in Bologna and properly credited in America as spaghetti alla Bolognese. There's Bologna's version of saltimbocca, known as *cotoletta alla bolognese*, or layered ham and veal breaded with an egg batter. More *caratteristico* is the turkey version, *petto di tacchino*. Then the most classical ring-shaped *tortellini di brodo* in Bologna is stuffed with prosciutto, veal and parmesan cheese, and served in a consomme, while the squarer-shaped *tortelli all'erbetta* of Parma is stuffed with ricotta and spinach, then flavored in the sweetest butter and parmesan. Very rich, indeed.

But there's more to the bounty of Emilia Romagna. In the delta region of the Po, near Ferrara, vegetables flourish and orchards thrive. Here you add the light element to the cuisine, the tomato and *zucca* (pumpkin that finds its way into gnocchi and tortelli), the apple, pear and strawberry. Nearby in Rimini the most succulent asparagus grows, often found wrapped in the tastiest piece of veal. Here, too, we find the fruit of Romagna's Adriatic sea, and the caviar of the Po, the eel of the delta. Around Modena are sweet Vignola cherries and peaches. In addition, imagine a few of the condiments, the almonds (delicious in desserts and found in Modena's amaretti macaroons) and nutmeg. Better yet, taste the dense earthy flavor of balsamic vinegar from Modena found in the preparation of many meat dishes.

Cuisine

Although the land no longer supports the noble olive tree, it being considered a waste to feed it with such fertile soil, it does yield grapes for **wine**. Sparkling Lambrusco, its most ordinary version made popular in the United States by Riunite, is the best-known Emilian wine. Its best quality, appropriately light for the heavy traditional cuisine, is perhaps found in the DOC Lambrusco di Sobrara from around Modena. Romagna offers a fruity white, the DOCG Albana, as well as its Trebbiano reds.

Travel Tips

Climate and Seasons

Elaborate irrigation is not the only source of water for the crops of the Po valley. Winter is foggy and often rainy, in addition to being quite chilly (Bologna's average low in January is 30° F, high 40° F). Summers are hot and humid (Bologna's average low in July is 68° F, high 86° F). The coast, however, is less humid and enjoys slightly milder temperatures. Obviously July and August are peak tourist months at the beach towns on the Adriatic, while summer is the least favorite time for the many trade fairs that take place in Bologna and other cities, such as Parma.

Arriving

Although Bologna airport offers some continental connections in addition to domestic ones, it is most likely that you'll be traveling through the region on the way between Rome and Venice, or Milan and Florence, and the like. The train connections between these cities are excellent, as are the highways; just Ravenna and the coast require transfers. Only if you approach through Umbria and Urbino (see that chapter) will the connections become more complicated. Fast trains to Bologna, in the center of the region, take about 3.5 hours from Rome, just over 1 hour from Florence, 2 hours plus from Milan, and a bit more from Venice. Autostradas make bus and car connections efficient to Bologna: A-1 from Milan (210 km, 130 mi.), Florence (104 km, 64 mi.), and Rome (380 km, 236 mi.) and A-13 from Venice (150 km, 93 mi.) as well as A-14 from the Adriatic.

Getting Around

Trains and buses efficiently connect the cities of the region and the car rentals are most easily arranged in Bologna.

Note: Avoid local roads near the coast during the summer beach scene. Traffic is snarled.

Bologna

Key to Bologna

Sights

The Basilica of San Petronio and other churches, paintings by the Bolognese school of the Carracci, and miles of arcaded old city streets.

Excursions

Excellent transportation system makes Bologna a convenient stopover or base for the region.

Shopping

Food is the specialty—just looking at the salumerias and fresh pasta shops is satisfying. (Many shops close Thurs.)

Accommodations

Good accommodations that are totally booked during trade fairs (least often in the summer).

Eating Out

Italians overnight here just to eat the Bolognese cuisine.

Getting Around

Traffic banned in very center, but walking is not only necessary but easy. Buses ply the main streets and taxis are available.

Arriving

Airport with European and domestic flights; frequent and fast train links with Florence, Venice, and Milan; superb highway links with region and with rest of Italy.

Bologna has a character all its own. Its broad streets and monumental Piazza Maggiore give it grandeur. Its nearly 22 miles of streets bordered by arcades give it distinction. Yet Bologna seems to be more down-to-earth, more lived-in than touristy. The prohibition of all but bicycle traffic from most of the historic center, now designated an urban park, has made the city more liveable, with outdoor cafes spilling out from the arcades onto the plazas and smaller streets for Bolognesi to enjoy themselves day and night. The wealth of its citizenry (among the highest per capita in Italy), the solidity and warmth of its brick and terra-cotta buildings, the finery in the shop windows, make it a city of comfort and substance.

But Bologna is more than a complacent bourgeois city. Its history of struggle against papal domination has given the Bolognese an air of determined independence and made the city a stronghold of the Communist Party in recent times. Even its arcades provide more than shade, and much like the city, they display the texture of history, from medieval wooden posts to those of Baroque marble, from the dreariest and poorest to the most elegant with frescoes, stucco and Corinthian columns. Middle class stolidness is broken,

Bologna

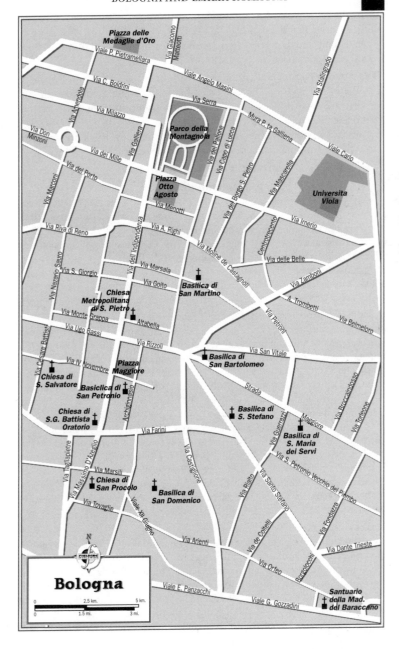

Bologna

too, by the presence of the oldest university in Europe (said to be founded in 1088), and one that has counted Dante, Petrarch, Copernicus, and, more recently, Fellini and Umberto Eco among its students in addition to those 65,000 currently enrolled.

The city of a half million, at the crossroads between Emilia and Romagna, is capital of the region. The tangential highway on the modern, high-tech outskirts anchors the food processing and distribution plants that have always made Bologna enviably rich. But the centro storico remains bustling and unmarred, home to medieval towers and churches, to paintings by the Carracci and Guido Reni, and, of course, to its arcades.

What to See and Do

Piazza Maggiore ★★

In the 13th century, Bologna was flourishing as one of the ten largest cities in Europe. Known as Bologna La Dotta, the learned, its university attracted students from all over the continent. And having just defeated King Enzo, son of Frederick II, the city celebrated its free *commune* status by planning this vast piazza. Construction continued over centuries alongside constant battles to retain independence from stronger neighbors. But when the last of the buildings around the piazza had been completed in the 16th century, Bologna was under papal rule and Charles V had been crowned Holy Roman Emperor in the basilica of patron Saint Petronio.

The piazza today remains in the center of the city, just as the area must have been in Roman times when the Via Emilia (now Via Rozzoli and its extensions) passed through ancient Boninio. The easiest way to orient yourself is by standing with the Basilica of San Petronio (south side of piazza) behind you. Flanking the street to the east is the **Palazzo Banchi** (1565) by Vignola, its harmonious Renaissance facade built to disguise the warren of medieval shops in the market behind. Next to it is the first permanent seat of the university, the Archiginnasio (1562). In front of the basilica is the **Palazzo del Podesta** (13th–15th-centuries) with its medieval bell tower to ring in the volunteer militia. To the left, or west, is the **Palazzo del Comune**, really two Gothic buildings linked by a 16th-century portal and anchored on the south end by a clock tower (1440). Next door, on what is technically the Piazza Nettuno, is the **Palace of the Notaries** (1381) and across from it, attached to the Podesta, is the 13th-century **Palazzo di Re Enzo**, where the captured Enzo was politely held prisoner until his death. On the piazza itself, near Via Rizzoli, is the **Neptune Fountain** with bronze sculptures (1566) by the Florentine-based artist, Giambologna.

Basilica di San Petronio ★★

Begun in 1390 on a scale that would have surpassed that of the cathedrals in Florence and Milan, this basilica is impressive, even though it never achieved its intended grandiose size and remains unfinished today. It is a masterpiece of Gothic brickwork, especially when viewed along its buttressed sides. In 1510 Michelangelo's colossal bronze statue of Pope Julius II was toppled from the facade and melted into cannon fodder during one of the many uprisings for independence. Despite this loss, the church retains around the main portal Jacopo della Quercia's

★ ★ bas reliefs of Old Testament stories (c. 1425) as well as sculptures (except for the figure of St. Ambrose). The heroic and muscular nude bodies of the Adam and Eve panels influenced Michelangelo, and the expressiveness of the expulsion scene embodies the realism of Early Renaissance art. The church *interior* is most notable for its space, open and soaring and pleasing. *Closed noon–3 p.m. in winter.*

Palazzo del Comune

The municipal government maintains its offices here just as it did in medieval times and just as the papacy did during its many centuries of rule. Above the portal is a statue of native son, Pope Gregory XIII, who reformed the Julian calendar; to the left is a lovely terra-cotta *Madonna and Child* (1478). Inside the palace, a staircase attributed to Bramante leads to a third floor Sala Farnese, fit to lodge Charles V during his coronation, as well as other opulent rooms that form the civic **galleria** *(10 a.m.–6 p.m.; till 5 p.m. in winter; closed Mon.; free)*, with Bolognese furnishings and paintings. **Cafeteria** (with views) off the Farnese rooms.

Archiginnasio

Via dell'Archiginnasio 2.
Now the town library *(9 a.m.–1 p.m. in summer; till 6:45 p.m. in winter; closed Sun.)*, this building was the first permanent seat of the university (1562-1800). Its walls are still emblazoned with 7000 coats-of-arms left by students and faculty, and the anatomy room from its renowned Institute of Science has been reconstructed to its 17th-century wood-paneled splendor. Next door is the **Museo Civico Archeologico** *(9 a.m.–2 p.m.; on weekends, 9 a.m.–1 p.m., 3:30-7 p.m.; closed Mon.);* with its display of some fine pieces from Bologna's predecessor, Etruscan Felsina (in Room X) and a state-of-the-art Egyptian exhibit in the basement.

Town Walks ★

Window shopping under a portico, or admiring the art in Bologna's many churches is especially pleasant on a stroll through the city. You can organize your walks around the following more important city sights.

San Domenico

Down Via Archiginnasio, then left onto Via Farini, you come to the Piazza Cavour with frescoes in its vaulted arcades. A right through this piazza, then another block brings you to the attractive surroundings of the Basilica of San Domenico, dedicated to the founder of the Dominican order who died in a convent at this site in 1221. The basilica has been reworked over the centuries, just like its masterpiece inside that is Domenic's tomb, the ★ *Arca di San Domenico* (central chapel). Like so much of Bologna's sculpture, this work is primarily Tuscan. The reliefs (1265) on the sarcophagus that depict scenes from the saint's life were carved by Nicola Pisano's workshop; the angel candlestick on the right and two saints atop the tomb (S. Petronic holding the city; S. Proculus, the right figure, back of tomb) are early works by Michelangelo. *Closed noon–3 p.m.*

Santo Stefano ★

Wind your way east from San Domenico to where Via Farini intersects Via Santo Stefano. Here was a Roman temple to Isis. Then the Early Christian bishop, St.

Bologna

Ambrose, founded a church. Over the next few centuries, as many as seven churches were built, churches preferred by the Lombards in the 8th-century and visited by Charlemagne soon after. Today, Santo Stefano refers to the surviving four churches, a maze of mostly Romanesque-style chapels and courtyards that is redolent with age. A visit to this intriguing complex begins in the **Church of the Crucifix** with its 11th-century crypt and continues (through a door on the left) into two of Bologna's oldest churches, both founded in the fifth century and both with ancient Roman capitals and fragments. The first, the polygonal **San Sepolcro**, was rebuilt in the 12th-century and, embedded in its Romanesque pulpit, is the curious tomb of San Petronio, which was supposed to look like the never-seen Holy Sepulcher in Jerusalem. Farther on is the church of the martyrs **SS Vitale an Agricola**, with three apses (renovated in the 11th century) and the original slits of alabaster windows. (Light machines for both churches are in San Sepolcro.) Retracing your footsteps to San Sepolcro, you find the door leading to the **courtyard di Pilato**, with walls of wonderful brick and terra-cotta chevron designs, but misnamed for its basin, which belonged to the Lombards, not Pontius Pilate. At one end is the 13th-century **Trinita** church, but through a door on the right you find another **cloister**, especially picturesque and with an 11th-century colonnade. *Santo Stefano is closed noon–3:30 p.m.*

Due Torri   ★

West on attractive Via Santo Stefano and you arrive at a complex of squares that forms the medieval heart of the city along with the Piazza Maggiore (just a block farther west). Anchored by the Merchant's Palace at one end and the soaring due torri, or two leaning towers, at the other, the area is architecturally quite rich. The fine Gothic ★**Merchant's Palace** (1382; at the end of Santo Stefano) is rich in brick and terra-cotta detailing. The loggia-style building was the settlement court for merchants and guilds. Other medieval palazzi front this Piazza della Mercanzia, but by now you will already be drawn to the towers. The one built by the Asinelli family (1109) being taller *(stairs for view; 9 a.m.–6 p.m., till 5 p.m. in winter; L3000)*, that by the Garisenda more tilted—it started sinking immediately, much like Pisa's, and was partially dismantled to save it.

Pinacoteca Nazionale ★

From the towers, you can follow Via Zamboni to the Piazzi Verdi with its **Teatro Comunale** (1756), its interior considered one of the finest Baroque theaters in Italy. Then turn left through the university area and you arrive at the Pinacoteca Nazionale. Along the way you might stop at the church of **San Giacomo Maggiore** *(Zamboni 15)* to see its ★ Cappella Bentivoglio (end of left aisle) with a lovely altarpiece of ★ *Virgin and Four Saints,* (1499) by Il Francia and, in front, the Bentivoglio tomb (1435) by della Quercia.

Pinacoteca Nazionale   ★

Via delle Belle Arti 56.

The considerable collection of Bolognese art here is interspersed with some masters from other regions. In medieval art, the works of Vitale da Bologna (c. 1330–60) can be found as in a Giotto school polyptych and a Lorenzo Monaco *Madonna Enthroned* (both in small room off second gallery). Il Francia (note ★ *Madonna*

with Child and Saints and Pala dei Manzuoli) is displayed along with Ferrarese works such as Cossa's *Madonna Enthroned*, as well as the Renaissance genius Raphael (★ *Santa Cecilia and Saints*). It is the Baroque hall where the Bolognese excel, with many works by the Carracci and Guido Reni, including large altarpieces such as Annibale's classical *Madonna and Child and Saints* (1593) and *Annunciation*, his cousin Ludovico's more passionate *Madonna dei Bergellini* (1588) and *Preaching St. John*, and Reni's *Beggar's Pieta*. Some smaller works are notable, too, such as Annibale's moody *Cristo Deriso*, Reni's *Portrait of Artist's Mother*, and Guercino's *St. William*. In the end, the gesturing and high drama of the style may tire you before you reach the last painting. *Open 9 a.m.–2 p.m., Sun. till 1 p.m.; closed Mon.; L8000.*

Where to Stay

Bologna has very comfortable hotels with central locations for sightseeing. But a number of days each month (except in summer, usually) are given over to trade fairs. Then, rooms are scarce and, when available, at their costliest—the high-end prices listed below are for doubles. On many weekends, holidays and in July–August, expect lower prices in singles and toward the lower price range in doubles. Reserve in advance.

Very Expensive

Grand Hotel Baglioni L310–620,000 CP ✿★★★★

V. Indipendenza 8, 40121; ☎ *225-445, FAX 234-840.*
Single L395,000 CP. Double L310–620,000 CP.
Just a block from the Piazza Maggiore on Bologna's main but traffic-free street, the Baglioni's location is superb. The hotel is elegant. Its common areas have stucco moldings and red carpet; its corridors are wide and furnished with antiques. Its 128 rooms have high ceilings and are attractively appointed. Good service. Restaurant. Bar. Parking.

Expensive

Royal Hotel Carlton L240–395,000 CP ★★★★

V. Montebello 8, 40121; ☎ *249-361, FAX 249-724.*
Single L311,000 CP. Double L240–395,000 CP.
Toward the stazione and in an area with little charm, the Carlton nonetheless is within walking distance of the sights. In exchange for ambience, it offers contemporary, subdued decor and the full services you expect of a Hilton-style hotel. The 250 rooms are more than comfortable. There's a restaurant, bar and garage.

Al Cappello Rosso L200–390,000 CP ★★★

V. de' Fusari 9, 40123; ☎ *261-891, FAX 227-179.*
Single L270,000 CP. Double L200–390,000 CP.
In the picturesque area just south of the Piazza Maggiore is this intimate hotel. Contemporary in decor throughout, the lobby opens to a tree-filled atrium and the 35 rooms are smartly furnished, graciously appointed with bathrobes, and include kitchenettes. Breakfast bar. Garage.

Corona d'Oro L280–420,000 CP ✿★★★

V. Oberdan 12, 40126; ☎ *236-456, FAX 262-679.*
Single L290,000 CP. Double L280–420,000 CP.

The handsome common areas of this hotel are full of architectural details from past centuries. The 35 rooms are carpeted and, though variable, somewhat small. Its location is on a quiet street near the Piazza Maggiore. Breakfast bar. Parking. Closed Aug.

Moderate

Roma   **L150–180,000**   √★★★

V. d'Azeglio 9, 40123; ☎ *226-322, FAX 239-909.*
Single L150,000. Double L170–180,000.

On one of Bologna's quaintest streets (a continuation of Indipendenza) and just south of the Piazza Maggiore is the Roma. This hotel is one of the best buys in Italy and offers an attractive lobby with comfortable bar and dining room, as well as boutiques. The 89 rooms are ample and decorated attractively with large, modern baths. Snappy service. A garage, too, as well as an excellent location.

Dei Commercianti   **L175–275,000 CP**   ★★

V. de' Pignattari 11, 40124; ☎ *233-052, FAX 224-733.*
Single L175,000 CP. Double L180–275,000 CP.

In a quiet corner near the west side of the San Petronio, this hotel offers an ultra-modern lobby and 31 rooms with servi-bar. Breakfast bar. Garage.

Inexpensive

Palace   **L100–150,000**   ★★

V. Montegrappa 9, 40121; ☎ *237-442, FAX 220-689.*
Single L100,000. Double L100–150,000.

Two blocks west of the Piazza Maggiore on Via U. Bassi and then a right takes you within sight of this old-fashioned hotel. Its high-ceiling lobby, furnished with armchairs, has a clubby ambience and many of its 117 rooms are quite large, with giant tubs for baths, carpeting, and air conditioning (fee). Breakfast bar. Garage.

Accademia   **L65–90,000**   ★

V. Belle Arti 6, 40126; ☎ *232-318, FAX 263-590.*
Single L65,000. Double L70–90,000.

In the university area near the Pinacoteca Nazionale, the Accademia offers 28 rooms, most with private baths, none with air conditioning. There's no elevator and there is some noise, so take heed. Breakfast bar. Limited parking.

Where to Eat

Since the 13th century, Bologna has been known not only as "the learned," but also as "la grassa," or the fat. Considering some of its contributions to cuisine, especially those that have permeated the New World—old standbys like spaghetti alla bolognese (really *al ragu*, or meat sauce) and bologna, or *mortadella* as the more ham-tasting version is known here—we might misinterpret this phrase that is meant as a compliment. Not only are ragu and mortadella better here than more familiar versions, but also, Bologna is considered by many to be the gastronomic capital of Italy. Bolognese fascination with food can be seen not only in the *salumerie* and restaurants, but even in paintings such as the great Annibale Carracci's *The Beaneaters*, and certainly on signs posted in the arcades for lectures on the history of food (we've seen one for the "ecology" of obesity). Bolognese willingly pay for quality—handstuffed tortelli being much preferred, though far pricier than the machine variety. With such discerning clients, the restaurants outdo themselves transforming the traditional tortellini, tagliatelle, and *petto di tacchino* (turkey breast) into something not simply good, but sublime. In recent years, however, critics have not been kind to Bologna; stars have been knocked off some of its formerly celestial restaurants so that now they're considered merely exquisite. If it's Emilian perfection you want, however, maybe you'll want to seek out the highly ranked **Antica Osteria del Teatro** in Piacenza or the **Fini** in Modena.

Elegant Dining

Franco Rossi $$–$$$ ★★★★

V. Goito 3; ☎ *238-818, FAX 238-818.*
Closed Sun.; reservation required. Meals L65–85,000.
Located just off Indipendenza, this intimate restaurant is one of the few to have retained its ranking among the city's best for many years. The *fagottino alla parmigiana*, or crepe filled with ricotta, mushrooms and chicory is ambrosial, and the bistecca aceto balsamico is densely flavorful, almost addictive; the salmon with red pepper, quite fine. The most traditional dishes are presented with flair: tortellini in brodo, but with tartufo; delicate tortelloni, with a filling of pumpkin squash and spring scallions; and the petto di tacchino, brightened with whatever inspires chef Lino Rossi. Even the crema caramelo is special. Attentive service overseen by Franco Rossi himself.

Pappagallo $$–$$$ ★★★

P. della Mercanzia 3; ☎ *232-807, FAX 232-807.*
Closed Sat. night, Sun. Meals L65–100,000.
Once one of Bologna's great restaurants, Pappagallo is now striving to regain its former accolades with its new chef. In an elegant medieval dining room, lightened with contemporary paintings and white walls, you can sample dishes that likewise combine the old with the new: avocado salad with shrimp and arugula or tagliatelle with oysters and porcini, veal with capers and Balsamic or rabbit with celery hearts and olives. Although the food is worthy of a visit, the service needs improvement.

Pure Bolognese

Gigina $ ★★

V. Stendhal 1b; ☎ *322-132.*
Closed Sat.; most of Aug.; reservation required. Meals about L40,000.
Bologna's secret bastion of traditional cuisine is located about a 20-minute ride north of the city (take exit 6 of the *tangenziale*) in a working class neighborhood. Gigina's is run by her big-hearted daughter, Nadia who good-naturedly bullies you into eating inordinate amounts. You come here, not for the nondescript setting, but to join the locals in consuming heaping plates of Mama Gigina's hand-made tortellini or tagliatelli. If you can eat more after the refills, there are those boiled Bolognese meats *(bollito)* to sample and roasted veal or rabbit. The prices are reasonable and the hugs and fussing from Nadia alone are worth a trip. Lunch is liveliest and best.

Diana $$–$$$ ★★★

V. dell'Indipendenza 24; ☎ *231-302, FAX 228-162.*

Closed Mon., early Jan., Aug Meals L50–80,000.

Another Bolognese institution, this one has refined ambience, a central location, and a more elegant presentation of its classic Emilian dishes to please its business clientele during the week, the Bolognesi on Sundays. The food is so traditional that crostini are spread with spuma di mortadella, rather than Tuscan chicken livers; and, of course, there's tortellini in brodo and lasagne verde as well as bollito misto (try the *magro*, or leaner version, with poultry and veal). If you save the tartufi and funghi porcini for dining adventures elsewhere, a very traditional meal will be almost moderate in price. In the summer, reserve a table on the outdoor terrace.

Trattorias

Leonida   **$$**   ★★

Vicola Alemagna 2; ☎ *239-742.*

Closed Sun., Aug., reservation required. Meals L40–55,000.

Just a block from Santo Stefano, this is where the Bolognesi send their out-of-town guests yet don't necessarily go themselves. It has the perfect rosey-warm ambience of an Italian trattoria with an outdoor terrace located on a quiet lane. The food doesn't match up to the ambience, however; avoid the disappointing pastas and try instead the more satisfying main dishes (rabbit in balsamic vinegar) and desserts.

La Columbina   **$–$$**   ★★

Vicolo Columbina 5; 231-706.

Closed Tues. Meals L35–50,000.

Follow the lane on the west side of the basilica to this convenient trattoria tucked away near the apse. Despite the Queen Victoria decor, the food couldn't be more Bolognese, especially the terrific *gramigna* (fat squiggles of pasta with ground sausage and peas.)

Simpler Meals

In   **$**   ★

P. Minghetti 2b; ☎ *226-646.*

Closed Mon. in winter. Main dishes L9–16,000.

For an al fresco lunch, join the office crowd at this trendy spot devoted to light eating. You can order just one course: a large salad *(insalatone)*, say, of *gamberetti e rucola* (ask for the extra virgin olive oil and balsamic vinegar), an antipasto or pasta.

Enogastronomia   **$–$$**   ★

Strada Maggiore 5.

10 a.m.–2p.m. only; closed Mon. Main dishes L10–20,000.

This is actually a wonderful food shop that serves some of its daily specials in a small dining area.

Da Ciro   **$**   ★

V. de'Gessi 5c.

Closed Wed., Aug. Pizza L7–15,000.

In a lane behind the Palace Hotel, this is a terrific choice for pizza and salad on a summer evening when you can sit on the terrace.

Da Pino   **$**   ★

V. Goito 2.

Closed Mon. Pizza L8–15,000.
Located just off Indipendenza, this is the place for pizza in the winter when you can settle into one of the cozy booths.

Snacks, Picnics, Caffe

Many cafes serve canapes with their apertivos. At some, the offerings have expanded so much the cafes have become places to eat, like **Il Calice** *(V. Clavature 13A; closed Sun.)* a tiny but sophisticated bar with an upstairs *sala da te*. Here you can sample caviar canapes, raw oysters, an excellent salad—not just the usual panini. **Enoteca Italiana** *(V. Malcontenti at Marsala)*, just off Indipendenza, offers panini and foccaci for lunch along with its extensive offerings of Emilia Romagnan wines by the glass. More grandly old world is **Caffè Zanarini** *(V. Farini near San Petronio, closed Mon.)* with its frizzante wines by the glass and excellent pastries. The **Caffè Palazzo Comune** *(2nd floor of Palazzo near Civic Museum; closed Mon.)* has terrific views of the P. Naggiore along with decent food and drink.

Food shopping is a delight even if you aren't buying. The **market** is just a block east of the Piazza Maggiore at Clavature and Drapperie, and nearby are many vegetable shops as well as **Melega Cesare** *(Calvature 12)*, with beautiful fruits as well a cold cuts and cheeses. The shops for your gourmet purchases, however, are the venerable **Tamburini** *(Caprari 1a, a block north on Drapperie)* with its wood oven roasting game hens, and its shelves, and even ceiling, jammed with delicacies; and **Paolo Atti** *(V. Caprari 7b)* with fresh pastas, pastries and prepared dishes, like stuffed red peppers. Your picnic shopping might expand to gift shopping at **Roccati** *(V. Fusari past Cappello Rosso Hotel)* for exquisite chocolates as well as **Scaramagli** *(V. Maggiore 31d)*, a supermarket devoted to wines, Modena balsamic vinegars, olive oils, and chocolates—all at good prices. *If you are picnicking, the benches at the nearby Piazza Minghetti (on V. Farini) might do, or the large La Piazzola park at the north end of town.*

Directory

Telephone Code 051   **Postal Code 40100**

Airport
> In Borgo Panigale, 7 km, 4 mi. northwest ☎ *311-578*, linked by bus #91 to train station.

Albergo Diurni
> P. Maggiore at Re Enzo (closed Sun.).

American Express
> **Big Tours**, *Independencia 12.*

Books in English
> **Feltrinelli International**, *V. Zambroni 7*, near P. Due Torre 1.

Bus
> **ATC**, local buses run the main streets; buy tickets at tabacchi. Pullman buses, *P. XX Settembre 6*, north end of Indipendenza ☎ *248-374* for regional destinations.

Car Rentals
> In city and at airport, such as **Avis** ☎ *551-528;* and **Budget** ☎ *358-480.*

Emergencies

Dial ☎ *113*.

Groceries

Just east of P. Maggiore, on Drapperie, Clavature, and Caprari, are the food shops and market.

Parking

Numerous private garages.

Police

Questura, ☎ *278-846*.

Post Office

P. VIII Agosto, with telegraph services.

Shopping

V. Indipendenza and V. Rizzoli, main commercial streets, but V. Stefano and V. D'Azeglio more picturesque, for window shopping or the passeggiata.

Swimming Pool

Stadio Comunale, *V. Costa 174*, indoor and out; fee.

Taxis

Dial ☎ *372-727;* or pick up at major piazzas.

Telephone

Telcom, P. VIII Agosto, in post office (open 8 a.m.–10 p.m.); and in train station.

Tourist Office

APT, Palazzo Comunale, west side P. Maggiore ☎ *239-660, FAX 231-454;* open 9 a.m.–7 p.m.; Sun. 9:30 a.m.–12:30 p.m. At stazione too.

Tours

CIT, V. Rizzoli, in Palazzo Re Enzo; **APT** tourist office *(☎ 239-660)*, for their 2.5-hour city tours (fee).

Train

On north edge of centro storico, just beyond (and west) of bus terminal; walk or take #25 bus to P. Maggiore.

On the Road

Small Emilian Towns

The well-tended fields, orchards and vineyards that mark the Po basin support the prosperous towns of Emilia just as they have since ancient times. Although agribusiness and agritechnology now send the products of Emilia to lands never conquered by Rome, its towns have a farming stolidity that reaches back to ancient times. Rome may have named the region with its Via Emilia, but later epochs have left more enduring marks on the cities. During the early Middle Ages, churches were built along the Roman road to accommodate the pilgrims winding their way to Rome and the crusaders heading for ships in Ravenna and Venice. The traffic along the old road produced solid brick Romanesque churches fronted by Emilian-style lion porches and decorated with Biblical stories carved by Wiligelmus in Modena, Benedetto Antelami in Parma, and an unknown master in Ferrara. Later, two duchies filled the towns with their palazzi and gardens, their libraries and art collections. Today, you can appreciate the legacy of the Farnese court in Parma and Piacenza and of the famous Este in Ferrara and Modena.

Whether you stop briefly in these towns for a glimpse of their admirable churches or for the pleasure of Correggio frescoes in Parma and Bernini's bust of Francesco I d'Este in Modena, or whether you decide on a more leisurely exploration, you'll find comfort and good hearty cuisine. Ferrara, off the Via Emilia, is a convenient stopover on the way to Venice; Modena, Parma, and Piacenza on the way to Milan. The Milan-Bologna train or the Autostrada del Sole can be taken in place of the Via Emilia, now SS 9.

Modena

Overshadowed by nearby Bologna, Modena seldom evokes any clear images. Yet it is a prosperous city of almost 180,000, famous for its opera singers (Luciano Pavarotti was born here and performs for his hometown once a year in the Piazza Grande) as well as balsamic vinegar, Lambrusco wine, amaretto cookies and Vignola cherries. And Modena is even more famous for its concentration of exotic car manufacturers (Maserati, De Tomaso, Lamborghini, Bugatti and, of course, Ferrari). Winding your way into the sizable city you find a surprisingly pleasant and compact historic center. The arcaded streets lead you by one of the great Romanesque squares of Italy and take you past the Baroque palazzi where the Este dukes resided after their expulsion from Ferrara in 1598. And with the Este came their library and art collection, treasures of modern Modena.

What to See and Do

Piazza Grande ★

Main street remains the Via Emilia. Just a few steps away is the heart of medieval Modena, the Piazza Grande with its town hall and, until recent decades, provincial market. But the eye-catcher here is Lanfranco's ★★**duomo** *(closes noon– 3:30 p.m.)*, begun in 1099 and the first Romanesque church with a lion porch. In fact, Lanfranco added considerable decoration to the serene Lombard-style exterior, as pilasters form patterns of arches that enclose blind arcades. The capitals of the pilasters, the roof, the portals—all are carved, even the solid brick wall is randomly punctured to hold bas reliefs. While there is constant delight in discovering these decorative details, the facade retains its Romanesque serenity. The 12th-century master Wiligelmus and his school created most of the ★facade sculptures, especially those on the south side, based on Arthurian legends as well as Biblical stories. Wiligelmus' masterpieces, however, are the wondrous main (west) portal carvings of vines and mythical animals and the panel scenes based on Genesis (left of portal). The set of four panels on the south side near the apse are devoted to Modena's patron S. Geminianus, carved by Agostino di Duccio (1442). The ★interior brick vaulting is impressive and the polychrome carvings of the pulpit of the raised choir are vigorous, if a bit stiff. (Light machine left aisle.) The patron saint is buried in the crypt amid slender Moorish columns with notable capitals. Casting its shadow over the duomo is the campanile, the **Ghirlandina Tower** (finished 14th-century), the symbol of Modena. One of Italy's tallest campanile (almost 300 feet), La Ghirlandina is best appreciated from behind the duomo on Via Emilia.

Palazzo Ducale

From the tower, cross Via Emilia and follow the series of traffic-free streets and squares that begin with Piazza Mazzini and end several blocks north at the **Palazzo Ducale**, begun by Francesco I d'Este in 1629 and now housing the West Point of Italy. Behind it are the public gardens. Or simply head west on Via Emilia until you arrive at the Palazzo dei Musei on the Largo Sant'Agostino. Here is the **Biblioteca Estense** *(second floor; 9 a.m.–7 p.m. except Fri. & Sat. till 2 p.m. and closed Sun.; free)* with some of the Este collection of manuscripts on display, including the extraordinary 15th-century ★ Bible of Borso d'Este, illuminated by Taddeo Crivelli and others. On the third floor is the **Galleria Estense** *(9 a.m.–2 p.m., except till 7 p.m. Fri.–Sat., till 1 p.m. Sun.; closed Mon.; L8000)*. Francesco I d'Este assembled most of the collection here, and he is seen most splendidly in Bernini's ★★portrait bust (1650), which so captured ducal pomposity that even the artist's later portrait of Louis XIV couldn't surpass it. Passing from the vestibule into a large gallery you find works by diverse artists such as Barnaba da Modena, Cosme Tura and Cima da Conegliano. In the next set of rooms are numerous works by Emilian artists, such as Dossi's portrait of the Ferrarese Alfonso I d'Este. The last rooms exhibit a collection from the Bolognese school of Baroque painting, including Guercino's ★ *Martyrdom of St. Peter* (1618).

Car Factories

As for seeing modern Modena, few of the car manufacturers open their factory secrets to outsiders. **Ferrari** does let car owners visit and, for the rest of us, has a gallery of vintage and modern cars near the factory in Marinello *(Thurs.–Sun. 10:30a.m.–1 p.m., 4–7 p.m.; L2000)*; **Maserati** *(☎ 21-760)* permits tours a few days a week by appointment only.

Where to Stay

So near Bologna, Modena is not usually an overnight stop. But if it suits you, there are hotels in the centro storico.

Canalgrande   L195–290,000

Corso Canal Grande 6; ☎ 217-160, FAX 221-674.
Single L195,000. Double L290,000.
The 80 air-conditioned rooms here occupy an 18th-century palace—located a number of blocks southeast of the duomo. The furnishings are lackluster, but there's a lovely garden and parking.

Liberta   **L95–135,000**   ★★

V. Blasia 10; ☎ 222-365, FAX 222-502; closed Christmas holidays and Aug.
Single L95,000. Double L135,000.

Right between the duomo and Palazzo Ducale. A modest but comfortable hotel near shops and restaurants and on a traffic-free lane, with 48 rooms (no air conditioning) and garage.

Where to Eat

Like many Emilian towns, Modena is noted for its good restaurants. Whether or not you want to sample the local *zampone* (stuffed pig's trotters), you'll find plenty to enjoy, especially entrées prepared with balsamic vinegar.

Fini   ★★★★

Largo San Francesco; reserve at ☎ 223-314, FAX 220-247.
Closed Mon., Tues., Christmas and Aug. L75–115,000.

Some blocks south of the duomo, Fini was founded in 1912 by the producer of the finest Emilian food products. These gourmet ingredients, from the salumi to the vinegar, are used in this highly regarded restaurant to create the best Emilian cuisine. The ambience is formal, the service as impeccable as the food, be it the extraordinary tortelli, the fritto misto (fried meats, fruits, vegetables), or a bollito misto that includes zampone.

Trattoria Bianca   **$$**   ★★★

V. Spaccini 24; ☎ 311-524, FAX 315-520.
Closed Sun., Sat. at lunch, Christmas season, Easter and Aug. Meals L45–65,000.

Just north of the centro storico (a somewhat pricey taxi ride) and just as authentic and traditional as Fini, Bianca offers a more relaxing ambience for enjoying your tortellini in brodo (or any of the freshly made pastas), beef prepared with the family-produced balsamic vinegar as well as a dessert of zuppa inglese made with the local amaretti. In the summer, reserve a table al fresco.

Forno San Giorgio

V. Taglio 6, just above P. Mazzini.

If all of this is more than you want, consider a visit to the bakery, where they are happy to warm a slice or two of artichoke and tomato pizza—the pastries are good, too.

Directory

Telephone Code 059   **Postal Code 41100**

Tourist Information

APT, V. Emilia, across from P. Mazzini ☎ 222-482; FAX 214-591.

Special Events

Antique Fair, in P. Grande, last Sunday of each month.

Arriving

Just a half hour by train or car from Bologna. Stazione connected to P. Grande by #7, 11 buses. • A-1 passes near on its way from Bologna (40 km, 25 mi.) to Parma (55 km, 34 mi.) and A-22 goes to Verona (100 km, 62 mi.).

Parma

Parma has more than hams and cheese. It claims Guiseppe Verdi as its own,
his birthplace being nearby, as well as Arturo Toscanini, and preserves this
musical tradition by the quality of opera in its **Teatro Regio** (1828). It also
preserves the greatest work of the Romanesque sculptor Antelami, the paintings of High Renaissance genius Correggio, and the Manneristic canvases of
Parmigianino. A modern, substantial city of nearly 180,000, Parma is pleasingly easy to explore, whether along the shady banks of the Po tributary that
divides it (usually the waters are diverted to more prized irrigation canals) or
on the broad neo-classical avenues that recall the reign of the royal Austrian
Marie Louise, Napoleon's wife, who arrived in 1815 after his exile to Elba.

What to See and Do

Piazza del Duomo   ★★

This magnificent medieval piazza once could hold the entire populace in its square.
Surrounded by easily defended buildings, the piazza was the very center of the fortified 11th-century city. When pink Verona marble arrived to begin the baptistery
in 1196, it was floated right to the square on a canal that connected the town to the
network of waterways in the Po valley. Today it remains the religious center of the
city. The ★ **duomo** *(closed noon–3 p.m.)* begun in 1090, is a fine example of Emil-
ian-Lombard Romanesque architecture, its brick austerity brightened by a double
lion porch and graceful arcades. Examination with binoculars of the arcades along
the roofline and around the east exterior can bring into focus the fabulous carvings
of gargoyles and beasties. Inside, the Romanesque is recalled in Antelami's bas relief
★ *Descent from the Cross* (1178; right transept, right wall; light machine), an early
work with Byzantine stiffness, but some of the new expressiveness too. Then leap
the centuries and enter the rapturous world of Correggio's dome fresco, ★★ *As-
cent of the Virgin* (c. 1526; light machine up steps from right transept, on left).
Considered by many to be the consummation of his style, the daring illusionism and
complexity of this work shocked many at the time it was created, but was later
embraced by the Baroque. ★★ **Baptistery** *(9 a.m.–12:30, 3–5 p.m., or 6 p.m.
April–June; in summer, 9 a.m.–12:30 p.m. and at 3:30–7 p.m.; closed Mon. Sept.–
Mar.; L3000)* is a landmark in Romanesque art because of its elaborate sculptural
decorations by Antelami and his workshop. Later than his *Descent*, the portal carvings and exterior animal friezes have almost Gothic fluidity, especially notable in the
fable told on the south, or rear, portal. On the west portal is the first *Last Judgment*
depicted in Italy. The lunettes of the interior and the niche figures (in the east loggia) representing the months, seasons, and zodiac continue Antelami's work, complemented by a wonderful ribbed dome and pleasing 13th-century frescoes.

Behind the duomo is the church of ★ **San Giovanni Evangelista** *(closed noon–
3:30)*, worthy of an admiring visit for another of Correggio's dome frescoes, this
one the earlier ★★ *Vision of St. John* (1520). Around the edge of the drum are
some very Michelangelesque apostles, one looking up, with us, into a seemingly
infinite celestial space through which Christ ascends (light in north transept). Also

by Correggio is the tympanum fresco of *St. John Writing*, over the sacristy door, in the north transept. Frescoes of various saints by Parmigianino are under the arches of the 1st, 2nd (light for both in 2nd) and 4th chapels on the north aisle. On the north of the church is the cloister with an original 16th-century **pharmacy**, complete with all its tidy jars *(hours similar to Baptistery; L3000)*.

Piazza Garibaldi

Via della Repubblica and Cavour.

Moving out of the Romanesque duomo piazza along the picturesque Via XX Marzo (turn right at Reppublica) you move along historically to the "new square" of the later Middle Ages when emerging free towns built Gothic town halls and commercial buildings to vie with those of the church. Although the Piazza Garibaldi has been revamped many times, it is today's true center of the city, where the locals take their *passeggiata* (a frenzied mess when cold sends them to their cars), sip tea with friends at the many cafes, and shop along Repubblica. In the northwest corner, near Via Garibaldi, is the church **Madonna della Stacchata** (1521) elaborately decorated by Parma artists, including Parmigianino's *Virgin* painted under the arch of the presbytery.

Palazzo della Pilotta ★★

Via Garibaldi.

Located amid some immense squares is the cold 16th-century complex built by the Farnese dukes. Whatever the architectural demerits of the building, it contains the **Teatro Farnese** (1619), an immense and intricate wooden theater built for ducal pleasure. Based on a Palladian design, it is said to be the first theater with moveable sets. The palazzo also contains a number of collections, among them the **Galleria Archeologico Nazionale** *(9 a.m.–1:30 p.m.; closed Mon.; L4000)* with some quality bronzes and sculptures from antiquity, as well as the ★★**Galleria Nazionale** *(third floor, entrance through the Teatro Farnese; open 9 a.m.–1:45 p.m.; L12,000)*. The high-tech exhibit spaces of this museum are themselves often stunning. Though the Farnese collection they display was greatly reduced when Charles the Bourbon carted them off with him to Naples, there remains enough to warrant a visit. Antelami is represented, as is Correggio, his ★*Madonna del Gerolamo* (1526) and ★*Madonna della Sodella* (1526) full of light, movement and innocence, and his intense *Pieta* (1524). Only a few Parmigianino remain, among them his ★ *Turkish Slavewoman*. There is a Leonardo ★sketch of a young woman, along with some works by the Bolognese CounterReformation school of the Carracci and Bartolommeo Schedoni.

With your ticket from the Galleria Nazionale you can enter the **Camera di San Paolo** *(V. Melloni 4, across V. Garibaldi and opposite post office; same hours as galleria)*. In the second sala, Correggio frescoed (1519) the vault with a mythological composition. The design is unusual, but more noteworthy for the fact that its completely pagan themes were painted for Giovanna da Piacenza, who was none other than the abbess.

Where to Stay

Except when the spring trade fairs fill up Parma, you should find the choice of hotels adequate.

Palace Hotel Maria Luigia   **L240–300,000 CP**   ★★★

V. Mentana 140; ☎ *281-032, FAX 231-126.*
Single L240,000 CP. Double L300,000 CP.

At the north edge of the historic district, near both the stazione and sights, is this modern hotel with 93 well-appointed rooms, restaurant, bar, parking.

Park Hotel Stendhal   **L170–255,000**   ★★★

V. Bodoni 3; ☎ *208-057, FAX 285-655.*
Single L170,000. Double L255,000.

Comfortable and right next to the Palazzo Pilotta, the Park has 60 modern rooms, restaurant, bar and parking.

Button   **L95–130,000**   ★★

San Vitale 7; ☎ *208-039, FAX 238-783. Closed mid July–Aug., 1st week Jan.*
Single L95,000. Double L130,000.

A few steps from the Piazza Garibaldi, the Button is bright and cheerful and in the heart of the historic district; there are 44 rooms (no a/c), many quite ample, with modern baths. Breakfast bar.

Where to Eat

If you can avoid thinking about your cholesterol levels for a day, you should do so in Parma. Even the butter here is exquisite. And when you combine it with parmigiano reggiano over the favorite pasta of tortelli, you have a simple but rich dish that is unforgettable. Here, too, you must try the *prosciutto crudo*, ("Parma ham"). With such sumptuous beginnings it hardly matters what follows.

Cocchi   **$$**   ★★★

V. Gramsci 16; ☎ *981-990.*
Closed Sat., Aug., and Christmas. Meals L45–70,000.

A wonderful spot for sampling the local cuisine is at this family-run and comfortable restaurant. Here the only formalities are with the food, and it is superbly prepared with the best ingredients, from the vinegars and oils for the salads and tortelli stuffed with spinach and ricotta to the lamb baked in rosemary and artichokes and ending with a reviving sip of the house *limonella*, or lemon liquor. (Located about 1 mi. from P. Garibaldi, across the bridge.)

Angiol d'Or   **$$–$$$**   ★★★★

Vicolo Scutellari 1; ☎ *282-632, FAX 282-747.*
Closed Sun. Fixed-price lunch L45,000. À la carte L55–90,000

This is Cocchi's new endeavor, a smarter restaurant located on the edge of the Piazza Duomo. Even if don't want to dine elegantly here (duck with red wine; veal medallions with porcini), you should succumb to lunching on their outdoor terrace for the fixed-price sampler of Parma's best (a plate of delicate prosciutto followed by rich tortelli sprinkled with the finest parmesan).

Parizzi   **$$**   ★★★★

V. della Republica 71; reserve at ☎ *285-952, FAX 285-027.*

Closed Sun. from June–Aug., Mon. Meals L45–70,000
In the opposite direction from Angiol d'Or, Parizzi is famous and bustling and serving equally wonderful tortelli all'erbette and delicate scaloppine.

Gallo d'Oro $ ★★

Borgo della Salina 3; ☎ 208-846;
Closed Sun. Meals L30–45,000
Good food and good ambience are featured at this location just south of Piazza Garibaldi (one block down Farini, turn left).

Gastronomia Garibaldi

Garibaldi 42; 8 a.m.–8 p.m.
Closed Mon.
For picnics or snacks or simply to salivate, go directly here where you can buy all that is delicious for take-out, from cured hams and cheeses to shrimp salad, from pizza slices to grilled vegetables, from regional wines to traditional *limoncino*, Parma's lemon grappa.

Directory

Telephone Code 0521   **Postal Code 43100**

Tourist Information
   APT, *P. Duomo 5* ☎ *234-735; FAX 238-605.*

Festival
   July concerts in Teatro Regio

Getting Around
   Town easily walkable.

Arriving
   Frequent trains to Milan and Bologna; convenient service to Florence; stazione north and walkable to center, but #1 bus to P. Garibaldi. •Pullman buses to provincial towns, leave from V. Toschi, behind Palazzo Pilatta. •Bologna is 95 km, 59 mi. and Milan, 120 km, 74 mi. on A-1.

Good Reading
   Stendhal's *Charterhouse of Parma* is partially set in Marie Louise's Parma.

Piacenza

   The terminus of the Via Emilia, Piacenza was founded at a critical juncture of the Po. Today its location continues to be important, creating not only a flourishing agribusiness in tomato canning, but also a methane gas industry. Though the entrance to town may not be inviting, the small medieval center of the modern city holds some gems of northern brick architecture. On the Piazza del Duomo is the Romanesque ★**cathedral** (1122–1233), its calm facade decorated with three Emilian porches, the middle one with traditional lions and the sides with variations. A few blocks west on the traffic-free Via XX Settembre, you pass the Gothic church of **San Francesco** just before entering the ★**Piazza dei Cavalli**. Here stands the quintessential northern town hall, the ★**Palazzo Comunale**. Begun in 1280, its harmonious facade is enriched by the contrast in texture of the marble loggia with the brick and terra-cotta of the upper windows, and enlivened by the gentle rhythm of six windows over five arches. In front of this palace stand two equestrian statues of Farnese dukes by Francesco Mochi (1580-1654), that of ★ *Alessandro* on the left remarkable for its early Baroque dynamism. Several more blocks north on Via Cittadella brings you to a piazza of the same name where the **Farnese Palace** (16th-century) has been restored and made into a museo civico *(9 a.m.–12:30 p.m., but also 3:30–5:30 p.m. Thurs., Sat., Sun.; closed Mon. i winter; L4500).* Although the assassination here of the first duke led the Farnese to establish their permanent court in Parma, where most of their art can now be seen, this museo contains works from a variety of periods, including the *Fegato di Piacenza*, an Etruscan bronze sheep's liver that was used in divination.

Where to Stay

Grande Albergo Roma   **L100–160,000**   ★★

V. Cittadella 14; ☎ 323-201, FAX 330-548.
Single L100,000. Double L160,000.
Just a half-block from the Piazza dei Cavalli is this substantial hotel with 90 air-conditioned rooms in modern decor, restaurant, bar and garage.

Florida   **L95–115,000**   ★

V. Colombo 29; ☎ 592-600, FAX 592-672.
Single L95,000. Double L115,000.
On the eastern outskirts is this plain motel with 40 a/c rooms, restaurant and parking.

Where to Eat

Antica Osteria del Teatro   **$$$**   ★★★★★

V. Verdi 16; reserve ☎ 323-777, FAX 384-639.
Closed Sun. dinner, Mon., Aug., early Jan. & Aug. Fixed-price meals L75 & 100,000. À la carte L70–130,000.
Some travelers find themselves here for reasons other than the architecture. These epicures come for this elegant restaurant with frescoes on its 15th-century walls, can be found in the historic section south of the Piazza dei Cavalli. While classic regional dishes such as tortelli are prized here, chef Filippo Chiappini Dattilo is more famous for his creative interpretations, like rabbit in olive vinaigrette and wild duck with peaches and porcini tarts.

Gotico   **$$**   ★

P. dei Cavalli 26; ☎ 321-940.
Closed Sun., Aug. Meals L35–55,000.
A convenient trattoria, this one also adds a Tuscan accent to the enjoyable cuisine.

Directory

Telephone Code 0523   **Postal Code 29100**

Tourist Information

P. dei Mercanti, near P. Cavalli *(☎ 29-324, FAX 334-348).*

Arriving

Trains from Milan (1 hour) and Bologna (2 hours) stop here and the stazione is walkable to the center, but connected by bus, too. • Pullman buses (P. Cittadella) are convenient to regional towns, Cremona, etc. • Milan is 68 km (42 mi.), Parma a little less, and Bologna 150 km (93 mi.) via A-1. Cremona and Pavia are close on A-21. • Parking: around old city walls.

Ferrara

Home to one of the great Renaissance courts, Ferrara had a rich cultural history for the centuries of Este rule. Surprisingly, some of the most famous names of the Este duchy belong to women—Isabella and Beatrice d'Este and their sister-in-law, Lucrezia Borgia. All three were among the most powerful women of the Renaissance, known for their intelligence, and, in the case of the sisters, great patrons of the arts at the courts of their spouses in Mantua and Milan. But their father, Ercole I, and the other male dukes set high artistic standards themselves, commissioning works by Piero della Francesca and Titian, providing hospitality to the likes of Petrarch and hiring the first Greek scholar of the Renaissance. Their patronage nourished a local school of Early Renaissance painting that included Tura, Cossa, and Roberti and resulted in two of the great epic works in Italian literature: *Jerusalem Delivered* (1575) by Torquato Tasso and Ludovico Ariosto's world classic, *Orlando Furioso* (1532), with many of the Este as characters.

Although many paintings and frescoes, palazzo furnishings and comforts have been lost, Ferrara retains the imprint of its ducal past. The delightful city is an example of early town planning by Ercole I and the local architect Biagio Rossetti. In the late 15th century they more than doubled the size of the city with broad symmetrical streets lined with gardens and handsome palazzi, a plan that today encompasses most of this city of 150,000. The more than five miles of fortified walls have now been converted into a park around the city; the streets are unusually peaceful, permitting only bicycles and pedestrians, not cars or even mopeds. The Sunday night passeggiata around the duomo is with families—on bicycles. An overnight here, on your way to Venice or other spots, can revive you for more demanding cities.

What to See and Do

Duomo

Anchoring the medieval center is the ★ **duomo**, its lower facade Romanesque, the upper facade Gothic, and the campanile, Renaissance. The three gables and screen form of the fabulous facade, all pink and white marble, which couldn't be more Italian. Over the elaborate main portal is an instructive ★ *Last Judgment* for potential sinners, with the condemned spilling off into a hell where they are devoured by monsters or boiled in a huge pot. The interior has been austerely renovated and is a disappointment except for the ★ **duomo museum** *(entrance left in atrium; 10 a.m.–noon, 3–5 p.m., closed Sun.; free)*. Here are wonderful ★ allegories of the months, reliefs removed from the church exterior, a Jacopo della Quercia sculpture, *Madonna of the Pomegranate* (1408), and Ferrarese master Cosimo Tura's organ decorations of the ★ *Annunciation* and ★ *St. George.*

Town Walk

Just a few steps north of the duomo is the **Castello Estense**, the first of the Este family monuments. Built in 1385 in response to an uprising, the castle is heavily fortified with moat, drawbridges and towers. But the interior was the lavish court of the Renaissance dukes, its spaces still grand and with traces of frescoes *(9:30 a.m.–5:30 p.m.; closed Mon.; L10,000).* Through the medieval city behind the duomo, east almost to the town wall, is the ★ **Palazzo Schifanoia** *(V. Scandiana 23; 8:30 a.m.–2 p.m., Sat.–Sun. till 5 p.m.; L6000).* Built by Borso d'Este in 1385 as a pleasure palace, the building contains significant, if damaged, frescoes of the Ferrarese school in the ★ Salone dei Mesi. Within the context of mythological and zodiacal scenes, Cossa, Roberti and others captured the carefree courtly routines of the fortunate Borso. A few blocks south on Via Mellone is the ★ **Palazzo di Ludovico Il Moro** *(V. XX Settembre 124; closed for restoration),* built by Rossetti in 1503 and named for Ludovico Sforza, the husband of Beatrice d'Este. The palace houses the **Museo Archeologico Nazionale** (closed for restoration) with its collection from Spina, an early Venice, but one built in the 5th century B.C. by Etruscans and Greeks for their port on the Adriatic. When Spina flooded in 390 B.C., its inhabitants relocated to what is now Ferrara. Exhibited are red figured vases, amber necklaces, and other tomb artifacts. Heading back toward the duomo, you can visit the **Casa Romei** *(V. Savonarola 30; 8:30 a.m.–2 p.m., Sat.–Sun. till 5 p.m.; L4000)* with its carved ceilings and frescoes, this 15th-century home of a *capitano* gives a more intimate glimpse than the grand palazzi into Ferrara's golden age. In the north section of town built by Ercole I, you find the family ★ **Palazzo Diamanti** *(Corso Ercole I at Corso Porta Mare; 9 a.m.–2 p.m., till 1 p.m. Sun., closed Mon., L8000),* designed by Rossetti in 1492 and covered with diamond motifs, the symbol of the Este. Inside is the *Pinacoteca Nazionale* with its collection of 15th- and 16th-century Ferrarese paintings. From here, it's a 10-minute walk past the Parco Massari to the **Jewish Cemetery** *(at end of V. Vigne; open till 6:30; closed Sat.;* ring for entrance; men must cover heads), a disturbingly tranquil spot with tombs of the Finzi and Contini.

Where to Stay

| **Duchessa Isabella** | **L330–410,000 CP** | |

V. Palestro 70; ☎ *202-121, FAX 202-638. Closed Aug.*
Single L330,000 CP. Double L410,000 CP.

Just several blocks north of the duomo, this elegantly renovated 16th-century palazzo retains its grand marble staircase, Venetian chandeliers and many antiques. The stairs lead to a lovely restaurant with soffit ceilings and frescoes. All 21 rooms are more than ample, the suites are grand indeed, and the baths are rather sumptuous; junior suites or full suites (very expensive) come with sitting rooms around a fireplace or a terrace over the large garden. The decor can be overstated, but the rooms never lack in comfort. Tours. Bar. Restaurant. Parking.

Ripagrande L225–310,000 CP √★★★

V. Ripagrande 21; ☎ *765-250, FAX 764-377.*
Single/double L225–310,000 CP.

In the medieval section a few blocks from the duomo is this renovated Renaissance palazzo with columns and quiet courtyards—one for summer dining. Most of the 40 rooms (primarily junior suites, both "superior" and "deluxe"; the doubles are moderate—a good buy) have steeple-high ceilings cleverly designed into traditionally furnished duplexes or triplexes. The top floor duplexes are the most romantic, with wood-beam ceilings and terraces. Restaurant, bar, free bicycles, parking.

Albergo S. Paolo L70–90,000 √★

V. Baluardi 9; ☎ *762-040.*
Single L70,000. Double L90,000.

On the market square of Piazza Travaglio and, in the back, overlooking a quiet medieval street, this inn is unusually pleasant for the price, with Oriental rugs in the small lobby, helpful service, and 31 shiny clean rooms (no air conditioning). Parking. Reserve in advance.

Ferrara

Where to Eat

Duchessa Isabella $$–$$$ ★★★

V. Palestro 70; ☎ *202-122, FAX 202-638.*
Closed Mon. dinner and Aug. Meals L65–100,000.

One of the few Emilian cities without a Michelin-starred restaurant, Ferrara does have exquisite dining at this hotel. With their Renaissance ceilings and Ferrarese school frescos, have become the place to go on special occasions—and there is a business lunch menu that is quite affordable. The antipasti (pancetta on a bed or arugula) and pastas (tortelli with walnuts and asparagus tips) are especially recommended. Otherwise try the trattorias.

Grotta Azzurra $–$$ ★★

P. Sacreti 43, a few blocks behind the Castello.
Closed Sun. dinner, Wed. Meals L35–55,000.

Reliable Trattoria fare with *al fresco* dining in the summer and pleasant service.

La Provvidenza $$ ★★

Corso Ercole I d'Este 92; ☎ *205-187, FAX 205-018.*
Closed Mon., part of Aug. Meals L50–70,000.

In a 17th-century palazzo and with garden dining, this restaurant is popular more for its ambience than cuisine, but the food is decent.

Orsucci $ ★★

V. Garibaldi 75, not far from duomo.
Open noon–3 p.m., 5–10 p.m., closed Wed. Meals L20–25,000.

For a late lunch or early dinner, head for the comfortable back room at Orsucci where, in addition to some of Italy's best pizza, you can sample the regional *ceci*, akin to a chickpea pancake, or a tasty platter of sausage and peppers.

Directory

Telephone Code 0532   **Postal Code 44100**

Tourist Information

Corso Giovecca ☎ *209-370, FAX 212-266*, just past main intersection on extension of Cavour.

Festival

Ferrara Estate, concerts in the piazzas July/August; Palio S. Giorgio, last Sun. of May, with a medieval procession.

Arriving

Excellent train connections to Venice, Bologna, and Ravenna—all under 2 hours away. Bus 3 connects stazione on west outskirts with center.

Pullman buses leave near stazione to Bologna, Modena, and other towns.

A-13 runs from Bologna, (48 km, 30 mi.) and Padua, from here A-4 goes to Venice (112 km, 69 mi.).

Getting Around

Walk or rent a bike (check tourist office).

Note

Shops close Thursday afternoons.

On the Road

The Central Adriatic

The central Adriatic can boast of art from medieval and Renaissance times—Rimini has the Tempio Malatestiano, and Ravenna, after all, gave refuge to Dante. Yet it is a region that backed off the historical stage after its initial importance in ancient times. No matter, what could be more appropriate than that Romagna should be the one area of the *regione* where substantial remains of the Empire can still be seen. Rimini continues to remind us of its early importance as an ancient town with the Arch of Augustus marking the crossroads of Via Emilia and Via Flaminia to Rome. Ravenna continues to overwhelm with its beautiful mosaics from the last days of the Empire.

Although Ravenna is a worthy tourist detour, the bustling modern beach resort of Rimini is quickly visited while traveling from Venice or Bologna, through Umbria and on to Rome. Many will be tempted to stop at Rimini or some of the similar towns to swim at the beach or just relax. In July and August, the congestion at these beaches, most covered with private lidos and often with limited public ones, can be off-putting. And in the summer of 1989, a yellow algae fouled the sea, putting most vacationers to flight. Although the government explained the algae were injurious only to those with open cuts, you might want to think twice before taking a plunge. Fertilizers from the Po and industrial waste from the northern Adriatic have made this part of the sea far from delightful.

Ravenna

While most of Italy was being ravaged by barbarian invasions, Ravenna experienced its greatest cultural flowering. While the Goths were sacking Rome, it was Ravenna that was the last capital of the Western Empire (A.D. 476), a capital that built its greatest monuments under the regency of Galla Placida, mother of the last emperor of the west. When much of Italy was subjugated by the invading Lombards, it was Ravenna that Justinian selected to revive the empire on the peninsula, and it was at Ravenna that this emperor from Constantinople left the most beautiful Byzantine art in western Europe (A.D. 526). Through most of these Dark Ages, Ravenna found itself fortunate. Even when conquered by the Goths, it was a civilized ruler like Theodoric (448–526) who not only maintained Roman institutions, but built a palace worthy of the King of Goths.

From the beginning of the Roman period, Ravenna's position protected it. An early Venice, the town was built on lagoons and naturally fortified. An important imperial city, its harbor at Classe anchored Rome's Adriatic fleet. Throughout the period of its apogee, Ravenna could be supplied and aided by sea from Constantinople. But, then, the Lombards finally conquered Ravenna in A.D. 751. The sea would recede as would Ravenna's importance. Venice, the new port to the East, would replace it.

Today Ravenna is 10 miles from the sea and surrounded by rings of industry. As you wind your way past the suburban refineries and into the modern town that has grown up around **Theodoric's Mausoleum**, you may have doubts about the detour here. But after visiting the Early Christian monuments in the centro storico, with the mosaic marvels that Galla Placida, Theodoric, and Justinian have forever graced the city, you'll doubt no more. Once you find the mostly traffic-free historic center *(around Via Roma, P. Kennedy, IV Novembre)* you'll soon stumble on the main square, the **Piazza del Popolo**. A large and pleasant square, lined with cafes and marked with the filigree windows and columns of Venice's brief domination in the 15th century, it is a good spot for beginning your tour of the mosaics.

Tip: A discounted ticket gains entrance to many of the following sights. Check at S. Vitale or the tourist office.

What to See and Do

San Vitale   ★★★

Follow V. Matteotti north out of P. del Popolo, turn left on Cavour, take second right for V. San Vitale.

While the brick facade and dome is Roman, the octagonal interior of San Vitale (526–547) is richly Byzantine. The dense and mystical space, the women's galleries, the carved columns, translucent marble, and alabaster windows remind you that the builder of the church was the same as Hagia Sophia's in Constantinople. As if being exotically Eastern weren't enough for a church, San Vitale also is dazzling. Set off the octagonal is the chancel covered with ★ ★ ★ mosaics that are the finest examples of Byzantine art in western Europe. In the apse are the most famous mosaics of the donors themselves in regal procession, the emperor Justinian with Maximian, the archbishop who consecrated San Vitale, and the empress Theodora with her court. As Byzantine as these mosaics are, the delightful elements of nature, in the dome vaults and under the arches, are Roman in origin. Although the details of the mosaics may be seen illuminated, they are perhaps more beautiful in natural light. Then the multifaceted surfaces, gilded and green and brilliant, catch the warm light from the alabaster, and, instead of glittering, they glow. In a courtyard behind San Vitale is ★ ★ **Galla Placida's Mausoleum**, built (c. A.D. 430) to hold her tomb as part of a church that no longer exists. Even though she may never have been buried here either, her mosaics are fortunately preserved. The earliest mosaics in Ravenna, the lapis blue and starry sky are spellbinding, and the figures are fine examples of the Hellenistic Roman style. (Light machine outside chamber.) *Both the basilica and tomb are open 9 a.m.–7 p.m.; 9:30 a.m.–4:30 p.m.Oct.–Mar. Admission L5000.*

Piazza del Duomo ★

Follow V. G. Rasponi south out of P. del Popolo for several blocks.

Next to the duomo is the freestanding octagonal ★ ★ **Battistero Neoniano** *(open 9 a.m.–7 p.m., 9:30 a.m.–4:30 p.m. Oct.–Mar.; L3000)* or the so-called orthodox baptistery. Another legacy from Galla Placida, the baptistery was appropriately built over a Roman bath. Its interior is a wonderful harmony of mosaics (post 452) and architecture. Following the Via Battistero east, you arrive at the Archbishop's palace with the **Museo Arcivescovile** *(same hours; L4000)*. Along with a mosaic-adorned chapel is a small exhibit of religious works that includes the ★ *Throne of Maximian*, that belonged to the bishop of San Vitale. Famous for the quality of its carvings in ivory, it is considered a masterpiece of Early Christian art.

Sant'Apollinare Nuovo ★

Southeast of P. del Popolo on V. Roma at V. Negri.

Exiting the Piazza del Popolo east on Via Diaz you pass near the ★ **Battistero degli Ariani** *(8:30 a.m.–noon, 2:30–sunset)*, built by Theodoric and used by the Christianized Goths who, by doubting the trinity, sparked the Arian heresy. In the dome are early 6th-century mosaics on the baptism of Christ and the Apostles, the reason for any visit. Continuing east to Via Roma, turn right for another legacy from Theodoric the Goth, **Sant'Apollinare Nuovo** *(9 a.m.–7 p.m.; Oct.–Mar. 9:30 a.m.–4:30 p.m.)*, flanked by an imposing round campanile of the 10th-century. In the interior the nave walls are adorned with ★ mosaics, most from c. A.D. 520 that legend claims the pope ordered blackened so their gleaming gold no longer would distract worshippers. On the right, a procession of martyrs dressed in very Roman togas proceed from Theodoric's palace (now destroyed save for some mosaics on the Palazzo Calchi a few doors away) to Christ enthroned. On the left, virgins proceed from the port of Classe, marked by its boats.

Nearby

City buses (#4 from stazione) and trains (less convenient) reach Classe (5 km, 3 mi. south on SS 16 to Rimini).

In Classe, the harbor built by Augustus is gone, but the second church built at Ravenna by Justinian can be seen. **★Sant' Apollinare in Classe** *(9 a.m.–noon and 2–6 p.m.; till 5 p.m. Sat.–Sun. and in winter; L4000)* shares its ground with an exceptional 10th-century campanile. A Roman basilica, unlike San Vitale, the interior is quite remarkable for its marble nave columns and, especially, for its apse ★mosaics with the saint surrounded by a lush green meadow.

Where to Stay

Most likely you'll be overnighting in Urbino, Ferrara, or Bologna. In case the mosaics do catch you in their spell there are two hotels to consider in the centro storico.

Bizanzio   **L140–200,000 CP**   ★★★

V. Salara 30; ☎ 217-111, FAX 32-539.
Single L140,000 CP. Double L200,000 CP.
Near San Vitale, this smartly furnished, contemporary hotel has 35 comfortable rooms (a/c) with well-appointed baths; only the "superior" rooms are really ample. Breakfast bar, garden and parking.

Centrale Byron   **L95–130,000**   ★★

V. IV Novembre 14; ☎ 212-225, FAX 34-114.
Single L95,000. Double L130,000.
Located a few steps from the Piazza del Popolo, this hotel offers 57 efficiently arranged, but bland rooms (a/c), and a breakfast bar.

Where to Eat

Metro   **$$**   ★★

V. Salara 20; ☎ 35-363.
Closed Sun. Meals L50–70,000.
For some of the wonderful local seafood in a soothing setting, try the risotto marinara or shrimp served with arugula and balsamic vinegar. Located not far from San Vitale.

Al Gallo   **$$**   ★★★

V. Maggiore 87; ☎ 213-775.
Closed Mon. night, Tues., and July–Aug. Sun. night, Mon., Tues.; Christmas and Easter; L45–65,000.
Just a few blocks from the centro storico and San Vitale. This venerable family-run restaurant serves artichoke tart appetizers and polenta with mushrooms, wonderful fresh pastas and rabbit stew or fish. In warm weather, dining is in a garden courtyard.

Ca' de Ven

V. Corrado Ricci 24; ☎ 30-163.
Open 10 a.m.–2 p.m., 5:30–10:30 p.m., Sun. 5:30 p.m.–11:30 p.m.; closed Mon.
For the most traditional fare of Romagna, walk just over a block south of P. Popolo to this enoteca. Offering wine tastings of the local Albana white and Trebbiano red in the rustic setting of a 16th-century palazzo. Snacks are served to accompany your

food, but the *piadina*, a kind of freshly prepared Syrian bread stuffed with cold cuts or cheese and greens, should be your choice here.

Directory

Telephone Code 0544   **Postal Code 48100**

Tourist Information

APT, *V. Salara 8* ☎ *35-404, FAX 35-094*, just off Cavour on way to San Vitale.

Festival

"Summer in Ravenna," can mean organ concerts in San Vitale, opera in the theaters, and international performers. For information, contact Ravenna Festival, *V. Mariani 2* (☎ *48-100*).

Shopping

Modern mosaics, many copies of the Ravenna's great ones, are made by *mosaicisti*. The most convenient place to shop or browse is that of the Signorini family around the corner from San Vitale at *V. Argentario 22*.

Arriving

Trains from Bologna, Ferrara (transfer for Venice), and Rimini, as well as pullman buses from Bologna

Ravenna lies 75 km, 47 mi. east of Bologna and south of Ferrara; 130 km, 81 mi. from Urbino and just a bit more from Venice, about 2 hours by the Via Romea, SS 309

Stazione is just east of P. del Popolo.

Parking lots marked near centro storico.

Rimini

Rimini is today known as a beach resort, the largest on the Adriatic. In peak summer months, chartered flights land here from all over Europe, but especially from London. Long and broad, the beach is hardly a place for solace in the peak season, and little of it is available for public use. And the sea, like the entire northern Adriatic, is far from pristine clean. Nonetheless, you might find the crowds, the discos, the beachiness of it all just the change of pace you need after a tour of the old city sights.

The old city of Rimini is about a half mile from the more famous modern resort, and its sights need not take up a lot of your time if you are yearning for the beach. The ★★**Tempio Malatestiano** (*V. IV Novembre; 7 a.m.–noon, 3-7 p.m.; more limited Oct.–Mar.*) is just a block east of the main avenue, Corso Augusto, and west from the stazione, walking on Via Dante. A seminal work of the Early Renaissance, Alberti's unfinished facade for this formerly Gothic church was the first based on classical forms. In this instance, the facade was inspired by Roman triumphal arches, such as Constantine's, with the details supplied by the nearby Arch of Augustus. Commissioned in the 1440s by Rimini's tyrant Sigismondo Malatesta (1417-68) as a temple to his love for his mistress Isotta, the decorations include their intertwined initials (S and I) forming friezes along with the Malatesta family symbols of roses and elephants. Pope Pius II was so outraged that Malatesta had converted a consecrated church into a personal memorial that he publicly condemned him to hell. The interior includes sculptural works and details by Agostino di Duccio and, in the second chapel left where postcards are now sold, Piero della Francesca's portrait of a kneeling Sigismondo (1451). In the next chapel, with Isotta's tomb (she eventually married her Sigismondo after he poisoned his previous wife), is a crucifix attributed to Giotto. Back at Corso Augusto, turn south through the Piazza Tre Martiri, once the ancient forum, and continue to the **Arco d'Augusto** (27 B.C.), at the juncture of Via Emilia and Via Flaminia.

Rimini

Where to Stay

Unless the yellow scum that appeared in the sea the summer of 1989 returns, you will have trouble finding a room during July and August. In winter, many hotels close. You might try the hotel service of Promozione Alberghieria *(P. Indipendenza;* ☎ *52-269; and at stazione; telephone fee).* Or come armed with a reservation.

Grand Hotel   **L285–450,000**   ❀★★★★★

P. Indipendenza 2; ☎ *56-000, FAX 56-866.*
Single L285,000. Double L450,000.
This is *the* deluxe hotel, all gingerbread Victorian and with 120 rooms and antique furnishings set amid a park and fronting a private beach. Restaurant, bar. Pool, tennis.

Lotus   **L90–110,000**   ★★

V. Rovani 3; ☎ *381-680, FAX 392-506; closed Oct.–Apr.*
Single L90,000. Double L110,000.
On the other hand, this hotel might do instead, with its pleasant garden and pool and 46 decent rooms (air conditioning) found out the Viale Regina Elena. Restaurant. Parking.

Where to Eat

Lo Squero   **$$–$$$**   ★★

Lungomare Tintori 7; ☎ *27-676.*
Closed Tues. in off-season, Nov.–Dec. L60–90,000.
For the freshest seafood along with views of the sea, this is a good choice though you pay for the location.

Ristorante Pic Nic   ★

V. Tempio Malatestiano 30.
Closed Mon. Entrées L7500–10,000.
If you're sightseeing, this might be more convenient. Also, its vast antipasto spread (the "bufet") is terrific, the pastas (try the *maccherone al astiche*) are very good, as are the pizzas at night. And the prices are low.

And, along the lungomari look for the *piadini* stands, that sell the flat, traditional bread baked fresh and then served wrapped around various cold cuts and cheeses.

Directory

Telephone Code 0541   **Postal Code 47037**

Tourist Information

> **APT**, next to stazione ☎ *51-331* and P. Indipendenza at beach ☎ *51-101, FAX 26-566.*

Arriving

> Trains on Bologna/Lecce line stop at Rimini Stazione, where town buses #10 and 11 go to P. Indipendenza at beach. Old city within walking distance of stazione.
>
> Pullman buses leave from next to stazione.
>
> Rimini is 62 km, 32 mi. south of Ravenna, 78 km, 48 mi. from Urbino.
>
> **Note:** *Off-season many hotels and restaurants close, especially Nov.–Mar.*

San Marino

Said to be the oldest independent republic in the world, diminutive San Marino was founded around A.D. 300 and exists today only by special dispensation from an Italy that completely encompasses it. The technical distinction of being independent gives this republic of 20,000 people the right to mint coins and print stamps—both of which have lucrative sales to collectors. Though easily visited by bus from Rimini (25 km, 16 mi. south and west into the mountains), the town of San Marino is ersatz medieval and touristy. When so many authentic towns can be visited, why come here unless you are a stamp collector?

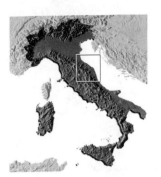

UMBRIA TO THE ADRIATIC

Santa Chiara Church graces Assisi, one of Italy's captivating hill towns.

History and Art

In the center of Italy is Umbria, so central it has no coastline or foreign frontiers. Hemmed in by the western slopes of the Apennines, with steep, forested hills and rugged terrain made fertile by rivers and lakes, Umbria is Gothic in its beauty. Mists rise from Lago Trasimeno, valleys narrow to ribbons, and the hills make for precipitous climbs to ancient towns. The Romans tried to broaden the plains by draining lakes and though they

287

succeeded in surrounding the hills of Perugia and Assisi with farmlands rather than water, they failed to tame this Umbrian land.

There is a wildness to the land. Perhaps it comes from the dangers that so often lurked along the course of the Tiber as it flowed toward Rome. Even centuries before the rise of that ancient city, the Umbri, Italic founders of Assisi, Spoleto, and Gubbio, combated the expansion of the Etruscans across the Tiber, at cities such as Perugia and Orvieto. Later, the intrusions came from the north, through the Tiber valleys that invited marching armies from the time of Hannibal and the Carthaginians, who, with their elephants, defeated the Romans at Lake Trasimeno in 217 B.C.

The Romans, too, found Umbria convenient for marching. Taking them to their wars in the north against the Gauls and Teutons was the Via Flaminia (built 200 B.C.) that passed near Todi and Spoleto, near Assisi, Gubbio and Urbino, then on to the Adriatic and the town of Rimini where it joined the Via Emilia. And the Romans found Umbria beckoning as well; patricians built their villas here and emperors visited springs and waterfalls praised by Virgil.

But with the fall of Rome, the northern barbarians once again reversed the direction of the armies going through the Tiber valley. First the Goths, who in 547 began a seven-year siege of Perugia, but more willingly bypassed Todi, aloof on its promontory. Then Justinian (552–565) brought a few years of Byzantine peace before the Lombards established the Duchy of Spoleto for centuries. Not even when Charlemagne regained control over Umbria (9th century) would the region find peace. As the core of the Papal States, Umbria was marched on by both Frederick Barbarossa and by Frederick II in the war of the Ghibellines against the pope's forces, the Guelfs. Throughout the centuries it was subject to the vicissitudes of the papacy—to its absence from Rome during the Avignon residence, to its expansionist trends during the Renaissance and Italian Wars.

Today, no longer ravaged by wars, no longer needing to hide atop fortified hills, Umbria still whispers danger, from the 11th-century castles that guard the passes of the Tiber to the Etruscan, Roman and medieval walls that so stolidly encircle the hill towns.

The mountains, streams and rushing Tiber attracted more than armies and despoilment. More quietly and gently, they brought Eastern monks who found the remote hillside caves perfect retreats from the church hierarchy at Ravenna. Around 480, in the small town of Norcia near Spoleto, would be born a man who followed this hermitic tradition of a life devoted to prayer. Yet St. Benedict would be remembered not for this austerity, but rather for the founding of the Benedictine Order that defined Western monastic experience with its daily schedule of prayer, study and manual labor. Centuries

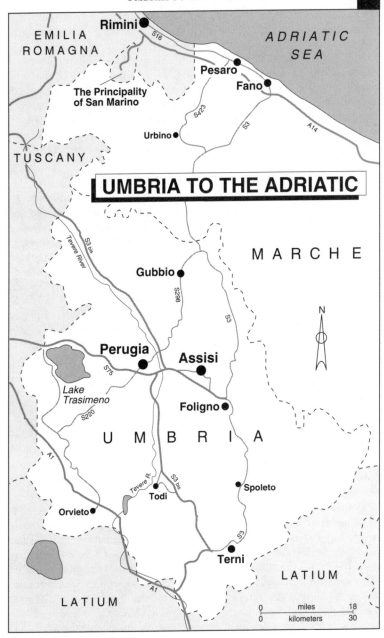

History and Art

later, another Umbrian saint would be born, this time in Assisi. Although he, too, would often retreat to mountain grottoes, renouncing the wealth of his family and the growing commercialism of the 13th century, St. Francis brought his message to the towns. Instead of isolated abbeys in the Benedictine tradition, town churches were built, preaching churches of the new Franciscan order that devoted itself to the urban poor. St. Francis touched not just neighboring Perugia or Gubbio (where he talked a terrorizing wolf into gentleness, so that the town wept when he died); he founded an order inspired by his own humility and kindness, one that would soon spawn the Order of St. Clare for women, and one that would spread around the world, retaining its vitality even today.

Umbria's religious history was not always so venerable. For most of the Western church's history, Umbria was part of its patrimony. Initially revenues from this region of the Tiber basin were distributed for the care of the poor. When the papacy emerged as a political power with its own armies, Umbrian monies funded the administration of the church and its troops. And when popes found themselves attacked in Rome, they retreated to their Umbrian towns—to Orvieto and to Perugia, where five popes were elected. The relationship was not always congenial, however. The popes in the late 15th century began exploiting the region for their own purposes—as Leo X summed it up, "God has granted us the papacy, let us enjoy it!" The popes assigned the various cities to the administration of their relatives: under Alexander VI, his son Cesare Borgia effectively controlled the region with his armies, and his daughter Lucrezia administered the city of Spoleto. Umbria didn't always take kindly to papal presumptions that, more often than not, interfered with local lords, such as the Montefeltro of Urbino and Gubbio, the Baglioni of Perugia. Some popes died of poisoning while visiting their Umbrian subjects. Perugia openly revolted in the 16th century against excessive taxation. Yet the region remained firmly part of the Papal States until Italian unification in 1860. Then, once again, Umbria fought against papal control, this time successfully.

Such intense religious history must leave its mark artistically, especially in Italy. It seems happily appropriate that Umbria flourished around the time of St. Francis. After his death (1228) and canonization, Assisi constructed a grandiose church (and for that reason one that was forever controversial among Franciscans) that would become the model for the Italian Gothic preaching church. Although Umbria offered the opportunity, Tuscany provided the painters for the church walls, making it one of the great treasures of Italy with its frescoes by Simone Martini, Pietro Lorenzetti, Cimabue and, of course, Giotto. Another great Gothic cathedral was built at Orvieto, under the order of Pope Urban IV (who was in Orvieto to escape a Ghibelline attack on Rome). Its most famous frescoes, once again by a Tuscan,

History and Art

were painted by a Signorelli—shaken by the destruction of Rome brought on by the Italian Wars.

Although much of its art is from Tuscany, Umbria produced a number of fine Renaissance artists. Il Perugino seems to have borrowed the softness of the local countryside for the backgrounds of his early 14th-century portraits. This poetic ambience continued through the work of the Umbrian School and can be seen in the early work of his pupil, Raphael. Umbrian, too, are the more decorative and Manneristic frescoes of Pinturicchio, though his best work is in Siena and Rome. Nowhere did the Renaissance flourish more, however, than across the modern Umbrian border in Urbino, where both Bramante and Raphael were born. These artists produced their greatest work elsewhere, but under Federigo da Montefeltro the ducal court of Urbino became one of the great centers of quattrocento art, second not even to Rome. Here the Laurana brothers worked as well as Botticelli, Piero della Francesca, and Alberti. As the region succumbed to stronger papal controls it lost much of its artistic vitality. Yet the Correggio-influenced Federico Barocci (1526–1612) produced in Urbino Early Baroque etchings and paintings while the town of Todi built the Bramante-inspired church of Santa Maria della Consolazione, a High Renaissance gem.

Modern Umbria

Umbria is primarily an agricultural region. Even its industries tend to relate to food: Perugia with its candies, Orvieto with its wines, Norcia with its salami and prosciutto, Spoleto with its black truffles. Terni, though, does manufacture plastics. Many of the hills remain covered with oak and evergreens, some of the passes are free of development (benefiting no doubt, from their preservation status as part of the historic Tiber valley). Although Lake Trasimeno is more polluted than when Hannibal's elephants watered there, and Perugia, the regional capital, has surrounded itself with modern buildings, Umbria has, for the most part, maintained its beauty. Travelers flock to the art cities of Orvieto, Perugia and neighboring Urbino. Students find the summer programs at both Urbino and Perugia delightful. Religious pilgrims from around the world pay homage to St. Francis at Assisi. And cultural aficionados plan around the summer festival at Spoleto. On the way from one town to the next, detours to smaller hill towns at Gubbio and Todi only add to the attractions of this small region that since prehistoric times has formed the land bridge between Rome and the northern Adriatic.

Cuisine

Umbria shares much in the way of cuisine with its Roman neighbor to the south and its Tuscan one to the west, but it adds a good dash of mountain robustness. Like Rome, it favors roast suckling pig, but here the *porchetta* often tastes of the wild fennel from the hillside. Like Tuscany, it roasts its pigeon and pheasant over wood fires and doesn't hesitate to use wild thyme and sage, but its *arista* pork is seasoned with fennel and lots of black pepper, not rosemary. It is a simple, hearty cuisine.

Chiana cattle graze around Lake Trasimeno, giving Perugia some fame for its beef along with Florence. Sheep feed on the wild herbs that cover the mountains, becoming the tasty, if simple spit-cooked *agnello all' arrabbiata*. Hogs favor Umbria and have given the area around Norcia fame for its pork products—its hams, salami, and especially its spicy *mazzafegati*, or pork liver sausage. Wild boar *(cinghale)* roam the forests, goats (for *capretto allo spiedo*) the steepest slopes. All in all, Umbria savors its meat.

Yet Umbrian streams and lakes produce fresh water trout and pike, crayfish and eel, and the *lasca* from Trasimeno. And the forests shelter quail and thrush as well as pheasant and wood pigeon. Such varied diet is given pungency by another product of the oak forests, the *tartufi* or truffle. The black truffle of Umbria is most famous, but the white is found here, too, to grate on the regionally preferred flat noodle *tagliatelle* or the commonsensical spaghetti. Olive oil is of high quality and mixed with garlic and tomatoes it makes the freshest sauce when poured over short noodles for the very Umbrian *strengozzi*.

Since Etruscan times, Perugia's cherries have been in high demand, and today Umbria's orchards produce considerable fruit, much of it dried for export, and the white figs stuffed with nuts. Desserts are often luscious, including Perugian chocolates and cheesecake *(torta con formaggio)* and the flaky pastries found at both Orvieto and Assisi. Another Etruscan tradition has been the **wines**, that of the smooth dry Orvieto Classico being the most famous from the region. The number of controlled labels is gradually increasing, resulting from a fair amount of experimentation with both vines and technique. The Torgiano area near Perugia produces some fine wines, and though the reds are most notable, particularly the Rubesca Riserva, the whites are interesting, too. Other DOC wines include Colli del Traimeno, producing vintage reds and good young whites, Colli Altotiberini, Colli Perugini, with decent reds and roses, and the most recent Montefalco. Assisi wines, both rosso and bianco, are light and pleasant.

Travel Tips

Climate and Season

For central Italy, Umbria has a particularly temperate climate. Its spring is glorious when wildflowers cover the hills; its summer is hot and dry in the valleys, but the hill towns provide refreshing retreats and have even made a go of being summer resorts; the lakes attract vacationing Italians, particularly in the hills around Trasimeno. Fall is wet; winter is damp and quite cold.

Arriving

The only routes into Umbria are by land and the best routes crossing the region approximate the ancient Via Flaminia: SS 3 from Rome to Terni, Spoleto, Gubbio, Urbino then Fano at the Adriatic; or the Rome-Ancona train that stops at Spoleto and is linked by bus to Urbino and Gubbio, and by train at Foligno to Assisi, and Perugia. Access from the southeast is difficult, because of the ruggedness of the Apennines, but from the west Orvieto is on the Florence-Rome rail line and just a brief detour off A-1; Perugia is linked to A-1 (60 km, 37 mi.) by superstrada 75bis and connected to Florence by train (change at Terontala). Bus connections link the region with major Italian cities.

Getting Around

Of course a car enables you to visit the towns in the least time. But train service between Perugia and Orvieto and between Perugia, Assisi and Spoleto (via a change at Foligno) is frequent. Only buses connect you with Gubbio and Urbino from Perugia, though the Rome/Ancona train links with these towns by special buses. Todi is best reached by bus from Perugia, though there is a connection with Orvieto. Buses ply the area and if their schedule suits you, consider the convenience they provide in dropping you off in the *centro*. Trains can take you only to the foot of these medieval hill towns, then a transfer to a bus is necessary to get you to town. If driving, expect to park, often for a fee, outside the medieval walls of the hill towns.

Special Tips

The universities at Perugia and Urbino are popular for foreign students wanting to study Italian language and culture. Hotels in small towns book up quickly spring through fall; reserve in advance or arrive at your destination early. The Spoleto festival requires advance planning to attend.

On the Road

Umbrian Towns and Urbino

Umbria has no large tourism cities to detain you or serve as your base of sightseeing. The regional capital at Perugia numbers more than 150,000 residents, but most live in the surrounding modern satellites rather than the smaller centro storico. Assisi and Orvieto, certainly the most popular tourist destinations, have permanent populations of under 30,000. Since all the towns have a range of good accommodations, you might find it easier to visit them on your way to other major destinations, dawdling along the way and spending nights as you desire. Urbino is a convenient stopping point across the peninsula; Assisi is a good place simply to relax, and there are thoroughly enjoyable country inns (see Orvieto and Perugia) to use as a base for exploration. But all the towns have a decent selection of accommodations and restaurants to make a stay pleasant. For this reason, the chapter is presented like an "On the Road" section. A route across the region is followed, from the west at Orvieto to Urbino near the Adriatic. Orvieto is an easy stopover between Rome and the north. Perugia or Assisi can be planned as day trips from Florence. Perugia, in the center, is 175 km, 109 mi. from Rome, a bit less from Florence, and 200 km, 124 mi. from Ravenna. **Note:** One of Italy's finest restaurants, Vissani, is on the Orvieto-Todi road (see "Orvieto")—a required detour for the serious eater who can afford it.

Orvieto

Orvieto's duomo is one of Italy's finest Gothic cathedrals.

Towering over 1000 feet above the Tiber valley, the old town of Orvieto adds considerable drama to any approach through the rolling hills to the west near Lake Bolseno. Its majestic position enabled it to dominate the valley in Etruscan times and to flourish until defeated and destroyed by the Romans in 280 B.C. Today ancient Volsinii can be discovered only in excavations under Early Christian churches, in tombs outside its many walls, and in museums on the Piazza del Duomo. It's fitting that in the town of Orvieto, so named after its revival by the church, that its glories are its duomo and Apocalypse frescoes, and that nearby Bolsena should be remembered not as the town of Etruscan retreat, but rather for its miracle of 1263. The miracle of Bolsena, said to substantiate that the wine and wafers of the eucharist are Christ's blood and flesh, has inspired many works of art, but certainly none greater than Orvieto's cathedral, built to commemorate the event. And it has inspired many a procession on the feast day of Corpus Christi, but the first was in Orvieto where it continues to be celebrated in full medieval costume and where the solemn tufa stone of its buildings is brightened by richly colored banners.

What to See and Do

Duomo ★★★

The cathedral (begun 1290) is set in the middle of a fine piazza lined with picturesque medieval homes, a papal palace, and a landmark clock tower. Whatever your approach to the Piazza del Duomo, you can't help but be impressed by this stripped travertine and granite church, which is one of the finest Italian Gothic cathedrals. The best approach is along the Via Maitaini, which suddenly opens up to the dazzling ★★★**facade** with its glint of gilded mosaics, pinnacles and gables, and sculpted marble. The facade, an immense triptych, wasn't completed until the early 17th century, or later if you consider the mosaics are reproductions and the bronze doors modern. Its design is attributed to Lorenzo Maitani (died 1330), a Sienese who was granted permission to bear arms in order to seduce him to Orvieto. However, there is no trace of those chaotic times in the harmony of the extraordinarily complex facade. Others worked on the facade, but Maitani was responsible for the ★★ bas-reliefs on the four piers of the lower facade (except the bottom sections of the two middle piers) as well as the bronze symbols of the evangelists above them. The reliefs, unusually realistic for the time, depict biblical stories, starting from the right with scenes from Genesis (note *Cain Killing Abel*) and ending on the left with an agonizing *Last Judgment*.

The beautiful space of the **interior** is decorated with masterpieces of the period, from the stained glass of the apse and the woodworking of the choir stalls, to the alabaster windows and the silversmithing of its tabernacles. One ★ tabernacle holds the bloodstained altar cloth from the miracle of Bolsena in the **Cappella del Corporale** (left transept) where Lippo Memmi's *Madonna della Misericordia* (1339) can be seen, too (on right). But the most famous art in the duomo belongs to another period, one of disillusionment and fear, resulting from the foreign invasions of the

Italian Wars. These ★★ frescoes of the Apocalypse (1499–1504) in the **Cappella Madonna di San Brizio** (right transept) are the most inspired work by Luca Signorelli, whose concern with male anatomy and agitated movement influenced Michelangelo. The chapel decorations were begun by Fra Angelico (ceiling frescoes, *Christ in Judgment* with assistance on the angels by Benozzo Gozzoli) and completed by Signorelli. On the left wall is *Preaching of the AntiChrist* with the devil whispering the words into the imposter's ear and Fra Angelico (in black) and Signorelli looking on (lower left corner). On the right is *Resurrection of the Dead*, a bleak landscape of male nudes, lost and directionless, and *The Damned Consigned to Hell*, with its writhing, chaotic mass of bodies and the torturing devil portrayed not as part animal, but as totally human. Signorelli also did the *Pieta* and the smaller frescoes flanking the entrance arch and altar windows. In the **nave**, near the font, is Gentile da Fabriano's resplendent ★ *Madonna* (1426).

The duomo is open 7 a.m.–1 p.m., and 2:30 p.m. till dusk. Access to newly restored Signorelli frescoes in the Cappella Madonna San Brizio requires a ticket (L3000; purchase at tourist office) and is restricted in number (20 at one time) and hours (Mon.–Sat. 10 a.m.–12:30 p.m., 2:30–5 p.m., Sun. 2:30–5 p.m. only; in summer, daily till 7:30 p.m.).

Museums

Three museums cluster in the Piazza del Duomo. To the right of the cathedral is the handsome, two-story Palazzi dei Papi (13th century; closed for renovation). Between the duomo and the palace is the modern display space of the **Museo Nazionale Archeologico** *(9 a.m.–1 p.m. and 3–7 p.m.; Sun. 9 a.m.–1 p.m.; L4000)* with exhibits from local Etruscan excavations. Across from the duomo is the private Etruscan collection of the **Museo Claudio Faino** *(9 a.m.–1p.m., 3–6 p.m. except Oct.–Apr. 1 2:30–4:30 p.m., closed Mon.; L4000)* with an emphasis on imported Greek vases and sarcophagi.

Town Walks

The Via del Duomo winds its handsome way out of the piazza past numerous ceramic shops and intersects with Corso Cavour, the main street running east and west through town. Just a block beyond the Corso is the old **Piazza del Popolo**, graced by the 13th-century **Palazzo del Capitano** with its stepped arcade and asymmetrical staircase and enlivened by a market Saturday mornings. Continuing northeast you come to the **Piazza XXIX Marzo** with the first church dedicated to **Saint Domenic** (begun 1233) and its convent where St. Thomas Aquinas taught. Inside the church is Arnofo di Cambio's tomb for Cardinal de Braye (c. 1282). From here, or along Corso Cavour, you arrive at the Piazza Cahen on the eastern edge of town next to the **public garden** with its views of the valley. Just north of the garden is the **Pozzo di San Patrizio**, a well designed by Sangallo the Younger on the orders of Pope Clement VII, who had retreated here during the Sack of Rome and wished to guarantee a local water supply in case of siege. For some reason, the dank well attracts any number of tourists down its hundreds of spiral steps that were carefully designed not to obstruct those climbing out *(fee)*. The most interesting walk, however, is west on the Corso to the ★ **Piazza del la Repubblica** and the nearby medieval streets like Via Commenda and Via Magalotti. As you approach the piazza, you can't help but note the 12-sided Romanesque ★**campanile** belonging to Sant'Andrea Church, founded in the 6th century and where Innocent III proclaimed one of the crusades. The square itself is built over a Roman forum, just as the church was built over Etruscan and Roman ruins.

Nearby

Even if you aren't visiting Todi you might plan a picnic in that direction along SS 79 bis. The hilly terrain offers fine views and the crossing of the Tiber is scenic.

Where to Stay

Villa Bellago　　　　　**L140–180,000 CP**　　　　　√★★★

Baschi-Todi Strada, SS 448, 05023 Baschi; ☎ *[0744] 950-521, FAX 950-524.*
Single L140,000 CP. Double 180,000 CP.
About 10 km north of the Porta Romana and just 10 km from the A-1 exit for Orvieto (turn left) the hotel is situated on a twelve acre spit of land jutting into the artificial Lake Corbara; the price for the 15 light and airy, fan-cooled and brand new rooms with either views (second floor, and larger) or terraces couldn't be more reasonable; good restaurant, poolside bar; large garden pool, a gym, tennis and game rooms; horseback riding arranged.

Maitani　　　　　**L120–190,000**　　　　　★★★

V. Maitani 5; ☎ *42-011, FAX 42-011; closed late Jan.*
Single L120,000. Double L190,000.
In town, the Maitani is just off the Piazza del Duomo, and offers 41 decent a/c rooms, and a terrace with good views. Restaurant.

Where to Eat

Vissani　　　　　**$$$**　　　　　★★★★★

12 km on ss 448 near Lake Corbara in Baschi; reserve at ☎ *[0744] 950-396, FAX 950-396.*
Closed Sun. dinner, Wed. Fixed-price lunch L100 & 140,000. Fixed-price dinner L140,000. À la carte L125–200,000.
There are any number of atmospheric trattoria in town, but consider dining along the country road to Todi where you find this Michelin-two-star establishment, one of Italy's best restaurants. Food is everything here, as demonstrated in the intimate and elegant dining room, separated from the kitchen of Gianfranco Vissani by only a glass wall. There's fine wine, attentive service and a large menu, but choose the degustazione menu (wines often included at lunch) with the day's creations (such as a soup of porcini with lobster, sun-dried tomato lasagne with black olive and hare sauce).

Il Padrino　　　　　**$$–$$$**　　　　　★★★★

☎ *950-206.*
Closed Sun. dinner, Wed. and July. Meals L60–85,000.
In the front room at Vissani is the original family restaurant. Its more traditional cuisine also is highly respected but overseen by Vissani's mother.

Villa Bellago　　　　　**$–$$**　　　　　★★

see hotel address above.

Closed Tues. & Jan. Meals L35–55,000.

If the above two are beyond your budget, head for pleasant al fresco dining by the lake and good seafood to complement its Italian menu. Located just over a mile before Vissani.

La Volpe e L'Uva   **$**   ★★

V. Ripa Corsica 1, toward San Domenic church; ☎ *41-612.*
Closed Wed. dinner. Meals L25–40,000.

In Orvieto proper, enjoy the eggplant rigatoni or the porchetta with fennel prepared by this trattoria.

Other Options

Right on the Piazza del Duomo, you can sample some of Orvieto's famous dry white wine along with a tasty wild boar sandwich (lombetto di cinghale) at **Cantina Foresi**. Or you can visit the cantina to buy wine for a picnic, shopping at the alimentari **Dai Fratelli**, around the corner on *Via del Duomo 10* and the pasticceria a few blocks behind the duomo at V. Postierla 18. The picnicking spots outside the walls (road to Todi and SS 71 west toward Bolsena) are plentiful.

Directory

Telephone Code 0763   **Postal Code 05018**

Tourist Information

   APT *P. del Duomo 24 (*☎ *41-772; FAX 44-433).*

Festivals

   Medieval procession for moveable feast of Corpus Christi (around early June); Musica Pro Mundo Uno, a late summer classical music festival. (Write Accademia Musicale Ottorino Respighi, V. Villa Maggiorani 20, 00168 Roma.)

Arriving

   Orvieto is 125 km, 77.5 mi. north of Rome, 170 km, 105 mi. south of Florence by train or A-1. It is linked by bus, train and the flat road SS 3bis to Perugia (85 km, 53 mi.); by bus to Todi (48 km, 30 mi.). A funicolar links the stazione with P. del Duomo. A few streets are closed to traffic; parking areas are most plentiful east side of town.

Todi

   Arriving along the scenic route from Orvieto (SS 79bis) Todi looms impressively from atop its steep Umbrian hill. Though off the path of modern highways, Todi once required Etruscan, Roman, and then medieval walls to protect it from the heavily trafficked Via Flaminia, marched by Carthaginians, Gauls, and the armies of Frederick II. Today it is small, tranquil and picturesque.

What to See and Do

Piazza del Popolo   ★

   Sightseeing need not be too organized. The medieval streets offer strolls that can quite easily encompass the several churches and squares of the town. A turn here and there offers breathtaking views of the Umbrian valley below. You can start in the 13th-century Piazza del Popolo, surrounded by all the important town buildings, from the **duomo** (closed 12:30–2:30 p.m.) on the north, to the fortress-style **Palazzo dei Priori** on the south, and the more accessible Gothic **Palazzo del Comune** and **Palazzo del Capitano** on the east with their striking loggia and external staircase. It is one of the most harmonious town squares, best appreciated from the duomo steps. The museum in the Palazzo del Comune may be closed for renovations, but the interior of the church, lit through its rosette window, is worth a look.

Town Walk

The narrow streets behind the duomo can be explored, or you can enjoy the fine views from the neighboring Piazza Garibaldi. A bit down Via Mazzini, just below the antique stores, is the Franciscan church of ★ **San Fortunato** (begun 1292) with its unusual soaring piers and vaulted ceiling. The main door is carved with a two-part *Annunciation* by Jacopo della Quercia and inside there's a fresco by Masolino (4th chapel, right). To the right of the church you climb to the old Rocca, and then continue up to a ★ **belvedere**. From here you can see the symmetrical central plan of ★ **Santa Maria della Consolazione** (begun 1508), but this church is worth the walk down the hill and outside the medieval walls. In the purest Renaissance style of Bramante, but said to be by Cola da Caprarole, the Greek cross plan is so perfect that the whole could be reproduced from any part. The impact is one of calm and harmony.

Where to Stay

For a lake setting, there's **Villa Bellago** (see "Orvieto" above), just 15 km away.

Bramante   **L185–210,000**   √★★★

V. Orvietana; ☎ *894-8382, FAX 894-8074.*
Single L185,000. Double L210,000.
Just below the Consolazione church and with a terrace for scenic views, the Bramante has the best in-town facilities. 43 air-conditioned rooms; restaurant; pool and tennis.

Where to Eat

For more spectacular dining on the Baschi road to Orvieto, see "Orvieto" above.

Umbria   **$–$$**   ★

V. San Bonaventura 13, just off P. Popolo; ☎ *894-2737.*
Closed Tues. and around Christmas. Meals L40–65,000.
The terrace with views at this cozy restaurant make it the favorite in-town dining spot; the pastas and antipasti are decent, but we found the traditional secondi mediocre.

Cavour   **$**   ★

1 block along V. Cavour from P. Garibaldi.
Closed Wed., Jan. Meals L20–35,000.
A lively trattoria full of locals, with pizza (till 2 a.m.) at night.

Directory

Telephone Code 075   **Postal Code 06059**

Tourist Information

Palazzo del Capitano (☎ 894-2526)

Festivals

In spring there is an antique fair, with emphasis on woodworking, a town specialty (look for shops around S. Fortunato); in Aug./ Sept., there's a national crafts fair.

Arriving

Todi is connected by frequent buses to Perugia (45 km, 28 mi.), an occasional one from Orvieto (48 km along scenic SS 79bis, less via Baschi). Spoleto is best by car, 45 km away on SS 3bis south, then on scenic SS 418 east.

Note

Weekends in season no traffic permitted beyond the foot of the hill (park here, take bus to center).

Spoleto

The medieval streets of Spoleto spill over the hillside. Sometimes they are still covered by vaulting and other times, of necessity, they turn into steps as they approach Romanesque churches and Roman arches as well as the rim of the Tessino river gorge. It is a memorable town to visit, but one made famous not by any artistic monument, but rather by the Festival of Two Worlds that once attracted the greatest performing artists and their admirers each June and July. The international competition in cultural festivals has eclipsed the importance of Spoleto's, but each year the concerts and ballets attract large crowds, especially for the final performance in front of the duomo.

An important Roman town, on the Via Flaminia, Spoleto has more than the usual ancient remains. The colonnade of a pagan temple is embedded in the Early Christian church of **San Salvatore** (across the river outside the Porta Garibaldi). Both Etruscan and Roman stones are visible in the town wall, and in about every major edifice, including the 14th-century castle, the Rocca. The forum, now the market square, is marked by the ancient **Arco di Druso**; the more recent replacement for Porta Fuga still commemorates where Hannibal was forced to retreat in 217 B.C. Although the amphitheater remains pretty much buried in the north (and lower) part of town, the **Teatro Romano** has been cleared and now forms the backdrop of the main Piazza della Liberta.

What to See and Do

In your wanderings up and down and, perhaps, even outside of town, there are several sights you'll want to seek out. Whether you walk to them or take a bus, you'll find the Piazza della Liberta the most convenient place to begin. Here the buses leave for the duomo and Monteluco and other spots, and the tourist office can arm you with a map as well as a relatively easy position for climbing through much of the town.

Piazza del Duomo ★

The Piazza del Duomo, approached by the stepped street Via Arringo, is stunning. Its major landmark is the ★**cathedral** *(closed 1–3 p.m.)* with a Romanesque facade and campanile now graced by a Renaissance porch (Ambrogio Barocci). Inside is a bust of Urban VIII by Bernini (over main door), two frescoes by Pinturicchio (1st tiny chapel, right; sacristan opens); and, in the right transept, there is *Madonna and Saints*, (16th C.) by Annibale Carracci and *Tomb of Filippo Lippi* (left wall), commissioned by Lorenzo de' Medici and designed by Lippi's son Filippino. In the apse are the frescoes on the life of the Virgin that Filippo was painting at the time of his death (1469), their softness and delicacy that so influenced Botticelli can still be discerned.

Other Sights and Views

As you exit the Piazza del Duomo on Via Arringo, you see the apse of **Sant'Eufemia** and can visit its exquisite Romanesque ★interior around to the right, through the courtyard of the Palazzo Arcivescovile. Also here, along Via Saffi-Fontesecco, are many art galleries and antique shops for browsing. Climbing up Saffi, you come to the papal fort, the **Rocca**, built by Gattapone who also constructed the nearby aqueduct and bridge, the ★**Ponte delle Torri** (1365), found just outside the portal along Via del Ponte. The views over the gorge and verdant hills are extraordinary as is the bridge that spans a 760-foot chasm at a distance 260 feet above the river. On the opposite side of the gorge is **Monteluco**, once the sacred grove of a Roman cult and, later, a favorite retreat of St. Francis. If the bridge is closed, the Franciscan monastery (8 km from P. della Liberta) is best reached by bus, but it is only a brief walk from Piazza della Liberta, across SS 3, to the base of the wooded Monteluco road where you find the ★**Church of San Pietro**, its wonderful Romanesque facade sculpted with lively animals and scenes of fables.

Where to Stay

During the festival, reservations should be made well in advance. Otherwise, hotels seem relatively plentiful and modestly priced.

Albornoz Palace   L135–160,000   ★★★

Viale Matteoti, 06049; ☎ *221-221, FAX 221-600.*
Single L135,000. Double L160,000.
A distinguished contemporary hotel located on the edge of town, but just a few minutes from Piazza della Liberta. Its pyramid shape is encased in glass to take full advantage of the country views (a cupola bar has 360° views). Inside, the decor includes smartly designed Italian furnishings warmed by Oriental rugs, and the 95 rooms are ample, even the standard doubles. Restaurant. Bar. Gardens. Garage.

Gattapone   L150–260,000   ⊛★★

V. del Ponte; ☎ *223-447, FAX 223-448.*
Single L150,000. Double/suite L185–260,000.

This dramatic inn consists of two cliffside villas and a garden built into the hill and overlooking the Ponte dei Torri; 14 tastefully furnished rooms and suites. Restaurant. (Always reserve).

Aurora   **L80–100,000**   √★★

> *V. Apollinare 3;* ☎ *223-004, FAX 221-815.*
> *Single L80,000. Double L100,000.*

This small, cheerful hotel is set back from the Piazza Liberta at Mazzini and overlooks the hills and the Teatro Romano. There are 14 ample, carpeted rooms (no air conditioning) and modern baths (unfortunately, they rain on everything). Reserve in advance. Restaurant. Breakfast bar. Parking.

Where to Eat

Il Tartufo   **$–$$**   ★★★

> *P. Garibaldi;* ☎ *40-236, FAX 40-236.*
> *Closed Wed., late July. Fixed-price meals L35 & 60,000.*

The most acclaimed restaurant in Spoleto serves deliciously refined Umbrian dishes, from the humble strengozzi to the local kid and lamb served with truffles (seasonal).

La Cantina   **$**   ★

> *V. Filetteria 10a.*
> *Closed Tues. L20–30,000.*

The tables at this centrally-located eatery function more as a trattoria than the indoor enoteca, but you can eat lightly at both—an antipasto of stuffed mushrooms, a spicy strengozzi alla Spolentino, or just a sandwich.

Snacks

There are many picturesque spots for a light meal. Near the duomo on V. Fontesecca, try a sandwich or soup at the **Enoteca Provinciale** *(closed at 7:30 p.m.);* and just as that closes, you can move next door to **Taverna dei Duchi** *(till 11 p.m.)* for a bruschetta or plate of prosciutto at one of the tables in the wine bar in front. And for a succulent sandwich of roasted pork, look for the *porchetta* stands in the **market** at midday *(closed Sun.).* Or shop at the market and picnic in the Piazza della Signoria (down steps left of cathedral) with its fine views, then have a coffee overlooking the gorge at **Caffe La Portella** *(V. del Ponte).*

Directory

Telephone Code 0743   **Postal Code 06049**

Tourist Information

> APT *P. della Liberta 7* ☎ *220-311; FAX 46-241.*

Festival of Two Worlds

In June and July it requires some advance arrangements. Check major travel agents for tickets or contact **Festival dei Due Mondi** *(*☎ *43-406),* Teatro Nuovo, 06049 Spoleto.

Arriving

Train connections are excellent. Spoleto is on the Rome (140 km, 81 mi.)/Ancona line and via Foligno (30 km, 19 mi.); there are frequent connections with Assisi and Perugia (65 km, 40 mi.). The stazione is on the north side of town, marked by an

Alexander Calder stabile and linked by bus to P. Liberta. Pullman buses link it with major cities, but only a car will take you to Todi (45 km, 28 mi.).

Assisi

Basilica of San Francesco contains numerous frescoes by famous artists.

The rose-hued stone of the 13th century buildings and the bright geranium pots on window sills make Assisi warmer and more welcoming than most medieval towns. It's almost as if this shrine to St. Francis is still imbued with his spirit. The small town is so picturesque it seems unreal at times and when night mists roll in from the surrounding scenic hills, enshrouding the narrow, winding streets, it becomes a movie set for the three musketeers. Despite the dreaded commercialism of such a pilgrimage site and despite the crowds of day tourists, Assisi is nonetheless delightful.

What to See and Do

Basilica of San Francesco

Whatever the purpose of a visit to Assisi, it includes a tour of St. Francis' church (1228–58). The grandiose proportions of this double church, one atop the other, and the lavishly frescoed walls, have troubled those Franciscans who live by their vows of poverty and humility. For those here to appreciate the art, there can only be a sense of gratitude to the controversial Fra Elia who planned the church in honor of the then newly canonized saint. The more influential **upper church**, with its wide, uninterrupted nave and simple progression toward the pulpit, defined the Gothic in Italy, an architecture created for the preaching Franciscan and Dominican orders that grew so rapidly in the 13th century. Beginning at the right transept and wrapping around the nave are the frescoes on ★★ *The Life of St. Francis*, long thought to be early works by Giotto and his school (c. 1295) and now considered by many scholars to be the work of three painters (perhaps from the Roman school of Pietro Cavallini), not one of them Giotto. Others believe scenes 2-19 are, in fact, by Giotto. Everyone agrees that these frescoes are important examples of early Gothic naturalism, full of St. Francis' love of nature and humanity. They also are the first attempts to narrate events in his life, from the first scene (in front of Assisi's Temple of Minerva) where his future is predicted by a humble man, through his renunciation of wealth (and his cloak) to his stigmatization (scene 19) two years before his death. Cimabue's frescoes in the apse and transepts have faded beyond visibility except for the remaining emotional power of his *Crucifixion* (post-1279; left transept).

In contrast with the light and simplicity of the upper church, the ★**lower church** containing St. Francis' crypt, is shadowy and mystical. Its nave is lined with numerous chapels, each frescoed, such as Simone Martini's ★★**Chapel of St. Martin** (first on left of long nave). Martini designed the entire chapel, from the inlay floors to the stained glass windows, making the whole unusually harmonious. The frescoes (c. 1328) are lyrical and rich in color. The faces in the lower panels are particularly expressive; the saints under the entrance arch, pure portraiture. Many followers of Giotto painted frescoes here, and his school was responsible for those in the ★**Magdalen Chapel** (third chapel, right); for the gilded *St. Francis in Glory* vault over the high altar, which when illuminated for service dominates the church and *Life of Christ* in the right transept, whose scenes are outshone by Cimabue's ★ *Enthroned Madonna with St. Francis and Four Angels*, and the nearby S. Martini (attributed) *Madonna, Child, and Two Saints*. The greatest masterpiece is in the left transept, where Pietro Lorenzetti and his workshop painted scenes from the Life of Christ, but only the master could have produced the brilliantly composed and moving ★★ *Deposition* (c. 1325).

The church dominates the lower end of Assisi, near the first gate, the Porta San Francesco, as you arrive. *Open, in summer, all day; closed 12–2 p.m. in winter. Bring coins to operate lights in lower church, and binoculars to see details.*

Town Walk

The extraordinary basilica alone is worth a visit here, but a leisurely walk through town is pleasant, from the church up to the top of Assisi where the Romans built their amphitheater, and numerous popes, the castle **Rocca Maggiore** (1367 and after), with its commanding views. Leaving the church along Via San Francesco you pass numerous ceramic shops and curio stalls as well as some fine buildings, such as the 15th-century pilgrims' hospice with frescoes still traced on the facade (at #13). Where the street climbs and changes its name to "Portica" is the **Museo Romano** (*10 a.m.–1 p.m.; 2:30–5:30 p.m., except in summer 3–7 p.m.; L4000*), which conceals ruins of the old forum. Then you arrive at the lively and handsome **Piazza del Comune**, surrounded with medieval civic buildings that share their space with the first-century **Temple of Minerva**, its Corinthian columns now the portico for a church. A detour on Corso Mazzini (the low street) leading out of the piazza quickly takes you to the Gothic austerity of **Santa Chiara** *(closed noon–2 p.m.)*, its facade pierced by a lacy rosette window and its interior graced by the 12th-century St. Damian crucifix (chapel to right) that informed Francis of his calling. Buried inside is St. Clare, founder of the Poor Clares. Back at the Piazza Comune, the high street *(V. San Rufino)* takes you to the **duomo** with its ★ Romanesque facade carved with symbolic animals of the evangelists and other Biblical themes. Continuing your climb, you arrive at the immense **Piazza Matteotti**; nearby you can discover remnants of the amphitheater or rest in the public garden. A farther climb takes you to the **Rocca** *(10 a.m.–dusk, L5000)*.

Nearby Sights

Each year, millions come to Assisi on a pilgrimage to St. Francis, visiting his church and birthplace as well as the simple chapel of Porziuncola where he died (now entombed in the massive **Basilica Santa Maria degli Angeli** (7 a.m.–noon, 2:30–dusk), a 5-km drive or bus ride south of town). Two other spots retain the beauty and solitude that appealed to the saint during his retreats: the **Santuario di S. Damiano** *(by steep footpath 2-km road outside Porta Nuova; 10 a.m.–noon, 3 p.m.–6 p.m.)* where the crucifix said, "Go, Francis and repair my church" and where St. Clare, in residence with the first Poor Clares, stymied an attack by an army of Frederick II; the **Eremo delle Carceri**, *(4 km outside Porta Capuccini; 8 a.m.–dusk)* the still-forested retreat where Francis preached to birds and creatures of God and where there is a convent built by St. Bernardine.

Where to Stay

There are plenty of facilities, including rooms in private homes and religious institutions (check APT office for listings), which isn't to say they don't fill up during religious holidays. Also, in the winter many inexpensive hotels close unexpectedly—arrive early or reserve in advance. Also none of the listings here include air-conditioned rooms, but then the evenings atop the hill are usually comfortable in the summer.

| **Subasio** | **L150–200,000** | ❀★★★ |

V. Frate Elia 2; ☎ *812-206, FAX 816-691.*
Single L150,000. Double L200,000.
A long-time favorite, with 70 charmingly furnished old-fashioned rooms (with modernized baths) near the basilica, some with wonderful views of the valley. There's a garden terrace with restaurant and good views. Bar, too.

| **Giotto** | **L120–195,000** | ★★★ |

V. Fontebella 412; ☎ *812-209, FAX 816-479.*
Single L120,000. Double L195,000.
This modern alternative is similarly located near the basilica and with fine views and gardens to go along with its 70 well-appointed rooms. Restaurant and lounge. Garage.

Umbra   L110–150,000   √★★★

> *V. degli Archi 6;* ☎ *812-240, FAX 813-653; closed mid-Jan.–mid-Mar.*
> *Single L110,000. Double L150,000.*
> Intimate and romantic, yet only a few steps from the Piazza del Comune. 27 rooms, a few with views, many furnished with antiques; a good restaurant with summer terrace. A good buy.

Dei Priori   L115–150,000   ★★

> *Corso Mazzini 15;* ☎ *812-237, FAX 816-804; closed mid-Nov.–mid Mar.*
> *Single L115,000. Double L150,000*
> Another intimate inn off the Piazza Comune, the 28 rooms here are comfortable; restaurant just for lodgers.

St. Anthony's Guest House   L50–75,000 CP   √★

> *V. Alessi 10;* ☎ *812-542; closed Dec.–Mar. 1.*
> *Single L50,000 CP without bath. Double L75,000 CP with bath.*
> A villa with countryside views, located between S. Chiara and the Giardini Pubblici. The Franciscan sisters who run the guest house add warmth to the comfort of their 15 rooms. Dining room. Gardens.

Where to Eat

Il Medioevo $$ ★★

> *V. Arco dei Priori 4;* ☎ *813-068.*
> *Closed Wed., most of Jan. and June. Meals L55–70,000.*
> One of Assisi's favorite restaurants, Il Medioevo is full of ambience and some of the restaurant walls actually date to Roman times. The food, like lamb spezzatino with artichokes, is Umbrian and good.

Umbra $–$$ ★★

> *In Hotel Umbra, near main square;* ☎ *812-240.*
> *Closed Tues. and mid-Nov.–mid-Dec. Meals L40–65,000.*
> This restaurant serves very Umbrian cuisine—lentil soup, cappelletti with black truffles, spit-roasted lamb and game. The setting is fine, too, an elegant dining room or, in summer, a tranquil terrace.

La Fortezza $ ★★

> *V. della Fortezza 2/b, just off P. Comune;* ☎ *812-418.*
> *Closed Thurs. Meals L25–40,000.*
> La Fortezza offers medieval ambience and modest prices for its decent seasonal Umbrian cuisine, including pasta with black truffles and duck with fennel.

Trattoria del Arco "Da Bino" $ ★

> *V. San Gregorio 8;* ☎ *812-383.*
> *Closed Tues., mid Jan.–mid Feb., early July. Meals L30–45,000.*
> Centrally located near the Minerva temple, below Via San Francisco, this trattoria serves excellent tagliatelli and other pastas; the house wine is good, and the ambience under its Gothic vaulted ceiling, pleasing.

Caffè and Snacks

The sweets, stuffed figs, and breads at **La Bottega del Pasticcere** *(V. Portica 7)* are irresistible and the lively character of the Piazza del Comune make its cafes an entertaining place to sit. At night, **Pizzeria Il Duomo** *(V. Porta Perlici 11; pizza L7–15,000)* serves antipasti and pasta along with pizza in its contemporary setting.

Directory

Telephone Code 075 **Postal Code 06081**

Tourist Information

    APT, *P. Comune 12* ☎ *812-534; FAX 813-727.*

Festivals

    All major religious holidays are honored with considerable care and attract great crowds, especially Easter Week, various holidays associated with St. Francis in August, and the commemoration of his death on October 3. In May, there's medieval pageantry associated with the Calendimaggio.

Books

    St. Francis' verses have been translated into English and can be found in shops of Assisi along with Le Fioretti (*"Little Flowers"*), an anonymous biography of the saint.

Arriving

    On a country road that runs off SS 75 between Perugia and Foligno, Assisi is 25 km, 16 mi. from Perugia and 50 km from Spoleto via Foligno, and well connected by bus (from P. San Pietro) to Perugia, Rome and Florence and train (stazione 5 km away; bus to center). Parking (fee) well-marked outside the medieval gates; Porta San Pietro is nearest the basilica; P. Matteotti is at the top.

Perugia

Bustling Perugia, the regional and commercial capital of Umbria, has an openness and cosmopolitanism unusual for a medieval hill town. Perhaps it's the diversity of its population that creates such an ambience, for Perugia is a center of learning with two universities including the Universita Italiana per Stranieri (for foreigners). Perhaps it is the pleasant cafe-lined streets, the park-lined boulevard with views of the Tiber valley below, or simply the size of this city that makes it seem sophisticated. Despite the depth of its history, from the encircling Etruscan walls and the Arco d'Augusto, with its Etruscan foundations, Roman additions and Renaissance loggia, there is an air of modernity. As if to impress this upon you, the main pedestrian approach to the centro storico from the bus terminal below is on escalators that take you through layers of the destroyed castle, the Rocca Paolina, decorated with contemporary art. Modern in spirit, but massively medieval in construction, Perugia is strikingly different.

What to See and Do

Piazza IV Novembre ★★

    North end of Corso Vannucci, the traffic-free street starting a few blocks away at Piazza Italia.

This magnificent square is flanked by the side of the Gothic duomo (north) and the fan-shaped steps of the Palazzo dei Priori (begun 1293). In the center is the symbol of medieval Perugia, the ★★Fontana Maggiore (1278), built at the apogee of Perugia's commercial success when it had just founded the university and completed the waterworks that this fountain commemorates. Sculpted by Nicola Pisano and his son, Giovanni, the fountain mixes secular themes with religious ones, showing the civic pride that led to its commission. On the bottom are 50 panels with scenes from the Bible as well as Aesop's fables and Roman history. Above are figures of prophets and saints as well as kings. Gloriously surmounting the fountain are graceful caryatids.

The ★**Palazzo dei Priori** has numerous entrances and separate chambers that contain the finest paintings the town offers of the Umbrian School, notable for its serene landscapes and poetic figures. Started by Pietro Vannucci (1445-1523), known as Perugino, the school ended with its second-best known artist, Pinturicchio. The school is best represented in the top floor ★**Galleria Nazionale dell'Umbria** *(entrance at Corso Vannucci 19; 9 a.m.–2 p.m., 3–6 p.m., till 7 p.m. Apr.–Oct.; Sun. till 1 p.m.; closed Mon. in winter; L8000).* The renovated museum reopened in 1994 with 13 rooms of regional art. Look for sculptures by the Pisani and by those who influenced the Umbrian School, such as Fra Angelico (a polyptyc) and Piero della Francesca (note the ★*Annunciation* above his polyptyc). Then, there is *Miracles of St. Bernardine*, a joint work by Perugino and Pinturicchio as well as fine works by both artists, particularly Perugino's landscape in ★*Adoration of the Magi.* Yet more paintings can be seen in the 15th-century banker's guild hall, the **Collegio del Cambio** *(Corso Vannucci 25; 9 a.m.–12:30 p.m., 3–6 p.m. in summer, 8 a.m.–2 p.m. in winter; Sun. 9 a.m.–12:30 p.m. year-round; L6000 includes della Mercanzia).* Here, in the Gothically handsome council chamber you find ★frescoes (c. 1500) by Perugino and his assistants, one of them the 17-year-old Raphael. Usually the Prophets and Sibyls (right wall) is attributed to Raphael; on the left wall is a Perugino self-portrait (middle pilaster). The fee from here also gains admittance to the **Collegio della Mercanzia** *(Corso Vannucci 14; same ticket, same hours as del Cambio)* with its 14th-century wood panelling covering even the vaults. Still exploring the palazzo, climb the fan-shaped steps to the **Sala dei Notari** with its Gothic period frescoes (free).

Town Walks

In almost any direction from the Piazza IV Novembre you can find interesting churches, vaulted streets and views of the countryside. One of the easiest and most picturesque walks is west along ★**Via dei Priori** to the Gothicized yet Etruscan Porta di San Luca and its medieval tower. Just beyond, toward the right is the ★**Oratorio San Bernardino**, with its pleasing Renaissance facade carved in bas relief. Another picturesque street, **Via Ulisse Rocchi**, leads north out of the piazza to the **Arco d'Augusto** before pushing on to the far north end of the city and the round church of **Sant'Angelo**, founded in the 5th century, its interior built with ancient columns.

South of the Piazza IV Novembre the Corso Vannucci leads to the Piazza Italia and the lovely **Giardini Carducci** with its views of the vast valley below. The gardens cover the ruins of the ★**Rocca Paolina** (1540 by Sangallo the Younger), which was built over a section of medieval Perugia in retribution for the town's rebellion against the papal salt tax. Excavations in 1963 revealed an entire street, complete with its 15th-century houses. Entry to this subterranean world can be gained through the *scale mobile*, or escalators in Piazza Italia (in the arcade across from Hotel Brufani) or by Via Marzia (follow V. Baglioni out of piazza, then turn right down Marzia) and the Etruscan gate that now gives entry to the surreal interior of the Rocca. Also in the south section of the town is the **Museo Archeologico** *(9 a.m.– 1:30 p.m. and, high-season only, 3-7 p.m.; Sun. till 1 p.m.; closed Mon. in winter; L4000)* housed in the ex-convent of San Domenico on Corso Cavour and exhibiting Etruscan and Roman art as well as prehistoric artifacts.

Nearby

Lake Trasimeno

If you need relief from sightseeing, you can follow the route of Hannibal's army west along the north shore of Lake Trasimeno. From the small resort town of Passignano (30 km, 19 mi.) a ferry quickly takes you to the Isole Maggiore where you can picnic and enjoy lake breezes.

Deruta

Since the 13th century, Deruta (20 km, 12 mi. on ss 3 bis from Perugia towards Todi) has been one of Italy's great centers for **majolica** ceramics. In the hilltop town, countless shops sell *maiolica*, jugs and plates decorated with medieval scenes or the Deruta classic design of spidery gold and blue against a white background. And at the foot of town, the prices can be quite good at the modern workshops and warehouses that line Via Tiburina (a street parallel with ss 3 bis); it is here where **G. Grazia** *(# 181)* produces some of the best contemporary work. Before buying, you can familiarize yourself with the tradition at the **Museo dello Maioliche** *(Tues.–Sun. 9:30 a.m.–12:30 p.m., 3–6 p.m.; L4000)*; afterwards you can relax on a terrace with panoramic views at ★**Fontanina** *(V. Solitara 14a; closed Tues. Meals L20–40,000)*, a hotel and trattoria found at the top of the centro storico. If majolica is something of a passion, visit **Torgiano** (6 km north) for the 16th-century Deruta drinking vessels exhibited in the **Museo del Vino** *(9a.m.–1 p.m., 3–6 p.m., in summer till 8 p.m.; L4000)*.

Where to Stay

Although there are numerous hotels in the wooded hills above Lake Trasimeno, most likely your visit is to Perugia itself.

Hotel Brufani   L390–425,000   ✿★★★★

P. Italia; ☎ 573-2541, FAX 572-0210.
Single L390,000. Double L425,000.
This is the favorite old hotel. Renovated in 1996, it offers modern conveniences, and many of its 25 rooms have wonderful views from the hotel's prime in-town location overlooking the Giardini Carducci restaurant and bar.

La Rosetta   L100–200,000   ★★★

V. Bonazzi 19; ☎ 572-0841, FAX 572-0841.
Single L100,000. Double L200,000.

Just off the P. Italia and set in a quaint courtyard, this hotel has 95 decent, if smallish rooms, with a variety of decors including just plain; some views. Restaurant.

Signa   L75–100,000   ★

V. del Grillo 9; ☎ 572-4180, FAX 572-2632.
Single L75,000. Double L100,000.

Past San Domenico and down a little alley off Cavour is this modernized hotel offering 21 small but bright rooms (no air conditioning), a garden and a breakfast room.

Where to Eat

Perugia is a major food producer and manufacturer, a reality that certainly benefits the
local restaurants. Look for the Torgiano wines produced nearby and save room for dessert: the almond tarts, the Perugino candies, the cheesecake.

Osteria del Bartolo $$–$$$ ★★★

V. Bartolo 30; ☎ 573-1561.
Closed Sun., mid Jan., late July. L65–85,000.

The place to enjoy Umbrian cuisine at its most polished is under the vaulted ceilings
of this former wine cellar. Just north of the duomo, the Osteria offers dishes richly
laced with truffles and artichokes and eggplant, and portions are more than ample.

La Taverna $$ ★★★

V. delle Streghe 8; ☎ 572-4128, FAX 573-5888.
Closed Mon. Meals L50–65,000.

A bustling spot, a block from the Corso Vannucci, with traditional rabbit and duck
as well as lighter fare, such as grilled fish with artichokes.

Le Tre Vaselle $$–$$$ ★★★★

V. Giuseppe Garibaldi 48, 06089 in Torgiano, 14 km on ss 3 bis towards Todi; reserve at
☎ 988-0447, FAX 988-0214.
Meals L65–85,000.

Out of town, but in Umbrian wine country, is this highly respected village inn (with
48 rooms; single L270,000 CP, double L295–335,000 CP) run by the Lungarotti
family, famous for their Rubesco wines. Among the offerings are chicory fried with
broad beans and bacon, risotto with radicchio and Rubesco, turbot with celery
sauce and veal with asparagus and wild fennel.

Cafes

For less costly fare back in Perugia, try any of the cafes along *Corso Vannucci*, a popular street for outdoor tables. **Bar Ferrari** *(at #43)* is a good choice here for its wide selection of food as well as its whipped cream delicacies and Perugian candies. **Pasticceria
Sandri** *(at #32)* has more traditional elegance for enjoying its pastries. And if you can't
get to Torgiano and its enoteca (**"Osteria del Museo,"** next to the museum on the main
street), you can taste and buy the regional wines at **Enoteca Provinciale Perugia** *(Ulisse
Rocchi 16; closed Mon.)*.

Directory

Telephone Code 075 **Postal Code 06100**

Tourist Information

> **APT**, *P. IV Novembre 4* ☎ *572-3327*.

Telephones

> **Telcom**, *P. del Comune II*, 8 a.m.–11 p.m., in winter till 7 p.m.

Festival

> In July, internationally famous musicians perform at the annual Jazz Festival. Check APT for information.

Arriving

> The stazione is outside town with bus connections to Piazza Italia. Trains via Foligno for Rome (175 km, 108 mi.; 3.5 hours) and via Terontola (Cortona) to Florence (155 km, 96 mi.; 2.5 hours). Pullman buses, leaving from P. dei Partigiani linked by stairs and escalators *(scala mobile)* up to P. Italia, are best for Siena (120 km, 74 mi.), Urbino (110 km, 68 mi.), Gubbio (40 km, 25 mi.), Todi (46 km), and Assisi (25 km, 15.5 mi.).

Getting Around

> For tours, check **CIT**, *Corso Vannucci 2* ☎ *572-6061*. Car rentals available.

Italian Study

> Universita Italiana Per Stranieri (Palazzo Gallengo, *P. Fortebraccio 4*, ☎ *576-4344*) is especially popular for its summer program.

Gubbio

Gubbio sits amid a truly Umbrian land, surrounded by ravines that are lush and green in summer, covered by periwinkle wildflowers in spring. Rising steeply against its backdrop of Monte Ingino, the medieval town is built of stone more ochre than Assisi's rose, warmer than Perugian gray. Its Gothic palazzi seem more picturesque than elsewhere, their asymmetry emphasized by the addition of the so-called "doors of death." These now-sealed doorways, found particularly on Via Baldassini below the Piazza della Signoria, have generated considerable speculation. Reachable only by ladder, some claim they were defensive retreats used during the constant feuding of the middle ages. Others say they were exits for death, based on pagan Umbrian rituals. Whether speculating on such details, or simply appreciating the portals and mullioned windows of the town, there really is nothing compelling to see. It's best to wander, beginning your visit by climbing the Via della Repubblica from Piazza 40 Martiri, and exploring the smaller streets around some of the following sights.

What to See and Do

Piazza della Signoria ★

> Jutting out from the hillside, this great stone plaza represents a considerable engineering feat for the Middle Ages. Begun after 1322, the piazza houses the civic pal-

aces and frames a fine valley view. The finest building here is the **Palazzo dei Consoli**, with its ceremonial steps leading up to the **Pinacoteca** *(9 a.m.–12:30 p.m., 3:30–6 p.m. tourist season; 9 a.m.–1 p.m., 3–5 p.m. winter; L4000)*. Even if you don't wish to see the Roman fragments or the ancient bronze tablets carved in the Umbrian language, you will want to glance at the majestic space of the single barrel-vaulted hall. And you might want to climb the stairs inside to look at some of the fine medieval crucifixes and art on your way to the framed ★ views from the second-floor loggia.

Duomo and Palazzo Ducale

Just off the piazza, follow the narrow, climbing, and often tunneled Via Ducale up to the next tier of town. Here are gardens and views as well as two other buildings to look through. Facing each other are the Palazzo Ducale *(9 a.m.–1:30 p.m. closed Mon. & Sun. off-season; L4000)*, the residence of the Montefeltros from Urbino, its elegant spaces and baronial fireplaces much inspired by the famous palace there; and the Duomo, consecrated in 1366 and with beautiful stone vaults leading unin-terruptedly to the altar.

Other Sights

On top of **Monte Ingino**, there's the basilica and monastery dedicated to Gubbio's patron Sant' Ubaldo. But the reason for a visit to the top is for the views on a clear day. You can hike, a mile or so up past the duomo. You can drive (5 km), perhaps taking in the **Roman theater** on the southern edge of town. Or you can pay for the funivia, or cable car *(closed 1–2:30 p.m., Oct.–Feb.)* that leaves from the Porta Romana on the southeast side of town.

Where to Stay and Eat

Bosone   L130–145,000   ★★

V. XX Settembre 22; ☎ *922-0698, FAX 922-0522.*
Single L130,000. Double L145,000.

There are a number of small, family-run hotels and pensioni, but this is the most favored for its garage, 33 renovated rooms (no a/c) with bath, and location in a medieval building near the P. della Signoria.

Fornace di Mastro Giorgio $$–$$$ ★★★

V. Mastro Giorgio 2; ☎ *927-5740.*
Closed Sun. night, Mon. except Aug.–Sept., and half of Feb. & July. Meals L60–80,000.
A handsome restaurant respected for its Umbrian specialities.

Pizzeria Il Bargello $ ★

V. dei Consoli 37, near fountain.
Closed Sun. Meals L25–40,000.
For simple dining or just pizza.

Cafés and Snacks

For snacks, consider the outdoor café and views at the **Garden Pensili**, just below the Ducal Palace, or shop at the alimentari *(V. della Repubblica 19, near tourist office, is one)* for sandwiches and enjoy them atop Monte Insino (where there's a café, too).

Gubbio

Directory

Telephone Code 075   **Postal Code 06024**

Tourist Office

    APT, *P. Oderisi 6*, at entrance to *centro storico* ☎ *922-0693, FAX 927-3409.*

Festivals

    May 15 is Sant'Ubaldo's feast day, celebrated joyously with morning festivities in P. della Signoria, followed in the afternoon by the Corsa dei Ceri, a race up Monte Ingino to the basilica, with teams carrying 16-foot contraptions crowned by small effigies of saints. Those carrying Ubaldo always win. The last Sunday in the month, medieval Gubbio takes on medieval Sansepolcro in the Palio della Balestra, a cross-bow tournament. During late summer, plays are performed in the Roman Theater.

Arriving

    Frequent bus service to the Fossato di Vico train station (19 km, 12 mi.) on Rome/Ancona line, to Perugia (40 km, 25 mi.) and to Assisi (46 km) as well as Urbino (70 km, 43 mi.).

Urbino

At the end of the 15th century, Urbino was the major power in this region, ruling over 50 towns from Gubbio in Umbria to the Romagna. The region was nonetheless squeezed by the truly great powers of the papacy in Rome and Venice to the north. Yet under Federigo da Montefeltro, Urbino not only maintained its independence, it also was one of the most cultured courts of the Renaissance, attracting Alberti and Uccello, Piero della Francesca and Botticelli, and the Laurana brothers, sculptor and architect. Federigo made his fortune, and the town's, by becoming the most respected condottiere of his time, leading the armies of popes, princes, and kings during a period of endless warfare. His enduring impact, however, was cultural. The youthful Raphael and Bramante grew up in the culturally rich atmosphere of the duke's palace, before taking their talents to Milan, Florence, and especially Rome. For centuries, young men from as far away as England were sent to Urbino to be educated and taught proper manners. And here Castiglione wrote *Il Cortegiano* ("The Courtier"), the classic book on style and conduct that the Emperor Charles V kept at his bedside. Today the humanist principles of the duke live on in his palace, a delight of open and well-proportioned spaces.

Urbino is a most pleasant mountain town tucked away in the Apennines. Not as picturesque as Gubbio or so medieval as Orvieto, its streets nonetheless climb to the **Fortezza dell'Albornoz** *(closed 1–4 p.m. and Oct.–Apr.)* now a park, and they twist past handsome homes, such as Raphael's birthplace, the **Casa di Raffaello** *(V. di Raffaello; 9 a.m.–1 p.m., also 3–7 p.m. except Sun.; closed Mon. in winter; L5000)* with period furnishings and a painting said to be an early work of the artist. In the morning light of summer, the town is its

loveliest for a stroll; at the end of the day, the Piazza della Repubblica is lively with conversation of foreign university students and old duchy descendants alike.

What to See and Do

Palazzo Ducale   ★ ★ ★

The reason to visit Urbino is the Ducal Palace. As you approach town, it dominates
all views, its walls seemingly grow from the hill itself. From the ★ **west facade**, its
beautiful, tiered loggia, gracefully carved by Ambrogia Barocci, are flanked by
spires. From the Via Veneto entrance, it diminishes even the duomo with which its
shares a piazza. **Inside**, its rooms are light and airy, unlike most Renaissance palazzi;
the staircases are majestic, yet human in proportion. The vast and ornate complex,
once home to a court of 500, lacks the pomp one might expect from generously
stuccoed ceilings and exquisitely detailed marble and wood fireplaces and door
frames all inscribed "FEDUX," for Duke Federigo. It seems liveable somehow, perhaps because of the charm of the tiny chapel tucked under the duke's apartments or
the intimacy of his ★ ★ studiolo, or study, with its fabulous intarsia woodwork.
Designed by Luciano Laurana (died 1479), this Renaissance palace is built over an
earlier castle and yet earlier Roman ruins (visible in basement). Nowhere is Laurana's success more visible than in the harmonious ★ ★ courtyard at the entrance.
Although two stories have been added to Laurana's design, his original scheme can
be easily appreciated, especially the lightness of the second story over the arcade,
achieved by pale Corinthian pilasters denying the darker walls supporting them.

On the *upper floor* is the ★ ★ **Galleria Nazionale delle Marche**, an extensive art
collection that ranges from the Byzantine style in the Marches through the Early
Baroque of Federico Barocci (1535–1612) on the top floor, and includes works by
the Venetian Giovanni Bellini as well as such Florentines as Luca della Robbia and
Verrocchio. Although the *Throne Room* with 17th-century tapestries after designs
by Raphael and the nearby *Sala degli Angeli* are impressive, the masterpieces of the
collection are in the ducal apartments, rooms clustered around Federigo's study and
beyond the Throne Room. Piero della Francesca's ★ ★ *Flagellation of Christ* is
remarkable for its perspective and concentration on color and composition, though
disturbing in its lack of emotion. This great artist also is represented by the ★ *Madonna di Senegalia*, almost secular save for the hint of wings on Gabriel, and perhaps by ★ *Citta Ideale*, as well based on architectural designs of Laurana. Look,
too, for Uccello's eccentric and colorful *Miracle of the Host*; Titian's Resurrection
and Last Supper; and Raphael's lovely and softly Umbrian ★ *Portrait of a Woman*
or "*La Muta*," as well as the predella *Scenes from the Life of the Virgin*, which may
have been done with Perugino.

*The palace and museum are open Monday-Saturday 9 a.m.–2 p.m., Sunday 9 a.m.–
1 p.m. In winter, accompanied visits only, beginning every 20 minutes. Ticket
(L8000) good also for* **Museo Archeologico**, *off the courtyard.*

Where to Stay

There are some modern hotels outside town; a few advertise pools. In town the hotels are not lavish but are certainly acceptable for a night.

Bonconte   **L125–180,000**   ★★

V. delle Mura 28; ☎ *24-63, FAX 47-82.*
Single L125,000. Double L180,000.
Immaculate with 20 smallish, but modern rooms with bath, no air conditioning. Breakfast service and limited parking.

Albergo Italia   **L50–80,000**   √★

V. Garibaldi 30; ☎ *27-01.*
Single L50,000. Double L80,000.
A few steps from Piazza della Repubblica, this aging hotel offers 30 sunny rooms with private baths, no air conditioning, but a pretty terrace for breakfast and low prices.

Where to Eat

Vecchia Urbino   **$$**   ★★

V. Vasari 3; ☎ *44-47.*
Closed Tues. in off-season. Meals L45–70,000.
A university town, Urbino has numerous places to snack but few fine restaurants. This is the most polished, with its homemade pastas, fresh fish and grilled game.

Rustica   **$**   ★

V. Nuova 3.
Closed Tues. Pizza L7–15,000.
A bustling trattoria, popular with locals for pizza.

Caffe Rinascente

P. della Repubblica.
Come here for the best coffee; there's also a tea room for snacks.

Directory

Telephone Code 0722   **Postal Code 61029**

Tourist Information

APT, *P. Duca Federico 35*, in front of palace ☎ *26-13; FAX 24-41* and map posted on wall P. della Repubblica at V. Garibaldi.

Courses in Italian

Corso Estivo per Stranieri, Universita degli Studi, *V. Saffi 2;* a summer program.

Arriving

Pullman buses and those from the stazione are in the Piazza Mercatale, below the palace. Here, there's parking and elevators (ascensori)—fees for both—up to town and the west facade of the palace. Buses to Pesaro (40 km, 25 mi.) on coast, to Gubbio and Perugia (110 km, 68 mi.), to Fossato di Vico train station on Rome/Ancona line, and to Rome (275 km, 171 mi.). Ravenna lies 130 km, 81 mi. away, via Fano. If driving the coast, take the A-14 autostrada to Rimini to avoid traffic.

Urbino

Urbino

FLORENCE AND TUSCANY

In Florence, don't miss the duomo, a gem of Renaissance architecture.

History and Art

Spreading between the forested Apennines and Italy's Tyrrhenian coast, the Tuscan land has always offered its people a diverse and rich environment. By the 7th century B.C. the Etruscans flourished here, using the wood from the forests for shipbuilding, the coast for ports and fishing, the mineral wealth for trade with Greece, the rivers, such as the Arno, for communication and irrigation, and the hills for defensively placed cities such as Volterra and Arezzo. Tuscany is, in fact, a swirl of hills, volcanic bubbles of hills, all oddly shaped, a few singularly dominating the landscape. Bare hills often, their forests long ago yielding to the geometry of tidy and square farms made in the style of the Etruscans and Romans. Soft green hills in the early spring when the young wheat, in fields of cut velvet, is ruffled by the wind. Bleached hills in the summer, carpeted by sun-ripened and tawny wheat, patterned by ridges of dark, wind-breaking cypresses and swatches of more delicately hued vineyards. Tuscany is a practical land. And in those regions where it remains most traditional, yielding the wheat, wine, and olive oil of ancient times, Tuscany is also a beautiful land.

Etruscans

Tuscany nourished the Etruscans. It accepted the Romans —though it never flourished under them despite two roads, the Via Aurelia on the coast and the Via Cassia inland, that linked such towns as Pisa, Florence and Siena, with the imperial capital in Rome. It suffered Arab attacks on its coastal cities and Lombard invasions until, in the 10th and 11th centuries, the most typical home of its people was no more than a mud hut. But from such wretchedness, Tuscany would revive, creating the great city states of the Renaissance on the ruins of the Romans and hilltops of the Etruscans.

Tuscan Revival

The Tuscan revival began with the commerce between Europe and the East that was renewed by the crusades. But the city states of Tuscany were destined to outstrip most rivals, giving birth to the leading financiers of Europe as well as to its leading artists. Even before the first crusade, the precocious port of Pisa had opened the Mediterranean to trade by sending expeditions to Sardinia (1015) and Africa to defeat the Moslems. Throughout the 12th century, Pisa and its neighbor to the north, Genoa, owned two of the three most powerful merchant fleets in the Mediterranean (the third, Venice, was Italian, too). Soon the trade of the ports of Genoa and Pisa would be facilitated by the first European banks, in Siena and Florence. And in 1252, Florence began minting the florin, which quickly became international currency. Further wealth came to the region through the textile industry: silk in Lucca and fine woolens in other towns. The transformation of Tuscany into prosperous, urban communities left the feudal years of serfdom and rural castles behind forever.

History and Art

Medieval Cities

The thriving cities grew beyond their ancient walls—if not their need for fortification. Tuscany saw town fight town in the struggles between the Guelphs and Ghibellines. In the process, Siena and Florence divided up most of Tuscany between them. The power struggles were repeated within the towns, noble family against noble family, and the emerging middle class

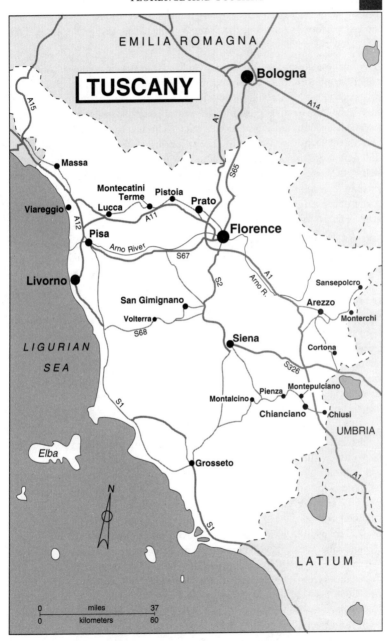

against them all. In Florence, the fighting between the factions was so intense that laborers repairing the Ponte Vecchio, damaged by floods, had to wear armor.

From these struggles, the towns would take on their medieval aspect of armed neighborhoods. Nobles constructed fortified palazzi with soaring towers to which they could safely retreat and from where their archers could survey the narrow streets. Families formed alliances, spanning the streets between their compounds and towers with archways. By 1200, Florence had about 100 such tower fortresses, the tallest measuring 65 meters, or nearly 250 feet. Until the middle of the 13th century, only the nobility could legally build towers. By then, however, the wealthy merchants had found their place in the *comune*, or municipal government. And in the end, only the bell tower of the *palazzo pubblico*, or town hall, would call the neighborhoods to arms. The bourgeois republics had been born.

As the Tuscan hill towns prospered and grew, great cathedrals, not just towers and wall fortifications, were built. The Romanesque duomo in Pisa that introduced the striped marble style of Tuscany came first and, then later, the more Gothic cathedrals in Siena and Florence. Stone symbols of mercantile success were built, too: guild houses, town halls and even universities in Siena, Florence and Arezzo. The Pisanos sculpted their magnificent pulpits, Giotto and Simone Martini frescoed church walls, and Ambrogio Lorenzetti painted the Palazzo Pubblico in Siena with tributes to civic life. Tuscany was changing, and the change affected literature, too. Dante, Petrarch and Boccaccio were Tuscan writers, and they created the language that would become modern Italian by writing in the local dialect rather than Latin.

The Black Death

Through its wealth and art, Tuscany had laid the foundation for the Renaissance by the early 1300s. But the Renaissance would be delayed. What war couldn't stop, the Black Death of 1348 would. Within a few months, half the population of both Siena and Florence died from the bubonic plague. Perhaps even more died, a stupefying number. Florence's population declined from 95,000 to half that number; Siena fared worse, declining from 50,000 to 15,000. Florence would recover; Siena never would. Siena abandoned work on its expanded cathedral, never to resume it. Many of its greatest artists died in the plague, including both the Lorenzetti. Out of the devastation grew religious fervor and mysticism, best personified by Catherine Benincaso of Siena, who would become the patron saint of Italy. The Renaissance would wait out this sad period of death and penance, until the 14th century ended.

History and Art

Renaissance Born

In the early 15th century, the Renaissance would finally be born. It would be born in Florence, a city that was soon to emerge as the major political force in the region, controlling all other Tuscan cities and ports, save Siena and Lucca. Yet Florentine power didn't go unchallenged, as other Italian states invaded Tuscany and laid siege to Florence. Mercantile Florence found its trade repeatedly disrupted, often by the Visconti of Milan, and it found itself paralyzed by states of siege. Despite the odds against them, the powerful wool merchant and banking guilds refused to submit to outsiders. These guilds, already in control of the government of the republic, rallied the populace, too, in the struggle for an independent Florence. They commissioned works of art that would extol the free and heroic citizen, works that would inspire resistance. Florence kept its independence. And in the process, it produced the art of Masaccio, Donatello and Brunelleschi.

Golden Years of Florence

The later 15th century brought the golden years of Florence, peaceful years in which the wealthiest of bankers and merchants took on the airs of a new nobility. They built Renaissance palaces inspired by the work of Brunelleschi and Alberti, and decorated their country villas with mythological scenes, such as Botticelli's *Birth of Venus*. They sent their sons to academies to study under the humanist poets and intellectuals. They were patrons of science as well as art, as interested in maps to the Orient (Columbus' chart was Florentine) as in the human anatomy painted by Signorelli and the Pollaiuoli brothers.

The Medici banking family ruled throughout the golden age power having become nearly hereditary despite the outward republican appearance of the *signoria*, or government. The two greatest Medici epitomized the age. Cosimo the Elder was founder of the Platonic Academy, patron to the architects Brunelleschi and Michelozzo, to the sculptors Donatello and Ghiberti, and to the painters Fra Angelico and Filippo Lippi. His grandson, Lorenzo de' Medici, known as "Il Magnifico," was a poet himself and diplomat, as well as patron to Botticelli, Ghirlandaio and the young Michelangelo, and founder of the world's first academy of art.

Golden Age Ends

The golden age would end, of course. Such wealth and sumptuous living produced charges of paganism and excesses from the fire-and-brimstone preacher Savonarola. He predicted the death of Lorenzo Il Magnifico and was proven right in 1492. He led the populace in expelling Lorenzo's son, the inept Piero, and creating a more republican government. He predicted foreign invasion, and was proven right again in 1494 when the French captured Florence. But for all his prophecies, Savonarola didn't foresee his own burning at the stake and didn't foresee that Florentine independence was soon to end forever.

Spain eliminated France from Tuscany, first defeating Florence with a nine-month brutal siege (1530) and then treating rebellious Siena to the same (1555). Tuscany became part of Spain, ruled again by the Medici, beginning with the first grand duke, Cosimo I. This time there would be no Medici pretense at republicanism. This time all Tuscany, even Siena (if not Lucca), would see the Medici coat of arms on their city gates. But the great European state of Florence no longer existed. Although the duchy would sponsor the sculptors Cellini and Giambologna, the Mannerist painters Bronzino and Pontormo, and the architect Vasari, the brilliance of the age would shine elsewhere. The Medici would endure until the 18th century.

Modern Tuscany

Tuscany (*Toscana* in Italian) is no less industrious now than it was during its heyday. Still manufactured are textiles, leather and paper; mined, too, are Elban iron, copper and mercury, and produced are wines, olive and sunflower oils, and wheat. Although the heavy industry concentrated to the west of Florence may interfere with your pleasure in visiting Prato, most of Tuscany remains easily recognizable as the background in a Giotto fresco or Botticelli painting. Not only is the countryside beautiful—despite the loss of so many silvery olive groves in the winter of 1985—but also the hill towns here preserve their greatest periods of history. San Gimignano retains a 12th-century ambience from its old defensive towers, Lucca and Pisa offer earlier Romanesque churches and campaniles, and Volterra, ancient Etruscan ruins. Siena and Florence are still competing after so many centuries despite their incomparably different characters— Siena so medieval with its archways and Gothic palazzi; Florence quintessential Renaissance with its heavy, rusticated stone churches and mansions. The number of the towns attests to the importance of the region, and each has its famous church, altar or fresco to entice you—from Arezzo and Cortona to Pienza and Montepulciano. Not surprisingly, tourism is one of Tuscany's greatest industries.

Cuisine

These days Tuscan food is considered the height of Italian cuisine. Mention of the *cucina Toscana* always is accompanied by the reminder that Catherine de' Medici took her chefs and recipes with her to the Paris court and thereby introduced France to the culinary arts. It is not surprising that the cuisine has taken on airs of refinement; yet many dishes show a less courtly side to the Tuscan temperament. *Ribollita* is, after all, leftovers brewed into a robust vegetable soup. And even the grilled meats *(arrosti)* of

Tuscany derive from the peasant lifestyle—pheasant, wild boar and hare hunted in the forests then cooked over a wood fire. Of course, with the addition of oil from the farm olive grove, and tarragon, rosemary and thyme from the hills, we're getting close to the Paris court again in terms of the sublime.

The truth is that the Tuscan food introduced by Catherine de' Medici was often as experimental for Tuscany as for the French court. Although wine sauces and wild mushroom sauces certainly were Tuscan, the creations of the pastry chef and Sicilian ice cream maker were innovations. Although *cacciucco* might have become bouillabaisse and duck in a sauce of those Arabic oranges, canard a l'orange, the more extravagant confections mirrored the grand duchy itself rather than Tuscany.

Tuscan food is simple, but wonderful. It derives from the frugality of the farmer, but also from the freshness of the farm's offerings and the heartiness of the hunt. From the simplest *fagioli all'uccelletto* (beans with sage, garlic and tomato), to roasted pork (arista) and soups thickened with bread, the food is always flavorful. When the local *funghi* (mushrooms), especially the pungent and aromatic porcini, are added to the hand-cut *pici* (thick spaghetti) of southern Tuscany or to fresh *pappardelle* noodles, the result is densely rich. Then add *cinghale* (wild boar) made into a sauce or sausage, the *crostini*, liver canapes of a gamey intensity, or even the salami spiced with peppercorns or fennel seeds, and you realize that the simple is far from insipid.

Tuscany's Vineyards

Throughout Tuscany you see the sheep grazing that give the region its ewe-milk cheeses, particularly *pecorino* which is most famous from around Pienza. Fortunately, the olive groves are still to be found, if less often, and Lucca and Chianti continue to produce their black-green extra virgin oils, if in more limited quantities than before. (Beware: much of the olive oil now sold in Tuscany is from Southern Italy and shouldn't fetch the prices of the finer Tuscan brands.) Most ubiquitous are the vineyards, for not only is Tuscany a major Italian producer of wines, but is second only to the Veneto in the number of controlled, quality wines. Chianti wines contribute the greatest number to this list. The best known chianti is the Classico from around Greve, symbolized by the *gallo negro* (black rooster) and include some fine *riserva* reds, capable of greater aging and complexity. (Antinori, Castello di Volpaia, and Ricasoli produce respected wines in this category.) But other valleys produce superb quality reds even if they aren't officially "chianti" (south around Montalcino and Montepulciano, and east in Rufina). One of the most respected, is *Brunello di Montalcino*, an austere red; if you can't afford it, the *Rosso di Montalcino* is the younger, lighter version. Nearby are the vineyards of Montepulciano that produces another controlled red, the

Cuisine

Vino Nobile (Poliziano and Fassati are among the many good estates). New, more experimental reds from cabernet additions to the traditional Tuscan grapes have been receiving the most acclaim (Antinori's *Tignanello*, Frescobaldi's *Pomino Rosso* and *Ornellaia*). And, of course, there are whites; in fact the bianco of the Val d'Arabia and Val d'Elsa is better than the red. The best known Tuscan white is *Vernaccia di San Gimignano*. For dessert wine, Tuscany produces its sauterne-like *Vin Santo*, produced by most estates, but the most refined is said to be the Avignonesi.

Travel Tips

Climate and Season

Tuscany is not far enough south to banish winter frosts, but such cold is unusual, though an extended spell of below freezing temperatures killed most of the region's olive groves in 1985. Damp, if not terribly cold in the winter (Florence has an average low of 35° F; high of 48° F in Jan.), Tuscany is most inviting May, June, and September when the temperatures aren't extreme and the summer horde of foreigners can be avoided. July and August can be searingly hot (Florence: average low 65° F; average high 87° F in July), but basically dry with some thunderstorms. The summer months are full of music and cultural festivals as well as medieval pageants—none more famous than Siena's Palio. The beaches along the Tyrrhenian coast are crowded with Italian families and the towns they've deserted become increasingly the domain of foreign visitors.

Arriving

The most direct transatlantic flights are those coordinated through London for landing at the Amerigo Vespucci airport at Peretola, just a few miles outside the center of Florence. The short Peretola runway limits the number of flights to 100-seater planes for European connections and 35-seaters for domestic service. The largest international airport is at Pisa (service to London, Frankfurt, Paris) where a fast train, coordinated with flights, connects with Florence (1 hour). However, one of the most convenient international arrivals to Florence is via the Rome airport, where you are transferred onto a special train for Florence that leaves from the airport (not the center of the city); on your return, luggage is checked through to the plane from the train station. At the moment, only Alitalia can book its passengers on these trains. Midway between Milan and Rome, Tuscany is well served by **toll roads** (A-12 from Genoa passes along the Ligurian coast and at Viareggio near Pisa connects with A-11 to Florence; A-1 from Milan to Rome has exits for Florence); **trains** (Milan to Rome line and coast line to Pisa with connecting, slow spurs to Siena, but efficient service between Viareggio and Florence and

Pisa and Florence); and long distance **buses** (the most efficient service for arriving at Siena).

Tuscany is well served by trains.

Travel Tips

Getting Around

In addition to the train and plane service described above, Tuscan towns are well-served by Lazzi buses that connect even small villages with the provincial capitals of Siena, Arezzo, Pisa and Florence. Car rentals and tours are available from the main tourist cities of Florence, Pisa and Siena. Florence as the regional capital has the most services for tourists, but the other two provide convenient jumping off points, too, for visiting the area. Tuscany is not large; it takes only two hours from Pisa to Siena and about one from each of them to Florence, but its small towns are popular detours and add time to any trip.

Special Tips

Tuscany is a difficult place to use credit cards. Although the best hotels and restaurants certainly accept them, be prepared with traveler's checks for other facilities. • If you're traveling here May through October, you might have an easier trip if you've reserved your hotels ahead of time. At festival times and in July and August, always reserve in advance. • Florence and Siena are popular centers for the study of Italian language and culture. Numerous institutions cater to this interest (see city directories and Practical Travel Information).

Florence

Key to Florence

Sights

The center for Early Renaissance art of such greats as Masaccio, Brunelleschi, Fra Angelico and Donatello as well as for High Renaissance works of Michelangelo— not to mention the numerous Raphaels, Titians and other masterpieces here. And then, there are the Mannerists.

Excursions

Most towns of Tuscany and even Umbria can be visited on one-day excursions from Florence. But the summer heat and crowds, as well as the higher prices, might be a factor in your decision whether to spend all your time here.

Nearby Waters

The famous spa at Montecatini Terme (west 51 km, 32 mi.), the Tyrrhenian coast at Viareggio (west 100 km, 62 mi. by A-11 or train); and the island of Elba off the Tyrrhenian coast, so popular with Florentines that in the summer there are special trains to the ferry terminal at Piombino Marittima (4 hours to Elba).

Festivals and Events

Music and film festivals from spring into the fall, both in Florence and nearby villages. All year, there are numerous concerts, art exhibits and films in this sophisticated city.

Shopping

Jewelry, leather goods, fashion, marbled paper, antiques and their reproductions.

Accommodations

From the sublime to the most basic, accommodations are plentiful and usually a bit costlier than elsewhere in Tuscany.

Eating Out

Tuscan food is favored by many, and the Florentine capital includes many fine restaurants as well as cantinas with wine tastings from nearby Chianti valley.

Getting Around

Residential and commercial properties are not numbered consecutively. Rather, commercial buildings have a separate red numbering system, indicated "r" in print. Residential numbers are black.

Walking through the historic center is the most practical way to sightsee. With the exception of mopeds, buses, taxis, and car access to hotels, vehicles are banned from central streets (not in the Oltrarno, however) from 7:30 a.m.–6:30 p.m. weekdays. And some streets and squares are totally free of traffic.

City bus (ATAF) routes can be obtained from the main office across from the train station or from tourist offices.

"Lungarni" are the variously named streets along the banks of the Arno; often they provide the best direction to follow when entering town.

Arriving

Pisa is the nearest large international airport and is connected to Florence by special fast trains (1 hour; gate 5 of stazione where you can check your baggage through to the plane). *Peretola* airport, 20 minutes from Florence's center (bus from P. Stazione), provides more limited service to domestic destinations such as Rome and Milan and international ones such as London, where connections are coordinated with transatlantic flights. A good alternative to either airport is the special train service between Rome's Leonardo airport and Florence's stazione.

The major train routes (fast trains to Rome 1 hour, 40 minutes; to Milan, 2.5 hours) buses, and autostradas connect this city with Rome (280 km, 174 mi.), Milan (300 km, 186 mi.), Bologna (110 km, 68 mi.), and Venice (275 km, 170 mi.).

Practical Tips

With so much to see, careful planning may be required to overcome the limits of Italian scheduling. Remember that most everything closes Sunday afternoon through Monday morning. Shops close 1–3:30 p.m. and Sunday through Monday a.m. Museums (except for the Uffizi, Museo del Duomo, Museo di Santa Croce, Palazzo Medici-Riccardi, and Palazzo Vecchio) have only morning hours, and most close Monday. Churches, however, usually reopen after a lunch break. Summer brings some extended hours; many shops stay open at midday and some shift their Monday closing to Saturday afternoon.

Florence may not be one of Italy's most expensive cities, but it certainly is Tuscany's. Also, it's steamier than most Tuscan towns because of its location in the Arno valley. (On the other hand, it's balmier when other spots are too cool.) For these reasons, many travelers prefer to split their time in Tuscany with other cities.

Good Reading: Vasari's *Lives of the Artists*, and Mary McCarthy's *Stones of Florence*.

As the birthplace of the Renaissance, Florence, or in Italian, *Firenze*, preserves some of the greatest art from the western world. Yet, if you expect an idyllic excursion through a city living in the past, you're in for a rude shock.

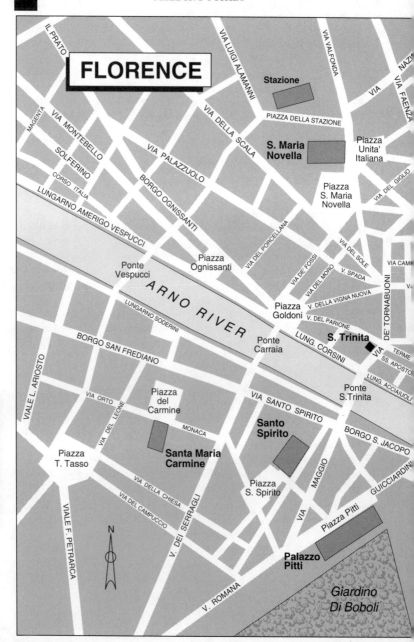

FLORENCE

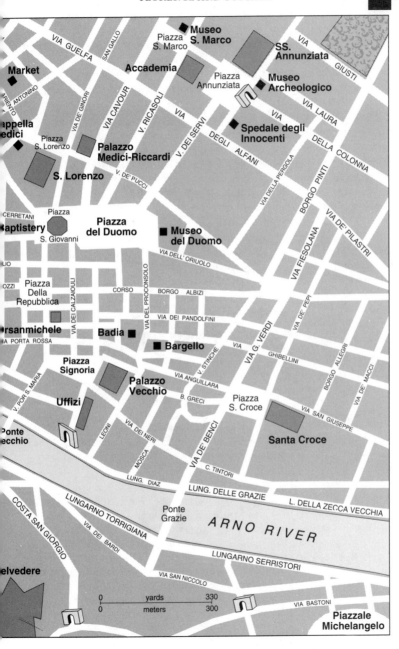

Florence bustles. It bustles today much as it did during the centuries that its currency was that of Europe, its Medici bank that of the popes, and its merchants, the wealthiest capitalists. Its rusticated stone buildings may contain the art of Michelangelo, Raphael and Leonardo—all of whom were working here around 1501—but these Renaissance facades define streets congested with modern activities. As one of the most powerful states in Europe, Renaissance Florence had a population of 100,000. Today the city counts nearly one-half million.

The 1988 restrictions on car traffic in the historic center have brought with them greater calm and pedestrian safety. Now you can concentrate on your sightseeing trying to not let it exhaust you. There is simply too much to see, if there is such a thing, or too much for the four days usually allotted to a visit. After you select the sights you most want to see, make sure you have time to add some variety to the museums and churches: Sit at a cafe and gaze at your favorite building. Walk somewhat aimlessly through the medieval streets around Via delle Terme or look at the antique shops in Oltrarno. Watch the sun set into the Arno, listen to Gregorian chants in San Miniato, or relax in the piazza of Fiesole. Better yet, break up the intensity of Florentine sightseeing with a visit to the Chianti valley or a quiet, less demanding Tuscan hill town, such as San Gimignano.

What to See and Do

Museum Hours

*In the summer, check for the museums participating in **Sera al Museo**, or extended opening hours from 8–11 p.m.*

Piazza del Duomo ★★★

There's no better place to begin your sightseeing than here where the streets radiate out in all directions and lead to the major sights of the city. And you can't miss the duomo—its cheerful colors and frothy facade are in unmistakable contrast with the surrounding web of sober Renaissance streets; its famous dome a landmark in any city view.

Duomo   ★★

In the early 14th century, the guidelines for the new cathedral dedicated to Santa Maria del Fiore were quite clear: build a church suitable to Florence, bigger and better than the great ones in Siena and Pisa. Florentine pride almost overreached itself; the duomo was so massive that a cupola couldn't be constructed to span the 140-foot opening that resulted. Not since the Roman Pantheon had such a ★★★ **dome** been built. Fortunately for Florence, it had the talents of Flippo Brunelleschi on hand in 1417 when the duomo was completed, save for its roof. The ribbed-style, double-shelled dome that he conceived not only solved the technical problems, but it remains one of the most beautiful in the world, rising magnificently above the bulky duomo, its graceful shape and 100-foot height dominating the city even today. Nearly every monumental dome since has been constructed with Brunelleschi's principles. The elaborate rib vaulting between the two shells of the dome can be observed on a climb up to the lantern for views. *(Entrance within duomo, north aisle; Mon.–Sat. 10 a.m.–last ticket sales 5 p.m.; L8000.)* Other views can be enjoyed from the lovely ★**campanile** *(9 a.m.–5 p.m., summer 8:30 a.m.–7 p.m.; L8000)* begun by Giotto during his term as the duomo architect. The sculpture for the facades of the duomo and campanile have been replaced by copies (the originals are in the museum, see below) and the neo-Gothic facade itself is a confection of the late 19th century that nearly turned the original Pisan-style colored marble into gingerbread.

The **interior** is in cold contrast to the warm colors of the facade, but the arches above the massive pilasters soar more than most Italian Gothic churches, and the intricate marble floors add interest. High on the wall of the west, and main, entrance is a mosaic of the *Coronation of the Virgin* by Gaddo Gaddi (14th C). Flanking it are joyous angel musicians by Santi di Tito (16th C) and above a wonderful ★clock with the four heads of the prophets by Paolo Uccello (1443). Uccello's fascination with realism can be seen in the ★equestrian portrait of the condottiere, John Hawkwood (1437, 3rd bay, north aisle). The mercenary war captain Hawkwood had switched allegiance from Milan to Florence on the condition that the city commemorate him with an equestrian statue. It did, but in fresco, not marble. Another such ★portrait to the left is one by Andrea del Castagno. Both Uccello and Castagno also designed some of the stained glass windows at the base of the dome, along with Donatello and Ghiberti. The dome itself is decorated with a fresco of the *Last Judgment* (late 16th C) by Vasari and F. Zaccari. The three apses are separated by sacristy doors over which are enamelled terracotta reliefs by Luca della Robbia—the fine *Resurrection* over the north sacristy is an early work in this medium (1442). (This is the same sacristy into which Lorenzo de'Medici escaped the murderous attack on him during mass by the Pazzi family.) In the central apse is a delicate reliquary urn by Ghiberti. *The duomo is open 10 a.m.–5 p.m.; masses are usually 7–10 a.m., 5–7 p.m.*

Baptistery   ★★

This jewelbox of a building, finely patterned in colored marble inlays and with the octagonal shape of a Byzantine royal chapel, dates from the 11th century. Although the baptistery was an early prototype for other Tuscan Romanesque churches, the 15th-century Florentines believed it was even older, surviving from the period when the main gate to the Roman military camp of Florentia stood near this spot. Mistaken as a symbol of Florence's classical past, the church inspired some of the first great works of the Early Renaissance—its **bronze doors.** Just as Florence was resisting the attacks of the Duke of Milan (and his condottiere John Hawkwood), its powerful banking guild commissioned a competition for a set of bronze doors that would make the citizens proud. Lorenzo Ghiberti and Brunelleschi each submitted bas reliefs (both their works are in the Bargello). Ghiberti won and, in 1423, completed the ★28 gilded bronze panels with scenes from the New Testament, now seen on the north door. Brunelleschi, in his loss, devoted himself to architecture. Pleased with the Ghiberti doors, the guild commissioned another pair with scenes from the Old Testament. Called worthy to be the *Gates of Paradise* by Michelangelo, these masterpieces took Ghiberti most of his life to complete, from 1425–52, and copies can be seen on the east door, facing the duomo. (**Note:** The panels are being restored; those already completed are on display in the Museo del Duomo.) A comparison of Ghiberti's two sets of doors shows the great changes in art during the Early Renaissance. The 10 Old Testament panels still are Gothic in their elegance, but new is Ghiberti's use of space. Complex narrative scenes, some in the same panel taking place at different times, are visually unified by the space created between the nearly freestanding foreground figures to the barest trace of the background landscape. The panels read two across, left to right, and portray: (1) Story of Adam and Eve; (2) Story of Cain and Abel; (3) The flood and Noah's drunkenness; (4) Abraham and the sacrifice of Isaac; (5) Jacob and Esau; (6) Story of Joseph; (7) Moses receiving the commandments; (8) Joshua and the fall of Jericho; (9) Story of David and Goliath; (10) Solomon receives the Queen of Sheba. The magnificent frame is Ghiberti's, too, with a self- portrait found in the classical medallion to the right, below panels. A third, earlier set of doors (1336) on the south by Andrea Pisano are simple by comparison, but the organization of the scenes from the life of St. John the Baptist in their quatrefoil frames is full of delicacy and clarity. The handsome **interior** of the baptistery (entrance south side) returns you to Byzantine tastes, if a very late evolution of the style. Some of the more intricate floor mosaics date from the early 13th century; the cupola mosaic, *The Last Judgment*, is later still. Also noteworthy here is the early Renaissance tomb (1429) of the antipope John XXIII, designed by Donatello and executed by Michelozzo. *Open Mon. –Sat. 1–6 p.m. and Sun. 9 a.m.–1 p.m. Admission L5000.*

Museo dell'Opera del Duomo   ★★

Located across the street behind the duomo at Piazza del Duomo 9, this museum houses a number of exceptional sculptures from the campanile, cathedral and baptistery. The most interesting are on the upper levels, particularly the landing with Michelangelo's ★★ *Pieta*, depicting a painfully expressive Christ figure, his body collapsed and broken. The sympathetic face of Joseph of Armathea is the artist's self-portrait. At one point, Michelangelo became angry with the intractability of the marble and smashed it. The sculpture was saved and repaired by his pupils. Up another flight of steps to the second floor you come to the playful and joyous ★★**Cantoria**, or marble choir stalls carved by Luca della Robbia (certainly his masterpiece) and Donatello. The Luca cantoria has been reconstructed (the original is below it) to better show the putti ecstatically singing their praises to God. Their innocence contrasts with Donatello's fleshy ones (opposite wall) whose wild antics look as if they're about to result in mayhem. Below Donatello's cantoria is his wooden statue, really a psychological portrait of an anguished ★ *Mary Magdalene*. This room also affords a chance to compare the differences in style and spirit between the medieval statues of Andre Pisano and the Renaissance confidence in those of Donatello. All these sculptures, like the reliefs in the next room (note those by Andrea Pisano), originally adorned the campanile. In the center of the last room are the restored panels of Ghiberti's ★★**bronze doors** (see "Baptistery" above). At

Florence

Santa Maria della Salute, Venice

Murano glassblower

Venetian glass

the rear of this room, a ★ silver altar shows the superb craftsmanship of the 14th and 15th centuries. Some of Florence's finest artists worked on it: Michelozzo carved the central statue of the Baptist, Verrocchio the scene of his beheading, and A. del Pollaiolo his birth. *Open holidays 9 a.m.–1 p.m.; closed Sun.; otherwise 9 a.m.–6 p.m., except till 7:30 p.m. in summer; L8000.*

Piazza Della Signoria ★★

The center of Florentine politics since the Middle Ages, the piazza remains even today the site of political speeches and demonstrations, as well as a gathering spot for Florentines and tourists alike. Some of the politics of the past can be read in the statuary here, from the republican ideals expressed in Michelangelo's *David* (original in the Accademia), slayer of tyrants, to the later and imperial portrait of Grand Duke Cosimo I in Giambologna's equestrian statue (1594). It was Cosimo I who commissioned the **Neptune Fountain** in an attempt to create some order in the irregularly shaped piazza, but instead he created Bartolommeo Ammanati's unsuccessful statue of the sea god that has since been the brunt of Florentine jokes. (The frolicking bronze nymphs by Giambologna, however, are delightful.) The sculpture continues in the **Loggia dei Lanzi**, the graceful structure on the south side of the piazza that exhibits, in its left arch, Benvenuto Cellini's confident bronze figure of ★ *Perseus* (1545), and, in its right arch, a copy of Giambologna's *Rape of the Sabines* (original in Accademia). Excavations beneath the piazza in recent years revealed not just earlier medieval buildings but also a Roman complex from A.D. 1.

Palazzo Vecchio ★★

Dominating the piazza is the somewhat squat yet powerful town hall begun in 1298. While the unusual shape of the palazzo was determined by the Roman theater over which it was built, its intimidating stone presence, its distinctive fortified tower with a bell to rally the citizenry against attack, resulted from the difficult times in which the urban and mercantile republic evolved. The facade remains much as it originally was, yet the interior has undergone numerous transformations, particularly in the 16th century when the Medici dukes commissioned Vasari and other Mannerists to turn the city hall into a regal residence. When Cosimo I moved into his new residence at the Pitti Palace, this one became known as *il vecchio*, or old one. Today the palazzo again functions as a city hall with many of its rooms, almost museums of Mannerist art, open to the public. The gilded and stucco elegance of the interior **courtyard** results from Vasari's work around 1565, when the Verrocchio fountain (1476) also was installed here (the original bronze putto and dolphin are upstairs). Upstairs, you come to the **Salone dei Cinquecento**, conceived in 1496 by Savonarola as the council hall for the highly representative, 500-member government, and later made more grandiose (by Vasari) as the audience chamber for Cosimo I. To the right of the entrance you can peek into that Mannerist gem, the ★ Studiolo (1570), with its Bronzino medallion portraits and Vasari decor. Here, Francesco I studied alchemy by candlelight. On the wall directly opposite the entrance is Michelangelo's sculpted and torso-twisted *Victory* (1527). On the next floor are the **Medici living quarters**, the Quartiere degli Elementi belonging to Cosimo I; his wife's Quartiere of Elenor di Toledo contains a chapel by Bronzino (1540). Farther along is the Chapel di Priori, painted by Ghirlandaio. Then, in

Florence

the Sala dei Gigli is Donatello's ★ *Judith with Holofernes* (c. 1460), once in the Piazza della Signoria with Michelangelo's *David. Open Mon.–Wed., Fri. 9 a.m.– 7 p.m.; Sun.8 a.m.– 1 p.m.; L8000 for upstairs galleries.*

Orsanmichele　　　　　　　　　　　　　　　　　　　　　　★

Walking along the now pedestrian street of Via del Calzaiulo that connects the city's two most important squares, those of the Signoria and the duomo, you pass Orsanmichele, symbol of a third power—the guilds. Built in 1337 as a granary and shrine, Orsanmichele included niches on the facade to hold sculptures of the patron saints of the most important guilds. Most of these niches weren't filled until the Early Renaissance, when Florence found itself besieged by foreign armies. The resultant sculptures are full of the heroic spirit of that time: Donatello's *St. George* (original in the Bargello) faces danger calmly and, in a ★marble relief below the statue, bravely slays the dragon (last niche on V. Orsanmichele), and Nanni de Banco's ★ *Four Crowned Saints* quietly consider the decision that will lead to their martyrdom. The evolving Renaissance style can best be seen in the contrast between Ghiberti's 1416 ★ *St. John the Baptist* (V. dei Calzaiulo at Lamberti), the first life-size bronze of the Renaissance, yet still International Gothic in style, and his later, very classical ★ *St. Matthew* from 1422 (rear of building, left niche). **Inside** is the exceptionally large and wondrous Gothic ★tabernacle by Andre Orcagna that encloses B. Daddi's *Madonna and Child* with stone frame and angels. Because of restoration, some of the exterior statues may be removed. *8 a.m.–noon, 3–6:30 p.m.; free.*

The Uffizi ★★★

In 1560, Cosimo I commissioned Vasari to design these government offices, or *uffici,* located between the river and the Palazzo Vecchio. The two resultant portico wings are united by an archway that frames a striking view of the Piazza della Signoria from the Arno. Vasari also designed, for the grand duke, a private and covered passageway to take him from the Uffizi over the Ponte Vecchio, and on to his Palazzo Pitti. (Guided visits to the **Vasari Corridor**, with its collection of artists' self-portraits, have been suspended since the 1993 bombing.) Cosimo's son turned the upper arcade of the Uffizi into a painting gallery for the Medici collection; subsequent generations added to it, until the last Medici left the collection to Tuscany in 1737. Although Napoleon lifted some important works for the Louvre, the Uffizi today still holds one of the most important painting collections in the world. To avoid exhausting yourself, try to be selective or divide your viewing into several visits. For the best short course in the history of Italian art, follow the galleries in their chronological sequence. At the end, you can rest in the terrace bar, where the views of Brunelleschi's dome, Giotto's campanile and the Palazzo Vecchio tower are worth the price of table service. **Note:** The Uffizi has reopened most of its galleries after a car-bomb damaged the museum in 1993; all those in the east wing are open and several in the west (including Room 25 and some of the Venetian rooms). Check for new, longer hours (till 6:30 p.m.) and for advance ticket purchase with time assignments—both in the experimental stage in 1996. *Open Tues.–Sat. 9 a.m.–7 p.m., Sun. 9 a.m.–2 p.m.; L12,000.*

Florence

The Uffizi contains Medici's Venus and portraits by Bronzino.

Museum   ★ ★ ★

The painting galleries are on the third floor, or *piano* 2. There is an elevator (reserved for handicapped) to the galleries, but the grand staircase provides the most fitting access. Midway up is the ★ **Print and Drawing Room** with its superb, temporary exhibits of Renaissance and Mannerist works. You enter the third floor at the tip of the **east arm** of the U-shaped floor plan (and you exit near the end of the west arm). Nearby, **Room 2** contains ★ ★ three great altarpieces of the Enthroned Madonna that show the transition in the late 13th C. from Byzantine, iconlike formality (though Cimabue's work does hint at the coming realism in comparison to the lesser works in this room), to the late Gothic interest in depth and portraiture (the Cimabue, 1280; Duccio, 1285; Giotto, 1310). Exiting through the left door, you see this trend toward realism more fully realized in **Room 3** with its Gothic-period works by Duccio's successors in Siena—the Lorenzetti brothers as well as Simone Martini, whose elegant ★ ★ *Annunciation* (1330) shows a shocked, recoiling virgin learning her destiny. **Rooms 5-6** are devoted to the International Gothic style (early 15th C.) that owed so much to Simone Martini. Here, Gentile da Fabriano's ★ *Adorazione dei Magi* is a complex yet graceful composition of the three exotic and splendid kings arriving in a very Tuscan-looking Jerusalem. **Room 7** contains Early Renaissance masterpieces, some secular in their subject matter like Piero della Francesca's highly individualized ★ portraits (1460) of Federico da Montefeltro, the prince of Urbino, with the sword-broken nose, and his translucent-skinned

Florence

wife, Battista Sforza. Uccello's ★ *Battle of San Romano* (1445) is medieval in its rich colors, Gothic in its pattern of lances and hedged fields, and purely Renaissance in its foreshortened, if carousel-like horses and its linear perspective. **Room 8** contains an exceptionally lyrical painting (second on left) of the Madonna in Filippo Lippi's ★ *Madonna with Child and Two Angels* (c. 1455). The fleshy Christ child, the diffused light, the naturalism of this painting, contrasts sharply with the Byzantine treatment of the same subject in Room 2. **Rooms 10-14** contain the most famous works of Botticelli. His ★★ *Allegory of Spring* (1482), with its diaphanously clothed graces dancing against a dense, mysterious forest, and his later ★★★ *Birth of Venus*, with its mesmerizing, nude Venus, her skin chalky and luminous, her neck elegantly elongated, are both dreamlike translations of the classical myths so popular during Lorenzo Il Magnifico's rule. Lorenzo himself is portrayed as the arrogant youth on the extreme left of Botticelli's ★ *Adoration of the Magi*; the artist, cloaked in yellow, confronts you on the right. In **Room 15** you find Leonardo da Vinci's ★★ *Adoration of the Magi* (c. 1481); unfinished and only an underdrawing, the work is no less than masterful, from the energy of the horses in the background to the pyramidal order of the transcendent virgin in the foreground. Leonardo's ★ *Annunciation* (c. 1473) is radiant with light, beautiful in its landscape details. And his hand can be seen in Andrea del Verrocchio's *Baptism of Christ* (c. 1470), where as that artist's apprentice, he executed the angel to the left, as well as parts of the landscape. Commissioned by the Medici and designed by Buontalenti, the octagonal **Tribunal** (1585) is itself a fine Mannerist work. It contains sculpture (including the Medici Venus, a Roman copy of a Praxiteles) and some ★ family portraits by Bronzino, including one of Cosimo I (to the right as you enter). Through the tribunal, you come first to a corridor with works by Signorelli and Perugino, then to a room containing exceptional Cranachs and Durers. In **Room 21** are several works by Giorgione and a serene *Sacred Allegory* by Giovanni Bellini as well as his *Composition with Christ*. Following a room with many Memlings is **Room 23** containing Correggio's ★ *Stay in Egypt* and Mantegna's ★ *Adoration of the Magi*, remarkably curved so as to insure depth of field.

The **west corridor** begins with two of the great artists of the High Renaissance. In **Room 25** is Michelangelo's ★ *Holy Family* (1503), painted in the somewhat strident colors now revealed on the cleaned ceiling of the Sistine Chapel. In **Room 26** are two important Raphael paintings, ★ *Madonna with Goldfinch* (c. 1506), heavily influenced by Leonardo, and ★★ *Portrait of Leo X* (c. 1518), a searching portrayal of the artist's papal patron, plus three other works including ★ *Portrait of Francesco Maria della Rovere*. Here, too, are paintings by Andrea del Sarto. The next few rooms exhibit other Florentine works from the early 16th century—the Mannerists Rosso Fiorentino, Pontormo and Bronzino. Confirming your impression that Florence no longer is the center of the artistic world is **Room 28**, full of the works of the Venetian artist, Titian. His ★★ *Venus of Urbino* (1538) presents an art form almost modern in its play of light and very Venetian in its sumptuousness. Titian's portraits show the same dramatic use of light and his ★ *Gentleman from Malta* seems a precursor of Rembrandt. Other Venetian works can be admired in

Room 34, with its ★ *Holy Family by Venese* (late 16th C.), **Room 35**, with its Tintorettos, and **Room 45**, with works by Tiepolo, Guardi and Canaletto. **Room 43** represents the late 16th century in Rome, and contains two self-portraits by Caravaggio, one as a sybaritic and saucy ★★ *Bacchus* (1595), who tilts his wineglass at you, the other as a terrifying ★ *Medusa* (1590), painted onto a shield. The three Rembrandt's in **Room 44** seem quite comfortable with all the paintings preceding them. In fact, 17th-century European art grew out of the Italian tradition. As you will already have observed in the **Sala di Rubens** (Room 41), the Venetian color and Roman monumentality of Rubens' works prove his eight years of study in Italy. But the dynamism of his crowd scenes in *Henry IV Enters Paris* and *Henry IV's Battle d'Ivry* come as something of a shock after so much Renaissance calm. The restless surfaces of the Baroque transformed Rome, then swept Europe. Soon after, artistic developments no longer centered on the Italian peninsula.

Piazza San Lorenzo ★★

The Piazza San Lorenzo bustles with crowds from the Central Market (up nearby Via dell'Ariento) and with tourists shopping for leather goods and whatnots at its open-air market. Although the piazza is unmissable at its location a short distance northwest of the duomo, some of the finest Renaissance architecture in Florence is hidden behind the fruit stands and unfinished facade of the Church of San Lorenzo. Brunelleschi, Michelozzo and Michelangelo worked here, each commissioned by the Medici, whose palace stands nearby and whose coat of arms of six balls can be seen everywhere, even in the nave of the church.

Church of San Lorenzo ★

The Medici paid for so much of this church that their tombs fill both sacristies and chancel; Cosimo the Elder merited a spot in front of the altar. Brunelleschi designed the church (1419-69), the first to be built in the Renaissance style. The harmonious proportions of the arcaded side aisles and the old sacristy, the perspective down the nave to the altar, the quiet repetition of details create a sense of both order and elegance. More expressionistic are the dramatic panels of ★★ two bronze pulpits, the last works by Donatello, that flank the nave near the transept. Brunelleschi's ★ **old sacristy**, at the end of the left transept, is decorated with bronze doors and medallions by Donatello (that Brunelleschi found disruptive of his design). Back in the transept, to the right, is Filippo Lippi's ★ *Annunciation* (1440) with its notable crystal vase. *See below for access to other parts of church. Closed noon–3:30 p.m.*

Biblioteca Medicea-Laurenziana ★★

Off the cloister of San Lorenzo (left of the church entrance) is the Laurentian Library (begun 1524) containing the Medici collection of rare books. Designed by Michelangelo, the building is a masterpiece. More sculptural than architectural, the vestibule is an agitated play of light and shadow created by recessed columns, broken pediments and voluptuous stairs. In contrast, the interior is appropriately restful for the study of illuminated manuscripts. At the rear of the library is an exhibition room displaying some of the collection. *Open 9 a.m.–1 p.m.; closed Sun.; free.*

Cappella Medici

Because the entrance no longer is from within the Church of San Lorenzo, it's hard
to realize that this chapel stands at the opposite end of the transept from Brunelleschi's old sacristy. In fact, Michelangelo designed this "new" sacristy (1520-34) to
balance Brunelleschi's and used many of his predecessor's Early Renaissance motifs,
particularly in the lower portion of the chapel. But the verticality of the chapel and
the slithery quality of the sarcophagus sculptures create an uneasy environment in
contrast to the serenity of Brunelleschi's. Michelangelo's sculptures for the chapel
are magnificent, even if incomplete. Lorenzo Il Magnifico and his brother Guiliano
are buried here, without tombs, in the wall graced with the ★ *Madonna and Child*;
their relatives, also named Lorenzo and Guiliano, are buried in the extraordinary
★★★ marble tombs with allegorical figures of *Dawn and Dusk* (to left as you
enter) and *Day and Night*. To reach Michelangelo's chapel, you must walk around
San Lorenzo to a rear entrance and then walk through the incredible marble mausoleum of the Medici grand dukes (Cappella dei Principi, begun 1604). *Open
9 a.m.–2 p.m.; closed Mon.; L10,000.*

Palazzo Medici-Riccardi   ★

Just off the piazza at Via Cavour 1, is this palace designed by Michelozzo in 1444.
Although the Medici later resided in the Palazzo Vecchio and Pitti Palace, this was
their primary residence and business office for nearly a century. The Riccardi
enlarged the mansion, yet it remains the prototype of Renaissance palaces with its
rusticated stone and classical cornice. The ★ **chapel** (up the first staircase to the
right in the courtyard) contains the original floor and ceiling as well as Benozzo
Gozzoli's delightful murals, ★ *Procession of the Magi* (1459), depicting the
Renaissance lifestyle of the Florentine elite. *Open 9 a.m.–1 p.m. and, except Sun.,
3–6 p.m.; closed Wed.; L6000.*

Santa Maria Novella ★★

This important Dominican church, begun in 1246, seems to stand apart from the rest
of Florence, just as it did at the time of its construction when it was outside the city walls.
The Dominicans sometimes preached to their followers in the spacious piazza fronting
the church, a good place to view the marble ★ facade that is Tuscan Romanesque on the
lower level, more Renaissance, but harmoniously so, on the upper level (by Alberti), with
its classical triangular pediment. Its **interior**, like Santa Croce, is Italian Gothic—that is,
not really Gothic, but rather an ample space for instructing the congregation. The austere
ambience may reflect the Dominican orthodoxy as much as the dreadful period after the
1348 Black Death when most of the chapels were dedicated. The ★ Strozzi Chapel (at
the end of the north, or left, transept) captures this period with its severe Andrea Orcagna
altarpiece and, behind it, the Last Judgment murals by his brother, Nardo di Cione.
Painted just a few years after the Black Death killed half of Florence's population, the murals show a wrathful Christ tormenting the wicked in a hell ghastly in its details. Paradise
is treated less obsessively: The composition is quite static, although the Strozzi must have
been reassured to find themselves included. Just to the left of this chapel is the door into
the sacristy where there's a ★ painted crucifix (attributed to Giotto) moving in its simplicity, as well as a fine terracotta *lavabo* by Giovanni della Robbia. To the right of the

Florence

Strozzi Chapel is a marble chapel with a dramatically lighted and ethereal ★ crucifix by Brunelleschi. Behind the main altar, the **chancel** *(open Mon., Wed., Fri.–Sat. 10–11:30 a.m., 4–6 p.m.)* is covered with frescoes, ostensibly on the life of St. John the Baptist and the Virgin, but really showing Florentine life in 1485 when Domenico Ghirlandaio painted them. Next to the chancel is another Strozzi Chapel, this one covered with murals by Filippino Lippi (1487). Up the nave, on the right, is Masaccio's ★★ *Holy Trinity* (1425), a fresco that introduces a Renaissance chapel into this Gothic church by means of the then new principles of perspective. The realism even pervades the skeleton in the tomb below who warns, "I was as you are, you'll be as I." Nearby is a carved pulpit, de-signed by Brunelleschi. *Tourist visits 7–11:30 a.m.; 3:30–6 p.m.; Sun. 3:30–6 p.m.*

Chiostro Verde

To the left of the church you enter the "Green Cloister," named after the mono-chromatic frescoes based on Genesis by Paolo Uccello (as you enter, straight ahead). Unfortunately, the most famous murals (the *Creation*, and *Flood and the Drunkenness of Noah*) are so damaged that you can just make out bits and pieces of his design—a serpent of temptation with a woman's head, apple trees, and the like. At the rear of the courtyard is the **Spanish Chapel**, used by the Spanish court in the 16th century and elaborately covered with frescoes (1365) on the glory of the Dominican Order by Andrea da Firenze. *Open 9 a.m.– 2 p.m.; Sun. 8 a.m.–1 p.m.; closed Fri.; L5000.*

Nearby Palazzi

Some of the wealthiest parishioners of Santa Maria Novella had their palaces just a few blocks away, down Via Belle Donne to the fashionable Via de' Tornabuoni (named after the patron of the Ghirlandaio frescoes) where it intersects with Via Strozzi. The ★ **Palazzo Strozzi** *(P. Strozzi 4; open Mon., Wed., Fri. 4–7 p.m.; free)* was begun late (1489) for such a wealthy, patrician family of bankers like the Strozzi, but then they had been exiled by the Medici for a good portion of the 15th century. Their grand palace is unusually massive, yet very Florentine with its three stories of rusticated stone. In a totally different Renaissance style is the **Palazzo Rucellai** *(V. della Vigna Nuova 48r)*, designed in the 1450s by Alberti for the same Rucellai wool merchant who later commissioned him to complete the facade of Santa Maria Novella. The interior is now the Alinari photography museum *(10 a.m.–7:30 p.m.; closed Wed., L5000)*, but it is Alberti's facade that is famous for its application of the classical orders to the decorative pilasters and capitals of the dif-ferent stories. Near the Strozzi is the 14th century Gothic **Palazzo Davanzati** *(V. Porta Rossa 13; by hourly guided tours in Italian only Tues.–Sun. 9:30 a.m.–2 p.m.; L5000)*, not the home of a Novella parishioner, but nonetheless interesting for the Museo della Casa Fiorentina Antica that it contains with period furnishings and exhibits on merchant lifestyle.

Other Churches

In this central area, two other churches had their wealthy patrons, including the Strozzi and Davanzati. **Santa Trinita** *(closed Sun. & noon–4 p.m.)*, at Tornabouni and Porta Rossa, contains Lorenzo Monaco frescoes, *Life of the Virgin* (1423), and the ★ *Annunciation* altarpiece (fourth chapel on the right), and Ghirlandaio's ★ St.

Francis frescoes (1485), and a copy of his *Adoration of the Shepherds* altarpiece *(Sassetti Chapel, right transept; original in Uffizi)*. The **Ognissanti Cenacolo** *(P. Ognissanti 42; open 9 a.m.–12 p.m. Mon., Tues., Sat.; donation)*, off the cloister of the church, contains noteworthy paintings: Ghirlandaio's *Last Supper* and *St. Jerome*, and Botticelli's *St. Augustine*.

Piazza San Marco ★★

Only a few blocks north of San Lorenzo and a block from the Annunziata, this piazza is framed on its east side by buildings of the university (founded 1321) with botanical gardens established by Cosimo I next to them. On the west side were the gardens of Lorenzo Il Magnifico, where it's said that Michelangelo studied sculpture as a boy. But the two major sights here are Michelangelo's sculptures themselves in the Accademia, and the works of Fra Angelico in the Museum of San Marco.

Museo di San Marco   ★★

In the convent designed by Michelozzo is this museum (n. side P. San Marco) devoted to Fra Angelico. Il Beato Angelico (blessed Angelico) was not only one of the most important painters in the Early Renaissance, he was also a devout friar in this monastery and painted in the service of his Dominican order. The cloister museum today preserves much of his work; it also gives a sense of life in the meditative orders—from the tranquil courtyard and refectory (with a rather stiff *Last Supper* by Ghirlandaio's workshop) to the dormitory upstairs of 44 cells, most painted by Fra Angelico with humble, contemplative works. The **museum** (to the right as you enter the cloister) contains Fra Angelico's more public and glorifying works, large altarpieces painted with his sparkling colors. His ★ *Descent from the Cross* (1434) is important for its early naturalism and its integration of the figures with the background landscape. At the opposite end of the hall is his famous ★ *Tabernacle of Linoioli* (1433) with its marble frame by Ghiberti and its *Virgin and Child* encircled by charming angel musicians. After you climb the stairs to the ★**dormitory**, you come to another famous Angelico, a fresco of the ★*Annunciation*. As you walk down the two corridors to look at the cell frescoes (most of the interesting ones, like cell 3, are along the corridor to left of the Annunciation), look for the ★**library** (down the other corridor), perhaps Michelozzo's best design (mid-15th C.). *Open 9 a.m.–2 p.m.; closed Mon.; L8000*.

Accademia   ★★

Just south of the P. San Marco, at Via Ricasoli 60, is the Galleria dell'Accademia and its Michelangelo sculptures. But it is Giambologna who is the show stopper in the first room, with the spiralling, seemingly liquid marble of his ★★ *Rape of the Sabines* (1583), a work that influenced Bernini. The Michelangelo hall is the second room on the ground floor and ends with a rotunda containing his colossal marble statue of ★★★ *David* (1504). Originally designed as a buttress sculpture for the duomo and meant to be seen from below, both front and back, this David would have looked out over Florence with his heroic gaze. But the statue so captured the republican spirit of the time that it was instead erected in the Piazza della Signoria. Contrasting with David's classical repose are Michelangelo's four ★★ *Prisoners*

(1520s), writhing and twisting to free themselves from their encasing stone. Originally planned as supports for the cornice of the tomb of Julius II, these figures are so moving in their present unfinished state, it's hard to wish them otherwise. The *Pieta* in this corridor probably is not by Michelangelo.

While the Michelangelo's are the primary cause of the long lines here in the summer, there are some fine paintings, too. If you have time, visit the rooms behind the Pieta where there is a delicate Mariotto di Christofano entitled ★ *Lo Sposalizio* (1457) and a Botticelli ★ *Virgin and Child* (1468) along with a Filippino Lippi, an Uccello, and other works. Toward the museum exit you find medieval altarpieces and the stairs to a second floor collection of Byzantine art from all over Christendom. *The Accademia is open 9 a.m.–7 p.m.; Sun. till 2 p.m.; closed Mon.; L12,000*.

Cenacolo Sant' Apollonia

Just over a block west of the piazza, at Via XXVII d'Aprile 1, is this refectory with a ★ Last Supper (c. 1445) by Andrea del Castagno. Ring bell for admission. *9 a.m.– 2 p.m.; closed Mon., L2500.*

Bargello ★ ★

Not too far along the Via Proconsolo from the P. della Signoria, you come to this austere fortress, begun in 1255, to serve as the official residence of the first governors. Later in the 16th century, it became the police headquarters and prison, or *bargello*. Contrasting with the impregnable, nearly windowless facade and tower is the light-filled courtyard with its colorful coats-of-arms of the neighborhoods and governors. It's easy to imagine lasting through a siege here, particularly with the well so strategically located inside. But the courtyard served also for executions; its walls, as well as the tower outside, served for humiliating paintings of the guilty, especially those who were so fortunate as to escape arrest.

Continuing the artistic tradition, but certainly in a more uplifting manner, the fortress today houses the ★ ★ **Museo Nazionale del Bargello**, with its important collection of Florentine Renaissance sculpture. The first floor exhibition room next to the entrance contains sculpture from the 16th century. Here are the original ★ pedestal bronzes from Cellini's *Perseus* as well as a few other examples of this artist's refined and stylized work. Along with works by Giambologna and other sculptors, there are studies from the school of Michelangelo, as well as a few of the master's own works, though not his most powerful. On the **second floor**, some pleasing *putti* and statues by Giambologna are displayed in the loggia; porcelains and other decorative arts are in rooms off to the left. But in the handsome exhibition hall to the right you find some of the museo's masterpieces. At the end of this room is Donatello's ★ ★ *David* (1430), not only the first lifesize nude sculpture since antiquity, but also a sensuously naked one, jauntily youthful and alive. There are other fine Donatellos here showing the diverse styles of his work, such as the classic repose of his ★ *St. George* (from Orsanmichele), full of determination yet reflective, and so unlike his David. On the right wall are the famous ★ ★ competition panels (1402) for the Baptistery doors. Although some have championed Brunelleschi's panel of the *Sacrifice of Isaac*, Ghiberti's still seems to be the winner. His composition is cohesive and pleasing, his classical figure of Isaac beautiful. Brunelleschi's panel is far less harmonious,

Florence

almost discordant, though it may be more expressive of the horrid moment when Abraham puts the knife to his son's neck. On the **third floor**, there are a number of rooms dedicated to the enamelled terracottas of the various members of the della Robbia family; in the one for Giovanni della Robbia is ★ *Bust of Costanza Bonarelli*, (1635), by the non-Florentine Bernini. Through these rooms you come to a sculpture room with Andrea del Verrocchio's ★ *David* (c. 1470); still youthful like Donatello's, but clothed and not nearly so triumphant. Also here are noteworthy sculptures by A. del Pollaiolo, Mino da Fiesole, and Verrochio's ★ *Bust of a Young Woman*. Above the loggia is a room of small bronzes, many by Giambologna, and in the back exhibition area is a collection of arms and armor. *Open Tues.–Sun. 9 a.m.–2 p.m.; L8000.*

Around the Bargello

In front of the Bargello on Via Proconsolo is the **Badia**, a Benedictine abbey with an attractive campanile and an interior graced by Filippino Lippi's ★ *Vision of St. Bernard* (1485; on left as you enter) and works by Mino da Fiesole. *(Open 9 a.m.–noon; in summer, 4–6 p.m. also, except Sun.; closed Wed.; free).* Although Dante's family home is gone from nearby Via Dante Alighieri, **Casa de Dante** *(V. Santa Margarita around the corner from the Badia; 10 a.m.–6 p.m., Sun. till 2 p.m., closed Thurs.–Fri.; L5000),* a 1905 house commemorating the great poet and his times, reopened in 1994. More authentic evocations of the past can be found in the old streets surrounding the Bargello: On Piazza San Firenze, just to the south of the Bargello, is the striking Renaissance **Palazzo Gondi**; in the opposite direction is the **Palazzo Pazzi-Quaratesi** *(V. Proconsolo 10);* and along the attractive street of Borgo degli Albizi are numerous 16th-century palazzi.

Santa Croce ★★

The huge square fronting this church is the center of one of Florence's oldest, if not richest, neighborhoods. Far enough from the center so as not to disturb the wealthy of the Renaissance, this district once bustled with textile workshops for the washing, combing and dyeing of wool. Around the piazza today are two of the finer palazzi, one still retaining its facade murals from 1619. The neo-Gothic, marble facade of Santa Croce dates from 1863, but the church was founded in 1294. As a Franciscan preaching church, its proportions are vast and open, horizontal rather than soaring. Nonetheless, the **interior** is majestic, its painted timber roof colorful, its altar and stained glass chancel framed by a triumphal arch, exquisite. The church contains burials of illustrious Florentines, such as Michelangelo, Ghiberti, Galileo and Machiavelli. Midway down the south, or right, aisle is a pulpit elaborately carved with scenes from the life of St. Francis by Bernardo da Maiana (c. 1475). Farther on, near the side door, is a Donatello ★ *Annunciation* (1435), very classically conceived. To the right of the chancel are the best that remain of ★ Giotto's frescoes that previously covered numerous chapel walls. First, in the Bardi Chapel are *Scenes from the Life of St. Francis,* (1315) and to the right, in the Peruzzi Chapel, *Scenes from the Lives of the Baptist and St. John the Evangelist.* The frescoes show Giotto's distinctive realism and monumentality, though they are not as compelling as his earlier works. In the end chapel of this transept is the *Coronation of the Virgin* a richly painted altarpiece by Giotto's workshop. A wooden Donatello crucifix (c. 1412) is displayed at

Florence

the end chapel in the left transept. *Open 8 a.m.–12:30 p.m., 3–6:30 p.m., Sun. 3–6:30 p.m. only.*

Cloister Museum ★

Exiting from the church, turn left for the entrance to this convent. Just to the right of the courtyard where you enter, is the former refectory, now the **Museo dell'Opera**. Santa Croce suffered severe damage from the 1966 floods, as can be seen in many of the works here. Despite the damage, Cimabue's ★ crucifix (13th C.) remains quite moving; Taddeo Gaddi's fresco of the ★ *Tree of Life* with a Last Supper beneath it still shows the strong, if simple forms of this follower of Giotto; and the scenes of Hell are just as poignant in the fragmentary state of A. Orcagna's *Last Judgment* (14th C.). Here too is a fine bronze *S. Louis of Toulouse* by Donatello. *Open 10 a.m.–12:30 p.m. year-round and 2:30–6:30 p.m. in summer, 3–5 p.m. Oct.–Mar.; closed Wed.; L3000.*

Pazzi Chapel ★★

At the rear of the cloister is the chapel commissioned from Brunelleschi by the Medici's enemies, the Pazzi. The portico probably was not designed by Brunelleschi, but the interior (1443) represents the consummation of his style and that of the Early Renaissance. Contrasting with the Gothic Duomo or even Santa Croce, this masterpiece totally redefines the vocabulary of architecture with elementary and pure geometric forms and with the simplicity of grey pietra serena on white stucco walls. The forms are classical but their treatment is unique. The pilasters flow through the frieze to form graceful arches that are repeated throughout the chapel. The blue glazed terracotta medallions by Luca della Robbia, and the clarity and proportions of the architecture combine into a serene and harmonious whole. *Access to the chapel is the same as the museum above.*

Casa Buonarroti

Near Santa Croce at Via Ghibellina 70 is the home built by Michelangelo's nephew on the site of the artist's original residence. Now a museum, the building contains the nephew's furnishings and only a few of Michelangelo's earliest works. *Open 9:30 a.m.–1:30 p.m.; closed Tues.; L8000.*

Piazza Santissima Annunziata ★

Just to the north of the duomo, up the Via dei Servi with its dramatic views of Brunelleschi's dome, is the Piazza SS. Annunziata. Although some of the porticos here were completed only in the 16th and 17th centuries, it's possible that this harmonious square was originally planned in its entirety by Brunelleschi, which would make it a very early example of modern urban planning. Giambologna began the equestrian monument to the Medici grand duke, Ferdinand I, but his student Tacca finished it and designed the fountains in the early 17th C. Important buildings stand at two sides of the plaza.

Spedale degli Innocenti ★

Flanking the east side of the square is the first truly Renaissance building (1419–29). This foundling hospital, designed by Brunelleschi, created the architectural vocabulary of the Renaissance: round arches supported on columns, squared and domed bays, pediment windows, and classical simplicity and proportion. Whether in the background of a Fra Angelico painting or recreated in the side aisles of later churches, these elements of the facade and loggia became standard Renaissance forms. In 1487, A. della Robbia added the enamelled medallions of swaddled infants. The building remains an orphanage, but the upstairs also contains a museum, its most famous work being Ghirlandaio's *Adoration of the Magi*. *Open 9 a.m.–2 p.m., closed Wed.; L3000.*

Church of SS. Annunziata ★

In 1314, this church was dedicated to a painting of the annunciation said to be miraculously completed by an angel. Even after Michelozzo rebuilt the church (1444–55), the painting attracted pilgrims who left hundreds of life-size images of themselves hanging from the rafters or crushed into the **Choistrino dei Voti**. Today this cloister (reached through the portico fronting the church) contains only frescoes, but a festa in the piazza each Annunciation Day (March 25) commemorates the centuries-old tradition. The cloister frescoes include a series by Andrea del Sarto on the Servite Order as well as *Visitation* (1516) by Pontormo (to the right as you enter atrium), a *Birth of the Virgin*, (1514) by Andrea del Sarto (toward church door), and a delicate ★ *Nativity* (1462) by Alesso Baldovinetti (left of church door). Inside the Baroque church **interior** are two psychologically haunting frescoes by Andrea del Castagno; his ★ *Vision of St. Julian* (1454) in the first chapel to the left and, next to it, his ★ *St. Jerome with Trinity and Two Maries*. In the unusual choir, designed by Michelozzo and modified by Alberti, are works by Perugino, Bronzino and Giambologna (for his own tomb). The Chiostro dei Morti is reached through a door in the left transept; to the left is a fine fresco by A. del Sarto, his ★ *Madonna del Sacco*.

Museo Archeologico

Across Via della Colonna from the Spedale is this archaeological museum with its extensive exhibits, including six rooms of Lorenzo de' Medicis collection of **antique gems** and cameos. The ★ **Etruscan section** includes reconstructions of tombs as well as masterpieces such as a 4th C. B.C. bronze ★ Chimera; the ★ Francois Krater (550 B.C.), an import from Athens; and the ★ *Arringatore* (100 B.C.), an Etruscan bronze that can't be distinguished from Roman ones save for its inscription in Etruscan. *Open Tues.–Sun. 9 a.m.–2 p.m.; L6000.*

Oltrarno ★★

Crossing the Arno to the Oltrarno, or south bank, you come to another Florence, one filled with artisans and students, with bicycles as well as cars. Here are the furniture and antique repair shops, the leather workshops as well as the elegant Borgo San Jacopo with its smart shops and restaurants. Here, too, are the collections of the Pitti Palace and two venerable churches to visit. But before you even get to the Oltrarno, you can enjoy walking along the *lungarni*, or broad avenues flanking the river and providing welcome relief from the more congested city streets. At sunset, many gather along the river and its bridges.

Buses (#15) from Fortezza da Basso and V. Tornabuoni stop at the della Grazia bridge and in Oltrarno at P. Pitti and Porta Romana.

Florence

Ponte Vecchio ★

Joining the two Florences are a series of bridges. The loveliest is the **Ponte S. Trinita**, with its three graceful arches that some believe were designed by Michelangelo, but executed by Ammanati. The most famous bridge is the Ponte Vecchio, or old bridge. A bridge has spanned this narrowest part of the river since Roman times; this Ponte Vecchio dates from 1345. Now limited to pedestrian use, the bridge retains the goldsmith shops that have operated here since 1592 when the Medici grand duke expelled the butchers and their smelly trade in order to make his daily walks in the Vasari corridor (above the shops) more pleasant. At night the closed shops look much like large wooden chests.

Palazzo Pitti ★★

Over the Ponte Vecchio and a few blocks farther along, you arrive at this grandiose palace. Begun in the 15th century, it was thereafter enlarged by subsequent generations of Florence's ruling families. The most remarkable addition was Ammanati's Manneristic ★**cortile**, or garden courtyard, built in 1617 for the Medici grand dukes. Today, the building contains many museums, among them: The **Gallery of Modern Art** (top floor; L6000) with Tuscan paintings, including works from the 19th-century impressionists school of the Macchiaoli (L12,000); **Appartamenti Monumentali** (middle floor), the furnished royal apartments; and Galleria Palatina (middle floor; L12,000). *All museums are open 9 a.m.–2 p.m.; closed Mon.*

The most famous of the Pitti museums is the ★★**Galleria Palatina**, containing the picture galleries of the Medici grand dukes—Titians, Raphaels, and other great works of the High Renaissance and Baroque periods, all scattered about courtly rooms among tapestries and sculptures and views of the Boboli Gardens. The lack of order in such a large collection can feel overwhelming. You can actually lose yourself if you permit your eyes to wander off the paintings themselves in order to explore the celestial regions of Pietro da Cortona's magnificent High Baroque ★ceilings of stucco and paint, artworks that were the forerunners of the Louis XIV style (found in each of the first five salas Venere, Apollo, Marte, Giove and Saturno). Fortunately, the curators have at least labelled the paintings so that you can feel somewhat grounded as you visit each room of this incredible collection.

Starting in the **Sala di Venere** (the first room on the left) there are four Titians, including the moody ★*Concerto*, the exhausted face of Pope Julian II in ★*Portrait*, and the opulent ★★*Ritratto di Donna*, also called *La Bella*. Here, also, are two landscapes by Rubens. The **Sala di Apollo** has two more Titians, ★*Portrait of a Gentleman* and *Mary Magdalene*, as well as portraits by Rubens and Van Dyck. Sala di Marte contains yet two more Titians, both portraits, as well as Van Dyck's ★*Cardinal Benivoglio* (1623) and Rubens' ★*Consequences of War* (1638) and *Four Philosophers*. The Raphaels begin in **Sala di Giove** with the sumptuous textures of ★★*Donna Velata* (1513) and continue in **Sala di Saturno** with three early works that are influenced by Leonardo—the two ★*Doni* portraits and the ★*Madonna del Granduca* (1505)—and a later, and absolutely wonderful tondo ★*Madonna della Seggiola*. There are seven of his works in all. **Sala dell'Iliade**, the last large room, contains Raphael's ★*La Gravida*, or pregnant woman, as well as two

Titian portraits. The **smaller rooms** are worth exploring if you're up to them. In the Sala dell'Educazione di Giove is Caravaggio's rather bizarre *Sleeping Cupid* (late 16th C.); in Sala di Ulisse is Raphael's *dell'Impannata*, and if you're continuing, stop in the Sala di Prometeo for Fra Filippo Lippi's tondo ★ *Madonna con Bambino.* Down the corridor, is the Sala della Guistizia with several unremarkable Titians. And with even more time you can seek out the exceptional works by Andrea del Sarto, Fra Bartolomeo, Tintoretto, Bronzino, Annibale Carracci and others.

Giardino di Boboli   ★

Behind the Palazzo Pitti (one entrance is through the cortile) are its formal gardens, among the most beautiful in Europe. Extending to the Porta Romana, they form a vast park in the urban center that contains a 16th-century version of a Roman amphitheater, grottos, fountains, sculpture, as well as shaded walks that make the hottest afternoon cooler. *Open 9 a.m.–sunset; L5000.*

Church of Santo Spirito   ★

The 18th-C. facade of this church watches over a wonderful little piazza located a few blocks from the S. Trinita bridge. Inside is a noble space created by Brunelleschi in 1434. The most logical of his works, this church is perfectly proportioned and arcaded, not just down the side aisles but around the transepts and end apse as well. Unfortunately, the Renaissance arcades culminate today in a jarring Baroque altar. In a middle chapel of the right transept is Filippino Lippi's ★ *Madonna and Child with Saints and Patrons* (1488).

Santa Maria del Carmine Church

Several blocks west of Santo Spirito, you come to this 18th-C. church, rebuilt after a fire destroyed it in 1771. Fortunately, the fire left for posterity the Brancacci Chapel in the right transept, where you find the ★★★**Masaccio and Masolino fresco cycle** on the Life of St. Peter (1425). Here Michelangelo, Fra Angelico, and other great painters came to study the seminal works of the Renaissance artist, Masaccio. Masaccio's accomplishments in perspective, in the play of light and shade to create convincing human dramas, can be seen by contrasting his powerful *Expulsion of Adam and Eve* (first fresco on left, upper tier) with Masolino's more Gothic and Linear *Temptation* (opposite wall). Next to the *Expulsion* is Masaccio's masterpiece *The Tribute Money* (the face of Christ is by Masolino); flanking the altar, the two lower scenes of S*t. Peter Healing with his Shadow* (left) and *Distribution of the Goods of the Church* movingly show us the crippled and the poor in Masaccio's Florence. Most of the remaining lower frescoes were painted later by Filippino Lippi. *Open 10 a.m.–4:30 p.m., except Sun. 1–4:30 p.m. and closed Tues.; L5000.* **Note:** *To protect the recently restored frescoes, visits are controlled and entrance permitted to a limited number at any one time. Arrive early in peak season.*

The Hills

Florence is beautiful from afar where an overview brings together its most famous monuments at a single glance. Whether sunset watching from the Piazzale Michelangelo, or cafe sitting in Fiesole, the short drives or bus trips are worthwhile.

Piazzale Michelangelo

One of the great tourist ★ viewing points, particularly at sunset, the piazzale can be reached a number of ways. The hearty can walk from the Oltrarno side of the Ponte Vecchio: One route goes along Costa San Giorgio to the Forte Belvedere, a 16th-C. fort now used for art exhibits, and then winds up the hill to the area of the piazzale; the other more difficult route follows Via dei Bardi through another gate of the fortifications before climbing to the open terrace of the piazzale with its steps, cafes, and, of course, great views. *The #13 bus runs from P. delle Stazione to Lungarno Acciaiulo and over the Ponte Grazie to the piazzale and then loops to Porta Romana on its return to the stazione. Or drive across the Ponte S. Nicolo and follow signs to Siena up the hill.*

San Miniato al Monte ★

Just up the hill beyond the piazzale is this famous Tuscan Romanesque church (begun 1090). Its steps not only afford a view of Florence, but a close-up of the marble inlaid facade. The interior, both its architectural detailing and marble floor, is Romanesque, too, but Renaissance works can be found in the Chapel of the Crucifix (end of nave) with its ★ Michelozzo tabernacle and the Chapel of the Cardinal of Portugal (north wall) with a fine Baldovinetti *Annunciation*. L. della Robbia has decorations in both chapels. The atmosphere becomes purely medieval when Gregorian chants are sung here. *Closed noon–2 p.m., Sun. 8 a.m.–2:30 p.m.*

Fiesole

Actually a separate town, 10 km, 6 mi., above Florence, Fiesole is too far away for the intimate views around the Piazzale Michelangelo. Yet the panorama of the surrounding Tuscan countryside with Florence nestled in the valley is most satisfying. More a village around a piazza than a true town, Fiesole provides refreshing breezes even in the summer and offers a tranquil *passaggiata* past villas and gardens, all overlooking the valley below. One walk winds off the west end of the piazza toward the Convent of San Francesco; an easier one leads off the east end to the right of the small church. Although you come here to relax and stroll, you might consider a walk through the Roman and Etruscan ruins *(open 9 a.m.–7 p.m. Apr.–Sept.; 10 a.m.–4 p.m. rest of year; closed Tues. in winter; L6000)* found behind the duomo. The Teatro Romano here still is used for performances, particularly during the Fiesole music festival in June and July. *The #7 bus from P. San Marco or P. Duomo or a drive past the Ponte Vecchio (then left onto Viale G. Amendola where you pick up Fiesole signs) will wind you up the hills to the main piazza.*

Festivals and Events

June 24 is the **Festa del Patrono**, feast day of San Giovanni Battista (St. John The Baptist), that concludes with the lights of Florence lowered so that showers of fireworks over the Arno can be all the more spectacular. During the day, a number of medieval traditions have been revived, with tourism somewhat in mind, around what is called **Calcio Storico**, or historical soccer. Said to be the predecessor to the game of soccer, this ancient game is played in the Piazza Santa Croce between the four traditional neighborhoods of Florence, and all players are in period dress. Since a few rounds precede the finals, other Calcio

Florence

Storico events usually take place in May and early June. *(Tickets should be obtained ahead of time; contact tourist information.)* Preceding the game on June 24 is a colorful procession of the medieval guilds. A very traditional Florence event is the **Scoppio del Carro** (explosion of the cart), on Easter Sunday. With much fanfare and ringing of church bells, a "dove" is set off from the altar of the duomo and rides a wire to the piazza and a gaily decorated cart, full of fireworks. If the dove successfully detonates the cart, it's a good omen. Sept.7 marks the **Rificolona**, an evening lantern-lit procession across the San Niccolo bridge into Florence, derived from the stream of women who once arrived from the countryside before the feast day of *The Virgin* in order to set up their stalls for the market in the P. Annunziata.

May and June is the time of **Maggio Musicale**, *(For advance tickets and information write the festival at Teatro Comunale, Corso Italia 16, 50123 Firenze)*, a series of classical music concerts, ballet and opera performed by leading artists. June through August, the Roman amphitheater in Fiesole sponsors more concerts in the annual **Estate Fiesolana**. Throughout the summer, classical music is performed in the courtyards of historic palaces as part of **Musicale nelle Piazze**.For all these events check with tourist information or the listings in *Florence Today*.

Shopping

In 1470, Florence had more woodcarvers than butchers. Though that startling ratio no longer holds true, Florence does retain its tradition of artisanry and is famous for its jewelry, marbled paper and leather products (especially shoes) among other crafts. The **Ponte Vecchio** is the centuries-old home for gold and silversmiths, even though the re-nowned firm of Settepassi has moved to plushier quarters on the Via Tornabuoni. Spilling off the bridge, along Por S. Maria and Lungarno Acciaiuoli, are numerous boutiques selling mosaics of semiprecious stones, the most supple of leather gloves, and linens. (**Cirri**, *Por S. Maria 38r*, is famous for children's wear; in other parts of town, **Pratesi**, *Lungarno Vezspucci 8/10r*, and **Garbo**, *Borgo Ognissanti 2r*, both have exquisite linens and lace.)

The *Oltrarno* is home to the cabinet makers and metal sculptors, the restorers and gilders. In the streets radiating from the antique stores on Via Maggio, you can see these *artigiani* in their workshops. Or you can visit the **Piazza Santo Spirito Market** on the second Sunday of each month to see them demonstrate their skills and to visit the stalls of the antique dealers. (Antiques abound on the other side of the river, too: There's another antique fair the last Sunday of each month at *Piazza del Ciompi*, north of Santa Croce; and fine shops cluster in the higher rent district of Borgo Ognissanti, such as **Romano** at *#20r*.) Also, in the Oltrarno is Florence's oldest paper-making concern, **Guilio Giannini & Figlio** *(P. Pitti 37r)*, specializing in marbled paper as well as desk sets covered with swirling designs. (**Note:** Flowered Florentine paper is manufactured, not handmade like the marbled item.) Another member of the Giannini family runs **Il Papiro** *(P. del Duomo 24r)*, with its various branches on the other side of the river.

Leather and fashions are best sought out on the right bank. *Via Tornabouni* is the *Fifth Avenue* of Florence, and here you can find **Ferragamo**, a Florentine company, right at its beginning *(2r)* and continue to its venerable jeweler **Settepassi** *(25r)*, and **Valentino**, **Beltrami**, **Gucci**, **Tanino Crisci** and **Armani** *(actually, around the corner on P. Strozzi)*—to name just a few. The high fashion spills over to neighboring streets, to the leather at **Gherardini** *(Vigna Nuova 13B)* and the shoes at **Pollini** *(V. Calimala 12r)*, **Ghirlandi** *(V. Cerretani 20r)*, and the branches of **Beltrami** everywhere *(including Calzaiuoli 50r)*.

Less pricey shopping is possible, too. For shoes, **Raspini** *(V. Martelli 1)* has a large selection in a range of prices; **Maraolo** *(V. Roma, off Piazza Republica)* sells discounted Joan & David shoes as well as other labels. The leather jackets and bags, as well as souvenirs and junk, attract many tourists to the **Mercato di San Lorenzo** *(P. San Lorenzo; 8:30 a.m.-6:30 p.m.; closed Sun. and Mon.)*. Or try the shops around Santa Croce, particularly the **Santa Croce Leather School** *(V. San Guiseppe 5r*, side entrance to church monastery). And you can shop with the Florentines for just about everything in **COIN** *(V. Calzaiuoli)*, a popular department store. Other affordable presents are art posters, found in the **museum shops**.

Where to Stay

Florence has a wealth of hotels in all price ranges, from the most modern deluxe hotel, through palazzi renovated into charming inns, to youth hostels and campgrounds *(one so convenient as Viale Michelangelo 80;* ☎ *681-1977* is **Italiani e Stranieri**, *open Apr.–Oct.)*. During Easter and summer months, you should reserve well in advance, especially if you have your heart set on one hotel in particular. For the smaller hotels and pensioni, always reserve in advance—most of the ones listed here book up early. To find an apartment for a longer stay, check with the listings in the bi-weekly *Le Pulce*, or the bulletin board at **Paperback Exchange** *(V. Fiesole 31r)*. Also, language schools usually can arrange housing for their students.

The better hotels along the Arno have triple-paneled windows to muffle the noise of the traffic below, but rarely do the more modest pensioni (below 3 stars). In the summer, you may find the lack of air conditioning and the need to open your windows results in sleepless nights at the simpler establishments. Even with the limitations on traffic, you might prefer a garden view to protect you if you're noise sensitive.

Many hotels have lower winter-and-August rates. High-season prices are listed below. All rooms are air-conditioned unless stated otherwise.

Very Expensive

Villa San Michele　　　　　**L700–1,300,000 MAP**　　
Via Doccia 4 in Fiesole 50014; ☎ *59-451, FAX 598-734.*
Single L700,000. Double L950–1,300,000 with two meals.
Just 5 km outside of Florence, is this former 15th-century monastery now refurbished into an exceptional inn with a facade attributed to Michelangelo (but revamped in the 17th century). The reception area once was the chapel. The 29 rooms, now with four-poster beds and tasteful furnishings and even, occasionally, a Jacuzzi, were the cells that then as now overlook beautiful gardens. Suites with private terraces are in a new garden annex. The entire estate has wonderful views of the Arno valley. Restaurant with indoor and terrace dining; lounges. Pool. Parking. Limo service to Florence. MAP required.

Grand Hotel　　　　　　**L480–595,000**　　❀★★★★★
Piazza Ognissanti 1, 50123; ☎ *288-781; FAX 217-400.*

Single L480,000. Double L595,000.

One of Florence's great 19th-century hotels located in a fashionable district by the Arno, the Grand has been exquisitely renewed from the crystal teardrop chandeliers of the foyer to the stained-glass roof of the winter garden and the splendor of its Baroque ballroom. More intimate than most in the Ciga hotels, the Grand has only 105 rooms, each spacious, some with balcony views of the Arno, and all now renovated in styles evocative of the quattrocento with sumptuous brocades, frescoes and antiques. Superb service. Restaurant. Garage.

Excelsior   **L410–615,000**   ★ ★ ★ ★ ★

Piazza Ognissanti 1, 50123; ☎ *264-201; FAX 210-278.*
Single L410,000. Double L575–615,000.

With the same excellent central location next to the Arno as its sister hotel, the Grand, the Excelsior also is one of the Florence's finest deluxe hotels. The lobby is paved with 16th-century marble inlay, and its high ceilings are coffered. Its 205 rooms range in decor from the comfortably sedate Imperial to brocaded Renaissance, many have Arno views and a few suites, private terraces; all are furnished with antiques and fine prints. The roof terrace bar and restaurant has been partially enclosed for year-round enjoyment of the stunning and unobstructed panoramic views. Off the lobby the stuffed armchairs of the Donatello Bar often are filled by Florentines. Superb service. Shops. Valet parking.

Helvetia e Bristol   **L370–575,000**   ✿★ ★ ★ ★

V. dei Pescioni, 50123; ☎ *287-814; FAX 288-353.*
Single L370,000. Double L575,000.

The reigning hotel of the late 19th century has been restored to its former period elegance, while the 50 rooms have been upgraded with modern conveniences (some with private Jacuzzi) and decorated with antiques, chandeliers and exquisite wall-coverings in a variety of styles from red-velvet Victorian to decorous Regency. The location near the duomo and just off fashionable Tornabuoni couldn't be more convenient. Restaurant and lounge.

Grand Hotel Villa Cora   **L430–650,000 CP**   ✿★ ★ ★ ★

Viale Machiavelli 18, 50125; ☎ *229-8451; FAX 229-086.*
Single L430,000 CP. Double L650,000 CP.

A neoclassical villa fit for the residence of Napoleon III's widow is now a splendid retreat for the traveler after a day's sightseeing in Florence. Located on a hill beyond the Piazzale Michelangelo, the Villa Cora is set amid gardens and offers marble drawing rooms with ornate ceilings, 48 Victorian style rooms—with modern comforts, restaurants and lounges, and a large swimming pool. Shuttle to centro storico.

Expensive

Lungarno   **L275–365,000**   ★ ★ ★ ★

Borgo San Jacopo 14, 50125; ☎ *264-211; FAX 268-437.*
Single L275,000. Double L365,000.

The Lungarno has a prime location in the Oltrarno near the Ponte Vecchio. On one side, the hotel opens to a fashionable shopping street; on the other, to the Arno free of any noisy and obstructive road. Not too surprisingly, many of the 66 rooms here have some of the best views in the city. The hotel is sleekly modern and subdued with a fine collection of contemporary art. The rooms are on the small side, but well appointed. Lounge. Roof terrace. Garage.

Berchielli   **L375–410,000 CP**   ★★★★

Lungarno Acciaiuoli 14, 50123; ☎ *264-061; FAX 218-636.*
Single/double L375–410,000 CP.
Conveniently located near the Ponte Vecchio and attractively situated facing the Arno on one side, the picturesque Piazza del Limbo on the other, the Berchielli is another choice hotel. The style here is smartly contemporary, with black and white marble floors, and slate grey detailing. The rooms are ample and attractive, those with river views special, and those duplex suites with piazza-side terraces especially tranquil. Restaurant. Lounge. Garage.

Croce di Malta   **L285–355,000**   ★★★★

Via della Scala 7, 50123; ☎ *218-351; FAX 287-121.*
Single L285,000. Double L355,000.
A few steps from Santa Maria Novella, the Renaissance exterior of this Best Western affiliate disguises a smartly modern lobby. The 98 well-furnished units are more traditional in decor; those with balconies over garden are best. Duplex suites available. You may have given up views of the Arno to come here, but you've gained a large garden for dining and sunning as well as a swimming pool. Restaurant. Lounge.

Bernini Palace   **L275–395,000**   ★★★★

Piazza San Firenze 29, 50122; ☎ *288-621; FAX 268-272.*
Single L275,000. Double L395,000.
Just behind the Palazzo Vecchio, this hotel occupies a Renaissance building pleasingly decorated with armchairs and brocaded fabrics. The traditional styling of the hotel includes broad halls, wrought iron staircases, and some antiques for character. The 86 rooms are ample and with modern comforts. Restaurant. Lounge. Garage.

Principe   **L270–355,000**   ✿★★★

Lungarno A. Vespucci 34, 50123; ☎ *284-848; FAX 283-458.*
Single L270,000. Double L355,000.
This elegant Renaissance palace faces the Arno and opens behind to a tranquil garden with fountain and lawn chairs. Its intimacy, modern comforts, and good taste make the 21 rooms (all varying; some with river views, others with garden quiet; some smaller ones with large terraces, larger ones with no terrace) a favorite choice for many. Handsome sitting rooms. Bar. Breakfast room.

Monna Lisa   **L270–350,000 CP**   ✿★★★

Borgo Pinti 27, 50121; ☎ *247-9751; FAX 247-9755.*
Single L270,000 CP. Double L350,000 CP.
Not far from the duomo, this very special hotel retains the ambience of the family home it once was. It's just that not many homes occupy Renaissance palazzi furnished with antiques and period pieces. The many sitting rooms open to the beautiful garden that by itself justifies the loyal following of this hotel. The 20 rooms vary, of course, but they are ample and with such charming touches as floral wallpaper and writing desks. The bathrooms often are old-fashioned. Bar. Parking.

Villa Belvedere   **L255–290,000 CP**

Via Castelli 3, 50124; ☎ *222-501; FAX 223-163.*
Single L255,000 CP. Double L290,000 CP.

On the Siena road at the edge of Florence, but connected by bus (#11), this family-run establishment clearly is not for those with limited time, but for those who wish to relax in the quiet garden, or to soak in the small pool and play tennis, the brief commute may be worth it. The 27 rooms vary in size, but those with balconies and views (a bit pricier) are the most highly recommended. Breakfast only. Garage. *Closed Dec.–Mar 1.*

Moderate

Loggiato dei Serviti   **L180–260,000 CP**

Piazza SS. Annunziata 3, 50122; ☎ *289-592; FAX 289-595.*
Single L180,000 CP. Double L260,000 CP.

This very special hotel has an excellent location that is not only central, but part of Brunelleschi's handsomely designed piazza. The hotel itself occupies a fine Renaissance building that has been modernized while carefully preserving Fra Angelico-style vaulting and other architectural details. The 29 rooms vary, but all are tastefully, if sparingly, decorated with antiques. Sitting room. Bar.

Morandi alla Crocetta   **L120–180,000**   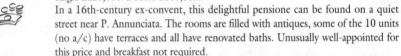

V. Laura 50, 50121; ☎ *234-4747; FAX 248-0954.*
Single L120,000. Double L180,000.

In a 16th-century ex-convent, this delightful pensione can be found on a quiet street near P. Annunciata. The rooms are filled with antiques, some of the 10 units (no a/c) have terraces and all have renovated baths. Unusually well-appointed for this price and breakfast not required.

Annalena   **L195–230,000 CP**

Via Romana 34, 50125; ☎ *222-402; FAX 222-403.*
Single L195,000 CP. Double L230,000 CP.

A few minutes beyond the Pitti Palace, this Renaissance palazzo retains its old-world ambience with numerous antique furnishings. Among its 20 comfortable and ample rooms (no a/c), those overlooking the lovely gardens and nurseries are highly recommended. Since this is really a pensione rather than a hotel, expect to take breakfast here.

Hermitage   **L215–265,000 CP**

Vicolo Marzio 1, 50122; ☎ *287-216; FAX 212-208.*
Single L215,000 CP. Double L265,000 CP

This homey pensione occupies the upper floors (elevator) of a palazzo near the Ponte Vecchio. The living room has overstuffed chairs and the roof terrace, used for breakfast in the summer, has views of the Arno. Those of the 14 rooms with baths rather than showers are considerably larger and some have river views. They also cost a bit more. No a/c.

Splendor   **L120–185,000 CP**

Via S. Gallo 30, 50129; ☎ *483-427; FAX 461-276.*
Single L120,000 CP. Double L185,000 CP.

Florence

Near San Marco, this former pensione offers sitting rooms with ceiling frescoes and period furnishings. The best of its 31 ample rooms overlook the quiet garden, but there's a pleasant garden terrace for everyone to share. Most rooms with baths; those without are inexpensive; no a/c. Elevator for luggage only.

Royal   **L155–240,000 CP**   ★ ★

Via delle Ruote 50, 50129; ☎ *483-287; FAX 490-976.*
Single L155,000 CP. Double L240,000 CP.
A little out of center, but just beyond San Marco, the Royal is a bit like an old-fashioned country house; its halls and common rooms are nicely proportioned, and there's a park-like garden in the back. Yet its 40 rooms, those preferred are in the back with garden views, have recently been modernized with a/c and hair dryers. Reading room. Lounge. Parking.

Le Due Fontane   **L140–245,000 CP**   ★ ★

Piazza SS.Annunziata 14, 50122; ☎ *280-086; FAX 294-461.*
Single L140,000 CP. Double L245,000 CP.
In a central location on a fine piazza, this commercial hotel has 48 decent rooms with modern baths, most with a/c.

Inexpensive
Calzaiuoli   **L160–175,000**   ★ ★

Via Calzaiuoli 6, 50122; ☎ *212-456; FAX 268-310.*
Single L160,000. Double L175,000.
Located between the duomo and Palazzo Vecchio, this commercial-style hotel offers 37 modern, well-maintained rooms. Small lounge; tiny lobby.

Villa San Girolamo   **L75–125,000 CP**   ★ ★

Via Vecchia Fiesolana 12, Fiesole, 50014; ☎ *59-141.*
Single L75,000 CP. Double L125,000 CP.
A 20-minute bus ride to Florence, but this tranquil 15th-century convent run by the Irish order of the Little Company of Mary has 50 clean, pleasant rooms with grand valley views. No religious affiliation necessary, but couples must be married.

La Scaletta   **L90–130,000 CP**   ★

V. Guicciardini 13, 50125; ☎ *238-028.*
Single L90,000 CP. Double L130,000 CP.
Right next to the Pitti Palace in the Oltrarno, this third floor pensione has 15 decent-size rooms (no a/c), most with good light, 3 with views of the Boboli Gardens, and all but 4 with private baths. There are pleasant sitting areas, a few antiques here and there, and a roof terrace with views over the gardens.

Albergo Firenze   **L75–95,000**   √

P. Donati 4, 50122; ☎ *214-203.*
Single L75,000. Double L95,000.
In a cul de sac off the Corso, this budget hotel has a spiffy and welcoming entrance and those of the 50 rooms renovated with private baths (no a/c) are bright and clean, if plain. A good buy for so central a location. Reserve in advance. Credit cards: None.

Where to Eat

Florentines take pride in their cooking, just as they take pride in everything Tuscan. It's hard not to come upon a hearty ribollita or diverse preparations of the ubiquitous bean, like fagioli all'uccelletto. Of course, the mushroom in its different guises is found in courses from antipasti through secondi. But Florence has added its own variations to a number of dishes. Fish or eggs may become Florentine by being served on a bed of spinach; *bistecca alla fiorentina* is simply a thick steak made local by its T-bone cut, unique in Italy. Split and grilled chickens are served with a ginger sauce, becoming *pollo alla diavola*; roast loin of pork is cooked with rosemary, garlic and cloves, becoming the popular *arista alla fiorentina*. Salami with fennel seeds is the popular *finocchiona*. Of course, the Chianti reds make fine accompaniments to such fare, as do the Brunellos, if you can afford them. The white Vernaccio, from San Gimignanol, is quite decent, and many of the house whites are light and pleasing.

Please note: Many restaurants close in August as well as on Sunday and Monday. Meal times are usually 12:30–2:30 p.m. for lunch with dinner beginning at 7:30 or 8 p.m. The menu turistico here often includes beverage—either mineral water or house wine. Reservations are always advised.

The Sublime

Enoteca Pinchiorri $$$ ★★★★★

> V. Ghibellina 87; reserve at ☎ 242-777, FAX 244-983.
> Closed Mon. & Wed. lunch, Sun., Aug., and Christmas. Fixed-price lunch L90–150,000. Fixed-price dinner L150,000. À la carte L130–225,000.
> Universally acclaimed as one of Italy's great restaurants. The setting, in an exceptional Renaissance palace with elegant and chandeliered interior dining rooms and a lovely garden courtyard for warm weather luncheons, is equal to the wine and food. Although some of the dishes may seem French-influenced Italian, many are creative reinterpretations of the most Tuscan fare. The offerings change constantly, from traditional grilled rabbit with fagioli to lasagne with crabmeat and wild fennel. The wine cellar is among the most extensive in Europe, and a special price can be paid for wine tasting to accompany each course.

The Superb

Il Cibreo $$–$$$ ★★★★

> V. dei Macci 118r, near Santa Croce; reserve at ☎ 234-1100, FAX 244-966.
> Closed Sun., Mon., late summer, and Dec. Meals L60–75,000.
> The traditional is also given a modern interpretation at Il Cibreo, but not so much as to permit pasta on the menu—it arrived in Italy too late to be authentically Tuscan. No matter how traditional this restaurant, the preparations are inventive and refined: artichokes, but as a flan appetizer; thick soup, but made of yellow peppers traced with parmesan; rabbit, but with lemon peel and egg. The day's menu is given verbally, in English if wanted; the prices for each course are printed. In summer, the tables spill over to the sidewalk and year-round you can try for one of the bare trattoria tables in a back room where the prices are more moderate.

Sabatini $$$ ★★★

> V. Panzani 9a; reserve at ☎ 211-559, FAX 210-293.

Florence

Closed Mon. Meals L70–120,000.

Forever the same, and for that reason pleasing to many, Sabatini serves completely traditional Tuscan dishes—bistecca alla fiorentina, pappardelle and rabbit—decently prepared and served in an elegant, yet unpretentious atmosphere.

The Very Good

Taverna del Bronzino ★ ★ ★

V. delle Ruote 25r; ☎ *495-220.*
Closed Sun., Aug. Meals L50–70,000.

A bit beyond the Piazza San Marco, this restaurant is comfortably housed in the Renaissance home of the Mannerist painter and now a popular spot for Florentines. The food is as pleasing as the easy ambience from the crostini of mushrooms on polenta and the Roman-style feast of vegetables (a plate of the day's contorni) to the secondi that include some seafood. But the unforgettable dishes here are the pasta del giorno, such as black truffle tortellini or artichoke ravioli.

Alle Murate $$ ★ ★ ★

V. Ghibellina 52r; reserve at ☎ *240-618.*
Dinner only. Closed Mon., Aug., and Christmas. Fixed-price dinner L60–65,000. À la carte L50–65,000. Wine bar about L30,000.

In the Santa Croce rione is this small restaurant of ten tables with polished service and wonderful food. The tasting menus, one Tuscan traditional, the other more southern Italian and creative, change daily and may include a cream of artichoke soup or a colorful beet tagliolini on a bed of arugula, stuffed pigeon in red wine sauce, or a very Tuscan rabbit stuffed with porchetta. There is also a wine bar here evenings, where you can sample the food inexpensively.

Dino $$–$$$ ★ ★ ★

V. Ghibellina 51r; ☎ *241-452, FAX 241-378.*
Closed Sun. night, Mon., Aug. Meals L45–70,000.

Also near Santa Croce, this intimate restaurant set under Renaissance arches has a soothing ambience and professional service. The food is Tuscan and prepared with some refinement: zuppa di farro (barley) made from an ancient recipe, beans with baby peperoncini, and stinco, or pork shank in green herb sauce.

More Moderate

Le Quattro Stagioni $$ ★ ★

V. Maggio 61; ☎ *218-906.*
Closed Sun., Aug., Christmas. Meals L45–60,000.

This is one of our favorites. Even the most traditional dishes, such as tagliatelle with porcini or grilled duck alla fiorentina, are prepared with sophistication, and the clientele often consult with the chef on seasonal specialties, like the gnocchi (even if you don't normally like it, try it when made of spinach and cheese and served with tomato and basil). The fish with sage, the crespelle with seafood, and the carpaccio are also good.

l'Toscano $$ ★ ★

V. Guelfa 70r; ☎ *215-475.*
Closed Tues. & Aug. Meals L40–60,000.

The ambience and menu are somewhat similar to Quattro Stagioni—a combination of Tuscan dishes with some lighter fare, including carpaccio. There's also an inexpensive fixed-price menu.

The Picturesque

Cantinetta Antinori   **$$–$$$**   ★★

P. degli Antinori 3, end of V. Tornabuoni; ☎ *292-234.*
Closed weekends, Aug., and Christmas. Luncheon L45–65,000. Dinner L65–75,000.
Several restaurants serve not only good Tuscan fare, but attract a satisfied following because of their settings, too. Among the more handsome in-town spots is the 15th-century palazzo of the wine-making Antinori family. In the tradition of a cantina, food is selected to complement the wines from the Antinori vineyards so that at lunchtime you need not partake of a full meal. Instead, you can sit in the elegantly panelled room, tasting some excellent wine to the accompaniment of tomato and mozzarella salad and cheese crostini or a pasta dish.

La Loggia   **$$–$$$**   ★★

Piazzale Michelangelo 1; ☎ *234-2832, FAX 234-5288.*
Closed Wed. and part of Aug.; reservation recommended. Meals L60–100,000.
In the summer the terrace here, overlooking the city, is understandably popular. Although tour buses bring crowds of diners, the service is good, the grilled fish and Tuscan meats flavorful, and the view fabulous.

Inexpensive But Good

Caffe Cibreo   **$**   ★★

V. dei Macci 114r
12-2 p.m., closed Mon. Fixed-price lunch L35,000.
Meals of some delicacy can be inexpensive when you choose a fixed-price option. Here you can simply sip some of the same sublime coffee served at the owner's more famous restaurant across the piazzetta or you can sit down to a lunch of antipasti or a shrimp and artichoke salad with soup and dessert.

Doney Caffe   **$**   ★★

P. Strozzi
Open till 8 p.m. Fixed-price lunch L35,000.
Next to the Emporio Armani, this stylish cafe is pricey unless you order the special three-course luncheon that may include sage tagliatelle, salmon and sorbet.

Trattoria Nella   **$**   ★★

V. delle Terme 19r; ☎ *218-925.*
Closed Sun. Meals L18–25,000.
Hearty fare can be found for inexpensive prices, none better than at the family-run and locally popular Nella, a few blocks from the Ponte Vecchio. The risotto is good, the mixed salad large, and the penne with artichokes great. There are fixed-price options at both lunch and dinner. Credit cards: None.

Trattoria Borgo Antico   **$**   ★★

P. Santo Spirito; ☎ *210-437.*
Closed Sun. Meals L18–25,000.

Florence

This popular eatery offers good pizza, good salads and good pasta (try the spaghetti di Borgo Antico) served al fresco in the pleasant square or, when cold or crowded, inside. Credit cards: None.

Trattoria Le Mossacce $ ★

V. Proconsolo 55r
Closed Sun., Sat. night and most of Aug. Meals L20–30,000.
This Florentine institution is well-located near the duomo. The food couldn't be more traditional—spaghetti with sugo, fagioli and arista. But it's chaotic at lunch. The food is decent, the prices are low (wine included), and if you don't have survival Italian, simply point at the dishes of those sharing the table with you. Credit cards: None.

Pizza I Ghibellini $ ★

P. San Pier Maggiore 8, off V. Borgo Albizi.
Closed Wed. Meals L20–35,000.
Near Santa Croce, this trattoria has okay pizza, a fine piazza for al fresco dining in good weather, and a more elaborate menu than the name suggests.

Picnics and Snacks

Although the cafes and cantinas mentioned below are good places to enjoy light meals, a more ambulatory lunch or picnic can be bought at one of the many *fornos*, or bakeries. Just before the lunch closing, these fornos usually have a wide choice of fresh pizza by-the-slice as well as pastries stuffed with meats or vegetables. Of course, the specialty food shops and alimentari sell delicious salami and prosciutto and cheese to eat with the bread coming out of the forno ovens. Two convenient places for shopping are the **Mercato Centrale** near San Lorenzo where the **Fornaio** *(Faenza 39r)* is complemented by the nearby **La Norcineria** *(V. Antonino 21r)*, with decent prices on cold cuts; in the Oltrarno, Borgo San Jacopo at Via Maggio is home to the elegant **Vera** with the makings for an antipasto as well as sandwiches. At the opposite end of San Jacopo near the Ponte Vecchio is **Il Fornaio** *(Guicciardini 5r)*. Take your purchases to the nearest garden or park, or save them for the views from the slopes around Piazzale Michelangelo. And for *gelati*, the fruity freshness of the ices at **Il Granduca** *(V. Calzaiuoli 57r)* and **Vivoli** *(V. della Stinche 7, behind the Bargello)* are justly famous.

Caffe and Cantina

Sometimes restaurants simply won't do. You just want to sit down and relax. You only want to snack or sip a glass of wine. The cafes and cantinas are your best retreat. Three of Florence's most famous cafes are conveniently located. At the **Rivoire** *(P. della Signoria 5r; closed Mon.)* preference for the paneled interior gives way in warmer weather to one of the best outdoor terraces for viewing the jugglers and orators of this famous piazza. The tea sandwiches, the pastries, and the spremuta di limone are quite good, but here it is the chocolate, both edible and sippable, that is the specialty. Leisurely sipping can be more difficult at **Giacosa** *(V. Tornabuoni 83r; closed Sun.)*, but if you are lucky enough to get one of the few tables, you can enjoy the tea sandwiches and other snacks at lunch, some hot, while watching Florence's most fashionable shoppers. **Bar Gilli** *(P. della Repubblica 39r; closed Tues.)* is fashionable, too, especially for cocktails; its Belle Epoque interior with frescoed ceiling makes it hard to join the sidewalk table scene. Not one of

Florence

Florence's most famous spots, but with superb pastries and coffee is **Robiglio** (*V. dei Servi 112r; closed Sun*).

Being in the heart of Chianti country, Florence has numerous wine bars, popular spots for a glass of wine accompanied by snacks or even more sophisticated fare. The *vanaini* are earthy and inexpensive, sometimes no more than a hole in the street wall where you stand for panini and wine (check out **Vinieri** at *V. de' Cimatori 38r, just off Calzaiuoli near Orsanmichele; open till 8 p.m.; closed Sun.*). Other vinaini have tables where you can eat antipasto or freshly made panini, such as **Vini** (*V. degli Alfani 70, near P. Annunziata; open till 8:30 p.m., closed Sat.*). The cantinas tend toward greater sophistication and are open evenings for snacks of crostini or light suppers of Tuscan specialties. A casual one on the Oltrarno is **Cantinone del Gallo Nero** (*V. Santo Spirito 6r; closed Mon.*). The ambience is that of a wine cellar, the food is stick-to-your-ribs Tuscan ribollita and open-faced sandwiches too hearty to be called "crostini." Better wines can be sipped at the elegant **Cantinetta Antinori** and fine foods accompany the wines at **Alle Murate** (see restaurants above for both).

Directory

Telephone Code 055   **Postal Code 50100**

Airlines

Alitalia, *Lungarno Acciaioli 10r* (☎ *27-888*).

Airport

In **Pisa**, connected by fast train to stazione centrale (flight information in Florence ☎ *27-88*); and **Peretola**, 5 km (☎ *333-490*) non-stop bus from P. Stazione.

Albergo Diurno

Near entrance to track 16 at stazione. Closed Sunday p.m. and Thursday.

American Express

V. Dante Alighieri 20 (☎ *50-981*), extension of V. Tavolini off Calzaiouli.

Books in English

BM Libreria, *Borgo Ognissanti 4r*, behind Hotel Excelsior: **Paperback Exchange**, *V. Fiesolana 31r*, north of Santa Croce; **After Dark**, *V. del Moro 86r*, near Santa Maria Novella; **Seeber**, *V. Tornabuoni, 68r*.

Bus Lines

ATAF, city buses, at *P. Stazione 2r* (☎ *580-528*); purchase tickets in tabachi. LAZZI, *P. Stazione 4-6r* (☎ *215-154*) for excursions to Tuscan towns.

Car Rentals

Avis, *Borgo Ognissanti 128r* (☎ *213-629*); **Europcar**, *Borgo Ognissanti 53r* (☎ *294-130*); **Hertz**, *V. Finiguerra 33* (☎ *218-665*).

Consulates

U.S., *Lungarno Vespucci 38* (☎ *239-8276*); **British**, *Lungarno Corsini 2* (☎ *284-133*).

Emergency

Medical emergency 24-hours: ☎ *477-891*.

Groceries

Mercato Centrale, near P. San Lorenzo; in Oltrarno, at end of Borgo San Jacopo.

Italian Courses

Centro Dante Alighieri *(V. De'Bardi 12;* ☎ *284-955)* is among the many reputable ones.

Parking

Main piazzas on perimeter of *centro storico*, such as P. Carmine, P. Stazione, Fortezza da Basso. On weekends, try closer to center.

Police

Dial *113.*

Post Office

V. Pellicceria, near P. della Repubblica.

Shopping

V. Tornabuoni is the major fashion avenue; Via Maggio and Borgo Ognissanti for art galleries and antiques; streets around Ponte Vecchio for linens, gems, stone work, etc.

Swimming Pools

Amici dei Nuoti, indoors, *V. del Romito 38;* **Costoli** *(*☎ *675-744)* at Campo di Marte, northeast part of city; **Bellariva** *(*☎ *677-521)* Lungarno Colombo 2. Fees.

Taxi

Dial ☎ *4798* or *4390.*

Telephone

Telcom, in stazione, near track 5; at post office; and V. Cavour (8 a.m.–9:45 p.m.).

Tourist Office

Informazione, helpful office outside train station entrance; **APT**, *Cavour 1r (*☎ *290-832, FAX 276-0383)*, mornings Mon.–Sat., 8 a.m.–7 p.m.; **Informazione Alberghiere**, hotel bookings for a fee, in stazione near track 16.

Tours

CIT, *P. Stazione 51r and Cavour 54r (*☎ *294-306).* Official guides, *Viale Gramsci 9a (*☎ *247-8188).* **Agriturist**, *V. Pronconsolo 10 (*☎ *287-838)* for spring garden tours, fall farm tours.

Train

Stazione Centrale, near Santa Maria Novella (☎ *278-785* for information). Stazione Rifredi, 15 minutes from the center, for fast trains from Rome and Milan (connected by #19 bus with stazione centrale).

Florence

Siena

Key to Siena

Sights

Exquisite medieval city of Duccio and Simone Martini with deservedly famous duomo, palazzo pubblico and art museums.

Excursions

Easy half-day trips to Montalcino and Monte Oliveto Maggiore as well as to San Gimignano. Many other Tuscan towns an hour or less away, including Florence. An excellent sightseeing base for Tuscany (and even Umbria).

Nearby Waters

Grosseto (85 km, 53 mi.), the beach for Sienese families; Chianciano Terme (74 km, 46 mi.), a 1930s-style spa with mineral waters for both bathing and imbibing (for the liver).

Festivals and Events

The famous Palio, July 2 and August 16, offers one of the most authentic medieval pageants in Italy combined with a thrilling horse race; July and August bring concerts, both classical and jazz, sponsored by the Accademia Musicale Chigiana.

Accommodations

A good range, from deluxe relais to youth hostels and camping, but numbers are limited. Most facilities located on the edge of the walled city where driving and parking are easier.

Eating Out

Pleasant trattorie, a number with fine, if not alta, cucina. Local sweets of panforte and ricciarelli and Sienese wines of Brunello, Nobile and Vernaccia as well as Chianti.

Getting Around

Park your car and walk, or be forever lost and entangled in no-traffic, medieval lanes. Taxis permitted even on pedestrian streets for hotel arrivals with luggage. Bus service around walls to the city gates; orange minibuses (called *pollicini*) go to the center of the city from Porta Pispini, Porta Romana, Certosa, P. San Marco and P. San Agostino until 8:30 pm. Car rentals, buses and tour agencies available for excursions.

Arriving

Pullman buses provide most efficient service from Rome (about 3 hours) and Florence (1 hour) and to nearby Tuscan towns. Some trains from Pisa are direct, but most require a change and delays because Siena is off the main line.

A raccordo, or 4-lane highway, off the A-1 autostrada at Florence, leads to Siena, as does SS 326 off A-1 from Rome, but beautiful drives through the Chianti Valley or Val d'Elsa from Florence (via San Gimignano) make this area worthy of a rental car.

Siena

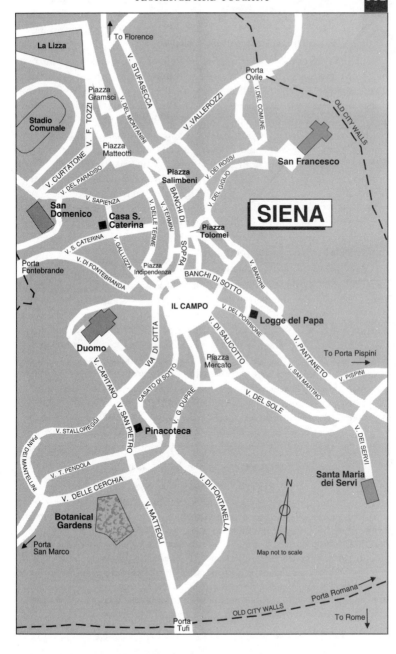

La Lizza

To Florence

Porta Ovile

V. STUFASECCA

V. DEL COMUNE

OLD CITY WALLS

Piazza Gramsci

Stadio Comunale

V. DEL MONTANINI

V. VALLEROZZI

V. CURTATONE

V. F. TOZZI

Piazza Matteotti

V. DEI ROSSI

San Francesco

V. DEL PARADISO

Piazza Salimbeni

V. DEL GIGLIO

SIENA

V. SAPIENZA

BANCHI DI

V. TERMINI

San Domenico

V. DELLE TERME

Casa S. Caterina

Piazza Tolomei

V. S. CATERINA

V. GALLUZZA

SOPRA

V. BANDINI

Porta Fontebrande

V. DI FONTEBRANDA

Piazza Indipendenza

BANCHI DI SOTTO

IL CAMPO

V. DEL PORRIONE

Logge del Papa

Duomo

VIA DI CITTA

V. DI SALICOTTO

V. PANTANETO

To Porta Pispini

VIA CITTA

Piazza Mercato

V. SAN MARTINO

V. PISPINI

V. CAPITANO

V. SAN PIETRO

CASATO DI SOTTO

V. G. DUPRE

V. DEL SOLE

V. STALLOREGGI

Pinacoteca

V. DEI SERVI

PIAN DEI MANTELLINI

V. T. PENDOLA

V. DELLE CERCHIA

V. DI FONTANELLA

N

Santa Maria dei Servi

Botanical Gardens

V. MATTEOLI

Map not to scale

Porta San Marco

Porta Romana

OLD CITY WALLS

To Rome

Porta Tufi

Siena

Special Tips

> Many restaurants and hotels do not accept credit cards. Reserve hotels in advance spring through fall, and many months in advance for the Palio.

Siena is a perfect medieval town. Its emblem of a wolf suckling twins may boast of the town's founding by ancient Rome, but its present appearance dates from the 13th and 14th centuries. Then Siena prospered as a financial center and vied with Florence for power, even defeating that city in battle. This period of Sienese glory produced an important school of Gothic art, founded on the elegant style of Duccio and his student Simone Martini. Sienese artists were in demand all over Tuscany and Umbria, and eventually their style evolved throughout Europe into the International Gothic. Such brilliance ended with the Black Death of 1348. Siena became more introverted and artistically conservative. Religious movements swept the town, led by the native Caterina Benincasa (who was to become patron saint of Italy) and the mystic Saint Bernardine. Siena never recovered from the devastation of the plague, and despite the talents of its artist Jacopo della Quercia, the Renaissance never really rooted here.

Today, the swirling streets lined with Gothic palazzi make Siena as lyrically beautiful as a Martini madonna. Within its still standing walls are powerful reminders of the elements of its medieval success—the church, the *comune* government, the banks, and, of course, the art. Siena has one of the great Tuscan cathedrals as well as great town halls. And on Piazza Salimbeni are the Gothic headquarters of Monte dei Paschi, the oldest bank in Europe, as well as the largest in Italy today. Everywhere are the paintings of the Sienese school, even on the covers of municipal registers, and their works are joined by those of other Tuscan sculptors, such as the Pisanos, Ghiberti and Donatello. Just in case the Medici coat of arms found on the town gates and the presence of the Medici fortress might suggest the defeat of independent Siena, such thoughts are banished twice each year in performances of the medieval Palio, an intense reaffirmation of the city's pride and former greatness.

What to See and Do

Piazza del Campo ★ ★ ★

One of the most beautiful plazas in the world, the Campo is intriguingly shaped like a shell (perhaps caused by the Roman ruins beneath it) and enclosed by gracefully curved, 14th-century buildings, the most notable being the Palazzo Pubblico. Set into its red brick and marble trimmed pavement is the **Fonte Gaia** (1419), a fountain carved by Jacopo della Quercia to celebrate the completion of the public water system in the city and now replaced by a reproduction. (The deteriorated original sculptures are in the top floor loggia of the Palazzo Pubblico.) From this center of the city radiate the major streets. At Palio time, Il Campo throbs with crowds and pageantry; at other times, people sit leisurely in the cafes or rush across the vast space as a short cut through the center of town. At all times, it is stunning.

Palazzo Pubblico ★★★

The pleasing facade of this town hall (1310) is complemented perfectly by the slender Torre del Mangia ("tower of the glutton"), its crown designed by Lippo Memmi in 1341 and named so incongruously after the vices of its first bell-ringer. At the base of the tower is the loggia-like chapel built in thanksgiving for the end of the Black Death that killed two-thirds of the populace. A comparison of this lovely town hall with the heavily stoned forcefulness of the Palazzo Vecchio sums up the artistic differences between Siena and its Florentine rival.

The interior is magnificently frescoed and carved by Sienese artists. Although the ground floor rooms that continue to function as offices for the municipal government are closed to the public, the upper story has been made into a museum and you can climb the several hundred steps of the tower for an exceptional ★ **view of Siena**. The most important **museum** works are found after the first few rooms and past the stairs to the upper loggia. You know you're near when you find the Sala di Balia painted with Spinello Aretino's naval battle (1408) and then enter the Sala dei Priori with murals dedicated to the life of the Sienese pope, Alexander III. Next comes the Sala di Cardinale with a marble-skinned *Madonna and Child* by Matteo di Giovanni (15th century; on left wall). From here you enter the ★ **chapel** with its every surface richly covered, from the frescoes of Taddeo di Bartolo (1407) to the choir stalls with inlaid wood scenes (1428). On the altar is a fine *Holy Family*, by Sodoma in the classical style, and surrounding the chapel is a lovely wrought-iron screen by della Quercia. A few steps away, you enter the **Sala di Mappamondo** where city officials deliberated between two famous frescoes attributed to Simone Martini, one offering them religious benediction, the other extolling Sienese military exploits. On the left is Simone's earliest known work, ★★ *La Maesta* (1315), that in its figural movement and illusion of space shows a strong shift away from Byzantine formalism. The graceful lines and patterns are pure Sienese Gothic; the great canopy unifying it all is Simone's genius. Across from the Maesta is ★ *Guidoriccio da Fogliano*, long thought to be the first equestrian portrait since antiquity, and now the subject of controversy. Some scholars believe this is not Simone's 1328 fresco of the condottiere, but rather a much later romanticized version. Whoever painted it left us an enchanting portrait of a medieval warlord parading on his horse. The **Sala della Pace** next door holds yet another Sienese masterpiece, Ambrogio Lorenzetti's ★★ *The Effects of Good Government* (1338), the first comprehensive landscape in the history of art. This delightful panorama leads you through a prosperous and peaceful Siena, rich with details of medieval life and surprisingly relaxed in composition for such an ambitious project. You're taken from the duomo through the streets and shops of town, with little pauses for a graceful composition of dancers and a realistic look at a shoemaker, and on through a town gate into the Tuscan countryside that looks much as it does today with its umbrella pines and cypresses, its rolling hills and its farmhouses. Accompanying this fresco is a deteriorated one of *Bad Government*, with Siena ravaged by robbers and war, and the *Allegory of Good Government*, showing the ruling council of the commune and their accompanying muses. In the final room are works of Sienese primitives, including a fine 13th-century *Madonna and Child* by Guido da Siena. *The museum is open daily 9:30 a.m.–6:15 p.m., except Sun. till 12:45 p.m.; mid-Nov. to mid-Mar. daily 9 a.m.–12:45 p.m.; L6000. The tower is open daily 10 a.m.–6 p.m., in winter till 1 p.m.; L5000.*

Nearby Sights

At *Banchi di Sotto 52*, is the fine Renaissance Palazzo Piccolomini, probably designed by Bernardo Rossellino and now housing the ★ **Archivo di Stato** *(9 a.m.– 12:45 p.m.; closed Sun.; free)*. These archives contain a public exhibit of the famous **tavolette di biccherna**, account books from 1268–1659, with wooden covers painted by such Sienese artists as Ambrogio Lorenzetti, Beccafumi and Sano di Pietro. Farther along Banchi di Sotto is a small piazza (to the right) with the **Logge del Papa** (1426), belonging to the Piccolomini, two of whom were popes. In the opposite direction, toward the duomo, the 15th-century international commercial tribunal, the **Loggia della Mercanzia**, marks the major pedestrian intersection where Banchi di Sopra joins Banchi di Sotto and its continuation around the outside of the Campo, Via di Citta. Along *Via di Citta*, you arrive at the handsome **Palazzo Chigiana** *(#89)*, a 14th-century building now home to a famous academy of music. Across the street are a number of notable palazzi, including another one belonging to the Piccolomini family and based on a Rosellini design *(at #126)*.

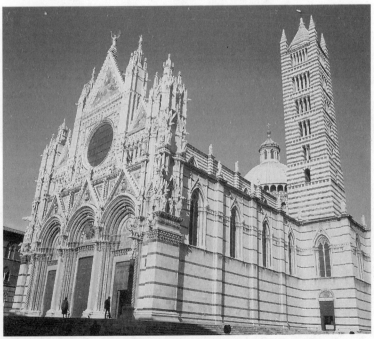

Sienna's duomo is noted for its interior sculptures as well as its facade.

Piazza del Duomo ★★★

Atop one of Siena's hills sits its fine Tuscan Gothic cathedral, so impressive and satisfying that it is hard to imagine the Sienese found it wanting. But they did, particularly after the duomo in Florence turned out to exceed theirs in size. At the apogee of Siena's power, it was decided that the church as we see it would become no more than a transept in a more grandiose cathedral. The Black Death of 1348 saved the Florentines from being outdone by the Sienese; construction stopped on the new duomo and all that remains of Siena's ambitious project is part of an aisle, now the Museo dell'Opera, and the towering facade called the *facciatone* (both outside the right transept).

Though not the largest church in Tuscany, the Siena duomo is particularly noteworthy for its sculpture, and in addition to its facade (now mostly copies) and interior sculptures, you can find a magnificent font in the baptistery, and other works (including the originals from the facade) in the Museo dell'Opera.

Duomo ★★★

Although the upper portion of the facade was fashioned after the successful one at Orvieto and the triangular paintings in the gables are 19th-century Venetian works, the ★ **lower facade** is distinguished by the design and sculpture of Giovanni Pisano (1284). The striped marble of the facade becomes even more remarkable in the **interior**, where its rich pattern covers the clustered columns converging on the altar and combines with masterful ★★ marble pavements and night sky- blue ceilings to create a dense, almost mysterious space. The pavements, designed from the late 14th to mid-16th century by many Sienese artists, especially Beccafumi, vary from simple ones of the prophets to elaborate ones such as Matteo di Giovanni's *Massacre of Innocents* (north transept). The oldest tablets, near the chancel, are covered except for a few weeks in August. In the **right transept** is the Bernini-designed Chapel of the Madonna del Voto, with two of the artist's sculptures flanking the door, ★ *St. Jerome* and *Mary Magdalene* (1661). The votive wall outside this chapel shows the veneration of the Sienese to its protectress, who has aided them against Nazi troops (1944) and Florentines (1260) alike. In the **chancel**, the inlaid woodwork of the ★ choir stalls dates from the 14th (on the sides) and 16th centuries; the stained glass window is by Duccio. At the **north transept** is the great octagonal ★★ pulpit (1268) by Nicola Pisano, who so masterfully fused ancient Roman narrative technique with the gracefulness of the Gothic style. Aided by his son Giovanni and Arnolfo di Campo, Nicola created a *Crucifixion* with a very human Christ and a powerful two-panelled relief of *The Last Judgment*, with a sculpture of God separating the panel of "the good," from a more dramatic one of "the damned." (Coin-operated illumination). Deeper into the north transept you find the Renaissance Chapel of St. John the Baptist with a ★ bronze statue of the suffering saint by Donatello in his late, expressive style. In the **north aisle** is the entrance to the ★ **Libreria Piccolomini**, pleasantly decorated with frescoes (1509) by the Umbrian Pintoricchio to house the beautiful hymnals collected by the famous Piccolomini pope, Pius II. Left of the entrance to the library is the Piccolomini altar, with four small, surprisingly lifeless statues by Michelangelo (1501–04). *The duomo is open 7:30 a.m.–5:00 p.m., except mid-Mar. to Nov. 1, when hours are 7:30 a.m.–7:30 p.m.*

Siena

The Piccolomini library is open 10 a.m.–1 p.m. and 2:30–5 p.m. in winter; in summer 9 a.m.–7:30 p.m.; L2000.

Museo dell'Opera del Duomo ★

Across from the south side of the duomo this museum displays some exceptional pieces from the cathedral's collection. Because it is housed in what remains of the never-completed "new duomo," it also provides access to the top of the facciatone with its ★ **view over Siena**. On the **ground floor** are some of the original ★ facade sculptures of prophets and symbolic animals by Giovanni Pisano. Animated stone, they are remarkable Gothic sculptures, even though seeing them at eye level probably distorts the manner in which they originally were intended to be seen. Also here is a bas relief ★ *Madonna and Child with Others* by Jacopo della Quercia. **Upstairs** is Duccio di Buoninsegna's ★★ *La Maesta*, (1308–11), once the high altar of the duomo. So respected was Duccio as a symbol of Sienese greatness, that when he completed this complex work, the entire town accompanied it in a procession from his workshop to the cathedral. The *Maesta*, despite its Italo-Byzantine formalism, shows Duccio's delicate patterning and jewel-like colors. The smaller panel paintings, particularly those of the Passion that used to form the rear of the altarpiece, display a more innovative Duccio, concerned with human emotion and the suggestion of space. These small, wonderful panels have led some Sienese to claim that Duccio, not Giotto, began the naturalism in art that would culminate in the Renaissance. Less controversial is the fact that the Sienese school evolved an early realistic style that can be seen in Pietro Lorenzetti's ★★ *Birth of the Virgin* (1342) found in the same room. On the **next floor** is the treasury that includes a wooden crucifix by G. Pisano. Up a few more steps, you find the panel painting *Madonna with Large Eyes*, the 13th-century, anonymous altarpiece from the duomo. Here, too, is the entrance to the **facciatone**, not a bad climb for the view. *Open 9 a.m.–7:30 p.m. mid-Mar.–Sept. 30; till 6 p.m. in Oct.; 9 a.m.–1 p.m. rest of year. L7000.*

Baptistery ★

Follow the outside of the duomo past the right transept, then go through a magnificent Gothic arch, and down steps to the separate entrance to the richly frescoed (1325) baptistery. The Early Renaissance ★★ **baptismal font** designed by della Quercia is most famous for its gilded bronze bas reliefs of the *Life of St. John the Baptist*. While Ghiberti's reliefs (*Arrest of the Saint, and* ★ *Baptism of Christ*) and della Quercia's *Annunciation to Zacharias* are more than of interest, it is Donatello's seminal ★★ *Feast of Herod* (1425) that is the most stunning. Not only may this relief be the first coherent example of vanishing point perspective, but its dramatic narrative technique (freezing the shocked reactions of the merrymakers upon the arrival of the Baptist's severed head) also had immense influence, even, according to art historian Frederick Hartt, on Leonardo's *Last Supper*. (Light machine to right of door). *Open 9:30 a.m.–1 p.m., 3–5 p.m., mid Mar.–Sept. 9:30 a.m.–7 p.m. and Oct. till 6 p.m.*

Pinacoteca ★★

Where Via del Capitano from the duomo intersects with Via di Citta coming from the Campo, you follow the continuation of Capitano called "San Pietro" until you find, on your left, this collection of Sienese paintings, housed in a 14th-century palace. Although the usual chronological arrangement here may be disrupted by renovations, you usually begin your tour on the second *piano* and to the right. A number of Duccio's paintings, including two ★ *Madonna with Child and Saints* and the *Madonna dei Francescani*, are preceded and followed by works in the flat, Italo-Byzantine style that, as fine as they are (especially those by Guido da Siena and Ugolino di Nero), certainly make Duccio's stand out as exceptional. The next rooms include works by the Gothic masters: the poetic Simone Martini (★ *Il Beato Agostino Novello* surrounded by four charming depictions of his miracles and ★ *Madonna and Child*); the more Giotto-like and dynamic Pietro Lorenzetti (★ *Madonna Enthroned*, ★ *Crucifixion*, ★ *Deposition* and others); and the softer Ambrogio Lorenzetti, fascinated by subjects unconventional for his time (★ *Madonna and Child* with St. Dorothy holding a lovely bouquet, two small experimental landscapes [c. 1325]—among the first since antiquity—and others). After these rooms the Sienese school continues the rich, elegant surfaces of its predecessors, but after a bit becomes too rich for many visitors—though Taddeo di Bartolo's *Crucifixion* and Barto di Fredi's *Adoration of the Magi* are among the many other works of interest. A bit more perspective finds its way into the paintings of Giovanni di Paolo, Matteo di Giovanni and the too-prolific Sano di Piero, yet the Gothic (and even Byzantine) style continue right through the quattrocento, finally emerging around the 16th century in the High Renaissance classicizing of Sodoma and the more Manneristic Beccafumi (both exhibited on the first *piano*). *Open 8:30 a.m.- 1:30 p.m., except Sun. and in winter 8 a.m.–1 p.m.; closed Mon.; L8000.*

Other Sights

A good deal of the pleasure of a Siena visit comes simply from strolling its streets as they wind past the arched entrances into once fortified *contrade*, or neighborhoods, areas still defined by their own fountains and churches, their own flags so ever present as the Palio draws near. They provide sudden views over the duomo or out into the inviting Tuscan countryside. Each of the following sights is a excuse for strolling.

San Domenico Church

On the northwestern edge of the centro storico, the massive unadorned brick walls of this Gothic church dominate the neighborhood below, where St. Catherine was born. *(Her home, now made into chapels, is open to the public.)* Here in San Domenico, she experienced many of her visions. Much of the art, including 16th-century frescoes by Sodoma (flanking the altar), is devoted to her life. Outside there is a superb ★ **view of the duomo**. From here, you can descend to **Casa S. Caterina** *(Costa S. Antonio; closed 12:30-3:30 p.m.)* through narrow streets to the duomo—one of Siena's most picturesque routes and one never more beautiful than at night when the churches are illuminated. Or you can walk several blocks along Via Curtatone to **La Lizza** park. Through La Lizza is the **Medici Fortress**, itself now a park and with a view of Siena's surroundings. To reach San Domenico from the Campo, climb the fashionable main street of Banchi di Sopra past the Piazza Tolomei, with its fortified palace (after 1267), and past the distinguished Piazza Salimbeni, to the top of the hill and the Piazza Matteotti.

Siena

San Francesco Church

Turning on Via del Moro next to the church on Piazza Tolomei takes you meandering through narrow streets that, if they don't get you lost, eventually lead you to the Piazza San Francesco. Here the city opens up to views of the countryside. And the cavernous interior of the San Francesco church, rebuilt after WWII bombing, provides a fresco of the crucifixion by Pietro Lorenzetti (first chapel left of altar). To the right of the church is an **oratorio** marking where St. Bernardine once preached. *Closed 1–4 p.m.*

Santa Maria dei Servi Church   ★

A brief walk begins along Via Salicotto, running out of the Campo from the left side of the Palazzo Pubblico. This street travels through the Torre contrada, passing its emblematic elephant fountain so scenically located, before approaching Via dei Servi. The walk continues on Servi through the ram contrada, and comes to the neighborhood park fronting Santa Maria dei Servi. From the steps of the church are good views over Siena; inside is Sienese art worth the walk. The second chapel, right aisle, contains the ★ *Madonna del Bordone* (1261) by Coppo di Marcovaldo (perhaps painted in exchange for that Florentine's release as a political prisoner) that was repainted in the Duccio style. In the right transept is a gloriously Byzantine ★ **chapel,** decorated with a 14th-century crucifix. The second chapel to the right of the high altar is painted with P. Lorenzetti's dramatic ★ *Massacre of the Innocents*, a daringly expressive work for the 14th century. The second chapel to the left of the altar contains his frescoes on St. John the Baptist with an interesting *Feast of Herod*. *Closed 1–4 p.m.*

Festivals: The Palio

Twice each year, Siena explodes with the color and excitement of the Palio. The most authentic medieval *festa* in all of Italy, the Palio dates back at least to the 13th century, when the town celebrated a victory over Florence with a wild horse race through town. In its present form, the Palio dates to the 16th century, when the Sienese decided to re-create life as it was before their defeat by Charles V and his Florentine allies, the Medici. Today, the 17 *contrade*, or neighborhoods—themselves legally constituted since the 12th century—continue this tradition twice each year on two feast days of the Virgin: July 2 and August 16. These two days represent the culmination of year-long Machiavellian plotting to win the *palio* (the banner given to the victor of the race) or, at the very least, to guarantee that one's enemy contrada loses, since only 10 contrade can participate in each Palio. On a more cosmic level, each contrada must outwit the forces of fate (the horses are assigned by lottery) and cunning (the non-Sienese jockeys, hired for their daring, ride bareback, and are viewed as untrustworthy mercenaries). The weeks before each Palio, the preparations intensify with trial races in the Campo, and flag-waving marches through town, and street festivals to earn money for Palio participation—maybe even to bribe the enemy's jockey. By the day of the Palio, Siena bristles with anticipation. Silk banners hang from the mullioned windows of its palazzi, contrade are brilliantly costumed to march in the historical procession accompanied by their flag-throwing pages. And everyone awaits the crazy, freewheeling race around the tortuous course of the Campo. Siena is never lovelier than on that night: torches illuminate the roofs of the palazzi,

Siena

the streets are filled with joyous participants, and those fortunate enough to find the victory banquet in the streets of the winning neighborhood will find the horse given the place of honor at the head of the table in night-long celebrations. The ideal way to witness the Palio is to begin at the duomo with the historical procession and then to follow the procession into the Campo, making a dash for a spot in the center. Sometimes, however, no spots are left, so that a more cautious approach is to grab your standing room by 4 p.m., when the police close off the Campo (save the one street—to right of palazzo pubblico—used by the historical procession). Or, if you're willing to pay a hefty price, buy tickets for the stands in front of the surrounding palazzi. (Contact tourist information *in early spring for a list of those selling seats.* ☎ *42-409, FAX 281-041*) The historical procession enters the Campo around 5:30 p.m. and is followed by the race two hours later on July 2; events begin about a half-hour earlier in August. A listing of Palio events can be obtained from the tourist office. If you plan to overnight in Siena, reserve your hotel room by March.

Where to Stay

Selvatellino Villa in Siena rents studios and apartments.

Many of the best hotels are a mile or so outside of town, linked by bus and taxi to the center. Most hotels are found on the edge of the *centro storico*, but within walking distance of the Campo. There are a few recommendable central hotels, though most are basic pensioni. If you are arriving by car and select a hotel within the walled town (most traffic banned, but hotel access permitted), you may find the winding medieval streets confusing, not to say frustrating. To help, we mention in our descriptions of the hotels the entrance to the city that gives easiest access. If you get confused nonetheless, just park your car and leave the baggage delivery to a taxi.

Although hotels clearly are not plentiful enough to meet demand during the tourist season, there is something for most tastes and budgets. Even the **Guidoriccio youth hostel** (☎ *52-212; take #15 bus*) and the **Colleverde Campground** with pool *(Strada di Scacciapensieri 47;* ☎ *280-044; Apr.–Nov. 10; take #8 bus)* are unusually fine budget options. If you haven't made a reservation well in advance for the season from April through October, check the hotel services of the tourist information booth in P. San Domenico. Unless otherwise stated, hotels are air-conditioned. For information on renting Italian villas or apartments contact **Italian Villas** ☎ *(206) 413-1343* or **The Parker Company** ☎ *(800) 280-2811, (617) 596-8282.*

Very Expensive

Certosa di Maggiano   L400–850,000

Strada di Certosa 82; ☎ *288-180; FAX 288-189.*
Single L400,000. Double L550–850,000.
Just over a mile outside Porta Romana in the Tuscan countryside, this exquisite Relais et Châteaux inn occupies a 14th-century renovated Carthusian monastery. The tranquil setting, with views of Siena and its famous towers in the distance, must have greatly facilitated the monks in their meditations. The library and sitting areas are furnished with fine antiques; the 14 units are far from cell-like; most are generous suites, all are well-appointed with modern comforts. Bus and taxi access to center. Excellent service. Good restaurant. Pool. Tennis. Garage.

Expensive

Park   L350–440,000

Via di Marciano 18; ☎ *44-803; FAX 49-020.*
Single L350,000. Double L440,000.
Commanding a hill and views two km north of the centro storico, this grand and formal hotel was designed as a private villa by the famous Renaissance architect, Baldassarre Peruzzi. The majestic common areas (including a 17th-century family chapel; a bar with baronial fireplace) have been decorated to the period with antique tapestries and paintings. The 70 rooms vary from traditional decor to sleekly modern; some are in new wings, some have views, all are sumptuously decorated, none is enormous. Polished service. Fine restaurants. Vast terraces and gardens; pool, tennis.

Villa Scacciapensieri   L200–380,000 CP   ❀★★★

Via di Scacciapensieri 10; ☎ *41-441; FAX 270-854.*
Single L200,000 CP. Double L200–380,000 CP.

An 18th-century villa with beautiful gardens and views and a relaxing ambience. Although in the hills above the stazione, the center (two km away) is reached easily by bus. The original villa retains its old-fashioned ambience despite a complete modernization: the reading room/lounge is inviting with a huge fireplace and the dining room is filled with light (although most dining is *al fresco*, weather permitting); the rooms have painted viga ceilings, hardwood floors and scalloped curtains. Other rooms in the gardens are of different vintage; all are large and comfortable; the few with showers but not baths are a bargain (moderate). Gracious service. Garden pool. Tennis. Parking. *Closed Jan.–Mar. 15.*

Jolly Hotel Excelsior   **L250–400,000 CP**   ★★★

Piazza La Lizza; ☎ *288-448; FAX 41-272.*
Single L250,000 CP. Double L250–400,000 CP.

Without the ambience or beauty of the previous hotels, this modern Jolly hotel offers a convenient location. The 126 units vary in size, only the larger ones are worth the price; those in the back are quieter. The lobby bustles. Restaurant. Bar.

Moderate

Palazzo Ravizza   **L155–200,000 CP**   ✿★★

Pian dei Mantellini 34; ☎ *280-462; FAX 271-370.*
Single L155,000 CP. Double L200,000.

This very atmospheric 17th-century private palazzo is located only a few blocks from the duomo, in the heart of the centro storico. Common rooms include ceiling frescoes and fine antiques, and there is a music room with a grand piano. Many of the 30 old-fashioned rooms open to a prized terrace and garden; most have private baths (those without are cheaper than the listed rates), many are very spacious; none have a/c. Still run by the original family, the Ravizza is more like a pensione than a hotel, and during the tourist season meal plans are required making it overpriced. In the off-season, it's a good buy. Limited parking. Reserve well in advance. Enter town by Porta San Marco.

Duomo   **L130–200,000 CP**   ★★

Via Stalloreggi 38; ☎ *289-088; FAX 43-043.*
Single L130,000 CP. Double L200,000 CP.

Slightly pricey (and with a car you'll have to pay for public parking), but worth it if you can reserve one of the rooms with a view of the hills and duomo (only two blocks away). Nothing fancy, the hotel is well-maintained with 22 modern rooms. Breakfast room. Enter by Porta San Marco.

Inexpensive

Il Giardino   **L95–150,000 CP**   √★★

Via B. Peruzzi 43; ☎ *285-290; FAX 221-197.*
Single L95,000 CP. Double L150,000 CP.

What a buy! Outside the walls near the Porta Pispina, this hotel has only a few rooms (7, all ample and modern) but a large terrace with stunning Tuscan views and a large pool. Decent restaurant. Free parking.

Antica Torre   **L80–120,000**   ★★

V. di Fieravecchia 7; ☎ *284-397; FAX 222-255.*

Single L80,000. Double L120,000.

Just off Via Pantaneto in the historic center, this tiny 15th-century tower has four floors (no elevator) with two pleasant rooms on each, one with panoramic views, all with nice touches like lace curtains; functional if small baths. Breakfast room. Public parking. Enter Porta Romana.

Chiusarelli   **L85–120,000**   ★★

Via Curtatone 9; ☎ *280-562; FAX 271-177.*
Single L85,000. Double L120,000.

On the edge of old Siena, between San Domenico and the Jolly Hotel, the Chiusarelli has a very convenient location. The rambling, renovated mansion has a living room-style lobby with a terrace overlooking the park grounds of the *stadio.* The 50 rooms vary in size, but all are immaculate and modernized, none with a/c, and a few cheapies without bath. Those in the back are quieter. Pleasant service. A good buy. Restaurant. Bar. Limited parking.

Alex   **L130,000 CP**   ★

Via G. Gigli 5; ☎ *282-338.*
Single/double L130,000 CP.

Clean and convenient, the modern Alex is just a block from the Porta Pispini. From its crossroads position, the hotel opens in the back to the countryside. Kindly owner oversees the eight rooms, each ample and sunny (small baths but with hair dryers no less); two units opening to street have air conditioning. Parking (free).

Where to Eat

Siena is quite traditional in its preparation of Tuscan food. Judging from its sole contributions to that cuisine, it seems to have a taste for rich sweets as well as for the frugal *fagioli all'uccelletto.* Sienese *panforte* is a Christmas treat throughout Tuscany, but this dense fruitcake with almonds, particularly good when flavored with chocolate, is available all year. *Ricciarelli* are oval-shaped little cakes, full of almond paste and dusted with powdered sugar. When fresh and not yet too hard, they are nice and chewy. Even if Siena has not contributed more substantial fare to Tuscan cuisine, the province is the heart of the wine country and produces white Vernaccios and ruby red Chianti to the north, as well as Brunello and Nobile reds to the south.

Fine Cuisine

An hour of south of Siena are two exceptional country restaurants each well-worth a dining excursion: **La Chiusa** (see "Montepulciano") and **Poggio Antico** (see "Montalcino").

Antica Hosteria Cane e Gatto   **$$–$$$**   ★★★★

V. Pagliaresi 6; reserve for lunch ☎ *220-751*
closed Thurs., part Jan. Fixed-price meal L50–70,000.

Our favorite in-town restaurant is on the Via di Pantaneto, an extension of Banchi di Sotto. Intimate and unpretentious, the owner/chef prepares a daily menu degustazione with quite a number of courses, each with a few satisfying choices. When available, the pennetto in walnut cream sauce or the fiochi with sage are wonderful, but then all the pastas here are delicate. The entrées can be exceptional, such

Siena

as any preparation of tagliata di vitello and the grilled beef with porcini. The wines are local and delightful.

Antica Trattoria Botteganova $$–$$$ ★★★
Strada Chiantigiana 29; reserve at ☎ 284-230
Closed Mon. at lunch, Sun., early Jan., early Aug. Meals L55–90,000.
About ten minutes from the center of town, this restaurant offers a touch of elegance to the traditional Tuscan food, be it ribollita or steak fiorentina.

Trattorias

Osteria Le Logge $–$$ ★★★
V. del Porrione 33; ☎ 48-013.
Closed Sun.; reservation recommended. Meals L35–55,000.
Casual and tolerant of light eating (and ordering) is this handsome restaurant. In good weather you may find yourself eating outside, just a few steps from the Campo. Although the menu changes often, the choices always are tempting, from the antipasti and pasta (particularly the house penne or the papparadelle with sausage), to a main dish of crisp duck a l'orange or delicious salmon carpaccio.

Da Mugolone $–$$ ★★
V. Pellegrini; ☎ 283-235.
Closed Thurs., late July. Meals L40–55,000.
Another attractive restaurant in the centro storico, a bit more formal than Le Logge and serving more traditional Tuscan fare along with a few fish dishes including pappardelle with salmon.

Da Enza $–$$ ★★
10 km, 6 mi. south on the Grosseto road; ☎ 342-040.
Closed Tues. L30–50,000.
Outside of Siena, this trattoria is a favorite family dining spot Sunday afternoons. The portions of the home-cooked food are ample, the daily fresh pasta and the superb arrosto misto (mixed grill of rabbit, pheasant, etc.) are justifiably sought after.

Pizza and Salads

Da Carlo e Franca $ ★★
V. di Pantaneto 138 at Pispini.
Closed Wed. Pizza L6–10,000.
A terrific neighborhood pizzeria! If the wait for tables is too long, you may never get a chance to try the whole pizza (the boscaiolo with sausage, garlic and mushrooms is delicious). But in the late afternoon and evening, you can always pick up their heartier, thicker pizza-by-the-slice.

Da Roberto $ ★
V. Calzoleria 26; ☎ 285-080.
Closed Tues. Pizza L10–15,000.
This trattoria has a romantic ambience with cozy indoor tables and, in the evening, outdoor ones. The wood-oven pizza is good, but avoid the watery wine and seafood.

Siena

Ristorante e Pizzeria   **$**   ★

V. Citta 20. Individual dishes L8–15,000.

Convenient for the tired sightseer, you can drop by at this upscale tavola calda for a variety of salads and vegetable plates.

Snacks and Picnics

Caffe Nanini *(Banchi di Sopra 99)* is where you must go, with all the Sienese, for your ice cream. **Pomo Oro** *(P. Indipendenza)* has *frulatti,* refreshing blended drinks of fruits and ice, as well as other light snacks. For picnicking, you might go to the Medici fort or join everyone eating right in the center of the Campo. The shops listed in the directory can provide you with excellent cheeses and cold cuts, and **Roticerria Monti** *(V. Calzoleria 12; closed Fri.)* sells spit-roasted chickens, arista, bean soup, panini and roasted chickens to go *(portare via).* In the Medici fort at the top of town is the **Enoteca Italia Permanente** *(3 p.m.–midnight, daily),* the national enoteca with an immense selection of wines and a terrace for tastings.

Directory

Telephone Code 0577   **Postal Code 53100**

Airport

In Pisa, a 2-hour drive.

Books in English

Feltrinelli, *Banchi di Sopra 66;* **Messaggerie Bassi**, *V. Citta 4.*

Bus

TRA-IN, P. Gramsci, near La Lizza park, for local buses (buy tickets at office or tabacchi); **LAZZI/SITA** *(☎ 204-245),* next to San Domenico church, pullmans to Rome *(P. della Repubblica;* ☎ *06-47941 in Rome),* Florence, S. Gimignano, and other Tuscan towns and villages.

Car Rentals

Hertz *(☎ 4-11-48);* others listed at tourist office.

Emergencies

☎ *113.*

Groceries

Saturday morning market behind Palazzo Pubblico; **Salumeria**, *V. di Citta 95;* **Pizzicheria Morbidi**, *Banchi di Sotto 27;* **Forno**, *P. Indipendenza,* makes good breads as well as their own panforte and ricciarelli.

Italian Courses

University of Siena, **Scuola di Lingua Italiana per Stranieri**, *Piazzetta Grassi 46* *(☎ 280-695)* has a famous summer language program July/August. The respected **Centro Linguistico Dante Alighieri** *(P. La Lizza 10)* offers 3-week intensive programs year-round.

Parking

Stadio Comunale, near San Domenico and La Lizza, is best bet (fee).

Post Office

Piazza Matteotti 37.

Shopping

Best antique and crafts shops (a few open Sundays) cluster on V. di Citta near Accademia Chigiana, and near the baptistry of duomo. Outdoor clothing market Wednesdays 8 a.m.–1 p.m., La Lizza.

Swimming Pools

Large outdoor pool at Colleverde Camping, 10 minutes from center. Outdoor pool in magnificent setting at Le Soline Camping (☎ *817-410)*, 18 km, 11 mi. south on Grosseto road in Murlo near Casciano. Fee for both; summer only.

Taxis

P. Matteotti and stazione; radio taxi, ☎ *49-222.* Service till 9 p.m. except summers till 11 p.m.

Telephone

Telcom, *V. dei Termini 40*

Tourist Office

APT, *Piazza del Campo 56* (☎ *280-551, FAX 270-676)*; in winter 8:30 a.m.–1 p.m., 3:30–5:30 p.m., Sat. 8:30 a.m.–1 p.m. only, closed Sun.; in summer, 8:30 a.m.–7:30 p.m., closed Sun.; kiosk on P. San Domenico books hotels *(288-084, FAX 280-290)* for fee (L3000).

Train

Stazione, *(☎ 280-115)* about 2 km north of center. Bus and taxi connections.

Pisa

Key to Pisa

Sights

Not just the Leaning Tower, but also the duomo and baptistery, masterpieces of Tuscan architecture; and the sculpture and two pulpits by the Pisanos.

Excursions

Easy visits to Lucca, Volterra, and other sights on the way to Florence and Siena.

Nearby Beaches

Only silting separates Pisa from the sea, so beaches are close, the most elegant at Viareggio, less than a half-hour by A-12.

Festivals

June festivities for patron San Ranieri with costumed processions and candlelight events on and around the Arno. Every four years, in June, the Old Republics Maritime Regatta celebrated with Venice, Genoa and Amalfi.

Accommodations

Decent selection, centered near P. del Duomo and P. della Stazione.

Pisa

Eating Out

Plenty of fine choices for Tuscan specialties, with a focus on seafood.

Getting Around

Major sights cluster in Piazza del Duomo, connected to the train station by taxi or bus (#1 or #3). The center, from the duomo to the train station, can be walked in under one-half hour.

Arriving

A very accessible city with the only major airport in Tuscany for both domestic and international flights. Autostrada connections, buses, and a train stop on the Genoa-Rome line as well as with train service to Lucca and Florence.

For centuries, Pisa was a port. It was a port for the Romans, and then it was a port for itself, one of the earliest maritime republics in Europe. In the 11th century, Pisa and Genoa joined their fleets to free the Tyrrhenian sea of Moslem pirates. In the process, Pisa conquered Sardinia, defeated Palermo and cities in Africa, and through the crusades, made itself wealthy off trade from Provence to Syria. The result was a glorious cathedral that created the Tuscan Romanesque style with its exotic stripes of marble, and a precocious humanism that would lead to the full-blown naturalism of the Renaissance through the sculptors Nicola Pisano and his son, Giovanni. Then Pisa's few centuries of glory were over. Genoa destroyed its fleet (1284). Silting destroyed its harbor. And Florence, conquering all in its path to the sea along the Arno, finally conquered Pisa after a nasty siege (1406). By the 16th century, Pisa was a university town, home to Galileo but no longer a maritime power.

What to See and Do

Piazza del Duomo ★★★

Since traffic has been banned, this huge, park-like complex with its mowed lawns seems isolated from the fabric of the city, making the medieval monuments more Disneyland than real. And the Leaning Tower, or *campanile*, does little to dispel the first impression, since it remains unbelievable no matter how many times seen. Of course, this is the real thing, despite its being called "Piazza dei Miracoli," place of wonders. It is wonderfully Italian in its trinity of separate church, campanile, and baptistery, and it is perfectly Tuscan Romanesque in its profusion of facade arcades and sculpture, in its rich inlays of colored marble. Joining the duomo complex is the camposanto with its frescoes, and two museums, but the most important indoor works are the Pisano pulpits, one in the duomo, the other in the baptistery.

Pisa

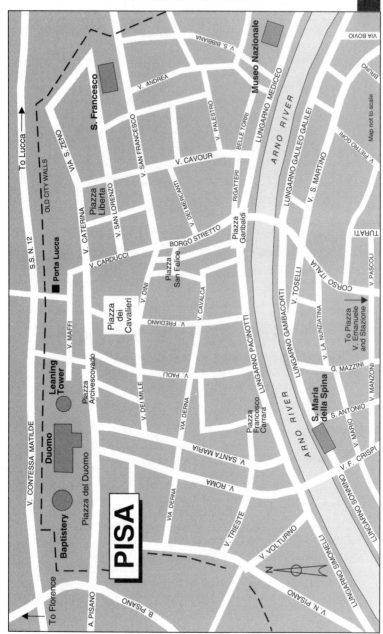

PISA

To Lucca →

OLD CITY WALLS

S.S. N. 12

Porta Lucca

V. MAFFI

V. CATERINA

VIA S. ZENO

S. Francesco

V. ANDREA

V. S. BIBBIANA

Museo Nazionale

VIA BOVIO

BRUNO

V. PIETRO GORI

Map not to scale

LUNGARNO MEDICEO

ARNO RIVER

V. PALESTRO

V. SAN FRANCESCO

V. CAVOUR

BELLE TORRI

RIGATTERI

LUNGARNO GALILEO GALILEI

V. S. MARTINO

Piazza Liberta

V. SAN LORENZO

V. DEI MERCANTI

BORGO STRETTO

Piazza Garibaldi

TURATI

V. CARDUCCI

Piazza San Felice

V. DINI

V. FREDIANO

V. CAVALCA

CORSO ITALIA

V. TOSELLI

V. PASCOLI

Piazza dei Cavalieri

LUNGARNO GAMBACORTI

LUNGARNO PACINOTTI

V. LA NUNZIATINA

To Piazza V. Emanuele and Stazione

V. PAOLI

G. MAZZINI

V. DEI MILLE

VIA DERNA

Piazza Francesco Carrara

ARNO RIVER

S. Maria della Spina

S. ANTONIO

V. MANZONI

Leaning Tower

Piazza Arcivescovado

V. SANTA MARIA

V. MARIO

V. CONTESSA MATILDE

Duomo

Piazza del Duomo

V. ROMA

VIA DERNA

V. F. CRISPI

Baptistery

To Florence

A. PISANO

B. PISANO

V. TRIESTE

V. VOLTURNO

LUNGARNO SIMONELLI

V. N. PISANO

N

Pisa

Visiting Schedules

The exterior of the buildings can be seen at any time of the day, and at night they are softly illuminated so that the white marble itself seems to glow. The hours for entering the buildings are, of course, more restricted. Between September and Easter, the visiting hours vary according to demand as well as the amount of daylight, but they invariably are shorter than during the peak tourist season. Check the current schedule upon your arrival at either the tourist office or in front of the Museo delle Sinopie.

Below are the two extremes for visiting, the most generous schedule of peak season and the most limited one for January.

Duomo • *10:45 a.m.–5:40 p.m.; in January, 10:45 a.m.–12:45 p.m., 3–4:45 p.m.*

Baptistery • *9 a.m.–5:40 p.m., in January, 9 a.m.–4:40 p.m.*

Camposanto • *9 a.m.–5:40 p.m.; in January, 9 a.m.–4:40 p.m.*

Tower • *Closed indefinitely.*

Museo delle Sinopie • *8 a.m.–7:40 p.m.; in January, 9 a.m.–12:40 p.m., 3:40–4:40 p.m.*

Museo del Duomo • *8 a.m.–5:20 p.m.; in January, 9 a.m.–12:30 p.m., 3–4:30 p.m.*

Admission Fees

Admission to the duomo is L2000 (except for Mass at 8 a.m. & 10 a.m.). All other monuments cost L6000. All-inclusive tickets are a bargain at L15,000. The duomo plus only three other monuments is L12,000. Tickets and details are available at the Museo delle Sinopie.

Leaning Tower   ★★★

So startling, so off the perpendicular (by over 16 feet), it is hard to notice what a fine *campanile*, or *bell tower*, this is. Just to the east of the duomo, the tower rises in repeated arcades, each one a different height to add interest, until it reaches nearly 180 feet. Hardly had the tower been started in 1173 when it started sinking. Each subsequent architect tried to correct the problem, but it continues, and even accelerated in 1992. Galileo climbed the tower for experiments that led to his principle that objects of different weights fall with equal velocity. More than 700,000 people used to climb the more than two hundred steps each year for the view, or simply for the odd, somewhat frightening, sensation of walking down the unrailed outside ramps, leaning with the tower. But, since 1990, the tower has been closed. A counterweight, installed at the base in 1993, seems to be successfully, if minutely, reversing the tilt and it is possible the tower will soon be open to a limited number of visitors.

The main facade of Pisa's duomo contains floriated columns and sculptures.

Duomo   ★★

Entrance through south transept in winter.

The church that created the style called "Pisan" was begun in 1063 and consecrated by 1118. The wonderful main facade with its floriated columns and sculptures of beasts inspired by crusades to the East, has later bronze doors from the school of Giambologna, added during the extensive renovations needed after a fire in 1595. Around the side, to the south transept facing the Leaning Tower, are Bonnano da Pisa's ★ bronze doors (1180), with scenes from the Life of Christ done in that artist's most refined style. The church **interior** is vast. Double columns, crowned with 11th-century capitals, divide the aisles. Gray and white marble patterns add solemnity. Though the dimness of the chancel makes it difficult to see the art, Giambologna's balustrade angels can be appreciated as well as Cimabue's ★ *mosaic* (1302) in the vault. Under the cupola is Giovanni Pisano's ★★ *pulpit* (1302–10), with its scenes from the lives of Christ and St. John the Baptist. Though more Gothic in his interpretation, Giovanni still followed his father's classicism, as can be seen in the deep relief of the panels and the nude figures of the *Fortitude caryatid* (more introspective than heroic, however) and *Prudence* (more virgin than Venus). The relief panels are most remarkable for their naturalism (note the landscape in the *Nativity*) and the expressive movement that unifies the individual figures (note the crowd of the *Crucifixion*, the horror of the damned in the *Last Judgment*).

Baptistery   ★

West of the duomo is the baptistery.

Although begun in 1152, the somewhat gingerbread aspect of this circular building results from 14th-century additions. However, Nicola and Giovanni Pisano made some modifications in the 13th century, including the main portal (facing the duomo; the original sculptures by Giovanni are in the Museo del Duomo). The crusades influenced the interior, which is based on the Holy Sepulchre in Jerusalem, its font elaborated with Moorish filigree. Pisa's victories also influenced Nicola Pisano's ★ ★ *pulpit* (1260), carved in the heroic style of antiquity over a century and a half before the official beginnings of the Renaissance. The figure in the round of *Fortitude* basks in its nudity. The New Testament reliefs show a *Last Judgment* like a Roman battle scene, the *Nativity* a reclining virgin as ancient as an Etruscan sarcophagus.

Camposanto

On the north side of the grassy piazza is the marble *camposanto*, or cemetery (begun 1278), built like a cloister and said to be filled with earth from the Holy Land. The rooms around this tranquil garden, surrounded by delicately traced windows, once were marvelously frescoed. But WWII bombings did terrible damage, though some of the paintings have been partially restored. Arranged along the corridors are Roman sarcophagi and sculptures, some studied by Nicola Pisano. At the left end, you see some old chains from the former harbor of Pisa and then enter a chapel in the northwest corner. Here are some of the best preserved frescoes, all dating from the late 14th century after the Black Death of 1348 had devastated Tuscany; ★ *Trionfo della Morte* (1350) captures this period with a nightmarish inferno in the Last Judgment scene.

Museo delle Sinopie

On the south side of the piazza is the medieval hospital now converted into a museum housing the sinopie, or underfresco drawings that have been removed from the Camposanto. When the frescoes were detached for restoration, these drawings were revealed and preserved. In some instances, such as Benozzo Gozzoli's work, they are the best way to understand what has been lost in the damaged frescoes.

Museo del Duomo   ★

Just east of the Leaning Tower and next to the tourist office on Piazza Arcivescovado is this handsome museum, opened in 1986 in a renovated medieval convent. Exhibited here are Giovanni Pisano's baptistery facade sculptures (room 5) and his famous ivory ★ *Madonna* from the duomo treasury (room 9). In fact, just about anything from the Piazza dei Miracoli no longer in use is preserved here and finely displayed, even Roman busts and marble mosaics from the duomo facade. The ground floor exhibits are especially intriguing with their loot brought back from Eastern battles, with Romanesque capitals by the early master Guglielmo, and with numerous Pisano school sculptures.

Around the Arno

A walk from the duomo to the Arno river can be very pleasant, mostly free of traffic and through the historic part of town. It's also not very time-consuming, as the walk can be forced into 15 minutes or so. Across the Arno, the Corso Italia, *the* spot for an evening *passeggiato*, leads through the more modern section of downtown, and in another ten minutes takes you to the grand Piazza Vittorio Emanuele and then on to the stazione. During the day, there are a few sights to see, a good museum, the scenic river; and both day and night this is the area to find the Pisans busily shopping, either at the food market off Piazza Garibaldi or at the smart shops in the tiny lanes intersecting Borgo Stretto.

The best walk begins by following Via Santa Maria out of the Piazza del Duomo. In a few blocks turn left at Piazza Cavalotti and continue on Via dei Mille to the striking 16th-century **Piazza dei Cavalieri**. Vasari carries much of the responsibility for the appearance of the square, from the church built according to his design to the Palazzo dei Cavalieri (left of church), as well as the palazzo covered with murals at #3. Via Dini leads out of this piazza and joins the historic street, Borgo Stretto, that leads past shops to the Piazza Garibaldi at the Arno river. Here you continue to the Corso Italia by crossing the Ponte di Mezzo, but it's best to turn left on the Lungarno Mediceo and visit the ★ **Museo Nazionale di San Matteo** *(a few doors past Piazza Mazzini; open 9 a.m.–7 p.m., Sun. till 1 p.m.; closed Mon.; L6000)*. This museum contains some fine works by exceptional artists such as Simone Martini's ★ polyptych, Nino Pisano's ★ *Madonna del Latte*, Masaccio's *St. Paul*, Fra Angelico's ★ *Redeemer*, and Gentile da Fabriano's *Madonna and Child*. For more of a river walk, go right at the Piazza Garibaldi onto Lungarno Pacinotti, pass Via Santa Maria and then cross over the bridge, Ponte Solferino. Now you can visit the **Santa Maria delle Spine** at its riverside spot. A small, but elaborate Gothic oratory, Santa Maria is like a jewelry box. Its many exterior sculptures are by the school of Giovanni Pisano (don't miss those along the street side).

Where to Stay

Within the central city there are numerous hotels, but very few are first- class. Many of the hotels cluster either near the train station or duomo; two locations that are adequately popular in the summer to require you to look elsewhere. In addition to these hotels, consider those in nearby Lucca. Outside of town on the beach at Marina di Pisa is **Camping Internazionale** *(☎ 36-553)*. Unless stated otherwise, rooms are air conditioned.

Grand Hotel Duomo	**L195–265,000 CP**	★★★

Via Santa Maria; ☎ *561-894; FAX 560-418.*
Single L195,000 CP. Double L265,000 CP
Our favorite option in Pisa is this hotel, with its location near the Leaning Tower. The lobby is large and attractive and there is a roof terrace with views over the Piazza del Duomo. The 94 rooms are comfortable, ample in size and with modern baths. Restaurant. Bar. Garage.

Europa Park	**L130,000**	√★★

Via A. Pisano 23; ☎ *500-732; FAX 554-930.*
Single/double L130,000.
Just one block away from the entrance to Piazza Miracoli, this quite elegant mansion with garden offers 25 good-size rooms (tiny baths; no a/c) that tastefully transcend the usual plastic decor for this price. Parking.

Royal Victoria	**L135,000 CP**	★

Lungarno Pacinotti 12; ☎ *940-111; FAX 940-180.*
Single/double L135,000 CP.
Built in 1839, this once grand hotel has been undergoing some necessary refurbishing, but could still use another coat of paint. Yet all has been furnished to period

and service is quite sprightly. The 20 rooms (no a/c) fronting the river have fine views and are quite large with modernized, tile baths. Restaurant. Bar.

Where to Eat

Though Pisa itself has created few Tuscan specialties (baby eels simply prepared and locally called "cee" is one), it nonetheless presents its Tuscan food with an unusual emphasis on Tyrrhenian seafood.

Sergio $$–$$$

Lungarno Pacinotti 1; ☎ 580-580.

Closed Mon. at lunch, Sun., Jan., and mid Aug. Meals L65–85,000.

Centrally located, Sergio's is recognized as the great restaurant for Pisan cuisine. The mussels with saffron, tagliarini with squid and vegetable sauces, or ravioli stuffed with fish, and any number of fish and shrimp dishes prepared magnificently with vegetables and herbs, are among the specialties.

Al Ristoro dei Vecchi Macelli $$–$$$

V. Volturno 49; ☎ 20-424.

Closed Sun. at lunch, Wed., and part of Aug. Meals L60–90,000.

Also near the Arno is Pisa's other respected restaurant. The dishes still take advantage of the nearby sea, with a magnificent *zuppa di pesce* (fish soup) and gnocchi with shrimp. The rabbit, or the pigeon with balsamic vinegar, the fine desserts, make this a close second to Sergio.

Da Bruno $–$$

V. Luigi Bianchi 12; ☎ 560-818.

Closed Mon. night, Tues., a few weeks in Aug. Meals L35–55,000.

Walk several long blocks east of the duomo and just outside the wall at Porta Lucca, you'll find this cozy trattoria serving Tuscan homecooking. Da Bruno offers thick ribollita, called *zuppa alla pisana* here, and hearty pappardelle alla lepre along with *totani ripieni*, stuffed calamari and *seppie*, or cuttlefish.

F. Salza $

Borgo Stretto 46. Meals L18–25,000.

Many needs can be satisfied at this elegant cafe and pasticceria: delicious sandwiches (such as the torta of caviar, salmon and egg), delicacies for a snack or picnic, as well as good pastries and gelati. At lunch, the tea room in the rear offers meals off its short but complete menu. If you want to **picnic**, you can join others on the Piazza del Duomo or seek out a bench in the Piazza Martire della Liberta park (on V. San Lorenzo a few blocks above Salza).

Il Montino $

P. San Felice off V. Mille.

Pizza L6–9000.

Not far from Salza, this trattoria is popular with locals for its pizza, served both at lunch and dinner.

Directory

Telephone Code 050   **Postal Code 56100**

Airlines

Alitalia/ATI, ☎ *48-027.*

Airport

Aeroporto G. Galilei *(☎ 500-707)*, 3 km south in San Giusto and with train service into the stazione centrale.

Bus

APT, P. San Antonio *(☎ 23-384)* near stazione, for Volterra, Tirrenia, Livorno (Leghorn); **Lazzi**, Piazza V. Emanuele *(☎ 46-288)* for service to most cities and Tuscan towns and with a convenient stop near P. del Duomo on V. Bonanno Pisano.

Car Rentals

Avis *(☎ 4-20-28)* and others.

Emergencies

Dial *113.*

Groceries

Market, off P. Garibaldi, behind Lungarno Pacinotti; **Salza**, *Borgo Stretto 46;* pizzicheria, V. Santa Maria 145, near duomo.

Parking

V. Contessa Matilde, outside wall near P. del Duomo; fee.

Police

Questura *(☎ 583-511).*

Post Office

Piazza V. Emanuele, near stazione.

Shopping

Boutiques on Rigattieri and Mercanti, off Borgo Stretto; shops along Corso Italia.

Taxis

Piazza del Duomo, near tourist office; P. Garibaldi; stazione.

Telephone

At stazione, open 24 hours, and Telcom, *V. Carducci 15.*

Tourist Office

APT, P. del Duomo, next to Museo del Duomo *(☎ 560-464; FAX 40-903);* open 9 a.m.–3 p.m., 4-6 p.m. and in summer, 9 a.m.–6 p.m., Sun. till noon; branch at stazione.

Train

Stazione Centrale *(☎ 4-13-85)*, south of Piazza V. Emanuele, linked to P. Garibaldi at Arno and P. del Duomo by #1 bus.

Pisa

On the Road

Small Tuscan Towns

The Tuscan countryside is unforgettable. No one can drive through the fertile vineyards of the Chianti valley, past the summer fields of marching sunflowers near Volterra, or around the clay hills south of Siena, without coming away with indelible impressions of cypresses and umbrella pines, of isolated hills crowned with the sunworn brick of a *fattoria*, or old farm-house. Such pleasures simply add to the delight of visiting the small towns, each with its artistic treasures and character, many with their famous wines to taste or local *pecorino* cheese to buy, all with their medieval fortifications built during the Guelf-Ghibelline conflict when each city struggled to maintain its independence from neighboring towns.

Some travelers spend an entire vacation visiting the small towns of Tuscany and enjoying country inns famous for their cuisine. How many towns you visit most likely will be decided by your means of transportation as much as the length of your vacation. Without a car, it is best to select a village or two to visit on a bus or tour from one of the Tuscan cities—Florence and Siena are both centrally located for such excursions. With a car, you can add the smaller towns on your way from Pisa to Florence, or Florence to Siena, and even Siena to Rome. And with a car and lots of time, you can comb Tuscany for 11th-century abbeys or mineral springs where Renaissance dukes once "took the waters." Or you can rent a country villa and enjoy the peace of rural life (see "Villas" in index).

SPECIAL TIP: The hill towns often permit only limited car traffic (access to hotels always permitted). If driving, it is best to continue until you can proceed no longer—usually just outside the medieval walls where there often is parking available. Or follow the blue "P" signs for parking to just within the *centro storico*. Train stations often are several miles *below* the hill towns and connected to the historic center by bus. Long-distance buses have stations right in the center.

Between Florence and Pisa

The sea, though not glimpsed on this route, has nonetheless played an important historic role. Pisa flourished early because it was a port. Florence, requiring a port for its vast trade throughout Europe, attempted to control its access to the sea by defeating the towns along the way. The area is certainly not the most scenic part of Tuscany, flattening out as it does from Pistoia toward the sea and bellowing smoke in the industrial ring around Prato. But the ebb and flow of Pisan, then Florentine influence, has left an unusually rich heritage of Romanesque and Early Renaissance architecture and sculpture, mostly Romanesque in Lucca, a hearty combination of both in Pistoia, and primarily Renaissance in Prato.

Lucca can be easily visited as an excursion from Pisa (or vice versa) and Prato is quickly reached from Florence. In fact, not much more than 100 km, 60 mi. separates Pisa from Florence. Whether you travel these miles by train (from Pisa to Lucca with a change there for the Florence line), bus, or car on the A-11 autostrada, a stop or two along the way is recommended.

Prato

In the 14th century, Prato was home to the self-made and wealthy merchant Francesco Datini. Beginning with the woolens manufactured here, he built himself a trading empire with branches in Florence, Pisa, Genoa, Barcelona, Venice and Avignon. A meticulous man, Datini kept all his personal letters and journals, all his account ledgers headed with "In the Name of God and Profit," and left the world one of the best documentary histories of a period. Today Prato is known as the "Manchester of Tuscany," and to reach the picturesque historic center once so familiar to Datini, you must now venture through the smokestacks and factories typical of 20th-century industrialization. The trip is worth it.

What to See and Do

Piazza del Duomo ★

The tiny center is easily walked. In the Piazza del Duomo is the handsome ★ **cathedral** *(closed noon–3:30 p.m. in winter; 4:30 p.m. summer)* with its Romanesque marble stripes and campanile. On the right side of the facade is the ★ Pulpit of the Sacred Belt by Michelozzo (original Donatello sculptures in Museo del Duomo). It is here that the sacred belt of the virgin, said to have been carried back to Prato from the Holy Land, is displayed on major holidays. Above the main door is A. Della Robbia's *Madonna and Saints* (1489). Inside, the ★ Chapel of the Sacred Belt (left aisle) is painted with the legend of this local cult (Agnolo Gaddi) and contains Giovanni Pisano's *Madonna and Child* (1317). The chancel is painted with Fra Filippo Lippi's fresco cycles ★ *Life of the Baptist* (1466), on the right, and ★ *Life of St. Stephen*. Fra Filippo hardly led a saintly life himself; in fact, he fathered Filippino Lippi who continued painting with the same rich textures and delicacy. Filippino's mother, Lucrezia Buti, was a nun in Prato, and her portrait is the basis for many of Filippo's madonnas, as well as for the Salome seen here (three times) in ★★ *Feast of Herod*. To tie together all of Prato's famous people, note that Herod sits under the Datini coat of arms, that family having commissioned the frescoes. In the right transept are frescoes by the school of Uccello. Next door is the ★ **Museo del Duomo** *(9:30 a.m.–12:30 p.m., 3-6:30 p.m.; festivi till 12:30 only; closed Tues.; L6000)*, housed in a fine cloister. In one room you find Donatello's exquisite, cavorting ★★ *putti* from the pulpit outside, Filippino Lippi's Saint Lucy, and Uccello's *Portrait of Jacopone da Todi*.

Prato

Other Sights

Via Mazzoni leads to the Piazza Comunale, with a statue of Francesco Datini in the center and the **Galleria Comunale** *(same ticket and hours as Museo del Duomo)* with the second piano display of della Robbi, Signorelli, and Filippini Lippi's *Madonna and Saints* (1503). A little detour along Via Guasti with a left at Via Ser Lapa Mazzei takes you by the **Palazzo Datini**, with its traces of facade painting. From here, Via Rinaldesco takes you into the Piazza San Francesco where Datini is buried in the church. A bit farther on is **Santa Maria delle Carceri** *(closed noon-4:30 p.m.)*, Guiliano da Sangallo's fine Early Renaissance church with interior terracotta decorations by A. Della Robbia. Dominating the piazza is the **Castello dell'Imperatore** (1248), the only castle by Frederick II built north of his Sicilian kingdom, and proof that since Florence was Guelf, Prato was sure to be Ghibelline if it wanted its independence—a hope soon dashed.

Where to Stay Eat

There are a few hotels in the centro storico, but most modern ones are in the commercial section of Prato.

La Veranda   **$–$$**   ★

Via dell'Arco 10; ☎ *38-235.*
Closed Sat. at lunch, Sun., Aug. Meals L35–55,000.
Conveniently located at the Piazza San Marco, near the Castello, La Veranda offers a wonderful antipasto table of salads and vegetables.

Caffe Brogi

In the Piazza del Duomo.
A good place to relax over a snack.

Directory

Telephone Code 0574   **Postal Code 50074**

Tourist information

Via Cairoli 48, near the castle *(☎ 24-112).* In the summer, Prato hosts a popular concert series that takes place in the castle. Contact tourist information.

Arriving

Lazzi buses stop in the Piazza San Francesco. The Florence-Viareggio train station is just a few blocks from the duomo. Lying near the intersection of A-1 from Bologna and A-11 between Lucca and Florence (20 km, 12.5 mi.), Prato is speedily reached by car. Pistoia is 16 km (10 mi.).

Reading

Iris Origo's **The Merchant of Prato**, for aficionados of the period.

Pistoia

Pistoia is a pleasant, flower-producing town situated below the Apennine mountains. Like most small medieval city states, Pistoia was alternately dominated by more powerful neighbors—in Pistoia's case, Pisa and Florence. Pisa has left its remarkable Romanesque imprint on the churches, but in the end it was, of course, Florence that was victorious. Pistoia has the odd distinction of being the namesake for pistols, not because it invented them, but rather, because it produced the concealable dagger, called "pistola" in medieval times.

What to See and Do

Piazza del Duomo

In the center of the historic area is this interesting square surrounded by Romanesque and Gothic buildings. The ★**Duomo** *(closed noon-4 p.m.)* with its campanile (originally a watch tower and later converted for church use) and Pisan Romanesque facade is complemented by Renaissance decorations on the main portal by Florentine Andrea della Robbia. The interior contains an extravagant ★ silver altarpiece in the Chapel of San Jacopo that was begun in 1274 and not completed until the early 15th century *(midway right aisle; fee)*. To the right is a ★ crucifix (1274), attributed to Coppo di Marcovaldo, but probably by his son, Guinta. Across from the duomo is the **baptistery** (1359), with very nice sculptures on its portal and tympanum, but most notable for the remarkable sweep of its red brick dome interior *(closed noon-3:30 p.m. and Mon.)*. Next to the baptistery is the old tribunal. Opposite the tribunal is the handsome Palazzo Comune containing the **Museo Civico** *(9 a.m.–1 p.m., 3–7 p.m.; festivi 9 a.m.–12:30 p.m.; closed Mon.; free)* with its exhibition of the work of native son Mariano Marini (died 1980) as well as medieval and Renaissance paintings. Actually, one of Marini's horse sculptures can be seen in the atrium whenever the town hall is open.

Town Walk

Follow the street along the side of the duomo and meander east for two blocks to the church of **San Bartolomeo in Pantano**, a pleasing enough church to visit if you have time. The Gruamonte sculpture (1167) on the facade is sadly worn, but there are fresco fragments and a Romanesque pulpit (1250) by Guido da Como inside. Returning to Via F. Pacino, behind the duomo, turn right for the **Ospedale del Ceppo**, with its colorful terracotta ★ frieze (1525), depicting acts of mercy, by the della Robbia workshop. A few blocks west to a small park, turn left, then right, and arrive at the ★ ★**Church of Sant'Andrea**. Its Romanesque facade is carved with Gruamonte's ★ *Journey of the Three Kings*, (1160). Inside is the real reason for coming to Pistoia, Giovanni Pisano's masterpiece, a hexagonal ★ ★ pulpit (1301). Pisano's Gothic expressiveness reaches its most agitated level in the relief panel *Massacre of the Innocents* and his angle statues are among his most sophisticated work, almost free-standing and exquisitely carved. Giovanni was pleased with this pulpit, too, and signed it "son of Nicola, and blessed with greater skill." The pulpit light machine also illuminates his ★ *Crucifixion*, (right aisle, in tabernacle) carved with no cross, but nonetheless expressive of the heavily hanging figure of Christ. Follow Via Rossi back toward the duomo, then take Via Roma and turn right on Cavour. Soon you arrive at the church of ★**San Giovanni Fuorcivitas**, its north facade intensely striped in marble and tiered with Pisan Romanesque arcades. In the middle of the interior is a *holy water stoup*, attributed to Nicola Pisano or his school, and in the right aisle is a ★ pulpit (1270) carved with Pisano assuredness by Nicola's student, Fra Gigulielmo da Pisa, but in the old-fashioned format already seen in Guido da Como's work. Opposite is Luca della Robbia's glistening white *Visitation*.

Where to Stay and Eat

Hotel Patria   **L80–125,000**   √★★

V. Crispi 8; ☎ *25-187, FAX 368-168; closed Christmas season.*
Single L80,000. Double L125,000.
On the flank of Fourcivitas, the Patria is all carpeted and surprisingly well-furnished for this category. The 25 rooms with private bath, no a/c, are a good buy. Restaurant. Bar.

Rafanelli   **$**   ★

Via Sant'Agostino 47; ☎ *532-046.*
Closed Sun. dinner, Mon., part of Aug. Meals L35–50,000.
Here you can enjoy the very Pistoian *maccheroni all'anatra* (duck) as well as other hearty Tuscan fare. All is well-prepared and reasonably priced.

Along the Corso Cavour near the duomo are several **cafes** with sandwiches, as well as pastry and food shops for a picnic on one of the benches in the part near the Fortezza, southeast of duomo. Also, most mornings there's a vegetable **market** in the Piazza della Sola, between the duomo and Fourcivitas.

Directory

Telephone Code 0573   **Postal Code 51100**

Tourist information

P. del Duomo, next to baptistery *(*☎ *21-622; FAX 34-328).*

Events

Luglio Pistoiese is a series of cultural events in July that culminates with the *Giostra dell'Orso*, a medieval jousting match once fought with a bear, now with just an effigy.

Arriving

Pistoia, surrounded by nurseries, is just off the toll-road A-11, 36 km (22 mi.) west of Florence, 42 km (26 mi.) east of Lucca, and 67 km (42 mi.) east of Pisa. On both the Florence-Viareggio and Florence–Bologna lines, the town is well served by trains. For bus service from Florence, look for the Lazzi buses in P. Stazione.

Montecatini Terme

Spas are popular throughout Tuscany, but none are so famous or sumptuous in Italy as those lining the Viale Verde at Montecatini. Since medieval times, Italians have come here to be restored, ingesting the mineral waters, soaking in baths, and enjoying the magnificent park surroundings. Montecatini, after a long slumber, currently is undergoing a revival. If you have time to pass through in season (spring through Oct.), visit the elegant ❀★★★★**Grand Hotel e Le Pace**, *(V. delle Torretta 1;* ☎ *75-801, FAX 78-451; with 150 lovely rooms, single L285,000, double L465,000, restaurant, lounges, gardens, pool, gym, and tennis, open May–Oct.)* or the neoclassical splendor of the Stabilimento (spa) Tettuccio, or take the funicular up to the old town for the views.

Directory

Tourist office

Viale Verdi 66; (☎ 772-244; FAX 70-109), information on walks through the wonderful gardens and parks.

Dining

If it's time to dine, consider ★ ★ ★ **Enoteca da Giovanni** (V. Garibaldi 25; closed Mon.; ☎ 71-695. Meals L55–80,000), which offers a fine wine list along with seafood specialties such as ravioli with shellfish sauce or an entree such as boned pigeon breast with pine nuts and grapes. Next door, the owner has a simpler trattoria, ★ ★ **Cucina da Giovanni** (V. Garibaldi 27; closed Mon.; ☎ 71-695. Meals L45–60,000).

Arriving

Montecatini is located just 15 km, 9 mi., west of Pistoia.

Lucca

Lucca is a delightful town to visit. Its people are animated, its Pisan Romanesque churches are wonderfully sculpted, and its streets are, on the whole, free of the jarring traffic found in so many medieval towns. Lucca is distinctive in other ways. Geographically, it is situated on a low-lying plain that does little to evoke the hilly landscape for which Tuscany is famous. Historically, Lucca succeeded in keeping its independence, save for a few years under Pisa, and eluded even the Medici grand dukes. After so many years of independence, however, it succumbed to Napoleon and became, in 1815, a duchy under Maria Luisa de Bourbon. Lucca was a major Tuscan power, made wealthy from its silk textiles. While today it is instead famous for its olive oil, the town is graced with the churches and palazzi built with the profits of its medieval industry. And thanks to Maria Luisa, its old walls have been transformed into a tranquil, nearly three-mile, tree-lined promenade.

What to See and Do

San Martino ★

From the large Piazza Napoleone follow Via Duomo east past the church of **San Giovanni** (on left) with its 12th-century portal and arrive at the ★ ★ **Cathedral of San Martino**, with its Pisan arcades. The sculpture of this facade is enchanting, from the carved columnettes—each unique, some with mermaids, others snarling tiger capitals, one a man hugging a bear—to the lower portion, parts of which may have been carved by Nicola Pisano, especially the ★ *Deposition* (left portal). The interior was renovated at a later time, from 1372 through the 15th century, but it retains the wispy tracery of a triforum that is Pisan Romanesque. Down the right aisle is a Tintoretto *Last Supper* (third chapel) and in the sacristy is Ghirlandaio's *Madonna and Saints* with its fine predella. In the left transept is Jacopo della Quercia's ★ *Tomb of Ilaria Carretto Guinigi*, showing the dead, but peaceful wife of a Luccan noble with her dog (light machine). In the chapel here is the lovely *Virgin of the Sanctuary* (1509) by Fra Bartolomeo, who provided so much inspiration to Raphael. In the left aisle is the 11th-century Volto Santo, or image of Christ, housed in an elaborate marble creation of the 15th-century Luccan sculptor Matteo Civitali. On the eve of the September 13th, the venerated statue is led in a procession through Lucca. *Closed noon–3 p.m.; in summer noon–3:30 p.m.*

Other Sights   ★

North of the Piazza Napoleone is the piazza and ★ **Church of San Michele**. Begun in 1143, the church and its facade provide another delightful example of the local Romanesque. The interior contains a pleasant Lucca della Robbia *Madonna and Child*, (first altar on right) Fillipino Lippi's *Four Saints* (right transept) and a dramatic 12th-century Lucca crucifix in the apse. Across from the church is **Museo Puccini** *(Corte S. Lorenzo 9; 10 a.m.–6 p.m., winter till 4 p.m., closed Mon.)*, commemorating the birthplace of the great composer. Leaving this piazza on the picturesque Via Fillungo, you make your way to Chiesa **San Frediano**, its facade remarkable for a 13th-century mosaic. The sturdy vaults of the 12th-century interior shelter an exceptional Romanesque ★ font, two pavement tombs by della Quercia (on left) and a Madonna with neon halo (unmissable when lit).

Town Walks

There are other fine walks if you have the time: down the medieval streets around the **Torre Guingi** *(open 9 a.m.–7 p.m., but 10 a.m.–4 p.m. Dec.–Feb.; L4500; follow sign off V. Fillunga)*; around the handsome northwest part of town where you find the restored **Palazzo Mansi** *(V. Galli Tassi)* with its small pinacoteca *(9 a.m.–2 p.m., Sun. till 1 p.m., closed Mon.; L3500)* containing some interesting Bronzinos; **shopping** around V. Battistero with its several antique shops or following the Lucchese to the boutiques hidden in the lanes off Via Fillunga (near Santa Croce); and joining in the evening *passeggiata* on Via Fillunga.

Where to Stay

La Luna   **L125–145,000**   ★★

V. Fillungo at Corte Compagni 12; ☎ *493-634 FAX 490-021; closed most of Jan. Single L125,000. Double L145,000.*

For an overnight, this charming hotel couldn't be more centrally located. Its 30 cozy rooms (no a/c) and sitting areas were renovated recently, but often retain such touches as exposed wooden beam ceilings. Limited parking.

Ilaria   **L90,000**   ★

V. del Fosso 20, ☎ *47-558. Single/double L90,000.*

Even less expensive, yet this centrally located family home desperately needs a coat of paint; 17 rooms (get an interior; no a/c), most with 4-star showers. Terrace. Parking.

Villa La Principessa   **L275–350,000**   ❀★★★★

In Massa Pisana 55050; ☎ *370-037; FAX 379-019; closed mid Jan.–mid Feb. Single L275,000. Double L320–350,000.*

There are first-class commercial hotels outside Lucca's walls, but why not drive 15 minutes more to enjoy the baronial splendor of Villa La Principessa. Found a few miles along ss 12 bis to Pisa and on the right. Surrounded by a park and fine gardens, this 14-century villa offers antique furnishings, painted viga ceilings and chandeliers, textured and brocaded wall coverings, great hearths, but all contribute to an utterly relaxed, country ambience. The 44 rooms are comfortably appointed. Lounges, bar, lunch al fresco. Large pool in garden. Main ★★★**Gazebo** restaurant *(Closed Sun. Meals L70–95,000)* is across the road in their very expensive annex (**Principessa Elisa**), which we don't like nearly as much.

Where to Eat

Lucca, birthplace to Giacomo Puccini, retains his favorite **Caffè di Sima** *(V. Fillungo 58)*, an old-fashioned tea room still popular for enjoying sandwiches and sweets. Of course, this town so famous for its olive oil can boast a finer cuisine than tea sandwiches.

Buca di Sant' Antonio   **$–$$**   ★★★

V. Cervia 1; ☎ 55-881, FAX 31-2199.
Closed Sun. night, Mon., most of July. Fixed-price meal L30,000. À la carte L35–60,000.
Everything from risotto with funghi to the traditional lamb with olives can be enjoyed at this country inn found right in the center of Lucca, just off Piazza S. Michele.

Da Giulio in Pelleria   **$**   ★★

P. San Donato; ☎ 55-948.
Closed Sun., Mon., early Aug. and Christmas season. Meals L30–40,000.
Without the tuxedoed waiters and artful menu of the Buca, this instead is a wonderful old-fashioned trattoria, with authentic Tuscan food and unusual quality for the price–from the antipasti and zuppa di verdura with pane (ribollita) to the spezzatino with olives. Don't miss it, at its location on the northwest corner just within the walls.

Picnics

If it's a picnic on the old walls or a light meal you want, head for **Piccolo Mondo** *(V. Cervia, next to Buca San Antonio; closed Thurs. afternoon.)*, a tavola calda with lots of take-out, or the fancier food store **A. Campione** *(V. Battistero 2, near San Martino)* and for wine and final local olive oils, **Vanni Enoteca** *(P. Miseracordia, just north of P. San Michele).* Or if it's a quick snack you want, join the Lucchesi at the counter of **Pizzeria Pellegrini** *(P. San Michele 25; closed Sun.)*, for a slice of delicious fresh pizza.

Directory

Telephone Code 0583   **Postal Code 55100**

Tourist information

APT *(☎ 419-689; FAX 490-766)*, at entrance gate of Vecchia Porta S. Donato on Piazzale Verde; 9 a.m.–7 p.m., but Nov.–Mar. till 1:30 p.m.

Arriving

Train and bus connections with Pisa, Viareggia on coast, and Florence. Located 18 km, 11 mi. from Pisa and 78 km, 48 mi. from Florence on A-11.

Events

Antique Fair each month on the third Sunday.

Between Florence and Siena

The region between Siena and Florence is considered the quintessence of Tuscany. Sheep graze the hills, vineyards cover the fields not now given to sunflowers. One of the favorite excursions, from either Siena or Florence, is to San Gimignano in the Val d'Elsa. With a car it's possible to add Volterra to the day excursion, enjoying the exceptional landscapes between the two medieval towns, and even to admire, if only from below, the 13th-century Sienese fort atop **Monteriggioni** (14 km from Siena on SS 2) whose towers so impressed Dante and whose purpose was to foil Florentine trade. This excursion is possible in a full day trip between Florence and Siena (157 km, 97 mi.) or a roundtrip from Siena (138 km, 86 mi.). Or you can prolong the enjoyment by staying overnight at either of the smaller towns.

Although the fastest route between Siena and Florence is on the *raccordo*, or superstrada (68 km, 42 mi.) by either car or express bus (about 1 hour), there is yet another route—the Chiantigiana. For those more interested in wine and the countryside than the medieval art of the Val d'Elsa, SS 222 through the heart of **Chianti country** might be the best choice. Here the hills become steeper and wilder and the world-famous wine business of the Chianti Classico flourishes. The road takes you through the Greve valley and into the tiny medieval village of Castellina in Chianti, passing on the way numerous wine estates, such as Rufino and Ricasoli, that are often open for tasting and sales. In Greve, you can visit the **Enoteca di Gallo Nero** *(P. Santa Croce 8.)* The 70-km, 43-m drive on winding scenic roads takes longer than the superstrada but is worth it.

San Gimignano

San Gimignano of the towers certainly deserves its popularity. Surrounded by ramparts, its narrow stone lanes shadowed by soaring defensive towers, it is the perfect fairy-tale illustration of a 13th-century town. While other medieval towns destroyed these bastions of warring family clans, for some reason, San Gimignano permitted 14 towers to survive, just enough to give the village distinction. It's hard to imagine that this picturesque town had more than 70 such towers flanking its palaces and that boiling oil, poured from their upper reaches on the enemy below, repeatedly set the town afire. Today, no longer a threat to civic harmony, the towers of San Gimignano attract busloads of visitors, who crowd into the town during the summer

months. *The all-in-one museum pass (L16,000) is a good buy if you plan to visit more than the Museo Civico and tower.*

What to See and Do

A walk around the town walls gives you a good perspective on the towers, as well as gentler views of the countryside. A visit to the six towers rising above the ★**Piazza della Cisterna**, with its well in the center, gives you a sense of why these fortified towns have been called "stone forests." Just through the piazza, the **Museo Criminologia Mediovale** *(10a.m.–1p.m.; 2–7p.m.; not on museum pass; L8000)* adds to the ambience with its displays of medieval tortures. But if the sun is shining, the stone walls turn warm and welcoming, and there are few more charming piazzas. A few steps away is the equally handsome ★**Piazza del Duomo**, center of the town's artistic treasures. Here, the interior walls of the **Romanesque church** are profusely covered with frescoes by Sienese artists of the latter part of the 14th century. The ★New Testament scenes (right aisle) by Barna da Siena reach a climactic *Crucifixion* (5th bay) and at the entrance (center aisle), is Taddeo di Bartolo's *Last Judgment* with a grizzly hell. Also here are polychrome sculptures of the Annunciation by Jacopo della Quercia. Off the end of the right aisle is the Renaissance ★**Cappella Santa Fina** *(open 9:30 a.m.–12:30 p.m. 3–5:30 p.m.; L3000)*, its architecture by Guiliano da Maiano, its frescoes by Ghirlandaio. In the courtyard next to the church (as exit, through archway on right), there's Ghirlandaio's *Annunciation* in the loggia, and two small local museums *(L7000)*. Also on the Piazza (left of church) is the 14th-century Palazzo del Popolo containing the ★**Museo Civico** in its tower, the tallest in town, by law. As you climb the stairs to the museum make sure you stop first in the Sala di Dante, where the great writer supposedly exhorted the town to ally itself with Florence. Here is Lippo Memmi's ethereal ★*Maesta*, clearly influenced by Simone Martini's in Siena. The museum on the upper floor has a fine collection of paintings by Benozzi Gozzoli, Fillipino Lippi, a crucifix attributed to Coppo di Marcovaldo, another to Guido da Siena, and Taddeo di Bartolo's *San Gimignano*, with the saint holding a model of the town with its many towers. On the opposite side of the stairs is a small room with Memo di Fillipuccio's pleasing *14th-century frescoes* of intimate domestic scenes. If you like, keep climbing to the top of the 117-foot tower for its ★**views**. *(Museum and tower hours are 9:30 a.m.–7:30 p.m. Apr.–Sept., otherwise closed Mon. and, Nov.–Feb., open only 9 a.m.–1:30 p.m., 2:30–4:30 p.m.; L7000 for museo; both L12,000.)* Via San Matteo leads out of the Piazza towards the opposite end of town where you find the **Sant' Agostino** church *(closed noon-3 p.m.; in winter, open 2–5 p.m. only)*, the only other church open in town and one with Gozzoli frescoes in the chancel.

Where to Stay

Pescille	**L100–130,000**	√❀★★

5 km south toward Castel S. Gimignano; ☎ *940-186, FAX 940-186; closed Nov.–Mar. Single L100,000. Double L130,000.*

Just 10 minutes by car from the center, but in another world of vineyards and rolling hills and country tranquility, this rustic inn has 35 rooms (no a/c; a few with terraces) with either views of hills or San Gimignano. Good restaurant, enoteca, large pool, and tennis.

Relais Santa Chiara	**L170–300,000 CP**	★★★

V. Matteotti 15; ☎ *940-701, FAX 942-096; closed mid Jan.–Feb. Single L170–220,000 CP. Double L170–300,000 CP.*

Just 5 minutes from the centro storico in a tourist village, the Santa Chiara is for those who want to be assured of their creature comforts. This brick, modern "farmhouse" doesn't have quite the perfect setting of the other hotels here, but half its 40 rooms do have views (reserve) of the Tuscan hills and the furnishings and bathrooms (some suites with Jacuzzi) are excellent; pool, garden terrace, breakfast room, bar.

La Cisterna   **L85–140,000**   ★★

Piazza della Cisterna 23; ☎ *940-328, FAX 942-080; closed mid-Jan.–mid-Mar.*
Single L85,000, double L105–140,000.

Right in town, this ivy-covered 14th-century palazzo with a prime location was recently tastefully renovated. The 46 units vary (no a/c) and so does the price, depending on whether there's a view, how stupendous it is and whether there's a terrace, etc. Good restaurant. Cafe.

Bel Soggiorno   **L90–135,000**   ★★

V. San Giovanni 91; ☎ *940-375, FAX 940-375.*
Single/double L90–135,000.

A smartly renovated 14th-century palazzo in the centro storico; reserve one of the 18 rooms in the rear overlooking the hills. Restaurant. Discounted parking.

Where to Eat

The farms around the hill town produce the popular white wine of Tuscany, *Vernaccia di San Gimignano*, easy to find as the house wine in local restaurants or to buy in the shops on the main streets.

Bel Soggiorno   **$$**   ★★

In the hotel.
Closed Mon. & mid Jan.–mid Feb. Meals L55–70,000.

This handsome dining room with country views serves traditional Tuscan pappa-radelle with cinghale and grilled game.

Le Terrazze   **$$**   ★★

In Hotel La Cisterna.
Closed Tues. and lunch Wed., and Nov.–Mar. Meals L55–75,000.

From the second-floor vantage point over the town and countryside, enjoy savory soups including ribollita, good rabbit and other main dishes prepared with mushrooms.

La Stella   **$**   ★

V. San Matteo 75; ☎ *940-444.*
Closed Wed. Fixed-price meal L25,000.

A trattoria with the local boar sausage on its *penne rustiche* and grilled quail.

Picnics

A good place to shop for a picnic is at the **alimentari** on San Matteo #5 or **La Buca** *(San Giovanni 16)*, not the cheapest salami (try the cinghale with fennel) in town but the only one with two stuffed wild boars guarding the door to prove they use the real stuff. Nearby the **Armando e Marcella** *(San Giovanni 88)* has the best pastry and tramezzi sandwiches; or taste the local wines while enjoying bruschetti or panini at **Gustano Enoteca** *(San Matteo 29)*.

San Gimignano

Directory

Telephone Code 0577   **Postal Code 53037**

Tourist information

P. del Duomo *(☎ 940-008)*; **UIT**, *V. San Giovanni 125 (☎ 940-809; FAX 940-809)*, for maps and hotel reservations. Both open 9 a.m.–1 p.m., 3–6 p.m.

Getting around

The main street begins at Porta San Giovanni and is called Via San Giovanni until it arrives at the famous piazzi; then it becomes Via San Matteo running between the Piazza del Duomo and the Porta San Matteo. The town is small; no traffic permitted inside the gates.

Arriving

Frequent tours and buses from both Siena (49 km, 30 mi.) and Florence (60 km, 37 mi.). The fastest route is along the superstrada to exits for Poggibonsi or Colle Val d'Elsa.

Volterra

Volterra is austere after San Gimignano's quaintness. Its massive walls and fortress are not simply picturesque, but menacing. A good deal of the stone solidity of the medieval town comes from its ancient past when it was one of the great cities of the Etruscan League dominating the Val d'Elsa all the way to Monteriggioni. Even today the walls of Etruscan Velathri still stand near Badia—outside the later walls of a smaller, medieval Volterra. The approach to the city is unforgettable with manicured Tuscan farms below and the powerful stone city above. Entering town you might encounter the Etruscan presence again at the **Porta all'Arco** (below the Piazza del Duomo) with its three distinctive sculpted heads. Or you might meet another power at Porta Selci where the **Medici Fortress**, finished by Lorenzo Il Magnifico, tells of Volterra's fall in 1361 to Florence.

What to See and Do

Town Walk

Medieval Volterra has its attractions. Narrow alleys, spanned by arches that once connected members of a clan to their shared tower, add to the ambience of any walk as do numerous substantial mansions. ★ **Piazza dei Priori** anchors this historic center with the oldest surviving municipal palace in Tuscany, the **Palazzo dei Priori** (c. 1208), model for the Bargello in Florence. Behind the palazzo is the Romanesque **duomo** and baptistery that are perhaps mustier than they are good. Opposite the palazzo is Via delle Prigioni leading to Via dei Sarti, lined with handsome palazzi. The handsomest is the Renaissance Palazzo Minucci-Solaini now housing the small **Pinacoteca** *(V. dei Sarti 1)* with its Signorelli, Ghirlandaio and Rosso Fiorentino's ★ *Deposition* (1520) *(9 a.m.–7 p.m.; off-season till 2 p.m. & closed Mon.; same ticket [L10,000] as Museo Etrusco)*. A longer medieval walk out of the central piazza is on Via Marchesi to Via di Castello, which takes you to the old ramparts, now the tranquil **Parco Archeologico** *(open till 5 p.m.)* with striking views of the Medici Fortress.

Museo Etrusco ★★

V. Minzoni 15, between the Medici Fortress and Piazza XX Settembre. Volterra has its Roman baths and amphitheater, but it is the Etruscans who win the day here. The astoundingly large collection of the Museo Etrusco Guarnacci helps you appreciate the number of Etruscans who were wealthy enough to pay for elaborately carved funerary urns. Even if you have time only to browse through this modern museum, you can enjoy the charming portraiture of domesticated couples carved atop their sarcophagus lids, and admire the elegant Giacometti-like bronzes as well as the alabaster reliefs of Greek myths. The last rooms on the top floor include some exceptional reliefs, as well as views from a terrace. In walking about Volterra, you can't help but notice that the Etruscan tradition of alabaster carving continues as a major crafts industry. *9 a.m.–7 p.m.; off-season till 2 p.m. & closed Mon. Same ticket (L10,000) as Pinacoteca.*

Where to Stay

| San Lino | L140–170,000 CP | ★★ |

V. San Lino 26; ☎ *85-250 FAX 80-620.*
Single L140,000 CP. Double L170,000 CP.
There are several small hotels, this being the best, with a convenient location, 43 rooms with bath, restaurant, garden, pool and garage.

La Paiola near Volterra is a restored 12th century farmhouse. (For rental information call ☎ *(800) 280-2811 or FAX (617) 596-3125).*

Volterra

Where to Eat

Osteria dei Poeti   **$–$$**   ★ ★

V. Matteoti 55; ☎ 86-029.
Closed Thurs., late Nov. Meals L30–65,000.
Decent Tuscan food served at a prime location for the Piazza dei Priori.

Da Beppino   **$**   ★

☎ 86-051.
Closed Wed., part of Jan. Meals L30–40,000.
Just up Via delle Prigioni, this trattoria is a bit cheaper and with outdoor tables for
enjoying the seasonal rabbit special or just pizza.

Via Gramsci is lined with alimentari and fruit stands, and at #64 you can buy *panini* for
a picnic in the nearby Parco Archeologico.

Directory

Telephone Code 0588   **Postal Code 56048**

Tourist information

Off P. dei Priori, V. Turazza 2 (☎ 86-150; FAX 86-150).

Arriving

Daily bus service from Pisa, Siena, Florence and San Gimignano. Infrequent train
service. Exit the superstrada or SS 2 at Poggibonsi or Val d'Elsa and continue on SS
68 for the 60 km, 37 mi. Siena trip, or 80 km, 50 mi., from Florence. San Gimignano is 30 km, 18 mi. northeast; Pisa, 65 km, 40 mi. northwest.

South of Siena

Since the 3rd century B.C., the Via Cassia has linked the land of the Etruscans with Rome. This ancient route, now SS 2, takes you through the often
treeless farmlands of the south, so remarkable for their rounded hills, their
grazing sheep, and their late-summer haystacks. Less than 25 miles away
from Siena, forks and splinters off this road take you to the traditional Tuscan towns of Montalcino and Montepulciano, and to the Monte Oliveto
abbey and the perfect Renaissance village of Pienza. A day excursion to the
abbey and Montalcino or to Pienza and Montepulciano is quite easy by car
from Siena. The bus service from Siena permits you to enjoy at least one such
spot in a day. And if you are continuing on to Umbria or to Rome by the autostrada, you might add the Etruscan museum in Chiusi to your itinerary.

Tip: La Chiusa near Montepulciano not only provides exceptional cuisine, in
case you want more than the local *pici* (thick, hand-cut spaghetti); it also has
some very comfortable rooms in case you want a more leisurely trip through
the area. **Poggio Antico**, outside Montalcino, is another worthy place to dine.

Monte Oliveto Maggiore

The wooded parklands and deep green cypress groves of this abbey are in
striking contrast with the surrounding ochre and clay hills that must constitute the Tuscan equivalent to the "badlands." In addition to the setting, you
can visit the cloister for the Sodoma and Signorelli frescoes on *The Life of St.*

Benedict. (The heroic style of Signorelli pretty much distinguishes his scenes from those of Sodoma). This Abbazia di Monte Oliveto Maggiore was founded in 1313 by Sienese aristocrats like the Tolomei and Piccolomini as a reform branch of the Benedictine order. It has been remodeled over the centuries, in some cases to near modernity, and includes a handsome refectory and a chapel with fine choir stalls and Baroque chapels. *Open 9:15 a.m.– 12:30 p.m.; 3–7 p.m., in winter till 5:30 p.m.; free.*

Practical Tips

Facilities

There is an unpretentious *restaurant,* ★**La Torre** *(closed Tues.,* ☎ *707-022),* on a lovely terrace near the entrance tower, that serves panini as well as meals (about L30,000); 40 rooms without private bath *(Write to Abbazia, 53020 Siena; closed off-season)* also are available.

Getting Around

To reach the abbey from SS 2, turn at the "abbazia" sign at Buonconvento (25 km, 15-1/2 mi. south of Siena) and continue for 9 km, 5.5 mi.

Montalcino

Montalcino's commanding position over the surrounding valleys assured it a place in the history of the Etruscans, Romans, and feuding city states of the middle ages. It is here, in 1555, that the Sienese retreated after the defeat of their city by Florence and managed to continue their independence as a republic in exile for four more years. Today Montalcino remains a fortified medieval *citta*, complete with stone gates and a 14th-century *rocca*, or fortress at its summit. A visit need not consume much time—a brief walk through the picturesque, but small village and a stop at the **rocca** *(9 a.m.–1 p.m., 2:30–6 p.m., till 8 p.m. in summer; closed Mon. except July 15–Sept. 15)* for its views. But then if you're interested in vintage wine, you'll want to sample the local *Brunello* that is one of Italy's finest reds, or the more affordable *Rosso di Montalcino.* Or you might even want to try the more experimental cabernets that have been coming out of this region. If you can, add a bit more time for the brief trip (10 km, 6 mi.) on the Castelnuovo Abate road to the ★**Abbazia Sant'Antimo**. This Romanesque church, built mostly around 1118, is beautiful, its alabaster interior radiant with the warm golden glow of sunlight. The carvings of the portal and the figured capitals are noteworthy *(11 a.m.–12:30 p.m., 2–5 p.m., but Apr.–Sept. 10:30 a.m.–12:30 p.m., 3–5 p.m.).*

Wine Tasting and Snacking

Inside the rocca is a handsome **enoteca** with good panini and other snacks to accompany your samplings of aged Brunello by the glass. The surrounding country roads are marked for many of the estates (look for "vendita diretta" or "cantina" signs). Or on your way to Sant'Antimo, you might stop at the famous vineyards of ★**Fattoria dei Barbi** *(*☎ *849-357; 5 km from Montalcino)* and sample their wines *(cantina 9:30 a.m.–noon,*

2–5:30 p.m., Sun. 2–5:30 p.m. only) and food *(taverna closed Wed. and, in off season, Thurs. night, late Jan. and early July. Meals L35–60,000).*

Poggio Antico   **$$–$$$**   ★ ★ ★ ★

localita Poggio; reserve at ☎ *849-200, FAX 849-200.*
Closed mid Aug.–Oct., Mon. except July–Aug. Fixed-price meal L60,000. À la carte L55–75,000.

If you want to dine well, then plan on a leisurely meal at this exceptional restaurant only five km south of Montalcino toward Grosseto. Here, on a wine estate with views over the Tuscan countryside, Roberto and Patrizia Minnetti have retreated from the pressure of keeping their Rome restaurant one of the top three. Rome's loss is your gain, at least temporarily, for the prices here are more affordable. A meal might begin with a mousse of the local goat cheese with tomato and basil accompanied by rosemary or truffle biscuits, and continue with *tagliatelle nero* with baby asparagus and other garden vegetables with slivers of parmesan, then a pigeon cooked crisp and wrapped in juniper leaves and pancetta, followed by a sublime and tart lemon gelato. There are only Poggio Antico wines, but they include brunellos.

Practical Tip

Montalcino lies about 40 km, 25 mi. south of Siena. Follow SS 2 just past Buonconvento then take the fork off that road for the remaining 14 km, 8.5 mi.

Pienza

This tiny Renaissance gem was designed and built in the years following 1458, the years in which its native son, Aeneas Silvius Piccolomini, was Pope Pius II. To elevate his birthplace, this perfect Renaissance man commissioned the perfect Renaissance *citta* from the Florentine architect Bernardo Rossellini. The scale is small, like the original village, the style is as grand as the classical Albertian principles on which it is based, and the result is somewhat unreal. In an early example of modern town planning, Rossellini designed the ★**Piazza del Duomo** with its cathedral and Palazzo Piccolomini; he even designed the picturesque well that makes it all look so much like a stage set. Although the price far exceeded Rossellini's estimate, Pius thanked him for being so deceitful about the actual cost: "If you had told us the truth... this fine palace and church, the loveliest in all Italy, would not now exist." The ★**duomo** is indeed fine and its light-filled, well-proportioned interior contains worthy Sieneseschool altarpieces *(closed 12:30–4 p.m.).* The right of the duomo is the **Palazzo Piccolomini** *(open 10 a.m.–12:30 p.m., 4–7 p.m. in summer, 3–6 p.m. winter; closed Mon.; L4000),* which offers guided tours through centuries of Piccolomini possessions. Far from museum-like, this home retains the intimacy of its owners—down to ripped upholstery and family snapshots—despite their demise a few decades ago. A fine view of the Val D'Orcia with Monte Amiatal can be enjoyed behind the duomo or from the loggia of the palazzo. And if you want, visit the **Museo della Cattedral** for a few Duccio-school paintings, tapestries, and a silver and silk cape of Pius II

(10 a.m.–1 p.m.; 4–6 p.m. in summer, 2:30–5:30 p.m. Nov.–Feb., 3–5 p.m. otherwise; closed Tues.; L3000).

Where to Stay

Il Chiostro   **L100–165,000 CP**   √★★

Corso Rossellino 26; ☎ *(0578) 748-400, FAX (0578) 748-440.*
Single L100,000 CP. Double L165,000 CP.
This is a small, tasteful hotel with 26 rooms (no a/c) in a restored 15th-century building. Restaurant; garden.

Where to Eat

Il Prato   **$–$$**   ★★★

Viale Santa Catarina 1; ☎ *(0578) 748-601.*
Closed Wed. Meals L35–55,000.
There are several decent trattorias, near the duomo, but Il Prato is the best in town with its rustic decor and sophisticated Tuscan country cooking. Located just outside Pienza's main gate.

Just as tempting are the *alimentari*, found to the right of the duomo on the Corso, where the famous local *pecorino* and the salami are plentiful. With a bottle of wine from nearby Montepulciano, you're set for a picnic. For the best accommodations and restaurants, see "Montepulciano."

Directory

Getting Around

Just an hour-drive from Siena, 42 km, 26 mi. south on SS 2, then east on SS 146 at San Quirico for 10 km, 6 mi. takes you to Pienza.

Transportation

There are daily buses from both Siena and Montepulciano (14 km, 9 mi. farther east).

Montepulciano

Both Siena and Florence may have fought over Montepulciano, but it was Florence that brought it glory. From Montepulciano, the humanist scholar Poliziano set off for Florence where he became the famous court poet of Lorenzo "Il Magnifico." In return, Florence sent Montepulciano its architect Antonio da Sangallo the Elder, who was followed by Sangallo the Younger, Michelozzo and Vignola—all of whom made their imprint on this town still full of Renaissance palazzi.

What to See and Do

A substantial, well-kept Tuscan town, Montepulciano offers a pleasant stroll from its lower Porta Prato up to its fortified Piazza Grande. Beginning at the Porta Prato, you pass in front of cantinas specializing in the hardy red **Vino Nobile di Montepulciano**, then arrive at Via di Gracciano lined with a series of impressive **mansions** (numbers 91 and 82 are by Vignola; on the curving facade at #73 are embedded Etruscan carvings). Just after #61 is Sant'Agostino church with its Michelozzo facade and an old tower with a Venetian style harlequin figure ready to ring in the festivities. Climbing farther, you come to Via di Voltaia (left after the archway), with the massive **Palazzo Cervini** (perhaps by Sangallo the

Elder) at #21, and the balconied **Palazzo Grugni** (Vignola) at #55. Continuing along this shopping street, you come to the point that its name changes to Via Poliziano; the birthplace of the poet Poliziano is marked at #5 and an interesting 16th-century portal is at #7. The **Santa Maria church** marks the visual end of this street; its piazza affords scenic views of the countryside and its interior contains a small Duccio-school *Madonna and Child* mounted in the center of a later, unworthy painting. The street climbs to the right and soon reenters the fortified walls before arriving at the **Piazza Grande**, literally the crowning glory of Montepulciano. It is surrounded by the duomo, town hall and palazzi by Sangallo the Elder, including his Palazzo Tarugi (opposite the duomo). Inside the **duomo** *(closed 1–3:30 p.m.)* is Michelozzo's ★ tomb for the Aragassi family and Taddeo di Bartolo's *Assumption* triptych behind the high altar. Below town (1 km) is the pilgrimage church of ★ **San Biagio**, the interior of which is considered Sangallo the Elder's masterpiece.

Where to Stay and Eat

You can make a picnic with the local ruby red Vino Nobile and foodstuffs from the *alimentari* at *Via di Gracciano 34*, taking your simple purchases to the countryside or to the bench near Santa Maria church.

Ristorante dal Cittino   **$**

> *Across from Palazzo Grugni.*
> *Meals L30–45,000.*
> Humble, but often crowded.

La Chiusa   **L240–300,000 CP**   ★★★★

> *Via Madonna, Montefollonico; reserve in advance* ☎ *0577-669-668, FAX 669-593.*
> *Single/double L240–300,000 CP.*
> *Closed Tues. and mid Jan.–late Mar. Fixed-price meal L130,000. À la carte L90–130,000.*
> Less than four miles away in Montefollonico (follow signs off SS 146 between Pienza and Montepulciano) is La Chiusa, one of the best restaurants in Italy as well as a country inn with ★★★ eight charming rooms *(no a/c)* in a thoroughly renovated farmhouse. The elegant meals consist of numerous courses, each a masterpiece of *nuova cucina* and each artfully presented, from the vegetable *flans* and *ravioli* with *truffles*, the goose breast with mushrooms and the duck with fennel, to the sinful desserts. Four hours can pass easily during a meal.

Directory

Telephone Code 0578   **Postal Code 53045**

Tourist information

> *Piazza Grande 9 (☎ 757-442).*

Arriving

> Buses from Siena and Chiusi; train stop on the Siena-Chiusi spur is 10 km, 6 mi. outside centro storico. Montepulciano is 66 km, 41 mi. from Siena, just 14 km farther east on SS 146 from Pienza.

Montepulciano

Chiusi

One of the 12 cities of the Etruscan Confederation, Chiusi today is of interest solely for its ancient past that flourished from the end of the 7th century B.C. and continued through the Hellenism of the 4th century B.C. and later. In a village where even the Romanesque duomo is built of Etruscan-cut stone, it's not surprising that its main sight is the ★ **Museo Nazionale Etrusco**, filled with locally discovered sarcophagi, canopic urns, and terra cottas. *(Open 9 a.m.–2 p.m.; festivi till 1 p.m.; closed Mon.; L12,000.)* Surrounding Chiusi are numerous Etruscan tombs such as the Tomba della Scimmia with Tarquinian style paintings and the later Hellenistic Tomba della Pellegrina. (Custodians living nearby unlock tombs; for details ask at museum.)

Practical Tips

Getting around

22 km, 13.5 mi. after Montepulciano, SS 146 joins the A-1 autostrada at Chiusi.

Transportation

Buses run regularly to Montepulciano (1 hour) and Siena (3 hours), and train service to Florence and Siena is available.

Arezzo and Environs

The area of Arezzo, called the Aretino, borders Umbria both physically and culturally. From Cortona in the south are views of the Umbrian mists of Lake Trasimeno; east toward the Apennines, the barren hills take on Umbrian steepness. Historically, the region has even been united with its neighbor, albeit involuntarily; and culturally, its greatest Renaissance artist, Piero della Francesca, fused Florentine concreteness with the softness of Umbrian light. But whether predominantly Umbrian or Tuscan, the Aretino is a must for those interested in Piero della Francesca's work, from his frescoes in Arezzo to the masterpieces in his birthplace of San Sepulcro and nearby Monterchi. And Cortona, more precariously situated on a narrow ridge than most hill towns, contains paintings by Fra Angelico worthy of a pilgrimage.

Arezzo is an easy stopover on the way between Rome and Florence. A round-trip sweep through Arezzo, Sansepolcro, Monterchi and Cortona can be made in a one-day excursion from either Florence (310 km, 192 mi.) or Siena (261 km, 162 mi.), but it's much better to enjoy yourself and be selective. You can also visit these towns on your way to the Adriatic Coast, perhaps viewing more Pieros in Urbino, or include them on your way into the heart of Umbria.

Tip: There are accommodations along the way, but for special food and ambience check the inns listed under Cortona.

Arezzo

From the top of historic Arezzo, you gaze down over the Aretino much as the Etruscans and Romans did, and even the Florentines, who later defeated the emperor-supporting Ghibellines of this city. Although views of modern Arezzo below banish any more romantic thoughts about this birthplace of Petrarch and Vasari, the centro storico offers some exceptional frescoes and fine architecture and a visit is always made pleasant by the friendliness of the Arezzani themselves

What to See and Do

San Francisco Church

The most remarkable frescoes (only partially visible during restoration) are Piero della Francesca's complex masterpiece ★ ★ *The Legend of the True Cross*, (1452–57) in the chancel of the San Francesco Church *(V. Guido Monaco and Cavour, midway up hill; closed noon–2 p.m.)*. The sequence starts on the right wall and depicts scenes from a rambling medieval fable about the life of the cross, from its beginning as a planting on Adam's grave through Sheba's recognition of it on her way to Solomon's court and its protection of Constantine in battle. Then Constantine's mother, Helena, searches for the cross and recovers it, but somehow it is stolen before being returned to Jerusalem after a battle. Under Piero's treatment, the story assumes a timeless simplicity. The colors are softly diffused with light, even in the night scene of Constantine's dream; and the shapes are sculpted, almost geometric, in a manner that later would influence the Cubists. As you exit the church, note the *stained glass* by Guillaume de Marcillat (1467–1529), a Frenchman whose works can also be found in San Domenico and the duomo.

Santa Maria Pieve

From the San Francesco Church, you can follow one of two streets that climb to the park at the top: Via Cesalpino leads to the duomo; and Corso Italia, just to the right on Cavour, which we follow, leads to ★ **Santa Maria della Pieve**. The Pisan Romanesque facade of Santa Maria climbs through three tiers of arcades, each formed by uniquely carved columns, one a human figure (top tier). Around the main inner arch of the main portal are fine carvings of the months of the year. The highlight of the impressive stone interior *(closed 1–3 p.m.)* is Pietro Lorenzetti's early Gothic ★ *Polyptych of Virgin, Child, and Saints*, full of Sienese color and texture as well as Giottoesque humanism. The best view of the apse and *campanile* is from the ★ **Piazza Grande**, to the rear of the church. The handsome piazza is surrounded by medieval and Renaissance buildings, including one with a loggia by Vasari.

Other Sights

Leaving the Piazza Grande in front of the loggia, you follow the Corso, now Via dei Piliati, past Arezzo's finest palazzi, curving your way up to the park and then left to the monolithic exterior of the **duomo** (begun 1277), that rises from its pedestal of steps on the Piazza della Liberta. The interior *(closed 12–3:30 p.m.)*, surprisingly lofty for a Tuscan church, houses in the left nave, a *Mary Magdalen* by Piero, and next to it the ★ *Tomb of Archbishop Tarlati* (1240), whose reliefs by Agostino di Giovanni and Agnolo di Ventura are remarkable for their boasting of the Ghibelline bishop's military exploits. Leaving by the opposite side of the piazza, the first right takes you by the **Casa di Vasari**, ornately frescoed by the artist in 1540 *(open 9 a.m.–7 p.m., festivi till 1:30 p.m.; closed Mon.; free)*, and ends at **San Domenico Church** *(closed noon–3:30 p.m.)*, with its powerfully moving ★★ crucifix (1370s) attributed to Cimabue.

Special Events

Arezzo is the location of a good *antiques fair* (first weekend of month, except Sept.) and the *Giostra del Saracino* (first Sun. in Sept.), when the different neighborhoods send costumed knights to take on a wooden effigy infidel for an old-fashioned jousting match. Both the fair and medieval festival take place in the Piazza Grande.

Where to Stay

Continentale   L100–145,000   ★★

Piazza Guido Monaco 7; ☎ 20-251, FAX 350-485.
Single L100,000. Double L145,000.
There are several acceptable moderate hotels near the stazione entrance to town. This is the most convenient, with 74 comfortable rooms with baths; restaurant.

Where to Eat

The **Caffé Costanti** *(P. San Francisco)* is popular for its faded turn-of-the-century grandeur and outdoor tables on the piazza; the snacks (in summer, brushcetti with fresh tomatoes and basil), the chocolate ice cream, the pastries all are good. The Saturday morning **market** *(left off the Corso at V. Garibaldi)* is a good place to look for panini of Aretino style *porchetta* (roast suckling pig).

Logge Vasari $–$$ ★★★

P. Grande; ☎ 25-894.
Closed Tues. L45–65,000.
Dining under Renaissance arcades designed by Vasari, sample the popular Tuscan specialties like steak fiorentino, but also try some of the wonderful dishes emphasizing color and vegetables: orechiette with broccoli and, in season, a great primavera pasta, risotto with asparagus and *straccetta alla rucola*. In the evening there's pizza.

Directory

Telephone Code 0575   **Postal Code 52100**

Tourist information

APT *(☎ 20-839)*, Piazza Risorgimento 116, second floor near Stazione; in summer, *P. Repubblica 22 (☎ 377-678; FAX 28-042)*, just to right as exit.

Arriving

Except for the Pendolino train, Arezzo is a stop on the Milan-Florence-Rome line. Or rely on car or bus from Florence (85 km, 53 mi.), Siena (65 km, 40 mi.), Sansepolcro (37 km, 22 mi.). An alternative route to A-1 from Florence is SS 69; a scenic route from Siena is SS 73.

Cortona

One of the most dramatically situated hill towns, Cortona seems to sit at cloud level. Whether driving the sinuous road up to its medieval walls or walking the narrow streets to the town perimeter, you can enjoy some of the greatest panoramic views in Tuscany. As one of the 12 cities of the Etruscan

League, Cortona can boast a long history, but its height failed to protect it from Roman and Florentine expansion. Today it is Cortona's medieval streets, its quaint, irregularly shaped piazzas, and its antique shops (there's a popular fair in September), that attract many visitors. The best sight of all is the ★ ★ **Museo Diocesano** *(P. del Duomo; Tues.–Sun. 9 a.m.– 1 p.m., 3–5 p.m., except till 6:30 p.m. Apr. to Oct.; L5000)*, and along the Giardino Pubblico. Plan for a stop at a small, but fine museum. Within are two Fra Angelico's, ★ *Madonna Enthroned with Saints*, and ★ ★ *Annunciation* (c. 1434), re-splendent in its blues and gold, and the prototype for his many later works on this subject. There are Sienese works, too: a fine Duccio school *Madonna and Child*, and Pietro Lorenzetti's early 14th-century ★ *Madonna and Child*, and *Calvary*. In addition, there are numerous late, rather stiff works by native son and early Renaissance master of anatomy, Luca Signorelli. Al-though the view from the piazza next to the duomo isn't bad, the best ★ view over the Val di Chiana and Lake Trasimeno is on the other side of town *(down Via Nazionale, the only level street)* at **Piazza Garibaldi** and along the **Giardino Pubblico**. Plan for a stop at the **San Domenico church** *(P. Garibal-di)* with its Fra Angelico fresco (on right as enter) and fine altar (triptyck by Lorenzo di Niccolo Gorini, 15th C) as well as a stop at the Palazzo Pretoria to see the Etruscan ★ bronze oil lamp with superbly carved animal designs surrounding a Gorgon's head (in the **Etruscan Museum**; *(10 a.m.– 1 p.m., 4–7 p.m. summer, 3–5 p.m. winter; closed Mon.; L5000)*.

Where to Stay and Eat

Hotel San Michele   **L110–145,000 CP**   ✿★ ★

V. Guelfa 15; ☎ *604-348, FAX 630-147; closed mid-Jan.–mid-Mar.*
Single L110,000 CP. Double L145,000 CP.

A tastefully designed hotel with 34 very comfortable rooms in a Renaissance palace, just off the P. della Repubblica and in the heart of the old center.

Il Falconiere   **L160–250,000 CP**   √✿★ ★ ★

loc. San Martino ☎ *612-679, FAX 612-927; closed early Nov.*
Single L160,000 CP. Double L250,000 CP.

If you're in the mood for the country rather than this fine town, with a car you can stay here, only a 10-minute drive from Cortona. A 1600s villa and chapel, set amid vineyards, olive groves and gardens, have been converted into a glorious restaurant and inn. The inn is the old villa with ancient stone lintels and wooden doors; 10 rooms (a/c) are decorated in provincial style, each sunny and with views of either Cortona and the countryside, some have frescoes. The ★ ★ ★ restaurant *(closed Wed. in winter; L60–80,000)*, whether in the beautiful lemon house or in the gar-den, is the perfect spot for a fine and leisurely meal (duck with peppercorns; steak with tartufo). From Cortona, the route to the inn is well marked from Via Roma; from Arezzo, it's just 26 km south on the Cortona road.

Cortona

Locanda dell'Amorosa   **L260–380,000 CP**   ❋★★★

2 km south of Sinalunga: about 20 km, 12 mi. from Cortona; 50 km, 30 mi. from Siena; must reserve ☎ 0577-679-497, FAX 678-216; closed Tues. at lunch and Mon., mid-Jan.–Feb.

Single L260,000 CP. Double L320–380,000 CP.

Fixed-price meal L65 & 90,000. À la carte L70–100,000.

Farther from Cortona, but within striking distance is another romantic spot to dine or overnight. This old farmhouse, now with all comforts, still rules a Tuscan estate that produces its own wines and olive oils. The setting is tranquil, the 10 rooms (some with a/c) very well-appointed, and the ★★★★food superb. Try the seasonal specialties—the thrush paté, the gnocchi, the lamb with thyme, and the quail with polenta.

Preludio   **$–$$**   ★★

V. Guelfa 11.

Closed Mon. Meals L35–55,000.

For dining in Cortona itself, Preludio is upscale, offering avocado salad with pine nuts and fontina, a carpaccio with pear and rucola, in addition to the usual pastas and main dishes.

Pub Fufluns   **$**   ★

V. Ghibellina 3.

Meals about L25,000.

Located just off the Piazza Repubblica the pub is locally popular for its pizza and, in summer, al fresco dining.

Right on the Piazza Repubblica is the **Caffe Signorelli**, where you serve yourself and then people watch with the locals at the outdoor tables. You can shop along Via Nazionale for a **picnic** in the Giardino Pubblici.

Directory

Telephone Code 0575   **Postal Code 52044**

Tourist information

V. Nazionale 72 (☎ 630-352).

Arriving

Cortona lies 32 km, 20 mi. south of Arezzo on SS 71 (follow "Perugia" signs) less than 70 km, 43 mi. from Siena and 55 km, 34 mi. from Perugia. Parking outside walls. Bus connections to Arezzo and Perugia and to Terontola and Camucia train stations.

Antique fairs

Weekends on P. Signorelli, the middle of each month; also, a two-week fair early in September.

Monterchi

On the edge of the tiny fortified hill town of Monterchi is a new little museum built just for Piero della Francesca's fresco ★★*Madonna del Parto* (c. 1458), recently moved from a nearby cemetery chapel. The subject, the virgin shown in the fullness of her pregnancy, is unique; the muted Tuscan col-

ors, the airy light and voluminous figures are pure Piero. *(Open 10 a.m.–
12:30 p.m.; 3–5:30 p.m., in summer till 7 p.m.; L5000.)*

Practical Tips

Transportation

Best visited by car, though there are buses from Sansepolcro.

Getting around

From Arezzo, travel east on SS 73 for 25 km, 15.5 mi., then turn right and follow
signs marked "Madonna" for 3 km. From Sansepolcro travel west on SS 73 for 12
km, 9 mi. before turning.

Sansepolcro

Sansepolcro is a pleasant town, its centro storico home of Piero della
Francesca, the modern town, home to Buitoni spaghetti. A brief stroll
through the traffic-free streets of the old, walled town, and you're ready for
the ★**Museo Civico** (also called "Pinacoteca"; V. Aggiunti 65). Head right
for the Piero room with the ★★*Resurrection* (1458), his famous fresco of a
spellbinding Christ gazing out over the brazenly foreshortened bodies of
slumbering soldiers. The simplicity of the geometry, the classicism of the figures, the stillness of the moment, emphasize the eternal significance of the
risen Christ. The revolutionary nature of Piero's early Renaissance style can
be seen by contrast with his ★*Madonna della Misericordia* (begun 1445), a
commission that fragmented his visual unity by requiring a Gothic polyptych
format and that flattened his monumental figures by its gold background.
Yet Renaissance symmetry and order and Piero's own solemnity of style pre-
vail. Also in this room is his lovely ★*Saint Julian. Open 9:30 a.m.–1 p.m.;
2:30–6 p.m., till 7:30 p.m. in summer; L10,000.*

Where to Stay and Eat

If you need to overnight, there are numerous modest, decent facilities.

La Balestra **L90–115,000** ★

V. dei Montefeltro 29; ☎ *735-151; FAX 740-370.*
Single/double L90–115,000.
On the edge of town, this modern hotel has 50 comfortable rooms and a good,
modest restaurant *(closed Sun. night and Mon.)*

Da Ventura **$–$$** ★★★

V. Aggiunti 30; ☎ *742-560.*
Closed Sat., Jan., and Aug. L30–55,000.
Only two blocks from the museum, this local trattoria serves wonderful regional
cuisine in an unpretentious setting.

Directory

Telephone Code 0575 **Postal Code 52037**

Arriving

Bus service to Monterchi, Arezzo, Perugia (70 km, 43 mi.) and other destinations.
Sansepolcro is 37 km, 23 mi. east of Arezzo on SS 73.

Sansepolcro

ROME AND LATIUM

Baroque fountains make the Piazza Navona one of Rome's great squares.

History and Art

Abandoned on a hill near a bend in the Tiber, the twin sons of Mars were suckled by a she-wolf. They later returned to the Palatine Hill, where they founded Rome in 754 B.C. As related in other stories of creation, the brothers fought, and Romulus killed Remus before becoming the first legendary king of Rome.

The story of Rome must begin with the demi-gods Romulus and Remus. Only a legend can explain Rome's rise from a rustic hamlet, really just one among the hundreds of such farming villages of Latin tribes, to an empire

409

that stretched from Mesopotamia to the British Isles. No archeological theory seems to suffice. Maybe the Palatine's location next to the Tiber could explain why Rome soon included all seven nearby hills. Maybe its strategic location where the Tiberina Island made the river easy to cross could explain how Rome soon conquered all its neighbors, including the civilized Etruscans, into a Latin province called "Latium." Even the ancients were somewhat baffled by their victories and attributed them to the intervention of another set of twins, the heavenly Castor and Pollux. But can even a legend convincingly explain how a humble village came to rule the world, imprinting its language, art, and law forever on the West?

Ancient Rome

Legends not history describe the first centuries of Rome's existence, a period when Romulus' monarchy continued. But there is little doubt that in the 6th century B.C., the Etruscans laid seige and ruled as kings themselves, bringing civic planning, literacy, and the arts to Rome—and even dress, for the toga was Etruscan. In 509 B.C., Rome declared itself a republic, overthrowing the Etruscan kings—but not before they had turned the Roman cemetery into what is now the Roman Forum, and had built the great temple to Jupiter on the Capitoline Hill. The Republic engaged in centuries of warfare—not all of its own choosing. After the Gauls invaded and burnt the Forum in 390 B.C., a defensive wall was built around the seven hills, a wall that needed patching when Hannibal led the Carthaginians in their 60-year Punic Wars against Rome. By 200 B.C., Rome had defeated the cities of Magna Graecia in southern Italy and was pushing against the Gauls in the north. Roman roads stretched across the peninsula carrying the legions to war, and, having defeated Carthage, Roman ships dominated the Mediterranean, ready to conquer the world.

By 200 B.C., Republican Rome had also taken on the civilized veneer of those it had conquered, the Etruscans and the Greeks. Roman towns followed the grid plan of the Greeks as well as the ritual organization of the Etruscans. Greek colonnades supplemented the raised podium temples of the Etruscans. Earthy realism in Etruscan portraiture complemented that of Hellenistic expressiveness. The auguries of the Etruscans joined the sibyls of the Greeks, the gods of all became Roman. And the bronze statues of Etruscan cities joined the hundreds upon hundreds of marble statues from Greek cities that were carried as booty in triumphal marches through the Forum of Republican Rome.

But the Romans themselves had much to contribute. They conquered the world, not just with armies, but also with their own unusual lack of exclusivity. Foreigners could become citizens, soldiers could become rulers, religious cults of all kinds were tolerated (to such an extent that at one point it was

TUSCANY

UMBRIA

ABRUZZO

A25

A25

A24

L'Aquila

A24

Rieti

S4

S4

Terni

Orvieto

A1

Lake
Bolsena

Vulci

S1

Tarquinia

Civitavecchia

Viterbo

S204

S2

Lake
Bracciano

Cerveteri

Tevere River

A1

S5

Tivoli

A24

A1

Rome

Frascati
CASTELLI
ROMANI
Castel
Gandolfo

Ostia

A12

Fiumicino

Cassino

Frosinone

A1

Gaeta

S213

Terracina

Latina

S148

Anzio

Orbetello

TYRRHENIAN
SEA

N

LATIUM

miles   24
0
kilometers   40
0

said there were more gods than people in Rome). The promise of upward mobility convinced conquered peoples to fight for Rome. Not only did warlords like Julius Caesar become rulers and soldiers receive land in new territories, but even slaves, once freed by a Roman, had the rights of citizenship. In this expanding Republic, bridges were built, towns created. The Romans not only had the political sense to make it happen, they were superb urban planners. Their forums and basilicas for courts and commerce became the benchmark of any respectable city. The inventors of concrete, their brick buildings soon had arches and vaults and domes, not the post and lintel of the Greeks.

In the late Republic, Rome was in considerable turmoil. Still at war in Greece and Asia Minor, it was weary. It was also experiencing internal turmoil, with rugged individualists vying for control of the Republic. These were Pompey and Julius Caesar (100–44 B.C.) and Anthony and Brutus, also part of our own legends, inspiring Shakespeare's dramas and untold numbers of bad movies. With the wealth brought by conquests, they lavished money on public projects. Caesar built his own forum next to the city's; Pompey, a great theater. They built country villas adorned with statuary, mostly Greek of course, and painting, Roman painting, that was becoming naturalistic, with an illusion of space. And sculptors produced their portraits in a new Roman style, penetrating psychologically, not just Etruscan in its frankness. Poets, like Catullus and Lucretius, wrote in the vernacular, making Latin literature as well as Roman art an accomplishment of the Republic.

The Republic ended, of course—even the assassination of the dictator Julius Caesar failed to revive it. His designated heir defeated the competition, including Anthony and Cleopatra in Egypt, and by 27 B.C. was granted imperial power by the Senate. Augustus, the first emperor (died A.D.14) promised the Romans peace both at home and abroad. It was time to consolidate the gains of centuries of war, time to impress the distant provinces with Roman brilliance. Augustus transformed Rome, his patronage probably unequaled again until the Medici of Renaissance Florence or Pope Julius II of Rome. He adapted the elegance of Hellenism to that of the imperial style. He covered the brick of Republican Rome with marble. His era produced Livy's histories, Vesuvias' principles of architecture, and Virgil's Aeneas; this of course, legitimized Augustus' rule by tracing his family back to the Trojan Aeneas as well as Venus. Later emperors would become even more grandiose, becoming living gods to be worshipped and building on a scale that transcended the monumental. Nero's statue was the largest bronze ever, taller than even the Colossus of Rhodes. Domitian's palace took over Romulus' Palatine hill. Their circuses, even their arenas, became colossal, and the domed spaces of some public baths could accommodate 3000. Under Trajan

(A.D. 98-117) the Empire covered its greatest territory, and Rome, with a population of one million, was the largest city in the world. Peace reigned for an interlude under Hadrian (A.D. 117–38) and Roman art reached another apogee, classically Greek in its sculpture but purely Roman in an architecture of enclosed space and light epitomized by the Pantheon.

The wars began again and eventually divided the empire. For the first time since Rome was a fledgling republic, it thought about reinforcing its walls. The originals were too small, so the Aurelian wall (A.D. 270s) wrapped around the outside of other hills—one, the Janiculum, across the Tiber, included more than the original Forum and encircled many markets, basilicas, temples, and palazzi, as well as five-story apartment houses. But by the 4th century, Rome no longer was a capital; Constantine had moved that to Byzantium. By the 5th century, barbarians from all directions sacked Rome, leaving its centuries of glory to be the marble quarries and artistic inspiration for later generations.

Christian Rome

It's hard to imagine a Rome without its aqueducts replenishing this city of fountains. Once the Roman aqueducts were blocked to prevent invasion in the 5th century, they weren't repaired again for 1000 years. Bone dry, the ancient baths fell into disuse and the circuses no longer were flooded for mock naval battles. The dark ages were grim indeed. But with pagan Rome dead, a new power emerged. The Catholic Church took over slowly at first, moving out of the catacombs in the 4th and 5th centuries to establish churches such as Santa Maria Maggiore, the magnificent rotunda of Santa Costanza, and the beautiful basilica of Santa Sabina. Pagan columns held their roofs aloft, and classical-style mosaics often decorated their walls. No matter that so much was borrowed, the triumphal arch of the church basilica framed the altar of Christ, not the emperor in his chariot.

Not only did the Church emerge triumphant over paganism, it filled the vacuum left by the removal of the capital to Constantinople. After Leo the Great confronted Attila the Hun (A.D. 455), convincing him to spare Rome, and Gregory the Great negotiated peace with the Lombards (A.D. 592), the papacy was on its way to assuming political, not just spiritual, power. When Charlemagne was crowned Holy Roman Emperor in (A.D. 800), he would be only the first of many emperors made and broken by the popes. Assuming control over parts of central Italy granted by the new emperor, the pope officially became the temporal ruler of the Papal States. Down to the 16th century, warrior popes like Julius II would lead their own armies.

Rome's fate would be that of the popes until 1870. The city would prosper with jubilees and mass pilgrimages, and it would be transformed by papal architects and sculptors whether Renaissance, Baroque or Rococo. And it would suffer when the Church did. In the tumultuous early centuries of the Church, the popes just managed to keep the city functioning between invasions of Moors, German anti-popes and Norman kings. Water remained limited to the Tiber or wells. Houses were mostly hovels amid the pagan ruins—ruins that, to the medieval Roman, were built by giants, not ancestors. Yet the popes did build churches, finding the necessary bricks from the spectator stands of the Circus Maximus. By the early 12th century, the Cosmati were paving the floors and pulpits of Romanesque churches like Santa Maria in Cosmedin with geometric patterns of colored marbles—once again supplied by the ancients. The glint of red porphyry and gold, the fragments of greens and blues, could also be found on campaniles and in the magnificent cloister of St. John Lateran.

A real Roman revival didn't occur until late in the 13th century when Nicholas IV, freed from the Guelph and Ghibelline wars, set out to glorify the city of the popes, now recognized as leaders of the Western Church. Only then did the subtlety of light and color from antiquity soften the rigid contours of Byzantine art; only then did the humanistic details of classical art break down the spiritual rigors of the icon. The beginnings of these changes can be seen in Jacopo Torriti's mosaics in Santa Maria Maggiore (1295) and in the tombs and tabernacles of the sculptor Arnolfo di Cambio, who fused the current Gothic taste with classical figures. But the real innovator was Pietro Cavallini (c. 1240–c. 1330) who explored space and movement in his mosaics at Santa Maria in Trastevere and in his frescoes at Santa Cecilia.

The revival was brief. In 1303, the papacy moved to Avignon, and Rome sank into chaos. The promise of a new naturalism in art would be realized in Tuscany, not Rome. It would be attributed to Cimabue, not Torriti, Giotto not Cavallini. As commerce stimulated other cities, Rome became the battlefield of warring noble clans like the Colonna (who claimed descent from the Etruscans) and the Orsini. The colosseum, the Teatro di Marcello, and the Castel Sant'Angelo became their forts; the population dropped to a mere 25,000. Not until the unified papacy returned and reestablished itself, did Rome rise out of its squalor. By then it was already 1420 and the Early Renaissance was in full swing–elsewhere.

Renaissance Rome

The return of the Holy See to Rome reunited the popes with their territories, the Papal States. Quickly, Rome became the equal to the other great Renaissance Italian states of Venice, Florence, Milan and Naples. And the pontiffs played power politics as intensely as any. They wooed Spain, then struck deals with France; they formed alliances to gain both territory and wealth. They used church appointments as bargaining chips, or sold them to enrich the papal coffers—or simply kept them within the family to spread the wealth. The power inspired Machiavelli to dedicate *The Prince* to Cesare Borgia, son of Alexander VI. The corruption led to anecdotes of princes, instructing sons, recently appointed cardinals, "to nonetheless be religious." Such papal abuses eventually would lead to the Sack of Rome and the rise of Martin Luther. But not before Rome itself was transformed into a capital fit, once again, for emperors.

Few *quattrocento* palazzi managed to be built following Alberti's principles, even though the Florentine had been inspired by the Colosseum. Florentines like Fra Angelico and Umbrians like Pintoricchio, though, were commissioned to refurbish churches as well as papal apartments in the increasingly grand Vatican Palace. Rome, however, in no way could be said to dominate Early Renaissance art. Yet nowhere did the rebirth of classical values strike a deeper, more harmonious chord. In Rome, art would quickly be elevated to the High Renaissance.

In 1503, Giuliano della Rovere became Pope Julius II. An imperial pope who wished to purge Italy of the French and Spanish, he at least succeeded in winning back the Papal States, and even enlarging them a bit. But Rome was foremost on his mind—it needed to be rebuilt to suit the increasing magnificence of the Church. First and foremost, old St. Peter's needed to be torn down and replaced with something more appropriate for the Vatican Palace next to it. And the palace itself was far from perfect. In the short decade of Julius' tenure, the Roman High Renaissance would be born, a style that matched antiquity in monumentality and vigor, but one that promoted the grandeur of the Church.

When Raphael arrived in Rome in 1508 to begin work on Julius' *stanze*, or apartments, Bramante already was working on St. Peter's, and Michelangelo was painting the Sistine ceiling. They created what many believe to be the golden age of Italian art. In architecture, Bramante breathed space between the walls, turning circles into spheres. In painting, Raphael, who would become the first truly wealthy artist, achieved an effortless harmony between his figures and the grand scale settings in which they moved. And Michelangelo forever changed art by the emotional intensity that animated his heroic figures, whether in marble or paint.

The High Renaissance witnessed the construction of lavish cardinals' palazzi, like that of Alessandro Farnese, and exquisite villas such as the Farnesina, built for the Chigi family. It produced gemlike churches, such as Santa Maria della Pace, as well as monumental ones that converted ancient baths into Santa Maria degli Angeli. It created entire streets lined with buildings and broad enough for splendid religious processions and grand pilgrimages. Raphael often had a hand in these designs, so did Bramante and Michelangelo—who also rebuilt the summit of the Capitoline Hill. But many other noteworthy artists participated, among them Baldassare Peruzzi

(1481-1536), a student of Bramante, and Giulio Romano (1499-1546), a pupil of Raphael. The golden age continued through the patronage of the Medici Leo X (d. 1521), and seemed capable of infinite projects as long as the Forum could supply the marble. Unfortunately, the Italian Wars intruded in 1527, when the troops of Charles V sacked Rome.

Counter-Reformation

The Sack of Rome sent the pope fleeing to Orvieto for refuge and dispersed the city's artists throughout Italy. Rome was burnt out by the Sack, its population cut in half. The confident age of the Renaissance was over. Weakened politically, the Church also found that moral corruption had reduced its spiritual authority. But the Catholic Church wasn't through, nor was Rome. Spain may have forced it into neutrality, Luther into the Counter Reformation, but Rome was on the rebound by the end of the century. The Church, after all, not only reformed itself, it zealously promoted its new virtue in Early Baroque projects. Michelangelo's weighty figures found themselves in the inspirational paintings of Annibale Carracci and Caravaggio, but now nudity was banished. Churches rose to house the new orders of the reformed church. The Jesuits' *Gesu*, designed by Giacomo dell Porta (1539–1602) and Vignola (1507–73), preserved Bramante's spatial volumes, but its emphatically Latin-cross shape denied any allusions to the pagan Pantheon.

Counter-Reformation Rome was not all austerity despite the Inquisition. The first aqueduct was repaired by Sixtus V in 1585, and as water flowed again through Augustus' Aqua Felice, fountains filled piazzas like St. Peter's and the Pantheon with their music. Not only did Sixtus construct fountains, he moved ancient obelisks to make grand urban vistas to accompany them. Inside private palazzi, the vistas were increasing too, as frescoes created mythological landscapes framed by elaborate ceiling architecture and trompe l'oeil devices. Those by Annibale Carracci for the Palazzo Farnese (1590s) were positively voluptuous. As the 17th century dawned, more aqueducts were repaired and water once again flowed in abundance through the city, its joyful movement an integral part of Bernini's sculpted fountains and the Roman High Baroque.

High Baroque

In the year 1600, a Holy Year, over a half-million pilgrims from all of Europe flocked to Rome. In preparation, the city had been beautified under Sixtus V, and merchants had built hotels and restaurants, and produced rosaries and other souvenirs. The Church had become big business, and it produced considerable prosperity in Rome, now grown to a city of over 100,000. In the off years, the more secular interests of those on the Grand Tour were served by the very same establishments, but with slightly different souvenirs. Gone were the defensive years of the Counter Reformation. The

Catholic Church was victorious. Its reformers became saints—Ignatius Loyola, Philip Neri, Theresa of Avila—and required new monuments to glorify them. Beginning with the Barberini pontiff Urban VIII (1623–44), Rome once again burst into creativity under papal patronage.

The 17th-century High Baroque had its big three, just like the High Renaissance. For architecture, there was Borromini, for sculpture, Bernini, and for painting Pietro da Cortona. Bernini did everything, from making stage sets to cake decorations. Cortona produced the first churches, like the rippling, ever curving surfaces of SS. Luca and Martina (1640). In fact, everything in the Baroque rippled and moved, whether in the spiraling dome of Borromini's Sant'Ivo (1642), in the fluttering draperies of Bernini's *St. Theresa*, or in the ceiling Pietro painted away into the heavens for the Barberini palace. No one defined the High Baroque more than Bernini, whose influence was so thorough that the name of Alessandro Algardi (1595–1654), his more conservative competitor, is barely known. Bernini captured individuality in his portrait busts, eternalized in marble the fleeting moment of Beata Ludovica's ecstasy, dramatized the colossal spaces of St. Peter's square with his colonnades, and created dynamic public squares with his fountains. Like Bernini himself, the High Baroque was exuberant and prolific.

Rome in the 17th century was the artistic capital of Europe. Spawned from the energies of the Early and High Baroque were the landscape paintings of Nicolas Poussin and Claude Lorraine and the Dutch genre paintings of "Il Bamboccio" or Van Laer. Peter Paul Rubens was in Rome in 1600, and Velasquez visited, too, in 1630. But the Baroque would be the last great artistic outpouring sponsored by the Church. It was not just that there were enough churches—over 300 during the 1725 Jubilee—but that papal resources were drained again by war (against the Moslems in the 18th century), and by the republican currents ushered in by Napoleon's troops in 1798. True, there was a brief flurry of artistic commissions that produced the Roman Rococo during the second quarter of the 18th century. However brief, the period left behind the memorable Spanish Steps (1726) and the Trevi Fountain (1732). And, perhaps because the coffers were poor, the stucco discovered by the Baroque to carve its fluid forms was increasingly applied to all manner of buildings and painted into the warm sienna and ochre of Rome. But with Napoleon's troops, and later with those of the Risorgimento, papal patronage finally came to an end.

For 2500 years, Rome has endured next to the bend in the Tiber that Romulus and Remus found so attractive. Each successive generation was built atop the former to create a city as extraordinary as it is long-lived. No wonder the French Senate declared it the second capital of their empire in 1810.

History and Art

And when Italy was reunified in 1870, the first time since antiquity, only Rome, the Eternal City, could be its capital.

Modern Rome and Latium

In less than a century, Rome grew from a city of a few hundred thousand to one of millions. Noble country estates were built into apartment complexes, and construction spilled outside the long enduring Aurelian walls and sprawled into the countryside of Latium (*Lazio* in modern Italian). As monumental as Rome has always been, it sometimes seems too small for its traffic, even with the straight avenues Mussolini paved through the old city. Despite these problems, typical of a large city, Rome seems to have weathered them well. Rarely is it ugly; most housing projects and light industries (electronics, pharmaceuticals, clothing, publishing, and engineering) remain on the outskirts. In the historic center, Rome remains vibrant and fascinating, and beyond the belt of development, Lazio is rural and agricultural.

Cuisine

Rome markets offer great delicacies for a picnic.

The cuisine of Latium is best considered Roman cuisine. Individual villages might be known for a particular dish, like Amatrice with its rich spaghetti sauce, and the countryside may excel in such treats as *porchetta*. But Amatrice's sauce is no longer its own, but Roman, served in every self-respecting trattoria in the city as *bucatini all'amatriciana* (hollow spaghetti with tomato, pecorino, and pancetta sauce laced with a few hot pepper flakes). And porchetta (roast suckling pig stuffed with rosemary and garlic, then carved into succulent slices to eat atop crusty, fresh pieces of bread) may always taste best alongside a rural road, but is considered by Romans to be theirs, too, a specialty item at every festival.

Not only does Roman cuisine dominate the region, it transcends the boundaries of Latium. Just as imperial Rome imported the black pepper and saffron of the East, so the contemporary capital borrows, too. It shamelessly shares the North's love of butter in creations of *fettucine all'Alfredo* and *saltimbocca* (veal scaloppine with prosciutto slices simmered in sage, butter, and white wine), and is just as likely to shave white truffles on fresh egg noodles, called *tagliolini*, as Milan. At the same time Rome consumes vast quantities of dried pasta, such as penne (short hollow tubes) with sauces typical of the south: simply olive oil, garlic, and, once again, those red peperoncini flakes that also appear in a zesty tomato sauce called *arrabbiata*.

Traditional Roman Cuisine

It is the countryside of Latium, however, that produced traditional Roman cuisine. To the south, where Latium overlaps the old Pontine marshes of Campania, fresh ricotta and buffalo mozzarella are still manufactured, and both find themselves fried in Roman cuisine, the mozzarella making a surprise appearance from inside *suppli*, or rice balls, the ricotta as *palle fritte*. To the east, in the Sabine Hills behind Tivoli, the best olive oil of the region is produced, just as it was in ancient Roman times. To the north, some of the best pecorino cheese in Italy is produced, so famous that its *piccante*, or aged variety, is known in America simply as Romano cheese. From Lake Bracciano to the Tyrrhenian coast, pecorino has been manufactured since the time of the Etruscans, when they, too, grazed their sheep here. Today sheep still graze over their ruins at Vulci, where you can snack on the local pecorino. But it is spring lamb, rather than mutton, that the descendants of the Etruscans prefer. Milk-fed, then roasted with rosemary, the lamb is called *abbacchio*; cut into chunks and braised with oil, garlic, white wine, egg yolks and lemon peel, it becomes *abbacchio brodettato*. Olive groves cover the hills in all directions, producing their delicious black fruit to be marinated (often with hot pepperoncini) for antipasti, or crushed into the oil for braising oxtail in celery *(coda alla vaccinaria)*, frying strips of codfish (filetti di baccala), or mixing with those pepperoncino flakes to pour into a thick *zuppa di ceci* (chick pea soup).

Perhaps what is especially Roman is the passion for vegetables and wild herbs. Although rugged Lazio is not fertile or large enough to be self-sustaining, it does produce some of the freshest items filling Rome's markets, from the delicate lettuce leaves for salads of such stunning variety that you wonder how only romaine was selected as a namesake, to winter's strangely lime-green and turreted *broccoli romaneschi* and fall's round *carciofi*, or artichoke. The hills produce wild mint and mushrooms, intense rosemary and deep green *cicoria* (chicory). Any weekend finds Romans searching for their wild greens and mushrooms around the lakes to the north or the Castelli Romani to the south. But no delicacy sets them on a more determined search in the fall than *rughetta*, known as *rucola* elsewhere in Italy and as arugula in English, but preferred wild here, whether harvested from along the ancient Appian Way or the surrounding hills.

Such devotion leads to great invention. The artichoke alone is made into soups, sliced with aged pecorino into a salad, stuffed into tomatoes, and braised with strips of beef into stew, or *straccetta*. But it is most Roman when prepared as an appetizer or contorni, and even then there are two competing traditions. *Carciofi alla romana* takes the artichoke with its stem, stuffs it with garlic, mint, and parsley, then steams it in oil and water; *carciofi alla guidea*, or the Jewish method, flattens the head of the artichoke into a flower, then fries it, rendering the heart tender and the surrounding leaves brown and crunchy.

The Jewish preparation of fried vegetables originated in the old ghetto in Rome. The tradition has nothing to do with kosher cooking, but everything to do with Roman cuisine where the *fritto misto di verdura* is a mainstay (and never better than when accompanied by one of those great Roman mixed salads or crisp green rings of *puntarelle* sauteed with anchovy paste and oil). One of the tastiest vegetables in this tradition is *fiori di zucca ripiena*, or fried zucchini flowers stuffed with mozzarella and anchovies.

Not everything is fried. Tomatoes are stuffed with mint and rice and stewed for *pomodoro con riso*; they are chopped with garlic, basil and oil and spread on a thick grilled slice of bread for *bruschetta*. Peppery *rughetta* finds its way onto carpaccio and into elegant salads. Whatever is seasonal, mushrooms or asparagus, radicchio or eggplant, makes its way into every course except dessert—unless we consider the fruits, those year-round strawberries and sweet *clementine*, tangerines so fresh they appear in the winter market with their leaves still waxy green.

Although not one of Italy's great **wine** producers, Latium nonetheless supports many vineyards. The vines seem to flourish in the volcanic tufa to the north, around Cerveteri where the Etruscans once found the same earth easy for carving their tombs, and south in the Alban Hills. Controlled content wines are prevalent from both areas, but particularly in the south where the DOC light, dry whites of the Castelli Romani find their way onto the tables of Rome. Frascati is the most famous of these, and the Fontana Candida label the most preferred. The reds are good, but hard to find, though we were fortunate to discover a rich red Colle Picchioni from Velletri in one of Rome's shops. A glass of Sambuca, an anisette produced in Latium, is best when a coffee bean or two breaks its intense flavor.

Cuisine

Climate and Seasons

Rome's climate permits tourism year long; however, July (88° F average high, 75° F low) and August can be debilitatingly hot, if conveniently without much rain; and freezing temperatures in January (54° F average high, 46° F low) and February are not impossible. On the whole, Rome is not especially wet, but the rains in November and December sometimes are persistent enough to interrupt the pleasure of your sightseeing. As usual in Italy, the spring and fall—especially May (73° F average high; 55° F low) and October (73° F average high, 64° F low)—offer the best weather. The surrounding hills of Latium, particularly the Apennine foothills to the east, are known for their cooling summer breezes. The Tyrrhenian sea, only 20 miles east of Rome, has a moderating influence on the weather of the region.

Arriving

Rome's Leonardo da Vinci airport in Fiumicino is the fourth busiest in Europe and certainly the largest in Italy, for both international and domestic flights. The airport is connected to central Rome in 25 minutes by train. Its coastal location near Ostia means that you could rent a car and head up the Etruscan coast to Tuscany and the north without entering Rome. Or you could take A-12 to the GRA beltway and pick up A-2 to the south. (**Note:** Before driving off while suffering from jet lag, check with airport tourist information about hotels at nearby seaside towns, like Fregene.) Rome is well connected by train and highway to major Italian (Milan 575 km, 347 mi.; Florence 270 km, 167 mi.; Venice 530 km, 329 mi.; and Naples 215 km, 133 mi.) and international cities. The fastest route to Rome is by the Autostrada del Sole, or A-1 from the north, A-2 from the south. One of the most scenic routes from the north is via SS 2 from Siena and past Lake Bolsena and Viterbo (3.5 hours). For further airport and train details see the Rome key and directory.

Getting Around

Trains and pullman buses connect central Rome with the towns of Latium; in fact, public transportation relieves you of the headaches of finding your way in and out of Rome by car. But to enjoy the countryside, or to visit more than one town on a day excursion from Rome, you might want to rent a car for the Etruscan ruins and Castelli Romani. *Avoid entering or leaving Rome during rush hours.*

Travel Tips

Rome

Key to Rome

Sights

The marble capital of Augustus' empire, the mosaics of Early Christian churches, the High Renaissance masterpieces of Raphael and Michelangelo, and the exuberant fountains of Bernini's Baroque, intermingle in surprising and wondrous ways that make Rome one of the great sightseeing cities of the world.

Excursions

Just an hour or so away are the ancient port of Ostia Antica, the fountains of Tivoli, the rolling hills of the Castelli Romani, and the Etruscan ruins of the coast.

Nearby Waters

Lido di Ostia, 28 km, 17 mi., by special train (departs from Line B "Piramide" stop), is Rome's disappointing beach with black sand, questionably clean sea, but plenty of breezes; *Lake Bracciano*, 35 km, 22 mi. by Viterbo train, by contrast is clean as well as refreshing.

Festivals and Events

Holy Week and *Christmas*, neighborhood religious festivals, such as Trastevere's *Festa de' Noaltri* (mid-July); Art festivals (July at Villa Medici; spring and fall, Via Margutta) and antiques fairs (V. Coronari in May); and grand summer events with the Santa Cecilia Orchestra (July), dance, theater and music on the Isola Tiberina (July–Sept.), and in just about any historic piazza or church cloister.

Shopping

While artisans and restorers still work in the old city around the Campo dei Fiori and in Trastevere, most of Roman shopping is devoted to the antique shops on *Via Babuino*, *Via Margutta*, *Via Coronari* and *Via Giulia* and the stylish designer boutiques near the foot of the Spanish Steps and around the Piazza Navona.

Accommodations

From the most deluxe hotels to pilgrimage pensioni, but seldom enough *(except, perhaps, Nov.–Feb.)* and never enough in the inexpensive categories.

Eating Out

Superb Roman, regional and international food, from the most experimental *nuova cucina* to the most traditional *spaghetti al carbonara*.

Getting Around

Once you see the traffic, the one-way maze of streets, the cars parked on sidewalks, you won't even dream of driving. Park your car at your hotel or a garage (see "Directory"), and forget it.

The most beautiful quarters of Rome either ban traffic or provide only limited access (to and from hotel, taxis, etc.), so only walking will introduce you to the real Rome.

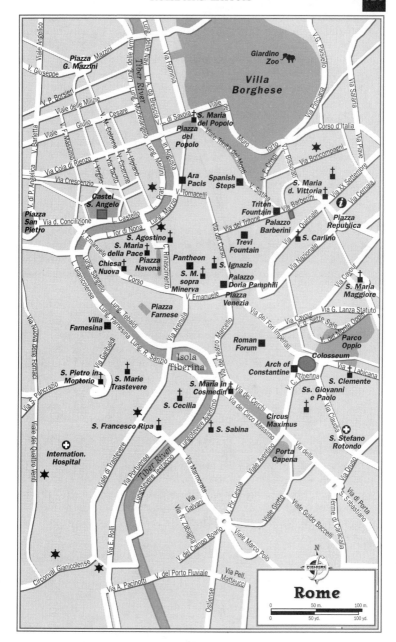

Rome

At times you'll tire, so public transportation is useful. Lines A & B of the subway, or **metro**, efficiently connect the edges of the historic center—the Stazione Termini with the Colosseum and Aventine Hill, as well as with the Piazza di Spagna and Vatican. Regular **buses** often have special lanes enabling them to negotiate traffic, but not along the *Lungateveri*, or riverside roads. Among the most useful bus routes are: #56, making a diagonal between the V. Veneto and Trastevere, passing the Triton fountain, the Corso, and P. Venezia; the pickpocket-laden #64 cutting east-west from the Stazione Termini to the Vatican via V. Nazionale and P. Venezia. The trolley #30, or **tram**, makes an immense time-consuming loop that can be useful on the short haul, as it travels from Viale Trastevere to the Celsius pyramid, Colosseum, Lateran and S. Maria Maggiore, to north of the Villa Borghese park, then over to P. Risorgimento near the Vatican. The *scenic Acquabus* rides the Tiber from Isola Tiburina to Ponte Duca d'Aosta with a stop at Ponte Cavour every day but Monday.

Maps • The EPT maps usually indicate the metro lines. Bus route maps are on sale at newsstands, but you might buy instead a street-indexed city map that also lists the routes of buses. The best aid to city exploration is *Tutto Citta*, published by the telephone company and found at hotels, cafes with public phones, etc. In addition to bus maps, it contains 64 street-indexed maps of the city, enabling you to find virtually any piazzetta or medieval lane.

Arriving

Two airports, *Fiumicino* (aka Leonardo da Vinci) for most international and domestic traffic and *Ciampino* (not as convenient) for charters and domestic flights. Fiumicino is connected to Rome by fast trains to the Stazione Ostiense annex (near metro B at Piramide) and Stazione Termini; Ciampino by bus to metroline A; taxis available too. *Rapid trains* to European as well as Italian cities (on the Pendolino 1.5 hours to Florence, 4 hours to Milan; 7.5 hours on the diretto to Venice; 2.5 hours to Naples); many *pullman buses* from smaller regional cities supplement the slower train service; and *highways* from every direction connect with the Grande Raccolta Annulare (GRA), or beltway that rings the city.

Driving Tips • If you are arriving on A-1 from the north follow "Via Salaria" signs from autotrada and GRA for the most direct route to Via Veneto area • On A-1 stop at the Salaria Ouest service area, or on A-2 from the south, stop at Frascati Est (May-Sept.), for maps of Rome and directions into the city given by EPT tourist offices of Lazio. • Make every effort to arrive early morning or between 1:30-3:30 p.m., Sun., or whenever you'll avoid traffic.

Special Tips

Great View • Rome offers many spectacular viewpoints from its hills, but a wonderful way of getting oriented is to climb to the top terrace of the Castel Sant'Angelo on a clear day. Here the panorama is accompanied by a graph identifying the places in front of you.

Sightseeing Tips • Binoculars can be essential for ceiling mosaics and frescoes as well as reliefs carved high on triumphal arches and columns. • Strict dress code enforced at St. Peter's and major basilicas. Visiting hours are seasonal, and may fluctuate gradually with the amount of daylight. Hours listed here are the longest (July-Aug.) and shortest (Dec.–Jan.). • *Most churches, but not St. Peter's and a few others, close noon–3:30 p.m., or 12:30–4 p.m.*

Museum Pass • The Museidon cards exclude many major museums and monuments, so check the details before buying one of these discounted one-price passes to city museums and archaeological sites.

Shop Hours • *Most close 1-4 p.m.*, all day Sun.,(however, quite a number now open on Sun., especially around the Corso, the Pantheon, and other lively areas; the V. Coronari antique shops open last Sun. of month) and Mon. morning; food shops close Thurs. afternoon or, in summer, Sat. p.m. instead.

Walking Tips • The frenzied traffic of main streets, like the Corso or V. Emanuele, or V. Trastevere, can be avoided by scenic detours through historic areas where traffic is restricted, so get a good map. • *Use official crosswalks* if you expect Roman drivers to notice you (California this is not, but we haven't yet seen a pedestrian run down either). • Beware of cars traveling in reverse. • Know that Romans do not curb their dogs.

Summer • It can be scorching, but weekends the Romans are at the beach and in Aug., especially the last two weeks, there's barely any traffic to mar your enjoyment of the city. (We still prefer the fall and spring.)

Crime • Not as dangerous as American cities, Rome does have thieves and most especially pickpockets. Be watchful around the P. della Repubblica and Stazione Termini, and in congested buses. Beware of the Gypsy children and begging women—one distracts you with a newspaper or doll-baby, the other picks your pocket. Really the best protection is prevention—use money belts, or put your money in unexpected places, like inside jackets or grocery bags, not in pants pockets.

Good Reading • Two historical novels on ancient Rome are *I, Claudius* by Robert Graves and *Memoirs of Hadrian* by Marguerite Yourcenar. Eleanor Clark's reflections in *Rome and a Villa* are the best in the genre of travel literature.

Rome, *Roma* in Italian, embraces so many icons of the past that it can be hard to think beyond the Colosseum and Pantheon, beyond Michelangelo's dome for St. Peter's and Bernini's Fountain of the Four Rivers to a modern city where three million now live. A city of two capitals, one of Italy, the other of the Catholic church, Rome hosts a worldly community of two separate diplomatic corps, seminarians and religious pilgrims, scholars at foreign academies for classics and arts as well as students at national institutes for drama and music. Considerable dash is added by the film industry, which thrives here. And sheer volume is contributed by the millions of tourists visiting the year round.

Despite the cosmopolitan air so many foreigners impart, the Romans themselves give the city its distinctive character. In fact, they seem pleasantly indifferent to the eccentricities of their visitors, perhaps from so much exposure over the centuries. Yet they are indifferent to little else. Full of zest, their driving, gesturing, and talking animates the city—or renders it chaotic, according to some. Unable to escape the constant presence of millennia of history, they have tamed it, hanging their laundry over monastic walls, washing their cars from marble fountains, defying the constraints of the ancient city by turning piazzas into soccer fields and nobles' villas into public parks.

However successfully the Romans have made the city theirs, it can be overwhelming on too brief a visit. Considering its museums alone (and Rome is more a great city than a city of great museums), the collections of Etruscan (Villa Giulia), Greek, and Roman art (Museo delle Terme and Capitoline museums) are not only among the greatest in the world, they are also immense. Then, in addition, a full day at the Vatican Museums hardly exhausts *them*. Moreover, there are Renaissance and Baroque collections at the Galleria Borghese and the Palazzo Barberini, but we haven't even begun to list the patrician galleries, like that of the Doria Pamphili. And you still haven't visited the Forum....

Yet it is Rome itself that is most beautiful—the glorious architecture and fountains, the meandering Tiber river, and the hills covered with cypresses and umbrella pines. *If you have time only for the major museums and the most monumental sights, then you might miss falling in love with Rome. It is the small streets, often winding and medieval or simply Renaissance straight, that can seduce you,* delighting you as they suddenly open to a beautiful piazza or frame an ancient obelisk. In truth it is the myriad of smaller churches, from Early Christian Santa Costanza with its 4th-century mosaics to Borromini's Baroque jewel Sant'Ivo, that thrill you upon discovery. It is the ancient columns embedded in a Renaissance facade, a Mithraic altar under a Christian church, or an antique sewer-cover honored as an oracle by busloads of tourists that can be most memorable.

Maybe, as they say, one lifetime isn't enough to know Rome. But you certainly can become acquainted. And any proper introduction should sample Rome's diversity, from its awesome monumentality to its most intimate *rioni*, or neighborhoods. Concentrate on those famous monuments and museums that you most want to see, but walk to them via the smaller back streets, stopping at a church or palazzo along the way. The Castel Sant'Angelo, for example, is most scenic when approached from the old pilgrimage street of Via Coronari, rather than on the Corso V. Emanuele; and Trastevere can be reached through the Jewish Quarter near the Teatro Marcello, then over Tiburina Island, rather than on the Via Arenula. Using the "Nearby Sights" sections under the following descriptions of the major monuments as well as the neighborhood walks, you can discover some of these more intimate parts of Rome. You might even make such detours to see your favorite art, plotting the Raphaels or Caravaggios, the Bernini sculptures, or Early Christian mosaics onto the map of your grand tour of the city. Then make sure you schedule in a picnic on one of Rome's hills after an exhausting visit to a museum. Or sip a *granita di caffe* in one of the many picturesque piazzas—and scheme your return.

What to See and Do

Piazza Venezia

This vast chaotic traffic circle can fortunately be avoided on most, if not all, walks through Rome. It is the center of the city through which cars and buses pass, and from where the "Colosseo" stop of Metro B is just a 10-minute walk. You can't miss it either, dominated as it is by that massive ungainly 20th-century monument to Vittorio Emanuele II, the white marble **Vittoriano**—its bronze triumphal chariots spotted from even across the city. Here, then, is a place to get your bearings. Behind the Vittoriano is the **Campidoglio**. In front, across the piazza, is the Corso, running north to the Piazza del Popolo and Villa Borghese. East, the Via Fori Imperiali runs past the Roman Forum to the Colosseum, and farther east is St. John Lateran Church. West, the Corso V. Emanuele skirts the Pantheon on its way to the Tiber, and continues to St. Peter's. South the Via Teatro di Marcello forms the edge of the old Jewish ghetto before approaching the Tiber with Trastevere on the far side.

Campidoglio ★★

One of the seven hills of ancient Rome, the *Campidoglio*, or Capitoline Hill, was the political and religious center of the Empire, the goal of every triumphal procession. Though the ancient temples and capitol buildings are gone, the Piazza del Campidoglio at the summit continues as the seat of the municipal government and the site of important public ceremonies. Though the Roman Forum once provided the sole access to the Campidoglio, today there is ★**Michelangelo's graceful ramp**, the *cordonata* ascending its west side next to the forbiddingly steep medieval stairs leading to Santa Maria in Aracoeli. In 1538, Michelangelo brilliantly redesigned the summit piazza, turning it into a public space befitting the grandeur of its history. The three palazzi facades are his design (only the Palazzo Nuovo, left, was new, added for symmetry) and form a trapezoidal perspective converging on the Palazzo Senatorio with its double staircase and fountain of the goddess Roma. Two-story pilasters were used to increase the monumentality of the palazzi, while ancient sculptures everywhere speak of Rome's heroic past, from the balustrade of the cordonata to the cornice sculptures of the palaces. No sculpture is more important to the design than the ★★bronze equestrian statue, *Marcus Aurelius* (A.D. 164) meant to be in the piazza center (original preserved in Palazzo dei Conservatori, to right; copy planned) on its Michelangelo-designed pedestal. A symbol of Rome, the statue was revered in the middle ages (it was thought to be the first Christian emperor, Constantine) and later became the inspiration for many Renaissance sculptors.

A visit to the piazza can be quite casual. You can enjoy the view out over the cordonata to the city, especially fine at dusk. You can glance into the courtyards of the side palazzi where there is della Porta's magnificent ★fountain made from an ancient river god (in the Palazzo Nuovo) as well as the ★★ *Colossal Head of Constantine* (in the Palazzo dei

Rome

Conservatori on right), its introspective gaze meant for the emperor's basilica in the Roman Forum, where it would have been part of a seated statue more than 30 feet high. And you certainly can enjoy the two ★ views of the Roman Forum behind the Palazzo Senatorio, breathtaking even at night when the Forum is illuminated: that to the right of the palazzo provides the best overview while that to the left leads down to the Forum. From this side you can see the ancient wall of the archives of Imperial Rome that literally forms the foundation for the Palazzo Senatorio, today's City Hall. With more time, your visit can include the museums and churches here.

On the P. Venezia, the Campidoglio is served by bus #64 to Vatican, #56 between Trastevere and V. Veneto.

Santa Maria in Aracoeli ★
Easiest access from rear of church, off east end of P. Campidoglio.
Since at least the 7th century, there has been a church here. Much of today's church, so elaborately hung with chandeliers, dates from the 13th century when the ★ Cosmati pavements, pulpits (at the crossing), and tombs (in the transepts) were crafted. Among the most cherished art here are Pinturicchio's ★ *Life of S. Bernardino*, (1485; 1st chapel, south aisle) and Cavallini's fresco ★ *Enthroned Madonna and Saints*, above the 1302 tomb of D'Aquasparta (end north transept).

Musei Capitolini ★★
9 a.m.–1:30 p.m. and also on Tues. & Sat. 5–8 p.m. (but Sat. till 11 p.m. Oct.–Mar. 30); Sun. and festivi till 1 p.m.; closed Mon.; L10,000.
The vast collections, mostly from ancient Rome, of the Capitoline Museums, are contained in the two flanking palazzi on Michelangelo's piazza. One ticket gains entrance to both.

Palazzo Nuovo
On the north side and with della Porta's river god fountain.
This museum contains Roman sculptures along with Egyptian ones, many from Hadrian's Villa. In the room at the top of the stairs, you'll discover the most famous work in the collection, the expressive ★★ *Dying Gaul*, a Roman copy of a 3rd-century B.C. bronze from Pergamon, as well as ★ *Satiro in Reposo*, (#7, copy of a Praxiteles). In Room 2, there's the marble ★ *Drunken Faun*, (copy of Hellinistic bronze) and in Room 3, the painfully arthritic ★ *Old Woman* (#22, copy of Hellenistic original) to see on your way to two rooms of portrait busts, Roman art at its best, whether of ★ *Cicero*, (Room 4, #56) or the young ★ *Augustus*, or the wondrous curls of ★ *Flavian Woman* (both Room 5, on columns). ★ Room 5 contains many other noteworthy works, among them in the center, a reclining ★ *Helena*, mother of Constantine. Across the corridor in a small room is the ★ *Capitoline Venus*, inspired by Praxiteles' Aphrodite; and in a room near the stairs, the mosaic ★★ *Doves*, lyrically executed.

Palazzo dei Conservatori
On the south side.
Unmistakable with Constantine's colossal head in its cortile, this palazzo holds a pinacoteca (2° *piano*) of Renaissance and Early Baroque paintings as well as extensive and important collections from antiquity (1° *piano*).

Piazza San Pietro, Rome

The Pantheon, Rome

Stone tablet, The Colosseum, Rome

The Colosseum, Rome

Climbing the stairs to the collections of ★★**ancient art**, you'll pass four ★relief panels from triumphal arches, three dedicated to Marcus Aurelius (on right wall, *Sacrifice to Capitoline Jupiter*–remnants of this temple found at rear of this palazzo), the fourth to Hadrian. Another fine Hadrian panel is seen at the next landing where you enter straight into Room 1 of the formal reception rooms of the Sale dei Conservatori, which hold the most famous works of the collection. From Algardi's *Innocent X* and Bernini's (with assistants) *Urban VIII* move on to Room 3. Here is the delicate bronze ★★*Boy with Thorn*, (1st century B.C.; center of room) perhaps a Greek original; the compelling bronze portrait bust thought to be the founder of the Republic ★★*Junius Brutus*, (3rd century B.C.); and the ★*Sarcophagus of Four Seasons*, (3rd century A.D.) In the center of Room 4 is the ★★*Capitoline Wolf*, symbol of Rome since ancient times. The she-wolf is an Etruscan statue (5th century B.C.) with the legendary twins added by A. Pollaioli in the Renaissance; against the rear wall is the stone list of consuls taken from Augustus' arch in the Roman Forum and framed by Michelangelo. Then you enter Room 5 with a 4th-century Greek ★statue of a dog, ancient ★bronze ducks, as well as Bernini's restrained bust of *Medusa*, (1636). If you want to see more, continue straight, until you are forced left through the Galleria Orti Lamiani, a passage overlooking the cortile on one side, a garden on the other, and with fine sculptures, like the ★*Esquiline Venus* (1st century B.C.). At the end, a left takes you to the stairs, a right through the rest of the collections, including the remnants of the Capitoline temple wall (end of corridor).

Upstairs, past a landing with 4th-century A.D. marble intarsias, is the ★**pinacoteca** with a small room of Venetian Renaissance paintings worthy of a detour (Room 2; Bellini, Veronese, and Tintoretto). Deeper into the gallery are Early Baroque (Caravaggio, Guercino, and some lesser Carracci works, most in the *salon*, midway through, then left) and Baroque paintings (concert hall at end, with Guido Reni, Pietro da Cortona).

North Side of Roman Forum

As you exit the northeast end of the piazza, with the Palazzo Senatorio on your right, a park on your left, you descend stairs that place you next to the fence of the Roman Forum near the Arch of Septimus Severus. You pass the **Mamertine Prison** (on left), now consecrated as S. Pietro in Carcere, a dungeon used in ancient times and according to Christian tradition, where Peter and Paul were imprisoned. Next to it is the first undulating church facade of the High Baroque, Pietro da Cortona's masterpiece ★★**Luca e Martina** (1640), its capitals echoing those of Septimus' arch and its coffered interior simply beautiful. *This path joins the Via dei Fori Imperiali and the Forum entrance.*

Roman Forum and Palatine Hill ★★★

All roads led to Rome, to this very spot where the ancient empire began, in the marshy strip of land at the foot of the Palatine and Capitoline hills. According to legend, Romulus founded the city on the Palatine in 753 B.C. And here the hillside village grew into the brick city of the Roman Republic, then the marble one of the Empire. Cicero gave his orations here on the Rostra. Julius Caesar was cremated here while Mark Antony came to

THE FORUM (WEST)

The Forum has survived fire, earthquakes, barbarian invasions and marble quarriers. Its temples have been transformed into churches, and colonnades lost under layers of time.

ARCH OF SEPTIMUS SEVERUS

Severus' elaborate monument (A.D. 203) is carved with the first historical narrative panels. They commemorate his battles with Partha, now eastern Iran.

Palazzo
Senatorio

Temple of
Concord

Rostra

Portico of Dii
Consentes

Column of
Phocas

VIA SACRA

TEMPLE OF VESPASIAN

Piransi did an 18th century engraving of the Forum from here. At one time its three columns were almost completely buried.

TEMPLE OF SATURN

Founded in 497 B.C. and rebuilt in 42 B.C., this was once the site of the state treasury.

BASILICA GIUILA

Basilica Giuila (54 B.C.) built by Caesar and Augustus, was used as a law court. It is located between the Temple of Saturn and the Temple of Castor and Pollux.

NEXT SPREAD

Basilica of Constantine

ROMAN

🏛
Temple of Saturn

FORUM

Colosseum

THIS SPREAD

Arch of Titus

SANTA LUCA E MARTINA

This medieval church was reconstructed by Pietro da Cortona in 1640.

Fora di Cesare

CURIA

The site of the Roman senate chamber was reconstructed in A.D. 203 as a Christian church.

BASILICA AEMILA

Once a large meeting area, this basilica was destroyed in the 5th century, A.D.

VIA DELLA CURIA

VIA DELLA SALARA VECCHIA

Forum Magnum

The Regia

Temple of Antonine and Faustina

Temple of Vesta

TEMPLE OF JULIUS CAESAR
Erected on the spot where Caesar was cremated.

VIA SACRA

TEMPLE OF CASTOR AND POLLUX

The three remaining Corinthian columns are capped by an entablature from the time of Augustus. The temple was dedicated in the 5th century B.C.

House of Vestal Virgins

Rome

THE FORUM (EAST)

Entering the ruins of The Forum provides a unique walk through ancient Rome and enables you to climb the magnificent Palatine Hill.

VIA DEI FORI IMPERIALI

TEMPLE OF VESTA

The Regia

VIA SACRA

TEMPLE OF ROMULUS

One of Rome's most sacred shrines, this was a temple dedicated to the goddess of the hearth. What remains is a section of circular Corinthian columns.

HOUSE OF VESTAL VIRGINS

ARCH OF TITUS

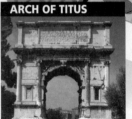

Priestesses who lived here were responsible for making sure the sacred fire dedicated to the goddess Vesta never went out. Several of the statues from the garden have survived.

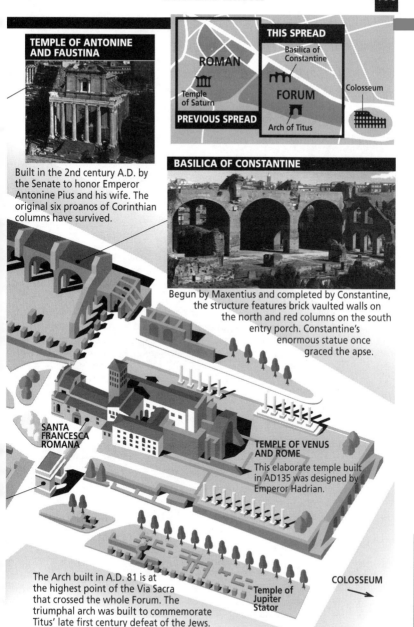

THIS SPREAD

ROMAN

FORUM

PREVIOUS SPREAD

Temple of Saturn

Basilica of Constantine

Arch of Titus

Colosseum

TEMPLE OF ANTONINE AND FAUSTINA

Built in the 2nd century A.D. by the Senate to honor Emperor Antonine Pius and his wife. The original six proanos of Corinthian columns have survived.

BASILICA OF CONSTANTINE

Begun by Maxentius and completed by Constantine, the structure features brick vaulted walls on the north and red columns on the south entry porch. Constantine's enormous statue once graced the apse.

SANTA FRANCESCA ROMANA

TEMPLE OF VENUS AND ROME

This elaborate temple built in AD135 was designed by Emperor Hadrian.

The Arch built in A.D. 81 is at the highest point of the Via Sacra that crossed the whole Forum. The triumphal arch was built to commemorate Titus' late first century defeat of the Jews.

Temple of Jupiter Stator

COLOSSEUM

Rome

bury him, "not to praise him." On the Via Sacra victorious emperors marched the Forum's length, displaying the booty from battles that made Rome *caput mundi*, capital of the world.

Here was the original Rome, its temples, triumphal arches, its law courts and senate. But here too were its markets, its social life, all crowded into the narrow streets lined with colonnades. Even the venerated Temple of Castor and Pollux stood atop a shopping complex where recent excavations have found evidence of 29 shops, one a combined barber-dentist shop where customers played dice games while waiting. Imperial Rome grew and expanded into new forums, but it is this one that maintained the Sacred Fire of the eternal city.

Incredibly, enough remains of the Roman Forum today for it to be evocative of the past. It has survived fire and earthquakes, it has survived barbarian invasions and Renaissance marble quarriers. Its temples have been transformed into churches, colonnades lost under layers of time. It was reduced to a cow pasture, only to be revealed again through the serious excavations that began in 1898 and continue today.

Visiting the Forum and Palatine

A visit need not be a formal walk through the ruins nor one confined to the official hours. The views from the Campidoglio (see above) are superb and night illumination makes it possible to see the site most dramatically. Not many reliefs or sculptures are left in the Forum and some—like the Arch of Septimus Severus, but not that of Titus—can be partially seen on the north path of the Campidoglio. But entering the ruins, even if you're not well versed in Roman history—for the history, audio tours in English can be rented—provides a unique walk through ancient Rome and enables you to climb the magnificent Palatine Hill. *Entrances are found on the north (V. dei Fori Imperiali) and east sides (V. San Gregorio). Open in summer 9 a.m.–6 p.m. (exit at 7 p.m.); in winter, till 2 p.m. (exit at 3 p.m.); Sun., festivi till 2 p.m. in summer, 1 p.m. in winter. L10,000. For buses, see "Campidoglio" and "Colosseum."*

Forum   ★★★

Entering from V. dei Fori, you are midway into the Forum at the foot of the ★ **Temple of Antonius and Faustina** (A.D. 141), since the 11th–century consecrated as the Church of San Lorenzo in Miranda, but retaining the beautiful frieze and porch of the deified emperor and his wife. To the right, you pass the ruined Basilica Emilia before arriving at the superbly preserved ★ **Curia** (rebuilt A.D. 203), the basilica of the Roman Senate that has survived because it was so early converted into a Christian church. The **Rostra**, or public speaking platforms, are found left of the triple ★ **Arch of Septimus Severus** (A.D. 203). Severus' grandiose monument is carved with the first historical narrative panels ever, albeit in a rather squat, unclassical style. They commemorate his battles with Parthia, now eastern Iran. At the foot of the Campidoglio, the tufa stone **Tabularium** (78 B.C.), archives for treaties and Roman laws, closes the western end of the Forum. In front are the marble columns from the ruined **Temple of Concord** (on right) and the **Temple of Vespacian**. Off to the extreme left is the **Portico of the Consenti** (rebuilt A.D. 367), a Corinthian colonnade dedicated to the 12 Olympian gods of the Romans and the last pagan monument erected.

The Roman Forum and Palatine Hill.

Beginning the Via Sacra on its route east, are the eight Ionic columns of the former ★ **Temple of Saturn** (founded 497 B.C., rebuilt 42 B.C.) where the state treasury was entrusted, followed by the ruins of the Basilica Giulia, built by Julius Caesar and Augustus and used as a law court. The next recognizable monument is the ★ **Temple of Castor and Pollux**, its three remaining Corinthian columns capped elegantly by an entablature from the time of Augustus. The venerated temple was dedicated in the 5th century B.C. when the Heavenly Twins are said to have fought side by side with the Romans in their defeat of the Etruscans. Just to the left, in what is now the center of the Forum, are the unrecognizable remains of the **Temple of Caesar**, where the famous ruler was cremated and later deified by his successor Augustus (whose own triumphal arch once stood here too). The circular, partially reconstructed ★ **Temple of Vesta**, originally a wooden hut in the 6th century, contained the sacred fire that symbolized Rome's continuity. Vestal Virgins, the only female priesthood in Rome, tended the fires under a vow of chastity that if broken, led to their burial–while alive. Their ★ house (rebuilt A.D. 64), behind the temple, encloses a garden courtyard where broken statues of important vestals can be found. Beyond the Temple of Antoninus, the Via Sacra continues past the monumental ★ ★ **Basilica of Constantine** (A.D. post 313), begun by Maxentius and completed by Constantine, and one of the last great buildings in Imperial Rome. All that remains are the magnificent brick vaulted walls of one aisle, the north, and the porphyry red columns of the south entrance porch, as well as part of the apse once filled by Constantine's colossal statue (see Campidoglio). Gone is the nave that soared even higher (114 feet). Marking the east end of the Forum is the ★ ★ **Arch of Titus**

(A.D. 81), celebrating the defeat of Jerusalem and famous for two reliefs in the passage that attempted a new form of illusionism. Accompanying you into the Forum is *Titus in Chariot* on one side, and on the other, the *Triumphal Procession*, carrying the menorah and other booty from the Temple of Jerusalem.

Palatine Hill ★★

Midway on the south side of the Forum, near Caligula's palace, you ascend the Palatine by way of the fountains, gardens and grottos of the fortunate Farnese family that had their 16th-century villa here. The ★ views from the top are fabulous, across to the Colosseum and, in the rear, over the **Circus Maximus** that once held 300,000 spectators at its chariot races. The tranquil country setting is wonderful, too, after the shadeless Forum below. And the ruins of imperial palaces amid such beauty makes the retreat here all the more romantic. Long before Vignola built the Farnesi their Renaissance villa, the emperors had built their palaces. And before them, in Republican times, so had the well-to-do. Even in the 8th century B.C. the Romans lived here, in wooden huts. Today, the Farnese gardens and villa sit atop Tiberius' unexcavated palace and just behind them, to the south, is the ★ **Casa di Livia** (1st century B.C.), named after Augustus' wife, but part of his house and with frescoes to reward a visit. The relative simplicity of this complex built during the transition from the Republic to the Empire contrasts mightily with the later ★ **Palace of Domitian** (end 1st century B.C.) that sprawls over most of the hill to the east. Proving why "palatial" derives from the Palantino, this vast complex includes the ruins of the state apartments and throne room (called "Domus Flavia," to north), Domitian's vast private residence (called "Domus Augustana"), and east beyond that, the stadium where he presided over games. One of the grand views is from a belvedere, south of this stadium.

Nearby Fori Imperiali

Via dei Fori Imperiali.

Built outside the Roman Forum by five rulers from Caesar to Trajan, the Imperial Forums accommodated the needs of Rome as it expanded from a Republic to an Empire. Later covered by Renaissance buildings, Mussolini cleared the area in 1924, exposed some of the *fori*, or forums, but paved over most of them when he constructed a massive avenue here for his military parades. Although these ruins are scattered on both sides of the street, a stroll along the north of the Via dei Fori Imperiali gives you ample opportunity to see the most interesting ones, in particular those of ★ **Trajan's Forum** (A.D. 113), near the Piazza Venezia and its two domed churches. Here you can see the ancient masterpiece ★★ **Trajan's Column**, its reliefs spiraling up in a narrative of the painful wars with Dacia (now Romania). The realistic scenes have been called the Roman equivalent to a documentary war film by scholar George Hanfmann, but you can't see them adequately without binoculars. On the north edge of this forum is the semi-circular brick ★ **Trajan's Market**, a three-story shopping mall ingeniously built into the Quirinal Hill. Behind it rises the massive medieval defense tower, the **Torre delle Milizie**. Next to Trajan's Forum is Augustus', with its ruined **Temple of Mars Ultor** (2nd century B.C.); then there's **Nerva's Forum** with its gigantic Corinthian columns and Hellenistic frieze.

Colosseum and Other Sights ★★★

So emblematic of Rome, it's said that when the ★★★**Colosseum** falls, so shall Rome. Fortunately an end was put to the Renaissance looting of its travertine marble facade—seemingly at just the right moment for achieving a picturesque broken profile. The monumental brick vaulted building is intensely Roman in design, but covered with a Greek veneer of different capital orders on its three tiers of arcades. The many arches formed the entrances to the arena, each numbered so that the 50,000 spectators could easily find their seats—considered a marvel of the time, though in some respects seating was preordained: senators on the first tier; citizens, the second; commoners on the third; and non-aristocratic women stuck off on the fourth with the workers holding up the awnings over the arena. In A.D. 80, when Titus dedicated the Colosseum, he sponsored 100 days of games in which 9000 animals were killed—leopards, lions, bears and a rhinoceros, though there is no historical evidence that any Christians were martyred then or later in the gladiatorial contests. The interior today exposes the underground passages where animal cages and machinery would have been kept. Originally there was a wooden floor covered with sand ("arena") to soak up the blood—and there are plans to recreate it (without the blood).

Admission to the arena is free, 9 a.m.–6 p.m. (exit 7 p.m.) May–Sept., and in winter till 2 p.m. (exit 3 p.m.); year-round Sun., Wed. exit at 1 p.m. Metro B stop "Colosseo"; buses (#85 runs from Colosseum to P. San Silvestre near Spanish Steps); trams (#30 behind Colosseum to Trastevere).

Arch of Constantine

Arch of Constantine   ★★

Far from being dwarfed by the Colosseum next to it, the triple arch of Constantine (A.D. 315) is quite stately. It commemorates a victory, of course, but really symbolizes the transition from pagan Rome to the Christian world. Erected by the Senate

Fielding
WORLDWIDE

ROME

THE COLOSSEUM

In A.D. 80 when Titus dedicated the Colosseum, 100 days of games were held in which hundreds of prisoners and slaves fought gladiators to the death and more than 9000 animals were killed. The wooden floor was covered in sand to soak up the blood.

Vomitorium

THE PODIUM

This platform terrace contained exclusive seats for the emperor and his upper class friends and guests.

Arena

INTERNAL CORRIDORS

Two corridors circled the ramps of seats and made it easier for people to reach their seats. The Colosseum could easily seat 50,000.

ENTRY ROUTES

Stairs were built leading to the seats at each level. Numbered levels and corridors helped people find their seats. People were seated according to their class or rank.

UNDERGROUND ROOMS

Excavations in the 19th century revealed the underground rooms where wild animals were kept. A winch brought the animal cages to the arena level and animals ran through long corridors to the arena.

COLOSSEUM ▶ RUINS

The colosseum's four story travertine marble facade was heavily looted during the Renaissance.

VELARIUM

A gigantic sailcloth awning sheltered spectators from the elements. Sailors, slaves, and lower class workers maintained the massive covering.

Fourth story added for more seating

Travertine blocks (later stripped and recycled by popes)

BOLLARDS

Bollards encircled the entire Colosseum as anchors for the Velarium.

80 arched entrances

Rome

to the first Christian emperor, it is a sculptural lecture (binoculars useful) to be like the great emperors who preceded him, for it is covered with old reliefs from monuments to Trajan (inside central arch and two side facades), Hadrian, who makes a pagan sacrifice (medallions on the facades), and Marcus Aurelius (eight reliefs across top of facades). The sorry little friezes over the arches belong to Constantine, an artful expression of the struggling empire, soon to end.

Nearby Hills and Churches

With the exception of a visit to the Michelangelo described below, most first-time visitors to Rome find it difficult to add the following sights to their itinerary—maybe a visit to one of the hills for a picnic, but otherwise they are rightly off to some of the more famous sights.

From the Oppian Hill north of the Colosseum, to the Celian south of it, Nero constructed his **Domus Aurea** (A.D. 65), or Golden House. If the size still isn't clear, consider that the Colosseum now sits on the landfill of his garden pond and probably is named after the Colossus of Nero, his 120-foot statue that graced the nearby vestibule. Upon completing his new home, the emperor reportedly sighed that at last he was housed like a human. Little of the Golden House remains, but the hills are lovely to visit, dotted with other ancient ruins in park-like settings. Yet it is Michelangelo who draws visitors to the **Parco Oppio**, one of the peaks of the Esquiline Hill and just a short walk northeast of the Colosseum. Climbing the Via delle Terme di Tito (down to the right are foundations of Nero's house), you turn left at the ruins of the *terme*, or baths, and deadend at the Piazza de **San Pietro in Vincoli** *(St. Peter in Chains; closed noon-3:30 p.m.)*. In the right aisle of the church is Michelangelo's powerful statue of ★★ *Moses* (1545), enthroned on the sadly incomplete Tomb of Julius II. (The "horns" are Biblical rays of light.) Only the two flanking figures of Leah and Rachel, earlier works, are also by the master. (Light machine.) Less often visited is the **Colle Celio**, behind the Colosseum and where the ruins of the Temple of Claudius mingle with those of Nero's nymphaeum. Atop the hill is the handsome church of **SS Giovanni e Paolo** *(V. San Gregorio, then left on Clivo di Scauro)* with its ancient columns, Romanesque lion porch and campanile (10th century) built on marble from Claudius' temple. Farther along, across the modern street of Via Claudia is the largest and oldest round church in the world, the compelling ★ **S. Stefano Rotondo** (A.D. 486).

To St. John Lateran

From the Colosseum it is only a ten-minute walk east (on V. San Giovanni Laterano) to the cathedral of Rome. Halfway there, you would be mistaken not to stop at ★★ **San Clemente**, a most intriguing medieval basilica. The lovely nave of the 11th-century church preserves a raised choir from its original 4th century church and culminates in the 12th century ★ *apse mosaics* with a Christ lost in a profusion of garlands and volutes (5th century style may indicate another borrowing from the earlier church) as well as an enchanting pastoral paradise. In the north aisle at the rear is the ★ *Chapel of St. Catherine of Alexandria*, frescoed by Masolino and perhaps Masaccio (the *Crucifixion* above altar) in the Early Renaissance style of Florence. As if this weren't enough for a visit, the church offers an Alice in Wonderland tour through the earlier, much damaged, 4th-century church over which it is super-imposed. Not only that, the *Early Christian church* with its fresco fragments is itself built over and around a Mithraic chapel and 1st-century Roman apartment house. The 60-foot descent into the past *(through sacristy; closed noon–3:30 p.m.; L2000)* is eerie, the exploration a confusing jumble of cultural artifacts, the impact unforgettable—especially the sound of water rushing through ancient Roman ducts.

Continuing to ★**San Giovanni in Laterano** *(open 7 a.m.–6 p.m.; strict dress code of St. Peter's*; metro A "San Giovanni" stop, bus 85 to Colosseum and P. Venezia and others) you arrive at the piazza of the same name so unmistakably marked with Rome's tallest and oldest (15th century B.C.) Egyptian obelisk. Here you face the baptistery and north side of the cathedral, founded by Constantine and considered the mother church of Catholicism. The 4th-century church was soon destroyed by the Vandals, then rebuilt and destroyed many times over. Only the separate octag-onal **Baptistery** *(8 a.m.–noon, 3–5 p.m.)* preserves any feeling of antiquity, and it is a 5th-century rebuilding that has undergone, like the church, considerable refur-bishing in papal pomp. A visit includes some fine 5th-century mosaics, however (1st and 2nd chapels left; ★apse, straight through, next to atrium). The main facade (1736) of the church faces east on the Piazza Porta San Giovanni, named for its 16th-century gate. The Baroque interior is appropriately impressive, its nave and four aisles redesigned by Borromini in 1645, its transepts earlier, by della Porta. In the crossing is the papal altar crowned with a Gothic tabernacle containing the silver reliquaries for the heads of saints Peter and Paul. Here only the pope says mass. The apse mosaics are poor reconstructions of Torriti's originals from 1291. In the south aisle, before the transept, is the entrance to the magnificent ★**Cosmati cloister** *(9 a.m.–5 p.m.; L2000)*, colored marble and inlaid gold chips glinting from its twisted columns and frieze (1220). Around the sides are artistic fragments from the medi-eval era of St. John Lateran.

Pantheon and Environs ★ ★ ★

The best preserved monument from antiquity, the ★ ★ ★**Pantheon** (A.D. 126) bridges the two millennia separating us in a way the ruined buildings of the Roman Forum cannot. If the Colosseum requires some effort of the imagination to recreate its former splendor, the impact of the Pantheon is immediate and awesome. Already famous in ancient times as a marvel of engineering, the temple has incomprehensibly survived whole. No matter that its bronze roof was carted off to Constantinople by an emperor. Or that the bronze fittings on the porch were taken by Urban VIII for Bernini's baldi-cchino in St. Peter's—giving rise to the barb "what the barbarians didn't do, Barberini (the pope) did." No matter that it was a medieval fortress or that a poultry market flour-ished on its porch in the Renaissance, a fish market at its steps until 1845. The Pantheon, with the great pagan emperor Hadrian himself as its architect, has survived, but as a church.

Approaching it from the narrow, picturesque streets around the Piazza della Rotonda, the Pantheon is surprisingly cramped in, just as it was when this was the Campo Marius, densely populated and full of temples, public baths and office buildings—columns and

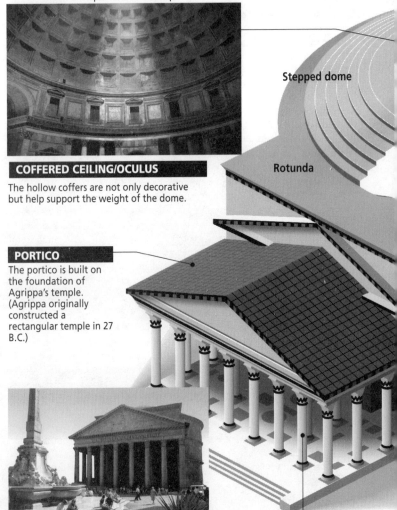

THE PANTHEON

The best preserved building in Rome is constructed of sixteen 10 meter tall columns topped by Corinthian capitals. The five register dome ends in a central nine-meter wide aperture at the top.

Stepped dome

COFFERED CEILING/OCULUS

Rotunda

The hollow coffers are not only decorative but help support the weight of the dome.

PORTICO

The portico is built on the foundation of Agrippa's temple. (Agrippa originally constructed a rectangular temple in 27 B.C.)

Granite columns

SHRINES/NICHES
The shrines that line the wall include the artist Raphael and numerous Italian royalty.

Oculus

Niche

Brick arches

Shrine

Marble floor

TOMB OF RAPHAEL
Raphael was buried here at his request upon his death in 1520. The remains of the artist rest below a Madonna by Lorenzetto.

WALLS
The walls of the drum that support the dome are 19 ft. thick.

◄ **Jefferson Memorial**
The Jefferson Memorial in Washington D.C. was modeled after the Pantheon.

fragments of which you suddenly come upon while wandering through the neighborhood. Originally all except the portico of the Pantheon was actually encased in the Basilica of Neptune built by Agrippa (27 B.C.). When Hadrian completely rebuilt and redesigned the Pantheon, he not only redid the basilica (friezes from it can be seen on the rear) but put Agrippa's name across the front of the Pantheon, leaving the world to mistake him for the architect for centuries.

From the outside, sitting on della Porta's Baroque fountain with its Ramses II obelisk, the Pantheon seems squat. It is, because the ground level has risen over the centuries, eliminating the original staircase up to the temple. Whatever disappointments you may feel from this perspective will vanish upon passing through the original bronze doors to the ★ ★ ★ **interior**. There's a timeless hush here. Little has changed. Much of the marble remains on the walls of the rotunda, the floor is Hadrian's design, the intricate coffered ceiling remains, if without its stucco and gilding. The hemispherical dome is still uncapped, its oculus letting in heaven's perfect circle of light. The dome spans a space larger than St. Peter's. The harmonious proportions are breathtaking, more so than the Palladian villas they inspired. There are later embellishments: Christian chapels, tombs for Italian kings and artists (Raphael's is between 2nd & 3rd chapel left). It's been said that the triumph of Roman architecture was its creation of interior space. In the Pantheon you understand.

The Pantheon, on the Piazza della Rotonda, is open 9 a.m.–6:30 p.m. in summer; till 4 p.m. late winter; year-round Sun. till 1 p.m. Free. In a traffic-free zone, the #119 minibus from P. Popolo gets closest, but other buses cruise the Corso to the east (#56 from V. Veneto, Trastevere) and the Largo Argentina south (#64 to Vatican). The area is best reached by scenic walks off the main thoroughfares, from P. Colonna to north, P. Navona west.

Nearby Churches ★

As you're walking around the area, the following churches and their piazzas are pleasant to explore. Just down the left side of the Pantheon is the Piazza Minerva with its delightful statue of ★ *Elephant Carrying Obelisk* (1666) by Bernini and the ochre facade of the ★ **Santa Maria sopra Minerva** (1280; *closed noon-4 p.m.*), built over an ancient temple to the goddess of wisdom. The wide spaces of its Italian Gothic interior are quite affecting and the ★ *frescoes* (1489) by Filippino Lippi in the Carafa Chapel (end right transept) as well as Michelangelo's *Christ with Cross* (1520; left side of choir; prudish drapery added later), are a few highlights of the artistic works here. Turning left along the side of the Minerva, the second right leads you to the busy square with **Il Gesu** church (1570; *closed 12:30–4:30 p.m.*), begun by Vignola, the facade finished by della Porta. Designed for the Jesuits, the plan became the prototype for the new order's expansion throughout the world. Although the too-familiar facade is austere, its exuberant High Baroque ★ *ceiling* by G. B. Gaulli (1674, with Bernini as advisor) simultaneously spills sinners over the vaults into our space in the church and expands into the nether regions of Christ. Retreating back up Via del Gesu, turn right in the Piazza del Collegio Romano, then left for a block to ★ **Piazza Sant'Ignazio** (1728), a beautiful Rococo stage set for the church of Sant'Ignazio (1626), whose undulating facade it echoes. The church interior is dominated by its ceiling, painted with one of the great trompe l'oeil of the High Baroque, A. Pozzo's ★ *Triumph of Ignazio* (1685; best seen from yellow disc in middle of nave). If you continue through this piazza (straight ahead, on left lane), you link up with the Piazza Colonna, then the Corso, not far from the Spanish Steps. Or you can retrace your steps to the following museum.

Palazzo and Galleria Doria Pamphili ★

P. Collegio Romano Although the Rococo facade of this palace faces the Corso, the entrance to the art gallery is from the piazza behind. The palace still belongs to the Doria-Pamphili family that produced Bernini's great patron, Pope Innocent X. In addition to visiting what is considered the best of the private patrician ★ art collections in Rome, you can also take a guided tour of their ★ apartments (*usually on the hour for half-hour; extra fee*) to see how descendants of princes of the Holy Roman Empire live. The collection includes: Titians (#10, ★29). Correggio (#20), a possible Raphael (★23), Caravaggios (★40, ★44, ★42), the Sienese G. di Paolo (#176), two portraits of Innocent X found together in a small enclave—a ★★Velasquez painting (#339) and a ★★Bernini bust (#VII)—and A. Carracci (★359). Other painters are represented, among the Dutch and French artists who were part of the 17th-century Roman art scene. The paintings are numbered, not labeled, but an identifying list can be purchased. *Open Tues., Fri through Sun. 10 a.m.–1 p.m.; L10,000 for museum; L5000 appartamenti.*

Around the Piazza Navona ★★

It's always a delightful surprise to enter the open space of the ★ Piazza Navona from the narrow maze of surrounding streets. Its oblong shape and monumental size date from Domitian's stadium in A.D. 86 (ruined entrance visible outside north end of piazza). Through the middle ages it continued to be used for sporting events, jousting and the like. Even in the last century, it was annually flooded in August for the cavorting of the Romans who drove carriages instead of chariots around it. Its present glorious appearance, however, dates from the 17th–century when the Pamphili pope, Innocent X, decided to spruce up his family's neighborhood and commissioned Borromini for the facade of the **Sant'Agnese** (1653; west side) and Bernini for his masterpiece ★★**Fountain of the Four Rivers** (1651; in the center). Given the simple task of raising an obelisk above a fountain, Bernini instead created a dynamic sculpture of rushing water and marble. He transformed travertine into a "natural" grotto where a lion roams and a palm tree grows as part of the four corners of the earth, represented by the encircling river gods. Although his assistants carved the river gods, his own hand enlivened the Nile (its face covered since its source was then unknown) and the Rio della Plata (with coins strewn at the base representing the riches of the New World), but not the Ganges with paddle (by Poussin) or the Danube. Bernini further animated the piazza when his composition of Neptune, nicknamed "Il Moro" (1653; copy) was added to della Porta's earlier, birdbath-style fountain (south).

The traffic-free piazza is just west of the Pantheon. Buses like the #64 to the Vatican run nearby on the Corso V. Emanuele to the south. This is an area good for scenic walks and links well with those around the Pantheon and the Campo dei Fiori.

Rome

Nearby Sights   ★

Almost an extension of Navona to the southeast is the piazzetta holding the painted rear facade of the ★**Palazzo Massimo** (1532), but it is the main facade *(V. Emanuele 141)* with its vestibule that explains why the palazzo is Peruzzi's masterpiece.

In the few blocks separating Piazza Navona from the Pantheon to the east are several churches. One is Borromini's tour de force, ★**Sant'Ivo** (1642), whose exotic spiraling dome (based on the papal crown) you may have already noticed on the Rome skyline (or *look from P. Sant'Eustacio,* behind church). Located inside the Palazzo Sapienza *(Corso di Rinascimento 40; Sun. 9 a.m.–noon),* the church forms a fascinating closure of the atrium, while its white interior soars and pulsates in the complex shape of the star of David (meaning "wisdom," appropriate to this former site of a university). On the south end of Rinascimento you can see **Sant'Andrea della Valle**, its dome by Carlo Maderno (1625) the second highest after St. Peter's. At the north end of Rinascimento bear right for **Sant'Agostino**; within is Caravaggio's barefoot *Our Lady of Pilgrims,* (1604; 1st chapel left), as well as Raphael's *Prophet,* (3rd pillar, left nave), inspired by Michelangelo. Just east of here, turn right for two blocks to **S. Luigi dei Francesi** *(closed 12:30–3:30, Thurs. p.m.),* famous for Caravaggio's ★★*St. Matthew Cycle* (c. 1599; 5th chapel, left; light machine on right). The three realistic paintings are elevated into the spiritual by the artist's characteristic abstract backgrounds and charged light.

To the west of Piazza Navona, the Via Coronari heads straight toward St. Peter's, the Renaissance pilgrimage route now a handsome street of antique shops. But instead of leaving the neighborhood, consider exploring its tangle of lanes and piazzettas. Off the northwest corner of Piazza Navona, hidden behind the Hotel Raphael, is the piazzetta designed by Cortona to complete the setting for his facade of ★**Santa Maria della Pace** (1656; enter by side door). You can enjoy this delightful example of Baroque urban planning even if the church, with Raphael's four ★*Sibyls* (1514; 1st chapel right, on arch) and a lovely Bramante ★cloister (1504; through sacristy) are under renovation. From here, with a map, you can angle southwest and arrive at the Piazza dell'Orologio with Borromini's **clocktower** at the rear of the **Chiesa Nuova** *(entrance V. Emanuele).* Before entering the Chiesa Nuova for its Cortona ceilings (apse and dome) and its two Rubens paintings (high altar) note another work by Borromini to the left—the facade of the ★**Oratorio**.

Campo dei Fiori: A Neighborhood Walk ★

The historic neighborhood wedged between the Piazza Navona and the Tiber offers a rich history and good strolls, but no major sights now that the Palazzo Farnese is closed to the public. Yet sooner or later you'll find yourself passing through here and wanting to return. Its most enchanting piazza is the ★**Campo dei Fiori**, filled in the mornings with a colorful food and flower market, its bustle overseen by the brooding statue of the philosopher Giordano Bruno, the most famous person burned at the stake here during the Inquisition. Other shadows lurk in the incomprehensible maze of medieval streets to the east—streets named after the goldworkers, locksmiths and crossbow makers who once lived here. Under their pavement lie the foundations of the Theater of Pompey where Julius Caesar was assassinated on the Ides of March in 44 B.C. To the west, some Renaissance order was imposed to facilitate the pilgrimages and processions between St. Peter's and the Lateran, and grand palazzi were built to accommodate cardinals and nobles with papal business. Just a block northwest of the Campo is the **Cancelleria** (c. 1486) one of the few Early Renaissance palazzi designed on Alberti's principles. But the most famous is the ★**Palazzo Farnese**, built for the cardinal who was soon to become Pope Paul III. It overlooks the quiet ★ **Piazza Farnese** with its two fountains made of marble tubs from the Baths of Caracalla. The palazzo was begun in 1513 by Sangallo the Younger, but its central window and cornice were by Michelangelo. Now the French Embassy, security prevents visits—even to Annibale Carraci's splendid ceiling frescoes. Turning left off this piazza (make sure you glance down the left side of the palace first to see the "mascher-one" fountain, assembled from an ancient Roman sewer cover), a 1.5-block walk brings you to the stucco ornamented facade of the ★ **Palazzo Spada** *(P. Capodiferro 3)*, built for yet another cardinal. Borromini added a delightful ★illusionistic colonnade in the east garden *(ask at ticket desk; no fee)* and there's a 17th-century art collection, unla-beled. *(Galleria open 9 a.m.–2 p.m., till 7 p.m. in summer weekends till 12:30 p.m., closed Mon.; L4000)*. Walking straight through the palace courtyards, you come to the ★**Via Giulia**, the magnificent 16th-century pilgrimage avenue designed by Bramante. To the left the Giulia ends near the Ponte Sisto river crossing to Trastevere. To the right, it passes the rear of the Farnese Palace, through a Michelangelo arch, and continues by handsome courtyards and churches as well as art gallery windows, on its path to the Tiber and St. Peter's.

This predominantly traffic-free zone is accessible by bus on its periphery: the #56 and #60 on the NE at Largo Argentina connect P. Barberini and Trastevere on the north; the #64 to the Vatican at V. Emanuele; and, on the south, the Lungotevere buses, like #280, connect Trastevere to P. Cavour, on the south.

Trastevere: A Neighborhood Walk ★★

Trastevere (meaning "across the Tiber") lies at the foot of the beautiful **Gianicolo** (Jan-iculum) hill and on the curving Tiber, where ancient Roman docks once received barges laden with Egyptian wheat and Egyptian obelisks alike. An ancient neighborhood, it also is said to be the most authentically Roman with its own dialect, piazzas filled with playing children, laundry hanging over medieval facades, and family-run trattoria serving home-cooking. But Trastevere is more than this. Just as it was the neighborhood of vernacular poets, like G. G. Belli, in the 19th–century, today the cafes and *moto* repair shops are cheek to jowl with experimental theaters, artisan shops, and an occasional avant garde gal-lery. Just as foreign merchants lived here by the ancient docks, so their descendants today live among a diversified international community.

Trastevere is very Roman indeed, so of course it has artistic treasures to enrich any walk through its lively streets. Our route continues from the Campo dei Fiori section, crossing the Ponte Sisto pedestrian bridge to Trastevere. At the fountain, angle to the right, then turn right through the old Porta Settimana that frames Via della Lungara. This street soon passes in front of the ★★**Palazzo Farnesina** *(9 a.m.–1 p.m., closed Sun., free)*, de-signed by Peruzzi in 1508, and with a ground-floor ★loggia painted with alluring gar-lands and themes suggested by Raphael. In a room off the loggia, Raphael himself painted the radiant ★★*Galatea* (1513; right wall, 2nd from left). Upstairs the trompe l'oeil

★paintings of Peruzzi turn an ordinary room into a colonnaded loggia overlooking Trastevere (ahead as you enter) and the Vatican (behind). Across the street from the Farnesina is the **Palazzo Corsini**, with its upstairs gallery *(9 a.m.–2 p.m.; till 1 p.m. Sun., closed Mon.; L8000)* of primarily 17th-century paintings. Walking back through the Settimana gate, continue straight, until you must turn. To the left is Trastevere's loveliest treasure, ★★**Santa Maria in Trastevere**, its delicate 13th-century facade mosaics creating one of Rome's great ★piazzas. The center of a swirl of picturesque streets, the church contains ancient columns along its nave that is paved with Cosmati work and opens to an apse covered with glorious mosaics (light machine front, left). In the apse below the precious Byzantine ★mosaics of the ★ *Virgin and Christ Enthroned*, (A.D. 1140), are six mosaic scenes from the ★ *Life of Mary* (1290s), by Pietro Cavallini, whose experiments in realism date before Giotto's. From here, you can climb the verdant Gianicolo (follow S. Cosimato east, turn right on Manara, which will dead end at the hill where, left of a fountain, steps ascend) to **S. Pietro in Montorio**. In a courtyard between the church and the Spanish Academy is Bramante's tiny, but seminal work of the High Renaissance, the circular ★**Tempietto** (1499; visible through gate, if not open; illuminated evenings). Across is a superb view of Rome, and an even grander one is a bit higher on the hill, across from the fountain of Paul V. The strong can continue up, then right across the ★**Passeggiata del Gianicolo**, picking up views of St. Peter's before descending to the Vatican itself. But really, it's too soon to leave Trastevere, for you haven't yet seen what many believe to be Bernini's consummate work, the sculpture of ★★ *Beata Ludovica* (1574) found in **S. Francesco a Ripa** *(last chapel on left; closed 12-4 p.m.; located east across Viale Trastevere on V. San Francesco)*, where the marble Ludovica, captured in the ecstatic moment of her death, glows in the natural sunlight Bernini planned for her. North from here, the streets lead to Via Genovesi, where you turn right and right again for ★**Santa Cecilia**. In the nun's choir here *(open to public Tues., Thurs., Sun. 11:30 a.m.–12:30 p.m., donation)* are the soft, beautiful colors of Cavallini's much destroyed masterpiece fresco the ★ *Last Judgment* (c. 1292). In the apse, note Arnolfo di Cambio's ★tabernacle (1293). North through the quaint streets, you emerge at the Tiber and Tiberina Island. South along Via di San Michele you approach the Porta Portese and come to the Complesso Monumentale de San Michele a Ripa exhibiting the ★★★ **painting collection of the Galleria Borghese** *(V. San Michele 22; Tues.–Sat. 9 a.m.–2 p.m., till 7 p.m. in summer, Sun. till 1 p.m.; L4000)*; walk through the entrance of the Instituto di Roma to the rear of the courtyard, then left for the exhibit. This renowned collection has been inaccessible for so many years that it caused a public outcry, resulting in the present exhibition opening in 1993 with the promise that it would remain here during the next few years of the Villa Borghese renovations. Not all 500 works of art are on exhibit (most notably missing are the Bellini and Botticelli paintings, Raphael's ★★ *Deposition*, Titian's ★★ *Sacred and Profane Love*, Antonella da Mesina's★★ *Portrait of a Man*), but there still are works by Giorgione, Titian, Raphael, Bernini's self-portraits, and all of the famous Caravaggios (among them ★★ *Madonna dei Palafrenieri*, 1605, rejected by the Vatican for its realism and ★ *David with head of Goliath*).

Both buses (#56 to P. Venezia, P. Barberini, V. Veneto; #75 to Largo Argentina, P. Venezia, Stazione Termini) and trams (#30 and #13 to Aventine, Colosseo, are especially convenient for the Borghese paintings), connect various parts of Viale Trastevere with the other side of the Tiber. But buses are not efficient for crossing the Gianicolo to the Vatican and a taxi tour can be made only from the Vatican to Trastevere. The modern Viale Trastevere cuts the neighborhood in half with Santa Maria in Trastevere on its west (connected most scenically by V. Lungaretta). A walk through the neighborhood is easily connected with the Vatican (V. della Lungara by the Farnesina is fastest), the Campo dei Fiori, the Jewish Quarter, and Aventine sections.

Jewish Quarter: A Neighborhood Walk

Originally, Jewish merchants joined many other foreign traders in Rome, living on both sides of the Tiber. But that was in ancient Rome when some also brought the practices of the new Christian sect with them. Subsequent practitioners of that religion, however, confined the Jews to this small quarter during the Inquisition (1555). Walls and guarded gates of this ghetto would endure until 1870, when all of Rome was liberated under the Risorgimento. Today the neighborhood is quite lively, and many Jews voluntarily reside here in what is the oldest Jewish community in the West. The Eastern-style **synagogue** *(1904; guided tours of temple and museum every morning except Sat.; L8000)* is now a landmark on the Tiber. Here it overlooks the beautiful ★ **Isola Tiburina**, the only island in the river. Once it was the property of a powerful Jewish family that, after conversion, produced a pope. Up the right side of the temple you pass the rear of the Teatro di Marcello completed by Augustus, who also constructed the **Portico d' Ottavia** (23 B.C.) as a "foyer" of 300 columns, temples, and libraries for the theater. Today the remnants of the portico form the porch of a church, which did little to prevent its use as a fish market until the last century. The heart of the Jewish Quarter is here on the **Via Portico d' Ottavia** as it stretches west past buildings marked in Latin with the names of their owners and embellished with ancient fragments. Here, too, are the shops, the Cafe Toto (midway) with its delicious cappuccino, and the restaurants specializing in *cucina alla giudea*, a Roman, not a kosher, tradition. Our tour continues "through" the Portico d' Ottavia (by an alley around the left and turning left up a street behind church) into the handsome **Piazza Campitelli**. Here you can make a brief detour a few blocks left to the ★ **Fontana della Tartarughe** *(in P. Mattei)*, a graceful fountain of dolphins, boys, and turtles. Or turn right through the Campitelli to the Via di Teatro Marcello. Left are the Campidoglio steps; right the frontal view of the ★ **Teatro di Marcello** (13 B.C.). Now you can see the tiered arches and rising capital orders that inspired the Colosseum. Since medieval times patrician families have found use for the building, first as a fortress, now as a palazzo built into the third tier. The elegant set of Corinthian columns rising amid the ruins belonged to the Temple of Apollo (32 B.C.).

Though traffic in this quarter is restricted, main thoroughfares bound it: Largo Argentina and P. Venezia on north (#64 to Vatican; #56 to P. Barberini), and Via Arenula (#75 Trastevere to stazione) and V. Teatro Marcello (#94 to top of Aventine). The Isola Tiburina and its ancient bridges are a favorite pedestrian crossing between Trastevere and the Jewish Quarter. The Campidoglio is only a few blocks north.

Rome

Around the Aventine Hill: A Walk ★

South of Tiburina Island rises the *Colle Aventino*, or Aventine Hill, an inviting hill with its shade trees and picturesque monastery. Even before lovely churches were built on its highest ridge, wealthy foreign merchants in ancient Rome had built their homes here above the busy cattle market and loading docks below. In fact, it is the ancient market area around the **Piazza Bocca della Verita** that attracts most visitors. Close to the Tiber is the oldest marble building in Rome, the delicately circular ★ **Temple of Hercules Victor** (end 2nd century B.C.) and next to it, the **Temple of Portunus** (100 B.C.), dedicated to the harbor god. Other ruins of the early Republican city abound nearby, often incorporated into later buildings. Nowhere is this truer than in ★★**S. Maria in Cosmedin** *(closed noon–3 p.m.)*, built within the arcades of the ancient market inspector's office. Some visit only the porch of this medieval church, placing their hands in the monster *bocca della verita*, or mouth of truth, said to bite the hand of liars. In truth, it is an ancient sewer cover. The church ★ interior, despite the glorious ★ Cosmati work (12th century) covering the floors, choir and ambos, feels simply ancient.

Behind S. Maria in Cosmedin stretches the **Circus Maximus** at the foot of the Palatine (left) and Aventine hills. From here, the Via Clivo di Pubblici winds right up the Aventine (there also are steps that lead up the front of the Aventine from the Lungotevere), past the well-marked gardens and churches with views over Rome toward St. Peter's. Here is ★ **Santa Sabina** (founded A.D. 422), one of the finest Early Christian basilicas, its noble interior graced with good proportions and Corinthian columns (2nd century A.D.). Its famous carved wooden doors *(facing side vestibule, not visible 12:30–3:30 p.m.)* include one of the earliest known crucifixion scenes (5th century). Farther up the hill the street

ends at the beautiful ★ **Piazza Cavalieri di Malta** (1765), designed by Piranesi. He also designed the facade at #3, the headquarters of the Knights of Malta. Even if you didn't stick your hand into the bocca della verita, you must peer through the keyhole in the green door for the most perfectly framed ★ view of St. Peter's. Out the other side of the piazza, you walk through one of Rome's wealthier neighborhoods while descending the Aventine. At the bottom, turn left on to Via Marmorata and you're heading toward Rome's most curious landmark, the **Pyramid of Cestius** (12 B.C.), not some modern Disney creation, but rather an ancient one, built as the tomb of a Roman official. Just before the pyramid, turn right for the **Protestant Cemetery** *(V. Cestius; 8–11:30 a.m. and 3:20–5:30 p.m., except Oct.–Mar. 2:20–4:30 p.m.; ring)*, a tranquil place full of flowers and stately cypresses and with the tombs of Shelley and Keats. Across from the Pyramid, on the Piazza Porta S. Paolo, rises the great **Aurelian wall** (3rd century). If you want, you can take a 15-minute walk along its impressive exterior east *(V. Giotto)* to the back of the ★ **Baths of Caracalla** (A.D. 212), and wander your way around the great brick walls of these best-preserved of the Roman baths to the entrance *(V. Terme di Caracalla; 9 a.m.–6 p.m. summer, till 3 p.m. winter, Sun. & Mon. till 1 p.m.; arrive an hour before closing; L6000)*.

A bit out of center, public transport is quite useful for the Aventino. Bus #94 runs across the hill near Santa Sabina, on its way between P. Venezia (V. Teatro Marcello) and P. Ostiense near the pyramid. Tram #13 runs from Trastevere to P. Porta S. Paolo to the east end of Circus Maximus, behind the Colosseum and just a few blocks west of the Ca-racalla ruins. The "piramide" stop on Metro A is convenient to the area.

Vatican City ★★★

Caligula, a great fan of sporting events, built his circus here and decorated it with an Egyptian obelisk, one that now adorns St. Peter's Square. Later, Nero executed Christians here. And later still Constantine built a church (4th C.) over the burial place of St. Peter.

In the 9th century a fortified wall was built to protect the area, one that was modified and rebuilt, and still stands. Later popes built a narrow passage through these walls, from their apartments to the thick walls of the Castel Sant'Angelo, where they could survive uprisings and even the great Sack of Rome in 1527. By then, of course, the popes ruled the Papal States that extended through central Italy and across the peninsula to Ravenna. All of Rome was their capital, their armies fought and at times allied themselves with Milan and Venice, and even, unfortunately for Italy, France and Spain. Since Risorgimento troops captured Rome in 1870, the fortunes of the Papal States have radically altered. Now confined to the old walls of the Vatican City, the Papal State is the smallest in the world. Yet it continues to mint coins, print stamps, and receive its own diplomatic corps. The army, however, was disbanded in 1970, except for its most famous mercenaries, the now very colorful Swiss Guards. Also confined to the Vatican City is the great art commissioned and collected over the centuries by the popes.

Visiting the Vatican

The sights and their visiting hours are described below, but a little strategy might be appropriate for planning your visit. • The Vatican is the destination of both religious and artistic pilgrimages. At Easter and during the summer, it can be uncomfortably crowded, especially in confined spaces like the Sistine Chapel. *Try to avoid Monday and free Sunday* (last one of the month) visits to the Vatican Museums; always be mentally prepared for the crowd—the Sistine Chapel can receive 161,000 a day. • It is easy to devote a day here, between St. Peter's and the Vatican Museums (with the Sistine Chapel), and looking over the exterior of the Castel Sant'Angelo. • The museums officially estimate five hours for the full tour, which is all they are usually open. Except in summer, it's necessary to arrive early and schedule St. Peter's for the afternoon. • Entrances to the Vatican Museums and St. Peter's are a 10-minute walk from each other, but a **Vatican bus** connects them *(except Wed. & Sun.; buy ticket on board)*, departing from the **Information Office**, south side P. San Pietro, and from a side entrance of museums. The chance to sit down is invaluable; the glimpses of the gardens and rear windows of St. Peter's (Michelangelo's) worthwhile. • **Tours** of the Vatican gardens require advance reservations through the Information Office *(☎ 6988-4466, FAX 6988-5100; L16,000).* • **Papal Audiences** *(usually Wed. 10:30 a.m.)* require advance application to the *Prefettura della Casa Pontifica 00120 Citta del Vaticano* *(☎ 6988-3017, FAX 6988-5378),* or drop off your request *(through bronze doors, north side P. San Pietro, Mon.-Sat. 9 a.m.–1 p.m.).* • **Dress Code:** Note strict code under St. Peter's. • Though walkable from most points across the Tiber, **public transport** might be helpful: bus #64 stops near St. Peter's after a run on Corso V. Emanuele

VATICAN CITY (NORTH)

The 108 acre Papal State is the smallest sovereign state in the world. It mints coins, prints stamps, has its own diplomatic corps and houses the great art commissioned and collected over the centuries by the popes.

This Spread

Next Spread

CASINA OF PIUS IV

This ornate structure was built by Pirro Ligorio in the mid-16th century as a summerhouse in the Vatican Gardens.

EAGLE FOUNTAIN

The Borghese crest is the eagle, and this fountain was built to commemorate the Acqua Paola aqueduct's first flow of water to the Vatican.

VATICAN RADIO

The Vatican broadcasts radio programs in 20 languages from a tower that is part of the Leonine Wall built in the 9th century.

Vatican Picture Gallery

PAPAL GARDENS

St. Peter's

VATICAN MUSEUMS

The Vatican has four color-coded paths through its vast collections. All go through the Sistine Chapel and have access to the Pinacoteca. Other must-sees are the Pio-Clementine Museum and the Stanze di Raffaelo.

GALLEON FOUNTAIN

This scale model of a 17th century ship is made of lead, brass and copper. It was constructed for Pope Paul V by a Flemish artist.

Entrance to Vatican Museums

Bramante Stairway

Belvedere Palace

Atrium of Four Gates

Vatican Library

Cortile del Belvedere

Raphael Loggia

St. Peter's Square

Rome

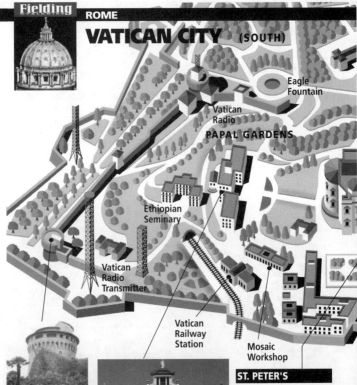

Fielding

ROME

VATICAN CITY (SOUTH)

Eagle Fountain

Vatican Radio

PAPAL GARDENS

Ethiopian Seminary

Vatican Radio Transmitter

Vatican Railway Station

Mosaic Workshop

Tower of St. John

Vatican Government Palace

ST. PETER'S

St. Peter's Basilica, begun in 1506, took over 100 years to complete. Bernini's bronze canopy rises six stories over the altar and crypt of St. Peter.

PAPAL GARDENS

Guided tours take visitors through the Papal Gardens which are spread over one-third of the Vatican's acreage.

Cortile del Belvedere

Information office

Obelisk

Papal Audience Chamber

ST. PETER'S SQUARE

Caligula's Egyptian obelisk (1586) adorns St. Peter's Square. On special occasions the Pope appears on the balcony over the square to bless the crowds.

MICHELANGELO'S SISTINE CHAPEL

Michelangelo labored painstakingly from 1508–1512 to depict elaborate scenes from the Old Testament on the chapel ceiling. All are now revealed in their original luminous colors after 10 years of cleaning completed in 1990. Benches are provided for viewing the ceiling from different perspectives.

Rome

from P. Venezia, while #492 makes a swing from the V. Veneto to P. Risorgimento; the "Ottaviano" stop on metro A is a 10-minute walk north of St. Peter's.

Special Tip

Beat the crowds to the Sistine Chapel by arriving early to the museums (8:20 a.m.), being among the first to enter; taking the elevator on the left as you pass through the main door, buying your ticket and, then, racing to the Chapel following any and all signs. Exiting the Chapel from the rear takes you to the Raphael rooms, still uncrowded.

Castel Sant'Angelo   ★★

Lungotevere Castello across Tiber.

Although the dome of St. Peter's is one of the most memorable silhouettes on the Rome skyline, the city of popes is best announced by the Castel Sant'Angelo. Sitting outside the official limits of the Vatican City, the castle nonetheless served the popes long and well as a fortress and a prison. It still looks impenetrable, though open to the public as a museum. The castle has dominated the Tiber since A.D. 130, when Hadrian began the building of his mausoleum here across the Tiber, connected by a specially constructed bridge. Much has changed, of course. The bridge, the pedestrian ★**Ponte Sant'Angelo**, still provides the most impressive approach to the castle, but now it is lined with angels carved by Bernini's assistants (two originals by Bernini were removed to Sant' Andrea delle Fratte). The monumental circular drum that was Hadrian's tomb, as well as the interior spiral ramp that led to it, remain. Soon after Hadrian's death they became part of the defensive works of the Aurelian wall, and were fought over and maintained as a fortress since. Although you may not be interested in the collection of arms or the elaborate papal apartments readied for emergencies free of any discomforts, you may want to enter the castle for its ★**views**, those through the parapets of the **pleasant cafe** or the great panorama from the top terrace under the gaze of the bronze angel. *Open 9 a.m.–2 p.m., Sun. till 1 p.m.; closed 2nd & 4th Tues.; L8000.*

Piazza San Pietro   ★★

The Viale della Conciliazione marches strong and wide to the famous Piazza of St. Peter, just as Mussolini wanted when he destroyed the tangle of medieval streets here. Unfortunately, what Mussolini thought befitting to St. Peter's diminished the impact of the piazza as planned by Bernini in 1656. The artist intended the elliptical arms of the colonnades to embrace visitors into the sudden open space of the piazza carrying them forward into the church. Although you can't enjoy it as it was meant to be, you can appreciate the swirl of columns (284) and wealth of statues atop them (140). And standing on the brown stones by the Early Baroque fountains, you can delight in Bernini's contrivance to make the colonnade appear a single row.

Basilica of St. Peter   ★★★

From the time Julius II began the construction of a new church (1506), it would take well over a hundred years to complete. Beginning with its monumental plan created by Bramante (inspired by Constantine's Basilica in the Forum and the Pantheon) and continuing to the lofty ★★ cupola, with the exquisite double-column design of its drum, by Michelangelo, the church grew until Carlo Maderno completed it, with the present, much criticized facade (1626). The now Baroque and pompous **interior** is vast enough for papal processions and pilgrimage-size crowds. In fact, it's hard to comprehend just how large the church is because it is so superbly proportioned. It's been said that it took the Cape Canaveral hangars to finally surpass the spatial volume of the basilica. And it took the genius of Bernini to fill the space below the cupola so effectively. Here over the high altar and crypt of St. Peter, his bronze canopy, or ★★ *baldacchino* (1633), rises the equivalent of six modern stories. At the same time it permits views through to the gilded rays and holy light of his ★★ *Cathedra* (1666; in apse), a fantastic High Baroque construction of marble, bronze, and stucco that frames what traditionally is held to be St. Peter's throne. The piers supporting the cupola are so immense that Borromini's San Carlo church would fit into one of them. A few of the other exceptional works clustered around the dome are Bernini's dramatic ★ *St. Longinus* (niche sculpture; 1st pier on right), his animated portrait of the Barberini pope on the ★ *Tomb of Urban VIII*, (1647; right side of apse) as well as his highly original design for the ★ *Tomb of Alexander VII* (1678; in aisle beyond left transept; executed by assistants), built around a preexisting doorway. More restrained are the lions of Canova's neo-classical ★ *Tomb of Clement XIII*, (1792; right aisle beyond transept). Though most of the decor now dates from the Baroque and later, the Renaissance still speaks to us through Michelangelo's early masterpiece, ★★★ *Pieta* (1499; 1st chapel, right aisle). The slightly tilted pyramidal ensemble is so compelling that you barely notice the madonna's strange youthfulness, much less her intentionally disproportional size.

The domes of St. Peter's Basilica.

ST. PETER'S BASILICA

St. Peter's is a wonder of architecture that took more than 100 years to complete. Originally designed by Bramante and with magnificent contributions from Michelangelo, Bernini and Carlo Maderno, its vast interior is large enough for pilgrimage-size crowds.

DOME

The majestic cupola designed by Michelangelo in 1574 is 435 ft. (132.5m) high. It was completed 16 years later by Fontana and Porta.

Tomb of St. Peter

BALDACCHINO

Bernini designed the gilded bronze canopy in the 17th century. It is supported by six-story high spiral columns.

Papal Altar

CHAPEL OF THE SACRAMENT

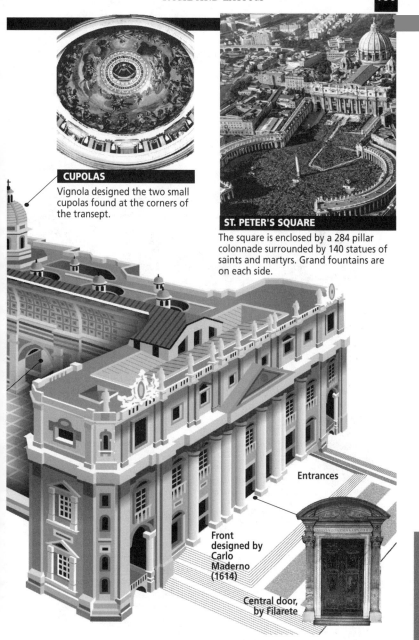

CUPOLAS

Vignola designed the two small cupolas found at the corners of the transept.

ST. PETER'S SQUARE

The square is enclosed by a 284 pillar colonnade surrounded by 140 statues of saints and martyrs. Grand fountains are on each side.

Entrances

Front designed by Carlo Maderno (1614)

Central door, by Filarete

THE ART OF ST. PETER'S

Some of the dramatic works clustered around the basilica are the bronze statue of St. Peter by Cambio, Michelangelo's "Pieta," Bernini's "St. Longinus" and bronze reliefs by Filarete.

ST. PETERS THRONE

Chapel of the column

Aspe

Chapel of St. Michael
St. Peter's Treasury

Baldaquin

Excavations beneath St. Peter's

Altar of St Thomas

Entry to Grottoes

Altar of the Crucifiction of St. Peter

Altar of Sts. Martial & Valeria

Clementine Chapel

Monument to Leo XI

POPE ALEXANDER VII MONUMENT

This work by Bernini, completed in 1678, sits in an alcove left of the transept near the sculptures of Truth, Charity, Prudence and Justice.

MOSAIC IN THE CHOIR CHAPEL

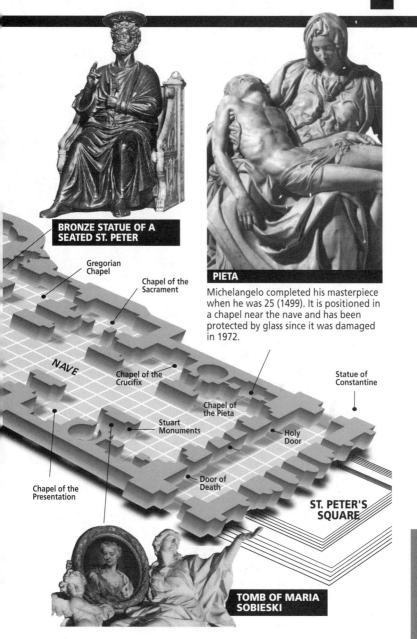

BRONZE STATUE OF A SEATED ST. PETER

Gregorian Chapel

Chapel of the Sacrament

PIETA

Michelangelo completed his masterpiece when he was 25 (1499). It is positioned in a chapel near the nave and has been protected by glass since it was damaged in 1972.

NAVE

Chapel of the Crucifix

Chapel of the Pieta

Statue of Constantine

Stuart Monuments

Holy Door

Chapel of the Presentation

Door of Death

ST. PETER'S SQUARE

TOMB OF MARIA SOBIESKI

St. Peter's is open 7 a.m.–6 p.m. (7 p.m. in summer). Visits to the dome and its
★ *views (partially by elevator, then steps; L6000) are permitted 8 a.m.–4:45 p.m.*
(6:15 in summer). Entrance from left aisle, past 1st chapel. **Dress Code**. *No*
shorts—not even for children, no mini skirts, no bare arms, etc. No photographs
permitted.

Vatican Museums   ★ ★ ★

Viale Vaticano, outside north walls.

The Sistine Chapel is here, as are papal apartments frescoed by the greatest artists of
the Renaissance. But before and after reaching these sights you walk through corridors and rooms full of other works, from frescoes and tapestries to old maps and
clocks. And along the way many museums tempt you: there are five alone on classical sculpture not including the Etruscan collections; others are as diversified as the
Egyptian, Modern Religious Art and Ethnographic collections. To help organize
the flow of visitors, the Vatican has developed four different color-coded paths
through the collections. All go through the Sistine Chapel, route A most directly,
and all have access to the Pinacoteca. But only the most expansive C and D routes
enable you to visit the other must-see art works here that are described below. On
a first time visit, you probably will want to limit the number of collections you
explore along your walk. Keys to the works are found on the walls of most rooms.

Pio-Clementine Museum   ★ ★

This first-floor museum of classical sculpture, the first you encounter, fills many
rooms and contains exceptional Greek and Roman works. Many of these works had
immense influence on later Renaissance and Baroque artists. The **octagonal courtyard** not only has the virtue of being easily identified, it also contains exquisite
works, including two masterpieces: the elegant ★ ★ *Apollo Belvedere*, (to left as
enter) a 2nd century Roman copy of a 4th century B.C. Greek bronze; and the tormented ★ ★ *Laocoon*, (also left; possibly a Greek original from Rhodes, 1st century B.C.), fighting off the snakes Athena sent to kill him and his sons. Through this
courtyard you enter the **Sala delle Muse** with the ★ ★ *Torso Belvedere* (1st century B.C.; center of room) by the Greek Apollonius—you almost want to say it's
Michelangelesque.

Stanze di Raffaelo   ★ ★ ★

On the second-floor, encountered after the corridors of tapestries and maps, are the
apartments of Julius II. Called the "Raphael Rooms," they contain that artist's
greatest works while in Rome. However, you visit them in the reverse order of their
development, and in fact, enter by the Sala di Costantino, painted after Raphael's
death (by Giulio Romano) and then enter yet another room in which his frescoes
were painted over. As compensation for the loss, the earlier ★ ★**Cappella del
Beato** (aka Cappella Nicolina) is preserved through a door here—a tiny chapel decorated by Fra Angelico (1448). After the refreshing delicacy of these Early Renaissance works, you finally plunge into the tumult of Raphael's late style, found in the
★ ★ ★**Stanza d'Elidoro** (1512–13). The second of his masterful rooms, this one
shows his rapid development from the quintessential High Renaissance painting
Miracle of Bolseno (over windows to left), with its rich Raphael colors and symme-

try, to the more powerfully dramatic one opposite (*Freeing of Peter*, famous for its play with light—from the natural glow of the sky to the spiritual), and the practically Baroque, almost Rubenesque ones to the sides. The first room, the ★ ★ ★ **Stanza della Segnatura** (1508–11) is the culmination of the classical painting style of the High Renaissance, full of spatial harmony, serene and static. Raphael's change in style in the two stanze is attributed to his first exposure (1511) to Michelangelo's Sistine Ceiling. In the most famous painting here, the *School of Athens* (left wall), Raphael recorded this experience by the late addition of a portrait of Michelangelo (the brooding figure seated in front of the steps, to the left). To the right of him, with a slate, is Bramante as Euclid; on the extreme right is Raphael next to Sodoma (dressed in white). Leonardo is portrayed as Plato (finger pointing up). All the walls, as well as the ceiling medallions, were painted by Raphael. Opposite the *School* is the *Disputa*. Here, the eternal repose in heaven is contrasted with the earthly arguments below.

Sistine Chapel ★★★

From the stanze, you descend steps and walk through the Museum of Modern Religious Art, before finding the well-marked entrance to the Sistine Chapel. On the ceiling, Michelangelo, who never before had worked in fresco technique, created what is said to be the greatest painting ever produced (1508–12). For more than 2 and a half years he stood on scaffolding, craning his neck, to create an elaborate work based on Old Testament scenes from the creation to Noah's salvation. Surrounding them are extraordinary figures of prophets and sibyls. All are now revealed in their original luminous colors after 10 years of cleaning, completed in 1990. Michelangelo began his monumental task near the entrance, and ended over the altar, behind which rises his later work *The Last Judgment*. Somewhere midway, experts agree that the great sculptor became more assured with his new technique, leaving behind the too-small scenes of the Flood, and producing his more famous heroic and highly expressive figures, none more famous than the *Creation of Adam*. To avoid the kind of neck cramps the artist suffered, you need to view the ceiling from the benches, and preferably from different perspectives. ★ ★ ★ *The Last Judgment*, (1536) was painted in an era of despair in Italy, after the Sack of Rome. Restored in 1994 to its original lapis blue background, the details of Michelangelo's expression of this despair now can be seen only too clearly. A stern god holds this painting together, almost as if by centrifugal force, the damned and wretched below on the right. At his feet is St. Bartholomew holding a flayed skin, in which Michelangelo has painted his own face.

Pinacoteca ★★

You can visit painting galleries at either the beginning or end of your tour, since the entrance is on the courtyard of the cafeteria, where you enter and exit the above galleries. Although the first galleries tempt you with P. Lorenzetti, S. Martini, a Giotto school altarpiece, and a lovely Gentile di Fabriano (all ★ Room II), usually you can resist until the show-stopper ★ ★ *Angel Musicians* (Room IV), detached frescoes by the relatively unknown Melozzo da Forli (1538-94). The end room (VIII) contains only Raphaels, including one of his first works, ★ *Coronation of the Virgin*,

(1503) and his last ★★ *Transfiguration* (1520), so much more monumental and theatrical and brilliant with color. In Room IX is the unfinished but riveting ★★ *St. Jerome* (1480) by Leonardo and a ★ *Pieta*, (1474) by Giovanni Bellini, while the 16th-century paintings in Room X include Veronese's ★ *Sant'Elena*. Room XII holds Caravaggio's ★★ *Deposition*.

The museums are open 8:45–1 p.m. (exit 1:45 p.m.) and closed Sun. except the last each month. The hours Mon.–Fri. are extended till 4 p.m. (exit 5 p.m.) Holy Week, July 1–Sept. 30. Closed holidays. (Ethnographic and Historical museums open Wed. & Sat. only.) There are head-set guides to the Raphael Stanze and the Sistine Chapel (fee; at museum entrance). There are museum shops, cloak rooms (free), and a cafeteria. Binoculars useful for Sistine Chapel. No flashes permitted on cameras. L15,000 except the last Sun. each month.

Villa Borghese ★★

This large public park also known as the Borghese Gardens, is named after the Borghese family who had their summer retreat here, just above the Via Veneto, outside the ancient Aurelian walls. The park itself is especially wonderful on Sunday mornings when Roman families take their strolls, but tourists are attracted by the museums.

The two most frequent approaches to the park are by the Via Veneto or from the Piazzale Napoleone (overlooking the P. Popolo) found along the Pincio passeggiato from the top of the Spanish Steps. Buses do run around the park, between P. Flaminio and V. Veneto (#490, #115) and an underground passage links the park with the "P. di Spagna" stop of Metro A.

Museo e Galleria Borghese ★★★

Housed in Cardinal Scipione Borghese's 17th-century villa and containing the family's private art collection, is this superb museum. Although the villa is undergoing repairs, necessitating the closing of the upstairs painting galleries (Temporarily on exhibit at S. Michele a Ripa; see "Trastevere"), a visit to the ground-floor sculpture galleries is a must. Here are Bernini's early sculptures (1619-24), displayed as centerpieces of many of the rooms. In the first sala (extreme left of temporary entrance) is ★★ *Apollo and Daphne*, as graceful as the wind blowing their hair, convincingly real, despite Daphne's fingers and toes turning into the gnarled roots of the tree she is about to become on Apollo's touch. In the next room, ★ *David* hurls his rock at us (the face is a Bernini self-portrait), but in the third sala, the centerpiece is Canova's sensuous and silky ★★ *Pauline Bonaparte*, (1805) Napoleon's sister, wife of a Borghese, depicted as Venus. Next is the magnificently grand sala, with Lanfranco's High Baroque ★ *ceiling fresco* (1624). Through to the next corner room you find Bernini's earliest sculpture ★ *Aeneas carried from Troy*, carved when he was just 20. Against the right wall is his unfinished *Truth* (begun 1645). Then, back in the entrance hall, you see the compelling *Rape of Prosperina*, Pluto's fingers sunk in her marble-defying flesh. *During renovations, visits are on the half hour and limited to 25 persons. The best strategy is to arrive around the half hour, then hope to wait only 1/2 hour for admittance. Open Tues.–Sat. 9 a.m.–2 p.m., till 7 p.m. in summer, Sun. till 1 p.m.; L4000.*

Villa Giulia and More   ★★

Two other museums are near each other in the north and opposite end of the park on the Viale delle Belle Arti. The ★★**Villa Giulia** *(9 a.m.–7 p.m. in summer; 9 a.m.–2 p.m., Wed. till 7 p.m. in winter; year-round Sun. till 1 p.m., closed Mon.; L8000)* houses a world-famous collection of Etruscan art, but holds more artifacts from nearby Cerveteri, Vulci and Veio than most could ever hope to absorb. But a selective visit, even for the Etruscan uninitiated, is enjoyable. The High Renaissance villa housing the collection is beautiful, designed for Julius II by Florentine architects (with a little help from Michelangelo), and with gardens (a replica of an Etruscan temple in one to right; a cafe in one at rear), a nympheum, and Pompeian-inspired frescoes under the arcades. Among the ground floor exhibits are large terracotta statues of ★ *Apollo* and ★ *Hercules* from the late 6th century B.C. temple near Veio (Room 7) and the ★★ *Sarcofago degli Sposi* (Room 8, 6th century B.C.), with a vivacious couple chatting atop their sarcophagus in what is an Etruscan masterpiece. Upstairs, the piece de resistance is the ★★ *Castellani Jewelry Collection* (Room 22; no more than 10 people at a time; tell guard you want to visit and leave a photo I.D.) containing exquisite work, from ★★ Etruscan lost-wax and beaded gold masterpieces to the crown of Umberto I (1888). Nearby is **Galleria D'Arte Moderna** *(V. Belle Arti 131; 9 a.m.–2 p.m., till 7 p.m. in summer and 1 p.m. Sun., closed Mon.; L8000)* with a permanent collection of Italian art from the last two centuries as well as temporary exhibits.

The Spanish Steps: A Neighborhood Walk ★★

The Spanish Steps

Every traveler soon encounters the shopping district bound by the Pincio hill and the Tiber. Since the 16th–century when the ancient aqueducts were repaired, bringing water to the depopulated area, this has been the *rione* of foreigners, whether Tuscan artists such as Peruzzi or French ones such as Poussin. In the 18th and 19th centuries the area became increasingly popular, especially with English and French writers and artists who frequented the **Caffe Greco** *(V. Condotti 86)*. The ★ **Scalinata di Spagna**, or Spanish Steps (1723; by Francesco de Santis), named after an ambassador's residence here, dates from this period. Slowly rising to the top of the Pincio with its obelisk and 16th-century church of **Trinita dei Monte**, the Rococo steps make an elegant curvilinear design. Although the ★ views from the top are superb, few are anxious to leave the ★ **Piazza di Spagna** at the foot of the Steps. Here they gather around the fountain by Bernini's father, Pietro, designed as a sinking boat to take witty advantage of the low water level here. To the right of the Steps is the **Casa di John Keats**, where the poet died in 1821.

There are a few other sights in the relatively modern neighborhood. Just a few blocks north of the Piazza di Spagna (along either Via Balbuino or, from the top of the Steps, the scenic *passeggiata* of the Pincio that borders the Villa Borghese park) is the vast yet pleasing ★ **Piazza del Popolo** (1816 by Giuseppe Valadier), with its Egyptian obelisk standing amid fountains and lions. On the north, next to the Aurelian wall punctured by a 17th-century gate, is ★ **Santa Maria del Popolo**. In its richly decorated interior, the first chapel (right) contains ★ Pinturicchio's best work here, from the frescoed walls to the altarpiece (1485), yet all the chapels on the right aisle as well as the ceiling vaults in the apse were painted by this Umbrian artist and his school. The chapel left of the apse explodes with Early Baroque energy. Opposite each other are two Caravaggio masterpieces (1601). On the right, ★★ *Conversion of St. Paul*, isolates the saint in spiritual light at the moment of his religious experience; ★★ *Crucifixion of St. Pe*ter, though dramatic with its diagonal composition, is realistic as only Caravaggio could be—from the dirt on the saint's feet to the fear on his face. By contrast, Annibale Carracci's contemporary ★ *Assumption* (in center) seems almost subdued. The ★ *Chigi Chapel* (2nd on left) was designed by Raphael (cartoon for dome mosaic; sculpture left of altar), but completed by Bernini (sculpture on right of altar; *Daniel and Lion*, on right as you exit). Via Ripetta runs south out of the Popolo and as it angles toward the river, it arrives at the Piazza Augusto Imperatore, an amorphous square created by Mussolini to display the earthlike mound of **Augustus' mausoleum** as well as the magnificent ★★ **Ara Pacis** (13 B.C.), now housed within modern glass walls *(open 9 a.m.–1 p.m., and also Tues. and Sat. 4–7 p.m.; closed Mon.; L4000)*. This "altar of peace," not only commemorated Augustus' return to Rome from battle, it established the exquisite Hellenized art style that was to become the hallmark of the Roman Empire during its Golden Age. Even when the monument is closed, you can see the delicately carved reliefs of imperial processions and acanthus scrolls on the exterior of the altar. Another ancient Roman monument lies several blocks south on the Corso, just below Via del Tritone. In the center of the **Piazza Colonna** is the ★ **Column of Marcus Aurelius** (A.D. 180), a stylistic contrast to the Ara Pacis. Too much warfare on the German frontier, not peace, produced the reliefs here. In a stark, expressive style, the column shows the brutality of war. Just behind this piazza is the **Piazza di Montecitorio**, with various legislative buildings (that on right designed by Bernini) enclosing an obelisk, while off the southwest corner of the Colonna you come to the **stock exchange** *(P. di Pietra)* with 11 massive columns from Hadrian's Temple that once stood here embedded in its facade. From the P. Colonna you can continue your walk through the sights near the Pantheon, or continue across the Corso to the Trevi Fountain and the sights of the Quirinal.

Although the Corso and V. Tritone can be quite busy with traffic, most of this neighborhood is a pedestrian zone. Metro A has stops at both P. di Spagna and P. Popolo, and bus #115 makes a loop around the edge of the district, up the V. Veneto and through the Villa Borghese to P. Popolo.

Around the Quirinal ★★

Although the *Colle Quirinale* was one of the original seven hills of Rome, its art dates primarily to the Baroque period. And while some travelers do climb the small hill to see the presidential palace, few visit the gemlike churches nearby. In fact, the most famous sights here lie at the foot of the hill near the Via del Tritone. The ★★**Trevi Fountain**, wedged between the Corso and Via del Tritone, is irresistibly excessive. Squeezed into a tiny piazzetta, the monumental fountain with its bounty of water creates so much excitement that tourists toss in their coins, hoping to guarantee a return to the Eternal City. Designed by Nicola Salvin in 1762, the fountain was developed from an earlier project by Bernini. Bernini's own ★**Triton Fountain** (c. 1637) is unfortunately overwhelmed by its location *(P. Barberini at V. Tritone)*, yet you can manage to appreciate the triumphant rise of the triton out of the sea and almost hear his shell trumpeting over the din of traffic.

Palazzo Barberini   ★★

V Quattro Fontane 13.

Just a bit up the hill to the right of the Triton Fountain is this palazzo, the **Galleria Nazionale d'Arte Antica**, with its collection of paintings from medieval through Baroque times. (Enter extreme left, up Bernini's double columned staircase to first floor). Even if you have no time for the galleries, you may want to see *the* High Baroque ceiling of them all, Pietro da Cortona's immense ★★ *Triumph of Divine Providence*, (1633; in Salone) depicting the glory of the Barberini pope, Urban VIII. In the galleries are fine works by Fillipo Lippi (Room 2), ★ Pietro di Cosimo (Room 4), ★ Beccafumi (Room 6), Raphael (★★ *La Fornarina*, Room 7), ★ Lorenzo Lotto and ★ Titian (Room 8), ★ Caravaggio (Room 15), ★ Guido Reni (★ *Putto Dormante*; Room 19), and a ★ portrait attributed to Holbein (Room 22). *Open 9 a.m.–2 p.m., except 1 p.m. Sun.; closed Mon.; L6000.*

Other Sights   ★

Exiting from the museum, continue left up the street to the first intersection. Here is another well-known fountain, the **Quattro Fontane** ("four fountains" 1593), one forming each corner, while the vistas down the streets are remarkable (the obelisks of the Pincio, Esquiline, and Quirinal hills and Michelangelo's Porta Pia). Sharing the corner with one fountain is Borromini's ★★**San Carlo alle Quattro Fontane** *(V. Quirinale; mid-1600s; closed 12-4:30 p.m. & Sat. p.m.)* fitted to this difficult spot without any loss of Baroque fullness and surmounted by a striking cupola. Inside the tiny church Borromini created a miracle of undulating space. Continuing down Via Quirinale toward the obelisk you find Bernini's ★**Sant'Andrea al Quirinale** *(on left, between the two small parks; 1678; closed noon-4 p.m. & Tues.)*, more sumptuous, but with space restrictions that resulted in an oval plan and an exquisite cupola. At the obelisk itself, surrounded by the ancient equestrian statues of Castor and Pollux, is the ★ **Piazza del Quirinale**. This is the summit of the hill, with a view of St. Peter's. On the right is the **Palazzo del Quirinale** *(Sun. 9 a.m.– noon; free)*, begun in 1574 and with a stately entrance by Carlo Maderno. Now the official presidential palace, formerly it was the summer residence of popes and is richly decorated. From here, you can descend the steps then turn right for the Trevi Fountain, left for P. Venezia, or straight for the Corso.

At the foot of the north slope of the Quirinal is V. Tritone with Metro A "Barberini" stop, the buses of the Spanish Steps neighborhood as well as #56 and #60 to P. Venezia and Trastevere.

Around Piazza Della Repubblica ★

This grand circular piazza of the turn of the century marks the eastern edge of Rome's center. Filled with traffic, the coming and going of long-distance buses, and the trainloads of people attracted to the Stazione Termini just south, the vast area is jarring. Even the elegance of the naiads frolicking with their horses in the **fountain** (1870) can't disguise that the area is a bit seedy. With your valuables tucked safely away, you can explore the sights, most of which are built in and around the ruins of the **Baths of Diocletian** (A.D. 298), the largest in ancient Rome.

The two metro lines intersect here at Stazione Termini, and buses #75 (P. Venezia and Trastevere), *#64* (P. Venezia, St. Peter's), *and others serve the area.*

Santa Maria degli Angeli

On the east side of the piazza, is this church built into the central hall of the Baths and retaining the original vaulting and red marble columns. Although Michelangelo designed the church, others so changed it (making the transept the nave), that it is disappointing. If you exit through the rear sacristy door, you see more ruins of the Baths.

Museo delle Terme   ★ ★

V. delle Terme.

Around the corner to the south, facing the stazione, is the entrance to this museum, officially called Museo Nazionale Romana. Comprised primarily of the ancient works discovered in Rome in the 19th–century, it is one of the great collections of the world for both Greek and Roman art. Unfortunately, most of the museum is closed for renovations, but some of the masterpieces can be seen. Only a few rooms are actually open on the ground floor, but the first (on right) includes the Greek original ★ ★ *Ludovisi Throne* (460 B.C.), magnificently carved with reliefs, the main one *Aphrodite Rising from the Sea* and a lovely side panel of a flute player. Through this room are other Greek sculptures, including two exceptional marble copies of Myron's famous bronze *Discus Thrower*. The ★ ★ *Lancelloti*, with its head intact, is the best-preserved in existence. Upstairs are the beautiful ★ ★ *frescoes* (c. A.D. 75) from Livia's (Augustus' wife) villa at Primaporta. Scattered around the delightful **great cloister**, once part of Santa Maria, are hundreds of sculptures. *The museum is open 9 a.m.–2 p.m., till 1 p.m. Sun.; closed Mon.; L12,000.*

Rome

Santa Maria della Vittoria   ★

Largo Santa Susanna.

Just north of the Piazza della Repubblica and only several blocks east of the Triton Fountain, is this church containing one of Bernini's best known works, ★ ★ *Santa Theresa in Ecstasy,* (1640; 4th chapel left). Bernini did more than carve the sculpture; he planned the entire chapel, including its ceiling and light, to enhance the impact of the saint's religious rapture. He even carved the chapel's patrons, the Cornaro family, as witnesses on a side wall. *Closed noon–4:30.*

Santa Maria Maggiore   ★ ★

Follow Via Cavour west for a few blocks, to the Esquiline Hill, with the obelisk and rear entrance of the great pilgrimage basilica, Santa Maria Maggiore *(7 a.m.–6 p.m.; strict dress code).* Although cloaked in an 18th-century facade, the church was founded in A.D. 432 and retains the classical proportions of the original basilica. The floor is a Cosmati mosaic (12th C.); the coffered ceiling is said to be gilded in the first gold brought back from the Americas. Above the Ionic columns of the nave and covering the triumphal arch behind the high altar are some of the finest Early Christian ★ ★ *mosaics* in Rome (5th C.). These small Biblical scenes require binoculars. Their naturalism contrasts with the Byzantine apse mosaics of the ★ ★ *Coronation of the Virgin,* (1295) by Jacopo Torriti. Standing in front of the main and *south facade* of the basilica, you see the fountain constructed from a gigantic fluted column from Constantine's Basilica in the Forum. Here the Esquiline slopes southwest to the Parco Oppio and the Colosseum, but before leaving consider a visit to the small, charming church of ★ **Santa Prassede** (A.D. 822; a block straight ahead, then right), with almost folkloric ★ *mosaics* in its south aisle chapel and apse (all 9th C.). *Between the Cavour and Termini metro stops, the church can be reached as well by Bus 70/71 from P. Flaminia via P. Berberini.*

Outside the Center

Catacombs and Appian Way   ★ ★

Via Appia Antica.

In ancient Rome, it was considered unhealthy to bury within the city walls, even though cremation was practiced. So Romans built their tombs along the roads outside the city. For the Christians, who didn't cremate, finding space for burials was a serious problem, especially during the second to fifth centuries after Christ, when hundreds of thousands converted. They discovered they could easily honeycomb the soft tufa stone outside the walls into underground, multi–layered cemeteries. (It is no longer believed that they were used as places to hide from Roman persecution.) The ★ ★ **Via Appia Antica** is one of the best-preserved ancient roads and preserves many of the Roman tombs (most reliefs now replaced by copies) and Christian catacombs. The catacombs, empty of their burials and only too rarely enlivened with Early Christian symbols such as Jonah and the whale, an Old Testament equivalent for the new resurrection, will probably disappoint all except religious pilgrims. The three Christian catacombs cluster together about 2 km from town, but to visit them all is very time-consuming, as you must wait for tour groups to form at each for the priest-guided visit. Save your time instead for a walk on the

Appian Way, and visit just one catacomb: **S. Callisto** *(V. Appia Antica 110; 8:30 a.m.–noon, 2:30–5 p.m., till 5:30 p.m. in summer; closed Wed.; L8000)* for its beautiful grounds; **S. Domitilla** *(V. Sette Chiese 283, a 10-minute walk off to west of Appian Way—be careful of speeding cars; 8:30 a.m.–noon, 2:30–5:30 p.m., closed Tues.; L8000)* for its ancient underground Christian basilica (4th century), and **S. Sebastiano** *(V. Appia Antica 136 at V. Sette Chiese; 9 a.m.–noon, 2:30–5 p.m., closed Thurs.; L8000)* for Giorgetti's moving Baroque statue of the saint (first chapel, left, in church). Continuing out on the Appian Way, on your left you pass the ruins of **Maxentius' Villa and Circus** *(V. Appia 153; A.D. 309)*, then at the top of a rise in the road is the ★ **Tomb of Cecilia Metella** (century A.D. 50), an immense round tomb retaining some of its frieze and marble facing. In the Middle Ages, the owners decided to fortify the tomb, so now it's crenellated like a castle. And then they charged tolls to all traffic on the road, thereby preserving the Via Appia Antica, because people soon found alternate routes and the ancient Roman way was buried by time. Just beyond the intersection with Via Cecilia Metella, begins the 1.5-mile-strip of the old road that archaeologists have revealed by excavations. There's little

traffic along the rugged stone pavement, and you can enjoy a ★ ★ **country walk** on the ancient road lined with cypresses and tombs, and past fields covered with wild flowers.

The Via Appia Antica begins at the Aurelian wall, just below the Baths of Caracalla, and runs about 2 km to the S. Sebastiano catacombs, then continues for another 3 km beyond that point. At the V. Cecilia Metella turnoff, the #118 bus that runs from behind the Colosseum must turn along with the rest of traffic, before making its return here into town. There are a few restaurants to sustain walkers; the **Hostaria Archeologia** *(V. Appia Antica 139; closed Thurs.;* ☎ *788-0494; moderate) across from S. Sebastiano, has a pleasant outdoor terrace and simple Roman food.*

Sant'Agnese Fouri Le Mura   ★★

V. Nomentana 2 km east of center.

This 7th-century basilica, much renovated save for the fine apse ★ **mosaic**, is our favorite of those found outside the ancient walls. It's set in a pleasing park and shares the grounds with the jewel-like ★ ★ **Mausaleo Santa Costanza** (4th C.), the circular tomb built by Constantine's daughter and decorated with delightful Christian ★ ★ mosaics that are, nonetheless, very classical with their Dionysian vines and fruits as symbols of renewal. (Those in the niches are 7th C.) *Santa Costanza as well as catacombs in the basilica are open 9 a.m.–noon, 4–6 p.m., closed Sun. morn. and Tues. p.m. Many buses run along V. Nomentana, #60 from P. Venezia and P. Barberini.*

Shopping

Shopping in Rome means browsing along some of the most picturesque streets of the city. And although Rome has an abundance of designer shops, it also has wonderful art galleries and antique shops to explore.

Spanish Steps

The most famous shopping area is in the streets at the foot of the steps. Here *Via Condotti* boasts some of the most renowned names in fashion—Gucci, Valentino, Ferragamo, and even the non-Italian Hermes and Cartier. It also has great Italian jewelers, among them the Roman **Bulgari** *(#10)* with his ornate creations, the exquisite antiques of **Carlo Eleuteri** *(#69)*, and the silver and gold of **Buccellati** *(#31)*. **Fendi** and **Ferre** are on Via Borgognona, **Benetton** seems everywhere, and the *Via Babuino* boasts **Missoni, Giorgio Armani**, and **Krizia**. In fact, the Via Babuino is even more famous for its shops of French and Italian antiques, and they spill over to Via Margutta. Babuina and Margutta also offer more contemporary choices; from the sumptuous fabrics of **Cesari** *(Babuina 18)* to stylish **Cassina** *(Babuina 100)* with the latest in Italian furniture as well as Frank Lloyd Wright designs and **Artemide** *(Magutta 108)* with Memphis style lamps, more witty than they are beautiful. Also, *Via Margutta* is full of art galleries and boasts a spring and fall **art festival**. Just off Babuino near the Spanish Steps is **Alinari** *(V. Alibert 16a)* with fine old photos of Rome. Not everything in this area is quite so expensive. For fashion, the most upscale block is *Via Bocca di Leone* (between Frattina and Carrozze) with **Valentino, Ferragamo, Ungaro, Gianni Versace,** and **Matassi** jewelry. For more affordable designer clothing and accessories (but not by much), check out **Discount dell'Alta Moda** *(V. Gesu e Maria 16)*. The jewelry at **Jako** *(V. Mario dei Fiori 57)* or **Clio Bijoux** *(V. Croce 53)* is emphatically and stylishly fake. The clothing is smart at the shops on *Via Gambero*, but more affordable, just as it is around the *Via Campo Marzio*, on the other side of the Corso, or in the **Rinascente** department store *(Corso across from P. Colonna)*. **The little outdoor market on Piazza della Fontanella Borghese** *(near end of Via Ripetta; closed Sat. afternoons, Sun.)* is highly respected for its antique prints and rare books. And at **Palazzo Ruspoli Art Gallery** *(Corso 418; fee)* you can admire a 16th-century mansion along with the special exhibits of world-famous artists, while the **Galleria Edieuropa** *(Corso 525)* often exhibits works by important Italian artists of this century.

Piazza Navona

Between the piazza and the Tiber are a multitude of shops, both the trendy and the stodgy, that give you an excuse for strolling through some of the most attractive streets of historic Rome. The galleries and English antique shops of **Via Coronari** are the most famous, but not far away is the most avante garde art gallery in town, **Ugo Ferranti** *(V. dei Soldati 25a)*. Around Via Scorfa there are nifty folding chairs and housewares (**Tradizione Casa**, *Scorfa 116*) as well as the jewelry creations of Carlo Vitali Orafo (**Bottega Orafa**, *V. Pianellari 24*) and the plaster busts of cupids and ancient Romans (**Beatrice Palma**, *Pianellari 17*). Just off the Piazza Navona, along Via Banchi Nuovi, there are antique shops (**Cose Cose** at #89 has Victorian earrings and silver) as well as up-and-coming clothing designers (**Luna e l'Altra,** *#105*).

Campo dei Fiori

Shops are plentiful in this neighborhood too, where the beautiful *Via Giulia* offers fine art and antique galleries like the **Galleria Giulia** *(#148)* as well as fine crafts, such as the Italian ceramics at **Ceramiche** *(#22)*. Nearby you can find those brass lion door knockers you've always wanted (**Handles**, *V. Pettinari at V. Giulia*) as well as beautiful old tiles and their fine reproductions at **Galleria Farnese** *(P. Farnese)*. Off Campo dei Fiori, Via dei Cappellari runs parallel with Via Giulia, and is crammed with shops offering furnishings, both antique and simply old, but less pricey. Around the Pantheon, there are the exquisite priests' robes, scepters and chalices at **De Ritas** *(V. de Cestari 48)* contrasting with the stylish plastic housewares of Guzzini at **Sodero II** *(P. Minerva 72)*. And **Dakota** *(V. Seminario III, off the P. Rotonda)* is a chic and witty Italian version of a U.S. Army-and-Navy store, complete with gas masks and vintage corduroy slacks.

Trastevere

If mainstream shopping isn't for you, then check out Trastevere. Funkier shops, many the workshops of artisans, are found here amid the fruit stands, especially in the streets around Santa Maria in Trastevere and on *Via della Lungaretta*. Just off Via del Moro is the **Galleria** *(V. Pelliccia 29)* with superb Italian folkart, including Pugliese ceramics. Contemporary art galleries are here, too, like the **Galleria Alessandra Bonamo** *(P. Sant'Apollonia 3, upstairs)*, **Il Ponte** *(Montoro 10 near Ponte Sisto)* and **Galleria Sales** *(V. San Francesco Sales 72, off the Lungara)*. Many curio shoppers trek to the Sunday morning **Porta Portese outdoor market** in Trastevere, but really it's hard to find anything here other than auto parts and cheap clothing.

Carnevale via Reggio

Festivals and Special Events

Religious events take on special intensity with the Vatican's presence as well as some of the major pilgrimage sites for the Catholic church. **Holy Week**, for example, includes a Good Friday procession of the cross from the Colosseum to the Palatine Hill and Easter the Pope gives his blessing to the city and the world. The **Christmas season** is marked by similar pilgrimages, but also by the delightful custom of children reciting poems and wishes to the **Santo Bambino**, sleekly wrapped in gold, at the Santa Maria in Aracoeli church on the Capitoline Hill (midnight Christmas Eve and on Jan. 6 the statue is moved with much fanfare to and from its chapel to the Christmas creche). Also for Epiphany, the kindly witch La Bufana pays a visit to Piazza Navona to give toys to the city's children. Although the *rione*, or neighborhood, around the Lateran church celebrates the **Feast of St. John** (June 20–24), no neighborhood celebrates more intensely than Trastevere for its **Festa de' Noaltri** (or "us others"), when the feast day of the Virgin of Carmel becomes part of a 10-day folk festival, with evening music, processions, fireworks, and much eating at tables set up in the middle of the streets (begins mid-July).

Cultural events are plentiful year-round, but when the weather warms up after March, they tend to take place in rather spectacular locations as well. July brings soloists performing with the orchestra of the **Accademia Nazionale di Santa Cecilia** (☎ *6880-1044 or 678-0742*) to the Villa Giulia gardens. The **French Accademia** sponsors a festival of the arts in July at its Villa Medici (☎ *676-1243*) on the Pincio Hill, while **Tevere Expo** sponsors a variety of shows along the banks of the Tiber (near the Cavour bridge), including one of regional arts and crafts with concerts in the evening (late June into July; ☎ *686-9069*). **Festa Musica Pro Mundo Uno** (V. Villa Maggiorani 20, ☎ *00-168*) sponsors concerts in churches late July into August. Also the **Palazzo delle Esposizione** (*V. Nazionale 194; open for exhibits 10 a.m.–9 p.m., except Tues.; restaurant, bar, museum shop; fee*) mounts blockbuster art exhibits worth seeking out as well as film retrospectives. Contact the EPT tourist office for information on these events, especially in its monthly publication, *Carnet di Roma*, or buy Thursday's edition of the newspaper *La Repubblica*, for its *Trova Roma* entertainment guide. But even *Trova Roma* doesn't list the **Pasquino** (Vicolo del Piede, just off flank of Santa Maria in Trastevere church) with its movies in English, the only ones not dubbed (*evenings only; closed August*).

Where to Stay

There are an enormous number of hotels in Rome, running the full gamut of the price range. Listed here are our favorites in convenient sightseeing locations in the city–a few slightly outside the center, in quiet garden settings are listed for those who prefer them. Many hotels cluster around the Piazza di Spagna and the nearby Via Veneto, an area with the most exclusive shops, the museums of the Villa Borghese, and many restaurants. (Be warned: Although most of this area is incredibly chic, the Via Veneto during late night hours has become a bit sleazy). Far fewer can be found in the historic heart of Rome, around the Pantheon and the Piazza Navona, though new hotels have opened recently in this most picturesque area that also happens to include some of the best restaurants and trattorias. Most of our recommendations are in these two areas, because we think they are the most convenient. But we did discover one in lively and convenient Trastevere to recommend, and we offer another in the Vatican. All of these areas are linked by good public

Rome

transport and taxis, and most are even within walking distance of each other. If you can't find a room in any of these hotels, try the Vatican or neighboring Prati district, where there are a number of good hotels, and where a walk across the Tiber can bring you into the center of things. For **apartment rentals**, check the biweekly publications *Wanted in Rome* and *Metropolitan*, found at newsstands and Anglo bookstores.

Reservations are a must at any time of year, since Rome's tourist season spills over into early spring and late fall, and religious holidays, with their attendant pilgrimages, fill in the gaps. Only late November/early December, as well as February, are somewhat off-season.

In the summer, you'll probably find air conditioning essential, if not for the heat, then for the noise. Although most of these hotels are in areas with restricted traffic (the hotels have double-glazed windows), the voices of those dining outside, or even the sudden blast of a moped, can keep you awake.

Very Expensive

Hassler   L470–900,000   ★★★★★

Trinità di Monti 6, 00187; ☎ *678-2651, FAX 678-9991.*
Single L470,000. Double L640–900,000.
It is hard to surpass the Hassler in comforts and convenience. The 19th-century hotel stands at the top of the Spanish Steps, commanding views over Rome. The self-assured atmosphere, the easy grace, and the elegance of the lobbies with their antiques, are supplemented by a garden terrace for summer dining, a club-style bar, and a famous rooftop terrace restaurant with spectacular views over Rome. The 103 units have been lavishly renovated (some with views of city, others of trees in the back). Even here, though, some rooms can be small, but there are a few U.S. $2000-suites with their private panoramic terraces, one with bullet-proof windows. No groups accepted. All these amenities and also a sun deck, tennis, bicycles and a garage.

Excelsior   L420–650,000 CP   ★★★★★

V. Veneto 125, 00187; ☎ *482-6205, FAX 484-0984.*
Single L420,000 CP. Double L650,000 CP
Both the Ciga's Excelsior and its Caffè Doney are among the most famous landmarks on the fashionable Via Veneto. The hotel is large and bustling, with high ceilings, chandeliers, and ornate decor in its lobbies. The 360 units include quite a number of suites as well as large (some very large) rooms decorated in a rococo gilded and mirrored style. Occasionally the marble baths almost match the rooms in size. Piano lounge. Solarium. Turkish bath. Garage.

Lord Byron   L420–560,000 CP   ❀★★★★

V. Notari 5, 00197; ☎ *322-0404, FAX 322-0405.*
Single/double L420–560,000 CP.
Situated on the northwest edge of the Borghese Gardens, perhaps a 10-minute taxi ride to the Via Veneto, this small, tranquil hotel offers all the grace and sophistication expected of Relais & Chateau affiliates. In a gleaming white art deco villa, the hotel has created 42 different rooms, some smallish, others suites, and all decorated tastefully but lavishly with priceless wallcoverings (a cashmere paisley in one suite),

paintings and antiques, baths of lovely marble and polished stone, and doors of burled rosewood. Rooms have lovely views of cypresses and umbrella pines. There's a comfortable living room "lobby," a few terraces, a piano bar and one of Rome's most elegant restaurants, Le Jardin. No groups. Garage.

D'Ingleterra — L330–560,000 —

V. Bocca di Leone 14, 00187; ☎ *69-981, FAX 6992-2243.*
Single L330,000. Double L500–590,000.

At the foot of the Spanish Steps and in the heart of Rome's elegant shopping district stands the welcoming ochre facade of the d'Ingleterra. Built in the 16th–century as a guesthouse for a patrician family, the palazzo didn't really become a hotel until the last century, when it catered to Franz Liszt, Henry James, and Ernest Hemingway. Although a favorite *pensione* of intellectuals and writers into this century, the hotel was recently renovated into a more sublime category. Despite the gleaming mirrors and mahogany, and the polish of the marble, the hotel has retained its 19th-century charm. Its 105 rooms remain old-fashioned rather than glamorous. Those on the fifth floor have terraces; on the sixth there are suites with views. All rooms have high ceilings and some antiques, though the baths vary from old-world marble opulence to more modern comforts. And size varies, too, but the price reflects this. The "Roman Garden" is a frescoed restaurant, complete with cumulus clouds painted on the ceiling. Handsome English bar. Arrangements for garage. No groups.

Holiday Inn Crowne Plaza — L410–600,000 — ★★★★

P. Minerva, 00186; ☎ *6994-1888, FAX 679-4165.*
Single L410,000. Double L545–600,000.

Locally known as the "Minerva" for its location on one of Rome's most character-istic piazzettas, this Holiday Inn has little about it, not even a sign, to remind you of its ordinary highway predecessors. After a renovation of this stately 15th-century palazzo, the *Minerva* opened in 1990 in our favorite neighborhood around the Pan-theon. Marble floors and original columns from the *cortile* grace the lobby; silk-covered walls and high ceilings create the pleasing setting for 135 quiet rooms (some with views of the ancient bricks of the Pantheon or Bernini's elephant sculp-ture in the piazza) with modern comforts. Restaurant and lounge. Airport pickup.

Hotel de la Ville — L530–650,000 CP — ★★★★

V. Sistina 67, 00187; ☎ *67-331, FAX 678-4213.*
Single/double L530–650,000 CP.

At the top of the Spanish Steps and next to the Hassler, this handsome hotel has many amenities in addition to its excellent location, not the least are the special prices often offered by its parent company, Inter-Continental hotels place it in the expensive category at times. In addition, the 19th-century lobby has high ceilings and traditional decor; the restaurant terraces overlook a patio garden; and the ser-vice is gracious. Some of the 195 units have balconies and/or views of the city, while others overlook the quiet patio and restaurant, some with large sunning ter-races. All are a good size and with modern baths. Piano bar. Garage.

Expensive

Borgognoni   **L380–475,000 CP**   ★ ★ ★ ★

V. del Bufalo 126, 00187; ☎ *6994-1505, FAX 6994-1501.*
Single L380,000 CP. Double L475,000 CP

A few blocks from the Spanish Steps, and just off the Piazza San Silvestro, the Borgognoni is a stylish hotel built around an airy, planted courtyard. Completely contemporary in decor, the hotel provides a pleasurable retreat after sightseeing in the city, especially when you're staying in one of the 50 rooms with a courtyard terrace. Lounge. Breakfast room. Garage.

Raphael   **L420–475,000 CP**   ✿ ★ ★ ★

Largo Febo 2, 00186; ☎ *682-831, FAX 687-8993.*
Single L420,000 CP. Double L440–465,000 CP.

Tucked in a piazzetta just a few yards away from the beautiful Piazza Navona, the Raphael's location is one of its greatest assets. It's charming too, with ivy draped over its facade and a cozy lobby full of paintings and some antiques. Although the 55 rooms and suites are modernized and well-appointed, they can be small. Roof terrace with fine views of Rome. Restaurant. Bar.

Moderate

Santa Chiara   **L220–290,000 CP**   ★ ★

V. Santa Chiara 21, 00186; ☎ *687-2979, FAX 687-3114.*
Single L220,000 CP. Double L290,000 CP.

With an unbeatable location on the Piazza Minerva behind the Pantheon, the Santa Chiara was renovated in 1989 and upgraded into a tasteful, contemporary hotel. The 95 rooms are no larger than they have to be, but they are comfortable, carpeted and well-appointed; the most tranquil overlook the *cortile*. Breakfast bar. Almost moderate.

Internazionale   **L200–290,000 CP**   √ ★ ★ ★

V. Sistina 79, 00187; ☎ *6994-1823, FAX 678-4764.*
Single L200,000 CP. Double L290,000 CP.

This family-owned hotel is a very special spot atop the Spanish Steps. A bit like Rome itself, the modern lobby leads to the unexpected—medieval-like hallways open to the Gothic wood ornamentation of a former convent or to the elegance of an 18th-century breakfast room. The 40 rooms vary, from suites with ceiling frescoes to modern 4th floor rooms with garden terraces. Even the smallest room (and it is small) has its compensation of a large balcony with Rome views. All the rooms are well maintained, with modern baths. The service is attentive and warm. No groups.

La Residenza   **L200–250,000 CP**   √ ★ ★

V. Emilia 22, 00187; ☎ *488-0789, FAX 485-721.*
Single L200,000 CP. Double L250,000 CP.

Just off the Via Veneto on a quiet street is this former villa, now a very comfortable, well-run hotel with homey sitting rooms and lounges. The 27 rooms have been pleasantly modernized with plaid carpeting and very good baths (hair dryers and even terry cloth robes). Summer roof terrace, bar, breakfast room, some parking. And good service.

Locarno   **L210–275,000 CP**

V. della Penna 22, 00186; ☎ 361-0841, FAX 321-5249.
Single L210,000 CP. Double L275,000 CP.

On a quieter street near the Piazza del Popolo and the Via Condotti shopping area, the Locarno is a small hotel with striking art nouveau highlights—on the doors, in the lobby, but especially in the bar. The 38 sunny rooms, with small baths, were renovated in'93. There's a comforting strip of garden for breakfast or relaxing. Nice service. Complimentary bicycles. Garage.

Columbus   **L200–275,000 CP**

V. della Conciliazione 33, 00193; ☎ 686-5435, FAX 686-4874.
Single L200,000 CP. Double L255–275,000 CP

For those wishing a Vatican location, the Columbus can't be beat. On the edge of St. Peters, this hotel began as a pilgrimage hospice in 1478 and elegantly housed visitors like Isabella d'Este and Alonso I of Naples. Today, this large and rambling palazzo somehow neatly maintains hall after Renaissance hall of frescoes, wooden beams, fireplaces, and hundreds of highbacked tapestry-covered chairs. The 100 rooms are carpeted and clean, the bathrooms are old-fashioned, but not worn. Rooms overlooking the vast inner *cortile* are quietest. Handsome bar. Breakfast room. Restaurant. Parking in *cortile*. Fee for a/c.

Trevi   **L210–260,000 CP**   ★★

Vicolo del Babuccio 20/21, 00187; ☎ 678-9563, FAX 684-1407.
Single L210,000 CP. Double L260,000 CP.

This is a smart new hotel in a quiet lane near the Trevi Fountain. (With your back to the fountain, walk straight ahead onto V. San Vicenzo, then left at Babuccio). The 15 carpeted and a/c rooms are smallish, but well designed and furnished with frigo bars, hair dryers and the like. Rooftop terrace for breakfast in warm weather and views. Inexpensive in the off-season.

Teatro di Pompeo   **L200–260,000 CP**   √★★

Largo del Pallaro 8, 00186; ☎ 6830-0170, FAX 6880-5531.
Single L200,000 CP. Double L240–260,000 CP.

Although just a block from the Campo dei Fiori and just two blocks south of the Corso Emanuele, this relatively new inn is on a tranquil piazzetta and many of its rooms are guaranteed quiet interiors. While the 12 rooms have modern decor and comforts, the breakfast room and bar are enclosed in the stone of Pompey's Theater where Julius Caesar was assassinated. Fee for a/c.

Madrid   **L190–260,000 CP**   ★★

V. Mario de Fiori 93, 00187; ☎ 699-1511, FAX 679-1653.
Single L190,000 CP. Double L260,000 CP.

At the foot of the Spanish Steps, the Madrid has 24 rooms, all carpeted, comfortable, and with good baths. The leather and beige lobby is small, the breakfast room decent, especially when it moves to the roof terrace in warm weather. Fee for a/c.

Gregoriana   **L250–280,000 CP**   ★★

V. Gregoriana 18, 00187; ☎ 679-4269, FAX 678-4258.
Single L250,000 CP. Double L280,000 CP.

With virtually no common areas (breakfast served in rooms), the Gregoriana never-theless competes in this category with its Spanish Steps location and 10 small, smartly decorated (with some tongue-in-cheek Italianate touches like bits of tiger-skin-patterned wallpaper) and comfortably modern rooms. Efficient service. Credit cards: None.

Inexpensive

Portoghesi   **L180–225,000 CP**   ★★

V. Portoghesi 1, 00186; ☎ *686-4231, FAX 687-6976.*
Single L180,000 CP. Double L225,000 CP.

In a quiet medieval corner just north of the Piazza Navona, the Portoghesi's loca-tion is its best asset. The furnishings are drab but there's an elevator, a roof terrace, a/c, and 27 quite ample rooms, not all have private toilets. The best rooms are "suites" (moderate) and open to a neighbor's flowering terrace.

Sant'Anselmo   **L100–200,000 CP**   ★★

P. Sant'Anselmo 2, 00153; ☎ *578-3214, FAX 578-3604.*
Single L100–150,000 CP. Double L160–200,000 CP.

When the city simply isn't what you want, perhaps this villa atop the beautiful (and quiet) Aventine hill is. There's a garden, a terrace on a piazzetta, sitting rooms and 45 rooms, all furnished eclectically in a rather rococo manner. There are two other villas surrounding the garden and under the same management: the **Aventino** offers plainer rooms, lower prices; the **San Pio** is similar to the Sant'Anselmo. Breakfast bar. No a/c. Parking.

Albergo del Sole   **L85–165,000**   √

V. Biscione 76, 00186; ☎ *6880-6873, FAX 689-3787.*
Single without bath L85,000. Double with bath L145–165,000.

Up the stairs from a street just off the lively Campo dei Fiori is this hotel with 50 decent-sized rooms at prices rarely seen in central Rome. The baths are basic (no shower curtains), but the beds are decent and there's a terrace and parking. Reserve in advance.

Margutta   **L140,000 CP**   √

V. Laurina 34, 00187; ☎ *322-3674, FAX 320-0390.*
Single/double L140,000 CP.

Just off the fashionable V. Babuina in the Spanish Steps area, this hotel offers 21 clean and ample, if simple rooms (no a/c) at a very low price given the location. A few rooms with terraces. Breakfast room.

Cisterna   **L130,000**   √★

V. della Cisterna 7, 00153; ☎ *581-7212, FAX 581-0091.*
Single/double L130,000.

Located just around the corner from beautiful Santa Maria in Trastevere, this fam-ily-run hotel is one of the few in this neighborhood. The 18 rooms (no a/c) are plain, but ample and fresh with decent baths; those overlooking interior garden patio are quietest. Breakfast room. Restaurant next door.

Where to Eat

Dining in Rome is not usually ranked as high as in the culinary capitals of Milan, Bologna or Florence, but that ranking, of course, doesn't mean you won't dine well. The most sophisticated food often ranges beyond the regional, finding inspiration not just from Tuscany and Emilia, but from France and Japan as well. Many restaurants in the capital specialize in the cuisine of other regions, from the risotti of the Veneto to the grilled eggplant of Sicily. It is the rare restaurant, however, that doesn't incorporate something Roman into its cuisine, if only an artichoke *alla giudea* or *spaghetti alla carbonara* (a sauce of eggs, bacon and pecorino). The local respect for vegetables and fruits enlivens even the seafood antipasti and results in a surprising array of vegetarian dishes, such as *rughetta* (arugula) with slivers of parmesan, or a pastry stuffed with zucchini flowers and cheese. Roman cuisine is abundantly available in elegant restaurants where the aroma of braised basil permeates delicate veal, in trattoria where *coda di vaccinara* prevails along with *gnocchi al ragu*. Seafood graces most menus, from the simple *spaghetti alle vongole veraci* (with maybe a dash of red peperoncini flakes) to magnificently succulent, ginger-flavored *mazzancolle*, or the local tender, large shrimps. Roman summer brings Roman relief, too, with the city's tantalizing gelaterias, its cafes serving refreshing *granite*, or ice drinks. The prevalent table wines are the whites from the Castelli Romani, but there is no lack of wines from other regions—the Tuscan reds tending to substitute for the rarer, but good, local ones.

Tips: Romans tend to dine late, between 1-3 p.m. for lunch, after 9 p.m. for dinner. The trattorias get lively earlier and even the best restaurants begin serving dinner by 8 or 8:30 p.m. • The city, fortunately, has many inexpensive trattorias and pizzerias, because most of its restaurants cluster in the moderately expensive to expensive range. (Remember you can usually lower the price category by making frugal selections, except at the best restaurants.) • As in all Italian cities, Sundays and August can be difficult times for dining out. If you find yourself stuck, the old ghetto has numerous restaurants open on Sundays as does Trastevere, which is your best bet in August, too.

The Superb

Rome's best known restaurants offer smart settings and excellent food. Typical of the city's diversity, each is distinctive from the other.

Relais Le Jardin   **$$$**   ★ ★ ★ ★ ★

> V. Notaris 5; ☎ 322-0404, FAX 322-0405.
> Closed Sun. and Aug.; reservation recommended. Meals L75–130,000.
> Sharing an Art Deco villa with the Hotel Lord Byron, this restaurant has Rome's most elegant setting. Its handsome piano bar and perfectly appointed rooms are the favorite spot for special celebrations—or if the budget permits, a simple celebration of the restaurant's superbly prepared international and Italian cuisine. The seasonality of the cuisine, as in all the best restaurants, makes for frequent changes in menu, but you might enjoy a flan of watercress and scallops or risotto with asparagus and lobster, a light pastry stuffed with funghi porcini, or a delicate quail with figs.

Convivio   **$$$**   ★ ★ ★ ★ ★

> V. dell'Orso 44; ☎ 686-9432, FAX 689-9432.

Closed Sun.; reservation recommended. Fixed-price meal L90–100,000. À la carte L70–110,000.

Located north of the Piazza Navona, this chic restaurant of ten Damask-covered tables in soothingly peach-colored rooms is the newest of the best. The food is excellent, the choices change seasonally (salads of fish, fennel and black truffles; rabbit stuffed with pâté and black olives; wonderful faraone and risotti) the wine list and service are very good, and the prices remarkably good for the quality.

La Rosetta $$$ ★★★★

V. della Rosetta 9; ☎ 686-1002, FAX 687-2852.
Closed Sat. lunch, Sun., & Aug.; reservation required. Meals L90–135,000.
Located just north of the Pantheon, the Rosetta is a restaurant with contemporary decor and clean, elegant lines. Famous for the freshness and inventive preparation of its seafood, Rosetta's signature dish is the cold antipasto called "marinati," with taste treats such as shrimp and rughetta salad, perch with orange slices. The dorado *(dorate)*, once memorably prepared with fresh anchovies, is worth asking for even when it's not on the menu. Fine service.

Papa Giovanni $$$ ★★★★

V. dei Sediari 4; ☎ 686-5308.
Closed Sun., Aug.; reservation recommended. Meals L80–115,000.
This intimate establishment, with old beams and stone walls, is located near the Piazza Navona, and serves traditional, but very refined Roman cuisine. Here, look for whatever is freshest—entire luncheons (but not dinners) can be chosen around the season's best, like artichokes or asparagus. Capretto is good, as are lamb, or veal, and game flavored with fennel or rosemary. Portions are somewhat small; service can be slow.

Agata e Romeo $$–$$$ ★★★★

V. Carlo Alberto 45; 446-5842.
Closed Mon. at lunch, Sun. Christmas season. Fixed-price meal L75,000. À la carte L60–85,000.
In a not so central location near Santa Maria Maggiore, this restaurant is well worth seeking out for its innovative cuisine. Although the menu changes with such regularity that your dining choices are hard to predict, you can rely on always finding a first-rate Roman bucatini all'amatriciana and excellent soups. Fish is featured throughout the menu, such as pasta with skate and broccoli, and the duck with porcini and rack of lamb are superb.

The Very Good

Fortunately, there are more moderately priced restaurants that combine ambience and fine cuisine.

Vecchia Roma $$–$$$ ★★★

P. Campitelli 18; ☎ 686-4604.
Closed Wed. & part of Aug.; reservation recommended. Meals L50–80,000.
In the old ghetto near the Capitoline Hill, this wonderful restaurant combines ambience and fine cuisine at somewhat moderate prices. Dining here is always pleasant, but never more so than outdoors, weather permitting, on one of Rome's quieter and lovely piazzas. The cuisine is Roman at its lightest and best. The antipasto

table may include a summery red pepper involtini or winter artichokes alla giudea accented by a crostino spread with caper pâté, but there are always seafood salads to choose from as well. The specials vary, and once included a knockout pappardelle frutti di mari with porcini and tomato, but usually you can rely on finding delectable *straccetta* (Roman braised meats and vegetables), served in summer with beef strips enhanced by herbs, radicchio and eggplant, or in winter with veal infused with the aroma of basil. Save room for the house-made fresh fruit granita, or sorbet.

Cornucopia $$–$$$ ★★★
P. in Piscinula 18; ☎ 580-0380.
Closed Sun., late Aug.-mid Sept. Meals L50–75,000.
Tucked to the side of one of Trastevere's most attractive piazzas (reserve an outdoor table in season), this small restaurant serves inventive preparations of seafood, from the ravioli neri with shrimp and the house-made fettucine Cornucopia, with tiny shrimp, tomato and funghi, to the stuffed calamari and seafood brochette. Add a salad and you're set.

Il Cardinale $$ ★★★
V. delle Carceri 6; ☎ 686-9336.
Closed Sun., July 15-Sept. 15; reservation recommended. Meals L45–70,000.
Just off Via Giulia, and rather overly decorated in posh Victorian (or "cardinal") red, this restaurant is a standout for its reasonable prices, given the quality of the food. Dine on good traditional Roman cuisine (ossobuco, grilled eels) prepared often with some new twists (chicken livers with anchovy and endive) as well as interesting salads—just what you would expect from the son of the more famous owner of Papa Giovanni's (see above).

Taverna Giulia $$ ★★★
Vicolo dell'Oro; ☎ 686-9768, FAX 689-3720.
Closed Sun., Aug. Meals L50–70,000.
Near the river end of the Corso Emanuele is this convenient, longtime favorite of travelers. There's a small outdoor terrace in season and superb Genovese cuisine. Of course, the pasta with pesto is dense and wonderful, but the panzotti salsa di noci (walnut sauce) is not to be missed, and the stinco, or veal shank roast, is juicy and full of flavor. We found the service to be indifferent, however, sometimes even grumpy.

Evangelista $$ ★★★
Lungoteveri Vallati 24; ☎ 687-5810.
Dinner only; closed Sun., Aug.; reservation recommended. Meals L45–70,000.
Located just west of Via Arenula, the Evangelista manages to offer sophisticated ambience and food at somewhat modest prices. The house specialty, year-round, is an appetizer of artichoke heart al mattone, but other dishes change with the season, from asparagus in spring to ovuli and porcini and truffles in fall, all served as salads, or showcased on pasta. Some of our favorite dishes have been tagliolini with porcini, pork with wild fennel and polenta and a light main dish of wild arugula leaves and thin parmesan slices. Credit cards: None.

Rome

Nino $$ ★★★

V. Borgognona 11; ☎ 679-5676.
Closed Sun. & Aug. Meals L45–70,000.
This regional restaurant, located near the foot of the Spanish Steps, serves reliable Tuscan cuisine. There's *pappardelle alla lepra* (thick noodles with hare sauce), spinach souffle accompanied by chicken livers, and grilled funghi porcini in season.

Piccolo Mondo $$–$$$ ★★

V. Aurora 39; ☎ 481-4595.
Closed Sun., Aug. Meals L50-75,000.
A bit pricey for its location near the Via Veneto, this lively Abruzzi restaurant has sidewalk tables as well as indoor ones. The antipasto array is extensive (make sure you point out your preferences to the waiter), the bucatini all'amatriciana is among the best in the city, and tacchino ai funghi (turkey with mushrooms) a traditional choice in addition to seafood.

In the Neighborhoods: Trattorias

Some restaurants will seduce you with their rooftop views or beckon you from their prized locations on Rome's most picturesque piazzas. Not too surprisingly, they usually are costlier than their food warrants. But yes, it's hard to resist them. We won't weaken your resolve by listing them, though, but instead point out that the same scene can often be enjoyed from a cafe or bar. Yet convenience is important when exploring a large city like Rome. So in addition to our recommendations above, here are some more modest establishments arranged geographically. (**Note:** Many do not accept credit cards.)

Near the Spanish Steps

Otello alla Concordia $–$$ ★

V. Croce 81; no reservations.
Closed Sun., Christmas season. Meals L35–55,000.
A delightful spot for summer dining alfresco. The food is good, too—try the cold pasta primavera or daily specials that may include *zucchini ripieni* (stuffed squash) or *vitello tonno*.

Buca di Ripetta $–$$ ★★

V. Ripetta 36; ☎ 321-9391.
Closed Sun. dinner, Mon., Aug. Meals L30–50,000.
A lively restaurant at lunch, filled with Romans enjoying the good traditional fare and large portions—stuffed tomato or a cold bean soup, saltimbocca and vegetable *fritto misto*.

Margutta ★★

V. Margutta 119; reserve at ☎ 678-6033.
Closed Sun., part Aug. L40–60,000.
Vegetarian fare served in a tranquil, contemporary setting; the *sformati* (flans) of mushrooms or cheese are good, as is the rigatoni with rughetta.

Near Campo dei Fiori

This area, including the Piazza Navona, has many fine restaurants (see above).

Grappolo d'Oro $–$$ ★

P. Cancelleria.

Closed Sun., Aug. Fixed-price lunch L30–50,000. À la carte dinner L35–55,000.
Few can equal the homey ambience of this trattoria that probably comes closest to what you've always imagined an authentic trattoria to be. Although we've found the traditional dishes uneven lately, we can recommend filling up from the antipasto table—one of the bargains of Rome.

Ar Galleto da Giovanni   **$–$$**   ★
P. Farnese 102.
Closed Sun. Meals L40–65,000. No credit cards.
When weather permits al fresco dining, we like Ar Galleto da Giovanni for its setting on one of the city's finest piazzas and its well-prepared Roman food.

Pierluigi   **$$**   ★★
P. de'Ricci 144; reserve at ☎ 686-8717.
Closed Tues. lunch & Mon. Meals L45–70,000.
Several blocks west of the P. Farnese on Monserrato, this eatery is best in warm weather when you sit in the piazzetta and enjoy the daily seafood specials—the *zuppa di cozzi* and the pasta with scampi are good, but the house wine is not.

Costanza   **$–$$**   ★★
P. Paradiso 63; ☎ 686-1717.
Closed Sun., Aug. Meals L40–65,000.
Located right off the Campo dei Fiori, you can enjoy professional service and a satisfying pasta (*alle vongole veraci* always is good) and salad under the arches of what once was the ancient Teatro Pompeo.

Trattoria Pallaro   **$**   ★
Largo del Pallaro 15.
Fixed-price L30,000.
When you're starving and funds are low, relax here at the outdoor tables and let Paola serve you her hearty, set-price meal from *arancini* to *torta di nonna*, wine included. Just a block off the Campo dei Fiori.

Near the Pantheon

Spiriti   **$**   ★
V. Sant'Eustacio 5.
Closed Sun. and 3–5:30 p.m.; L5–15,000.
Restaurants like Papa Giovanni and La Rosetta (above) are supplemented by the simpler fare here. Just one-half block west of the Pantheon, a small pub serving many wines by the glass along with hearty soups, good salads, and hot "sandwiches" like melted scamorza cheese in radicchio leaves. Avoid the 1 p.m.–lunch crowds.

Le Maschere   **$**   ★★
V. Monte della Farina 29; ☎ 687-9444.
Open 7:30 p.m.–midnight; closed Mon., late Aug. L25–40,000.
A popular Calabrese trattoria, several blocks south of the P. Rotonda and just west of Largo Arenula. The antipasto table is vast, with five varieties of eggplant, the pastas, like *pappardelle alla gondoliere* (with seafood) and the swordfish are good, but the pizza is a favorite here.

Rome

Cul de Sac #1   **$**   ★
> *P. Pasquino 73; closed Mon. lunch & Aug.; meals about L30,000.*
> Close to the P. Navona. An informal wine bar serving a light lunch.

Near the Capitoline Hill

The offerings of the Pantheon area are pretty close, but the Jewish Quarter is too, including the Vecchia Roma (see above).

Da Giggetto   **$–$$**   ★ ★
> *V. Portico d'Ottavia 21; closed Mon.; July; reserve at* ☎ *686-1105; L40–60,000.*
> In summer, Da Giggetto shares a sidewalk with the broken columns of Augustus' ancient portico and serves the traditional cuisine of the old ghetto—artichoke alla giudea, vegetable *fritto misto*, filetti di baccala.

Around the Colosseum

There is little to choose from here but it's a good area for a picnic.

Antica Hostaria da Franco   **$–$$**   ★
> *V. San Giovanni Laterano 48;* ☎ *735-876.*
> *Closed Mon. Meals L35–50,000.*
> A bright and cheerful restaurant, just a bit east of the monument, that serves acceptable seafood—try the spaghetti with clam sauce and a salad.

Taverna del Quaranta   **$**   ★
> *V. Claudia 24.*
> *L25–40,000; no credit cards.*
> On the street running along the top of the Colleo Celio. Decent pub-style food.

In Trastevere

Not only are some of the city's finer restaurants here (see above) but so are most of its small trattorias and pizzerias, many of which spill out onto the sidewalks and piazzettas in summer. Although the area is liveliest in the evening, you'll never starve in Trastevere.

Taverna della Scala   **$**   ★
> *P. della Scala; closed Tues.; no reservations; meals L40–50,000.*
> Sample hearty Roman *cucina casalinga* (homecooking), that may include gnocchi a ragu and certainly bucatini ala'amatriciana or spaghetti all'arrabbiata along with *coda alla vaccinara*. Just west of Santa Maria in Trastevere with summer outdoor dining.

La Fraschetta   **$**   ★ ★
> *V. San Francesco a Ripa 134; closed Sun.; reserve at* ☎ *581-6012; pizza L10–15,000.*
> Near Viale Trastevere. Although both it and Taverna della Scala serve pizza in the evening Fraschetta's is better.

Ivo a Trastevere   **$**   ★ ★
> *V. San Francesco a Ripa 159;* ☎ *581-7082.*
> *Open 6 p.m.–2 a.m.; closed Tues., Aug.; pizza L9–13,000; no credit cards.*
> A Roman institution for pizza and bruschetta. It's starkly plain and always thronged with people. Come early.

La Gensola   **$–$$**   ★ ★
> *P. della Gensola 15; reserve at* ☎ *581-6312.*
> *Closed Sat. lunch, Sun. L40–60,000.*

On the opposite side of Viale Trastevere, near the Piazza in Piscinula, is one of our favorite trattorias, not for the ambience, but rather for the lively patter of the owner and his freshly prepared Sicilian cuisine. Do not miss the *pasta con brocoletti* with a cream tomato sauce and a few sprigs of fresh basil or the big dish of mussels and clams marinera. Even the insalata mixta is good.

Vatican Area

This is such a culinary wasteland—you might want to remember that it's not far across the river to the **Taverna Giulia** (above). On the other hand, if it's a light lunch you want, the ★ cafe at the **Castel Sant'Angelo** *(follow signs to bar; admission fee plus L8–12,000 for pasta)* is good and the views are grand.

Picnics, Snacks, Shops

When restaurant options are limited or when you want a quick meal, you always can find a *tavola calda*, or sandwich shop–even near the **Vatican** *(Via Cesare Battista*, just two blocks from the Vatican museums, is lined with such places) and the **Colosseum** (sandwich trucks pull in behind Constantine's Arch). Some places are better endowed than others. At the foot of the Spanish Steps, you can enjoy a sandwich at the outdoor cafes on the quiet **Via Frattina** (**Vanni** at #94 has focaccia with speck ham and parmesan slices) or in the traffic-free **Piazza San Lorenzo in Lucina** (across the Corso from V. Frattina). Near the Triton fountain is the vast array of panini and tramezzini offered by **Pepy** *(V. Tritone and V. Fontane)*, and near the Pantheon are the cafes rimming the piazza and lining Via Maddalena to its north (**della Palma** at #23 has decent prices). Off the Piazza Navona, **Fratelli Paladini** *(V. Governo Vecchio 28)* makes great sandwiches with pizza dough. At the foot of the Aventine, **Volpetti Piu** *(V. Alessandro Volta 8, just off Mamorata)* serves pizzas and salads cafeteria style. But there is no snack more Roman than bakery pizza, especially *pizza bianca*—baked dough brushed with oil, sprinkled with salt and maybe rosemary. Midmorning to 12:30 p.m., the bakeries are jammed with Romans demanding their slice (priced by weight), whether in the **Campo dei Fiori** *(the forno at west end of piazza)*, **Trastevere** *(the forno on east side of P. San Cosimato)*, or the **Spanish Steps** *(Fior Fiori, V. Croce 17, open till 2 p.m.)*.

The **picnic options** are even better. You may enjoy your fruit and cheese while looking at St. Peter's from the patio of the Vatican Museums' cafeteria, but the view is never better than from the Santa Sabina park on the Aventine Hill. You can sit on the grass behind the Castel Sant'Angelo, but there are spectacular views from atop the Janiculum Hill. In fact, all the hills provide great picnicking options, from the Borghese Gardens atop the Pincio to the tiny parks on the Quirinal (along V. Quirinale), from the glorious Palatine at the Forum to the Celio behind the Colosseum (in the *Villa Celiamontano* park near V. Claudio), and the Colle Oppio in front of it that stretches to Santa Maria Maggiore as the Parco Traiano. And we haven't even begun on the fountains, where you can sometimes find a ledge to sit near their refreshing waters.

There are plenty of shops to supply you. Near the Spanish Steps, the *Via della Croce* is the main grocery street, with its small vegetable market and the famous deli **Fratelle Fabbri** *(at #28)*, but **Torrefazione Teichner** *(P. San Lorenzo in Lucino 17)* has more prepared foods, such as marinated porcini or shrimp salad, and **Gargani** *(V. Lombardia 15)* near the Via Veneto is famous for its cheese. The **Campo dei Fiori market** *(till 1 p.m. week-days, 3 p.m. Sat., closed Sun.)* has all the fruits and vegetables, plus the nuts, pickled sun-dried tomatoes and marinated artichokes for a feast while **Salsamantaria Ruggeri** (S.E. corner) and the **Forno** (west end) can supply you very well with deli and bakery needs. There's a smaller **market in Trastevere** *(P. San Cosimato)*, where the fruits and vegetables and deli stands, as well as surrounding shops, give you plenty of choice. Two other note-worthy gourmet food shops are **Volpetti** *(V. Scrofa at Portoghesi and V. Marmorata 47b, at the foot to the Aventine)*, and **Franchi** *(V. Cola di Rienzo 204)*, in the Prati district to-wards the Vatican.

Gelato, Granita and Grattachecca

Gelato, or ice cream, is not uniquely Roman, but the passion with which Romans pur-sue their enjoyment of it has led to unusual variations on the intensely fresh flavors of Ital-ian gelati. **Fiocco di Neve** *(V. Pantheon/Maddalena 51)* adds the crunchiness of *riso* (rice) to many of the traditional flavors while **Tre Scalini** *(P. Navona; closed Wed.)* has carved an international niche for its *tartufo* of sinfully rich chocolate ice cream with choc-olate chunks and a cherry all frozen together, then when ordered, flattened and topped with *panna*, or whipped cream (carry-out service half the price of table service). In fact, *panna* toppings and ice cream sundae-style combinations are popular, especially at one of the oldest gelaterias, **Giolitti** *(V. Uffici Vicario 40, near end of Maddalena; closed Mon.)*. While **Della Palma** *(V. Maddalena 23; closed Wed.)* is the third gelateria we recommend at this location near the Pantheon, its beautiful array of exotic fruit flavors and its choco-late-rimmed cones are among the best. Of course gelato is everywhere; try it in Trastevere at **Sacchetti** *(P. San Cosimato 61; closed Mon.)* where the gianduia (hazelnut chocolate) ice cream with panna is nearly as good as its morning *sfogliatello di ricotta*.

Ices are a favorite too, and as the warm weather arrives the cafes bring out the *granita*, frozen juice or coffee, crushed, then sipped slowly while the flavored ice melts. The re-freshing lemon granita is accompanied by a pitcher of water to adjust the flavor or simply prolong the pleasure; the coffee comes with whipped cream. Again the Pantheon area is blessed with these summer concoctions, as the **Caffe di Rienzo** *(P. Rotonda, west side; closed Mon.)* serves an elegant *granita di limone* (at a cost you may not want to pay for table service) along with their delicious pastries, and the **Tazza d'Oro** *(V. Orfani 86; closed Sun.)*, just east, adds whipped cream to the bottom as well as the top of its portable cup of *granita di cafe* (no table service). But look for these *granite* at all the best cafes; and check the restaurants for exotic fruit-flavored granite to be served as dessert sherbets.

And, then there is *grattachecca*, or ice shaved then topped with syrup or juice. Some-how American "slush" doesn't quite match the homemade syrups and slices of fresh fruit or bits of coconut found in the Roman versions at the tiny kiosks along the Tiber river. Look for the one on the Trastevere side of the Tiberina island bridge, another near the Ara Pacis and Ponte Cavour.

Enotecas and Famous Caffes

Although famous cafes, like **Doney's** (closed Mon.) and the **Paris** (closed Sun.), where film stars lived the *dolce vita* in the Sixties, have experienced something of a revival with the closing of traffic on the Via Veneto, the glamorous also frequent the now more fashionable area at the foot of the Spanish Steps. The elegant **Caffè Rosati** *(P. del Popolo at V. Ripetta; closed Tues.)*, with its prime sidewalk location and good pastries, is one of *the* places to be seen. The **Caffè Greco** *(V. Condotti 86; closed Sun.)*, founded in 1760, is a handsome *sala da te* where waiters in morning coats serve you, just as they served Liszt, Byron and other foreign luminaries. Remember that at cafes, the price *al banco* will bring you the same ambience and the same *granita di limone* at a third to half of the table price.

Enoteca bars, or wine shops with bars and a few tables for sampling their wares, can be found in most Roman neighborhoods. **Enoteca Antica** *(V. Croce 76A; closed Sun.)* near the Spanish Steps, has a comfortable bar with sophisticated wines by the glass and wonderful snacks, even light meals (smoked fish, quiche-like *spuntini*) to accompany your tastings. (There's actually a decent, small restaurant here, but the bar is best for wine). **La Bevitoria** *(P. Navona 72, east side; evenings only; closed Wed.)* has only a few spuntini, or hor d'oeuvres, but the choice of wines is as superb as the location.

Directory

Telephone Code 06   **Postal Code 00100**

Airlines

Alitalia, *V. Bissolati 13 (☎ 460-881).*

Airports

Leonardo da Vinci Airport at Fiumicino, 25 km, 15.5 mi. west of A-12 *(☎ 60-121* for information, *☎ 223-640* for domestic); train (6:30 a.m.–9:30 p.m.; bus service off-hours) connects airport with Stazione Ostiense annex (25 minutes; Tiburtina-Fiumicino line) and Stazione Termini (buy tickets next to Track 22; Termini-Fiumicino line); taxis, car rentals available. **Ciampino** airport *☎ 794-941*, 15 km, 9 mi. southwest at SS 7 and GRA beltway, for some domestic and charter flights; COTRAL bus connects with metro line A at Anagnina.

Albergo Diurno

Public baths at Stazione Termini, underground halls, 7:30 a.m.–8:30 p.m.

American Express

P. di Spagna 68 (☎ 72-282).

Books in English

American Book Shop, *V. della Vite 57;* **Lion Bookshop**, *V. Babuino 182;* used and new, with trade-ins at **Economy Book Center** *(Torino 136),* **Open Door** *(Lungaretta 25).*

Buses

ATAC, for city service, P. Cinquecento *(☎ 46-951)* across from Stazione Termini, for day and weekly passes; route maps sold at newsstands; buy tickets in advance at tabacchi or newsstands and cancel on board; tickets permit 2 transfers, including the subway; 24-hour service, but after 10 or 11 p.m. servicio nottorno is limited; see "subway." **COTRAL** *(591-5551),* Latium regional service; check EPT for different departure points.

Car Rentals

Avis, *P. Esquilino 1* (☎ *470-1400*); **Europcar**, *V. Lombardia 7* (☎ *475-0381*); **Hertz**, *V. Sallustiana 28* (☎ *463-334*); and others, at airport and in town.

Consulates

Canada, *V. Zara 30* (☎ *445-981; after hours, 033-722-7195*), 10 a.m.–noon, 2–4 p.m., except late summer, 10 a.m.–2 p.m.; **Great Britain**, *V. XX Settembre 80a* (☎ *482-5551*), 9:30 a.m.–12:30 p.m., 2–4 p.m.; **United States**, *V. Veneto 119* (☎ *46-741*), 8:30 a.m.–noon, 2–4:30 p.m. Service at all three Mon.–Fri. only, but with 24-hour emergency telephone response.

Emergencies

Dial ☎ 113; **Tourist First Aid**, (☎ *118 or 462-371*); 24-hour pharmacy, **Antonucci**, *P. Barberini 49* (☎ *462-996*).

Groceries

Campo dei Fiori hosts a beautiful market, **Enoteca Cavour** *(V. Cavour 313)* is a respected wine shop, and others, along with gourmet shops, are listed in text.

Italian Courses

Italiaidea, *P. della Cancelleria 85* (☎ *654-7620*); **Dante Alighieri Society**, *P. Firenze 27* (☎ *675-1105*); **Dilit** *(V. Marghera 22;* ☎ *678-1105*); and many more.

Parking

Garages are rarities, except those associated with hotels. Two are near the Via Veneto: at Porta Pinciana, under the Borghese park; on V. Ludovico, across from the Hotel Eden.

Police

Questura, foreign office, *V. San Vitale 15* (☎ *46-86*).

Post Office

P. San Silvestro, main office with 24-hour telegraph service and postal service 8:30 a.m.–7:30 p.m. Mon.-Fri., Sat. till 11:50 a.m.; *Vatican Post*, P. San Pietro, main office on south side; for international mail only; considered more reliable than the government's. Open Mon.-Fri. 8:30 a.m.–7 p.m., Sat. till 6 p.m.

Subway

Metropolitana or the "metro" with two lines intersecting at Stazione Termini; tickets sold at tabacchi, newsstands, and automatic change machines in stations; service 5:40 a.m.–11:30 p.m.; BIG daily pass purchased at ATAC, shared with buses.

Swimming Pools

Piscina Olimpica, Foro Italico on Lungotevere M. Cadorna *(*☎ *360-8591)*, indoor lap swimming; **Piscina delle Rose**; EUR on V. America *(*☎ *592-6717)*, outdoor pool; some private fitness centers, like *Roman Sport Center* (under Borghese park, ☎ *361-4358*) offer day passes for all activities, including 2 pools.

Taxis

Yellow or white, metered cabs (with many authorized surcharges) with stands at major piazzas; or call (☎ *35-70 or 49-94*).

Telephones

Telcom, Stazione Termini; Villa Borghese underground parking, access from V. Veneto (8 a.m.–9:30 p.m.); P. San Silvestro 20 (8 a.m.–11:30 p.m. except Sun. 9 a.m.–8:30 p.m.).

Tourist Office

EPT, *V. Parigi 5 (☎ 4889-9200, FAX 481-9316)*, across from side entrance to Grand Hotel, just outside P. della Repubblica; open Mon.–Sat. 8:30 a.m.–7 p.m.; branches with hotel reservations (fee) at Stazione Termini (between tracks 2 and 3; ☎ 487-1270) and Fiumicino airport (international arrivals; ☎ 6501-0255). **Vatican Information**, P. San Pietro (south side); *(☎ 6898-4466, FAX 6988-5100)*; Mon.–Sat. 8:30 a.m.–1 p.m., 2–6:30 p.m.

Tours

Secret Walks *(☎ 3972-8728)*, for specialty tours led by U.S. residents in Rome; *ATAC*, (see "buses"), 3-hour city bus tour at 3:30 daily, Apr.–Sept., 2:30 on weekends Oct.-Mar.; American Express (above), **CIT** *(P. della Repubblica 68, ☎ 474-6555, FAX 481-8277)*, and others, offer city and regional tours; Vatican Gardens tours, reserve through Vatican Tourist Information, above; the historic Tiber river aboard Tiber II, Tourvisa *(V. Marghera 32, ☎ 493-481)*; authorized guides *(Rampa Mignanelle 12, ☎ 678-9842)*.

Train

Stazione Termini, P. dei Cinquecento (☎ 47-75 information), with links to peripheral stazioni, is centrally located with subway (lines A & B), bus (#64 Colosseum, P. Venezia, Vatican; #75 to Trastevere; #492 Villa Borghese), airport train (buy tickets next to Track 22) and taxi connections. Downstairs, there's a fast train ticket service (fee) and an *albergo diurno* (day hotel).

On the Road

Excursions in Latium

Travelers have heard of the hills of Tuscany, the Greek temples of Sicily, but certainly not much about Latium, or *Lazio*. Since the 4th century B.C. when Rome conquered its neighbors—the Sabines in the Apennines to the east, the Etruscans north, and the Latin tribes in the Alban Hills south—the region has been overshadowed by its capital. The volcanic hills and lakes of Etruscans and Latins alike became summer retreats for Roman patricians and later, the papal court. So many popes built summer castles in the Alban Hills that the region became known as Castelli Romani. Where the Sabines watered their flocks in spring-fed valleys, Hadrian built his villa as did Cardinal d'Este, and Tivoli's gardens became renowned. Even the Tyrrhenian sea of the Etruscans was tamed, dredged, and reshaped into Ostia, a port adequate for ancient Rome. Today, Ostia's beaches are the local beaches for Romans.

Excursions in Latium

Lake Bracciano is a favored resort, as well as the major reservoir for the city. Latium continues to be conquered by Rome.

The castles, villas, and ancient ruins of Etruscans and Romans alike make Latium as interesting to explore as better known regions. But it is an area more likely to be filled with Roman villas and weekend vacation homes rather than the hotels of international travelers. And although the rolling hills covered with vineyards and grazing sheep remain as they were millennia ago, the city of Rome has grown and expanded, turning rural areas into suburbs and making most of these sights just a brief trip outside the city limits. For these reasons, we approach Latium as excursions from the city rather than overnight explorations. Because it can be time consuming to exit the city, unless by train or during off-hours, most travelers limit their excursions to Tivoli or Ostia Antica. But Viterbo and the lakes make a scenic route into Tuscany, as do the Etruscan sights, while the Castelli Romani can mark the beginning of a journey into Southern Italy.

Tips: There are tourist information offices for Latium along the Autostrada del Sole, to the north on A-1 at the Salaria Oueste service area, to the south on A-2 at Frascati Est (high season only). The Grande Raccolta Annulare or *GRA*, makes an immense loop around Rome connecting the state roads and autostradas with various routes into the center.

Tivoli

The Aniene River drops from the Apennines through the ravines of beautiful ★★ Tivoli. Abundant with water and cooled by mountain air, the gardens of Tivoli are as popular today as they were when Julius Caesar and Hadrian followed the Via Tiburtina past the travertine quarries to their villas.

Right off the main piazza of Tivoli is the ★ **Villa d'Este** *(9 a.m. to 1 hour before sunset; L10,000 when water jets full, L5000 otherwise)*, the 16th-century estate of Cardinal Ippolito d'Este, renowned for its terraced gardens and fanciful fountains, none more frivolous than the monumental Fountain of the Water Organ that imitated the cries of screech owls in its repertoire. Although the villa at the top of the terraces need not take your time, views over the symmetrical gardens and countryside are superb from its windows. On the upper ridge of Tivoli, above the Rocca Pia fort, is the **Villa Gregoriana** *(9:30 a.m.–4:30 p.m. winter, 10 a.m.–7 p.m. summer; L3000)* a pleasant park with walking paths and picturesque views across a gorge to the ancient **Temple of Vesta** (can be seen from entrance gate). About 5 km before you reach the town of Tivoli is the turnoff to the ★★ **Villa Adriana** *(9 a.m. to an hour before dusk; 7:30 p.m. in summer; L8000)*, the vast ruins of Hadrian's 2nd-century villa. Hadrian, the great architect of the Pantheon, built the estate of his dreams here. Paths through the lovely grounds, so evocative of the past, take you around the great baths, covered with Pantheon-like domes, to temples and complexes inspired by the buildings Hadrian had admired on his travels through the Empire, like the *Canopis*, based on a sanctuary near Alexandria, its nymphaeum facing a pool surrounded by classical statuary. Also, there's the *island villa*, the emperor's retreat within his own massive palazzo. Aimless strolling is most pleasurable here, but a model of the villa at the entrance can give you some orientation. Next to some very stately cypresses, there are picnic grounds.

Where to Eat

Adriano   ★★★
> V. Villa Adriana 194; ☎ (0774) 382-235.
> Closed Sun. dinner. Meals L55–85,000.
> Picnicking at Hadrian's Villa is ideal, but this restaurant is near the entrance and, in season, offers lovely alfresco dining on fresh pastas, abbacchio, and *stinco* (veal stew).

Cinque Statue   ★★
> V. Quintilio Varo 1; ☎ (0774) 20-366.
> Closed Fri., Sun. dinner, Mon., late Aug. Meals L40–55,000.
> In Tivoli, there are a number of cafes and trattorias around the Villa Gregoriana. Just across from the entrance is this comfortable restaurant, its food a bit uneven, but the meat antipasto is immense, the crespelle and lamb *(abbacchio)* quite good.

Practical Tips

Arriving
> Tivoli is 35 km, 21.5 mi. east of Rome on Via Tiburtina (SS 5). The COTRAL bus leaves from Rebibbia, the last stop on Metro B, and can drop you off at the intersection for Hadrian's villa (1 km away) before continuing 5 km into Tivoli. The #4 bus (not 4/) passes near Hadrian's Villa from central Tivoli.

Ostia Antica

One of the easiest excursions from Rome is to the well-preserved ruins of ★★Ostia Antica, its ancient port city. Certainly the most traditional way to visit, much like a load of wheat from Egypt, is on a boat tour down the Tiber in warm weather. The ruins are extensive, but pleasantly parklike with shrubs and umbrella pines rustled by the wind of the nearby sea. Founded in the 4th century B.C. to protect the mouth of the Tiber, Ostia later became an important city for the supply of Rome. Here ships would unload grains from around the world, and merchants would store them and arrange for shipment on barges up the Tiber to Rome. A very international community of navigators, merchants, and the like joined the more local society, and archaeologists have excavated Mithraic temples from Syria and ones to Serapis from Egypt, as well as a very early synagogue. After the Goths sacked the city in the 5th century, Ostia was abandoned. Along the Decumanus Maximus, the main street that runs through the city for almost a mile, the sights are well marked. On the right, the ★**Baths of Neptune** are worth a look for their mo-

Ostia Antica

saics, and the ★**theater** (2nd century; performances of classical plays in summer) is in good condition. Behind the stage you can see the two columns of the Temple of Ceres that stand in the ★**Piazza delle Corporazione** where mosaic pavements still proclaim the nature of these former offices of navigators (the towers symbolize lighthouses) and shipbuilders, as well as their nationality (the elephant symbolizes Africa, "Narbonenses," Carthage). Farther down the Decumanus is the ★**Forum** with its temples and basilica. On the right is the **Capitoline Temple**, and continuing down a lane on its right you come to the intersection of Via dei Dipinti and Via di Diana. On the corner is a typical four-story **apartment house** of the middle class. Around the corner on Diana, on the right, is a ★**thermopolium**, a very *caratteristico* Italian bar with a stand-up counter on the street and a more relaxing space inside for enjoying a warmed wine with honey. At the end of Dipinti is the **Museo Ostiense**, while just before its steps, to the right, are traces of the synagogue. Back on the Decumanus, the road to the old port (the sea has receded) is to the left, but instead, follow Via della Foca heading toward the river (to the right). Along here you'll see temples (on right) and behind them some upper-class homes, such as the **Domus Amore e Psiche**, named after its statuary (now in museo). Back on Foca, turn through the Casa Serapide (on left), to the mosaics and paintings of the ★**Baths of Sette Sepienti**. And there's even more.

Stone masks from theater stage, Ostia

The ruins are open 9 a.m. till 6 p.m. in summer, 4 p.m. in winter with exit 1 hour later. L10,000. Parking available.

Where to Eat

In the ruins, at the theater, is a *caffè* for snacks. Just outside the ruins, around the 16th-century castle, are a number of trattorias such as **Al Monumento** (moderate) for grilled fish.

Directory

Tourist Information

EPT in Rome has a map brochure on Ostia Antica; a souvenir shop at the theater sells guidebooks.

Arriving

Ostia Antica lies 25 km, 15.5 mi. west of Rome along the Via del Mare (SS 8), an unusually benign exit from the city. • The Magliana stop of Metro B connects you with the Lido di Ostia train, which stops at the ruins. • Mar.–Nov. contact **Tourvisa** (*V. Marghera 32 in Rome;* ☎ *493-481*) about their boat tours. **Lido di Ostia**: Just 4.5 km away on the Via del Mare (or by train, or #4 bus) are the black volcanic sands of Rome's beaches. The sea has recently been pronounced "bathable" once again. The beaches certainly will be crowded in summer, but a seafood lunch and sea breezes may be appealing.

Etruscan Ruins

Etruscan civilization flourished through its trade with the Greeks, especially from the 7th through 5th centuries B.C. The ports where the Greeks and Etruscans exchanged the iron ore, silver and copper of what is now Tuscany for the gold of the east could be found along Latium's coast. The Tyrrhenian Sea, named by the Greeks, meant "Etruscan", and the ports where they traded are now the modern towns of Cerveteri and Tarquinia (whose kings ruled Rome in the 6th century B.C.), while inland Vulci controlled the routes to the mines in northern Etruria. The Roman occupation of Etruscan cities pretty much destroyed traces of their earlier culture. Because the Etruscans built elaborate tombs and "took it all with them," archaeologists have been able to reconstruct a great deal from their necropolises. Two of the most important cemeteries are found at Tarquinia and Cerveteri (both bus accessible), while the setting and museum at Vulci make a delightful ending to a car excursion along the Via Aurelia.

Cerveteri   ★

Exit SS 1 or A-12 about 50 km, 31 mi. from Rome and turn inland; COTRAL bus from V. Lepanto at Metro A "Lepanto" stop.

Cerveteri, or ancient Caere, is best known for the ★**Necropoli Etrusca** *(9 a.m.–7 p.m., May–Sept.; 9 a.m.–4 p.m., Sun. 11 a.m.–4 p.m. in winter; closed Mon. year-round; L8000)* found at Monte Banditaccia about 1.5 km north of the medieval hilltown. Designed much as a city with fountains and conveniences for mourners, but with tombs, not shops, lining its streets, the necropolis is quite picturesque—a delightful spot for picnicking rather than morbid reflections. Along the main street look for **Tumba dei Rilievi** (ask custodian to open), dating from the 4th century

B.C. and painted with a wide variety of household items. There's the **Museo Nazionale** *(9 a.m.–6 p.m.; in winter 9 a.m.–2 p.m., closed Mon.; free)* in town, but the most interesting works from Caere are seen in Rome, at the Villa Giulia and in the Vatican Museum.

Tarquinia

100 km, 62 mi. on SS 1 or A-12, then turn inland; COTRAL bus from V. Lepanto at Metro A "Lepanto" stop.

Although the setting of the ★**Necropoli Etrusca** *(Tues.-Sun. 9 a.m.–2 p.m.; in summer, till 7 p.m.; L8000 includes town museum)* is quite bleak compared to the charm of Cerveteri, the tomb paintings make up for it. You can visit only with a guide (and must wait for a group to form—not long even in off season) and, in order to protect the tombs, may visit no more than five (of the 5000 excavated) chosen for that day. The earliest paintings date from 540 B.C. and continue to the 2nd century B.C. with considerable variety—from delightful dancing and hunting scenes to the later (4th century B.C.) more sinister, allegorical scenes about death. The cemetery is almost a mile from the walled medieval town (turn right at wall as entering, then left at sign). In the town, just as you enter, is the Piazza Cavour (information office here) dominated by the Palazzo Vitelleschi (1436), now the ★**Museo Nazionale** *(9 a.m.–2 p.m.; in summer, till 7 p.m., closed Mon.; L8000 fee includes tombs)*. The museum is being reorganized, but look for the pair of terracotta ★*Winged Horses* (4th century B.C.) that crowned an ancient temple (last seen, top of stairs, left). If something non-Etruscan is needed, a 15-minute walk through medieval Tarquinia to its towers and castle might be in order (left off P. Cavour, next to the museum).

Vulci

118 km, 73 mi. on SS 1 and/or A-12 from Rome, then turn right at sign for another 12 km.

Vulci was so wealthy that an amazing number of the Greek vases found in museums around the world came from its tombs. Yet the few visible ruins here (at Casale) are actually Roman, and the fabulous humped **bridge** was rebuilt by them from Etruscan foundations. Even the most famous **Francois Tomb** (late 4th century B.C., a bit farther down the road from bridge; may be under restoration), painted with allegorical battle scenes, probably expressed the Etruscan preoccupation with an increasingly powerful Rome. What remains is both in the Villa Giulia in Rome and here in the **Museo Etrusca** *(9 a.m.–1 p.m., 4-7 p.m. in summer; 9 a.m.–4 p.m. winter; closed Mon.; free)*, housed in the moated and medieval ★**Castello dell'Abbadia** next to the bridge. (Downstairs are the earliest Villanovan artifacts; upstairs those from the height of the city 7th century—4th century B.C.—look for ★fibula sanguisuga, a pin of gold bead work with tiny winged lions). The rural setting, dotted with ruins and grazed by sheep, is enchanting, especially if you lunch here at the "snack" bar (see below).

Where to Eat

A picnic at the Cerveteri necropolis or a snack at the cafes near the Tarquinia museum can be just fine, but try to have lunch at the farmhouse at Vulci.

Casale d'Osteria **$–$$** ★ ★

Turn right before the Roman bridge on country lane that leads to Roman ruins of Casale;
☎ *0766-898247.*
Meals L40–50,000.

This unpretentious spot, with outdoor tables in summer, a roaring fire in the hearth
in winter, serves wonderful country food—fresh pecorino laced with red peppers,
olives marinated in orange rind, delicious bruschetta and antipasti, as well as hearty
pasta dishes.

Practical Tips

Arriving

You can visit all the sights only by car, picking up the Via Aurelia (SS 1) exit from
near St. Peter's. If you leave early in the morning, you'll arrive at Vulci by lunch.
You might consider looping back to the city via Lake Bracciano, or continuing on
to Tuscany through Viterbo (see below). Or if you'd like the beach, consider the
fashionable resort of **Orbetello**, just 30 km, 18.5 mi. farther north along SS 1 from
the Vulci turnoff. A COTRAL bus visit to the area is most feasible if you visit either
Tarquinia or Cerveteri.

Viterbo and the Lakes

This region north of Rome is a world unto itself. Crenellated castles and
Renaissance villas grace the ancient land of the Etruscans. Lakes and gentle
hills covered with orchards and olive groves make for refreshing summer
swims and pleasing drives. Anchoring this attractive province is medieval
★**Viterbo**, once the refuge of popes. Picturesque walks down narrow lanes
spanned by arches and flanked by rough stone walls (around ★ P. San Pellegrino especially) are enhanced by such Gothic delights as the ★ Papal Palace
(on the P. San Lorenzo). From Viterbo you might continue north to Lake
Bolsena, where you can easily continue on to Siena in Tuscany or Orvieto in
Umbria. Or you might overnight in Viterbo, before completing a loop back
to Rome through Etruscan ruins (see above), making sure you stop on the
way at **Tuscania** (24 km, 15 mi. west of Viterbo; 24 km east of Tarquinia), to
see the fascinating Romanesque churches on the hill outside its walls (★ S.
Maria Maggiore with its carved portals and ★ San Pietro built atop an Etruscan acropolis, both begun in the 8th century and renovated through the
early 1200s). To visit only Lake Bracciano and Viterbo makes for an easy excursion. Better yet is a leisurely drive to Viterbo through the Latium countryside (about 100 km, 60 mi.): As you begin on the old Via Cassia (SS 2)
through suburbs that almost obliterate the remaining remnants of the ancient Etruscan city of Veio, you despair of the congestion. But suddenly
Rome is left behind, and before you lie country roads and interesting detours
on your way to Viterbo. The most scenic route takes you first to **Lake Bracciano** (20 km off SS 2 on SS 493). Overlooking the lake is the small medieval
town of **Bracciano**, remarkable for its picture-perfect baronial castle, the

★Castello Orsino-Odescalchi (1470), still occupied by its princely owners. Dipping down to the water and continuing along the western shore of the lake to picturesque **Trevignano**, you then head north to **Sutri**, passing at the foot of the medieval town where Etruscan tombs and a Roman amphitheater speak of distant ancestors. The rolling hills grazed by sheep lead on to Ronciglione, then north on the Via Cimino that skims above the eastern edge of **Lake Vico**. From here you might take a 3-km detour into **Caprarola**, a narrow village built onto a ridge with views of the Apennines. Here Vignola built the High Renaissance ★Villa Farnese (1559) and G. Rainaldi, the Baroque church, San Silvestre (1621). Back on the road above Lake Vico, the combination of lake and mountain scenery speeds you along the final 16 km to the impressive Porta Roma and medieval walls of Viterbo.

Where to Stay

Tuscia   **L75–120,000**   ★★

V. Cairoli 41; ☎ 344-400, FAX 345-976.
Single L75,000. Double L120,000.
In Viterbo, there is the modern and functional Tuscia, conveniently located near the edge of the old town and with 45 small, carpeted rooms with tiled baths.

Where to Eat

Richiastro   **$–$$**   ★★★

V. Marrocca 16; ☎ 236-909.
Open Thurs.–Sun. except July–Aug. Meals L35–50,000.
In Viterbo, you can't go wrong with the traditional cooking here. Just below the market square (P. delle Erbe) off the main pedestrian street of Corso Italia.

Snacks

For snacks, try the pastries and sandwiches at the 19th century **Gran Caffe Schenarde** (Corso Italia 11).

Directory

Telephone Code 0761 in Viterbo   **Postal Code 01100 in Viterbo**

Tourist Information
EPT, P. Caduti 14 (☎ 304-795).

Arriving
Train from Rome stops at Lake Bracciano and Viterbo, but for Viterbo the COTRAL bus service (Lepanto stop of Metro A) takes under 2 hours and is more frequent. Off the GRA, SS 2bis, the Via Cassia Nuova, is the most direct route for Viterbo (85 km, 53 mi.); SS 2, the Via Cassia, is the most direct route to Bracciano.

Castelli Romani

The Alban Hills just to the south of Rome can be idyllic, but arriving in the snarled traffic that lasts almost the entire way and, in summer especially, that can clog the narrow roads between towns, makes us want to discourage you. It's really more relaxing to simply picnic on the Aventine Hill or stroll the

Via Appia Antica. However, if the wines of **Frascati** entice you to that pretty town, or the pope's summer residence at **Castel Gandolfo** intrigues you, then by all means make the trip, but make it by car. The sights aren't grand, but if the traffic isn't too bad, the meandering along country roads can be pleasant. Only in a car can you wind your way around the Monte Cavo to the **Rocca di Papa**, with its panoramic views once shared by the ancient Latins' Temple to Jupiter. Only in a car can you stop for strawberries at Nemi or wild mushrooms along the forest roads, or pull into estates marked *produzione propria* for Frascati whites, Velletri reds. At the lakes, **Albano** and the smaller **Nemi**, you might want to take a stroll.

Where to Eat

Before settling into a restaurant, look for a roadside *porchetta* stand, preferably one stationed with a lake view for enjoying your sandwich of roast suckling pig—considered its tastiest when from these hills.

Cacciani   **$$–$$$**   ★ ★ ★

V. Armando Diaz 13; ☎ *(06) 942-0378.*
Closed dinner on Sun. except Apr.–Oct., Mon., part of Jan., & late Aug. Meals L50–70,000.
In Frascati (just right of the main square of P. Roma; enter from the rear). The lovely terrace overlooking the gorge and park make the pleasant food here special, whether a tasty artichoke soup or traditional *frittura di vedura*.

Practical Tips

Tourist Information
   EPT in Rome has maps of Provincia di Roma, including one on agritourism.

Arriving
   Following the wretched Via Appia Nuova (SS 7) out of Rome for 23 km, 14 mi., turn left on SS 217 just beyond the Ciampino airport and the GRA. Soon you come to a critical intersection (about 1 hour from Rome *centro*) where straight ahead is the Rocca di Papa and Nemi (11 km), left is Frascati (7 km) and right is Castel Gandolfo (2 km). From the autostrada (A-2) there's an exit to Frascati. From the Stazione Termini, Laziali section, there is a train for Frascati (half-hour), if you want to forego the drive through the hills.

Castelli Romani

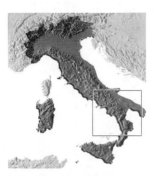

NAPLES AND
SOUTHERN ITALY

Byzantine villages cling to the rocky Amalfi coast.

History and Art

Exactly where Southern Italy begins may be a bit uncertain—it is definitely below Rome and just as unquestionably encompasses Naples at the ankle of the Italian boot. It spreads southward to the tip of the toe across from Sicily, up the instep and around the high Apulian heel across from Albania. It has a vast coastline (greater still if that of Sicily is included), drawn on maps with

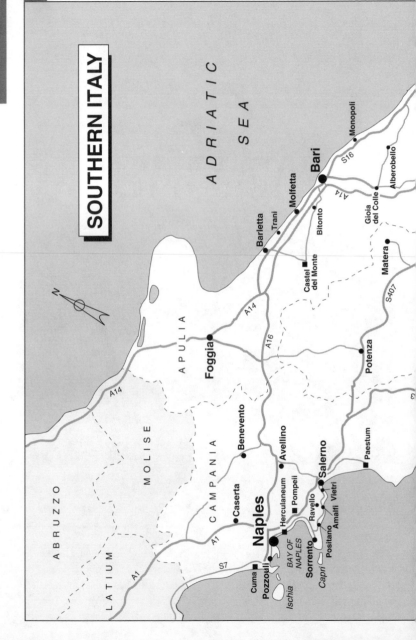

SOUTHERN ITALY

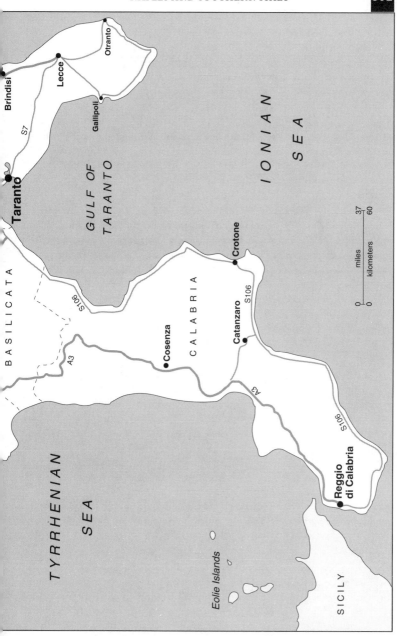

long stretches free of any names. Although the Adriatic heel is unusually flat, the remainder is rugged highlands and cliffs falling to meet the sea.

In the South, the first great civilization took root along the coasts. Greeks, seeking maritime trade or simply needing land, established colonies and exchanged goods with the native peoples, from the Apulians along the Adriatic to the Samnites and others around the Bay of Naples. From the first settlements in the 8th century B.C. through succeeding centuries, these cities flourished in what is now called Magna Graecia, or greater Greece. It is here in the instep that the voluptuaries at the town of Sybaris have given us the word "sibaritic," while Pythagoras and his school of followers practiced asceticism at nearby Crotona. From Paestum and Neapolis (Naples) on the west to the wealthiest city, Tarentum (Taranto), on the heel, Greek culture wedded with the Italic in a marriage that would endure more than a millennium.

Nowhere did the geography and culture unite more dramatically than around the Bay of Naples. The beauty of the natural harbors, the steep mountains with their volcanic silhouettes, the looming shapes of the bay islands of Capri, Ischia, and Procida inspired Greek mythology. It is here the Sirens sang so irresistibly that even those who knew the danger set ashore and lost their lives. Only Ulysses could resist the enchantment of the bay, and he had to seal his sailors' ears with wax and have himself tied to the mast. *Herakles,* the Roman Hercules, stopped on these shores, too, after the 10th of his 12 labors, just as he seems to have passed wherever Greek civilization spread.

The earliest Greek settlers on the bay chose the volcanic island of Ischia (8th century B.C.). When the island's volcano erupted they learned why their ancestors had identified the entrance to Hades nearby, at the deathly still waters of Lake Avernus on the mainland. Surrounding this entrance are the Phlegrean Fields where the scorched earth bubbles and smokes. Around this bay the earth's plates crash, the ground swells and subsides, earthquakes and volcanic eruptions are as integral to the setting as its beauty. Across these fields walked gods and heroes—both Ulysses and Hercules explored the underworld crowded with ghosts. Later these burning fields would inspire Roman poets as they had inspired Homer, and Virgil would have Aeneas descend into the underworld accompanied by the fearless Sibyl from Cumae.

The threatening volcanic region did little to deter settlers. In fact, they fought over it. The Etruscans from their inland city at Capua challenged the Greeks. Then, in a war immortalized by Pindar, the united Greek forces dealt them a lethal blow in 474 B.C. But then the local Samnites challenged the Greeks, and with the support of the fellow Latin-speaking Romans, took over everywhere but at Naples. The Romans set siege to Neapolis for three years until in 328 B.C., they established themselves on the bay. Eventually, they would replace the Greeks and Samnites on both sides of the bay, finally spreading to Pompeii around 80 B.C.

Whoever struggled for supremacy over the Greeks always fell victim to their culture, so the region remained Hellenistic. Noble Romans came to Neapolis to study Greek literature and art. Patricians adorned their villas, whether on the west near the baths of Baia or east near Herculaneum, with Greek sculptures, often carved by Greek artists. They painted the walls of their homes and country estates with scenes from Greek mythology, and they practiced cults inspired by the Greeks themselves, changing only the names, perhaps, from Dionysus to Bacchus. And here the Romans spoke Greek. Although the Romans had already been exposed to Hellenistic culture through the Etruscans, it is around the fabulous bay that they first directly encountered it. Through the Late Republican period and into the Imperial Age, the Romans first copied and absorbed Greek culture here, before transforming it into their own.

The Naples melting pot produced more than Greco-Roman culture. Its Phlegrean Fields continued to boil, but the empire builders still came. The sulfurous muds at Baia attracted the wealthiest Romans for cures—the emperor Hadrian, on his death bed, was carried from Tivoli to Baia in one last desperate effort at salvation. The volcanic ash around the great commercial port of Puteoli (Pozzuoli), the Tyrrhenian coast's equal to the Adriatic's Ravenna, led to the discovery of the cement that enabled the Romans to develop their vaulted architecture. But in A.D. 79, Pliny the Elder would be disturbed from Rome's naval station at Misenum with reports of a strange cloud covering the far side of the bay. Dashing off to observe this phenomenon, the great naturalist died, as did so many others on this day. Vesuvius, so long dormant as to be forgotten as volcanic, had erupted from its slumbers.

The destruction of Pompeii, Herculaneum and other towns yet unrecovered did not end Roman dominance of the region. The Imperial Age was just beginning, and the forces that would culminate in the fall of Rome lay elsewhere. In fact, the Phlegrean Fields and often erupting Vesuvius still have not prevented settlement, so that great cities and ports have disappeared under modern ones—the classical city of Neapolis with its aqueducts and streets can best be only glimpsed in the excavations under its Gothic duomo. Yet ruins of amphitheaters and vaulted baths dot the landscape; the Sibyl's cave at Cumae can still be found under a Greek acropolis. Vesuvius itself preserved the greatest legacy: under its deep layers of ash and lava Pompeii and Herculaneum have revealed themselves as time capsules of the ancient world.

While northern Italy suffered its way through the invasions of the Dark Ages, the South experienced its share, too—the Lombards made it to Salerno on the west, to Bari on the east; and the Arabs, who actually conquered Sicily in A.D. 800, often set ashore here, leaving behind their watchtowers and even their labyrinthine town plans, which could be as effective as any fort in confounding enemies. But even while the North was held by the barbarians and Sicily by the heathens, the southern peninsula flowered under Byzantine rule and traded with the East, and even with the infidels. Like Venice, the ports of Amalfi and Bari flourished. And when Byzantine rule was replaced by the Normans in the early 1100s, the South once again was united with Sicily, just as it had been when part of Magna Graecia. Along the Amalfi Coast churches were built in a local style called "Arabo-Byzantina," that fused Eastern arabesques with the Norman Romanesque. Around Bari, the Norman merged with the northern lion porch and a strong sculptural tradition in the Apulian Romanesque. And when Frederick II inherited this Kingdom of Sicily in the 13th century, he strengthened the Norman forts at Naples and throughout the peninsula, but saved some of his most original designs for Apulia, his beloved hunting ground and the land where he entrusted his heir and wife.

Although somewhat fortunate in the early middle ages, the South was soon to become a great backwater, save for the royal court at Naples. Under Frederick II, the united Ghibelline south had fought against the Guelf forces of the popes. With Frederick's death in 1250, the Kingdom of Sicily was offered up by the pope to whoever could conquer it for him. And thus began the uncomfortable centuries, when the French and Spanish divided the kingdom, then united it and fought, but seldom did anything but exploit and overtax it into feudalism.

There were a few enlightened periods. The Angevin king, Robert of Anjou (1309–43), known as "the Wise," created a period of great culture in Naples. French Gothic taste prevailed, but most often as interpreted by Tuscan artists such as Tino di Camaino and Simone di Martini. Robert was a patron of literature, too, and both Petrarch and Boccaccio lived in Naples for periods under his rule. During the Renaissance, the Aragon king, Alfonso the Magnanimous (1442–58), patronized some of the finest artists of the period, including Antonella da Messina and Francesco Laurana.

It was not until the Baroque, however, when the region had long slumbered under Spanish viceroys, that local schools of art were inspired. The wealthy church and land barons had money to spend and encouraged two provincial schools, one in Lecce in Apulia, the other more influential one in Naples. With so much money for patronage available, Roman artists were attracted to Naples, among them the Early Baroque artist Caravaggio, who left an entire, if secondary, school behind him; the High Baroque painter Lanfranco; and the more Neoclassical architect Domenico Fontana. They brought a style that kindled something in the Neapolitan spirit. The result was more decorative than organic, however, and quite distinctive from that of Rome. In the 17th century, Cosimo Fanzago (1591–1678) created his inlaid marble designs, while Luca Giordano's (1632–1705) paintings were in such demand that his best work is found outside the South. And Salvatore Rosa (1615–73), Naples' greatest artist, painted so much in the Roman tradition that his romantic landscapes are seldom seen in his native city. During the 18th century, the movement intensified with architects like Ferdinando Sanfelice (1675–1748), who began a tradition of ornamental staircases and portals, although few of his own works survive, and Antonio Vaccaro (1678–1745), who created a confectionary lightness that still delights in his cloister at Santa Chiara. The Accademia founded by Francesco Solimena (1657–1747) trained painters who worked in all the great courts of Europe.

The virtuosity of the Neapolitan Baroque tends toward the vapid and cluttered in its late phases. Perhaps it was in response to this trend that Charles the Bourbon, upon assuming power in 1734, imported two Roman architects to build his Palazzo Reale at Caserta. With the Bourbons and their artists Ferdinando Fuga (1699–1782) and Luigi Vanvitelli (1700–1773), Naples witnessed a return to the more classical. With the arrival of Napoleon's armies at the end of the century, the Neoclassical was firmly rooted.

Having mentioned the Greeks, Romans, the Normans and Arabs and Swabians, having considered briefly the Anjou and Aragon, and other of the various faces of the French and Spanish, we have left out mention of yet others who, however briefly, took much from the land but left little behind. When Garibaldi's troops finally unified the South with the rest of Italy in the middle of the 19th century, they unfortunately would not bring prosperity along with independence. The land of Magna Graecia and medieval maritime cities still had earthquakes and hardships to endure.

The Modern South

Italians always refer to the South as *Il Mezzogiorno*, or place of the noonday sun. Such a poetic name in fact connotes nothing but trouble to northern Italians. After decades of funding special development projects throughout the South, the region still remains well behind the North—the per capita income of Naples is half that of Milan. Part of the problem has been bad central planning—the magnificent coast of Calabria was selected for a steel mill, not tourism, for example. And organized crime—the Camorra around Naples and Campania, the Ndrangheta in Calabria—certainly shares a good deal of the responsibility, as its tactics have chased industry away and corrupted more local governments than anyone can enumerate.

But history also reveals how deeply rooted the plight of the Mezzogiorno is. Modern Italy has increasingly focused toward northern Europe, and in so doing has turned away from its most ancient ties in the Mediterranean—the very ties that created Magna Graecia as well as the thriving Byzantine and Norman seaports of the region. Later, the feudalism of French and Spanish rule retarded the South just at the time the Renaissance city states in the north flourished through capitalism and industry.

All these problems have delayed the development of the South. Yet the South has improved. Apulia, in particular, is one region where the standard of living and the economy have outstripped its neighbors. For one reason, the greatest aqueduct in the world now irrigates the formerly parched region and has made agriculture a profitable enterprise—Apulia now produces more olive oil and wine than any other area. For another, the region has never been afflicted by organized crime, the only section of the South for which this is true. And finally, the capital at Bari has revived its traditional ties to the East and developed itself into a modern wholesale trading port on the Adriatic. Although Bari is something of a success story and can boast major publishing houses as well as the primary hi-tech center of the South, it still suffers high unemployment. And Naples, despite its oil refineries, automobile assembly and food processing plants, struggles even more, with an unemployment rate of 30 percent.

For the traveler, the undeveloped Mezzogiorno presents both delights and difficulties. Away from the popular destinations around the Bay of Naples, the region sees far fewer tourists than the rest of Italy. In Apulia, your search for a Norman castle or Romanesque church will be warmly aided by locals; small towns will feel very traditional, and there, the prices are more reasonable than in the North. But, on the other hand, the facilities at both the deluxe and modest end of the spectrum are not as plentiful in the cities, and illegal building and housing projects can mar the setting of historic sights.

Cuisine

Campania

The countryside of Naples, the *regione* of Campania, has many rugged stretches away from the sea where the Apennines continue their march down the Italian peninsula and bring winter cold. Along the Amalfi Coast, the mountains crash to the sea, but here the benign climate has inspired farmers to terrace the cliffs into year-round citrus and olive groves. But if much of the Campania is difficult to farm, its strip, along the Tyrrhenian Sea between Rome and Naples, is legendary for its fertility. In ancient times, multiple crops were produced each year, and today, great fruit orchards and vegetable crops still cover the fields—the tomatoes from San Marzano are so succulent that canned foods boast they use nothing else. And when the Pontino swamp has been drained and controlled, as it was under ancient Rome and as it is today, it too is valued land. Since Byzantine times, the buffalo have grazed here, their milk used to make the local mozzarella cheese.

From the simplest ingredients of the Campania, its olives, tomatoes and cheese, comes Neapolitan cuisine. Although cows are now replacing the buffalo, the mozzarella is no less popular. Unlike the highly processed version found in the U.S., mozzarella here is dayfresh, delicious when just sprinkled with black pepper, and wonderful whether in an *insalata caprese* (with some of those San Marzano tomatoes, olive oil, and basil) or on a steaming portion of spaghetti with fresh tomatoes, or even on eggplant parmigiana. When oregano and garlic are added to the tomatoes, some mozzarella placed on top and a pie crust underneath, you have a *pizza Margarita*—one of the most traditional versions of this dish that comes with a slightly thicker crust and a bit more cheese than found to the north. (Since a pizza oven was excavated at Pompeii no one has bothered to dispute Naples' claims to originating this dish.) Even without the mozzarella, the olives and tomatoes and some anchovy paste combine into a lively *puttanesca* sauce for spaghetti. Then there is *bistecca alla pizzaiola*, the tomatoes, garlic, and wild oregano disguising the stewed sadness of the meat from this region.

Although the Campania has had little meat with which to create culinary thrillers, it does have more than enough seafood. Now the garlic and bits of tomato find themselves lacing a shellfish stew, or adding zest to a *zuppa di cozze* (mussels). Clams are as likely to appear on spaghetti as tomatoes, and *alici* (anchovies) are such a highlight of Neapolitan cuisine that dishes containing them almost always are called *alla Neapolitana*. Here the *alici* often are served fresh with some of those lemons and pressed olives that grow along the coast, but they can be found on pizza too, and as we've already seen, they add flavor to the *puttanesca* sauce. Whether large, sweet scampi (here called *mazzancolle*), squid, or fresh tuna or sea bass, the seafood finds its way into soups, pasta and lasagna. Or it's simply grilled (with garlic) for a main dish. Add to this pleasing cuisine a few more of the vegetables so loved in the Mezzogiorno—eggplant grilled or marinated, sweet peppers made into *peperonata* (like the Sicilian eggplant *caponata*), *scarole Natale* (Christmas escarole with raisins, pine nuts, and capers), or spinach with slices of garlic—and you have the flavors of the Campania. For dessert, you might try a ricotta cheesecake with dried fruit, called *pastiera*. Or maybe a good old-fashioned *cassata*, or *spumone* will do.

The art of **wine** making is as ancient as the civilization here. The Greek vines are still recorded in the name of many white "greco" wines, and Pliny recorded his pleasure in those from Falerno. Today, the region is not one of the great wine producers, though fresh and fruity whites are readily available as refreshing accompaniments to the local seafood—the *bianco superiore* from Ischia, the Greco and others from Ravello among them. There are even some controlled label wines, such as Fiano di Avellino and Greco di Rufo, both from the interior of the Campania, as is the red DOC Taurasi—all recommended. Most famous, and in some years deservedly so, is Lacryma Christi de Vesuvio. Its name "the tear of Christ," referring to Christ's reaction when he saw how Lucifer had stolen this part of paradise, probably accounts for its popularity, but both the reds and whites are DOC controlled content. From the Beneveneto interior is the famous Strega liqueur.

Apulia

Apulia shares the southern preference for garlic, a spicy touch of *peperoncini* and dry pastas (here they are madly shaped into ears of *orecchiette*, intensely twisted into screw-shaped *fusilli* or wadded into little balls of *cavitelli*). And the long sea coast also enhances the cuisine with fish, *gamberoni rossi* (a kind of shrimp), lobster and crab, mussels certainly, as well as the famous oysters from Taranto. The fish might be laced with the excellent local olive oil, or cooked with saffron, or sprinkled with basil or the local almonds, or mixed together into a spicy seafood stew called *ciambotto* that is used as a sauce over spaghetti.

But Apulia's landscape, though formerly harshly dry, is flat and easy to till. Its few rolling hills have long been used for grazing, so that the sheep add much lamb to the diet as well as ewe's milk to the pecorino and ricotta cheese (aged and served sharp as an appetizer). With the new aqueduct and irrigation system, the region has added cattle to its grazing herds, and around the town of Gioia del Colle produces Italy's finest non-buffalo mozzarella and ricotta. The cheeses find their way into the filling of a rich *lasagna*, such as we know it in the U.S.; they are stuffed into little ravioli called *panzerotti*, and made into dessert cakes of ricotta spiced with the local dried fruits also produced here.

Apulia shares the South's love of vegetables, but even adds to the usual repertoire of eggplant, zucchini, and the like with its own wild mushrooms, chicory and arugula, and *lampasciuni* (a mild onion) and asparagus. Most traditional is a dish of *orecchiette al rape*, a sauce of turnip greens and garlic. And there's a soup of fava beans and chicory. The antipasti are superb, and the soups can be unusually hearty (we once had one just heaped with artichokes).

Instead of Naples' passion for pizza, Apulia has one for all manner of breads. *Focaccia*, that quilted pizza-like bread, is folded over a filling of black olives, aged ricotta, tomatoes, and anchovy for *focaccia barese*; it is sprinkled with tomato, garlic, and oregano for Lecce's *puddica*, and is used for sandwiches and all manner of snacks throughout the region. The breads don't end with these variations, but continue with the hard ring-shaped *taralli* of Bari, the kneaded olive bread of Lecce, and the like. The interest in dough extends to desserts where it is cut into strips flavored with wine, fried and drenched in honey for Christmas *cartellate.*

Not only does Apulia produce much of Italy's olive oil and almonds, it is the largest **wine** producer. The robust reds of the Salerno peninsula have long been used for blending more famous wines produced in the North, but only recently has local production developed controlled label wines. Il Falcone is a DOC red wine worth seeking out, the Castel del Monte is best when red or rose, and Locorotondo's white is dry but pleasantly fruity as is Salice Salento. But not all the good wines have DOC controls—there is the wonderful rosé of Rosa del Golfo, the smooth but light reds and whites of Dona Marzia, and table wines that repeatedly surprise you with their character.

Travel Tips

Climate and Seasons

Southern Italy can be scorching hot in summer when sea breezes aren't near enough to make the weather tolerable (in Naples, the average high in July is 86° F, low 77° F), but the weather is more often quite temperate in the winter (in Naples, the average January high is 54° F, the low 48° F). Apulia on the Adriatic is drier than other regions from November into February; in Campania, however, drizzle and clouds can add some chill to the air. Despite the chill, the olives along the Amalfi Coast don't even ripen until November, and forsythia and roses bloom along the coast into the "winter" of December. But Campania, notable for its sea resorts and islands, definitely has its tourist season. The busiest months are July and August, although peak season prices are in effect in June too, and September, as well as the week before Easter. Although the "season" is from Easter through October, some hotels remain open throughout the year and many reopen for the Christmas season. The best time to travel is in the spring and fall, when the crowds are gone and the weather is quite fine—both October and May are very mild (in Naples, the average high for both is 72° F, the low 64° F).

Arriving

Naples is the major city of the South, so that its airport actually includes some European flights in addition to domestic ones, which also link Rome with Bari and Brindisi. However, *some transatlantic flights* (for the moment Alitalia only, but check with your travel agent) *link up with downtown Naples by special, nonstop trains from the Rome airport.* If your plans don't include Naples and you are picking up a rental car for travel farther south, the airport 5 km outside the city is more convenient. Naples is the most accessible city of the South, connected by train from Rome in under 2 hours by the *rapido* and just 7 to Milan. From Naples, trains continue south to Sicily (Messina, 9 hours). Bari and Brindisi (only two hours to the south by train) are the major ports for ferries to Greece, and also are well-connected by train to the rest of Italy, such as the fast Pendolino from Bari to Rome. And the *autostrada* network runs down both coasts; A-14 along the Adriatic to Bari connects with A-24/25 to Rome (465 km, 288 mi.); the Autostrada del Sole (increasingly called A-2, not A-1, along this stretch) connects Rome and Naples (215 km, 133 mi.). Despite the many connections through Naples, many prefer to avoid it entirely and do so by driving around it to the Amalfi coast or by taking the hydrofoil to Capri from Fiumicino (Medmar, ☎ *[06] 858-767;* summer only), near Rome's airport.

Getting Around

The cities of Southern Italy are not always efficiently linked to each other, but a train from Naples ties in at Caserta for Bari (3.5 hours) and Brindisi (5.5 hours) on the Rome to Lecce train, and the cross-peninsular highway A-16 connects with other highways to make for an efficient drive between Bari and Naples (265 km, 164 mi.). The decent but more local SS 379 covers the 155 km, 71 mi. between Bari and Brindisi. Car rentals are available in the cities; buses and tours provide service within the regions. Driving around Naples, including A-3 to Pompeii, can be nerve-racking. If you are not visiting the bay area, consider avoiding it entirely. A-30 near Caserta connects with A-3 near Salerno, where you can pick up the Amalfi Drive or continue to Paestum and points farther south.

Special Tips

The earthquake that shattered this region in 1980 converted many modest hotels into refuges for the homeless. As a result, the large cities of Apulia and Campania have a limited selection of hotels. Expect to pay more in Naples and Bari, for example, and reserve ahead. Naples, Bari, Brindisi and Taranto (if you find yourself there) are all port cities with considerable unemployment and crime. Take sensible precautions against theft and park your car in a garage.

Naples

Key to Naples

Sights

Two not-to-be-missed museums are the Capodimonte collection of Renaissance paintings and the Museo Archeologico Nazionale with paintings and mosaics from Pompeii among its extensive collection of antiquities. The San Martino monastery, the churches around Spaccanapoli, and the bay itself, dominated by Vesuvius, add to the sightseeing pleasures.

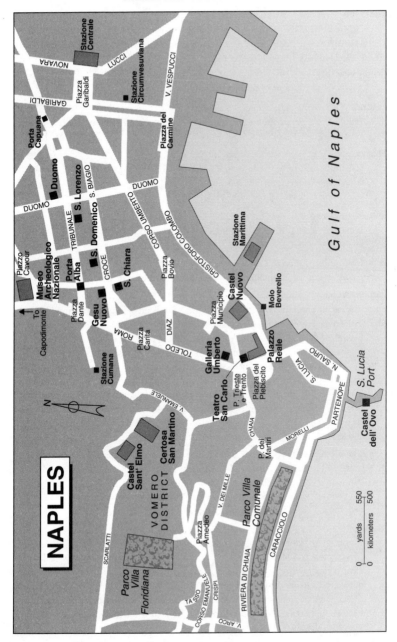

Excursions

Naples is the major crossroads for the great sights around the Bay of Naples, from Pompeii to Italy's equivalent of Versailles at Caserta. Nearby Sorrento, however, is a more congenial overnight base.

Nearby Beaches

Amalfi Coast, Sorrento, and the islands of Capri and Ischia.

Festivals

Luglio Festivale, or July music festival at Capodimonte; Festa of the patron San Gennaro, Sept. 17; opera season at Teatro San Carlo (☎ *797-2370*), Dec.-June.

Shopping

Christmas *presepi*, or creche scenes, some so elaborate that they are villages in miniature, have been a speciality of Naples since the 18th century and are still made and sold around the end of the year.

Accommodations

Limited, without the range you might want—safe, moderate and inexpensive establishments are in low supply.

Eating Out

Hearty and good Neapolitan fare, from pizza to *zuppa di cozze*.

Getting Around

A great diversity of transportation is available from *funicolari* to the hilltop of Vomero and ferries to the islands and Sorrento, to trams (#4) running along the bay from the Stazione Centrale to Mergellina on the opposite side of the city and the subway (Metropolitana) running more inland between those points with a stop near the Museo Archeologico. There are taxis. There are city tours and excursions. And there are buses, of course, running along the main drag Via Toledo (changing names to V. Roma and others) to the Archaeology Museum and on up to Capodimonte. **Warning:** Buses can be useless during rush hour when they also are overly crowded and dangerous—it is not unheard of that people are injured in the pushing and shoving. • The funicolari often are closed for repairs.

The suburban trains, such as the Circumvesuviana to Pompeii, Herculaneum and Sorrento (1 hour), are invaluable means of sightseeing without a car. Cars are only a burden in Naples itself, where they should always be put in a garage—preferably one belonging to a reliable hotel. For connections to bay excursions and nearby beaches and islands, see those destinations elsewhere.

Arriving

European and domestic flights; trains from Rome (2 hours on a *rapido*), Brindisi (5.5 hours), and Messina (9 hours); ferries to Sicily and Sardinia make Naples the crossroads of the region. Naples is 215 km, 133 mi. south of Rome on A-2 (also named A-1 on older maps), 55 km, 34 mi. north of Salerno by A-3 (but more beautifully by the Amalfi Drive). **Note:** Arriving by train, check to see if you can disembark at the Stazione Mergellina, more convenient to hotels as well as some ferry lines than the Stazione Centrale.

Special Tips

The poverty in Naples is quite palpable, and for the unsuspecting tourist, so are its consequences. Everything here is something of a hassle (settle taxi prices in advance—or ask for the meter, if you can; make sure you're not given and charged for a hotel suite when all you want is a standard; etc.). And Naples is notorious for its *scugnizzi*, or street kids. Theft is so rampant that evening shopping brings out hundreds of special police to line the streets. Motor scooterists are adept at grabbing the necklaces and bags of both pedestrians and those seated in cars.

Tuck your valuables away. Don't carry a handbag.

Leave what you can in the *cassa di sicurezza* of your hotel.

Park your car in a hotel garage—better yet, if you're staying in Sorrento, leave it there and take the Circumvesuviana to Naples for the day.

Stay away from the Spaccanapoli area at night and be on the lookout for thieves even around Santa Lucia. Avoid the Montecalvario area (west side of V. Roma around P. Carita) at all times.

What to See and Do

Castel Nuovo has a spectacular triumphal arch entrance.

The majestic bay is still majestic. Modern-day Ulysses find it hard to resist the scenic Sorrento peninsula. The perfectly conical Vesuvius sends out thin ribbons of smoke reminding all of the ruined cities of Pompeii and Herculaneum at its foot. Across the bay, the lively Mergellina port nestles at the foot of Posillipo, where Augustus had a villa. And connecting these two mountainous arms of the bay is Naples itself, the former Greek port of Neapolis now crowned with the medieval **Castel Sant' Elmo**, and further protected by two more castles at its feet, the Norman **Castel dell'Ovo** at Santa Lucia harbor, and the Angevine **Castel Nuovo** at the Beverello.

Ancient mysteries, natural beauty, and ruined cities are the stuff of the Grand Tour. Understandably, Naples was a primary stop along the way, from the 17th century on. However, the modern urban sprawl of Naples has forever scarred the scenic bay, and the belching smoke of its industry obscures that of Vesuvius. With a population of 1.2 million, Naples is the most densely populated city of Italy, as well as one of its poorest. It is not picturesque. Illegal buildings, earthquakes (as recently as 1980), and massive WW II bombings have destroyed the cohesive character of its historic center. Crime and squalor has chased today's travelers away.

Despite all these off-putting realities, it would be a mistake not to visit Naples—at least for a day's sightseeing, if not the month-long sojourn of Edwardian travelers. The Capodimonte must be visited by anyone who cares about Renaissance painting, the Museo Archeologico by all who have come this far to see Pompeii. And San Martino or the churches and palazzi of the Spaccanapoli can be visited, if you have time. A lunch along the bay, maybe at the bustling hydrofoil port at Mergellina, a drive on the Lungomare (or sea promenade), shopping for antiques and designer clothes around the elegant Piazza dei Martiri, are the pleasures of Naples. And if you can swing a night here during opera season, a performance at the 250-year-old Teatro San Carlo should be your reward.

Assuming that you might be using nearby Sorrento as your base, or that you are just stopping briefly on your way to Capri or the Amalfi Coast, we emphasize a tour of Naples that can be managed in just a day—especially a summer day when both visiting hours and daylight are prolonged. In winter, you'll have to hustle to fit in the two major museums in the morning, and then the churches in Spaccanapoli will be closed until late afternoon. A few other sights as well as accommodations are listed as well, for the convenience of those staying in Naples. Some people actually fall in love with Naples—despite its difficulties. Taking the proper precautions against theft, they venture out into the city to enjoy the operatic energy of the Neapolitani and the theatrical street life that is endlessly unfolding.

Author's Tip

Always check museum openings with the tourist office: longer hours are as common in the summer as sudden closings are during holiday season.

Museo Archeologico Nazionale ★ ★ ★
V. Roma at P. Museo.

Housed in an immense 16th-century palazzo is the National Museum, one of the greatest collections of Greco-Roman art in the world—it also happens to contain an Egyptian collection and the fabulous Farnese jewel collection (Sala di Venere). Recent decades have seen nearly continuous restoration and remodeling, so that often parts of the sculpture collections aren't on view and other sections have temporary installations. There is always enough to see to make a visit more than worthwhile, especially for the masterpiece mosaics and paintings from Pompeii. The **ground floor** is devoted to sculpture. Here in the grand entrance hall are Imperial Roman works. In the rooms located through the first door on the right, you can usually find some of the best Roman copies of Classical Greek sculptures, among them ★ *Aphrodite Sossandra* (Room I, 2nd statue, right), ★ *Slayers of the Tyrant*, (Room I, center), the bronze ★ *Ephebus* (Room VII at end) from Pompeii, and the best extant copy of Polycleitus' ★ *Doryphorus, the Spear-Thrower*, as well as a copy of Pheidias' ★ *Athena*, (both in rooms off to the right of Room I).

Up the staircase at the end of the entrance hall, you come to the **mezzanine level** and on the left, the ★ ★ ★ **Rooms of Pompeii Mosaics**, a treasure trove of wall and floor decorations. Beginning with the typical country house "beware of dog" mosaic in the first room (Room 57), you pass between mosaic-decorated columns into a room with nymphaneum niches. The next room (59) contains mosaics of the folksy ★ *Consulting a Witch* and ★ *Itinerant Musicians* as well as the painterly ★ *Portrait of a Woman* (#124666). If you aren't yet convinced of Roman virtuosity in this medium, Room 61 will cast away all doubts. Here is one of the great works from antiquity, the ★ ★ *Alexander Mosaic*, (1st century. B.C.), once a floor in the House of the Faun. Inspired by a Hellenistic painting of Alexander's battle at Issus, the action, depth, and color are created out of four basic colors of tesserae, or tiny chips. Also in this room is the bronze statue, *Dancing Faun*, from the atrium of the same villa.

Once again, climb the stairs. At the **top**, on the right are rooms with small ★ bronzes and marble statues from the elaborate garden and atrium of Herculaneum's Villa Papiri, named after the thousands of charred scrolls painstakingly excavated from its library. But the real sights here are found in rooms to the left, where there are all sorts of items from Pompeii—from cameos and crystal jewelry to ivory and glass. The most important ones are the wall paintings—the exceptionally delicate four small ★ panels of women representing the seasons (Room 74 in center; note *Spring Gathering Flowers* #8834); the girls playing, or ★ *Le Giocatrici* (Room 72 in center); and the ★ *Portrait of the Baker and his Wife*, (Paquius Proculus e la Corsorta, #9058) and the famous ★ *Sappho*, or woman writing (#9084), both in Room 78. From Paestum, is the strikingly Greek ★ *Danza Funebre* (Room 67). And notable works from Herculaneum can be seen in the center of Room 73.

The museum is open 9 a.m.–2 p.m. Tues.–Sat.; Sun. 9 a.m.–1 p.m.; closed Mon.; L12,000. Located just above P. Dante on the corner of V. Roma, the museum can be reached by any bus running north-south along the main street, such as #24, or by subway at P. Cavour, just a few blocks east.

Capodimonte ★ ★

Capodimonte means "top of the hill," and this is where you find the Bourbon royal estate at the north end of Via Toledo/ Roma and its extensions. The Neo-classical palace (begun 1738) is surrounded by a delightful park, once the king's hunting grounds. The north wing of the palace houses two museums: the Royal Apartments (2nd floor) with a porcelain room displaying the 18th-century Sevres-like china once manufactured on this hill; and the air-conditioned ★ ★ **Galleria Nazionale** (top floor) with its exceptional collection of Italian paintings. Although many of the rooms exhibit works to reward the patient visitor, be sure not to miss the following highlights. Simone Martini's ★ ★ *St. Louis Toulouse Crowns Robert of Anjou* (1317; Room 4) not only is painted with the Sienese artist's sinuous lines and richness, but its five predellas are the first since antiquity with vanishing point perspective. Masaccio's ★ ★ *Crucifixion*, (1427; Room 6) may have a gold leaf background, but the expressive composition of this Early Renaissance work is anything but Byzantine. Room 7 contains Botticelli and other Tuscan works, while Room 8 includes Giovanni Bellini's mysterious ★ ★ *Transfiguration* (late 1480s), with a very human figure of Christ set in an elaborate and bleak landscape. There is a drawing each by Michelangelo and Raphael in Room 12 and a number of Correggios in Room 14, including the evanescent ★ *Zingarella*, or Gypsy Woman (1516). Room 18 contains Titian's ★ *Penitent Magdalena* (1565), while Room 19 contains three superb Titians from the mid-1540s: ★ ★ *Portrait of Pope Paul III and Two Nephews*, its unfinished state perhaps adding to the sense of spontaneity; another ★ ★ *Portrait of Paul III*, pure Venetian in its color; and ★ ★ *Danac*, a classical nude cloaked in Venetian luster. Flemish works are in Room 20, including Breughel's ★ *The Blind Leading the Blind* (1568), and Room 25 holds Early Baroque works from the Carracci school, but Room 29 contains Caravaggio's powerful ★ ★ *Flagellation* (1607). The Neapolitan Baroque artists, including Salvatore Rossi, are represented in Rooms 32-39.

The park is open 9 a.m. to dusk (free); *the museums; in summer, 10 a.m.–6 p.m. Tues.–Sat., till 2 p.m. Sun.; in winter, 9 a.m.–2 p.m. Tues.–Sat., till 1 p.m. Sun.; closed Mon.; admission L8000. Located north of the P. Dante and the Museo Nazionale, and best reached by taxi or bus: #110 and 127 from Stazione Centrale; any like #160 from P. Plebiscito, but #24 takes you farthest up the hill, to the main entrance.*

Spaccanapoli ★

Not to be found on any map, "Spaccanapoli" refers to the decumanus of ancient Neapolis that split the city in half. Today this narrow but straight street has many names as it cuts east from Via Roma to the Piazza Gesu Nuovo and on to the Via Duomo. Two of its easier-to-find names are Via Croce and V. San Biagio dei Librai. The approximately mile-long daytime walk takes you through the *centro storico*, full of churches and *caratteristico* palaces, but also through Naples' worst slum. When the churches are closed *(noon–4:30 p.m.)*, there is not much rewarding to see. If you are uncomfortable at the thought of this walk, you might just want to visit the sights at Piazza Gesu, on the edge. Here, around a typically outlandish piece of Neapolitana Rococo called a *guglia*, or a free-standing ornamental spire (this one dates to 1747), are two important churches. Disguised by the diamond-rusticated facade of a former palazzo (1470), **Gesu Nuovo** invites you through its elaborate portal and treats you to a very Baroque interior dancing with colored marbles and frescoes (that above the entrance portal by Francesco Solimena, 1725). Just beyond the piazza is the entrance gate to ★ **Santa Chiara**, founded in 1310 and later revamped into the Baroque. Since its interior was destroyed by firebombs in WW II, it was restored to the original simplicity of the French Gothic and contains beautiful medieval sculpture, none more sublime than the 14th-century ★ ★ *Angevine tombs* around the high altar: Tomb of Mary of Valois (right wall; by Tino di Camaino from Siena), that of Charles, Duke of Calabria (right of Altar; by Tino), and Tomb of Robert of

Angou (behind high altar; Florentine). To the left and rear of the church is the entrance to the ★ *Chiostro delle Clarisse*, designed by the 18th-century artist Vaccaro into a confection of a garden filled with orange trees and majolica tiles. East on Spaccanapoli you arrive at the Piazza San Domenico with another guglia in front of **San Domenico Maggiore**. Rebuilt many times since its Gothic beginnings, the church contains a ★ candelabra with caryatids by Tino di Camaino (left steps of high altar), and a high altar and choir seats with inlaid marble designs by the Baroque artist Fanzago as well as many Tuscan sculptures in its chapels. You can turn left up the side of San Domenico onto Via De Sanctis, where you'll find the Baroque sliding into the technical bravura of the marble *Veiled Christ* (1753) in the **Cappella San Severo** *(10 a.m.–1 p.m. daily; also 5–7 p.m. except Sun. and Tues.)*, or continue straight on the Spaccanapoli where you first pass **S. Angelo a Nilo** (on your right), then, marking the corner at the left, the ancient sculpture of the river god Nile. Passing Rococo palazzi, you come to **Via San Gregorio Armeno**, where turning left through a sienna archway, you come to the San Lorenzo church (on the right) where the poet Boccaccio met his "Fiammetta," daughter of Robert of Anjou. Around the Christmas season this is the street of the *presepio*, or creche makers, and you can find all kinds of specialty scenes, from the three kings to market scenes. After San Lorenzo is Via Tribunale. A left takes you to the Porta d'Alba (by Vanvitelli) and back to the Piazza Dante; a right to the Via Duomo. Although no longer in Spaccanapoli, this is a convenient time to visit the ★ **cathedral**, just to the left on Via Duomo. Founded by the Anjou in 1294, the duomo now is more Baroque than Gothic. Its most famous chapel (the *Tesoro* of the patron San Gennaro; right aisle, 3rd chapel; *8:30 a.m.–noon*) was adorned by some of the best Baroque artists: Fanzago designed the gilded bronze grill, Solimena the silver altar front, and Lanfranco painted the dome. And even the *Basilica of S. Restituta* (entered center, left aisle), a 4th-century church built over the Temple of Apollo and incorporated into the duomo, is mostly remarkable for its ceiling painted in the virtuoso manner of Luca Giordano. However, in the crypt under the high altar are sublime Renaissance marble bas reliefs in the ★ *Sepolcro di San Gennaro* (by Tommaso Malvito, 1497–1506). **Underground Neopolis** You can walk the streets of the ancient city by taking a weekend tour into the excavated area under the cathedral. Check with the tourist office at P. Gesu for information.

Certosa Di San Martino ★

If you have only one day, you might substitute a visit here for the sights of Spaccanapoli. Located on the Vomero hill, a pleasant residential area of the city, the beautiful monastery of San Martino shares the summit with the **Castel Sant' Elmo** (14th century, rebuilt 16th century) and its ★ **views** of the bay. The Carthusian monastery was originally built in the 14th century, but was remodeled during the Baroque. Even if you are not especially interested in the **Museo Nazionale di San Martino** with its exhibits on local history and culture, you might want to visit for the *presepio* rooms, with "nativity" scenes from the heyday of this art form, and the ★ **Chiostro Grande**, with each of its four corners boasting doorways ornamented by Fanzago (1631). And the Gothic church is cloaked in some of Naple's finest Baroque work, from the choir (Lanfranco's *Crucifixion*) into the nave (marble inlaid work by Fanzago, ceiling by Lanfranco) and chapels (west end by Vaccaro; east end grills by Fanzago).

The monastery is open Tues.–Sat. 9 a.m.–2 p.m.; Sun. 9 a.m.–1 p.m.; closed Mon.; L12,000. The Funicolari Centrale runs from the Via Toledo (across from the Galleria) up to the Vomero.

Other Sights

As you're making your way around Naples, you'll inevitably pass through the downtown area. Here you are at the south end of the Via Toledo/Roma, between the Castel dell'Ovo and the Castel Nuovo. (Embedded in the 13th-century Nuovo fort is a ★ fine Renaissance **triumphal arch** by Francesco Laurana, 1455). On the massive **Piazza del Plebiscito** is S. Francesco di Paolo (1817) an unharmonious church inspired by the Pantheon and Bernini's colonnades for St. Peter's. Across from it is the **Palazzo Reale** (1600), the Spanish viceregal palace built by Domenico Fontana, now housing government offices. The main wing *(inside courtyard, entrance on left; 9 a.m.–2 p.m. Tues.–Sat., Sun. till 1 p.m.; fee)* has a chapel by Fanzago at the foot of the majestic staircase (both mid 17th century), while upstairs is the Court Theater (1768) by the Roman Ferdinand Fuga. At the back of the palace is a small park looking over the Castel Nuovo. Around the corner from the Palazzo Reale is the largest and most sumptuous opera house in Italy, the **Teatro San Carlo** *(V. Vittorio Emanuele at P. Trento e Trieste; 1737; visits by appointment ☎ 797-2111; ticket information, Tues.–Sat. ☎ 797-2331)* built for the Bourbon king, Charles. Across the street is the 19th-century shopping mall called the **Galleria Umberto** *(V. Emanuele at V. Toledo)*, more ornate than Milan's, of course, though built 10 years later. As Via Toledo stretches up to the Capodimonte past the city's major sights, you might just head in the opposite direction and round the point of Santa Lucia with the Castel dell' Ovo, where the long sea promenade stretches to Mergellina.

Where to Stay

Travelers on a modest budget should plan to upgrade from their usual accommodations. *There are just too few reliable hotels to recommend in the lower price ranges—*most are in a sleazy cluster around the Stazione Centrale. The majority of the better hotels can be found on the seafront *(V. Partenope and V. N. Sauro)* near the Castel Sant' Ovo in the area called Santa Lucia. Though these hotels often command views, the traffic can be quite intense, so you might want an interior room. We mention a few others scattered in the better neighborhoods. If you have a car, choose a hotel with a garage and expect to pay big city prices. All hotels listed have a/c.

Expensive

Vesuvio   **L290–420,000 CP**   ★★★★

V. Partenope 45, 80121; ☎ 764-0044, FAX 589-0380.
Single L290,000 CP. Double L420,000 CP.

A fine hotel, its interior a bit more traditional and pleasing than the modern facade. The 180 rooms, many with views, have high ceilings, stucco moldings and parquet floors plus all modern comforts. One suite, complete with piano, was the residence of Enrico Caruso, the famous tenor. Rooftop restaurant and lounge terrace (enclosed in winter). Good buffet breakfast. Garage.

Santa Lucia   **L270–395,000 CP**   ★★★★

V. Partenope 46, 80121; ☎ 764-0666, FAX 764-8580.

Single L270,000 CP. Double L360–395,000 CP.

Completely renovated in 1989, this bayfront hotel is very contemporary in its elegance, but quite traditionally Italian in its use of gilded furniture and ceramic tiles. Many of its 130 tasteful rooms have views, all are ample and modernized. Terrace restaurant, piano bar and garage.

Moderate

Paradiso L175–275,000 CP ★ ★ ★

Via Catullo 11, ☎ 761-4161, FAX 761-3449.
Single L175,000 CP. Double L275,000 CP.

If you want to relax in Naples and your funds don't permit a stay at the more deluxe hotels, there is no better choice than the Paradiso. From atop Posillipo. the Mediterranean white hotel affords fabulous views of Vesuvius across the bay. There's a rooftop terrace restaurant and half the comfortable 70 rooms have views (reserve one in advance). Posillipo is lovely and tranquil, but apart from being next door to Naples' best restaurant, the hotel is a bit inconvenient. (Take the funicolare or bus from Mergellina 10 minutes up to the Orazio stop.) Limited parking.

Majestic L190–280,000 CP ★ ★ ★

Largo Vasto a Chiaia 68, 80121; ☎ 416-500, FAX 416-500.
Single L190,000 CP. Double L280,000 CP.

Located near the fanciest shopping district, within walking distance of the sights, and near the Amedeo subway stop, the modern, first-class Majestic offers 130 carpeted, color-coordinated and comfortable rooms, along with a pleasant lobby. Restaurant. Garage.

Inexpensive

Rex L100–140,000 ★

V. Palepoli 12, 80132; ☎ 764-9389, FAX 764-9227.
Single L100,000. Double L140,000.

In Santa Lucia, just a block off Via N. Saura, the Rex is plain but acceptable, and offers 40 a/c (fee) rooms. Breakfast room. No garage.

Where to Eat

No matter what everyone says, Neapolitan cooking will not remind you of your neighborhood pizzeria. It is just too good, the ingredients too high in quality and too fresh to be so ordinary. Even the simplest pizza Margarita can be elevated by the flavor of the local San Marzano tomatoes and the freshness of real buffalo mozzarella. And whether you try your linguine with the tomatoey *alla puttanesca*, or with the freshest clams still in their shells, *alle vongole veraci*, you'll know that you're dining in Italy. To end your meal, choose a *pastiera napolitana*, the traditional ricotta cake with orange rind.

La Sacrestia $$$ ★ ★ ★ ★

V. Orazio 116; reserve at ☎ 761-1051, FAX 764-8769.
Closed Sun. in July, otherwise Mon., closed Aug. Meals L65–100,000.

Set above Mergellina on Posillipo and with stunning views from the garden terrace and elegant indoor dining rooms, the Sacrestia is Naples' most beautiful restaurant. It is also considered its best, offering traditional Neapolitan cuisine along with more *nuova cucina*. You might try a simple pasta with provolone and tomatoes, or ravioli

stuffed with eggplant; a delicate veal, or fresh anchovies stuffed and fried with mozzarella. In the afternoon, you can arrive by the Mergellina funicolare (the restaurant
is just across from the Orazio stop), but a taxi is easiest.

Ciro a Santa Brigida $$ ★★★
V. Santa Brigida 73; ☎ *552-4072.*
Closed Sun., mid July–late Aug. Meals L40–65,000.
Just off V. Toledo past the Galleria, this cozy restaurant bustles, from lunch until
after the opera. Air-conditioned and with good service, Ciro's is popular for its
wood-oven pizza at both lunch and dinner. But it also is a restaurant respected for
its Neapolitan cuisine. The vegetable appetizers and pastas are excellent, the fritto
misto of seafood is prepared with a light touch, and when accompanied by a salad,
is a satisfying meal. The fish can be perfectly prepared, such as a baked sea bass, but
the shellfish stew, *pignatiello e vavella*, is the favorite here. Leave room for the pastiera.

Mimi alla Ferrovia $$ ★★★
V. Alfonso d'Aragona; ☎ *553-8525.*
Closed Sun. and mid-Aug. Meals L35–60,000.
In the seedy area around the Porta Capuana (take a taxi, particularly at night), this
comfortable restaurant is famous for its authentic Neapolitan cooking. The antipasto Mimi, with everything from stuffed peppers to squash blossoms, is ample
enough to prevent you from proceeding to the seafood specialties caught by Mimi's
fishing fleet.

Don Salvatore $$ ★★★
V. Mergellina 4; ☎ *681-817, FAX 761-4329.*
Closed Wed. Meals L45–65,000.
Not only is it open in August, it's air–conditioned and comfortable, and some of the
tables have views over the port. Although you may come for the pizza at night, the
seafood at both lunch and dinner is prepared with a knowing and creative hand,
worthy of the degustazione menu or the more straightforward spaghetti "cosa nos-
tra" (with shellfish) and *insalata caprese* (tomatoes, mozzarella, basil and oil).

La Cantina di Triunfo $ ★★
Riviera di Chiaia 64; ☎ *668-101.*
Open 8:30–11 p.m., closed Sun., Aug. Dinner L35–45,000.
One of the most popular of Naple's trattorias, La Cantina offers more sophisticated
dining than that label usually suggests. Even such familiar dishes as spaghetti frutti
di mare and baccala transcend their simple Neapolitan origins. Daily menu (limited)
is recited. Credit cards: None.

Da Giovanni $$–$$$ ★★
V. Morelli 14; ☎ *764-3565.*
Open 8 p.m. Closed Sun. and in Aug. Meals L55–75,000.
The ambience is soothing and the service is refined at Giovanni's, located on a street
lined with antique shops and just off the elegant Piazza dei Martiri. The gnocchi
with mozzarella and tomato or the artichokes grilled with radicchio are great beginnings, and the seafood (best choice at lunch) is fresh and often includes the traditional *pignatiello*, or shellfish stew with slices of garlic and tomato.

Ristorante 53 **$–$$** ★★

P. Dante 53; ☎ *341-124.*
Closed Thurs., late Aug. Meals L40–55,000.
Though the busy intersection of Piazza Dante is totally resistible, its location is convenient for sightseers and its trattorie serve good Neapolitan food. Here, sample the antipasto table and pasta frutti di mare.

Snacks

In addition to Ciro's and Don Salvatore for pizza, there are other snacking options. **Caflish Caffe** *(V. Toledo 253, near the Galleria; closed Sat.)* not only has a much respected counter with pastries stuffed with mushrooms and cheese and the like, but in back there is a cafeteria where you might just select some salad and soup or a plate of escarole. The **Gran Caffe Le Caffetiera** *(P. Martiri 26; closed Mon.)* is on the city's most elegant square, with outdoor tables in warm weather, and good pastries the year round. Nearby is **L.U.I.S.E.** *(P. Martiri 68)* an excellent gourmet shop with traditional *pastiera*, or ricotta cake.

Directory

Telephone Code 081 **Postal Code 80100**

Airport

In Capodichino *(*☎ *709-2815)*, 5 km, 3 mi. NW of city; connected by #14 bus with P. Garibaldi; taxis charge double fare. Rome's Fiumicino airport (for Alitalia passengers) is connected by fast train to the Naple's Stazione Centrale.

American Express

Ashiba Travel, *P. Municipio 1 (*☎ *551-5303)*.

Books In English

Guida, *V. Porta d'Alba 20*, off P. Dante, superb books in Italian, too.

Bus

Regional buses SITA *(*☎ *552-2176)*, V. Pisanello at P. Municipio for Amalfi; **Capolinea** to Caserta, from Porta Capuana. *Local*: Remember to purchase tickets in advance at newsstands or *tabacchi*.

Car Rentals

Avis *(*☎ *407-333)*; **Europcar** *(*☎ *401-454)*, and others, at airport, some at stazione, too.

Consulates

United States, ☎ *583-8111* with 24-hour emergency lines.

Emergencies

☎ *112* or *113*.

Ferries

From Mergellina: SNAV *(*☎ *761-2348)* and **Alilauro** *(*☎ *761-1004) aliscafi*, or hydrofoils to Sorrento, Capri, Ischia. From Stazione Maritima at P. Municipio: **Tirrenia** *(*☎ *551-2181)* ferries to Palermo (10.5 hours) and other Sicilian cities, and Cagliari, Sardinia (16 hours); **Siremar** *(*☎ *551-2112)* to Isole Eolie (Lipari Islands) in summer; and at nearby Molo Beverello **Caremar** *(☎ 551-3882)* and others with ferries and *aliscafi* to Capri, Sorrento, Ischia.

Funicolar

For Vomero, 3 lines including the Centrale (most reliable service), across from Galleria, to San Martino; for Posillipo, from Mergellina.

Groceries

Alimentari behind Galleria on V. Santa Brigida; and around P. Martiri on V. Cavallerizza.

Opera

Teatro San Carlo *(V. San Carlo 93;* ☎ *797-2331)*, open Tues.–Sat. 10 a.m.–1 p.m., 4:30–6 p.m. (till 8:30 p.m. on performance days) for tickets during Dec.–June opera season.

Police

English spoken at ☎ *794-111.*

Post Office

P. Matteotti, off V. Toledo.

Shopping

Antiques, V. Morelli between Santa Lucia and P. Martiri; *presepi*, or nativity scenes, V. San Gregorio Armeni in Spaccanapoli; most exclusive boutiques, P. Martiri to V. dei Mille.

Subway

Metropolitana, from Stazione Centrale, to P. Cavour (Museo Archeologico), P. Amedeo (Via dei Mille), Mergellina, Pozzuoli.

Taxi

Stands near subway entrances, P. Plebiscito, stazione, P. Gesu, or call ☎ 556-4444.

Telephone

Telcom, 9 a.m.–5 p.m. in Galleria; **ASST**, Stazione Centrale, 7 a.m.–9 p.m.

Tourist Office

EPT, *P. Martiri 58 (*☎ *405-311)* and airport; **AAST** Palazzo Reale *(*☎ *418-744; FAX 418-619)*, and P. Gesu (open festivi, too, 9 a.m.–2 p.m.; in summer, 9 a.m.–7 p.m., Sun. until 2 p.m.; ☎ *552-3328)*, stazione, Mergellina (seasonal).

Tours

For city tours, excursions around bay and to Amalfi Coast, as well as for ferry reservations, etc., contact **CIT** *(P. Municipio 70;* ☎ *552-5426)*, or **Aritur** *(P. Trieste e Trento 7;* ☎ *400-487)*. Harbor tour, 1-hour, contact "Love Boat" *(*☎ *573-1532)*. For weekend tours to churches and into the now underground streets and aqueducts of Naples' past, contact AAST *(*☎ *552-3328)*.

Train

Stazione Centrale, P. Garibaldi on east side and well-connected by bus, subway, and tram, information ☎ *553-4188*; **Stazione Mergellina**, often the first stop in Naples on trains from the north, is more pleasant and usually more convenient for the tourist; tram #4, the subway, and taxis provide connections. **Suburban Trains** Ferrovia Circumvesuviana, V. Garibaldi, one block below Stazione Centrale (☎ *779-2444),* for Pompeii, Herculaneum, Sorrento; Ferrovia Cumana *(*☎ *551-3328),* P. Montesanto, near P. Dante.

Sorrento

Il Miramare, Sorrento, offers sea view apartments.

Key to Sorrento

Sights

A lovely resort, with good connections to nearby sights.

Excursions

Pompeii (28 km, 17 mi.), *Herculaneum* (42 km, 26 mi.), even *Naples* (52 km, 32 mi.) and *Amalfi* (35 km, 22 mi.) and *Paestum* (85 km, 53 mi.).

Festivals

Good Friday procession; July classical music concerts in the San Francesco cloister; October film festival.

Shopping

Intarsia, or inlaid wood furniture, is a centuries-long crafts tradition of Sorrento.

Accommodations

A fuller range of choice than in Naples.

Eating Out

Ample choice, from seafood to pizza, but many resort hotels require meal plans.

Getting Around

A small town, buses run the main Corso Italia and elevators ply the cliffs down to the sea.

Arriving

European and domestic flights from Naples' airport connected by 1-hour bus or by the Circumvesuviana train departing from the central stazione in downtown Naples. Bus service from Amalfi Drive. Also ferry and Aliscafi connections from Naples, Capri, and Ischia (in season). By car, exit A-3 at Castellamare for Sorrento, 27 km, 17 mi. away.

Special Tips

A relaxing base for exploring the sights of the Bay of Naples.

What to See and Do

The dramatic beauty of the Sorrento peninsula certainly must have been the source of the ancients' belief that the Sirens lured sailors to their death here by the loveliness of their song. From the time of Augustus through the Belle Epoque of the Astors, the wealthy have suffered little by giving in to the natural allure of this spot. Their villas, some in ruins, others still lived in, command the views over the sea to Capri and Naples. Orange and lemon groves cover their cliffside terraces, roses bloom in their gardens year round. One, the 18th-century **Villa Correale** *(V. Correale, east of main piazza)* now is a museum with art and artifacts from Sorrento history. Another, from ancient times, is in ruins on the **Punta del Capo** to the west (3 km out on Corso Italia by bus or car, then a 20-minute walk), a ★ scenic spot where the winds have carved arches into the rocks called "Bagno della Regina Giovanna."

Like the many international travelers who find their way to Sorrento, you're probably not here for local sightseeing, but for the convenient base the resort provides for exploring the region. Simply wandering around town, you'll find a few medieval streets flanking the Corso Italia (west of P. Tasso), you'll enjoy the **views** from the belvedere near the Villa Correale or the Punta del Capo, and you'll find the Moorish 14th-century cloister of **San Francesco** (next to the public gardens, or "Villa Comunale," where the elevator leads down to the ferry dock).

Where to Stay

Although demand is most intense in July and August, the high season stretches from April to October, when reservations are recommended and many hotels require that you take meal plans. It is not unusual that hotels on the breezy promontories above the sea don't have air-conditioning, as you'll see indicated below. All of these hotels are within walking distance of the main piazza; those on Via Califano are closer to the public tennis courts. Il Miramare offers sea view apartments. Call ☎ *(800) 280-2811* or *(617) 596-8282*.

Very Expensive

Grand Hotel Excelsior Vittoria   L320–520,000 CP

P. Tasso 34; ☎ *807-1044, FAX 877-1206.*
Single L320,000 CP. Double L400–520,000 CP.

This wonderful Victorian hotel is full of old-fashioned ambience and graceful furnishings. Its beautiful gardens stretch from the main piazza to a great terrace above

St. Peter's central cupola, Rome

Emilia Romagna

Quirinal, Rome

Rome corner market

the sea. The comforts here are modern, with 120 large, airy rooms (no a/c), with gilded touches and many with terraces and views. Restaurant, handsome bar. Elevator to port; good pool. Parking. Open year-round.

Expensive

Grand Hotel Ambasciatori   **L260–310,000**   ★ ★ ★ ★

V. Califano 18; ☎ *878-2025, FAX 807-1021.*
Single L260,000. Double L310,000.
A bit east of the central square, this tastefully modern hotel offers a lovely terrace and garden overlooking Vesuvius and the sea, and 103 comfortably appointed rooms (a/c), many with the same views. Restaurant, lounge. Elevator to sunning terrace. Pool. Parking. Open year-round.

Imperial Tramontano   **L245–280,000**   ★ ★ ★ ★

V. Vittorio Veneto 1; ☎ *878-2588, FAX 807-2344.*
Single L245,000. Double L280,000.
With a fine location near the center but commanding views of the sea, this hotel has gardens on the street side and all sea cliffside. Although the entrance atrium is modern, most of the 105 ample rooms are more eclectic, and the sitting rooms are elegantly old-fashioned with intarsia tables, frescoes and ornately tiled floors complementing the sea views. Restaurant. Lounge. Elevator to beach. Pool. Parking. Closed Jan.-Feb.

Moderate

Bellevue Syrene   **L195–255,000**   ★ ★ ★

P. Vittoria 5; ☎ *878-1024, FAX 878-3963.*
Single L195,000. Double L255,000.
Just down the street from the Imperial, the Bellevue offers fine gardens, sea views and 50 a/c rooms of varying size in the converted 18th-century villa. Restaurant. Elevator to beach. Parking.

Inexpensive

Regina   **L80–110,000**   ★ ★

V. Marina Grande 10; ☎ *878-2722, FAX 878-2721.*
Single L80,000. Double L110,000.
In the same enclave as the preceding hotels, but across the street from the sea, the Regina offers 36 plain rooms (no a/c), with balconies overlooking the garden and a top-floor restaurant and terrace with sea views. Closed Nov.–mid-March.

Villa di Sorrento   **L85–150,000**   ★ ★

V. Fuorimura 4; ☎ *878-1068, FAX 807-2679.*
Single L85,000. Double L150,000.
Just a few steps off the Piazza Tasso, this in-town mansion offers no views, but it is one of the few modest establishments open in the offseason. The 19 homey rooms (no a/c) are decently furnished and have modern baths; those in the rear are quieter. Breakfast room. Nearby pay parking.

Loreley et Londres   **L100,000 CP**   ★

V. Califano 2; ☎ *807-3187.*
Single/double L100,000 CP.

With the same striking views as the better hotels along this strip, this pensione-style villa has a garden, 23 rooms (no a/c)—get the ones facing the sea—a restaurant and a sunning terrace. MAP required Aug. Closed Nov.–Feb.

Where to Eat

Don Alfonso $$–$$$ ★★★★★

P. Sant' Agata in Sant' Agata sui Due Golfi; ☎ *(081) 878-0026, FAX 533-0226.*
Closed Mon.–Tues. (Mon. only, June–Sept. 30) and mid-Jan.–Feb.; reservation recommended. Fixed-price meals L75–100,000. À la carte L50–130,000.

For one of Italy's most acclaimed restaurants (three stars from Michelin), you need travel only 10 km, 6 mi. south of Sorrento on SS 145 to the stunningly situated village of Sant' Agata sui Due Golfi. The menu is created according to seasonal ingredients, many from the owner's farm. The wine cellar is good. A table can choose one of two degustazione menus, traditional or innovative, or you can order à la carte. Along with the traditional antipasti, there's foie gras with walnuts and hazelnuts, and in addition to a sublime gnocchetti, there's oyster risotto; then choose from lobster salad, lamb or rabbit in herbs, and stuffed calamari. In summer, there is garden dining. There are 3 suites (single L160,000 CP, double L250,000 CP) for those who don't want to travel after feasting.

La Favorita O' Parrucchiano $–$$ ★★★

Corso Italia 71; ☎ *878-1321.*
Closed Wed. in off-season; reservation recommended. Meals L30–55,000.

In the center of Sorrento, this is the place for Neapolitan specialties. You can enjoy a stupendous antipasto table with marinated and stuffed vegetables and seafood salads, as well as the Sorrentine's favorite pasta, gnocchi (potato dumplings), and all manner of seafood. Not only is the food good, the garden dining is delightful.

La Lanterna Mare $$ ★★

V. Marina Grande 44; ☎ *807-3033.*
Closed Jan.–Feb. & Mon., except July–Aug. Meals L45–70,000.

This pleasing restaurant, with al fresco dining in season, is a good choice for vegetable and seafood antipasti and a hearty meal of fish soup.

Snacks

In the medieval Via Pieta is the vast **La Stalla** (#30; evenings only; moderate), a pizzeria where you share long wooden tables and listen to live music. We enjoyed the pasta chitarra with fresh tomatoes and mozzarella more than the pizza. Or plan a picnic—the shops along Via Cesarea and the **Salumeria** at Corso Italia 63, have the necessary provisions.

Directory

Telephone Code 081   **Postal Code 80067**

Airport

In Capodichino (☎ *081-709-2815*), outside Naples, with bus connections to Sorrento.

American Express

Acampara Travel, *P. Angelina Lauro 13* (☎ *878-4800*).

Bus

Local: Along Corso Italia to Punta di Capo. **Pullman**: From stazione, SITA buses run to Amalfi (1.5 hrs) and Salerno; CITAL to Rome's Tiburtina station.

Car Rentals

Sorrento *(Corso Italia 210/A;* ☎ *878-1386);* or at Naples airport and stazione centrale.

Ferries

Marina Piccola, below the Villa Comune park (elevator and road access). Aliscafi *(Alilauro,* ☎ *807-3024; FAX 807-2009)* and ferries *(Caremar,* ☎ *807-3077; FAX 807-2479)* to Capri and Naples year-round; to Ischia, in season.

Groceries

Salumeria, *Corso 63;* wine shops and fruit stalls along V. Cesarea.

Parking

Around edge of town and one block south of P. Tasso, off V. Fuorimura.

Post Office

Corso Italia 210.

Shopping

Wood inlaid furniture, corner of P. Tasso and Fuorimura.

Taxis

P. Tasso or dial ☎ *878-2204.*

Telephones

Telcom, P. Tasso, 9 a.m.–1 p.m., 4-9 p.m.

Tourist Information

AAST, *V. Luigi di Maio (*☎ *807-4033; FAX 877-3397)*, inside the Bar dei Forestieri. Open 8:30 a.m.–2 p.m., 4–7 p.m.; July-Sept. 8:30 a.m.–12:30 p.m., 4:30–8 p.m. closed Sun.

Tours

Many agenzie di viaggio, clustered in the center, offer tours to Paestum, Pompeii, etc.

Trains

Stazione, Corso Italia, a few blocks east of P. Tasso, for the Circumvesuviana to Pompeii (half-hour), Ercolano (Herculaneum, 45 min.), and Naples (1 hour).

Excursions

Around Naples Bay

The great classical sights around the Bay of Naples and its extension to the west, the Bay of Pozzuoli, include some of the great ruins of the Greco-Roman world. We can only wonder what has been lost when we consider that the ancient cities of Herculaneum and Pompeii were quite minor settlements in their own time. The imperial family had villas not at Herculaneum, but at Baia and thereabouts on the opposite side, and Augustus actually enjoyed his time at the one he built on Capri. The most important Roman port was also across the bay at Puteoli, or today's Pozzuoli, not at Pompeii. Virgil lived at Neapolis, or Naples, and Pliny wrote from his naval station at Misenum. Even in pre-Roman times, it seems that the Greeks might have been kept to this far away side of the bay, near the Phlegrean Fields, for evidence shows that the local Pompeiian peoples were allied with the Etruscans, not the Greeks, and Herculaneum may have been founded as late as the 4th–century B.C., perhaps by the local Samnites, and not the Greeks either. But even if Pompeii and Herculaneum were not the great Roman or Greek cities of their time, their tragic preservation under the ash and lava of Vesuvius' eruption has left the modern world its most vivid picture of life then.

These excursions can be made from either Sorrento or Naples, although some are slightly more convenient from one than from the other. Dining facilities are more often touristy than fabulous, so you might bring a lunch with you. But a visit to the islands can be for a day of relaxation by the sea, or longer, as the facilities are excellent. Caserta, actually off the bay, can be visited on your way to and from Naples, as well as on a special excursion.

Pompeii

... the courtyard on which his room opened was being choked by a rising layer of cinders and ash, so that if he delayed any longer it would have become impossible to escape ... They discussed whether to remain in the house or go outside. The walls of the house were swaying with repeated violent shocks, and seemed to move in one direction and then another, as if shifted from their foundations. Nevertheless they dreaded the rain of pumice stones, though small and light, in the open air.

Pliny the Younger
(As translated by Joseph Jay Deiss in *Herculaneum*)

On that August day in A.D. 79 more than 17 feet of ash rained down on Pompeii, burying the city of 20,000 for centuries. Initially, some citizens returned, looking for lost loved ones, definitely digging through ash for valuables left behind, and perhaps themselves getting caught in the final devastation of Vesuvius' eruption. Most escaped, but Pompeii didn't. Covered and forgotten, it wasn't until 1748 that the town was rediscovered. Since then excavations have continued until today, exposing 100 of the walled city's 163 acres frozen in a moment of time. Once again, sunlight strikes the snack bars and bakeries lining the Via Abbondanza, the main street, as well as the gardens of private homes. Town walls proclaim political campaign slogans and announce gladitorial contests. Home interiors are richly painted with mythological scenes, and brothel ceilings are decorated with erotic ones. From the most public squares to the busiest streets still screeching of commerce with their rutted pavements, and still splashing water with their pedestrian stepping stones, Pompeii reveals itself—a provincial city involved in the thriving commerce created by the great Roman port at what is now Pozzuoli. From its theaters and large amphitheater (the only one this side of the bay), from its many bars, inns and brothels, Pompeii shows how people from surrounding towns came here for weekends of gladiatorial bloodbaths and debauchery. But it is from their homes that the Pompeiians speak most intimately, the windowless facades protecting the cherished privacy of their innermost recesses adorned with a *lararium*, or altar to household gods. For the wealthier, a Greek-style peristyle, or cloister, surrounds tranquil family gardens. All that is missing is the Pompeiians themselves; only those luckless few remain, eternally captured in their death throes by the plaster casts formed of rain and Vesuvian ash.

What to See and Do

Pompeii Ruins   ★★★

While much of the art as well as the housewares and jewelry are in the National Archaeology Museum in Naples, there is much left here to see. The west, or Porta Marina, entrance is the most frequently used, and a short walk takes you to the edge of the ★★**Forum** with the Basilica of Justice (2nd century B.C.), the largest building in Pompeii on your right, and the pre-Roman ★**Temple of Apollo** on your left (statues of Diana and Apollo are copies). At the north end is the ★**Temple of Jupiter** flanked by two triumphal arches. Dominating this public square, the best preserved outside of Rome, is villainous Vesuvius. Although the scale after Rome is definitely provincial, there is an immediacy to this Forum, perhaps provided by the traces of its market functions along its west (now with exhibits) and east sides. Also on the east side is the **Temple del Genio di Augustus** (begun A.D. 69), enclosing a ★carved marble altar where bulls were sacrificed. Next door was the wool market with carved marble door. From the mix of buildings, it's easy to conclude that the Forum was the true heart of the city, for religion and government as well as commerce. From here, it is easy to orient yourself for a visit to the site. Running off the east side is the main street of Via Abbondanza, leading to important public buildings, and off the northside, Via di Mercurio, leading to some of the most important houses and villas.

Down Via Abbondanza, you soon turn right to the ★★**Foro Trianguolo**, an older, irregular section of the city with a small Doric temple (6th century B.C., dating from when the Hellenized city was under Etruscan, not Greek, influence). From here you enter a shady forum, then turn left into the picturesque ★**Teatro Grande** (2nd century B.C.). At the end of the forum, you can look over into the **Gladiators Barracks** and then walk down to the ★**Odeon**, or formerly covered theater (80 B.C.), built by the Romans. Left up V. Stabiana you'll see a Roman ★**Temple of Isidis** (Isis) to the left, but to the right, at the end, is the ★**Casa di Menandro**, a rich, two-story home with its own baths, elaborate lararium, or shrine, and frescoed peristyle in the rear. Turning left, you again reach Abbondanza. Around this intersection are walls covered with slogans, chariot ruts in the street, a *thermopolium*, or snack bar much like the ones seen throughout Italy today, and the nearby **baker's shop** and home of Paquis Proculus, whose compelling portrait with his wife is in the Naples museum. Since both of these are to the right, you can just continue beyond them. At the right turn for the amphitheater, continue straight on Abbondanza and visit the ★**Casa di Loreius Tiburtinus** (the first on your right) with its elaborate frescoes of scenes from the *Iliad* (off the loggia), as well as the ★**Villa Giulia Felice** (last on right), perhaps an inn, and still retaining its lovely peristyle and gardens. Now turn right off Abbondanza and head down to the **Amphitheater** (begun 80 B.C.), that attracted 12,000 spectators and much business to Pompeii. Next to it is the **Palestra**, where the youths of town exercised. Passing the Palestra, then right and left onto Abbondanza, you are heading back toward the Forum, but just before it you'll find the ★★**Terme Stabiane** (V. Stabiana and Abbondanza). The men's baths are found through the first door on the right, with marble floors and stucco ceiling; the women's dressing rooms are at the far end on the right. After the baths, Vicolo di Lupanari leads off to the brothel district.

Back in the Forum, you can follow Via di Mercurio to some of the most elaborate homes of Pompeii. The ★★**Casa dei Vettii** (turn *right onto Vicolo di Mercurio, then left on V. Vettii*), a wealthy merchant's home, is one of the most interesting to visit in Pompeii because of its excellent condition (reconstructed) and lavish frescoes. (Note those on right of peristyle.) Upon leaving, turn right, then left, and then another left for the **Casa del Fauno** (House of the Faun), one of the largest in Pompeii, with two atriums and two peristyles. But its fame rests on its art, especially the Alexandrian mosaic, now in the Naples museum. Leaving here, walk right to the end, then turn right up Via Consolare to what was the main gate, and exit the walled city. You pass along a lane lined with cypress and tombs, go through a ticket booth, then turn right to the ★★**Villa dei Misteri** (just over a five-minute walk from central Pompeii). A room of this villa is beautifully painted with a nearly life-size initiation rite into the secret cult of Dionysus—the exhausted, sometimes frightened expression of the bride is haunting, and the modeling and rich color make it one of the great Roman paintings (1st–century B.C.). To find it, walk along the outside of the house with the road on your right, then enter the last door.

The ruins are open 9 a.m. until 1 hour before sunset (in Jan. till 3 p.m., June till 7 p.m., exit 1 hour later). In 1996 the ruins were closed Sun. & holidays, but call the tourist office to see if protests have reversed this cost-cutting measure. Admission fee L12,000. Cafe in shady grove near west entrance; pricey cafeteria just off north side of Forum. Off-season, you may need to ask to guard to open some homes you wish to visit (no tip required).

Pompeii Terzo Millennio (*V. Plinio near entrance to ruins; weekdays 8:30 a.m.–7:30 p.m. in summer, shorter hours off-season; fee*) is a 25-minute film with a computer simulation of the final days of Pompeii. It plays continuously in five languages.

Foro Trianguolo at Pompeii dates from the 6th century B.C.

Where to Eat

Cafes and simple trattorias, even a few simple hotels, can be found in and around the two entrances to the ruins, but you might just want to settle for a simple sandwich, and make plans to stay elsewhere overnight. There's nothing worthwhile here except the ruins.

Directory

Tourist Information

In the piazzas near the two main entrances are kiosks with maps of the ruins (☎ *[081] 861-0913; FAX 8632-1101; closed Sun.).*

Arriving

By car on A-3 or by the Naples-Sorrento Circumvesuviana train (about a half hour from either city; Pompeii Villa dei Misteri stop), you arrive almost in front of the Porta Marina entrance to the ruins, 28 km (17 mi.) from Sorrento, 24 km from Naples. By the Naples-Salerno FS or the Circumvesuviano Naples-Poggiomarino (get off at Pompeii Santuario), you have a brief walk to the Porta di Nucera entrance near the amphitheater.

Festivals

July–Sept. classical concerts take place in the Teatro Grande.

Herculaneum

Only six square blocks of Herculaneum (*Ercolano* in Italian) have been excavated against Pompeii's vast acreages, and these have been excavated only since 1927 rather than over centuries. An aristocratic seaside resort and fishing village of under 5000, Herculaneum was buried not under ash, but rather mud avalanches that effectively sealed the town in solidified muck sometimes 85 feet deep. In the 18th century, tunnels were dug down to the fabulous suburban Villa dei Papiri (still submerged, but its library of 2000 carbonized papyrus scrolls and elaborate peristyle sculptures are in the Naples museum) that inspired the Getty Museum in California. Despite its early rediscovery, Herculaneum lay inaccessible. Instead of the picks and shovels used at Pompeii, power saws, compressed-air drills, bulldozers and the most modern excavating technology have been necessary to expose the site. Then, too, a modern town has limited the extent of the digging, and the pyroclastic flow forced the sea to recede and has left a towering wall separating the ancient settlement from its former marina. It is under this marina that the skeletons of 150 residents were discovered as recently as 1980, found in family groups, clinging to each other as they and their town were obliterated on the second day of Vesuvius' eruption:

*[There]...loomed a horrible black cloud, ripped by sudden bursts
of fire, writhing snakelike and revealing sudden flashes larger
than lightning...*

**Pliny the Younger
(Translated by Joseph Jay Deiss)**

The mud may have delayed excavations. The modern town may prevent all
of Herculaneum from being known—no temples have been found, or even
brothels, and the theater is presently inaccessible. Excavations continue, but
what has been exposed already is even better preserved than at Pompeii.
Nothing was stolen from the site, so that jewelry and money and valued possessions were left untouched. The fiery mud slide carbonized and preserved
wood beams, wood furniture and storage bins; it left the houses intact with
their two stories, their balconies, and picturesque overhanging roofs. From
the grain in the storage vats to the flowers in the garden and the undamaged
bronze statuary in the peristyles, Herculaneum has vividly revealed the details of daily life. Not a commercial town, its streets aren't rutted. Better
planned, perhaps, than Pompeii, its drainage system made pedestrian stepping stones unnecessary. Wealthier than Pompeii, its houses are more sumptuous, often with finer frescoes, mosaics and statuary, and their gardens have
been accurately recreated. Not surprisingly, Herculaneum is preferred over
Pompeii by many travelers.

What to See and Do

Herculaneum Ruins   ★★★

As at Pompeii, the bronzes and valuables have been removed to the Museo Archeologico in Naples, and often have been replaced with copies here. But it is quite easy
to spend more than two hours exploring the fascinating and often lovely details of
the many homes and few public areas. Your best orientation is along the entrance
path that overlooks the site. Immediately below you is the Palestra. Running north
and south are three long streets (the carda, numbered V, IV and III) and across
them are the Decumanus Maximus, on the north where excavations are just beginning to explore a forum at the foot of the modern town, and the Decumanus Inferior. To the south, and no longer visible, was the marina.

The entrance path now takes you into the town on its southwest side at Cardo III.
There are houses here with peristyles and mosaics, but the first one on your right is
the largest at the site, if not in the best condition. Just a block ahead, turn right onto
the Decumanus Inferior, with the men's baths and gym running a full block on your
left. A left onto Carda IV takes you to the **★Casa Sannitica**, a Samnite house with
a traditional atrium and carved oculus. Across the street, you can enter the **Men's
Baths** (c. A.D. 1), continuing almost back to Cardo III, where you descend marble
steps to the circular and domed frigidarium (cold water bath). Back on Carda IV,
you enter the **★Women's Baths** at #8, also well preserved even down to the original
glass window. There are numerous buildings opposite, preserving such antique rar-

ities as carbonized furniture, but the ★ ★ **Casa di Nettuno ed Anfitrite** is the most remarkable. From the street, furniture can be seen in its exposed second-story room, and below is a well-preserved shop retaining even a coil of rope. Inside, in the rear of the house, is the brilliantly colored wall mosaic that gives the house its name, as well as a mosaic covered nymphaneum. At the present end of Cardo IV is the Decumanus Maximus, with the usual public well, or fountain, at the intersection. While excavations are beginning to explore buildings on the north side, turning right, you pass shops on the south. Straight ahead is the ★ **Palestra**, used for public games and graced with a bronze fountain, but the entrance is at the Decumanus Inferior on Cardo V. Heading down Cardo V, you'll see many shops, including a *pistrinum*, or bakery (at #8), complete with grinding mills and pans. Below the Decumanus Inferior are other shops and houses; the ★ **Casa dei Cervi** (#21), or House of the Deer, is one of Herculaneum's most elegant. The rear peristyle has become a garden surrounded by enclosed corridors. The center room was used for summer dining with views over the sea (now there's the lava-like wall). In a room to the left is a lewd statue of a drunken Hercules. But if you have little time, you should schedule in our last block early in your visit because Cardo IV below the Decumanus Inferior has some of the finest homes. The facades at ★ #11 (with a lovely covered atrium, too) and the balconied ★ #3 are in superb condition, and #2, the ★ ★ **House of the Atrium Mosaic**, has not only a grand tufa-buckled geometric mosaic, but also a fine peristyle and garden.

Open 9 a.m.–one hour before sunset (in Jan. 3 p.m., June till 7 p.m., exit 1 hour later). There are places near the entrance gate for a snack, but why not bring a sandwich with you? **Tip:** *In the off-season in particular, you may need to request the guards to open some buildings. Admission fee L12,000.*

Excursions to Vesuvius

The Solfatara Crater, Mt. Etna in Sicily, and Vesuvius are the only active volcanos in Europe. Granted that Vesuvius last erupted in 1944, the smoking volcano is merely dormant, not harmless, as a visit to its crater will convince you. (Best on a clear day for views of the bay). You can exit A-3 at the "Vesuvius"signs near Torre del Greco, or you can take a blue SITA bus from the Circumvesuviana train stop in Ercolano, to a point marked for the crater. From there, it is about a 45-minute walk on a path to the summit (fee for requisite guide to top and around the crater).

Practical Tips

Arriving

The modern town of Ercolano is reached by the exit of the same name from A-3, 10 km (6 mi.) from Naples, 42 km (26 mi.) from Sorrento, and 14 km from the Pompeii exit. The Circumvesuviano train from Naples (20 minutes) to Sorrento (40 minutes) provides frequent and rapid service, and drops you off about a 10-minute walk from the ruins (just walk downhill). By car or train, follow signs for *Scavi di Ercolano* to reach the ruins. Pay parking is to the left of the entrance.

Phlegrean Fields

Everything about the Phlegrean Fields (*Campi Flegrei* in Italian), or those flaming fields of Homeric myths, sounds terrific. The fire and brimstone, the smoking earth of the ancient underworld, are still recalled by the landscape west of Naples around the Bay of Pozzuoli. Seismic shakes called bradyseism submerge ancient pillars only to shake them to the surface again, this time covered with the shells and telltale marks of life under the sea (at the **Serapeum** in **Pozzuoli**). Here too, is the mysterious cave of the Cumae Sibyl, the sybaritic spas of the Romans at Baia. But you can comb this territory, digging into reminders of the classical world, and your discoveries seldom measure up to the effort required. Naples has sprawled here, too. The baths (called temples) and amphitheaters have to be tracked down in congested towns. **Lake Avernus**, the entrance to Hades, can hardly divert your attention from the surrounding traffic jams. Our advice is to save your time for the previously described sights, but if you're still in the exploring mood, then the trip to Cumae and Solfatara can be recommended—both are sufficiently untouched to brush you with the past. And with a car, you might also drive down to the rocky cape of Misenum, still scenic and once the Roman naval port where the two Plinys initially witnessed the eruption of Vesuvius.

Solfatara ★

Although modern apartments have been built on part of the rim, the Solfatara Crater is the best preserved part of the Phlegrean Fields. A shady park provides the entrance, then a marked path leads you around the crater of this semi-dormant volcano on safe but spongy ground. All around you is a hellish landscape of chalky ashy, eerie smoke holes and vile sulfurous fumes. You literally walk on bubbling earth and pass pits of boiling water. This is all that's left of Homer's inspiration—and it's enough. *The park is open 9 a.m.–1 hour before sunset; L5500; picnic grounds and cafe, parking inside gate.* **Arriving:** The Ferrovia Cumana train (departure from Montesanto funicular, near P. Dante) goes to Pozzuoli, and Solfatara is about 1 km away. By car, exit the tangeziale west at Agnano Terme, and follow signs to Pozzuoli. Solfatara is 1 km on SS 7 before Pozzuoli, on your right, about 11 km, 7 mi. from Naples. If you visit **Pozzuoli**, you'll see one of the largest extant Roman amphitheaters at the entrance to town. The Serapeum (see above) really an ancient market place, is down by the port.

Cumae ★

Now called Cuma in Italian, this ancient town was one of the first Greek settlements in Italy, founded c. 750 B.C. It is a place of tremendous appeal, with ruins scattered on a majestic site, forested and tranquil with views over the sea. Here at the park is the ★ **Sibyl's Cave** (6th–5th-century B.C.), a trapezoidal gallery hewn out of the rock and ending in a three-niched cave where the prophetess spoke to Aeneas. Walking through the gallery even today, you can imagine the mystery of the spot when enclosed by ancient darkness. The sibyl was one of the two most venerated oracles in the classical world. Following steps above the cave, you can visit temple

Capri

ruins on the acropolis and look over the farms below that now certainly cover the ancient city. *Open 9 a.m.–2 hours before sunset; L4000; parking.* **Arriving:** Ferrovia Cumana trains (departure Naples from Montesanto funicolar, near P. Dante) bring you to Fusaro (35 minutes) and a 15-minute bus ride to the ruins. The tangenziale exit at Lake Averno takes you to SS 7 and the nearby ruins, (just before the ruins you pass the **Arco Felice** on the ancient road built at the time of Domitian). Or you can follow SS 7 from Solfatara and Pozzuoli. Naples is 16 km, 10 mi. east.

Capri

Only several miles long, less than a few wide, the island of Capri may be small, but its beauty is legendary. Grottos and natural rock formations form its east coast; mountains and donkey paths cover most of its interior. Fragrant, semi-tropical vegetation transforms it into the paradise Lucifer is said to have stolen and planted here. Such beauty attracted Augustus, who bartered Ischia for Capri from the Neapolitans. And his successor Tiberius retired here, according to Tacitus, to lead a life of debauchery and eccentricity. Other eccentrics have followed over the centuries, as well as ordinary folk, so that it is now an international resort. Visitors walk the countryside looking for remnants of Tiberius' Villa Jovis or visit fabulous villas like that at San Michele, or simply take a boat trip to the Grotta Azzurra (Blue Grotto), or a bus to the swimming at the rocky Marina Piccola. You can come for the day or stay for months, but if it's relaxation you want, avoid July and August.

Where to Stay

The fame of Capri makes for numerous distinguished hotels, but few inexpensive ones. And few remain open in the off-season, from November to Easter. Because of the steep cliffs of the island, the hotels are found considerably above the sea, most near the picturesque town of Capri.

Grand Hotel Quisisana   **L350–650,000 CP**   ★★★★★

V. Camerelle 2; ☎ *837-0788, FAX 837-6080. Open Easter–Oct.*
Single L350,000 CP. Double L400–650,000 CP.
This is the grand dame of all the hotels, dating from the 19th century. Located in the center of the town of Capri, the Quisisana still commands sea views and envelops its privacy in extensive interior gardens. The marble lobby is opulent, the 150 rooms have all modern conveniences. Restaurant, popular terrace cafe, American bar. Pool. Tennis. Sauna.

Scalinatella   **L440–650,000 CP**   ★★★★

V. Tragara 8; ☎ *837-0633, FAX 837-8291. Open mid-Mar.–Nov.*
Single L440,000 CP. Double L500–650,000 CP.
This splendidly tasteful villa contains 28 rooms, many with two baths, plus terraces and grand views. Breakfast terrace, lounge, gardens, small pool.

Punta Tragara   **L315–500,000 CP**   ★★★★

V. Tragara 57; ☎ *837-0844, FAX 837-7790. Open Easter–late Oct.*
Single L315,000 CP. Double L430–500,000 CP.

Terraced into the cliffs, this former villa offers 33 suites, all enjoying panoramic views from either a private terrace or balcony. There also are 10 lovely rooms (expensive). Fine restaurant, breakfast terraces, lounge, gardens, whirlpool, pool.

Villa Brunella   **L295,000**   √★★

V. Tragara 24; ☎ *837-0122, FAX 837-0430. Open mid-Mar.–Nov.*
Single/double L295,000.
A tranquil inn that has sea views, 18 rooms, gardens, restaurant and small pool.

Villa Sarah   **L140–240,000 CP**   ★★★

V. Tiberio 3/a; ☎ *837-7817, FAX 837-7215. Easter–Oct.*
Single L140,000. Double 240,000 CP.
This hotel has a lovely, quiet park setting and 20 rooms (no a/c), with views from the hill leading to Tiberius' villa.

Florida   **L100–130,000**   ★

V. Fuorlovado 34; ☎ *837-0710, FAX 837-0040. Open Mar.–Nov.*
Single L100,000. Double L130,000.
There are 19 rooms (no a/c) in this plain, comfortable hotel with a fine garden, breakfast terrace and access to pool (fee).

Where to Eat

Unless otherwise indicated, the restaurants are located in or around the picturesque village of Capri.

La Capannina   **$$–$$$**   ★★★

V. Le Botteghe 14; reserve at ☎ *837-0732, FAX 837-6990.*
Closed mid Nov.–mid Mar., Wed. except in Aug. Meals L60–85,000.
One of Capri's most popular dining spots offers gardens and superb service to complement its ravioli alla caprese (cheese filled and fried), its fresh stuffed anchovies and zuppa di pesce.

La Savardina-Da Eduardo   **$**   ★★

V. Lo Capo 8; reserve at ☎ *837-6300.*
Call for off-season closings. Meals L30–50,000.
Near Tiberius' Villa Jovis dine in a lovely citrus grove on vegetable antipasti and pastas, followed by seafood. An incredible bargain for both the food and the setting. Credit cards: None.

Buca di Baco-Da Serafina   **$–$$**   ★★

V. Longano 25; ☎ *837-0723.*
Closed Wed. & Nov. Meals L25–60,000. Pizza L8–12,000.
Near the main piazza, this small restaurant stokes up its wood ovens at night and serves the best pizza in Capri on long, shared tables. There is also a full trattoria menu for lunch and dinner.

Canzone del Mare   **$$–$$$**   ★★

Marina Piccola; ☎ *837-0104, FAX 837-0341.*
Closed Nov.–Easter and evenings. Fixed-price meal L70–80,000. À la carte L65–110,000.
Down by the sea is this stylish bathing club with its own pool and beautiful restaurant by the sea.

Snacks

Up around the main Piazza Umberto in Capri, you must spend part of your time nursing a drink or snack at one of the four cafes. And shop for a picnic at the gourmet deli of **La Capannina**.

Directory

Telephone Code 081   **Postal Code 80073**

Tourist Information

P. Umberto 19 (☎ 837-0686) and at dock, Marina Grande *(☎ 837-0634).*

Getting Around

You'll have little use for a car here (they're often banned in peak season) and buses ply the few roads that can be driven, from Marina Grande to Capri and from Capri to Marina Piccola and to Anacapri. Also there is a beautiful funicular from Marina Grande to Capri, and there are taxis and boats for tours.

Arriving

Marina Grande, on the north side of the island, is the main ferry and hydrofoil port. The better hotels have representatives meet you to take your luggage; official porters also are available. • Ferries cost less than hydrofoils and take twice as long: Caremar *(☎ 837-0700)* has ferries to Naples' Molo Beverello (1.5 hours) and Sorrento (45 minutes); Navigazione Libera del Golfo *(☎ 837-0819)* has ferries to Naples, Sorrento, and Jun.–Sept. to Ischia (1.5 hours). Caremar also has *aliscafi*, hydrofoils, to Naples (45 minutes); Alilauro *(☎ 837-6995)* and SNAV *(☎ 837-7577)* have aliscafi to Mergellina in Naples as well as Sorrento (30 minutes). Also, in season, there is service to Positano and Amalfi that permits one-day excursions; and hydrofoil service from Fumicino near Rome's airport *(Medmar ☎ [06] 858-767).*

Seasons

Capri functions Easter until early Nov.; its highest hotel prices and its most frequent boat connections are June–September and Easter.

Ischia

Perhaps suffering from Augustus' ancient rejection, Ischia remained a very local spot, industriously producing some of the best wine of the region and fishing the blue-green waters of the seas. Occasionally, writers from afar, such as Ibsen, would come for the thermal baths and warm muds of its spas, and other visitors would rent villas for summer stays. Although not yet caught up to the neighboring island of Capri, Ischia is shedding some of its much vaunted simplicity. A volcanic island of 18 square miles and still bubbling with sulfurous springs for its spas, Ischia now offers fancy boutiques and luxurious accommodations, especially at the chic spa of Lacco Ameno and the main harbor and settlement of Porto Ischia. You can take boat tours around the island, pulling into wine centers such as Florio, and swim at the sandy beaches of picturesque Sant'Angelo. You can drive through the pine groves searching out spas and grand views of the sea. And certainly, you'll want to visit the magnificent **Castello Aragone** *(closed Jan.–Mar.)* at Porto Ischia, crossing the bridge to the 15th century Spanish fortress island that stands where the ancient Greeks before them built theirs.

Where to Stay

Regina Isabella e Royal Sporting L320–650,000 CP ★★★★★

80076 Lacco Ameno; ☎ *994-322, FAX 900-190. Open mid Apr.–mid Oct.*
Single L320,000 CP. Double L340,000 CP (Reginella)–L650,000 CP.
The most luxurious hotel has entertained royalty and movie stars at its spa and in its extensive gardens. Along with 133 impressive rooms, some with spectacular views, and the restaurant and elegant lounges, are a private beach, 3 pools, sauna, gym and tennis. The hotel owns **La Reginella** *(*☎ *994-300, FAX 980-481)* across the piazza from it, where you stay for less but still have access to many of the facilities.

Grand Hotel Punta Molino L315–650,000 CP ★★★★

80077 Ischia Porto, Lungomare Cristofo Colombo 25; ☎ *991-544, FAX 991-562.*
Open mid-Apr.–Oct.
Single L315,000. Double L650,000 CP.
Convenient to the marina, this former villa sits most delightfully in a park overlooking the sea. There are 80 rooms, restaurant, bar, 2 pools (1 thermal; 1 indoors), tennis and gym.

San Montano L235–310,000 CP ★★★

80076 Lacco Ameno; ☎ *994-033, FAX 980-242. Open Apr.–Oct.*
Single L235,000 CP. Double L310,000 CP.
On a hill above the bay, this pleasing resort has 65 rooms, many with views. Restaurant and bar, 2 pools (1 thermal); tennis and sauna.

San Michele L100–165,000 ★★

80070 Sant'Angelo; ☎ *992-276, FAX 999-149. Apr.–Oct.*
Single L100,000. Double L165,000.
More in keeping with an older Ischia is the southern fishing village of Sant'Angelo. This hotel is a good place to enjoy the tranquility and views; there are 50 rooms (no a/c), a restaurant, garden and pool, as well as thermal waters.

Where to Eat

Giardini Eden $$–$$$ ★★★

V. Nuova Porta Romana; reserve at ☎ *993-090.*
Closed dinner & Oct.–May. Meals L60–85,000.
A mile east at Ischia Ponte, near the castle, are the cliffside gardens and fabulous views of this restaurant. The seafood and pasta are wonderful.

Gennaro $$ ★★★

V. Porto 66; ☎ *992-917.*
Closed Tues. (except July–Aug.) & Oct.–Easter (except Christmas season). Meals L50–65,000.
Lining the waterfront of the Porto Ischia are many trattorias, but none better than Gennaro.

Da Peppina $–$$ ★★

V. Bocca 23 in Forio; ☎ *998-312.*

Caserta

Closed Nov.–Feb., at lunch & Wed. except June–Sept. Meals L35–55,000.

On the western part of the island, Peppina's has a terrace overlooking the sea and the village of Forio, with its churches and towers. Much of the food comes from the owners' farm and there are grilled meats and rabbit to enjoy.

Directory

Telephone Code 081

Tourist Information

V. Jasolino at Porto Ischia (☎ 991-146).

Getting Around

Boat tours, buses, taxis and cheaper mini taxis (motorbike driven), and car rentals are all available.

Arriving

Ferries from Naple's Molo Beverello (1.5 hours) on Caremar (☎ 991-781) and to Capri (1.5 hours) only Jun.–Sept. on Libera del Golfo (☎ 984-028); aliscafi to Naples' Mergellina (40 minutes) on SNAV (☎ 991-215) and Alilauro (☎ 991-888).

Seasons

Apr.–Oct. is the tourist season, but peak hotel prices and most frequent boat service occur June–Sept.

Caserta

Really inland rather than part of the bay, Caserta is famous for the ★ **Reggia di Caserta**, the 18th-century Bourbon palace and gardens called the "Versailles of Italy." Built for Charles III by Luigi Vanvitelli, the neoclassical palace (1752-74) is one of the largest in Europe, with 1200 rooms. From the magnificent octagonal vestibule, follow the grand staircase up to the many sumptuous and marble rich *appartamenti* of the Bourbons. (Guided visits to other areas, including the Teatro di Corte and Palatine Chapel, take place on school holidays, Mon.–Sat. before 11 a.m.) But it is actually the formal ★ **park**, also designed by Vanvitelli and also much inspired by Versailles, that brings the crowds. The 250 acres of gardens are arranged around a one-kilometer long avenue that runs from the rear of the palace, proceeds past pools and fountains of mythological creatures, and ends at a great waterfall where marble figures of Diana and Acteon and others hunt and run over the rocks. To the right of this fountain is the entrance to the English Garden, quite romantic and arranged around ruins and a small lake. Up and above the Diana waterfall is a great viewpoint, reached by steps. To take best advantage of the gardens, pay for the bus that runs the avenue almost to the waterfall. Get off when the sculpture fountains begin, saving your energy for strolls in the **English Garden** or climbs to the viewpoint (last entrance to both, an hour before closing). *Open 9 a.m.–1:30 p.m., till 7 p.m. July–Oct., except Sun. till 12:30 p.m. (2 p.m. in summer) for the appartamenti; the park closes at* *dusk (3 p.m. in winter) and the waterfalls may be operating only 11 a.m.–3 p.m.; admission to palace L8000, grounds L4000.*

What to Eat

Although there's a cafe near the waterfall, you might want to bring a picnic with you. Two blocks toward the center of town is the convenient **Paninoteca Losfizio**—try the eggplant and tomato panino, or sandwich. In the town center, **Antica Locanda Massa** *(V. Massini 55; closed Sun. dinner, Fri., part of Aug.;* ☎ *321-268; meals L45–60,000)* is a good choice.

Practical Tips

Arriving

By train from Naple's stazione, or by bus from P. Porta Capuana (1 hour). The palace is across a vast square from the stazione and bus stop. By car, exit Caserta Nord from A-2 (28 km, 17 mi. from Naples; 200 km, 124 mi. from Rome), then continue 2 km to the "reggia." Parking across street.

On the Road

The Amalfi Coast

From Sorrento south to Salerno, the Littari mountains and the sea create one of the world's most dramatic coastlines. The limestone cliffs survive in their primordial state as mysterious massifs rising from the sea. More often, their rocky surface has been wind-and water-carved into stalagmite formations, or hand cut into terraces of Andean intensity for groves of lemon and olive trees, bougainvillea and nopal cactus. Medieval villages such as Amalfi and Ravello, graced by the churches and palazzi created in the local Byzantine-Moorish style, have wedged their way into the mountains. Promontories carry watch towers built by 9th-century Arab pirates. Through this extraordinary setting threads the ★★★**Strada Amalfiana**, winding its way like a narrow ribbon up and down the mountains, tunneling its way through the sandstone at times, dipping to the Mediterranean-blue sea streaked with turquoise, pausing at tiny, but nonetheless world-famous resorts such as Positano, and passing that of Vietri, where all manner of majolica ceramics are made and sold. After Salerno, the mountains retreat, the flat peninsula continues to stretch south, and a highway serves fine where before only a great engineering feat would do. But if the scenery doesn't carry you on, the promise of Greek ruins at Paestum might.

Practical Tips

The Amalfi Coast is just 50 km, 31 mi. long, and the addition of Paestum is only another 35 km, 22 mi. The trip is often made in a day, with a return to Naples or Sorrento by the faster autostrada route of A-3. Regular buses from Sorrento and Naples ply the Strada Amalfiano (SS 163) with stops at Positano, Amalfi and Salerno, but you have to pick up local buses to Ravello and Paestum. Many people rent a car in Naples or Sorrento for the drive, pulling into the charming towns to eat and explore, staying overnight at some of the excellent accommodations available. The region certainly warrants the more relaxed pace.

Driving

The Amalfi Drive is narrow, and on its most southern stretch, occasionally without guard rails. Oncoming cars, especially oncoming buses, seem ready to push you into mountain or sea as they round hairpin curves. Not only should you drive carefully, using your horn at blind spots, but you might want to plan a drive at offhours, during lunchtime, say, and certainly not during weekends in July and August.

Reaching the Strada Amalfiana

The road is not clearly marked until you are well on it. You definitely don't want to follow signs to Salerno, which are always for the autostrada A-3, as are the Amalfi signs on occasion. Positano is a safer destination to look for, as it can be reached only by the Amalfi Drive. From Naples, follow A-3 to Castellamare (25 km, 15.5 mi.), then continue toward Sorrento until you see the sign for Meta (about 20 km, 12 mi. from Castellamare; 7 km from Sorrento). From Sorrento, you have the additional option of first driving south to Sant'Agata sui Due Golfi and then following signs to Positano from there—you'll soon pick up the Amalfi Drive.

Seasons

High season and high prices are encountered June into September as well as around Christmas and Holy Week. But spring and fall are popular times too, so reserve in advance.

Positano

This resort village is so dramatically crowded by the mountains that it seems scratched out of the cliffs themselves. From the beach cove at the bottom, two roads make their serpentine way up through the town and hills, one ascending (*V. Colombo*, Amalfi side), and the other descending (*V. Pasilea*, Naples side), till they join the two-way Strada Amalfitiana. Clinging to the cliffs are schools, churches, villas, hotels and stylish boutiques. Where a broad enough limestone shelf can be found, there's always a piazzetta and cafe with a gathering of people pausing during their climbs on the hundreds of steps cascading down the hillside. Positano is beautiful and it is chic.

Where to Stay

Le Sirenuse   **L490–650,000 CP**   ★ ★ ★ ★ ★

V. Colombo 30; ☎ *875-066, FAX 811-798; open year-round.*
Single L490,000 CP. Double L 650,000 CP.
Positano offers two of Europe's finest hotels, sophisticated retreats around which many plan entire vacations. The first one is this 19th-century villa terraced into five levels above the Positano cove, with a smattering of antiques among the serene contemporary furnishings, a library as well as gardens, a terrace restaurant and 58 distinctively furnished rooms, each with sea view, many with private balconies, some

with Jacuzzi. Le Sirenuse offers the most romantic setting in Positano. Excellent service, good restaurant, heated pool and elevator to beach.

San Pietro   **L675,000 CP**   ❀★ ★ ★ ★ ★

84017 Positano; 1 mi. east of Positano; ☎ *875-455, FAX 811-449; open Apr.–Nov. Single/double L675,000 CP.*

Part of the Relais & Chateaux network and outside the town, this is the other great Positano hotel. Also terraced into a cliff, its modern architecture is indiscernible through walls of bougainvillea. Superb views and service, 55 suite-like rooms, restaurant, gardens, tennis and an elevator to the private beach and bathing cove, all these are merely the basic elements of this romantic retreat.

Palazzo Murat   **L275,000**   ❀★ ★

V. Mulini 23; ☎ *875-177, FAX 811-419; open Easter.–Nov. and Christmas. Single/double L275,000.*

In Positano, this is a charming 18th-century villa with a modern annex (air conditioning available in this wing only; fee) around a heavenly garden. The 25 rooms have views of flowers or sea. Breakfast bar.

Casa Albertina   **L165–195,000 CP**   ★ ★

V. Tavolozza 4; ☎ *875-143, FAX 811-540; open year-round. Single/double L165–195,000 CP.*

Higher up the Positano hillside and about 20 steep steps from the road are the 21 delightfully furnished rooms here, each with a balcony and views. Restaurant.

Pasitea   **L135–170,000 CP**   ★ ★

V. Pasitea 137; ☎ *875-500; open year-round. Single L135,000 CP. Double L170,000 CP.*

Even higher on the Positano hillside, but more conveniently located on the road and with some parking (fee), is this friendly hotel, white, modern and immaculate, if a bit plain; its 18 rooms open to furnished balconies and views. Restaurant with outdoor terrace, bar; sunning terrace.

Where to Eat

The food at its best is the local seafood, clams over spaghetti, mussels sprinkled with cheese, marinated swordfish, or maybe a brochette of shrimp with white wine from nearby Ravello. Not only do the restaurants have similar food, but their prices don't vary a lot either. So look for location.

Chez Black   **$$–$$$**   ★ ★

in Positana; ☎ *875-036, FAX 875-789. Meals L40–70,000; closed Jan.*

A very popular and breezy spot near the beach that serves local seafood and, at night, pizza.

La Cambusa   **$$–$$$**   ★ ★

in Positana; ☎ *875-432, FAX 875-432. Meals L45–80,000*

Another popular seafood restaurant near the beach.

Il Capitano   **$$–$$$**   ★ ★

V. Pasitea; ☎ *811-351.*

Meals L45–80,000; closed Nov.–Dec. 26.

For more panoramic views, climb midway up the hill and, in summer, enjoy the good seafood on the outdoor terrace.

Caffe La Zagara

on square next to beach; open all year

A good place for pastry and focaccia sandwiches, as well as the cozy fire in winter, the refreshing iced cappuccino in summer.

Directory

Telephone Code 089   **Postal Code 84017**

Tourist Information

V. Pasitea entrance to town (seasonal) and center (☎ *875-067; FAX 875-760).*

Getting Around

A bus makes the road loop through town (buy tickets on board), but hillside steps provide shortcuts and are easy on the descent. There are taxis, too. Down at the center, there are **parking** lots. Leave your car here if you're staying in a small hotel without parking. Later, the hotel can send a porter to pick up your baggage.

Arriving

By car or bus from Naples, Sorrento or Salerno (40 km, 25 mi.), and by boat from Capri and Amalfi in season. Positano is just 11 km from the Meta turnoff for the Amalfi Road.

Amalfi

Today Amalfi is one of the larger resorts along the coast, with a bustling ferry port near its beach and a grand population of 6000. Amalfi's size today is nothing compared to its heyday as one of the first great maritime republics of Italy. Then its population was 70,000! Amalfi first began to flourish under Byzantium, but by the 8th century, it was an independent republic with trade far into the Orient. Its naval commerce led to the invention of the compass and the codification of the first maritime laws. But in the 12th century the Normans from Sicily conquered Amalfi, and soon after, its major rival on the seas, Pisa, sacked it repeatedly.

Amalfi's medieval period is quickly discovered by anyone with a little time to explore the town and not just its coast and grottoes. A few blocks from the sea is the striking ★**duomo**, founded in the 10th century, but often remodeled and an exotic blend of styles—from the powerful Norman facade and the bronze doors cast in Constantinople (11th century) to the Moorish arches found around the ★**Cortile del Paradiso** *(entrance to left of bronze portals; 9 a.m.–1:30 p.m., 3–8 p.m.; L3000).* The Cortile, originally a cemetery for nobility but later incorporated into the church, is now almost a museum of Amalfian art, from classical sarcophagi to Renaissance chapel frescoes. The town itself is something like an Arab souk when you start exploring its alleyways. Leading off the left of the duomo, is a covered walkway that soon joins with a medieval arcade lining the modern main street of Via Genoa. Off to the sides, climb narrow steps and whitewashed covered alleyways that lead to homes, convents and viewpoints above town—all completely unmarked. You might try to follow such a path to the Cappucine Convent (founded 1212), now a hotel near the tunnel entrance to town. Or simply wander about the small piazzas found on either side of Via Genoa. And in case you're still thinking about the grottos, the **Grotta Esmeralda** can be visited by motorboat *(10 a.m.–5 p.m.; Oct.–Feb. till 4 p.m., weather permitting)* from the docks, or by driving (taxis available) four km toward Sorrento, then descending on an elevator and paying for a boat into the colorful cave waters.

Where to Stay

Santa Catarina | **L370–490,000 CP** | ★★★★

SS Amalfitana 9; about 1/2 mi. on the Sorrento side of town; ☎ *871-0121, FAX 871-351; open all year.*
Single/double L390–490,000 CP.

This lovely cliffside resort is surrounded by terraced gardens on both sides, and has an elevator down to the sea where there are sunning terraces, a pool and seasonal restaurant. Above the sea are verandas, a restaurant and sitting rooms, as well as 54 rooms tastefully furnished and with views of the sea. There is also an "annex" of nine so-called villas scattered about in the gardens that are least pricey units (no a/c). Meal plans encouraged in season.

Luna Convento | **L195,000** | ★★★

SS Amalfitana; ☎ *871-002, FAX 871-333; open all year.*
Single/double L195,000.

On the Salerno edge of town, this hotel combines a convenient location with some views of the sea. Even better, the hotel is a converted 12th-century convent with a lovely cortile as its lobby and an antique-filled sitting room. Off the rear is a chapel and, like a secret passageway, a covered alleyway to the center. The 42 rooms (those with sea views and balconies preferred) have been totally modernized since St. Francis Assisi and Ibsen stayed here. Restaurant with views. Across the street at the medieval tower is the sea, sunning beach, and snack bar. Garage.

Miramalfi | **L155–195,000 CP** | √★★

SS Amalfitana, ☎ *871-588, FAX 871-588; open year-round.*
Single/double L155–195,000 CP.

This modern hotel with somewhat plastic furnishings is located out toward the Santa Catarina. It may be without charm, but it does have a cliff setting with sea views, steps leading down to a pool and sunning terraces near the sea. And the prices are very good for the 44 rooms. Parking.

Where to Eat

La Caravella | **$$** | ★★★

V. Matteo Camera 12; closed Nov., Tues. in low-season; ☎ *871-029, FAX 871-029.*
Meals L45–70,000

There are plenty of spots for enjoying the local seafood, but this restaurant overlooking the port is considered the best for its good wines, fresh ingredients and interesting pesto made of olives and capers. And the prices are good for the quality.

Da Gemma   **$$–$$$**   ★★★

V. Cavalieri di Malta; ☎ *871-345.*
Meals L45–75,000; closed Wed.,except July-Aug., at lunch during Aug.,& mid-Jan.–mid-Feb.

Found to the left of Via Genoa, just past the duomo, this simple trattoria is a local favorite. In warm weather, you can take a table on the roof terrace and enjoy well-prepared seafood—large and succulent grilled shrimp, garlicky *zuppa di pesce.*

Zaccheria   **$$–$$$**   ★★

Strada Amalfiana in Atrani; located just before the tunnel to Ravello; no phone.
Meals L55-80,000; closed Mon. (not July–Aug.), Nov.

Also called La Cantina del Nostromo, this restaurant has a spectacular location, with a cliffside terrace for enjoying its mixed grill of shellfish.

Snacks

The **Rendezvous** bar *(overlooking port toward Hotel Luna; closed Tues. except July-Aug.)* makes good sandwiches; ★ **Marina Grande** *(V. delle Regione;* ☎ *871-129; closed Nov.–Feb. & Wed. except July–Aug.),* right on the beach, is recommended in the evening for pizza; and the **Green Bar Taverna** in the arcade along Via Genoa *(Supportico Rua 44)* has calzoni and panini.

Directory

Telephone Code 089   **Postal Code 84011**

Tourist Information

AAST Across from the Marina Grande, on waterfront *(*☎ *871-107; FAX 372-619)*

Arriving

Bus and car from Naples (76 km, 47 mi.), Sorrento, and Salerno. Amalfi lies just 16 km (10 mi.) from Positano, 27 km (17 mi.) from Meta, 25 km (15.5 mi.) from Salerno. Amalfi also can be approached by A-3 from the Angri exit. There is ferry and hydrofoil service to Positano and Capri in season.

Ravello

Perched high above the sea, at the end of a road zigzagging past vineyards and orchards and around steeply cut ravines, is this picturesque medieval village. Founded in the 9th century by Amalfi, the town has its share of the same exotic architecture and is famous for its gardens and views. The simple facade of the ★**duomo** (1086) belies the fineness of its bronze doors (1179; by Barisano da Trani; shown by sacristan) and the 13th-century Arabo-Byzantine pulpits in the nave, the most magnificent held aloft by twisted columns and lions, a simpler one with a delightful Jonah and the whale mosaic. In the crypt is an attractively arranged *museo (9 a.m.–1 p.m., 3–5 p.m. except, June–Oct. till 7 p.m.; free)* with Romanesque sculptures, mosaics, and a lovely bust of Sigilgarda Rufolo (1272). And just off the south side of the church

Ravello

is the romantic ★ **Villa Rufolo** *(9:30 a.m.–1 p.m., 2–4:30 p.m., but 3–7 p.m. in season; L4000)*, also in the local Moorish style, especially the columnettes of the small courtyard. Here Wagner found his inspiration for the magic garden in *Parcifal*. You can understand why, as you walk amid the gardens and ruined villa and gaze out at the magnificent panorama of sea and countryside. Through the picture window walls of the former chapel is an exhibit of antiquities. A 15-minute walk east of the Piazza del Duomo takes you to the turn-of-the-century **Villa Cimbrone** *(9 a.m.–dusk; L5000)* with gardens and an even greater panorama of the coast from its celebrated belvedere.

Where to Stay and Eat

Palumbo   L470–600,000 CP   ★★★

V. San Giovanni del Toro; ☎ *857-244, FAX 858-133; open all year.*
Single/double L470-600,000 CP.
An exquisite villa built around a 12th-century mansion is now a hotel that offers not only garden terraces and grand views, but also a Romanesque cortile and Baroque frescoes. In this Palazzo Confalone are eight rooms furnished with antiques. But in case these are out of your price range, you might consider the "Residenza,"or annex across the way, where seven rooms, a few with sea view, have more modest tariffs (L250–300,000 CP.) Good restaurant on terrace in season (meals L85–125,000; closed Jan.–Feb.).

Rufolo   L165–250,000 CP   ★★

V. San Francesco; ☎ *857-133, FAX 857-935; open year-round.*
Single L165,000 CP. Double L200–250,000 CP.
Near the villa of the same name, this hotel and some of its 29 rooms (no a/c) also share its views. Restaurant (in season) and pool.

Ristorante Garden $ ★

Strada Panoramica; ☎ *857-226.*
Meals L25–50,000; closed Tues. in off-season.
Through the tunnel near the duomo, look for this spot serving good food at modest prices and with stupendous views for enjoying the gnocchi alla Sorrentina and the shrimp brochettes. There are a few rooms (single L75,000CP; double L100,000 CP) with the same views.

Directory

Telephone Code 089   **Postal Code 84010**

Tourist Information
P. Duomo *(*☎ *857-096; FAX 857-977)*.

Arriving
Turn off Amalfi drive 1 km from Amalfi, 22 km (13.5 mi.) from Salerno, then wind your way up for 5 km. Also, Ravello is accessible by A-3, from the Angri or Nocera exit and continuing by the Chiunzi pass. There's bus service from Amalfi and Salerno.

Festivals
In early July, *Festival Musicala* in the Villa Rufo.

Vietri Sul Mare

Since Etruscan times Vietri has been a ceramic center. Today it produces all manner of colorful tiles and plates, some handsome copies of 17th-century majolica, others the pasta bowls you've always dreamed of owning. The *ceramiche* shops are densest in the upper city around the main square. But if you've already made your purchases in Amalfi or along the drive, then just continue on.

Practical Tips

Vietri marks the end of the Amalfi Drive, 22 km, 13.5 mi. from Amalfi, and just 3 km to Salerno on SS 18. If you're continuing to Paestum, we recommend you avoid the congestion of Salerno by picking up A-3 (direction Reggio di Calabria).

Salerno

The *centro storico* hides another one of those pleasing Arabo-Byzantine churches, so typical of this coast. And the broad and palmlined Lungomare is quite stately. But if you're traveling by car, it's best to bypass Salerno—the industry and gnarled traffic on its southern outskirts is nerve shattering after the beauty of the Amalfi Drive. It's best to pick up A-3 in Vietri or Battipagli, depending on your direction. Salerno, capital of the province that includes the Amalfi Coast and Paestum, also is a major terminus for pullman buses and trains on the Naples to Reggio di Calabria route as well as local buses up the Amalfi Coast and down to Paestum ("Sapri" bus, departs from P. Concordia). The stazione and nearby bus stations are a healthy distance from the centro storico. Car rentals available around stazione.

Practical Tips

DISTANCES: 25 km, 15-1/2 mi. from Amalfi, 35 km, 22 mi. from Paestum, 55 km, 34 mi. from Naples by autostrada. • SITA buses (*Corso Garibaldi 117*, ☎ *(089) 226-604*), for Sorrento and Naples via Amalfi coast.

Paestum

This ancient Greek city, founded in the 6th century B.C., was famous for its roses that bloomed twice a year. The benign Mediterranean climate that permitted such ancient wonders also brought the malaria that depopulated the city in late Roman times. By the time the Arabs sacked Paestum in A.D. 877, it already was greatly diminished and soon was forgotten. Today, three grand Doric temples stand amid fields of wildflowers swept by the winds of the nearby sea. Parts of the ancient walls still enclose it, and the Forum of the Romans who conquered in 243 B.C. can be discerned at its sunken spot where ruins of an amphitheater now jut into the modern periphery road on the east. There are several entrances to the sight, but a convenient beginning is through the Porta della Giustiza on the south. Following the Via Sacra, which runs the length of the site, you pass the first and earliest temple on your right, the so-called ★**Basilica** (mid-6th century B.C.), the proportions and taper of its fluted columns a bit crude compared with the next one, the ★★**Temple of Neptune** (5th century B.C.), likewise misnamed, as both temples were dedicated to Hera. The Neptune is one of the three best preserved temples in Europe, along with Theseus in Athens and Concord at Agrigento. Its monumental majesty is unrivalled. Continuing north, you cross the Roman main street of the Decumanus Maximus, flanked by columns. Here is the sunken Forum, while to the north is the ★**Temple of Ceres** (6th century B.C.), originally dedicated to Athena, and probably built sometime between the other two. Exiting to the east, crossing the periphery road and walking a bit to the right, you come to the ★**Museum**. In the main hall are ★34 metopes carved with Homeric scenes (6th century B.C.; best seen from upstairs) that once covered a nearby temple. At the rear of the ground floor are extremely rare ★★Greek paintings (480 B.C.) from the *Tumba del Tuffatore*, or Tomb of the Diver. The deceased dives the Underworld while a very Greek banquet is depicted on the walls. Perhaps like Plato's Symposium, the discussion is about immortality.

One ticket (L8000) gains entrance to both the ruins and the museum. The ruins open 9 a.m. till 90 minutes before sunset, the museum (closed Mon.) till 1 hour before sunset. (For example in July, the ruins close at 6:30, the museo 7 p.m.; in Jan. the ruins at 3, the museo at 3:30 p.m.)

Where to Stay and Eat

At the beach just 1 km southwest of the ruins, there are seasonal snack bars, restaurants, and hotels. There are cafes near the museum. And just at the south edge of the site are year-round facilities:

Hotel Martini   **L150,000 CP**   ★★
84063 Paestum; ☎ *811-020, FAX 811-600.*
Single/double L150,000 CP.
This modern hotels has gardens, access to beach club, restaurant, parking and 13 convenient units (no a/c).

Ristorante Nettuno   **$–$$**   ★
☎ *811-028, FAX 811-028.*
Meals L40–70,000; except during July and Aug. closed evenings and Mon.
Views over the ruins and a very pleasant beflowered terrace compensate for the basic menu.

Directory

Telephone Code 0828

Tourist Information
V. Magna Graecia 151 (☎ *811-016; FAX 722-322)*, at ruins.

Arriving
By car, exit A-3 at Battipaglia and continue 20 km, 12 mi. to Paestum. The bus to Sapri from Salerno, stops at Paestum as does the *locale* train from Salerno to Reggio

Calabaria. The ruins are 35 km, 22 mi. from Salerno; 100 km, 62 mi. from Naples by A-3; 120 km, 74 mi. on A-3 and A-30 to Caserta, another 200 km (124 mi.) on A-2 from Caserta to Rome; Reggio Calabria is just under 400 km south on A-2.

On the Road

Southern Adriatic Towns

The sights of Apulia (*Puglia* in Italian) include little from its ancient past. Exceptional Hellenistic statuary can be found in some of its museums—the **Museo Nazionale** in Taranto is in fact the only reason to consider visiting the once great Greek port. Travelers still follow the Appian Way to Brindisi for ships to Greece and other destinations in the East, just as the Romans did, and a few amphitheaters, a column, or statue speak the empire's domination of the region. But, unlike the Bay of Naples, the presence is definitely muted—the vineyards and olive groves first planted by the Greeks make the most eloquent statement of their presence. And the Romans, normally so generous with their monuments, tell of struggles here with the absence of such memorials. For it was Apulia that invited Pyrrhus to defeat the upstart Romans, a defeat that has become notorious in history, but which nonetheless left the Romans initially without control of the region. And it is in Apulia that Hannibal thrashed the Romans in 216 B.C. during the second Punic War.

Without the grand classical monuments so typical of the rest of the South and Sicily, Apulia has not attracted as much tourism as other areas. Many know it from a dash across its flat plain to the discomfort of a ferry wait in Brindisi. But the region has definite attractions. During the 12th and 13th centuries when its ports sent crusaders to the East, towns such as Bari flourished, building fabulous Romanesque churches and impressive forts. In Lecce to the south, the 16th and 17th centuries spawned some wondrous Baroque architecture. And geographically in between, the farmers of the Murge developed a curious conical architecture of *trulli* that now delights many travelers.

For the traveler looking for less-frequented parts of Italy, Apulia should be a primary *regione* to explore. For anyone making the trip to the Greek ferries, an extra night or so to see some of the sights will be amply rewarded. The region is decently served by inter-city buses and by train (especially along the coast), but if you really want to explore the churches and Frederick II castles that seem to mark each town around Bari, then a car would be most efficient.

North of Bari

The province around Bari was a favorite area of Frederick II. From 1214 to 1250 he spent considerable time here when he wasn't fighting the pope's forces in the north or managing affairs at his capital in Palermo. Like the Normans who preceded him, Frederick also set off for crusades from here, a business that brought considerable prosperity to the region. He also loved to hunt in Apulia, although today it hardly seems possible that the denuded farmland could have satisfied him. Although the story of the Normans and Frederick is found under Sicily, here their exotic Eastern preferences once again surface in the arabesques carved on pulpits and Norman Romanesque church facades, in the Moorish vaults of their crypts, and in the octagonal shape of some of Frederick's castles or even his choice of the elephant as his emblem—found on many churches. Although both the Norman kings and the Swabian Frederick traveled with opulent courts and harems, their architecture also shows northern influences—here, the Norman churches have Lombard lion porches as well as women's galleries, and under Frederick especially, the sculpture shows the sturdy figures of ancient Rome.

What to See and Do

Each town in this area seems graced by a church or castle, or both—there are too many to list them all. But an excursion to one or two of the following, or even a loop tour encompassing them all (145 km, 90 mi.), will introduce you to the finest ones outside of Bari itself. Exiting A-14 for **Trani** (36 km, 22 mi. north of Bari), you come to the magnificent seaside setting of this medieval port that seems too small to have vied with Bari in its importance. Although Frederick's castle has been rebuilt too often, the ★ **cathedral** (begun late 11th century) couldn't be more striking, its powerful Norman walls bleached white and set against the blue sea. The facade carvings and rosette windows, the portal with its bronze doors cast by Barisano di Trani, and its intriguing crypt are all notable. Farther up the coast is the port of **Barletta** (16 km, 10 mi.), not as pretty, but with an impressive ★ **Castello** (*9 a.m.–1 p.m., 3–4 p.m., but 4–7 p.m. Apr.–Sept.; L3500; closed Mon.*) built by Frederick and his heir Manfred, who maintained his court here, and later enlarged by the Anjou. The nearby **duomo**, on the edge of a small medieval centro storico, is said to have been partially built by Richard the Lion Heart. A few more blocks away from the sea, the Anjou built **San Sepolocro** with a fine Gothic interior. In front is the **Colosso di Barletta**, a 5th-century bronze representing a Byzantine emperor, left in Barletta by a Venetian shipwreck. Exiting town inland for **Andria**, you then pass through Andria and continue until you sight Frederick's most magnificent work, the ★ ★ **Castel del Monte** (begun 1240; *9 a.m.–1 p.m.; check for longer summer hours; L4000*). Crowning one of the few hills of this wine region and surrounded by woods, the octagonal castle is majestic in its isolation. The detailing of the second floor apartments and the Roman triumphal arch entrance can only suggest its former appearance, when coral and marble decorations could be found throughout. Now beginning the loop south toward Bari, follow the country road, past the vineyards for which Castel del Monte is famous, to the bypass around industrial Ruva, and continue to **Bitonto** (40 km, 25 mi.). Following signs for "la cattedrale" you come to the Piazza Cavour with its arches and medieval tower, and then plunge into the *centro storico*. Rising in its center is the finest example of Apulian Romanesque, the Bitonto ★ ★ **cathedral** (*closed midday*; begun 1175), much inspired by the San Nicola in Bari. The facade is richly carved, from the lunette over the main portal, down its right flank, and around the apse window. In the interior, on the right is a carved pulpit and an ★ ambo with a relief of Frederick II and his family. The crypt includes some finely carved figural capitals (left aisle). The last leg of the loop is Bari, less than 20 km, 12 mi. away.

Where to Stay and Eat

There are some hotels and restaurants near the Castel del Monte as well as near the Trani cathedral. The best facilities are probably in Barletta, but dine with a Castel del Monte red or rose.

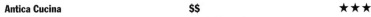

| **Antica Cucina** | **$$** | ★★★ |

V. Milano in Barletta 73; reserve at ☎ (0883) 521-718.
Closed Sun. night, Mon., late July & late Jan. Meals L40–70,000.
Only several blocks from the Colosso is this wonderful restaurant serving regional delights such as eggplant with crab, beef stew with escarole and aged ricotta.

| **La Casaccia** | **$–$$** | ★ |

V. Cavour 40 in Barletta; closed Mon.; ☎ 0883-33719; meals L40–60,000.
A more modest family-run spot for good regional food, but with air-conditioned comfort. Pizza, too.

| **Artu** | **L115–170,000** | ★★ |

P. Castello 67, 70051 Barletta; ☎ (0883) 332-121, FAX 332-214.
Single L115,000. Double L170,000.
If you need a place to stay, this is a good convenience hotel, across from the castle and with 32 carpeted, plain but air–conditioned rooms. Restaurant. Garden. Parking.

Practical Tips

Arriving

A car can make this into a day trip, but any other means of transport is more limiting. Regular buses run from Bari to these towns, and there are trains to Bitonto and Barletta. Castel del Monte is best by car or tour.

Bari

An ancient port and then a Byzantine one, Bari flourished through the crusades and the Norman and Swabian periods of Apulia's history. Like many cities of the South, the capital of Apulia is more modern than historic, its streets crowded (population around 400,000) and its outskirts industrialized. But the main shopping area, anchored by the pedestrian Via Sparano that connects the stazione with the old city, is pleasant enough, and the sea breezes of the Lungomare promenade are even more so.

You may come here only for the ferries that cross to Greece (a longer trip than from Brindisi, but Bari is nicer). Yet a walk through the souk-like *citta vecchia*, or old city, can be quite exotic. It is a tangle of streets, often covered and alley-like, designed to confound medieval invaders who, once lost, could easily be captured or killed. Leaving such thoughts behind (but not entirely—thefts are common here), you can find your way along the edge, entering the arch at Corso V. Emanuele and soon arriving at the Romanesque **duomo**. You wind a bit more and might become distracted by shops selling local ceramics, plates, pitchers and the like with the province's distinctive blue *fleur de lis* and rooster pattern. Then you'll find the handsome Norman Romanesque church of ★**San Nicola** (begun 1087; *closed noon–3:30 p.m.*) with its influential three-part facade and unusual main portal (here, docile bulls replace Emilian lions), and far richer one on the north side with its ★lunette relief. San Nicola stands in a complex of courtyards, once the seat of Byzantine governors. The interior, with 15th-century arches, holds a Byzantine tabernacle on the high altar, and the crypt below, with carved capitals, mosaic floor and a most Byzantine ambience, holds the remains of the generous St. Nicholas. Just outside the *citta vecchia*, near the duomo, is the **Castle** *(9 a.m.–1 p.m., 3:30–7 p.m.; in winter Sun. mornings only, closed Mon.; L4000)*, its present appearance resulting from renovations by Isabele of Aragon, but its trapezoidal center by Frederick II. It looks impressively romantic when bathed in nighttime illumination.

Where to Stay

The choice is limited, so try to reserve in advance.

Palace Hotel L200–265,000 ★ ★ ★ ★

V. Lombardi 13 at Corso V. Emanuele; ☎ *521-6551, FAX 521-1499.*
Single L200,000. Double L265,000.
A good first-class hotel right near the Castle offers an attractive modern lobby and 200 rooms that vary a bit in age, size, and price, but are all among the best in the city. Good Restaurant. Lounge. Garage.

Villa Romanazzi-Carducci L155–240,000 CP ★ ★ ★

V. Capruzzi 326; ☎ *522-7400, FAX 556-0297.*
Single L155,000 CP. Double L240,000 CP.
A good choice if you don't mind being a bit out of the center. Set in a park, the 18th-century villa has 89 suites, a dining room, pool, gym and garage.

Grand Hotel e D'Oriente L160–230,000 ★ ★ ★

Corso Cavour 32; ☎ *524-4011, FAX 524-3914.*
Single L160,000. Double L230,000.
Just across one of the main streets from the Sparano shopping area, this older but renovated hotel has a contemporary lobby and gentle ambience, its 140 rooms ample (and away from the main street, very quiet) and carpeted. Restaurant. Lounge. Access to garage.

Boston L120–160,000 ★ ★

V. Piccinni 155; ☎ *521-6633, FAX 524-6802.*
Single L120,000. Double L160,000.
Right in the center, this '50s-style hotel, renovated in 1989, offers 70 up-to-date rooms, breakfast room and garage.

Where to Eat

Although you'll want to explore the restaurants on excursions to the North and in the Trulli District, there are some decent ones in Bari. A good food store is the **Salumeria** *(V. Emanuele 28)*, not far from Cavour.

Ai Due Ghiottoni   **$$–$$$**   ★★★

V. Putignani 11; ☎ *523-2240.*
Closed Sun., most of Aug. Meals L50–75,000.
In the Sparano shopping district. This favorite spot serves the traditional orecchiette with turnip greens as well as a northern tagliatelle con funghi, local seafood as well as veal and rabbit.

Taverna Verde   ★★

Largo Adua 18; ☎ *554-0870.*
Closed Sun. & Aug. L30–45,000.
A popular trattoria near the Lungomare N. Sauro with local seafood and Barese vegetables combining for a good meal.

Directory

Telephone Code 080   **Postal Code 70122**

Tourist Information

EPT *P. Moro 33*, across from stazione but entrance around corner *(*☎ *524-2244; FAX 524-2329).*

Arriving

Airport with domestic flights, 9 km from Bari; connected by bus to stazione. Stazione Centrale with trains to Naples via Caserta (3.5 hours), Rome (on the fast Pendolino) and Bologna (7.5 hours), as well as more local connections especially to Brindisi (2 hours). • Buses to towns north of Bari (AMET, Corso Cavour 2). • Highways from Naples (265 km, 164 mi.), Rome (465 km, 288 mi.), and Bologna (680 km, 422 mi.), but the southern region is linked mostly by state roads. • Stazione Maritima (just north of *citta vecchia*) for ferries to Greece: Corfu (11 hrs.) and Igoumenitsa (12 hrs.) via Brindisi, and Patras (15 hrs.); **Ventouris Ferries** *(*☎ *524-4364)* and **Morfimare** *(*☎ *521-0022)* daily in season, less Nov.–Mar.

Getting Around

Car rentals (airport and stazione), taxis, and CIT tours *(Principe Amadeo 92).*

Beware

Avoid the port area at night and don't visit the old city alone, especially at night.

Park your car in a garage.

Try to reserve ferries well in advance through travel agents.

The Trulli District

Down the coast from Bari, past the sea town of **Polignano a Mare**, you turn inland at **Monopoli** to the Trulli District, anchored by the village of Alberobello. Here, the Pugliese flatlands rise and roll into hills, plump cows graze in green pastures, and from the deep red earth grow olive trees and grapevines. Adding to the picturesque aspect of this very pastoral landscape are the *trulli* themselves, stone buildings shaped into cones, often whitewashed with stone peaks and crowned with crosses. Clusters of them form farmhouses, single ones shelters and storage bins in the fields, some seem brand–new, but others have been worn down to stone like prehistoric tumuli. The trulli originated here centuries ago, not millennia as some have imagined, perhaps as granaries. Their cool interiors became favored for houses, some quite elegant, others organic and compelling. You can simply enjoy the scenery by driving the 12 miles to Alberobello, then continuing to **Locorotondo** (15 km, 9 mi.), and finally drive to the top of the old city for the view out over the Valle d'Istria. You also might stop here at a cantina to buy some of the good local white wine. Fewer than another 10 km takes you by more trulli to another wine town, that of **Martina Franca**. But you'll definitely have to explore **Alberobello**, even if you don't drive the full 45 km road between Monopoli and Martina Franca. Embedded in modern Alberobello is a town of trulli, its streets are lined with townhouse trulli, shops peak out from trulli, there is even a trulli church and a trulli hotel. It is all quite excessive and charming at the same time.

Where to Stay and Eat

Trullo d'Oro $–$$ ★★

V. Cavallotti 29, Alberodello; ☎ *(080) 932-3909.*
Closed Mon. except in summer and Jan. Meals L30–65,000.
You probably would like a restaurant more than a hotel, but in Alberobello you can want both and find them in trulli. Here's a chance to test the interior of a trullo, while serving authentic Pugliese cuisine, from the focaccia barese to the local lamb and *salsiccia* (sausage). And try the local cheeses (pecorino, mozzarella and ricotta) and wines.

Hotel dei Trulli L240–265,000 ✿★★★

V. Cadore 2, 70011, Alberodello; ☎ *(080) 932-3555, FAX 932-3560.*
Single/double L240–265,000.
In a park atop a ridge of the town's trulli district. This intriguing hotel offers 28 trulli bungalows arranged around a pool. Restaurant. Parking.

Grotta Palazzese $$–$$$ ★★★

V. Narcisco 59, 70044, Polignano a Mare; ☎ *(080) 740-677, FAX 770-767.*
L50–90,000.
But you may want to take advantage of your proximity to **Polignano a Mare** *(just off SS 16; 35 km, 22 mi. south of Bari, and about the same distance north of Alberobello).* The spectacular setting of this warm-season restaurant is in the natural hollow of a cliff above the Adriatic next to a tiny whitewashed medieval town. The food includes wonderful pastas with Pugliese vegetables, but also the likes of ravioli stuffed with oysters. There is scampi cooked in spumante, fish stuffed with mushrooms, and the like. It also offers a daily degustazione menu. The restaurant has a ✿★★**hotel** *(single L115,000, double L155,000)*, its 20 rooms smallish, but tastefully furnished, some with porthole views of the sea.

Il Melograno L300–500,000 CP ★★★

Contrada Torricella 345, 70043 Monopoli; ☎ *(080) 690-9030, FAX 747-908; closed Feb.;*
Single L300,000 CP. Double L465–500,000 CP.

Monopoli *(on SS 16, 20 km east of Alberobello and 15 km south of Polignano)* is where you should seek refined accommodations. Just 3 mi. south is this tranquil small inn found just 3 mi. south of Monopoli, with 30 antique-filled rooms (a few with Jacuzzi), a ★★★ fine restaurant in a garden *(meals L45–75,000)*, pool, gym, tennis and shuttle to beach.

Practical Tips

Arriving

Alberobello is just over an hour south of Bari, on SS 16 (divided most of its length) and on a country road picked up at Monopoli. The Bari-Taranto train of the Ferrovie del Sud-Est, with stops at the towns in the Trulli district and in Lecce, is a good way to sightsee.

Brindisi

Despite its long history, Brindisi has little to see. Most travelers find it an unpleasant interlude on their way to Greece and points farther east. We can only wonder what the Roman emperors thought of it as they set off for their vast territories. All that remains is one of the markers for the terminus of the Appian Way, which began at the gates of Rome, wandered past now famous tombs and what would become Christian catacombs, and continued south to this port. The column marker, with a capital carved into four deities, can be seen at the harbor. There's a castle, and a *centro storico* that doesn't warrant the effort.

Where to Stay

If you can, plan your arrival to coincide with your day of departure. Certainly an overnight at the other places mentioned in Apulia will be more interesting.

Majestic L140–190,000 CP ★★★

Corso Umberto 151; ☎ *222-941, FAX 524-071.*
Single L140,000 CP. Double L190,000 CP.

This hotel is first-class and very modern. Near the stazione, with 68 well appointed rooms, restaurant and garage.

L'Approdo L100–150,000 ★

V. del Mare 50; ☎ *529-667; FAX 526-398.*
Single L100,000. Double L150,000.

Convenient for the ferries and fine for a night, with 23 rooms (no air conditioning), breakfast bar, garage.

Where to Eat

La Laterna $–$$ ★★★

V. Tarantini 14; ☎ *564-026.*
Closed Sun. dinner, Mon., Aug. Meals L40–65,000.

Near the Piazza Duomo in a 15th-century palace, La Laterna has an even nicer garden setting when weather permits. The pastas are good (especially ravioli with lobster), as is the fish that prevails on the menu.

La Nassa $ ★★

V. Colonne 57; ☎ *526-005.*
Closed Mon. L30–40,000.

An attractive restaurant near the ancient column, specializing in seafood—try the *risotto frutti di mare.*

Directory

Telephone Code 0831 **Postal Code 72100**

Tourist Information

EPT, *Lungomare Regina Margherita 5 (*☎ *521-944)*, near the Stazione Marittima and kiosk at P. Cairoli, a few blocks from the train station towards the port.

Ferries

Brindisi is the major embarkation point for Greece. There's regular service to Corfu (about 9 hours), Igoumenitsa (11 hours), Patras (16 hours or so) and Cefalonia (16.5 hours; Adriatica lines only). You will want to reserve before arriving in Brindisi, especially if you are transporting a car and particularly in the summer. Use one of the CIT agencies or a travel agent. If not, purchase your tickets from one of the authorized agencies lining the Corso Umberto between the train station and port. The two major companies are Adriatica *(*☎ *523-825)* and Hellenic Mediterranean Lines *(*☎ *528-531).*

Arriving

Brindisi is 115 km, 71 mi. south of Bari on SS 16 and its 4-lane, limited access continuation SS 379. Bari trains from Rome and Bologna link up to Brindisi in 2 hours. There's an airport, just outside the center, with some domestic flights.

Lecce

Just from its nicknames—the "Apulian Athens" and the "Florence of Apulia"—you know that Lecce is special. Although it flourished under the Romans when Hadrian built a major port here (at San Cataldo), as well as under the Normans, Lecce is a Baroque town. Within its old walls and gates, and lining its often winding streets are Baroque palazzi and churches, ornately and idiosyncratically carved with just about anything—Renaissance loggias over Gothic pointed arches, fruit trees and even fish scales, and Byzantine arabesques as well as classical foliation. Unlike Roman Baroque, the interiors and architectural forms are not themselves interesting, but the style shares the exuberance of the era. In addition to the delightful facade sculpture, the local stone itself, soft and easily carved, is warm ochre and welcoming in tone. Perhaps even more enchanting is that no one can really explain the origin of the style or why little Lecce, hidden away in the heel of Italy, so energetically redesigned itself from the mid-16th century until the 18th.

What to See and Do

Any tour of the town begins in its main square, the **Piazza Sant'Oranzo**, where one of the earlier and more eccentric Baroque buildings, the Sedile, or town hall (1540s; by Gabriele Riccardi) rises next to the ruins of a Roman amphitheater (1st century B.C.). A few blocks north on Via Santa Croce is the ★**Santa Croce** church and ex-convent (now Palazzo dei Celestini), harmonious yet built over the full length of the Baroque period, from Riccardi's lower facade of the church to Giuseppe Zimbalo's more ornate upper portion (1679). West out of Piazza Sant'Oranzo, Via Vittorio Emanuele brings you to the entrance gate of the ★**Piazza del Duomo**, probably the only duomo square in Italy that is basically enclosed. The gate, the rebuilt cathedral, and the seminary were all designed by Zimbalo and his followers, though others had a hand in the 17th-century complex. At the rear of the piazza is the fine Bishop's Palace, and to the right the wonderful portal and atrium well of the ★ Seminario. South out of the piazza Sant'Oranzo is the Via Imperatore that passes **Santa Chiara** on the right before arriving at that of ★**San Matteo** on the left, with the reverse curvature of its facade that may or may not have been inspired by Borromini, and with fish scales that only its Leccese architect Archille Carducci (1644-1712) could have invented. There are many more churches, many palazze that a walk around town will quickly reveal. On the southern edge of the centro storico is the **Museo Provinciale** (*V. San Francesco Re at Gallipoli; 9:30–1:30 p.m., also, except Sun., 2:30–7 p.m.; free*) has a pinacoteca and a fine archeology collection that indicates how long the ceramics tradition has existed in this region. Apulian ceramics constitute one of the rare folk art traditions still surviving in modern Italy. To learn what's available, include the government-run **Artigianato** shop (*V. Rubichi 21, just off P. Sant'-Oranzo*) on your tour.

Where to Stay

Facilities in the *centro storico* are very limited.

Presidente   L120–190,000   ★★★
> *V. Salandra 6; ☎ 311-881, FAX 372-283.*
> *Single L120,000. Double L190,000.*
> Only a 15-minute walk east of the Piazza Sant'Oranzo, in the modern downtown, is this large, '50s-style glass hotel with a tasteful lobby and the most comfortable rooms (155) in town. Restaurant, lounge, garage.

Cote d'Est   L85–120,000   ★★
> *Lungomare in Melendugno San Foco 73026; ☎ (0832) 881-146; open year-round.*
> *Single L85,000. Double L120,000.*
> If you have a car, you might consider the Cote d'Est, 25 km, 15.5 mi. south of Lecce on the coast. Across the road from the beach, some of the 37 rooms of this modern hotel have sea views. Restaurant. Lounge. Parking.

Where to Eat

The choice of restaurants is a little better than the choice of hotels, and local Salerno wines, such as the red Salice Salento, the white Salice Salento and rose Rosa del Golfo, are good.

Barbablu $-$$ ★★★
> *V. Umberto I #7; ☎ 241-183.*

Closed Mon. Meals L40–55,000.

Across from Santa Croce church, this polished restaurant is the best in the centro storico. The Pugliese dishes and seafood are brightened by the inventive accents of its chef.

I Tre Moschettieri   **$$**   ★★

V. Paisiello 9/A; ☎ *308-484.*
Closed Mon. & late Aug. Meals L50–65,000.

Located a few blocks from the castle, this restaurant features al fresco dining in warm weather and local dishes prepared with fresh ingredients. There's pizza at night, too.

Guido e Figli   **$**   ★

XXV Luglio 18; ☎ *305-868.*
Closed Mon. except in summer. Meals L20–35,000.

One of the cheapest trattorias in Italy, yet we can vouch for the vegetable antipasto as quite good and the pizza as okay. (Located just 2 blocks east of P. Sant'Oranzo.)

For some homemade focaccia ripiena, try the **Paisello Caffe** *(V. Palmieri 73 at V. Prato)*; for traditional olive bread, **Panetteria Valentina** *(off V. Emanuele on V. Petronelli near duomo)*, and for good breakfast pastries and a quiet break, **Caffè del Duomo** *(V. Emanuele across from duomo).*

Directory

Telephone Code 0832   **Postal Code 73100**

Tourist Information
    AAST, *V. Rubichi 25 (*☎ *304-443).*

Getting Around
    Only walking will do in the centro storico, but there are taxis to help and buses that run the streets of the modern city.

Arriving
    Lecce is 40 km, 25 mi. south of Brindisi by the "Superstrada Lecce" highway and a 1-hour train ride (stazione on south edge of *centro storico*, about 15-minute walk or take bus to P. Sant'Oranzo). Rome is 6 hours via Bari on fast Pendolino train.

Beware
    If your car has a radio, park it in a garage.

Salento Peninsula

Lecce is a good base for explorations to the south, where the Salentine peninsula makes its final stretch into the heel of Italy. Olive groves and vine-yards grow profusely in this rugged flat land. Peasants, speaking a dialect traceable to ancient Greece, work the orchards much as they have for millennia. Spanish watchtowers and undateable stone dolmens dot the vast, long curve of coast. When summer sun-worshippers abandon the beaches here, the peninsula is quiet, and the few thousand inhabitants of each village settle into age-old rhythms of fishing and farming.

What to See and Do

An excursion along the Adriatic coast to the tip of the peninsula can be quite aimless as long as you succumb to a swim now and then or seek the high ground for a clear view of Albania's mountains just 60 mi. across the sea.

Otranto

One place to plan a stop should be **Otranto** *(45 km, 30 mi. south of Lecce on the coastal road SS 611)*, a pretty seaport looking much like a Greek village. White cubical houses climb medieval lanes up to an Aragonese **castle** (1485); the blue sea, green shutters, and flowerfilled balconies add colorful accents. If Otranto were nothing more than a few scenic walks, sea, and beach, it would still be a pleasant stopover. Yet this port has something more—its **cathedral**. Down the lane across from the castle, you find the church, a capsule of local history. Begun by the Normans in 1080, the very Eastern-style crypt includes carved columns from ancient, Byzantine and Romanesque times. Upstairs, the Chapel of the Martyrs (end of right aisle) recalls Turkish raids when Otranto was a Venetian port. And covering the floor of both the aisles and the nave is a delightfully folkloric ★ **mosaic pavement** by Pantaleone (1163) with mythological beasties, a tree of life, and biblical scenes.

Around the Tip

A dip farther down the rocky Adriatic coast might include a few picturesque resorts. Not far south of Otranto is **Santa Cesarea Terme** (16 km, 10 mi. on SS 173) with thermal grottos and hot springs *(open mid-May to mid-Nov.)*. Then there is fortified and medieval **Castro** (6 km farther south), commanding great views from its cliff location, while below at **Castro Marina** are tantalizing blue waters and the Zinzulsa Grotto. Those with cars may want to continue down the coast to its tip at **Capo Santa Maria de Leuca** (95 km, 59 mi. from Lecce), where the views from the white cliffs are panoramic and the swimming good in the sea at the resort below. To continue around the peninsula to **Gallipoli** (85 km, 53 mi.) can be monotonous, and Gallipoli, despite the allure of its name and ancient Greek founding, is not nearly so pleasing as Otranto. If you do plan to visit the Ionic coast at Gallipoli, you might simply save it for another day trip from Lecce (45 km, 28 mi. on SS 101) or head there directly from Otranto (50 km, 34 mi. on SS 459), forgoing the southern coast. Although no British embattlements (1809) are here to remind you of a recent grim movie, you do have to drive through the disappointing modern Gallipoli before arriving at the bridge that leads to the old island city. A road rims the labyrinthine centro storico of the island, passing its crumbling churches and still impressive castle.

Where to Eat

Both Otranto and Gallipoli have good restaurants.

Acmet Pascia   **$–$$**   ★★

Lungomare degli Eroi 21, in Otranto;  *(0836) 801-282.*
Closed Mon., except July–Aug., Oct. Meals L40–55,000.

A great terrace restaurant along the port wall offers fresh pasta "mitiche," fish soup and lots of seafood along with the view.

Marechiano **$$** ★★★

Lungomare Marconi in Gallipoli; ☎ *(0833) 266-143.*
Closed Tues. except in summer. Meals L40–60,000.
Found on the mainland side of the bridge (to the right, down by the water), and
with views over the old city, Marechiano has delicious seafood, from zuppe di pesce
(but the artichoke soup is good, too) and *orecchiette frutti di mare* to the sea bass
in salsa verde.

Practical Tips

The coastal road can be unpleasantly congested in the summer, especially on week-
ends, when you might want to take the inland highways to a few selected destinations.
Buses run from Lecce to both Otranto and Gallipoli as well as to Leuca; there are other
local buses out of Otranto. From Lecce to the tip of the peninsula by coastal road is about
100 km, 62 mi.

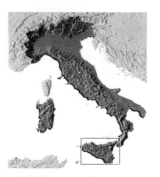

SICILY

The Norman Church of San Giovanni, Palermo, sits amid a romantically tangled garden.

History and Art

Sicily, land of oranges and almonds, island of rocky coves and spits of sandy beaches, of rolling hills and castle-crowned promontories, is also the summer land of hot sirocco winds and winter snows on fiery Mt. Etna. It is the island of legends where Demeter, goddess of the harvest, dropped her scythe and formed the harbors of Trapani and Messina. It is here that Homer's Ulysses encountered the wind god and Cyclops hurled his deadly rocks into the sea. An ancient land, Sicily is where Phoenicians built their ports and Greeks their temples, where Plato struggled to create his ideal republic, and where Aeschylus saw his plays so successfully performed. Here, where Vikings took on Oriental harems and splendor in a culture called Norman, common criminals assume mythic roles as *mafioso*.

Since 1860, when Garibaldi landed at Marsala, Sicily has been part of a unified Italy. Yet the union has often baffled both parties. Although Sicily is only a few miles from the toe of the Italian peninsula, only a brief ferry crossing of the Straits of Messina from the continent of Europe, it has been as much a part of Africa and the East. For over a thousand years, Sicilians spoke Greek; for hundreds, they spoke Arabic. Not until A.D. 1200 did they join Europeans in speaking Latin. For millennia, Sicily was a bridge between continents, a link between the East and West.

Although today Italy plans to attach the island to the mainland by a tunnel or bridge across the Messina straits, in the past Sicily was at the Mediterranean crossroads of many civilizations, and vulnerable to attachment by a dizzying number of them. By the 9th century B.C., the Phoenicians had established their trading outposts around Trapani and Palermo, convenient locations for setting off for Iberian metals. In the 8th century B.C., crowded conditions in Rhodes, Corinth, and Chalcedon led Greek colonists to settle on the fertile lands of the east coast. Eventually, the Carthaginians, North African heirs to the Phoenicians, found themselves at odds with the ever-expanding Greeks, resulting in clashes between Hannibal and the Syracusan Dionysus for dominion of the island. Both remained, however, the Carthaginians keeping to the west coast. They remained, that is, until 241 B.C., when Rome required Sicily as its jumping-off point for ruling the Mediterranean. Later still, in the 5th century of our era, the Vandals and Goths, who seem to find their way everywhere, also found their way to Sicily. They were followed by the Byzantines, the Arabs, the Normans and the Swabians. Then the unpopular Angevine French arrived, only to be ousted in the bloody uprising of the Sicilian Vespers (1282) commemorated in Verdi's *I Vespri Siciliani*. The Spaniards settled in for centuries of rule from Palermo, only occasionally disturbed by Piedmontese and Austrian usurpers. Next, the Spanish Bourbons from Naples ruled before England held the island as a protectorate at the beginning of the 19th century. Even with its unification with Italy, Sicily's peace was far from guaranteed, for in the 20th century it was once again used as a springboard, this time by the allied forces attacking Hitler. Perhaps the only conqueror who failed to gain Sicily was Napoleon.

Despite such a turbulent history, there were periods—under the Greeks, the Arabs, the Normans, and the Swabian Frederick II—when Sicily was not simply an outpost of an empire, but rather the seat of great culture and a flourishing Mediterranean power. The Greek tyrants of Syracuse, like Dionysus and Agothacles, managed to create the largest empire in the Western

History and Art

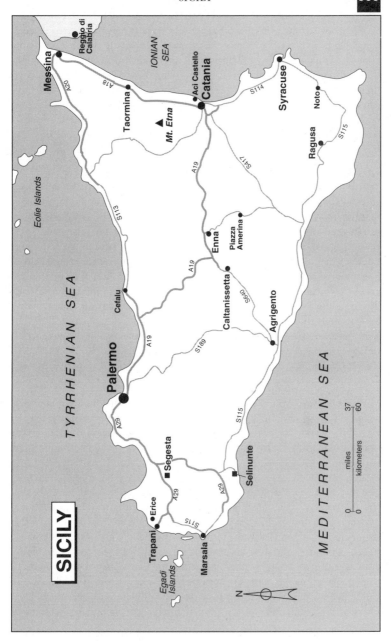

History and Art

world by conquering most of Sicily, parts of Southern Italy, and North Africa. So great was the power of Syracuse that Athens repeatedly tried to challenge it, and in 415 B.C. was humiliated in a great defeat thoroughly described for posterity by Thucydides. Not only successful at conquest, Greek Sicily produced the great philosopher Empedocles, the celebrated rhetorician Georgias, and the scientist Archimedes, whose clever defensive works of Syracuse are said to have kept the Roman legions at bay for two years. Perfect Greek cities were built all over the east and southeast of the island, at Agrigento as well as Syracuse, at Selinunte and Gela, so that today their Doric temples still stand, their masterfully painted vases and minted coins filling museums.

With the Arab invasion of A.D. 800, the power shifted in Sicily from Syracuse on the east coast to Palermo on the west. In an example of tolerance that was to continue even during the Christian rule of the Normans, Palermo bustled with an amazing array of peoples—Greek Christians and Jews, Berbers, Tartars, Africans and Persians. While Sicily became an important trader in the Islamic world that dominated the Mediterranean from Spain to Syria, Palermo was a great city with hundreds of mosques and a population exceeded in Christendom only by Constantinople. For more than 250 years, the Arab emirs ruled a prosperous Sicily. Yet they left few tangible remains, even though their impact on the language and cuisine endures today. Perhaps the accomplishments of this period are best reflected in the next centuries, for it is the Arabs who were the artisans, administrators and financiers to the Norman kings.

In 1160, Norman mercenaries under Roger landed at Messina the request of the pope, who hoped to win Sicily not only from the "infidels," but also for the western church. Roger found Sicily so much to his liking that he ceased the wandering of his Viking ancestors and established a dynasty in the opulent style of the Arab emirs who had preceded him. Having few followers with whom to colonize the island, he initially relied on the Arabs and Greeks, who were already in charge, and thereby created a unique culture, one that could hardly please the pope. His son Roger II accepted the Byzantine concept of divine ruler and lived sumptuously, attended by eunuchs and a harem. Far from slothful, however, he maintained a professional army that conquered much of North Africa and all of Italy north to the Papal States. When excommunicated by the pope, Roger convinced him to reverse his decision by kidnapping him. The Normans left a rich legacy. The tolerance of their court led to the sharing of scientific and scholastic ideas by diverse cultures, and the first Latin translations of Plato, Euclid and Ptolomey. Their splendid cathedrals and churches display the same co-mingling of cultures—the Greek, Arabic and Latin.

Frederick II, Swabian and German king, Holy Roman Emperor, "inherited" the throne to Sicily though he nonetheless had to fight for it upon assuming his augustan authority in 1220. Part Norman, Frederick preferred Sicily to any other possession, and maintained his court at Palermo while engaging in the Ghibelline wars and power struggles in Italy against three popes and their Guelf allies. If his ventures had succeeded, he would have been the first to unify Italy since Roman times. Certainly, because of the trouble he gave the popes, he was known as something of a heretic. But his learning also earned him the title "stupor mundi," wonder of the world. He himself spoke six languages, and his court was renowned for its vernacular poetry (which inspired Dante), as well as for its scientific learning (from here Arabic numerals were introduced into the West). At the time of the intolerant crusades, he permitted Arabs and Jews to practice their religions within his domains. Although continuing much of the Norman tradition, even to maintaining a harem for himself in Apulia, he devoted himself to building castles rather than cathedrals. Even today, these forbidding fortresses dominate the hills of Sicily.

Two conquests, those of Rome and Spain, endured for many centuries, but hardly contributed to the well-being of the island. Both empires conducted their main business elsewhere, and simply used the island to help pay for their various wars and exploits. Rome broke the economy of Sicily by waging the prolonged and brutal Punic wars against Carthage here. Then it enslaved much of the population, expropriated their land, overtaxed its people and, impressed by the island's Hellenistic culture, pillaged its temples and carried off hundreds of sculptures to Rome. Spain, with only 400 rather than 600 years to rule the island, was less brutal. Nonetheless, its conquests were across the Atlantic so that the Mediterranean island never figured centrally in its plans. And while the Italian mainland flourished with mercantile city-states during the Renaissance, Sicily under Spain was isolated intellectually by the Inquisition and crippled in commerce by the expulsion of the Jews and their capital. Rome left its monuments, amphitheaters and the pleasure palace of Piazza Armerina; Spain, Baroque churches and baronial mansions. But under both empires, Sicily was cut off from the mainstream of history. Under both, it was left a wretched legacy of huge landed estates that impoverished most Sicilians. It was too bad, perhaps, that Napoleon's revolutionary army never arrived.

Modern Sicily

Sicily today still lives off the land and sea. Its fishing fleet is one of the largest in Italy, and it produces vast quantities of the nation's fruits, wine and olives. Yet modern Sicily continues to struggle with its inheritance. Millennia of farming have led to deforestation and long summers when the rivers run dry. Different outlooks from the rest of Italy led to Sicily fighting for and becoming the first semi-autonomous *regione*. Unfortunately, the mafia infiltrated the regional government in Palermo, so that national efforts to industrialize and diversify the economy were often frustrated by corruption. Nonetheless, even before recent efforts to purge organized crime from Sicily, there was some success at modernization. Industry thrives at Gela, in Porto Empedocle, above Syracuse, and even in Palermo. New highways connect the coasts and irrigation helps the farmers. Whether future efforts will erase the poverty that has too long afflicted the region remains to be seen. For the thousands of tourists, who represent a source of considerable income to the island, the Greek and Norman sights remain fascinating. And even though the beaches near the few industrial areas have become somewhat polluted, Taormina remains one of the great European resorts and the sea around the Lipari and Egadi islands, near Cefalu to the north and Selinunte to the south, remains clear and beckoning.

Cuisine

Sicilian food is the same rich blend as its history and geography. From ancient and fertile Sicily comes the wheat still grown in its interior, the vineyards and wine along the coasts, the olives and oil of Ragusa, and the wild fennel covering its hills. The mild climate produces vegetables year round: the tomato, artichoke, and the purple cauliflower called "broccoli." The sea—be it the Ionian to the east, the Tyrrhenian to the north, or the Mediterranean—produces most of Sicily's preferred dishes. Catania cultivates mussels and clams on its Ionian coast and Messina hauls in great quantities of delicate tasting swordfish. Trapani, in the late spring, takes advantage of the tuna migrating through its part of the Mediterranean. And the anchovies that flavor so many local dishes are harvested everywhere.

From North Africa comes the couscous of Trapani, where it is transformed by seafood. From the Arabs comes the luscious *melanzana*, or eggplant that finds itself grilled and marinated into many forms of pasta sauces (such as the island's hearty and flavorful *pasta alla Norma* with tomatoes, eggplant, and the pungent grating cheese *ricotta salinata*) and antipasta (such as the sublime *caponata*, a blend of eggplant that just begins with capers, tomatoes and olives). In fact, it was the Arabs who contributed so much to what is now Sicilian cuisine. They brought the pine nuts and currants that flavor just about everything, including the filling of rolled *involtini di spada*, or stuffed swordfish; the capers that flavor a *risotto marinera*; the sesame seeds found on Sicilian bread; the almond trees that bloom each February in Agrigento and yield their fruit to marzipan, or *martaban* in Arabic; the oranges of every variety, especially the blood or "Sicilian" orange.

It was the Arabs, too, who brought sherbet from China to Sicily and began the passion for ice cream in the western world. Perhaps the Arabs also left their taste for sweets along with the ingredients, for Sicily uses every opportunity for creating new confections. Two of the most popular pastries are the cannoli, those hollow pastry tubes filled with sweetened ricotta cream, and the *cassata siciliana*, a cake of many forms that most often has a ricotta and cream filling, lots of candied fruits, and a green pistachio icing.

Although we don't know the origin of *arancini*, Sicily's most prevalent snack of fried rice balls filled with ragu or cheese, the manufacture of *marsala*, its famous aperitif and dessert wine, began in the town of the same name under the hopeful eye of an 18th-century Englishman. (Try Marsala Vergine or Vergine Riserva.) Sicilian **wines** have enjoyed a longer history and are known to have been favorites of ancient Rome. Among those wines that today can be found everywhere on the island is the consistently decent red or white *Corvo di Salaparuta* and the pleasant white *Rapitala*.

Travel Tips

Climate and Season

Sicily has little rainfall, but November and December are its rainiest months. January and early February are mild for winter—you can find swimming pools operational in balmy Agrigento—but cold for Sicilians (average high 60° F). The summer can be exceedingly hot (average high 87° F) with hotels very crowded. Try traveling March through early June, September through October for the most comfortable climate and best conditions.

Arriving

Palermo and Catania have major **airports** with daily flights from Rome and Milan, and less frequent flights from other Italian cities. Summer season brings international flights as well, from Paris and London. The Trapani/Marsala Airport has service from Rome.

Long-distance buses and trains (many with sleeping cars or couchettes) reach Palermo, Catania, and Messina via the ferries across the Messina straits. Rome (12 hours to Palermo) and Milan are the major departure points for trains; Rome (9.5 hours to Messina) for the bus route *(Sais (06) 4825684 from P. della Repubblica 42 for reservations)*.

Ferries to Messina leave from Villa San Giovanni (20-minute crossing) and both ferries (30 minutes) and hydrofoils (20 minutes) leave from Reggia di Calabria. Service is frequent, though not continuous from 5 a.m.–10 p.m. Overnight car ferries depart daily from Naples for Palermo (9 hours). Once a week, there's a car ferry from Genoa to Palermo (23 hours) with cabins available. Except during July and August, half the cost is refunded upon purchase of your return ticket if you stay at least 6 days in Sicily and have foreign license plates. There's also a ferry from Cagliari to Palermo (14 hours).

Autostrada del Sole is the **highway** to take to the ferry for the Messina straits. South of Salerno there are no tolls. Between Salerno and Reggio Calabria, this highway has recently been plagued by bandits. *Do not drive it at night and use towns, not highway gas stations, for refueling and food.*

Getting Around

Car rental agencies operate at the airports, major cities, and the resort of Taormina. Tour agencies also are plentiful, including the economy-style of CIT and those by larger international agencies. Only local flights connect Trapani and Palermo, and both with the island of Pantelleria. The major train routes are Messina to Palermo; Messina to Catania and Syracuse. Because of the completion of several highways, buses are often faster. Autostradas connect Palermo and Catania in less than 3 hours; Palermo and Trapani (2 hours) and Mazara del Vallo; Messina to Palermo (about 3.5 hours); and Messina to Catania to Syracuse (about 3 hours, but the leg to Syracuse has more gaps than pavement).

Special Tips

Sicily is quite affordable compared to other parts of Italy. Museum fees are half those of Florence; the autostradas are more often than not free; and hotels and restaurants offer you more for your money. • Taormina is an especially comfortable base for exploring much of Sicily (except in the summer high season).

CRIME: The mafia might be the best known Sicilian organization, but its presence is usually unfelt by the traveler. Unless you count the names of towns like "Corleone," the sightseer looking for signs of the mob will most likely be disappointed. But, of course, there is crime in Sicily and of the type that concerns tourists. Like urban centers throughout the world, Palermo and Catania, Sicily's two largest cities, experience a fair amount of street theft. • The Reggio Calabria-Salerno highway to the Messina ferry and some Sicilian roads have been subject to banditry. Trucks are the primary targets, but it is best not to drive at night.

Palermo

Key to Palermo

Sights

Extraordinary Norman churches—including the duomo in nearby Monreale; fine regional museums of art and archaeology.

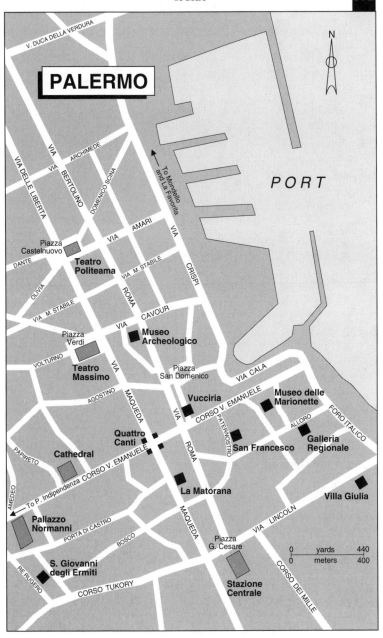

PALERMO

V. DUCA DELLA VERDURA

VIA DELLE LIBERTA

VIA

VIA BERTOLINO

ARCHIMEDE

DOMENICO SCINA

VIA AMARI

VIA

DANTE

Piazza Castelnuovo

Teatro Politeama

VIA M. STABILE

VIA M. STABILE

OLIVIA

VOLTURNO

ROMA

VIA

CAVOUR

CRISPI

PORT

To Mondello and La Favorita

Piazza Verdi

Museo Archeologico

Teatro Massimo

VIA

MAQUEDA

Piazza San Domenico

VIA CALA

AGOSTINO

Vucciria

VIA

CORSO V. EMANUELE

Museo delle Marionette

FORO ITALICO

PATERNOSTRO

ALLORO

Quattro Canti

Cathedral

PAPIRETO

ROMA

San Francesco

Galleria Regionale

To P. Indipendenza CORSO V. EMANUELE

La Matorana

AMEDEO

Villa Giulia

Pallazzo Normanni

PORTA DI CASTRO

BOSCO

MAQUEDA

VIA LINCOLN

Piazza G. Cesare

S. Giovanni degli Ermiti

RE RUGERO

CORSO TUKORY

Stazione Centrale

CORSO DEI MILLE

0	yards	440
0	meters	400

Palermo

Excursions

Easy half-day trips to Segesta, Erice, Cefalu; Selinunte and Agrigento within striking distance.

Nearby Beaches

Mondello Lido, 10 km (6 mi.); Cefalu, 70 km (43 mi.).

Festivals

Festival of Santa Rosalia, July 10-15; Festival of Dance and Music, July/August by sea at Villa Castelnuovo; annual puppet theater festival, November.

Accommodations

Decent selection in all categories.

Eating Out

Superb Sicilian cuisine in both elegant and rustic restaurants. *Pasta alle sarde* is unique to Palermo.

Getting Around

Snarled traffic and snarling drivers make tours, buses, and taxis a wise alternative to driving yourself. Walking the best bet for most in-town sights.

Arriving

Airport with daily domestic flights and, in summer, a few international; train and bus service from Rome (12.5 hours) via Messina straits; overnight ferry from Naples. Train and bus connections with rest of Sicily.

Special Tips

Purse and camera snatching and pick-pocketing are common crimes but not violent ones. Sightsee with as few valuables as possible. Park your car in a garage. • The old sections around Corso and stazione are deserted after 8 p.m.; consider taking taxis at night.

Good reading

The Leopard, by Guiseppe Tomasi de Lampedusa.

What to See and Do

The capital and main port of Sicily has been a colony of Phoenicia, Rome, and Byzantium, as well as an Arab city rivalling Cairo and Cordoba. It was the most cultured and most lavish court of Europe under the Normans and Swabians, and for centuries it was the seat of Spanish viceroys, the city of wealthy land barons and counts. Under the eternal, looming presence of Monte Pellegino, Palermo has grown and changed until now, its old city is decayed by the weight of history, and its streets entangled with traffic like so many centuries of bureaucracy. More modern tastes have moved the center to broader, tree-lined avenues, while industry and car exhaust have added to the thickness of the air, and housing projects have scarred the golden hills of Conca D'Oro. A modern city plagued by the usual urban problems, Palermo simultaneously offers a unique, even exotic, blend of cultures. No matter the traffic hassles, the disconcerting ill-repair of former baronial palaces, Palermo's sights are worth the inconvenience, for here are the masterpieces of Norman architecture and art, here are fine regional museums boasting Greek

Palermo

sculpture from the 5th C. b.c., and Renaissance paintings from the hand of Antonello de Messina.

Center of Old City ★★

Quattro Canti

Corso Vittorio Emanuele at Via Maqueada.

For most of Palermo's history, the Corso was the main thoroughfare of the city, leading west from the palace, past the cathedral, and on to the port. While the city grew to the north in recent centuries, the palaces along the Corso decayed, never to recover after WW II damage. Here, at the center of the old city, the Baroque intersection of the Quattro Canti retains some of the former opulence of the Corso. Its curved facades and sculptures are designed as a four-part fountain dedicated to the seasons. And just south on Maqueada is an even more ornate relic, the 16th-century fountain of the **Piazza Pretoria**.

A few more steps south, and you come to the adjoining Piazza Bellini, a fine spot overlooked by two small Norman churches that show the Norman blend of the Byzantine, Saracen, and Romanesque. **★La Matorana**, with its superb campanile, also retains its original Norman dome, with a Greek hymn in Arabic lettering around its base, and some of the oldest mosaics in Sicily (note Roger II being crowned, not by the pope or an emperor, but by Christ, in the mosaic panel on the right, near entrance). After leaving the appealing intimacy of this church, note its neighbor **San Cataldo**, also from the 12th century. Although the interior (with Roman columns) was never completed, the three red domes and the Arabic facade, with lacy crenellations and window screens, are pleasing. *La Martorana is open 8:30 a.m.–1 p.m. and 3:30–5:30 p.m., till 7 p.m. in summer; festivi 8:30 a.m.–1 p.m. Ask there for the key to San Cataldo if it's not open. The #1 and #77 bus, and others, stop at P. Bellini.*

Cathedral

Corso Vittorio Emanuele at Via S. Agata.

Though an imposing structure, the cathedral has perhaps suffered too many additions over the centuries. With round arches and pointed ones, with arabesques and crenellations, all topped by a Baroque dome, the cathedral is a bit ungainly. The exterior of the apse shows its Norman origins, but the facade is mostly from the 14th and 15th centuries. Inside, there are six royal tombs in the right aisle, including those of Frederick II and Roger II. *Closed noon–4 p.m. Bus 27, 38, or 4.*

Palazzo dei Normanni ★★

Corso Vittorio Emanuele at Piazza della Vittoria.

This highest point in the city is also one of the most historic. Fortified in ancient times (Roman house ruins can be seen under their protective covers in the piazza), the Arab Emirs next built here, then the Norman kings built over their constructions, and later the Spanish viceroys added their own enlargements. The palace facade is primarily of Spanish origin, but the towers are Norman. And although the eccentric 16th-century Porta Nuova that spans the Corso recalls an old war victory, the peaceful palm garden of this handsome piazza indicates more accurately the parliamentary functions now taking place in the palace. It is the 12th and 13th centuries that were the heyday of this palace, centuries when the Palermo royal courts of the Normans and of Frederick II dominated Europe culturally. And it is the Norman artistic achievement that rewards today's visitor. *Bus 27, 38, 4 and others.*

Access to the ★ ★ **Cappella Palatina** is found left and around to the rear of the palace. Started by Roger II in 1132, the lavish interior of this chapel benefits what was then the wealthiest court in all of Europe. Here Byzantine gold ★ mosaics glimmer in a dense, almost mysterious space. Colored marbles decorate walls in intricate patterns and both Greek and Latin calligraphy contribute to the opulent design. An extraordinary ★ ★ Moorish stalactite-style ceiling, deeply carved and painstakingly painted with saintly portraits and abstract motifs, crowns the nave. In the apse, the madonna mosaic dates from the 19th-century, but the opposite west wall is purely 12th century, with the Norman throne under that of the Omnipotent. (On request, the caretaker can turn on lights.)

The regional legislature occupies the top floor of the palace, formerly the location of the Royal Apartments with the **Sala di Re Ruggero**. The ★ mosaics (1170) in this king's salon are among the few secular ones remaining from the Norman period. Although 19th-century mosaics can be seen here, the almost Persian scenes of graceful peacocks and pussy-cat lions that cover the walls date from the Normans.

Because of official functions at the palace, it's possible to find both the Sala and chapel closed. For the Royal Apartments wait at reception desk for escort (Mon., Fri.–Sat. 9 a.m.–noon or make an appointment (☎ 656-1111); for the Cappella Palatina, 9 a.m.–noon and 3–5 p.m., Sat.–Sun., 9–10 a.m., and noon–1 p.m.

San Giovanni degli Ermiti

A half-block down Via del Benedettini (leading out of the left side of the Normanni palace).

This picturesque Norman church has red oriental domes and a romantically tangled garden. It is built over an earlier mosque, and now is desanctified. There's little to see in the interior fortunately, since the hours are irregular. *Officially opens 9 a.m.– 1 p.m., but also 3–5 p.m. Tues., Wed., Fri.*

Port Area

East, the Corso Vittorio Emanuele crosses a main intersection with Via Roma, skirts the famous **Vucciria market** on its left and the **Chiesa San Francisco** on its right (down V. Paternostro), with its elaborate rose window and Gothic portal. Straight ahead, through the Porta Felice, is the **Foro Italico**, a once elegant boulevard by the port that now runs past amusement parks and outdoor gelati shops. At Via Lincoln, the Foro reaches the **Villa Guilia**, an elaborate, if somewhat rundown 18th-century-style garden. Next door are the subtropical splendors of the **Orto Botanico**. *(closed Sundays and every afternoon).* The area still hasn't quite recovered from the heavy bombing it suffered in WWII, and is somewhat impoverished. However, weekends and the Sunday passeggiata bring the Foro to life with the bustle of children playing and families enjoying themselves. In the vicinity are two museums. *Buses 3, 5 and 24 are convenient.*

Galleria Regionale di Sicilia   ★

Via Alloro 7.

Just a few blocks off the Foro in the 15th-century Palazzo Abatellis is the museum of Sicilian sculpture and painting. The collection is definitely worth a visit, and some of the relatively unknown works, such as *S. Nicole in Cattera* (1300s' upstairs) and the 15th-century sculptures of Antonello Gagni (ground floor) provide interesting surprises. Among the masterpieces here are Francesco Laurana's late 15th-century ★ *Bust of Eleanor of Aragon* (ground floor) and a roomful of Sicily's Renaissance master, Antonello de Messina. His ★ ★ *Virgin Annunciata* (c. 1465) is deceptively simple, built out of geometrical forms and beautiful light to create a compelling image of the Virgin against a stark background. His other paintings include ★ *Portrait of S. Augustin. Open 9 a.m.–1:30 p.m.; Tues., Thurs., Fri., also 3–6 p.m. (but 2–7:30 p.m. in summer); Sun. 9 a.m.–12:30 p.m.; L2000.*

Museo Delle Marionette

Via Butera 1; ☎ *328-060.*

Just off the end of the Corso are these quarters for the museum and its Sicilian puppet collection, used during weekly theatrical performances of the traditional Carolingian tales of knightly heroism and chivalry. *Open 9 a.m.–1 p.m. and also 4–7 p.m. Mon., Wed., Fri.; closed Sun. L5000.*

North of the Corso ★

Both Via Roma and Via Maqueada head north from the Corso Vittorio Emanuele and pass through numerous shops and offices of the more modern city. Some of the grandest structures of 19th-century Palermo line Via Maqueada and its extensions. As V. Maqueada leaves Quattro Canti, it pauses in front of the neo-classical **Teatro Massimo** (Piazza Verdi; closed), before continuing to the vast piazza Castelnuovo/Politeama with its **Teatro Politeama Garibaldi** crowned with rearing bronze horses and chariot driver. From here, the street becomes the fashionable Viale della Liberta lined with cafes and boutiques. While browsing and strolling, be sure to visit the Museo Nazionale. *Buses 101 and 107 are among those circling in this area.*

Museo Archeologico Nazionale ★ ★

Piazza Olivella 4.

Wedged between the Via Roma and Maqueada near the Teatro Massimo, the museum is pleasantly housed in a former 16th-century monastery. Contained here are the rare sculptural adornments of Sicily's Greek temples, the famous frieze panels, or ★ metopes from Selinunte dating from the 6th and 5th century B.C. The Selinunte room is on the ground floor, at the rear of the second courtyard. The exhibits are well-marked and include some delicately carved heads and the bronze Ephebus, in addition to the metopes. At the end of this room is the entrance to the ★ Etruscan collection that contains elaborately carved sarcophagi from Chuisi, some of reclining figures with the sinuous grace of Buddhist art. The bronze room (upstairs, entrance end of museo) contains two exceptional sculptures: ★ *Ram*, 3rd Century B.C., a realistic work from Syracuse; and ★ *Hercules and Stag*, a Roman work from Pompeii. And there's much more. *9 a.m.–1:30 p.m., and also 3–6 p.m. Tues. and Fri.; Sun. till 1 p.m.; L2000.*

Outskirts ★★

Palermo

Monreale's cloisters features 228 distinctly different columns.

Monreale   ★★★

8 km, 5 mi. SW of Palermo.

The last and, for many, the greatest accomplishment of Norman art, the cathedral
and Benedictine cloister of Monreale were begun in 1174 by William II and pretty
much completed before his death 15 years later. The rapidity of construction
resulted in an exceptional unity of style.

The ★★**cathedral** facade (may be covered for restoration) offers pleasing Arabic
designs in contrasting limestone, lava and brick, particularly on the three apses. The
main portal has bronze doors carved by Bonanno da Pisa shortly after he completed
his work for the Pisa cathedral. The interior shimmers with more than 6000 sq.
meters of ★mosaic—second in extent only to Hagia Sophia in Constantinople.
Despite the wealth of detail depicted in the scenes from the Old Testament (above
the nave) and the New, the overall clarity of the design leads the eye inexorably to

the apse, where a glowing Christ casts his blessing. While the floors date from the 16th century, the columns are from antiquity, and some of the capitals are carved with Roman gods. The stalactite-style wooden ceiling over the choir is worthy of note as are the royal tombs of the two Norman Williams. Coin-operated lights available.

On the south side of the church is the entrance to the ★★**cloisters**, so Arabic in their delicacy and inventiveness, so European in their narrative reliefs. Here, 228 slender columns form the cloister, and not one is like any other. Their shafts are plain or inlaid, twisted, zigzagged, or foliated. Their carved capitals relate both Biblical stories and allegories; they represent warriors, kings and fighting animals. As you approach the SW corner with its small square enclosure and delightful fountain, you see the dedicatory capital with William II offering the church to the Virgin. In the NE corner group of four you find a superb Annunciation.

The cathedral is open 8:30 a.m.–noon, 3:30–6:30 p.m.; L2000 for access to roof and views of cloister and valley. Cloister hours are 9 a.m.–7 p.m. except weekends till 1 p.m. Apr.–Sept.; 9 a.m.–1 p.m., but Sun. till 12:30 p.m. Oct.–Mar.; L2000. The 389 bus, from P. Indipendenza, and the 8/9 bus, departing from V. Stabile near Ruggero Settimo and continuing out on Corso Calatafimi and across Viale della Regione, take you to the village of Monreale and its cathedral. Driving the same route, you pick up SS 186 and signs to Monreale.

La Zisa

Piazza Guglielmo i Buomo, northwest of Palazzo Real.
William the Bad would never believe the seedy surroundings of what was formerly his earthly paradise, this pleasure palace built in the 12th century. Although medieval crenallations fortified it and later residents transformed it according to their own tastes, the Sala della Fontana retains the original gold mosaics, stalactite ceiling and fountain. Other rooms display a small collection of Islamic art. *Open 9 a.m.– 1:30 p.m. weekdays, and also 3–5:30 Tues. & Fri. Bus 24 from Castelnuovo.*

Museo Etnografico Pitre & La Favorita

7 km north of old center.
A refreshing drive toward the base of Monte Pelligrini and through the calm of La Favorita Park brings you to an enchanting, if bizarre Bourbon villa called the **Chinese Palace** (late 18th C.; closed to public) and its next door neighbor, the Ethnographic Museum. Although the museum displays are a bit musty, the small collection of colorful ★ Sicilian carts, elaborately painted with historical and political scenes, and the ex-voto miracle paintings, some from the 19th century, might appeal to you. *Open 9 a.m.–1 p.m.; closed Fri.; L2000. Bus 14, 15 and 101 from Stazione and V. Roma.*

Mondello Lido

10 km, 6 mi. north.
Over a mile of beach stretches between the two promontories Monte Pellegrino and Monte Gallo, forming one of Sicily's best known beaches. The scene is typically Italian, with most of the sandy expanse covered with neat rows of beach chairs. You might want to pay your admission fee to one of these clubs that has a pool, since the

Palermo

condition of the sea in this increasingly industrialized area is somewhat suspect. In the summer, some prefer to use Mondello as their base, but the traffic congestion between here and the city makes this option a cumbersome one for the sightseeing traveler. *Bus 14 or 15 on V. Maqueda and Liberta.*

Festivals and Entertainment

In addition to the special events mentioned in the Key, it is worth elaborating on the folk tradition preserved in Palermo's *teatro dei pupi*, or puppet theaters. Since the Normans introduced the chivalric tales of Roland and other legendary knights of Charlemagne, the Sicilians have been retelling and reinterpreting them. Today, the heroic feats of these knights are still told in the puppet theaters. The most authentic performances are at Museo delle Marionette (Sat. or Sun. usually; ☎ *328-060).* For information on these theaters and the other festivals, contact the AAPIT tourism office.

Where to Stay

Apart from a few seaside establishments, most of the better hotels are found in the modern part of the city, around P. Castelnuovo/Politeama and along V. della Liberta. Although requiring a good walk or ride to the sights of the old city, these hotels are well-placed for dining and evening walks. A few hotels in Mondello are listed in case that's your preference, but be sure to reserve way in advance for summer accommodations. Unless otherwise stated, rooms are air-conditioned.

Expensive

Villa Igiea   L240–360,000 CP

Via Belmonte 43, 91042, 4 km north; ☎ *543-744, FAX 547-654.*
Single L240,000 CP. Double L360,000 CP.
Overlooking the sea, this hotel is an extraordinary villa designed by Palermo's great art nouveau architect Ernesto Basile. The dining room best preserves Basile's style, but all the common areas and antiques, the quiet terraces, are quite remarkable and grand; the 100 rooms also show their age, but less pleasingly. Small pool.

Moderate

Excelsior Palace   L170–220,000 CP   √★★★★

Via Marchese Ugo 3, 90141; ☎ *625-617 6, FAX 342-139.*
Single L170,000 CP. Double L220,000 CP.
Near the north end of Via della Liberta, this recently renovated palazzo retains its old world charm with antique furnishings and new, yet extravagant Venetian glass chandeliers. The 86 rooms are adequate in size with modern baths, interiors are best for quiet. Handsome old bar and good restaurant. Parking.

Jolly Hotel   L180–240,000 CP   ★★★★

Foro Italico 22, 90133; ☎ *616-5090, FAX 616-1441.*
Single L180,000 CP. Double L240,000 CP.
The city has turned away from this neighborhood; the sea-walk with its neoclassic wall has become an amusement park. Yet the gardens of Villa Guilia and other sights are nearby, the lobby bustles with local functions and visitors on business. The 300 rooms are modern and adequate and there is a pleasant garden and pool. Shuttle to Teatro Politeamo, under 10 times daily.

Politeama Palace Hotel   **L160–220,000 CP**   ★★★

Piazza Ruggero Settimo 15, 90124; ☎ *322-777, FAX 611-1589.*
Single L160,000 CP. Double L220,000 CP.

Facing the multiple piazzas more often known as Castlenuovo, this modern hotel with small lobby has a commercial efficiency improved by its tone of sophistication. The 100 carpeted rooms have snazzy tiled baths and are decently insulated against noise. Coffee shop.

Inexpensive

Europa   **L100–140,000**   √★★

Via Agrigento 3, 90141; ☎ *625-6323, FAX 625-6323.*
Single L100,000. Double L140,000.

Just off Via della Liberta, this modern, commercial hotel has 73 well-appointed rooms that are as comfortable as those with higher prices. Restaurant. A good buy.

Albergo Liguria   **L70–95,000**   √★

Via M. Stabile 128, 90139; ☎ *581-588.*
Single with bath L70,000. Double with bath L95,000.

Its card says central and all modern comforts, and for the budget price, this is surprisingly true. Really a small pensione, there are only 16 bright and clean rooms, half with private baths. No a/c. Reserve well in advance.

In Mondello Lido

Mondello Palace   **L180–265,000 CP**   ★★★★

Viale Principe de Saclea, 90151; ☎ *684-0001, FAX 450-657.*
L180,000 CP. Double L265,000 CP.

Palermo's favorite beach hotel offers 83 comfortable rooms with bath, gardens, pool and tennis, and private beach. Restaurant. Bar. Garage.

Splendid La Torre   **L145,000**   √★★★

V. Piano Gallo 11, 90151; ☎ *450-222, FAX 450-033.*
Single/double L145,000.

At the far end of Mondello Lido but on the Palermo bus line, this 117-room hotel is on the beach, with tennis and pool, and considerable comfort. Restaurant. Bar. Parking.

Where to Eat

It's hard not to be pleased eating in Palermo. The pine nuts and currants, and the eggplant and olives of the Arabs must have first mingled with the seafood of its great capital at Palermo before spreading through the rest of Sicily. A few dishes, Palermo kept to itself—*pasta con le sarde* (fresh sardines seasoned with fennel), a form of caponata in which shellfish or tuna roe is mixed with the eggplant, and *panini di panelle*, or fried chick pea squares. In Palermo, marzipan, known as *pasta reale*, is also called *frutte di Martorana* in honor of the church and convent where it is claimed these almond paste fruits were created and hung as decorations on trees in order to welcome a visiting bishop. Lunch, the main meal, is eaten usually around 1:30 p.m. or so, dinner not before 8 p.m.

Approdo da Renato   **$$–$$$**   ★★★★

V. Messina Marina 224; ☎ *630-2881.*
Closed Sun., late Aug.; reservations advised. Meals L50–90,000.

On the extension of Via Foro Italico, the dignified L'Approdo, in an antique-filled mansion, is Palermo's best. There is a superior wine cellar, refined Sicilian cuisine: wonderful pastas with shellfish, fish in sweet and sour marinades, fabulous fish soup.

Charleston $$$ ★★★
P. Ungheria 30 near P. Verdi; ☎ *321-366.*
Closed Sun. July–Sept. Meals L65–100,000.
For elegant dining, don't miss this highly regarded restaurant. Here Sicilian and international dishes share the menu. The antipasti are especially good and the eggplant Charleston is popular, as is the grilled involtini di spada.

Le Terraze $$$ ★★★
V. Regina Elena in Mondelo; ☎ *450-171.*
Open daily June–Sept. Meals L65–100,000.
In the summer, the Charleston moves to this seaside restaurant in Mondello.

La Cuccagna $–$$ ★★
V. Grantelli 21a; ☎ *587-267.*
Closed Fri. (except June–Sept.), late Aug. Meals L35–65,000.
Cozy rather than elegant, this is where you can enjoy fresh artichokes with garlic from the antipasto table, and *zuppa di cozze* and *involtini di spada*. The *pasta con le sarde* is strong with fennel. The location is convenient, off V. Roma near the Grande Albergo.

Sapori di Mare $$ ★★
V. Mondello 52 in Modello; ☎ *684-0623*
Closed Mon. off-season. Meals L50–70,000.
Lobsters swim in a tank, the day's catch is in the refrigerated display case and the food couldn't be more satisfyingly prepared, from the lobster sauce on the pasta to the seafood couscous.

Hotel Patria $–$$ ★
V. Aragona 6; ☎ *616-1136.*
Closed Sun. Meals L25–50,000.
The hotel is gone but this difficult-to-find tiny restaurant, also known as Trattoria Stella, engagingly spills onto a small piazza when the weather permits. The daily offerings, like the wooden tables, are simple but good. (Look for V. Alloro off V. Roma between Lincoln and the Corso, then wind your way for a few blocks.

Osteria da Ciccio $ ★
V. Firenze 6.
Closed Sun. Meals L25–45,000.
Across V. Roma and behind #178 is this storefront restaurant where you start with wonderful roasted red peppers *(peperone)* and follow with a savory swordfish marinera, spiced with hot peppers, garlic and oregano.

Market and Food Shops

Sneaking its way behind the boulevards of Roma and V. Emanuele and ending at the Piazza San Domenico is the famous central market of **Vucciria**. In full swing with the fishermen's catch and continuing throughout the day, the market offers all variety of color and sounds and smells along with its delicious fruits, its barrels of Sicilian olives, and its tempting goods for snacking and picnic-making. More elegant are the shops along **Via Villareal** *(running diagonally from V. Stabile to just west of P. Castelnuovo)* particularly **Cappuccio** *(#20)*, with its prepared foods—stuffed sardines, torta rustica—and excellent salumeria (there's a stand-up bar, too). The marzipan is good at **Pasticceria La Preferita** *(#47)* and the pastries and marzipan at nearby **Extrabar Olimpia** *(V. Ruggero Settimo 99)* are famous. **Note:** Food shops usually close Wednesday afternoons: summer they might switch to Saturday p.m.

Caffè and Snacks

One of Palermo's oldest snacking establishments is ★ **Antica Focacceria** *(V. Paternos-tro 58, in front of San Francisco church; closed Mon.; meals about L20,000)*, with its tra-ditional tavola calda and marble tables for eating arancini, panini di panelle (weekends only), and even pizza. One of the city's most fashionable cafes is **Roney's** *(V. della Liberta 13; closed Mon.; moderate-inexpensive)* with a terrace bar where Palermites meet to be seen and discuss the world's events at one of the best stand-up counters—calamari fritti and other delights in addition to the panini and arancini, and good pastries. In the area of Quattro Canti is the **Trattoria Bernini** *(P. Bernini; closed Tues.; pizza L7–12,000)*, the favorite spot for evening pizza, especially in the summer when dining is al fresco. And nearby, convenient for snacks while sightseeing, is **Caffè Quattro Canti** *(Corso V. Eman-uele 315)*, where you can enjoy a hot, open-face sandwich called Crostino Quattro Canti in the rear tea room. In the summer, make sure you have your gelati at **Ilardo** (Foro Ital-ico), particularly during the Sunday passeggiata.

Directory

Telephone Code 091   **Postal Code 90100**

Airlines
>   **Alitalia**/Ati, *V. Mazzini 59 (☎ 601-9333)*.

Airport
>   **Punta Raisi** *(☎ 591-690)*, 45 minutes from Palermo on Trapani road, with car rentals, taxis, and connecting buses (Stazione Central and behind Teatro Politeama at V. Lumia).

American Express
>   **Ruggeri Giovanni & Figli**, *V. Amari 40 (☎ 587-144)*.

Books in English
>   **Feltrinelli** *(P. Verdi);* **Flaccovio** *(V. Ruggero Settimo 37)*.

Bus
>   **AMAT** city buses leave from in front of stazione. (Buy tickets at tabacchi). **SAIS** *(☎ 616-6028)* pullman service to other parts of Sicily as well as to Rome leave from V. Paolo Bolsamo near the stazione.

Car Rentals
>   **Avis** *(☎ 333-806)*, **Europcar** *(☎ 321-949)*, and others.

Consul
>   United States, *V. Re Frederico 18* bis ☎ *611-0020;* for traveler services, contact Naples consul.

Emergencies

Dial 113.

Ferries

Tirrenia, *V. Roma 385 (☎ 602-1111).*

Groceries

Vucciria market, between V. Roma and Corso.

Police

Questura ☎ *210-111;* for Polizia Turistica, dial ☎ *113.*

Post Office

V. Roma, south of Cavour.

Shopping

Via della Liberta for the most fashionable shops; the Corso up Via Roma and Via Maqueada and the small streets in between are Palermo's downtown; the Corso around Quattro Canti has numerous old and used book shops.

Taxis

Major piazzas and hotels; meter-operated.

Telephone

ASST, V. Lincoln in front of stazione, open 24 hours. **Telcom**, P. Ungheria north of P. Verdi. 8 a.m.–1 p.m., 4–8 p.m., Sun. 8 a.m.–noon, 4–5:30 p.m.

Tourist Office

AAPIT, *P. Castelnuono 34 (☎ 583-847; FAX 331-854),* 8 a.m.–8 p.m., Saturday a.m. only; Sunday, closed. Very helpful office. Airport *(☎ 591-698)* and stazione *(☎ 616-5914),* too.

Tours

CIT, *V. della Liberta 12 (☎ 586-333),* for city and island bus tours; also see American Express above.

Train

Stazione Centrale at V. Roma and Lincoln *(☎ 616-1806).*

On the Road

Western Sicily

Most often bypassed by the highway from Palermo to Agrigento, the western part of Sicily has a number of interesting sights for the leisurely traveler. Here in the province of Trapani is the coast so long dominated by Carthaginians and Arabs. Away from the coast, the land remains sparsely populated and tranquil, yet two of the great warring factions of ancient times have left their temples behind, at Segesta and Selinunte, the most dramatically situated Greek ruins in all of Sicily. Those looking for seaside vacations, might head for the islands off the town of Trapani. Other travelers might visit Segesta and Erice on a day excursion from Palermo or whip through

Selinunte on the way to Agrigento. But if you're looking for overnight facilities, those at Selinunte and the hill resort of Erice are the most convenient.

Segesta

In 416 B.C., Segesta asked Athens for help against its enemy, Selinunte. According to Thucidydes, Athens sent Alcibiades to look over Segesta and he returned reporting its great wealth. Since Segesta was never particularly wealthy, historians believe the ancient city tricked the Athenians into an alliance by building a grandiose ★**Doric temple**. This unfinished temple, majestically isolated on a hill, still commands respect nearly 2500 years later. While the temple can be glimpsed from all over the valley, closer views are to be had along the access road that climbs to the amphitheater. To actually reach the temple (no carvings), a hike is necessary.

A 1 km access road climbs Monte Barbaro, site of the ancient, if unexcavated, city of Segesta. You can drive or hike the road to the 3rd century B.C. Greek **amphitheater** at the top. Carved out of the mountainside, the amphitheater has a ★magnificent setting with views of the distant sea and ancient hills. Usually, you share the amphitheater with just the wind and the grazing goats, but every odd-numbered year during parts of July and August, classical plays are performed here and should not be missed. For the schedule, contact *AAPIT in Trapani. Open 9 a.m.–sunset; no fee; cafe at entrance to access road.*

Practical Tips

Segesta is a few km off A-29 at A-29dir (extension) to Trapani, 65 km, 40 mi. south of Palermo and 40 km, 25 mi. east of Trapani. The Trapani-to-Palermo train stops a 20 minute walk away. AST buses from Trapani provide service Mon.–Sat. Special buses run from Trapani and Palermo for performances.

Erice

Rising nearly 2500 feet above Trapani harbor, the rocky hill of Erice was an important landmark to sailors in ancient times. It also was a legendary spot, where Trojan heroes wandered and pilgrims stopped to participate in a Carthaginian fertility cult at the Temple of Venus Erycina. So great was the following of this cult that centuries later, the conquering Romans felt obliged to rebuild the temple. Though the town **museum** (on the tiny main square of P. Umberto; 9 a.m.–2 p.m.) holds a few works from the Roman temple, and some of the cyclopean town walls date from the period of Carthage, Erice today has an overwhelmingly medieval character with narrow cobbled streets and thick stone walls. In winter, the town is often enshrouded in mist and cold; in summer, delightful gardens and a picturesque setting attracts so many European travelers that the town takes on an international aspect. A good place for strolling, take Viale Conte Pepoli from Porta Trapani to the Villa Balio gardens where a Norman castle sits on the former site of the Temple of Venus. On a clear day, the views reach all the way down the coast to Africa.

Where to Stay

All the hotels are a good buy.

Elimo   **L100–150,000**   ★ ★

> *V. Vittorio Emanuele 75;* ☎ *869-377, FAX 869-252.*
> *Single L100,000. Double L150,000.*
> Just off P. Umberto is this strikingly attractive hotel with 21 rooms, a good restaurant, bar, roof terrace.

Moderno   **L100–140,000**   ★ ★

> *V. Vittorio Emanuele 63;* ☎ *869-300, FAX 869-139.*
> *Single L100,000. Double L140,000.*
> Cozier than Elimo and also known for its restaurant, the Moderno offers 40 comfortable rooms and a bar.

Ermione   **L115–165,000**   ★ ★ ★

> *V. Pineta Comunale;* ☎ *869-138, FAX 869-587.*
> *Single L115,000. Double L165,000.*
> Erice, cooler than the coast below, has only this one hotel with air conditioning. Outside the walls and ugly-modern in style, it has fine views and a pool along with 48 rooms and decent restaurant

Where to Eat

Hotel Moderno   **$–$$**   ★ ★ ★

> *Meals L40–60,000.*
> One of the best places to dine on local fare—fish couscous or pesto made of almonds, tomato and eggplant—is in this hotel.

Monte San Giulano   **$–$$**   ★ ★

> *Vicolo San Rocco 7;* ☎ *869-595.*
> *Closed Mon. & mid Jan.–mid Feb. Meals L40–60,000.*
> The well prepared local cuisine here is enhanced by a more stunning setting.

Maria Grammatico

> *Corso Emanuele 14.*
> Don't miss the marzipan shaped into beautiful peaches and other fruits or the *buccellati di fichi* (fig cookies).

Directory

Telephone code 0923   **Postal code 91016**

Tourist Office

> *V. Conte Pepoli 11 (*☎ *869-388, FAX 869-544);* a town map is located on V. Antonio Carlin just above the P. Umberto.

Arriving

> Bus service from Trapani (40 minutes) leaves from near train station. Erice is 15 km, 9 mi. from Trapani center; 30 km, 19 mi. from Segesta and reached by an exit off A-29dir.

Trapani

Just as in ancient times and again in medieval times, Trapani today is a major port between Tunis and Europe. Although you might find yourself here to take a boat to the Isole Egadi or Pantelleria, there is no strong reason to visit. Trapani is capital of this province, the poorest in Sicily. Its people are pleasant, its seafood good, and its *centro storico*, the part that survived WWII bombs, quite interesting for a stroll. The Corso Vittorio Emanuele runs down the center of the old promontory with the port just a few blocks away on each side. Yet rather than warehouses and fish shops, the Corso passes boutiques (halfway down, look for Libreria Best Seller with beautiful books on Sicily) and Baroque mansions and churches. The duomo, like many of the white cubical houses piled near the sea, shows the traditional influences of North Africa with its Moorish cupola and campanile.

Where to Stay and Eat

Astoria Park   **L115–170,000**   ★★★

Lungomare D. Alighieri in Erice-San Cusumano 91020; ☎ *562-400.*
Single L115,000. Double L170,000.
A comfortable hotel 3 km on the Lungomare toward Erice and situated by the sea with modern facilities including 90 rooms, with a/c, a restaurant, bar, tennis and pool. Buses from the center stop in front of the hotel.

P & G Ristorante   **$$**   ★★★

V. Spalti 1, reserve at ☎ *547-701.*
Closed Sun., Christmas season and Aug.; L45–65,000.
The large park of Villa Margherita marks the beginning of the centro storico and here is this wonderful casual spot to try the local seafood. In season, the *triglie* (red mullet), the *neonata* (newborn sardines), or any fish on display are a good choice. The *risotto marinara* provides a flavorful beginning and the Trapani-style fish *cuscus* is particularly good, when available.

Islands and Beaches

The **Isole Egadi** lie 7 to 23 miles off the coast and can be quickly reached by hydrofoil. All three islands can be visited in a day, if you want, but **Favignana** is commercial enough to forego, and you might want to bring a picnic to the others. **Marettimo** (1 hour by hydrofoil) is the most beautiful, with clear grottos for skin diving and hiking trails. **Levanso** (20 minutes) offers paleolithic art in its *Cava del Genovese* along with swimming coves. **Pantelleria** is halfway to Africa, more than 4 hours away by ferry but just a quick plane ride from the Trapani terminal. Isolated and austere, it has a loyal summer following.

Directory

Telephone code 0923   **Postal code 91100**

Tourist Offices
   AAPIT, *V. Sorba 15 (*☎ *27-077; FAX 2-94-30)*, a handsome building found 3 blocks behind train station (exit terminal to right and take first right); at airport and port, too.

Arriving

Train from Palermo takes 3 hours; bus or car of A-29/A-29dir takes 2 hours for 105 km, 65 mi. Birgi airport lies a half-hour to south on Marsala road, connections to Rome and Pantelleria. Ferries and hydrofoils *(Siremar,* ☎ *540-515)*, from port.

Motya

The coastal road to Marsala from Trapani (also known as the Birgi airport road) skirts the salt beds of the local saline industry. Nowhere is this industry more picturesque than at the dock for the boat to Motya. Turning at the sign for Motya, you leave the road (about 7 km, 4 mi. outside Marsala) and take a 1.5 km detour that skirts by **Stagnone Lagoon**, piled high with salt colorfully protected by tiles. Windmills stand among the mounds, grinding salt. To the north looms Monte Erice, straight ahead the island of Motya with its 8th century B.C. ruins of Phoenician Mozia and ancient Carthaginian walls. Here, Dionysus, the Syracusan tyrant, defeated Carthage, but not before his fleet became mired in the lagoon. Your detour can be as quick as a drive through, or it can continue on a 1 km boat ride to visit the island where a museum of sorts holds the finds from excavations.

Marsala

Marsala is an easily managed town, made pleasant by the ochre and warm colors of its buildings and by the park connecting its ancient promontory and 16th century town. The promontory is the site of Lilybaeum, founded in 396 B.C. by Carthage to replace Motya. So well fortified, it took the Romans 10 years of Punic wars to capture the port, and then they occupied it themselves for centuries. Not until the Arabs settled here was the city renamed to Mars-al-allah (harbor of God). Today, **Lilybaeum** is an archaeological park, with some Roman mosaics of tigers chasing antelopes (open during tourist season by custodian). More interesting is the nearby **Museo Archeologico di Marsala**, located in a refurbished marsala wine warehouse. Among its attractive exhibits is the 5th century B.C. ★marble statue of a haughty charioteer, found recently in the sea near Motya and probably sculpted in Greece. Here also are some of the ★Roman mosaics from Lilybaeum. In a second room is another recent underwater find, all that remains of a Punic galley, or for that matter, any ship from the 3rd century B.C. *(open 9 a.m.–2 p.m.; festivi till 1 p.m.; also 3–6 p.m. Wed., Sat.–Sat.; free).*

The town seems full of life, still prospering from the marsala wine business that began in the 18th century. Its old section requires only a short walk, down Via 11 di Maggio from the Porta Nuova up to the Piazza della Repubblica with its Baroque cathedral. Behind the duomo, toward the Porta Garibaldi, is the **Museo degli Arazzi** with eight Brussels tapestries from the 16th century, depicting the "Capture of Jerusalem." *(Open 9 a.m.–noon and 4-6 p.m.; by guided tour; L1000.)* Following the Lungomare Mediterraneo past the port and 2 km south of the center, you come to the marsala distillery and warehouse called **Cantina Florio**, open to the public for tasting of this fortified and sweet wine drunk as an aperitivo or with dessert. The *Marsala Vergine* is considered superior. *(Mon.-Fri. 10 a.m.–1 p.m., 3:30–6 p.m.; closed Aug. ☎ 781-111).*

Where to Stay and Eat

You can shop in the **market** (near Porta Garibaldi) and at **Alimentari D'Amico** *(across from Museo Arazzi)* to stock up for a picnic in the park or the lido at the tip of the promontory. In the attractive setting of the Piazza della Vittoria just outside Porta Nuova, is **Caffe Kalos** *(closed Wed.)* with sandwiches, pastries, and good *arancini*.

| **Trattoria Garibaldi** | **$–$$** | ★ |

V. Garibaldi.
Meals L25–50,000.
A few steps from the Porta Garibaldi, this cozy spot serves a bargain-priced menu turistico and plenty of seafood, including the regional cuscus and a risotto marinera.

| **Hotel President** | **L85–150,000** | ★★ |

V. Nino Bixio 1; ☎ 999-333, FAX 999-115.
Single L85,000. Double L150,000.
To overnight, you'll have to go outside the centro storico a bit to this comfortable hotel with 85 rooms (a/c), restaurant, pool, and parking.

Directory

Telephone code 0923   **Postal code 91025**

Tourist Information
 Pro-Loco, *V. Garibaldi 45* near duomo *(☎ 714-097).*

Arriving
 Located 19 km, 12 mi. south of Trapani and within easy striking distance of the Birgi airport. Buses provide the best connections here, but there is a train from Trapani. It lies 20 km west of A-29 and is less than an hour's drive to Selinunte.

Selinunte

Few ruins are so evocative of the past, long lost and forever destroyed. The acropolis of Selinunte, with the crashing surf of the Mediterranean below it, is strewn with hundreds of megalithic stones and rock-hewn columns, some nearly seven feet in diameter. Dramatically rising amid these Greek ruins are the colossal columns of Temple C, and even they had to be resurrected a few decades ago. One of the most prosperous of Greek cities in the 5th century B.C., Selinunte has suffered the ravages of war and nature, first at the hands of Hannibal and his Carthaginian armies who, at the request of Segesta, conquered the city and sacked it in 409 B.C. Though rebuilt, Selinunte was then destroyed to avoid capture by Rome. Even then, some of Selinunte's temples, its defensive walls, its many homes and shops must have been left standing. Then earthquakes felled whatever was left.

What to See and Do

Today, Selinunte is still being excavated and, in some instances, its temples or parts of them, have been reconstructed, though it remains uncertain as to which gods they were dedicated. A number of the temples here had metopes on their friezes, a rare occurrence in Sicily; all these sculptures have been removed to the Museo Nazionale Archeologico in Palermo. In the **East Group** (10-minute walk from the stazione, now used for buses) are three temples. To the left is Temple E, dating from 488 B.C., reconstructed in 1958 and considered an exceptional example of the Doric style. Nearby is the **antiquarium** with exhibits on the reconstruction of the temple. Next is Temple F, perhaps the oldest, and begun in 560 B.C.} Then there is Temple G, never completed, but an ambitious project begun at the end of the 6th century and the second largest temple in Sicily. Only one column now stands. The **Acropolis**, seen in the distance, is at the end of a mile-long road running parallel to the tiny beach resort of Marinella di Selinunte. Covering a vast hilltop terrace overgrown with scrub and clover, and with the wild parsley that gives the site its name, are the ruins of the fortified city. Below it were the harbors for its fleets that traded with North Africa. You can wander for quite a while here, admiring Temple C, discovering the grid of streets and the north gate of the defensive wall (the round base of a tower remains). If you're staying for a few days, you can walk to the north and to the west and still cross over ancient Selinunte.

The **parco archeologico** opens 9 a.m.–6 p.m.; fee (L2000) for the Acropolis. In August there are concerts and plays performed at the East Group.

Where to Stay and Eat

Although Castelvetrano used to provide most of the facilities for a visit to the ruins, *Marinella di Selinunte* has been busily making itself a far more convenient base. Along the stretch of beach, you can find numerous pizzerias and trattorias as well as pensione-style hotels. There's a campground 1 mi. away.

Pierrot   **$–$$**   ★

Closed Jan.–Feb. Meals L40–55,000.

An especially pleasant trattoria with its views and terrace, over the beach.

Lido Azzurro   **$**   ★

Meals L30–45,000.

Nearby is this longtime favorite trattoria.

Hotel Garzia   **L125,000**   √★★

V. Pigafetta; ☎ 46-024 FAX 46-196.

Single/double L125,000.

Located near the acropolis. We not only had a good meal and great cappuccino here, but we found the 70 rooms (a/c) modern and well-appointed, many with balconies and views of the acropolis. Restaurant, bar and lido bar.

Directory

Telephone code 0924   **Postal code 91020**

Tourist Information

In Castelvetrano, P. Garibaldi across from duomo; in Selinunte at East Group.

Arriving

Castelvetrano is the crossroads for Selinunte which lies 11 km, 7 mi. south and is connected by bus. Driving to Selinunte is quick and easy; from Palermo via Alcamo on A-29 it's 110 km, 68 mi. to Castelvetrano; from Agrigento on SS 115, it's 90 km, 56 mi. But bus travel to Castelvetrano can require numerous changes and delays.

Tip

If you find yourself with some time in **Castelvetrano**, don't fail to walk the few blocks of the old city (most was destroyed in the 1968 earthquake) and look for the Auditorio *(V. Garibaldi)* with its facade carvings of two people boiling in purgatory.

Agrigento

Key to Agrigento

Sights

Sicily's finest Greek temples and a medieval "old" town that's good for strolling.

Excursions

A day trip to Selinunte on the coast (90 km, 56 mi.) or an inland loop to Enna and Piazza Armerina (240 km, 149 mi. round trip).

Nearby Beaches

Around Eraclea Minoa (30 km, 19 mi.) and San Leone (6 km, 4 mi.) from Valley of the Temples.

Festivals

Summer plays and concerts in the Valle dei Templi and theaters in town; Pirandello Festival in August at that dramatist's birthplace of Kaos, on the sea near Porto Empedocles; February Almond Blossom Festival.

Accommodations

Decent selection, but few centrally located.

Eating Out

Fine restaurants.

Getting Around

A car is useful here, as the town with its facilities lies 3 km from the Valle dei Templi and some hotels are another 3 km east on SS 115 in a commercial section called Villagio Mose. Without a car, you can manage from town by taxi or by buses running to San Leone and Porto Empedocles, asking to be dropped off at the ruins.

Arriving

Pullman buses from Palermo (2.5 hours) and Catania (4.5 hours); trains from Palermo (almost 3 hours), Syracuse via Caltanisetta (5.5 hours) and Catania (4.5 hours). Palermo (via SS 121 and SS 189 is 130 km, [81 mi.]); Syracuse (via Gela on SS 115) is 215 km (133 mi.); Catania (via A-19, then south at Enna) is 170 km (105 mi.).

What to See and Do

Crowning the lower hills of Agrigento are the proud temples of ancient Akragas, founded in 580 B.C. By exporting wine and olives to North Africa, Akragas grew to a city of 200,000 and became wealthy enough to be praised by the poet Pindar as the "most beautiful city of mortals." During the relatively brief span between 480 and 410 B.C., Agrigento built at least eight temples. Only Athens built more. And while Athens awaited Socrates, Agrigento produced the philosopher Empedocles who identified the four basic elements of the universe: the earth, air, fire and water that dominated scientific thought until the Renaissance.

So famous are the ruins of this Greek city, you expect to see them just as they are pictured in travel brochures—solitary and looking out toward the sea. It comes something of a shock to see the looming monotony of modern Agrigento apartment complexes on the ridge above. And the sea, perhaps because of pollution from Porto Empedocles, often seems nothing more than haze on the horizon. But if you give yourself some time, at least an overnight, you block the modern city from your vision, much like the promoter's camera, and Agrigento becomes better than its photographs. Here you can experience the temples, etched by the morning light and warmed into a golden glow by the setting sun, then starkly illuminated against the night sky. Walking among them you breathe the surrounding orchards and gardens, full of wild thyme, snowy white with almond blossoms in the early spring, and bright with roses and silvery olive groves. And when you tire of the temples, the medieval section of the town of Agrigento, built atop the acropolis of Akragas, offers its parks and winding streets.

Valle Dei Templi ★★★

The valley of the temples covers a large area below the modern city and its ruins span the Greek era through the Roman one, and even include some Christian catacombs. You might want to get an overview along a circular drive on the **Strada Panoramica** to SS 115, then back up Via dei Templi, a drive made most dramatically at night, when many of the monuments are illuminated. (If you can't arrange the drive, the view from Viale della Vittoria in town isn't a bad substitute.)

Those monuments that can be easily visited are along Via dei Templi. Across this road from the parking area next to the Bar Posto di Ristoro, you enter the ridge where three Doric temples so majestically dominate the valley. The **Temple of Hercules**, to the right, is the oldest in Agrigento, built in 520 B.C. and much in ruin today. Commanding your attention to the left is the **★★ Temple of Concord**, the best preserved Greek temple in the world, except for the Theseion in Athens. Dating from 430 B.C., the temple's conversion into a Christian church in the 6th century saved it from destruction. A 10-minute walk beyond the Concord is the more damaged and slightly older **Temple of Hera**, mistakenly known as the Juno Lacinia. From here you can see some of the ancient wall. Returning to the parking lot, you find the entrance to the **★ Templo di Giove**, or the Olympian Zeus, once the largest temple in Sicily before earthquakes and modern building projects stripped it of its grandeur. Most unusual was the facade of this temple, supported by 38 gigantic telamones, or Atlantean figures, each 25 feet high. (A reproduction of one is here, an original in the museum.) Just beyond are the four-column remains of the **Temple of Castor and Pollux**. *The temples are open from 9 a.m. to sunset and are free.*

Toward town on the V. dei Templi (about 1 km from the Posto di Ristoro) is the **Museo Regionale Archeologico** *(open 9 a.m.–1 p.m., Tues. & Sat. till 5 p.m.; closed Mon.; no fee)*. The number of exquisite 5th-century B.C. ★Attic vases on display here would dispel anyone's doubts about the wealth of Akragas. On the lower level are models of the Temple of Zeus, and farther along are a few marble sculptures from the Greco-Roman period. In the neighboring **Church of San Nicola** is the 3rd-century B.C. ★ *Sarcophagus of Phaedra*, a delicately carved scene of Phaedra's grief at the loss of her lover, Hippolytus. Across V. dei Templi is the **Quartiere Ellenistico Romano** *(open 9 a.m. to an hour before sunset; no fee)*, part of the Roman town that flourished when Agrigento was the center for the Sicilian sulfur industry. Many homes were paved with patterned mosaics; the best ones here can be found in the glass enclosures.

Agrigento

Town

The main medieval street of Via Atenea leads out of the main park and plaza of Piazza Moro and wanders through the medieval town built on the acropolis of Agrigento. As you wander through, note **Piazza Purgatorio** where, to the left of the church, a lion sits atop the entrance to the Greek underground water system. Continue strolling to **Piazza Pirandello** and its theater, then if you feel like a 10-minute uphill walk, follow V. Bac Bac (across from the Gothic church, now a bank), to V. Matteoti and V. Sapanera. At the dead-end turn right and you arrive at **Santa Maria dei Greci** church, built around a 5th-century B.C. temple. (Custodian shows remnants of six fluted Doric columns in the foundation; tip.)

Nearby Beaches

A long stretch of beach runs in front of **San Leone** *(below the SS 115 traffic circle all the way to Villagio Mose, below the Jolly Hotel)*. Whether the sea here is clean, we don't know, but the beach is breezy. If you can, drive to **Eraclea Minoa** *(toward Sciacca on SS 115 for about 30 km [19 mi.] then 4 km on access road)*, an archaeological park with Greek ruins that are most noteworthy for their fabulous situation above white sand cliffs and a beautiful part of the Mediterranean. There is a campground nearby and an access road to the beach. You can picnic at the ruins. *(Open from 9 a.m. to sunset.)*

Where to Stay

If you are without a car, you should consider either the Villa Athena or the in-town hotels. Otherwise, you will find getting around by taxi a bit cumbersome. All hotels have air-conditioned rooms.

Moderate

Villa Athena	L150–220,000	❀★★★

Via dei Templi; ☎ *596-288, FAX 402-180.*
Single L150,000. Double L220,000.
If you can, stay right here in the valley of the temples with the Templo Concordia almost within touch and certainly within view. There are 40 rooms, not large but handsome, some with views and two with terraces. Fine gardens. Outdoor terrace restaurant and bar. Pool. Parking.

Jolly dei Templi   **L180–240,000 CP**   ★★★★

Villaggio Mose, SS 115 3 km, 1.5 mi. east of ruins; ☎ *606-144, FAX 606-685.*
Single L180,000 CP. Double L240,000 CP
A well-run and well-maintained hotel with a huge lobby, often lively with meetings
and conventions, and 146 comfortable rooms. Large pool and sunning area. Restaurant and bar. Parking.

Inexpensive

Tre Torri   **L130,000**   ★★

Villaggio Mose, SS 115 2 km, 1 mi. east of ruins; ☎ *606-733, FAX 607-839.*
Single/double L130,000.
A modern hotel with full services and 120 rooms. Restaurant and bar. Pool. Parking.

Concordia   **L65–85,000**   ★

Piazza San Francisco 11; ☎ *596-266.*
Single with bath L65,000. Double with bath L85,000.
A good in-town location, just below V. Atenea and only several blocks from the
train station, this hotel is clean and bright with 18 rooms with tiled baths and even
a/c. Its prices are budget low. Restaurant next door.

Where to Eat

The restaurants are as spread about as the hotels. At the ruins, you have the bar for
snacks or the terrace restaurant at the Villa Athena. In town, a number of decent trattorias
make it a pleasant dining spot. Our favorite is on the Strada Panoramica, closer but still
requiring transportation from town or Villaggio Mose. For price categories, see "Introduction".

Le Caprice   **$–$$**   ★★★

Strada Panoramica 51; ☎ *26-469.*
Closed Fri. and early July. Meals L35–65,000.
If you have one meal to eat in Agrigento, try to enjoy it here. In fact, if you have
two meals to eat, you might just as well return. You can eat at modest prices—the
involtini di spada costs no more than at the town trattoria. The problem is resisting
the antipasto table and the shellfish, the artichokes and eggplant, the stuffed mussels
and delicate gamberoni. Not only is the seafood among the best in Sicily, but the
service is unpretentious and good.

Kalos   **$$**   ★★

P. San Calogero; ☎ *26-389.*
Closed Tues.; reservation required. Meals L45–65,000.
Off Piazza Aldo Moro in the town, this restaurant specializes in seafood and it's all
fresh and well-prepared.

Trattoria Black Horse   **$**   ★

V. Celauro 8, right off V. Atenea not too far from P. Moro; ☎ *23-223.*
Closed Sun. and Christmas. Meals L20–35,000.
In town, this small, family-run restaurant offers a specialty of lasagna made with
bechamel and prosciutto, and a low-priced tourist menu that often includes fish.

Snacks

For snacks and the like, there are several spots in town. **La Corte degli Sfizi** *(walk along V. Atenea to a fork, look up steps to the right; closed Wed.; pizza L7–10,000)* has an up-scale ambience and, in the evening, good pizza and a garden in the back. The **alimentari** *(V. Goeni 23)* on P. Moro is good for shopping and the **Caffè Amato** nearby at the corner of V. Atenea has pastries and gelati. Along the lovely Viale della Vittoria, just a block from the train station, is the **Story Bar**, a popular place for arancini and pizza slices as well as sweets.

Directory

Telephone Code 0922   **Postal Code 92100**

Bus

Pullman Service from Piazzale Rosseli near post office; San Leone and Porto Empe-docle buses from Piazza Moro, down V. Crespi, then along Via dei Templi.

Emergencies

Dial ☎ *113*.

Groceries

Alimentari *(V. Goeni 23)* on Piazza Moro is of high quality; fruit vendors and salumeria, across from ASST tourist office.

Police

Questura, *(☎ 25-922)*.

Post Office

Piazza V. Emmanuele.

Taxi

Piazza Moro and Piazza Stazione; *(☎ 26-670)*.

Telephone

Telcom, *V. Atenea 96*, open 8 a.m.–8 p.m.

Tourist Office

AAST, right between train station and Piazza Moro *(☎ 2-03-91)*; **EPT**, V. Battisti *(☎ 20-454, FAX 20-246)*.

Train

Stazione Centrale, a block from main square of Piazza Roma *(☎ 20-989)*.

On the Road

The Interior

Arabic, Norman and Swabian castles, abandoned and crumbling, manage to still keep watch from the hilltops of the interior. In this quiet region, al-ways important farmland for wheat, but never very populated, you see farm-houses on rocky perches, no longer in use, but once so hopefully placed out of harm's way. Here are the mountains of Sicily, its deep valleys and its few remaining woodlands. Wild herbs and fennel cover the hills and sheep graze.

The Interior

In this fertile landscape was born the legend of Persephone, daughter of the harvest goddess Demeter, who was kidnapped by Pluto and taken down into Hades through a rift now covered by Lake Pergusa. Though kidnapped in the fall, Persephone returned in the early spring, symbolizing the planting cycle so critical to the earliest inhabitants, the Siculs, who made a cult of the legend before the arrival of the Greeks. Two medieval towns warrant a visit here: Enna, the most picturesque hill town in Sicily, and Piazza Armerina, with its Roman villa, justly famous for mosaics. The region can be visited by detours off the Palermo-Catania *autostrada*, or by excursion from Agrigento. Facilities in the region are limited, but an overnight is best made at Enna.

Enna

Towering nearly 3100 feet above the Sicilian landscape, the hill town of Enna attracts tourists for its panoramic views that on clear days stretch out over Lake Pergusa and all the way to Mt. Etna. Enna's position has long been admired, more for its fortifications, however, than its beauty. First the Greeks took it from the Siculs, then the Greeks fought the Greeks over it and the Romans thought it worth a two-year siege. The Arabs took it from Byzantines, but only after crawling through the sewers for a surprise attack. Frederick II found it an easily defensible location for one of his castles and further fortified the hill with a series of watchtowers, most now functioning as church *campaniles.*

What to See and Do

Today, the town streets and plazas make a picturesque setting for enjoying the views. After climbing to the town, you arrive at the large Piazza Vittorio Emanuele dominated by the rough and monolithic church of San Francisco. From a belvedere off to the left, there are views out toward Etna. The main street of Via Roma diverges from P. Emanuele; going downhill, it arrives at a public park with the octagonal **Torre di Federico II** *(V. IV Novembre, open till dusk; free);* going straight, it takes you to the major sights of this old city, past a series of small piazzas to the duomo. The **cathedral**, its old facade looking like a *campanile* without a church, was founded in 1307 by Eleanor of Aragon, Frederick II's wife, and is thought to have been built over an ancient temple dedicated to Persephone. Around the Piazza del Duomo are two small museums: **Museo Alessi** *(Tues.–Sun. 9 a.m.–1 p.m., 4-7 p.m.; free)*, with the rich treasury of the duomo as well as Greek coins and other objects from the town's past; and **Museo Archeologico** *(9 a.m.–1:30 p.m. and also 3:30-6:30 p.m. except Sun.; free)*, with fine displays of regional artifacts, including a few kraters. Continuing on Via Roma, you come to the promontory totally dominated by the awesome **Castello di Lombardia**, built by Frederick II as both a fort and residence. Only six of the original 20 towers remain; the ★ **Torre Pisano** is the favorite for its views. In the atrium, concerts take place during the summer. *(Open in summer 9 a.m.–6 p.m.; in winter 10 a.m.–12:30 p.m.; 3–5 p.m.; closed Mon.; free)* The town is attractive for evening strolls, when many of the monuments are illuminated and a *passeggiata* takes place on V. Roma *(closed to traffic 6-9 p.m.).*

Where to Stay

Check with tourist office for other hotels, 8 km away near Lake Pergusa (said to be polluted).

Hotel Sicilia   **L80–150,000 CP**   √★★

P. Napoleone Colanjanni 7; ☎ 500-850, FAX 500-488.
Single L80,000 CP. Double L150,000 CP.
Also known as Grande Albergo Sicilia, this hotel is just a few steps from the duomo. The 80 rooms are quite comfortable and with tiled baths and hair dryers. Restaurant, bar. Parking.

Where to Eat

The food of the interior is especially pungent with the local *maccheroni alla Norma* enriched by wild greens and fennel and the sharp *ricotta salata* made from ewe's milk. Another dish, spiedini di salsiccia, is lamb marinated with oregano, garlic and hot pepper flakes, then rolled around bits of cheese before being skewered and grilled. *Bruschetta*, better than any garlic bread you've tasted, is a specialty, too.

La Griglia   **$–$$**   ★★

V. Falantano 19, between the Municipio and P. Garibaldi.
Closed Mon. in winter; L30–55,000.
All the above dishes can be enjoyed at this family-run restaurant.

Centrale   **$–$$**   ★★

P. 6 di Diciembre 9.
Closed Sat.; except in summer. Meals L35–55,000.
A bit more upscale, but without any improvement in the food. Although we found the salsiccia disappointing, the pastas were good and the *melanzane arrosti* delicious.

Directory

Telephone code 0935   **Postal code 94100**

Tourist Office

AAPIT, *V. Roma 413 (☎ 500-544; FAX 500-720)* with good maps and brochures on both Enna and Piazza Armerina.

Note

The altitude of Enna makes it cooler than most of the island and in winter it is quite misty.

Arriving

Enna lies 85 km (53 mi.) from Catania, 135 km (84 mi.) from Palermo, and 95 km (59 mi.) from Agrigento. It is on the same train line as Agrigento (stazione at foot of hill town) but delays are likely. Buses provide the best connections, including Piazza Armerina.

Piazza Armerina

Although the various piazzas and churches that climb the hills of this medieval town make for enjoyable walks and impressive views—particularly from the duomo at the highest point, it is the ★★**Roman villa at Casale** (5 km (3 mi.) on the outskirts to the southwest) that provides the real attraction for visitors. Dating primarily from the 4th century A.D., this villa is so extraordinary with its countless rooms and courts, with peristyle and pool and perhaps even a throne room, that some scholars believe it was the retirement estate of the emperor Maximilian, who co-ruled with Diocletian. Although the villa was buried by a landslide in the 12th century so that its partial walls must now be roofed with plastic, most of its miles of ★ ★ ★ **mosaic pavements** are intact. Nowhere else are there so many Roman mosaics to be seen, nor so many so exquisitely preserved. They are everywhere, from the latrine to the throne room, from the grand reception corridor to the nursery. And they include just as great a variety of themes, from massage scenes in the baths to chariots being pulled by ducks in the nursery, from fabulous hunting scenes with delightful birds and animals (in the grand corridor) to women in bikinis working out with weights (room south of peristyle). In a separate building to the south, are dramatic scenes of the labors of Hercules, finely executed with sophisticated use of *chiaroscuro. Open 9 a.m.–one hour before sunset; L2000; restaurant facilities. May–Sept. a shuttle bus links ruins to centro storico.*

Where to Stay and Eat

Da Battiato $ ★

> *Contrada Paratore 11;* ☎ *685-453, FAX 685-453.*
> *Meals L25–35,000.*
>
> Just where you turn onto the 1.5-km access road for Villa Casale is this convenient and comfortable cafe and restaurant. In addition, there are ★ 13 simple rooms (single L50,000, double L70,000), most with private bath.

La Tavernetta $–$$ ★

> *V. Cavour, 1-1/2 blocks up from the main square of P. Garibaldi;* ☎ *685-883.*
> *Closed Sun. and Jan. Meals L30–50,000.*
>
> In the old center of Piazza Armerina. An intimate *trattoria* with a fresh pasta *alla Tavernetta,* typical of the region with its eggplant and wild herbs.

Directory

Telephone code 0935   **Postal code 94015**

Tourist Office

> **AAST**, in old center, *V. Cavour 15 (*☎ *680-201; FAX 684-565).*

Arriving

> Piazza Armerina lies 37 km, (23 mi.) south of Enna on SS 117. There are buses from Enna, trains from Palermo and Catania. From Agrigento, it's 110 km (68 mi.). Approaching town on SS 191 from Caltanisetta you come to Villa Casale first.

Syracuse

Key to Syracuse

Sights

Picturesque Ortygia, the old town of Syracuse; the Archaeological Park with its ruins of ancient *Siracusa*; the fine archeology museum.

Excursions

Magnificently Baroque towns of Noto and Ragusa.

Nearby Beaches

Fontane Bianche, 16 km, 10 mi. south; congested in season.

Festivals

Classical drama festival in the Greek Theater, even-numbered years, May/June; Patron Saint Santa Lucia is honored each December 13 and first Sunday in May.

Accommodations

Few that are convenient.

Eating Out

Wonderful seafood; restaurants cluster in *Ortygia*.

Getting Around

Ortygia and the Archaeological Park are separated by a 40-minute walk or a bus ride through the modern commercial city. Taxis and car rental available, too. For Ortygia and the Park, walking is a necessity.

Arriving

Well-connected by bus, particularly via Catania, only 1.5 hours away. Once A-19 is completed north to Catania and south to Gela, access should be easier.

Warning

Ortygia has become depopulated on the north side toward the tip, where it can be too isolated for comfort. Stay on the more crowded streets near the sights and restaurants.

Good reading

Mary Renault's *Mask of Apollo* is set here, during the time of Dionysus.

What to See and Do

Founded by colonists from Corinth in 743 B.C., Syracuse (*Siracusa* in Italian) grew into the greatest city in Europe and one of the most feared powers in the Greek world. Its harbor witnessed the landing of Pyrrhus with his elephants, of Plato bent on educating Dionysus II into a philosopher king, of Aeschylus and Pindar bringing their talents to the court of Hieron. And it witnessed the total defeat of the Athenian navy in 413 B.C. when, according to Thucidydes, 7000 Athenians were captured and imprisoned in the stone quarries of Syracuse. Under Gelon in the 5th century B.C., Syracuse expanded from the easily defended island of Ortygia to the mainland. The ancient city covered the same area it does today: the island, the central commercial district where Gelon built the angora, or market, and the neapolis with its theater and new residences, now the Archaeological Park. Its population was much greater.

Since the Romans conquered Syracuse in 212 B.C. and inadvertently killed its great inventor and scientist, Archimedes, Syracuse hasn't been the same. It's been sacked by northern vandals and Arabs alike, stripped of Greek finery by admiring Romans, and felled by earthquake and plague. Only a few columns remain from the angora and no other period has filled the commercial district with better architecture. To the east, across a bridge, remains Ortygia, still tantalizing, and to the west lies the ancient ruins of the neapolis.

Ortygia   ★

Syracuse

Crossing the bridge to this island, you come to the few remaining columns of the **Temple of Apollo** (565 B.C.), believed to be the oldest in Sicily. Glances into the back courtyard of the **municipio** (next to the duomo) show excavations into the city's past, other Greek relics can be spotted here and there, including the spidery alleyways that reflect the plan of the original Greek city. Yet despite the Greek remnants and despite the massive 13th-century Castello Maniace (closed to public) that Frederick II built on the tip, Ortygia today is predominantly baroque with wrought-iron balconies, palazzi, and churches. It also is overwhelmingly Mediterranean, the sea almost always within sight, and the buildings bleached whitest of whites. Whether Ortygia captivates you may depend on the time of your visit—whether the sun creates romantic patterns on the facades, and whether balmy breezes entice you to sit at a cafe around the **Fonte Aretuso**, a legendary spring said to link Syracuse to its ancient homeland in Greece. Perhaps there is no more picturesque time in Ortygia than early evening when the baroque facades are softly illuminated and the shoppers bustle in the Piazza di Archimedes or stroll along the sea on the Foro Vittorio Emanuele. You might even discover an organ rehearsal in the ★★**duomo**, at that hour all mysterious with shadows. Encased in the 18th-century baroque facade of the cathedral, is the 5th-century B.C. Temple of Athenia, built in commemoration of a Syracusan victory over Carthage. The nave columns were actually carved out of the cella of the temple, and the original peristyle columns line the aisles. Nowhere are the contrasts of Sicilian history better witnessed than in the Spanish Chapel here, where an ornate iron door, opening into a rococo chapel, is flanked by towering Doric columns. More of the ancient temple can be seen on the side street, Via Minerva. *(The duomo closes noon-4 p.m.)* Several blocks away is the **Museo Regionale** *(V. Capodieci, up a few blocks from the Fountain of Arethusa; 9 a.m.–2 p.m., Sun. till 1 p.m.; L2000)*, housed in the handsome medieval Palazzo Bellomo, a pleasant place for this collection of Early Christian art as well as regional folk art. Upstairs are the two great paintings of the museum: ★*Annunciation* (1474) by Antonello da Messina, a work much damaged but preserving the artist's subtle treatment of light and space (note the pages of the book); and, in contrast, ★ *Burial of Saint Lucy* (1608) by Caravaggio, full of dramatic light and emotion.

From the Archaeological Park, all buses running toward town on Viale Teracati go to Ortygia.

Archaeological Park ★

The former neapolis is now an attractive park with numerous ruins from ancient times. Viale Rizzo practically encompasses the park, and from its upper reaches provides a panoramic view over the ruins and all the way out to the harbor. The main entrance on Via Augusto, off Viale Teracati, brings you to the **Roman Amphitheater** on your left. Probably constructed around the 2nd century, most of the amphitheater is hewn out of the natural rock. It is superbly constructed and unusually large, vying with that in Verona. Still remaining are some of the vaulted corridors under the seats where gladiators and animals entered the arena. Farther along, again on the left, is the **Altar of Zeus the Liberator**, built by Hieron II in the 3rd century B.C. Though much destroyed by Spanish recycling of the stone, its immense size—large enough for the sacrifice of 450 oxen—is still discernible, if not its grandeur. Across the road from the altar is the pay booth into the ★ ★ **Greek Theater** and quarries *(fee)*. Following a path to the left, you come to the Greek Theater, one of the largest known, with a seating capacity of 15,000. Since the 6th century B.C., a theater has been here, though only a wooden one. Over the centuries it was improved and enlarged until the present one, which dates mostly from the 3rd century B.C. The seats were carved entirely out of bedrock. Above them were porticos for shelters in bad weather. And farther above, was a grotto sacred to the muses. Here, Aeschylus produced *Prometheus Bound* and *The Persians*. And here, quite probably, Plato attended a morning performance, enjoying the view out to the great harbor, a view somewhat obstructed today. Retracing your steps, you follow the right branch of the path and arrive at the lovely gardens of the **Latomia del Paradiso**, the largest quarry of a system that once extended all the way north to the sea. The most famous cave here is called the **Ear of Dionysus**, so named by the artist Caravaggio for its shape and acoustical properties. *Open 9 a.m. until 2 hours before dusk. Fee L2000. From Ortygia, buses numbered 1, 3, 4, or 19 run near the Archaeological Park, via Corso Umberto and Corso Gelone.*

Museo Regionale Di Archeologico ★ ★

Viale Teocrato. A 15-minute walk from the park, this handsome museum opened in 1988 to replace the former Museo Nazionale in Ortygia. It displays many exceptional Greek artifacts from the region's past, beginning with the late bronze age and ending with the Roman era. Among the many works worth seeking out are the 6th-century B.C. ★ *Torso From Lentini* and a ceramic ★ *Goddess Suckling Twins*, from Megara Hyblaea (both in Section A). Temporarily in Section B, is the famous marble statue of ★ ★ *Venus Anadyomene*, a Roman version of a Hellenistic statue, and in Section C is the ★Adrano bronze, a 5th-century B.C. statuette of a male athlete. Eventually, an upper floor will display Roman and Hellenistic objects. *Open 9 a.m.–1 p.m., Tues.–Sat., 1st & 3rd Sun. Fee L2000.*

Catacombe San Giovanni

Via San Sebastiani.

About a half-block off Viale Teocrato, midway between the museum and park and across from the APT office, are these Christian catacombs from the 3rd to 6th centuries. Among the oldest in Europe, these are second in extent only to those in

Syracuse

Rome. *The entrance is down the side of the church. Pull bell handle. If visits are in progress, you may have a wait. Open mid Mar.–mid Nov. 9 a.m.–1 p.m., 3–6 p.m.; in winter 9 a.m.–1 p.m. Fee L2000.*

Nearby

In 1693, an earthquake devastated much of southeastern Sicily. Where once stood ancient and medieval towns, there was nothing. Towns were built and the result was a completely fresh style more *rococo* than *baroque.* Two towns to the south are particularly fine examples of this Sicilian *baroque.*

Noto   ★

35 km, 22 mi.

An easy half-day excursion by car or bus, Noto is well worth so small an effort. Its *centro storico* is tiny and self-contained, a jewel of 18th-century town planning. As you walk the Corso with its stately, ochre buildings, notice how each side street ends in an interesting facade, and that the architecture harmoniously incorporates the slope of the surrounding land. A brief walk up Via Nicolaci to see the ★ balcony carvings of the **Palazzo Nicolaci**, maybe a stroll on elegant Via Cavour in addition to the Corso, and you're done. Even if you aren't hungry, stop at **Pasticceria Corrado Costanzo** *(V. Spaventa 7, behind the municipio; closed Wed., early Sept.)* and sample the jasmine and rose petal marzipan of the world famous confectioner.

Ragusa

60 km, (37 mi.) farther towards Gela.

Ragusa might be best approached by a car trip to Agrigento. Although the approach from the west is confusing and unpleasantly industrial, from the east you can get a stunning overview without even leaving your car. But the overview is of Ragusa Ilba, the partially abandoned, but impressive medieval section that is dominated by the Sicilian *baroque* church of ★ **San Giorgio**. After the earthquake, most building occurred on the other side of a gorge, in modern Ragusa. The easiest sampling of Ragusa's offerings is to exit the highway for Ragusa Ibla, drive past it, and then snake your way up to the newer Ragusa on Via Massini. Here you can park your car near **Santa Maria delle Scale** (the steps link modern Ragusa with Ibla) and enjoy more views of Ibla and the neoclassical dome of San Giorgio. Then climb the handsome Corso Italia with its baroque mansions, and arrive at the duomo and surrounding buildings, the heart of baroque Ragusa. Ragusa has considerable presence, and in case that intrigues you into a longer stay, the **tourist office** *(next to S. Giorgio;* ☎ *621-421; FAX 622-288)* has good maps and there is the comfortable ★★**Hotel Montreal** *(Corso Italia 70; 50 modern rooms with baths and a/c; restaurant, bar;* ☎ *[0932] 621-133, FAX 621-133; single L75,000, double L110,000).* **Caffe Trieste** *(Corso Italia 76; closed Sun.)* not only is attractive, it has a very good stand-up bar with snacks.

Where to Stay

Syracuse doesn't have a lot of choice for hotels. Those listed below have the most convenient locations. Unless otherwise specified, the rooms are with air conditioning.

Moderate

Grand Hotel   **L200–275,000 CP**   ★★★★

V. Mazzini 12; ☎ *464-600;FAX 464-611.*
Single L200,000 CP. Double L275,000 CP.
Finally a first-class hotel has opened in Ortygia. Overlooking the port, it's nor far
from the bridge (turn right after crossing). Once a musty, old hotel, the 19th-cen-
tury Grand has been completely renovated; architectural traces of its former glory
days remain to give it character. Although only a few of 40 rooms have port views,
they all are well-appointed. Restaurant. Bar. Parking.

Jolly   **L200–230,000 CP**   ★★★

Corso Gelone 45; ☎ *461-111, FAX 461-126.*
Single L200,000 CP. Double L230,000 CP.
Located in the heart of the shopping district and midway between the sightseeing
areas, the Jolly offers a pretty convenient location with a pleasant lobby and bar, 100
decently appointed rooms and parking. Taxi stand, too.

Grand Villa Politi   **L140–245,000 CP**   ❀★★★

Via M. Politi Laudien 2; ☎ *412-121, FAX 36-061.*
Single L140–160,000 CP. Double L215–245,000 CP.
Surrounded by gardens and overlooking the beautiful Latomia dei Cappuccini, the
quarry where thousands of Athenians were imprisoned so long ago, the setting of
this hotel couldn't be finer. A marble staircase leads to a veranda and up into the old
world elegance of the lobby where Winston Churchill passed his vacations. Many of
the 96 rooms (renovated ones pricier) have views of the quarry and the sea beyond,
others of the large pool; some are quite large and with balconies. The rooms are a
little spartan, but undergoing renovation, and time has worn the grandness of the
lobby, but only a bit. This is a wonderful place. Easy to stay here if you have a car,
but buses do pass into town and the Museo Nazionale is a 20-minute walk.

Forte Agip   **L160,000 CP**   ★★

Viale Teracati 30; ☎ *463-232, FAX 67-115.*
Single/double L160,000 CP.
Despite its location in the parking lot of a gas station (rear rooms preferable), this is
one of the most convenient hotels for sightseeing in the area of the Archaeological
Park. The 83 rooms are modern, the style and service functional. Restaurant.

Where to Eat

Syracuse is well-known for its shellfish, particularly oysters and mussels and that delicious species of shrimp called *gamberoni rossi*. It produces numerous wines: the white
Eloro is light and especially good with seafood, the red is full-bodied; the Val d'Anapo
white is good and dry, the red is light.

Minosse   **$$**   ★★★★

V. Mirabella 6; ☎ *66-366, FAX 66-366.*
Closed Mon. and late Nov. Meals L40–60,000.
In Ortygia, this fine restaurant is acclaimed for its interesting regional cuisine. The
house specialties—meats, not just seafood, and good desserts—are enjoyed in an
elegant wine cellar setting.

Jonico—a Rutta e Ciauli   **$$**   ★★★
> *Riviera Dionisio il Grande 124;* ☎ *65-540.*
> *Closed Tues., major holidays, Aug. Meals L45–65,000.*

A fine setting with a terrace overlooking the sea is matched by good Siracusan seafood (spaghetti with anchovies, swordfish) inventively prepared by Pasqualino Giudice.

Rossini   **$$**   ★★★
> *V. Savoia 6;* ☎ *24-317.*
> *Closed Tues., major holidays, Aug. Meals L40–65,000.*

In Ortygia and run by the same family as the Jonico, this restaurant has more authentic Sicilian cuisine, including a good antipasto buffet, fritti misti of fish as well as stewed meatballs and lamb.

Darsena   **$–$$**   ★★
> *Riva Garibaldi 14;* ☎ *66-104.*
> *Closed Wed. Meals L35–60,000.*

Near the bridge in Ortygia, this restaurant has some tables overlooking the water. Although the preparations here are quite simple, the gamberoni we tried practically wriggled with freshness.

Trattoria Il Teatro   **$–$$**   ★
> *V. Agnello 8;* ☎ *21-321.*
> *Closed Mon. and Nov. Meals L25–50,000.*

In the Archaeological Park at the Viale Rizzo entrance, you can dine in this pleasant garden restaurant. There's a budget-priced menu turistica in the afternoon; in the evening the food and service are more refined.

Snacks

On your way from the Museo Nazionale, you can find the makings for a picnic in the park at **Gastronomia** *(V. Teocrito 127)*. In the evening, **Baccho Pizzeria** *(Teocrito 113; pizza L6–9,000)* has delicious, thick slices of pizza for stand-up snacks, and pretty good spaghetti and whole pizzas for dinner.

Directory

Telephone Code 0931   **Postal Code 96100**

Airport
> In Catania, 1.5 hours by bus.

Books
> **Libreria Editrice**, *V. Maestanza 56*, Ortygia, for lovely books on Italy (in Italian).

Buses
> City buses leave Ortygia from the Column of Apollo (buy tickets in tabacchi); pullman bus depot is near post office, V. Trieste 28.

Car Rentals
> **Avis**, *P. della Repubblica 11*, **Maggiore**, *V. Terrere 14*; and others.

Emergencies
> Dial ☎ *113.*

Groceries

Morning market in Ortygia; **Salumeria Barreca**, Corso Gelone across from Jolly, and nearby vegetable shop and bakery. **Gastronomia**, *V. Teocrita 127.*

Police

Dial ☎ *113.*

Post Office

Ortygia near bridge.

Taxis

Ortygia, Column of Apollo; stazione; etc.

Telephones

Telcom, V. Tercati near Hotel Agip, 8 a.m.–8 p.m.

Tourist Office

AAPIT, across from catacombs on *V. San Sebastiano 43* (☎ *67-710, FAX 67-803)*
AAST, *V. Maestanza 33*, 1.5 blocks from P. Archimede in Ortygia *(☎ 464-255, FAX 60-204)*, Parco Archeologico, and, in summer, stazione.

Train

Stazione Centrale, in commercial downtown off Corso Umberto; *(☎ 67-964).*

Catania and Mt. Etna

Key to Region

Sights

Mt. Etna, forever smouldering, and sometimes erupting; Catania, with its 18th-century Sicilian baroque buildings.

Nearby Beaches

Riviera dei Ciclopi.

Festivals

Processions in honor of Catania's Santa Agata, Feb. 3-5.

Accommodations

Limited.

Eating Out

Good selection of restaurants.

Getting Around

Snarled Catania traffic makes walking best for sightseeing. Buses, taxis, car rentals available. Special trains, tours, and buses for Mt. Etna exploration.

Arriving

Airport with domestic flights from mainland cities; major bus and train connections; A-18 and A-19 converge here, but linking highway and access road into city not complete, making for considerable confusion; ferries to Naples, Reggio Calabria, Malta.

Special Tips

> Though Etna excursions are convenient from beautiful Taormina, Catania is best for those intent on reaching the main crater. Warm clothes and sturdy shoes are necessary for a visit to the crater. They can be rented on site at the Rifugio Sapienza. *Specialty tours available (see Directory).*

What to See and Do

The largest and most active volcano in Europe, Mt. Etna dominates the Ionian coast, rising strikingly above the surrounding low mountains. Thick at its base, Etna deceives you into thinking it's just another mountain; not until you notice its smoking crater or snowcovered cone rising above the clouds do you appreciate its grandeur. Named by the ancients, the volcano also figured in Greek myths and histories. Pindar described one eruption of spouting, "unapproachable fire," and Aeschylus told of another of the more than 100 that have been recorded. But Etna's violent history is far from over. Explosions near its main crater killed two people in 1987, and there have been serious eruptions in the past two decades, most recently in 1992. Fortunately, the lava has usually flowed into a vast pit called Valle del Bove, not over towns, as it had in the past. Catania has been a frequent victim of the volcano, situated as it is right below. The city witnessed its greatest devastation in 1669, and not long after, it experienced the dreadful earthquake of 1693. Although Catania has been settled since prehistoric times, its broad boulevards and Sicilian *baroque*, really *rococo*, churches and palaces date from its reconstruction in the 18th century, a vast project that used lava stone as the main building material.

Catania Sights

The second largest city of Sicily shares the same traffic congestion as the larger Palermo. Car exhaust has added a grunginess to the already gray volcanic tone on the *baroque* buildings, but the quality of the architecture, the ease of walking, and the pleasantness of the city gardens and tree-lined boulevards like Viale XX Settembre make for a decent half-day of sightseeing. The major *baroque* buildings, many of them designed by G. B. Vaccarini, can be seen on a loop tour from the fine gardens of Villa Bellini to the duomo and back. From Villa Bellini, you can follow Via Sant' Euplio to the Corso Sicilia where, depressed in the middle of the traffic circle, are the few remaining ruins of an immense **Roman amphitheater**, second in size only to the Colosseum. Once it was faced in white marble, but now only lava stone is left. Crossing the circle pick up ★ **Via Crocifieri**, the most beautiful street in Catania, lined with Sicilian baroque churches and convents. At Via Vittorio Emanuele, you can turn right for a few blocks if you want to see the **Teatro Romano** *(entrance at #266; if closed, walk a few doors farther for a glimpse)*, built over its Greek predecessor and still offering performances. Turning left on Via *V. Emanuele*, you come to the **Piazza del Duomo**, centered by Vaccarini's fountain, now the symbol of Catania. Inspired by Bernini, the fountain is composed of an ancient, lava elephant carrying an Egyptian obelisk. The rebuilt facade of the *duomo*, although sporting Corinthian columns from the Teatro Romano, is also the work of Vaccarini. Some of the interior chapels show the Norman influence from the time of the cathedral's founding. You can continue up Via Etnea toward Villa Bellini again. You'll pass on your right the **University**, partially designed by Vaccarini. There are more churches as well as many shops along this bustling main street. At the end looms Mt. Etna.

Catania and Mt. Etna

Touring Mt. Etna ★★★

The layers of lava around Etna have created an extremely varied landscape, from subtropical orchards and banks of bougainvillea, up to the pine forests beyond Linguaglossa, and on to surreal lava formations. Springs push their way through the surface, rivers add to the fertility, and vineyards and pistachio trees thrive. The towns and villages that have survived the centuries of Etna's violence proclaim their presence with medieval castles and churches, with Roman shrines, and with Greek walls. A trip around the base takes you through much of this variation, and the most classic way of enjoying it is by the **19th-century railroad Circumetnea** *(see "Directory").* (The train leaves Catania and ends at Giarre by way of Randazzo 3.5 hours later; buses from the main piazza in Giarre take you back to Catania along the sea coast of the Riviera dei Ciclopi.) You can drive around the volcano yourself, following signs for Misterbianco, then picking up the towns of Paterno, Adrano, Randazzo, Linguaglossa (a beautiful, crumbling centro storico; hotels and facilities), and Fiumefreddo, before heading back to Catania by the coast or on to Taormina.

The thrill of seeing a volcano, however, can only be satisfied by a trip to its crater. Most of the year, you can drive or take the special 8 a.m. AST bus from the train station to the Rifugio Sapienza for a 1-day roundtrip excursion. Depending on conditions, you may be able to go no farther, but from the town of Nicolosi (facilities and hotels) and above, you'll see extinct craters and lava beds. During the winter when there is enough snow for skiing, you can take the cable cars from Sapienza for exceptional views of the summit. In better weather, when Etna permits it, you can take a jeep or bus from Sapienza to within a half-hour's walk of the main crater and from May to October, you can even arrange a night visit to see the red-glow of the burning crater and the sunrise over Sicily.

WARNING • Etna has been erupting regularly the past several years. Always check conditions with the Alpine Club or AAPIT offices (see directory) for both the road conditions and volcanic activity. If you are planning a night trip or a hiking trip, you must inform the Alpine Club in advance. **Special Tip** • The Rifugio Sapienza is run by the Alpine Club and offers overnight facilities, a restaurant, and rentals for warm clothing and sturdy shoes.

Nearby Beaches

Between Catania and Giarre to the north is the beautiful rocky coast called **Riviera dei Cyclopi**. Massive rock formations create tiny swimming coves and, everywhere, Mt. Etna is dominating. The coves were formed by Cyclops, of course, who in his jealousy over a nymph's love for the shepherd Acis, hurled rocks from his perch on Mt. Etna and struck the shepherd dead. The main towns—**Aci Castello** (9 km, [5.5 mi.]), where a castle dramatically commands the little bay, and **Acitrezza**, with its fishing harbor surrounded by trattoria and pensioni—are the favorite resorts of the Catanese. Even if you aren't looking for a swim, you might enjoy a trip through this area either on a base tour of Mt. Etna or on your way to Taormina.

Where to Stay

The best facilities are the beach hotels along the Riviera dei Cyclopi, but Catania, with limited facilities, is the most convenient base for making arrangements to visit Mt. Etna and for traveling to the beaches if you don't have a car. The hotels are air-conditioned unless otherwise indicated.

Grand Hotel Baia Verde   L280–310,000   ★★★

V. Angelo Musco 8, 95020 Catania-Cannizzaro; ☎ *491-522, FAX 494-464.*
Single/double L280–310,000.
With a fabulous setting on a volcanic cliff overlooking the sea, this fine hotel is only 4 km (2.5 mi.) from Catania (towards Aci Castello) and provides a morning bus service into the city. There are 130 spacious rooms; a highly praised restaurant (meals about L60,000); a pool, tennis, and access to the sea. Parking.

Jolly   L190–235,000 CP   ★★★

Piazza Trento 138, 95129; ☎ *316-933, FAX 316-832.*
Single L190,000 CP. Double L235,000 CP.
A pleasant stroll from Villa Bellini, but quite a hike from the duomo, the Jolly is at Viale XX Settembre and faces a busy square in the fashionable shopping district. The lobby areas are contemporary in decor and the 160 rooms comfortable. Restaurant Bar. Parking.

Albergo Moderno   L125–140,000   ★

Via Alessi 9, 95124; ☎ *325-309, FAX 326-674.*
Single L125,000. Double L140,000.
Recommendable modest hotels are scarce. This hotel, between Crocifero and Etnea streets, at least has a quiet and convenient location, but the 47 bright rooms are worn. No restaurant, no a/c.

Where to Eat

Catania claims to be the birthplace of that wonderful Sicilian eggplant concoction, *caponata*. And here it is lovingly addressed in the diminutive as *caponatino*. The fish, like everywhere, is well prepared, but the anchovies from Catania's bay are often found in pasta sauces and other preparations. The most prevalent wines come from Etna, usually white and somewhat dry and acceptable.

La Siciliana $$–$$$ ★★★★

V. Marco Polo 52a; ☎ *376-400, FAX 722-130.*
Closed Sun. evening, Mon., early Aug.; reservation required. Meals L50–70,000.
One of the most popular restaurants is a bit inconvenient to reach without a car, but it's worth the effort to take a taxi from the center for the 4 km, 2-1/2 m. Once it must have been a country trattoria. Although surrounded by modern buildings today, it remains *caratteristica*, its summer garden is inviting and its regional food is some of the best in Sicily. Of course, there's *pasta alla Norma*, and pasta with fresh anchovy sauce. The *insalata di mare* is delicious, as is all the fish, especially when prepared with pine nuts and scallions. The menu changes frequently, but always ends satisfyingly with the ice cream cassata.

Ristorante Selene $$ ★★★

V. Mollica 24-26 in Cannizzaro; ☎ *494-444, FAX 492-209.*
Closed Tues. and Aug. Meals L45–65,000.
Just south of Aci Castello near the Sheraton Hotel, this restaurant is right on the sea with a breezy terrace as well as an attractive indoor dining area. The setting is beau-

tiful, the food very *tipico* and good. You can choose (or create) a full-course meal complete with wine and always with seafood, for a sensible price. Worth the 4-km ride from Catania.

Pagano $-$$ ★★★

V. de Roberto 37; ☎ *537-045.*
Closed Sat. lunch, Sun. dinner and Aug. Meals L40–55,000.

In town, you won't feel at all deprived dining at the reputable Pagano, conveniently located just behind the Excelsior *(near the Jolly Hotel)*. The Sicilian cuisine, from the antipasti with caponata and spaghetti nero with seppie to rigatoni alla Norma and the popular seafood and meat secondi, is very good—and the prices, very reasonable.

Caffè Dining

Fresh seafood salad, homemade pasta, and chocolate mousse can be enjoyed at the attractive **Giardino d'Inverno** *(V. Asilo S. Agata 34; closed Mon. and Aug.; reserve at* ☎ *532-853; meals about L45,000)*, located just south of the Corso Italia at Liberta. Our favorite spot for stand-up eating is **Caffè Le Caprice** *(V. Etnea 30; closed Mon.; meals L25–35,000)*. You can select an entire meal or just a salad or the traditional arancini. You can eat just what you want. And if you want to sit down, there is a pleasant tea room. In the evenings, there's only pizza and arancini for substance, but gelati and pastries are always available.

Directory

Telephone Code 095 **Postal Code 95100**

Airlines
   Alitalia, Corso Sicilia near P. Repubblica *(*☎ *327-555)*.

Airport
   5 km, 3 mi. south in Fotanarossa *(*☎ *252-111);* bus 24 from V. Etnea.

Alpine Club
   C.A.I., *V. Vecchia Ognina 64* in Catania; Refugio in Sapienza; other locations on Etna.

American Express
   V. Etnea 65 (☎ *316-155)*.

Buses
   City buses run from P. del Duomo along V. Etnea; SAIS, *V. Teatro Massimo 41* *(*☎ *536-168)*, to Rome, Sicilian cities including Piazza Amerina, Riveria dei Ciclopi. ATA bus to Sapienza, from Stazione Centrale at 8 a.m.

Car Rentals
   Hertz, airport *(*☎ *341-595);* **Maggiore**, P. Verga *(*☎ *310-002)*, and others.

Emergencies
   Dial ☎ *113*.

Ferries
   Tirrenia, *P. Grenoble 26 (*☎ *316-394)*.

Catania and Mt. Etna

Groceries

Market, a few blocks off V. Etnea on V. Pacini, and below P. del Duomo.

Post Office

V. Etnea 215, near Villa Bellini gardens.

Shopping

Via Etnea, the main downtown street; and smartest shops on Viale XX Settembre.

Taxi

In major piazzas (☎ *328-455*, ☎ *330-966*).

Telephone

Telcom, *Corso Sicilia 67*, *Tues.–Sat. 9 a.m.–1 p.m., 4–7 p.m., Mon. 4–7 p.m., V. San Euplio 116*, across from Villa Bellini.

Tourist Office

AAPIT, V. Pacini at Largo Paisello 5, next to Villa Bellini gardens (☎ *310-888; FAX 316-407)*, very helpful; at airport and stazione.

Tours

CIT, airport and *V. di Sangiuliano 208* (☎ *317-393)*, and many others. **ETNA tours**: SITAS (☎ *914-141)*, for dawn and sunset tours to crater; **Pianeta Etna** (☎ *731-2711)*, walks or treks with botanists, geologists.

Trains

Stazione, P. Giovanni XXIII; and to Etna, **Ferrovia Circumetnea**, *Corso delle Provincie 13* (☎ *541-250)*, off V. Leonardo da Vinci, runs many trains daily (you can get on and off for village visits) as well as train-bus tours (mid-July–Oct.) that permit add-ons to the summit. (☎ *541-246*, tour reservations).

Taormina

Key to Taormina

Sights

Exquisite sea resort with Greek theater and medieval town.

Excursions

Mt. Etna is near, and the sights of the entire east coast and interior are easily reached.

Nearby Beaches

Mazzaro, at the foot of Taormina, reached by road (3 km) or *funvia*. Giardino Naxos, 10 min.

Festivals

Folk festival, end of May. Performances in the Greek Theater, July-mid-September.

Accommodations

Extensive offerings from the most deluxe hotels to simpler pensioni.

Eating Out

Excellent selection of restaurants.

Getting Around

The town must be walked, since its main street is closed to traffic and its others are mere alleyways leading through hillside gardens. Parking can be a problem; leave your car, if you can, near the lots at either end of town or at the Mazzaro *funvia* lot. Walking paths, *funvia* (cable cars), and roads lead down to beaches; buses and taxis run to *stazione* at foot of Taormina.

Arriving

Airport one hour away at Catania, with shuttle bus (1-1/2 hours) and car rental connections; train and bus service connections with major cities of Messina (50 km, 31 mi.) and Catania (50 km, 31 mi.).

Special Tips

Taormina is balmy year-round, good for outdoor tennis in January, if not for swimming. But many facilities close November through February, so if you visit off-season you might want to explore the area between the public garden and the Greek theater for restaurants and shops, as this area seems to serve residents as well as tourists.

What to See and Do

Set 700 feet above the blue sea, the medieval town of Taormina is warmed by the Mediterranean sun, its hills terraced with tropical palms and bougainvillea, and with cypresses, and almond and orange trees. Walking along the picturesque **Corso Umberto**, climbing the footpaths to the 16th-century castle at **Castel Mola**, and driving along **Via Roma** or **Via Pirandello**, you constantly glimpse the sea and gardens and mountains. And everywhere is the mesmerizing presence of Mt. Etna, looming through the clouds, snow-covered and glistening half the year, or just as often ominously hidden in its own thick, gray, billowing smoke. So magnificent is the setting, that it's hard to believe that Taormina wasn't found by Greeks before 403 B.C. Apparently the Romans agreed, for Taormina was a favorite vacationing spot for partrician families. By the 18th century, Goethe had described its beauty, and by the end of the 19th century it was a well-established international resort.

Taormina today is an elegant resort, its medieval town linked to the sea below at Mazzaro by a cable car. While the beaches rim some quiet coves for swimming, the town itself provides art exhibits and concerts, and most of the hotels, restaurants, and shops. The traffic-free Corso Umberto runs from the town's old gates at Porta Messina and Porta Catania, passing along the way some Gothic churches and Roman remnants, as well as antique shops, boutiques selling lace and linen, and fine food stores. At a 12-century watchtower, the Corso widens to form the **Piazza IX Aprile** with its panoramic views and fancy terrace cafes, all carpeted inside. Farther along, near the Porta Messina, is the handsome **Palazzo Corvaja**, its 14th-century courtyard worth a glance and its rooms often filled with art exhibits. Outside the Porta and leading to the right, is Via Teatro Greco, which takes you to the most famous and breathtaking ★★ view in all of Taormina, that from the **Greco-Roman Theater** (open 9 a.m. to one hour before sunset; L2000). The theater was the second largest after that in Syracuse, built by the Greeks but later modified by the Romans. Walking back on Via Teatro Greco, the streets to the left lead to the lush, tropical

★**Public Gardens**, a large, wonderful park with its own fine views looking out toward Mt. Etna. You can drive (5 km, [3 mi.]) or climb to the delightful **Castel Mola**, sitting so high above Taormina. You can discover the Gothic Badia or the old Roman thermae at the **Naumachie**, just below the Corso. You can take in the modern resort of **Giardino Naxos** only a few kilometers away, and maybe even visit the tiny museum in that port, with its exhibits on Naxos, the first Greek settlement in Sicily. But none of this matters as much as the sense of well-being this relaxing resort provides.

Where to Stay

For its small size, Taormina has an enormous number of hotels and pensioni, and the AAST also lists furnished rooms and apartments. But late June through August, it can be difficult to find a room unless you've made advance reservations. Also remember that many establishments close from November to March. Unless otherwise stated, rooms are air-conditioned.

Please note: During the Taormina peak season (April/May and July to mid-September), many, but not all hotels charge for full (AP) or partial (MAP) meal plans. These hotels may cost only a moderate amount off-season for a room, but the price of the meals can easily upgrade them into a higher price category, especially when two or more people are involved. The prices considered here are simply peak season room prices. If meal plans are required, expect the price to jump up a category.

Very Expensive

San Domenico Palace   **L350–650,000 CP**   ❀★★★★★

Piazza San Domenico 5; ☎ 23-701, FAX 625-506.
Single L350,000 CP. Double L650,000 CP.

One of the great hotels of Italy, the San Domenico occupies the tranquil gardens and cloisters of a 15th-century monastery. Exquisite antiques, including old choir stalls and paintings, adorn the lobby and refectory, the lounge, and the corridors. The 117 rooms vary from monastic cells to large suites, all tastefully furnished, but sometimes a bit worn. The more modern units are in the newer wing. The atmosphere is somewhat formal, and the gardens are extensive and terraced on a hillside dominated by views of the sea and Mt. Etna. Here there are some restaurants and lounges as well as a heated pool. Garage.

Expensive

Grande Albergo Capotaormina   **L275–355,000 CP**   ★★★★★

In Mazzaro, 98050; ☎ 24-000; FAX 625-467.
Single L275,000 CP. Double L355,000 CP.

This ultra-modern hotel, designed by one of Italy's foremost architects (Minoletti) is dramatically situated above the sea 1 km above the village at Mazzaro. Its salt-water pool is built right into a cliff, and an elevator takes you down to a private beach. All 208 rooms have private terraces and sea views. Good restaurants, lounges, entertainment, shops. Garage. Closed Jan.-Mar.

Villa Sant'Andrea   **L220–300,000 CP**   ★★★★

Via Nazionale 173, Mazzaro, 98030; ☎ 23-125, FAX 24-838.
Single L220,000 CP. Double L300,000 CP.

On a shady cove and with a pebbly, but private beach with good swimming waters, this gracious, old mansion, now a hotel, offers a relaxing atmosphere and fine accommodations and service. The 48 rooms are comfortable. The restaurant is very good. Lounge. Pool. Garage.

Moderate

Excelsior   **L180–255,000 CP**   √★ ★ ★ ★ ★

Via Toselli; ☎ *23-975, FAX 23-978.*
Single L180,000 CP. Double L255,000 CP.
Occupying a promontory that juts out near the Porta Catania, the Excelsior has a five-star location. Extensive gardens cover its grounds, and the heated pool, at the tip of the promontory dominated by Mt. Etna, is exceptional. Although the facade is neo-Moorish, the interior is pure British Empire, with many comfortable sitting rooms furnished with wing-back chairs. This fine hotel has 89 rooms, some with extraordinary views. Restaurants. Lounges. Private beach club. Parking. The price varies with season, but can be surprisingly modest given its luxury.

Jolly Diodoro   **L220–255,000 CP**   √★ ★ ★ ★

Via Bagnoli Croce 75; ☎ *23-312, FAX 23-391.*
Single L220,000 CP. Double L255,000 CP.
The architecture of this Jolly is a bit bland, but the full window sweep in the dining area and many of the 102 rooms result in good views of the hills, sea, and Mt. Etna. The hotel location is excellent, next to the public gardens, and its rooms are all comfortably appointed. Restaurant, lounge. Good pool area with deck and views. Jacuzzi. Parking. Price category is for room with breakfast.

Villa Paradiso   **L150–250,000 CP**   ★ ★ ★

Via Roma 2; ☎ *23-922, FAX 625-800.*
Single L150,000 CP. Double L250,000 CP.
Next to the public garden, this small hotel offers some great views of Mt. Etna and the sea from its living-room style lobby, its top-floor restaurant, and its front junior suites with balconies. There are a total of 33 rooms. Transportation to beach club with pool and tennis in Letojanni. Closed Nov.–mid-Dec.

Inexpensive

Villa Belvedere   **L150–225,000 CP**   √★ ★

Via Bagnoli Croci 79; ☎ *23-791, FAX 625-830.*
Single L150,000 CP. Double L225,000 CP
Not far from the public gardens and with a number of its 41 rooms with balconies and views, this hotel is very comfortable. Breakfast bar. Good pool. Parking. Closed mid-Jan.–mid-Mar and mid Nov.–mid Dec. A good buy.

Villa Fiorita   **L150,000 CP**   √★ ★

Via Pirandello 39; ☎ *24-122, FAX 625-967.*
Single/double L150,000 CP.
Just a block away from the center, this small inn has 24 pleasant rooms, many with balconies. There is a garden, a pool, a sauna. A considerable bargain given the attractiveness and hospitable service.

Villa Nettuno   **L100,000 CP**   √★

Via Pirandello 33; ☎ *23-797, FAX 626-035.*
Single/double L100,000 CP.

This pensione sits a bit above the road and offers its charming ambience along with 12 rooms, all with bath and balconies, most with sea views. No a/c. Fine garden. In the budget range with breakfast.

Where to Eat

   Taormina's many gardens and panoramic views are shared by the restaurants. Even the plainest spot on the Corso may open up to a garden terrace.

The Beautiful

Les Bougainvilles   **$$$**   ★★

San Domenico Palace Hotel; ☎ *23-701, FAX 625-506.*
Reservation required. Meals about L95,000.

The panoramic views and beautiful dining terraces at the San Domenico Palace are well-known, and the indoor dining rooms, furnished with antiques, are equally lovely, but you might confine a visit to the afternoon tea as we've had sad reports about the uneven yet very pricey food. Perfect service, of course.

Oliviero   **$$–$$$**   ★★

Villa Sant'Andrea, V. Nazionale in Mazzaro; ☎ *23-125, FAX 24-838.*
Evenings only. Meals L60–70,000.

This hotel restaurant has a lovely seaside terrace and offers delicious seafood risotto and candlelight dining to the accompaniment of piano music.

La Giara   **$$–$$$**   ★★

Vico La Floresta 1; ☎ *23-360, FAX 23-233.*
Late dinner; closed Mon. except in season. Meals L55–80,000.

Just down from the Corso, La Giara is the new stunning place to be seen for dinner and dancing, especially in the summer when dining is on a candlelit terrace. The food includes the most popular of Sicilian dishes (smoked fish, involtini of swordfish) as well as international ones.

Pleasant and Good

Giova Rosy   **$$**   ★★★

Corso 38; ☎ *24-411.*
Closed Mon., except July–Sept., and Jan./Feb. Meals L50–65,000.

More modest in price than beautiful, the Giova nonetheless has its own attractive garden terrace and serves excellent seafood, including spaghetti del Presidente, with frutti di mare.

La Griglia   **$$**   ★★

Corso 54; closed Tues., mid-Nov.–mid-Dec.; ☎ *23-980, FAX 626-047.*
Meals L40–60,000.

Another good choice, La Griglia also has garden views, a fine antipasto table and well-prepared seafood.

Da Lorenzo   **$–$$**   ★★

V. Amari 4; ☎ *23-480.*
Closed Wed. (except June–Sept.) and early Nov. Meals L30–60,000.

A comfortable restaurant with just a small outdoor terrace, not a panoramic one, but the service is good and so is the food, especially the smoked swordfish appetizer and the fusilli with fresh artichokes.

The Convenient

La Ginestra $–$$ ★★

V. Crocifisso in Contrada Fontanelle; ☎ *625-751.*
Evenings only except Sun.; closed Wed. Meals about L45,000; pizza L9–15,000.
A 10-minute walk downhill from Taormina, this good trattoria serves tasty pasta and excellent pizza as well as daily fish specials and homemade ice cream.

Il Delfino $$ ★

V. Nazionale Mazzaro; ☎ *23-004.*
Closed off-season. Meals L40–55,000.
This beach club and restaurant offers dressing rooms and swimming as well as decent seafood.

Caffè

Numerous ice cream and pastry shops line the Corso, but you might want to seek out **Pasticceria Etnea** *(Corso 112)* for its fabulous concoctions, particularly the marzipan. **A.Chemi** *(Corso 102)* makes fabulous confections of orange peel and shaved and flavored ices called, *granita*. **Mocambo** *(Corso at Piazza IX Aprile)* is the place to people watch and sip a Campari. Piano music in evening.

Directory

Telephone Code 0942   **Postal Code 98039**

Airport

In Catania.

American Express

La Duca Viaggi, P. IX Aprile *(☎ 625-255).*

Bus

SAIS *(☎ 625-301)* V. Pirandello, outside walls.

Car Rentals

Avis, *V. San Pancrazio 6;* **Europcar**, *V. Pirandello 33A;* **Maggiore**, at train station; and others.

Funvia

Cable cars: V. Pirandello, outside Porta Messina in Taormina; near Mazzaro Sea Palace in Mazzaro.

Groceries

Along the Corso.

Newsstand

Corso 51.

Post Office

P. San Antonio near Porta Catania; open mornings.

Taxis
　　P. Duomo *(☎ 23-800)*; in Mazzaro *(☎ 21-266)*.

Telephones
　　Telcom, in Avis office (see above) outside Porta Messina.

Tennis
　　Circolo di Tennis, Public Garden *(☎ 23-282)*.

Tourism Office
　　AAST, Palazzo Corvaja on Corso, near Porta Messina *(☎ 23-243, FAX 24-941)*.

Tours
　　CIT, *Corso 101 (☎ 23-301)*; **SAT**, *Corso 73 (☎ 50-198)*, and others, to Mt. Etna, Agrigento, Piazza Armerina and other major Sicilian sights.

Train
　　Stazione Taormina/Giardini *(☎ 51-026)*, 10-minute taxi ride.

On the Road

North Coast

　　The Tyrrhenian coast is the most scenic in Sicily. With only a few industrial developments to mar the landscape, you can set out from Messina and follow the foothills of the great eastern mountain range before skimming along the rocky coast. Greeks and Romans have left their remains at Termini Imerese. The Normans built their great cathedral at Cefalu. Frederick II defended the coast with his castles, including his favorite at **Castroreale**, and the Spaniards set up watchtowers. Reminders of this past are everywhere perched safely on promontories and hills. At Tindari, there's a fine view of Etna, its snow-capped cone unmistakable half the year, and overlooking the sea is the sanctuary to the Madonna of **Tindari**, a pilgrimage site since the 16th century. Whether you're simply traveling from Messina to Palermo (235 km, 146 mi.), or whether you plan to stop at the Lipari Islands or Cefalu, the trip is a most pleasant one. The train and SS 113 run almost parallel to each other; the *autostrada* A-20 is sometimes tunneled, but is also scenic. (A-20 is unfinished for the 75 km (47 mi.) between Rocca di Caprileone and Cefalu.)

Messina

　　Dominating the narrow straits separating Sicily from the Italian mainland, Messina has forever been the gateway to Sicily. Even the ancient Greeks explained their peopling of the island through the legend of Hercules' swim across the straits. Today the ferries and hydrofoils constantly ply the waters where Ulysses struggled with Scylla and Charybdis, bringing tourists and residents alike from Calabria on the other side. Unfortunately, Messina has few historic sights, since most of the city and more than half of its population was destroyed in the earthquake of 1908. The straits themselves afford beautiful views of Sicily's east coast and the mountains of Calabria, and a ride across them to see the famous Greek ★★bronze warriors of Raice (5th century B.C.) in the **Museo Archeologico** in Reggio di Calabria *(Tues.-Sat. 9 a.m.–1:30 p.m., in summer also 3:30-7:30 p.m.; Sun. 9 a.m.–1 p.m.; L2000)* is time well spent.

In Messina there is the **Museo Regionale** *(V. della Liberta; open 9 a.m.– 1:30 p.m. Tues.-Sat., also Thur. & Sat. 4–6:30 p.m., Sun. till 12:30 p.m; L2000)*, housing the works of art salvaged from the earthquake. The collection includes a fine 13th-century *Portrait of Placido* and Bellini-influenced works by Vicenzo Catena. In addition, there are the better-known pieces— Antonello da Messina's very Flemish-style ★ *Polytych di San Gregorio*, as well as Caravaggio's ★ *Adoration of Shepherds*, and his powerful ★★ *Raising of Lazarus* (1609), bathed in mysterious light. *It's located 2 km north on the Villa S. Giovanni car-ferry terminal and reached by following the harbor or taking the #7 or 8 bus on Via Garibaldi.* A km south of the car-ferry terminal is the **Piazza del Duomo**, center of one of the older, more charming parts of the city. The *duomo* was first built by Roger II in the 12th century and included Norman embellishments of gold mosaics, reused granite columns from antiquity, and frescoes. Collapsed by the earthquake, it was rebuilt. Then destroyed by fire, it was again painstakingly recreated, though most of the mosaics and frescoes are gone forever. The *campanile* is remarkable at noon, when cannon shots begin a grand display in what was the largest mechanical clock early in this century. *Duomo closed noon-4 p.m.; #7 and 8 buses bring you near on Via Garibaldi.*

Where to Stay

Jolly   **L185–225,000 CP**   ★★★

V. Garibaldi 126; ☎ *363-860, FAX 590-2526.*
Single L185,000 CP. Double L225,000 CP.

A bit simpler than most in this chain, the Jolly's 100 rooms are smaller too, but its lobby overlooks the Straits and its location is convenient.

Where to Eat

Pippo Nunnari   **$$**   ★★★

V. Ugo Bassi 157; ☎ *293-8584.*
Closed Mon. and early July. Meals L50–70,000.

Messina is a great center for swordfish, and cultivates clams and mussels. The pride it takes in its seafood can be judged at this restaurant in the business section below Via Garibaldi. Despite their tuxedos, the expert waiters don't interfere with the cheerful and informal ambience of this superb restaurant. From the succulent insalata di mare to the pasta alle vongole, the involtini di spada wrapped around capers, tomatoes, and olives, and the light, crabcake-like *frittata di neonato* (newborn sardines), the food is superb.

Trattoria Da Mario   **$**   ★

    Lungomare V. Emanuele next to the Jolly Hotel.
    Closed Wednesday; pizza L7–12,000.
    Popular in the evenings for wood-oven pizza.

Directory

Telephone Code 090   **Postal code 98100**

Tourist Office

    ASST, *P. Cairoli 45, 5th floor (*☎ *293-5292, FAX 694-780)* and outside Stazione
    Centrale *(*☎ *674-236).*

Arriving

    Frequent crossings of the Straits from Villa di San Giovanni (15 minutes) and Reg-
    gio Calabria. Long-distance trains and buses from Rome arrive first in Messina
    before making connections to Palermo and Catania.

Isole Eolie

At Milazzo, just 32 km, 20 mi. to the A-20 exit from Messina, you catch
the ferries and hydrofoils to the Aeolian Islands, named by the ancient
Greeks for Aeolus, god of winds, and now also known as the **Lipari Islands**
(pronounced LEE-pah-ri). This group of seven volcanic islands is a favorite
summer resort area and was designated a natural park in 1989. Their geolo-
gy fascinates many, just as in the past it did the Greeks, for whom Homer
called these "the floating islands" because the number of their rock formations baffled sailors. **Vulcano** island has a number of craters, one somewhat
easily (if there's no sudden disaster) hiked in an hour, and **Stromboli** island is
a perfectly shaped cone, so quintessentially volcanic that it continuously (if
only mildly) erupts. The archaeology of this archipelago attracts others, for
since neolithic times the islands have been inhabited. Today, there are archaeological sites to visit, and a fine museum *(Mon.–Fri 9 a.m.–2 p.m. and,
in summer, 4–7 p.m.; free)* on the largest island of **Lipari**. Then there are the
picturesque villages and breathtaking landscapes of islands like **Panarea**, the
beaches of **Salina**, the scuba diving near the farthest islands of **Alicudi** and **Fi-
licudi**.

Where to Stay

    For a brief tour of the islands, use lovely Lipari as your base. Here there are numerous
hotels as well as a hostel in the island's castle.

    NOTE: If you plan a vacation on the islands, you should get a full listing of facilities
from ENIT in New York or London. The AAST in Lipari has listings of rooming houses
and apartment and house rentals. Reservations should be made well in advance for summer bookings. Many of the facilities close November through March and most of them
are quite simple, which is how most of the visitors here like them.

Carasco   **L160–260,000 CP**   ★★★★

    Porto delle Genti, Lipari; ☎ *981-1605, FAX 981-1828; closed Oct. to Apr.*

Single L160,000 CP. Double L260,000 CP.

Lipari's best hotel is on a cliff by the sea, 89 rooms, restaurant, bar, and pool.

Villa Meligunis   L210–270,000   ★★★

Via Marte, Lipari; ☎ *981-2426, FAX 988-0149; closed Oct.–Mar.*
Single L210,000. Double L270,000.

This inn is without beach and swimming pleasures, but instead offers the ambience
of a 17th-century villa and views from its rooftop terrace. 32 rooms and suites.

Oriente   L100–135,000   ★

Via Marconi 35, Lipari; ☎ *981-1493, FAX 988-0198; closed off-season.*
Single L100,000. Double L135,000.

A central hotel with 25 plain and clean rooms, no a/c, and a garden.

Sciara Residence   L130–270,000 CP   ★★

In Piscita, Stromboli; ☎ *986-005, FAX 986-284; closed Nov.–Apr.*
Single L130,000 CP. Double L270,000 CP.

If you're among the adventurous planning the nighttime climb to the Stromboli's
crater, then you'll need this tranquil spot set in a flower-filled park near the sea with
60 rooms and terraces and fortunately, since meals are required, a decent restaurant,
pool and tennis court.

La Piazza   L130–260,000   ★★

Panarea; ☎ *983-176, FAX 983-003; closed Oct.–Mar.*
Single L130,000. Double L260,000.

If you're vacation bound for the crystal-clear swimming coves and lusher setting of
tiny Panarea, the isolated La Piazza provides 30 romantic rooms, gardens and sea
views as well as a restaurant and pool on this island increasingly dotted with the
whitewashed villas of the Milanesi.

Where to Eat

For eating, the fish, including lobsters and oysters, are wonderful when freshly caught,
and they're well accompanied by the local Malvasia wine produced on Salina.

Filippino   S–SS   ★★★

P. Municipio; ☎ *981-1002, FAX 981-2878.*
Closed mid-Nov.–mid-Dec., Mon. off-season. Fixed-price meals L35–45,000. À la carte
L55–70,000.

In the port of Lipari, Filippino provides the finest cuisine on these islands. Try the
seafood antipasto or soup, the pasta—especially the ravioli, along with local wines
and cheeses.

La Nassa   S–SS   ★

V. Franza 36; ☎ *981-1319.*
Closed Thurs., Nov., Jan–Feb. Meals L30–60,000.

Just out of the town this simple trattoria ia a local favorite for seafood.

Da Vicenzino   S   ★

Near Porto di Levante.
Meals L30–50,000.

On Vulcano. Simple fare.

Da Zurro   **$$**   ★★
>*In Piscita;* ☎ *986-085.*
>*Closed Oct.–Apr. Meals L45–65,000.*
>In Stromboli, convenient to the ferry landing of the main port, Zurro's offers good
>food, from the housemade pasta to the eggplant and seafood dishes.

Trattoria Maria e Nunzio   **$$**   ★★
>*Near beach before Cala Junco;* ☎ *983-018.*
>*Closed off-season. Meals L45–65,000.*
>This scenic spot on Panarea can be reached by boat or 1/2-hour walk from the port.
>Plan your visit to include the nearby Milazze ruins (14th century B.C.).

Directory

Telephone code 090   **Postal code 98055**

Tourist Office
>**AAST**, Corso V. Emanuele 202 on Lipari *(*☎ *988-0095 FAX 981-1190).*

Arriving
>Year-round there are ferry and aliscafi connections to the islands from Milazzo, not
>far from Messina by train or highway; by bus from Catania airport (Jun.-Sept.). In
>the high season, there are sea connections from Palermo and Messina, too, but also
>from Naples. From Jun.-Sept., the Naples hydrofoil takes 4 hours to Stromboli, 6
>to Lipari *(Aliscafi SNAV, V. Caraccoiola 10, 80122 Naples;* ☎ *[081] 761-2349);*
>from Jun.-Sept., the Naples ferry travels overnight (sleeping cabins available) to
>Lipari in 12 hours *(Agenzia Carolo Genovese, V. de Pretis 78, 80133 in Naples;*
>☎ *[081] 551-2112).*

Getting Around
>Lipari and Vulcano are the easiest islands to reach for a short visit, each being under
>an hour from Milazzo. Filicudi and Alicudi are too far away for casual visits. • Lipari
>is your best base for a brief stay because of its tourism office, island bus service and
>car rentals, and hydrofoil service to the other islands. (*Aliscafi,* or hydrofoils, take
>about half the time of ferries but cost more. The ferries often stop at numerous
>ports on each island.)

Note
>Many of the islands, such as Panarea and Stromboli, don't permit autos.

Seasons
>Many facilities close November to Easter, and those that continue to function do so
>on a more limited schedule.

Cefalu

A towering outcrop of rock almost seems to push Cefalu, the small medieval town at its base, into the sea. Fishing boats fill the cove east of town; on
the west stretches the Lungomare and beach. Cefalu is a thriving beach town
in summer, but it is best known for its 12th-century ★★**duomo** *(closed noon-
3:30 p.m.),* one of the three great works of Norman architecture. The cathedral, begun by Roger II in 1131, is a powerful architectural accomplishment,

strongly vertical despite being Romanesque, imposing yet subtle, and well worth a walk around the right to the rear apses. The somber interior is most striking for its ★ **mosaics** (central apse) among the oldest in Sicily, but with magnificently well-preserved colors.

Leaving the duomo behind you, walk toward the sea on Via Mandralisca and look for the **museum** at number 13. Though it is tiny and eccentric, you can easily work your way through this collection of Greek vases and seashells to the Flemish-influenced painting of Antonello da Messina, ★ *Portrait of a Man* (1465). In the painting gallery, it's worth looking for *Sacra Familia* by Vicenza Catena, a follower of Bellini. *Open 9 a.m.–12:30, 3:30–6 p.m. (in summer, 4:30–7 p.m.), Sun. only till 12:30 p.m.; fee.*

Where to Stay and Eat

La Villa del Vescovo   **$–$$**   ★★★

> *Contrada Santa Lucia, off ss 113;* ☎ *921-803, FAX 921-803.*
> *Closed Mon. in off-season & lunch July–Aug. Meals L35–65,000.*
> With a panoramic view of Cefalu from its hillside location 3 km from town, this restaurant offers fine food, like taglierini in a shellfish sauce and seafood salad with lobster.

Osteria del Duomo   **$$**   ★

> *V. Seminario 5;* ☎ *21-838.*
> *Closed Mon. except summer, and Christmas season; L45–60,000.*
> A pleasant place to dine on pasta and seafood in the summer when the tables spill onto the main square.

Da Nino   **$$**   ★

> *Lungomare 11;* ☎ *22-582.*
> *Closed Tues. in off-season. Meals L45–65,000.*
> Just a few steps from town. Unpretentious but good trattoria with an abundant antipasto table, local seafood done Sicilian style, and pizza in the evening.

Riva del Sole Hotel   **L150,000**   ★★

> *Lungomare 25;* ☎ *21-230; FAX 21-984.*
> *Single/double L150,000.*
> Just outside town, this modern hotel is both convenient and comfortable for the sightseeing visitor with 28 (a/c) rooms with bath, restaurant and bar; garage. Reserve well in advance for summer.

Baia del Capitano   **L150–200,000**   ★★★

> *Contrada Mazzaforno, 4 km, 2.5 mi. west;* ☎ *20-003, FAX 20-163.*
> *Single L150,000. Double L200,000.*
> More resort-like hotels can be found several miles west of town (where there are also campgrounds). Look for this one, a good choice with its pool, private beach, tennis and restaurant in addition to 39 rooms, most with sea views.

Directory

Telephone code 0921 **Postal code 90015**

Tourist Information

 AAST, *Corso Ruggero 77 (☎ 2121-050, FAX 22-386).*

Arriving

 An easy half-day excursion from Palermo or a pleasant stop between Palermo and
Messina, Cefalu is 2 km off A-20 and 70 km (43 mi.) from Palermo. Buses, trains,
and, in summer, hydrofoils (to Palermo) connect Cefalu with other parts of Sicily.

FOOD GLOSSARY

Meals (Pasti)

cena	supper, dinner
colazione	breakfast. In some regions, it can mean lunch, and *la prima colazione* then indicates breakfast.
pranzo	lunch. In some regions, it may mean dinner, and *la colazione* indicates lunch.
spuntino	snack

Menu

antipasti	appetizers
contorni	salads and vegetables
coperto	fee for dinnerware and bread
dolci	desserts
menu degustazione	a special set-priced meal arranged by chef
menu prezzo fisso	a fixed-price meal, usually not as elegant as a menu degustazione
menu turistico	the most basic of the fixed-price meal options
minestre	soups, but in the South may mean antipasti
pietanze	main courses, entrees
primi piatti	first course options, usually pasta, risotti, or soup
secondi piatti	main course options

Cooking Methods

affumicato	smoked
ai ferri	grilled
al cartoccio	baked in paper
al forno	baked
alla griglia	grilled
a piacere	cooked as you wish
arrosto	roasted
a scelta	cooked according to your choice
bollito	boiled meats
cotto	cooked
crudo	raw, cured
cucina casalinga	homecooking
del giorno	daily special
della casa	house specialties
farsi	prepared at table
fritto	fried

Cooking Methods

in brodo	in broth
in umido	stewed
involtini	thin slices of fish or meat rolled and stuffed
lesso	boiled
ripieno	stuffed
sformato	molded, like a flan

Meat (Carne)

abbacchio	milk-fed lamb
agnello	lamb
arista	roasted pork
bistecca	steak
braciola	chop
capretto	kid
costoletta	cutlet
fegatini	chick livers
fegato	liver, usually calves
maiale	pork
manzo	beef
nodini	veal chops
ossobuco	veal shank
pancetta	unsmoked bacon
polpette	meatballs
prosciutto	ham
cotto	baked ham
crudo	cured ham
salsicce	sausages
salame	salami-style dried sausage
salumi	processed pork; cold cuts
vitello/a	veal

Poultry and Game
(Pollame e Cacciagione)

anatra	duck
cinghiale	wild boar
faraone	guinea hen
coniglio	rabbit
lepre	hare
oca	goose
palomba	wood pigeon
piccione	pigeon
pollo	chicken
petto di pollo	chicken breast
quaglia	quail
tacchino	turkey

Seafood (Frutti di Mare)

acciuga	anchovy
alici	anchovy
anguilla	eel
aragosta	spiny lobster
astice	Maine-type lobster
baccala	dried salt cod
bottarga	pressed tuna roe
branzino	seabass
brodetto	fish stew
calamari	squid
capesante	scallopes
capitoni	large eels
cernia	sea bass
coda di rospo	toadfish tail
cozze	mussels
gambero	shrimp
gamberoni	large shrimp
gamberini	small shrimp

Seafood (Frutti di Mare)

granchio	crab
lumache	snails
mazzancolle	large shrimp, scampi
merluzzo	cod
moscardini	tiny octopus
neonate	new born sardines
orata	bream
ostriche	oysters
pesce	fish
polpo	octopus
rombo	turbot
rospo	monkfish
salmone	salmon
sarago	bream, firm white fleshed fish
sardine	sardines
scampi	prawns
seppia	cuttlefish, squid
sogliola	sole
spada	swordfish
spigola	seabass
storione	sturgeon
tonno	tuna
triglia	red mullet
trota	trout
vongole	clams

Pasta

agnolotti	half-moon shaped ravioli
bucatini	hollow spaghetti
cannelloni	fresh pasta squares rolled around meat or cheese, covered in sauce, and baked
capellini	hair-thin noodles
crespelle	crepe-like pasta, usually fresh

Pasta

fettuccine	flat egg noodles
fusilli	corkscrew-shaped pasta
gnocchi	small dumplings of flour or potato meal
lasagne	sheets of pasta, most often layered with sauce and baked, but sometimes filled with ricotta or meats
linguine	thin spaghetti
orecchiette	ear-shaped pasta
panzerotti	like ravioli, usually fresh
pappardelle	broad and flat noodles
penne	short tubes, cut diagonally at ends
ravioli	stuffed pasta squares, best when fresh
rigatoni	grooved pasta tubes
tagliatelle	wide fettucine
taglierini	narrow fettucine
tortellini	small stuffed rings, best when fresh
trenette	similar to fettucine
vermicelli	very thin spaghetti
ziti	pasta tubes

Sauces (Salse)

agli'olio	garlic and oil
al burro	cooked with butter
all'agro	cold vegetables tossed with lemon
amatriciana	tomato, pancetta, and pecorino cheese sauce
arrabbiata	tomato sauce laced with pepper flakes
marinera	seafood and tomato sauce
pesto	basil, pine nuts, garlic, and cheese
puttanesca	tomatoes, olives, capers, and traces of anchovies
ragu	basic meat sauce
sugo	basic tomato sauce, sometimes the same as ragu

Sauces (Salse)

vongole	clam and garlic sauce
vongole veraci	sauce with clams in shells

Vegetables (Verdure)

barbabietole	beets
bietole	chard
all'agli'olio	sauteed in olive oil and garlic
carciofo	artichoke
ceci	chick peas
cipollo	onion
fagioli	beans
fagiolini	green beans
finocchio	fennel
funghi	mushrooms
insalata	lettuce, salad
melanzana	eggplant
ovoli	wild mushrooms, either orange or red
patate	potatoes
peperone	sweet peppers
piselli	peas
pomodoro	tomato
polenta	cornmeal
porcini	wild mushrooms
porro	leeks
puntarella	asparagus chicory
radicchio	bitter red lettuce
riso	rice
risotto	rice casserole
rucola	arugula
rughetta	arugula
scarola	escarole
sedano	celery
spinaci	spinach

FOOD GLOSSARY

Vegetables (Verdure)

tartufo	truffle
zucca	pumpkin
zucchini	squash

Fruit (Frutta)

ananas	pineapple
arancia	orange
banana	banana
ciliegie	cherries
fichi/fico	figs/fig
fragole	strawberries
frutta di bosca	wild berries
macedonia	fruit salad
mandarina	tangerine
mele	apples
melone	melon
pera	pear
pesche	peaches
pompelmo	grapefuit
uve	grapes

Spices/Condiments

aglio	garlic
aceto	vinegar
basilico	basil
burro	butter
capperi	capers
maggiorana	majoram
olio	oil
olive	olives
verde	green
neri	black
origano	oregano

Spices/Condiments

pepe	black pepper
peperoncino	dried, hot red pepper
prezzemolo	parsley
rosemarino	rosemary
sale	salt
salvia	sage
senape	mustard
zafferano	saffron
zenzero	ginger
zuccero	sugar

Cheese (Formaggio)

dolce	not aged or sharp, but mild
fresco	fresh
mozzarella	a mild, soft fresh cheese of cow or buffalo milk
padano	a grating cheese like parmesan
parmesana	a hard, sharp cheese considered the finest for grating, but when less *stagionato*, or aged, used for eating, too
pecorino	ewe's milk cheese that, depending on age, is eaten (*dolce* or a bit *piccante*) or grated (very *stagionato*) when it is better known in the U.S. as *romano* cheese
piccante	aged or sharp
ricotta	fresh cow or ewe's milk cheese, similar to cottage cheese
scamorza	a mozzarella-like cheese encased in a hard skin and often smoked
stagionato	aged or dried to varying degrees, from simply sharp to grating quality

FOOD GLOSSARY

Pizza

funghi	with mushrooms
margarita	the classic tomato, garlic, basil, and mozzarella
napolitano	with capers, tomatoes, and anchovies
peperoni	with roasted sweet peppers
quattro stagioni	each quadrant with a different topping —usually artichoke, mushroom, prosciutto, and the fourth, more variable
salsicce	with sausage. When salsicce calabrese or piccante, it is usually like our pepperoni

Drinks (Bevande)

acqua minerale	mineral water
gasata	carbonated
mezza bottiglia	half-liter bottle
bibita	soft drink
birra	beer
alla spina	draft
scura	dark
caffe	coffee
frulatta	milk and fruit shake
Hag	decaf
latte	milk
magro	skim
limonata	lemonade
granita	shaved, flavored, ice drinks
spremuta	fresh juice
succo di frutta	canned or bottled juice
te	tea
vino	wine
bianco	white
caraffa	carafe

Drinks (Bevande)

da tavola	table wine
DOC/DOCG	regulated grape content
frizzante	slightly sparkling
mezza bottiglia	half bottle
rosato	rose
rosso	red
spumante	sparkling

Desserts (Dolci)

biscotti	cookies
cannoli	pastry shells stuffed with custard or sweetened ricotta cheese
cassata	spumone-like ice cream or, particularly in Sicily, cake and cream combinations
crostata	fruit pie
gelato	ice cream
panna	whipped cream
profiterole	small whipped cream puff
semifreddo	frozen dessert of ice cream, custard, or cream
tiramisu	chocolate and coffee flavored pastry with whipped cream
torta	cake
zabaglione	warm dessert of marsala, egg yolk, and sugar that often is poured over other desserts
zuppa inglese	a trifle, or rum-soaked cake layered with cream

Ice Cream Flavors (Sapori di Gelato)
also, see "*Fruit*"

amarena	black cherry
castagna	chestnut
cioccolato	chocolate

FOOD GLOSSARY

Ice Cream Flavors (Sapori di Gelato)
also, see "Fruit"

cocco	coconut
cono	an ice cream cone
coppa, coppetta	a cup, small cup of ice cream
crema	cream and egg yolk
gianduia	hazelnut chocolate
lampone	raspberry
limone	lemon
malaga	rum raisin
mandorla	almond
menta	mint
mirtilli	blueberry
more	blackberries
nocciola	hazelnut
noce	walnut
stracciatella	chocolate chip
uva secca	raisin

Useful Phrases

a puntino	medium rare
al sangue	very rare
ben cotta	well-done
caldo	hot
congelato	frozen
freddo	cold
in scatola	canned
mangio subito	to eat immediately, like a slice of pizza, not wrapped for take-out
mezza porcione	half portion
portare via	take out, usually wrapped for eating later
una fetta	a slice
un assaggio	a taste or sample

HOTEL QUICK-REFERENCE TABLES

Prices given below can only be approximations as explained on pages 4 through 5. There is no regulation of hotel prices in Italy, so there are no official prices. *Prices are in Italian lira.* They should be expected to fluctuate due to seasonal variations and unpredictable inflation rates during the year-long life of this guidebook. Better rates often are available when corporate or promotional rates are requested.

Except as otherwise noted, rates are for a double room on the European Plan (EP), without meals, but including tax and, technically, service fees. **These rates reflect high-season prices**. However, in addition, you may pay more for breakfast—an item that can range in price from L5000 for a skimpy continental at a simple pensione to L30,000 per person for a buffet breakfast at a first-class hotel. Where CP (Continental Plan) is indicated, breakfast, usually a continental, for two is already included in the price; AP (American Plan) includes continental breakfast, lunch, and dinner; MAP (Modified American Plan) includes continental breakfast and either lunch or dinner.

LAND ROUTES INTO ITALY			
	Phone	**Rate (in lire)**	**Rating**
ITALIAN RIVIERA & GENOA			
Genoa (Telephone Code 010)			
Agnello d'Oro	*246-2084*	**115–150,000 CP**	★
Europa	*246-3537*	**150–200,000 CP**	★★
Jolly Plaza	*839-3641*	**290–365,000 CP**	★★★★
Savoia Majestic	*261-641*	**230–330,000 CP**	★★★

LAND ROUTES INTO ITALY

	Phone	Rate (in lire)	Rating
Portofino (Telephone Code 0185)			
Hotel Splendido	*269-551*	**560–915,000 MAP**	❀★★★★★
Hotel Eden	*269-091*	**180–260,000 CP**	★
Portovenere (Telephone Code 0187)			
Grand Hotel Portovenere	*792-610*	**165–225,000 CP**	★★★
Royal Sporting	*790-326*	**160–290,000 CP**	★★★
Cinque Terre Telephone Code (0187)			
Barbara (in Vernazza)	*812-201*	**45–70,000**	–
Ca' d'Andrean (in Manarola)	*920-040*	**75–95,000**	★
Colonnina (in Monterosso)	*817-439*	**105,000**	★
Marina Piccola (in Manarola)	*920-103*	**75–95,000**	–
Porto Roca (in Monterosso)	*817-502*	**210–295,000 CP**	❀★★
PIEDMONT & VAL D'AOSTA			
Aosta (Telephone Code 0165)			
Europe	*236-363*	**180–255,000**	★★
Turin	*44-593*	**85–120,000**	★
Turin (Telephone Code 011)			
Astoria	*562-0653*	**120–155,000 CP**	★
Jolly Principi di Piemonte	*562-9693*	**365–440,000 CP**	★★★★
Victoria	*561-1909*	**180–250,000 CP**	√★★★
Verduno (Telephone Code 0172)			
Real Castillo	*470-125*	**115–170,000 CP**	❀★★★
Barolo (Telephone Code 0173)			
Hotel Barolo	*56-354*	**110,000**	★★
Alba (Telephone Code 0173)			
Savona	*440-440*	**95–135,000**	★★
THE DOLOMITES			
Bolzano (Telephone Code 0471)			
Asterix	*273-301*	**120,000**	★★
Park Hotel Laurin	*311-000*	**250–315,000**	★★★★

LAND ROUTES INTO ITALY			
	Phone	**Rate (in lire)**	**Rating**
Trento (Telephone Code 0461)			
Accademia	*233-600*	**185–255,000 CP**	★★★
America	*983-010*	**115–160,000**	★★
Cortina d-Ampezzo (Telephone Code 0436)			
Da Beppe Sello	*32-36*	**125–200,000 CP**	★
Menardi	*24-00*	**229–400,000 MAP**	❀★★
Miramonti Majestic	*42-01*	**500–900,000 (w/two meals)**	❀★★★★★
Panda	*860-344*	**115–190,000**	★
THE FRUILI			
Cormons (Telephone Code 0481)			
Hotel Felcaro	*60-214*	**70–120,000**	★★
Udine (Telephone Code 0432)			
Astoria Hotel Italia	*505-091*	**190–255,000**	★★★
Quo Vadis	*21-091*	**60–90,000**	★
Trieste (Telephone Code 040)			
Al Teatro	*366-220*	**95–115,000**	★
Duchi d'Aosta	*73-51*	**250–330,000 CP**	★★★

MILAN AND LOMBARDY			
	Phone	**Rate (in lire)**	**Rating**
MILAN			
Milan (Telephone Code 02)			
Antica Locanda Solferino	*657-0129*	**165,000**	√★
Bonaparte	*85-60*	**370–445,000 CP**	★★★
Casa Suissera	*869-2246*	**200–246,000 CP**	★
Duomo	*88-33*	**370–550,000**	★★★★
Europeo	*331-4751*	**200–245,000 CP**	★★
Excelsior Gallia	*67-85*	**485,000**	★★★★★
Four Seasons Milano	*77-088*	**610–725,000**	★★★★★
Grand Hotel et de Milan	*723-141*	**550–700,000**	❀★★★★

MILAN AND LOMBARDY

	Phone	Rate (in lire)	Rating
Gran Duca di York	874-863	140–185,000	★
London	7202-0166	115–165,000	★
Manin	659-6511	250–315,000	★★★
Manzoni	7600-5700	160–210,000	√★★
Principe di Savoia	62-30	615–700,000 CP	★★★★★
Ritter	2900-6860	170–220,000 CP	★★
Spadari al Duomo	7200-2371	390–425,000 CP	✿★★★
Star	801-501	130–190,000	★

LAKE MAGGIORE

Stresa (Telephone Code 0323)			
Des Iles Borromees	30-431	345–580,000 CP	✿★★★★★
La Fontana	32-707	90–110,000	√★★
La Palma	933-906	230–260,000	★★★
Pallanza/Verbania (Telephone Code 0323)			
Majestic	504-305	170–285,000 CP	★★★

LAKE ORTA

Orta San Giulio (Telephone Code 0322)			
La Bussola	911-913	160–250,000	★★
Orta	90-253	95–145,000	★
San Rocco	911-977	225–350,000 CP	★★★★

LAKE COMO

Como (Telephone Code 031)			
Barchetta Excelsior	32-21	235–255,000	★★★
Metropole & Suisse	269-444	170–230,000	★★★
Tre Re	265-374	75–125,000	★
Cernobbio (Telephone Code 031)			
Miralago	510-125	115–160,000 CP	★★
Villa d'Este	34-81	570–750,000 CP	✿★★★★★
Bellagio (Telephone Code 031)			
Belvedere	950-410	135–215,000 CP	√★★★
Grand Hotel Villa Serbelloni	950-216	320–650,000 CP	✿★★★★

MILAN AND LOMBARDY			
	Phone	**Rate (in lire)**	**Rating**
Varenna (Telephone Code 0341)			
Du Lac	*830-102*	**140–230,000 CP**	★★
Menaggio (Telephone Code 0344)			
Grand Hotel Victoria	*32-003*	**190–265,000 CP**	★★★★
LAKE ISEO			
Iseo (Telephone Code 030)			
Ambra	*980-130*	**90–120,000**	★
Erbusco (Telephone Code 030)			
Gualtiero Marchesi L'Alberto	*776-0550*	**240–350,000 CP**	❀★★★★
LAKE GARDA			
Sirmione (Telephone Code 030)			
Eden	*916-481*	**100–155,000**	★★
Ideal	*990-4243*	**85–150,000**	★
Olivi	*990-5365*	**115–165,000**	★★★
Villa Cortine Palace	*990-5890*	**300–500,000**	❀★★★★
Gardone Riviera (Telephone Code 0365)			
Grand Hotel	*20-261*	**170–290,000**	★★★★
Montefiori	*290-235*	**80–125,000**	★★
Riva del Garda (Telephone Code 0464)			
Bellavista	*554-271*	**135–175,000**	★★
Hotel du Lac et du Parc	*551-500*	**160–390,000**	★★★★
LOMBARD HISTORIC TOWNS			
Bergamo (Telephone Code 035)			
Arli	*222-014*	**95–145,000**	★★
Excelsior San Marco	*366-111*	**210–290,000**	★★★
Il Gourmet	*437-3004*	**90-135,000**	★★
San Vigilio	*253-179*	**145,000**	★★
Brescia (Telephone Code 030)			
Hotel Vittoria	*280-061*	**290–395,000**	★★★★
Master	*399-037*	**125–185,000**	★★★

MILAN AND LOMBARDY

	Phone	Rate (in lire)	Rating
Mantua (Telephone Code 0376)			
Broletto	*326-784*	**95–140,000**	★
Mantegna	*328-019*	**95–145,000**	★★
San Lorenzo	*220-500*	**230–265,000 CP**	❀★★
Cremona (Telephone Code 0372)			
Albergo Duomo	*352-242*	**90–130,000**	★
Astoria	*461-616*	**75–110,000**	★
Continental	*434-141*	**100–160,000**	★★

VENICE & THE VENETO

	Phone	Rate (in lire)	Rating
VENICE			
Venice (Telephone Code 041)			
Agli Alboretti	*523-0058*	**135–200,000 CP**	√★
Bauer Grunwald	*523-1520*	**360–650,000 CP**	★★★★★
Cipriani	*520-7744*	**995–1,200,000 CP**	★★★★★
Da Cici	*523-5404*	**85–115,000**	√
Danieli	*522-6480*	**400–765,000**	❀★★★★★
Des Bains	*526-5921*	**420–500,000 CP**	❀★★★★
Do Pozzi	*520-7855*	**185–235,000 CP**	❀★★
Excelsior Lido	*526-0201*	**375–685,000**	★★★★★
Flora	*520-5844*	**195–250,000**	❀★★
Gabrielli Sandwirth	*523-1580*	**350–430,000 CP**	❀★★★
Gritti Palace	*794-611*	**570–900,000 CP**	★★★★★
La Calcina	*520-6466*	**110–165,000 CP**	★
La Fenice et des Artistes	*523-2333*	**195–310,000 CP**	★★★
Londra Palace	*520-0533*	**350–425,000 CP**	★★★★
Metropole	*520-5044*	**410–525,000 CP**	❀★★★
Pausania	*522-2083*	**190–275,000 CP**	❀★★
Pensione Accademia	*523-7846*	**150–235,000 CP**	❀★★

VENICE & THE VENETO

	Phone	Rate (in lire)	Rating
San Stefano	520-0166	170–230,000 CP	★★
Saturnia International	520-8377	385–520,000 CP	❀★★★★
Padua (Telephone Code 049)			
Albergo San Antonio di Padua	875-1393	80–100,000	★
Donatello	875-0634	135–210,000	★★
Leon Bianco	875-0814	125–155,000	★★
Majestic Toscanello	663-244	170–260,000 CP	❀★★★
Plaza	656-822	175–255,000 CP	★★★
Verona (Telephone Code 045)			
Accademia	596-222	220–370,000 CP	★★★
Antica Porta Leona	595-499	150–170,000	★★
Aurora	594-717	75–100,000	★
Bologna	800-6990	150–175,000	★★
Colombo d'Oro	595-300	195–300,000	★★★
Due Torri Baglioni	595-044	485–580,000 CP	❀★★★★
Giulietta e Romeo	800-3554	100–145,000	★★
Victoria	590-566	220–350,000 CP	★★★★

SMALL TOWNS OF VENETO

Vicenza (Telephone Code 0444)			
Campo Marzio	545-700	185–220,000	★★★
Cristina	323-751	120–145,000	★★
San Raffaele	323-663	95,000	√★
Bassano del Grappa (Telephone Code 0424)			
Belvedere	529-845	150–200,000 CP	★★★
Brennero	228-544	70–100,000	★★
Asolo (Telephone Code 0423)			
Duse	55-241	200–250,000 CP	★★
Villa Cipirani	952-166	325–450,000	❀★★★★
Treviso (Telephone Code 0422)			
Albergo Beccherie (Campeol)	540-871	85–100,000	★★
Continental	411-216	170–220,000	★★

BOLOGNA & EMILIA ROMAGNA

	Phone	Rate (in lire)	Rating
BOLOGNA			
Bologna (Telephone Code 051)			
Accademia	*232-318*	**65–90,000**	★
Al Cappello Rosso	*261-891*	**200–390,000 CP**	★★★
Corona d'Oro	*236-456*	**280–420,000 CP**	❀★★★
Dei Commercianti	*233-052*	**175–275,000 CP**	★★
Grand Hotel Baglioni	*225-445*	**310–620,000 CP**	❀★★★★
Palace	*237-442*	**100–150,000**	★★
Roma	*226-322*	**150–180,000**	√★★★
Royal Hotel Carlton	*249-361*	**240–395,000 CP**	★★★★
SMALL EMILIAN TOWNS			
Modena (Telephone Code 059)			
Canalgrande	*217-160*	**195–290,000**	★★★
Liberta	*222-365*	**95–135,000**	★★
Parma (Telephone Code 0521)			
Button	*208-039*	**95–130,000**	★★
Palace Maria Luigia	*281-032*	**240–300,000 CP**	★★★
Park Hotel Stendhal	*208-057*	**170–255,000**	★★★
Piacenza (Telephone Code 0523)			
Florida	*592-600*	**95–115,000**	★
Grande Albergo Roma	*323-201*	**100–160,000**	★★
Ferrara (Telephone Code 0532)			
Albergo S. Paolo	*762-040*	**70–90,000**	√★
Duchessa Isabella	*202-121*	**330–410,000 CP**	★★★
Ripagrande	*765-250*	**225–310,000 CP**	√★★★
THE CENTRAL ADRIATIC			
Ravenna (Telephone Code 0544)			
Bizanzio	*217-111*	**140–200,000 CP**	★★★
Centrale Byron	*212-225*	**95–130,000**	★★
Rimini (Telephone Code 0541)			
Grand Hotel	*56-000*	**285–450,000**	❀★★★★★

BOLOGNA & EMILIA ROMAGNA			
	Phone	**Rate (in lire)**	**Rating**
Lotus	*381-680*	**90–110,000**	★★

UMBRIA TO THE ADRIATIC			
	Phone	**Rate (in lire)**	**Rating**
Orvieto (Telephone Code 0763)			
Maitani	*42-011*	**120–190,000**	★★★
Villa Bellago	*(0744) 950-521*	**140–180,000 CP**	√★★★
Todi (Telephone Code 075)			
Bramante	*894-8382*	**185–210,000**	√★★★
Spoleto (Telephone Code 0743)			
Albornoz Palace	*221-221*	**135–160,000**	★★★
Aurora	*223-004*	**80–100,000**	√★★
Gattapone	*223-447*	**150–260,000**	❀★★
Assisi (Telephone Code 075)			
Dei Priori	*812-237*	**115–150,000**	★★
Giotto	*812-209*	**120–195,000**	★★★
St. Anthony's Guest House	*812-542*	**50–75,000 CP**	√★
Subasio	*812-206*	**150–200,000**	❀★★★
Umbra	*812-240*	**110–150,000**	√★★★
Perugia (Telephone Code 075)			
Hotel Brufani	*573-2541*	**390–425,000**	❀★★★★
La Rosetta	*572-0841*	**100–200,000**	★★★
Signa	*572-4180*	**75–100,000**	★
Torgiano (Telephone Code 075)			
Le Tre Vaselle	*988-0447*	**270–355,000 CP**	–
Gubbio (Telephone Code 075)			
Bosone	*922-0698*	**130–145,000**	★★
Urbino (Telephone Code 0722)			
Albergo Italia	*27-01*	**50–80,000**	√★
Bonconte	*24-63*	**125–180,000**	★★

FLORENCE & TUSCANY

	Phone	Rate (in lire)	Rating

FLORENCE

Florence (Telephone Code 055)

	Phone	Rate (in lire)	Rating
Albergo Firenze	214-203	75–95,000	√
Annalena	222-402	195–230,000 CP	❀★★
Berchielli	264-061	375–410,000 CP	★★★★
Bernini Palace	288-621	275–395,000	★★★★
Calzaiuoli	212-456	160–175,000	★★
Croce di Malta	218-351	285–355,000	★★★★
Excelsior	264-201	410–615,000	★★★★★
Grand Hotel	288-781	480–595,000	❀★★★★★
Grand Hotel Villa Cora	229-8451	430–650,000	❀★★★★
Helvetia e Bristol	287-814	370–575,000	❀★★★★
Hermitage	287-216	215–265,000 CP	❀★★
Le Due Fontane	280-086	140–245,000 CP	★★
Loggiato dei Serviti	289-592	180–260,000 CP	★★★
Lungarno	264-211	275–365,000	★★★★
Monna Lisa	247-9751	270–350,000 CP	❀★★★
Morandi alla Crocetta	234-4747	120–180,000	❀★★
Principe	284-848	270–355,000	❀★★★
Royal	483-287	155–240,000 CP	★★
La Scaletta	238-028	90–130,000 CP	★
Splendor	483-427	120–185,000 CP	❀★★
Villa Belvedere	222-501	255–290,000 CP	❀★★★
Villa San Girolamo	59-141	75–125,000 CP	★★
Villa San Michele	59-451	700–1,300,000 MAP	❀★★★★★
Siena (Telephone Code 0577)			
Alex	282-338	130,000 CP	★
Antica Torre	284-397	80–120,000	★★
Certosa di Maggiano	228-180	400–850,000	❀★★★★
Chiusarelli	280-562	85–120,000	★★

FLORENCE & TUSCANY

	Phone	Rate (in lire)	Rating
Duomo	*289-088*	**130–200,000 CP**	★★
Il Giardino	*285-290*	**95–150,000 CP**	√★★
Jolly Hotel Excelsior	*288-448*	**250–400,000 CP**	★★★
Palazzo Ravizza	*280-462*	**155–200,000 CP**	❀★★
Park	*44-803*	**350–440,000**	❀★★★★
Villa Scacciapensieri	*41-441*	**200–380,000 CP**	❀★★★
Pisa (Telephone Code 050)			
Europa Park	*500-732*	**130,000**	√★★
Grand Hotel Duomo	*561-894*	**195–265,000 CP**	★★★
Royal Victoria	*940-111*	**135,000 CP**	★
SMALL TUSCAN TOWNS			
Pistoia (Telephone Code 0573)			
Hotel Patria	*25-187*	**80–125,000**	√★★
Montecatini (Telephone Code 0572)			
Grand Hotel e Le Pace	*75-801*	**285–465,000**	❀★★★★
Lucca (Telephone Code 0583)			
Ilaria	*47-558*	**90,000**	★
La Luna	*493-634*	**125–145,000**	★★
Villa La Principessa	*370-037*	**275–350,000**	❀★★★★
San Gimignano (Telephone Code 0577)			
Bel Soggiorno	*940-375*	**90–135,000**	★★
La Cisterna	*940-328*	**85–140,000**	★★
Pescille	*940-186*	**100–130,000**	√❀★★
Relais Santa Chiara	*940-701*	**170–300,000 CP**	★★★
Volterra (Telephone Code 0588)			
San Lino	*85-250*	**140–170,000 CP**	★★
Pienza (Telephone Code 0578)			
Il Chiostro	*748-400*	**100–165,000 CP**	√★★
Montefollonico (Telephone Code 0577)			
La Chiusa	*669-668*	**240–300,000 CP**	★★★★

FLORENCE & TUSCANY

	Phone	Rate (in lire)	Rating
Arezzo (Telephone Code 0575)			
Continentale	*20-251*	**100–145,000**	★★
Cortona (Telephone Code 0575)			
Hotel San Michele	*604-348*	**110–145,000 CP**	★★
Il Falconiere	*612-679*	**160–250,000 CP**	√❀★★★
Sinalunga (Telephone Code 0577)			
Locanda dell'Amorosa	*679-497*	**260–380,000 CP**	❀★★★
Sansepolchro (Telephone Code 0575)			
La Balestra	*735-151*	**90–115,000**	★

ROME & LATIUM

	Phone	Rate (in lire)	Rating
ROME			
Rome (Telephone Code 06)			
Albergo del Sole	*6880-6873*	**85–165,000**	√
Borgognoni	*6994-1505*	**380–475,000 CP**	★★★★
Cisterna	*581-7212*	**130,000**	√★
Columbus	*686-5435*	**200–275,000 CP**	❀★★
Hotel de la Ville	*67-331*	**530–650,000 CP**	★★★★
D'Inghilterra	*69-981*	**330–560,000**	❀★★★★
Excelsior	*482-6205*	**420–650,000 CP**	★★★★★
Gregoriana	*679-4269*	**250–280,000 CP**	★★
Hassler	*678-2651*	**470–900,000**	★★★★★
Holiday Inn Crowne Plaza	*6994-1888*	**410–600,000**	★★★★
Internazionale	*6994-1823*	**200–290,000 CP**	√★★★
La Residenza	*488-0789*	**200–250,000 CP**	√★★
Locarno	*361-0841*	**210–275,000 CP**	❀★★
Lord Byron	*322-0404*	**420–560,000 CP**	❀★★★★
Madrid	*699-1511*	**190–260,000 CP**	★★
Margutta	*322-3674*	**140,000 CP**	√

ROME & LATIUM

	Phone	Rate (in lire)	Rating
Portoghesi	*686-4231*	**180–225,000 CP**	★★
Raphael	*682-831*	**420–475,000 CP**	✿★★★
Sant'Anselmo	*578-3214*	**100–200,000 CP**	★★
Santa Chiara	*687-2979*	**220–290,000 CP**	★★
Teatro di Pompeo	*6830-0170*	**200–260,000 CP**	√★★
Trevi	*678-9563*	**210–260,000 CP**	★★
VITERBO			
Viterbo (Telephone Code 081)			
Tuscia	*344-400*	**75–120,000**	★★

NAPLES & SOUTHERN ITALY

	Phone	Rate (in lire)	Rating
NAPLES			
Naples (Telephone Code 081)			
Majestic	*416-500*	**190–280,000 CP**	★★★
Paradiso	*761-4161*	**175–275,000 CP**	★★★
Rex	*764-9389*	**100–140,000**	★
Santa Lucia	*764-0666*	**270–395,000 CP**	★★★★
Vesuvio	*764-0044*	**290–420,000 CP**	★★★★
Sorrento (Telephone Code 081)			
Bellevue Syrene	*878-1024*	**195–255,000**	★★★
Grand Hotel Ambasciatori	*878-2025*	**260–310,000**	★★★★
Grand Hotel Excelsior Vittoria	*807-1044*	**320–520,000 CP**	✿★★★★
Imperial Tramonto	*878-2588*	**245–280,000**	★★★★
Lorely et Londres	*807-3187*	**100,000 CP**	★
Regina	*878-2722*	**80–110,000**	★★
Villa di Sorrento	*878-1068*	**85–150,000**	★★
NAPLES BAY			
Capri (Telephone Code 081)			
Florida	*837-0710*	**100–130,000**	★

NAPLES & SOUTHERN ITALY

	Phone	Rate (in lire)	Rating
Grand Hotel Quisisana	837-0788	350–650,000 CP	★★★★★
Punta Tragara	837-0844	315–500,000 CP	★★★★
Scalinatella	837-0633	440–650,000 CP	★★★★
Villa Brunella	837-0122	295,000	√★★
Villa Sarah	837-7817	140–240,000 CP	★★★
Ischia (Telephone Code 081)			
Grand Hotel Punta Molino	991-544	315–650,000 CP	★★★★
Regina Isabella e Royal Sporting	994-332	320–650,000 CP	★★★★★
San Michele	999-276	100–165,000	★★
San Montano	994-033	235–310,000 CP	★★★
AMALFI COAST			
Positano (Telephone Code 089)			
Casa Albertina	875-143	165–195,000 CP	★★
Le Sirenuse	875-066	490–650,000 CP	★★★★★
Palazzo Murat	875-177	275,000	❀★★
Pasitea	875-500	135–170,000 CP	★★
San Pietro	875-455	675,000 CP	❀★★★★★
Amalfi (Telephone Code 089)			
Luna Convento	871-002	195,000	❀★★★
Miramalfi	871-588	155–195,000 CP	√★★
Santa Catarina	871-0121	370–490,000 CP	★★★★
Ravello (Telephone Code 089)			
Palumbo	857-244	470–600,000 CP	❀★★★
Rufolo	857-133	165–250,000	★★
Paestum (Telephone Code 0828)			
Hotel Martini	811-020	150,000 CP	★★
SOUTHERN ADRIATIC TOWNS			
Barletta (Telephone Code 0883)			
Artu	332-121	115–170,000	★★
Bari (Telephone Code 080)			
Boston	521-6633	120–160,000	★★

NAPLES & SOUTHERN ITALY

	Phone	Rate (in lire)	Rating
Grand e D'Oriente Hotel	*524-4011*	**160–230,000**	★★★
Palace Hotel	*521-6551*	**200–265,000**	★★★★
Villa Romanazzi - Carducci	*522-7400*	**155–240,000 CP**	★★★
Alberobello (Telephone Code 080)			
Hotel Dei Trulli	*932-3555*	**240–265,000**	✿★★★
Polignano a Mare (Telephone Code 080)			
Grotta Palazzese	*740-677*	**115–155,000**	✿★★
Monopoli (Telephone Code 080)			
Il Melograno	*690-9030*	**300–500,000 CP**	✿★★★
Brindisi (Telephone Code 0831)			
L'Approdo	*529-667*	**100–150,000**	★
Majestic	*222-941*	**140–190,000 CP**	★★★
Lecce (Telephone Code 0832)			
Cote d'Est	*881-146*	**85–120,000**	★★
Presidente	*311-881*	**120–190,000**	★★★

SICILY

	Phone	Rate (in lire)	Rating
Palermo (Telephone Code 091)			
Albergo Liguria	*581-588*	**70–95,000**	√★
Europa	*625-6323*	**100–140,000**	√★★
Excelsior Palace	*625-6176*	**170–220,000 CP**	√★★★★
Jolly Hotel	*616-5090*	**180–240,000 CP**	★★★★
Mondello Palace	*684-0001*	**180–265,000 CP**	★★★★
Politeama Palace Hotel	*322-777*	**160–220,000 CP**	★★★
Splendid La Torre	*450-222*	**145,000**	√★★★
Villa Igiea	*543-744*	**240–360,000 CP**	✿★★★
Erice (Telephone Code 0923)			
Elimo	*869-377*	**100–150,000**	★★
Ermione	*869-138*	**115–165,000**	★★★

SICILY

	Phone	Rate (in lire)	Rating
Moderno	*869-300*	**100–140,000**	★★
Trapani (Telephone Code 0923)			
Astoria Park	*562-400*	**115–170,000**	★★★
Marsala (Telephone Code 0923)			
Hotel President	*999-333*	**85–150,000**	–
Selinunte (Telephone Code 0924)			
Hotel Garzia	*46-024*	**125,000**	★★
Agrigento (Telephone Code 0922)			
Concordia	*596-266*	**65–85,000**	★
Jolly dei Templi	*606-144*	**180–240,000 CP**	★★★★
Tre Torri	*606-733*	**130,000**	★★
Villa Athena	*596-288*	**150–220,000**	✿★★★
Enna (Telephone Code 0935)			
Hotel Sicilia	*500-850*	**80–150,000 CP**	√★★
Piazza Armerina (Telephone Code 0935)			
Da Battiato	*685-453*	**50–70,000**	★
Syracuse (Telephone Code 0931)			
Forte Agip	*463-232*	**160,000 CP**	★★
Grand Hotel	*464-600*	**200–275,000 CP**	★★★★
Grand Villa Politi	*412-121*	**140–245,000 CP**	✿★★★
Jolly	*461-111*	**200–230,000**	★★★
Ragusa (Telephone Code 0932)			
Montreal	*621-133*	**75–110,000**	★★
Catania (Telephone Code 095)			
Albergo Moderno	*325-309*	**125–140,000**	★
Grand Hotel Baia Verde	*491-522*	**280–310,000**	★★★
Jolly	*316-933*	**190–235,000 CP**	★★★
Taormina (Telephone Code 0942)			
Excelsior	*23-975*	**180–255,000 CP**	√★★★★★
Grande Albergo Capotaormina	*24-000*	**275–355,000 CP**	★★★★★
Jolly Diodoro	*23-312*	**220–255,000 CP**	√★★★★

SICILY			
	Phone	**Rate (in lire)**	**Rating**
San Domenico Palace	23-701	350–650,000 CP	★★★★★
Villa Belvedere	23-791	150–225,000 CP	√★★
Villa Fiorita	24-122	150,000 CP	√★★
Villa Nettuno	23-797	100,000 CP	√★
Villa Paradiso	23-922	150–250,000 CP	★★★
Villa Sant'Andrea	23-125	220–300,000 CP	★★★★
Messina (Telephone Code 090)			
Jolly	363-860	185–225,000 CP	★★★
Lipari Islands (Telephone Code 090)			
Carasco	981-1605	160–260,000 CP	★★★★
Oriente	981-1493	100–135,000 CP	★
La Piazza	983-176	130–260,000	★★
Sciara Residence	986-005	130–270,000 CP	★★
Villa Meligunis	981-2426	210–270,000	★★★
Cefalu (Telephone Code 0921)			
Baia del Capitano	20-003	150–200,000	★★★
Riva del Sole Hotel	21-230	150,000	★★

HOTEL INDEX

RESTAURANT INDEX

INDEX

D

H

I

J

L

Order Your Guide to Travel and Adventure

Title	Price	Title	Price
Fielding's Alaska Cruises and the Inside Passage	$18.95	Fielding's Las Vegas Agenda	$14.95
Fielding's The Amazon	$16.95	Fielding's London Agenda	$14.95
Fielding's Asia's Top Dive Sites	$19.95	Fielding's Los Angeles	$16.95
Fielding's Australia	$16.95	Fielding's Malaysia & Singapore	$16.95
Fielding's Bahamas	$16.95	Fielding's Mexico	$18.95
Fielding's Baja	$18.95	Fielding's New Orleans Agenda	$16.95
Fielding's Bermuda	$16.95	Fielding's New York Agenda	$16.95
Fielding's Borneo	$18.95	Fielding's New Zealand	$16.95
Fielding's Budget Europe	$17.95	Fielding's Paris Agenda	$14.95
Fielding's Caribbean	$18.95	Fielding's Portugal	$16.95
Fielding's Caribbean Cruises	$18.95	Fielding's Paradors, Pousadas and Charming Villages	$18.95
Fielding's Disney World and Orlando	$18.95	Fielding's Rome Agenda	$14.95
Fielding's Diving Indonesia	$19.95	Fielding's San Diego Agenda	$14.95
Fielding's Eastern Caribbean	$17.95	Fielding's Southeast Asia	$18.95
Fielding's England	$17.95	Fielding's Southern Vietnam on 2 Wheels	$15.95
Fielding's Europe	$18.95	Fielding's Spain	$18.95
Fielding's European Cruises	$18.95	Fielding's Surfing Indonesia	$19.95
Fielding's Far East	$18.95	Fielding's Sydney Agenda	$16.95
Fielding's France	$18.95	Fielding's Thailand, Cambodia, Laos and Myanmar	$18.95
Fielding's Freewheelin' USA	$18.95	Fielding's Vietnam	$17.95
Fielding's Hawaii	$18.95	Fielding's Western Caribbean	$18.95
Fielding's Italy	$18.95	Fielding's The World's Most Dangerous Places	$19.95
Fielding's Kenya	$16.95	Fielding's Worldwide Cruises '97	$19.95

To place an order: call toll-free 1-800-FW-2-GUIDE
(VISA, MasterCard and American Express accepted)
or send your check or money order to:
Fielding Worldwide, Inc., 308 S. Catalina Avenue, Redondo Beach, CA 90277
http://www.fieldingtravel.com
Add $2.00 per book for shipping & handling (sorry, no COD's), allow 2–6 weeks for delivery

Fielding's
Budget Europe

The penny pincher's guide to great times, great buys and discoveries in 18 countries!

In this all-new Fielding tight-budget guide to Europe, readers learn how to get maximum mileage for their dollar. The most exciting cities in 18 countries are covered, with more than 2600 tough, but fair reviews of hotels, restaurants and attractions.

With 46 maps, tour guides and b/w photos.

$17.95

Fielding's
Europe

The 49-year-young classic, totally updated every year.

This is the classic guidebook to the best of Europe, featuring secret spots, fabulous resorts and romantic hideaways. It is written in an entertaining style by experienced travelers with intimate knowledge of each of the 16 countries covered. With an emphasis on the little known or unexpected, it is intended for both the first-timer or the savvy traveler back for more!

With hotel quick-reference charts, 111 detailed maps, plus 3-D tour guides.

$18.95

Fielding's
European Cruises

The indispensable guide to Europe's most popular cruises.

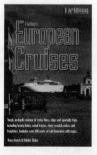

As many as 80 ships and 74 ports of call are covered, enabling readers to make the best choices in touring Europe this elegant and hassle-free way! This highly informative handbook is written in an engaging style by Shirley Slater and Harry Basch, the husband-and-wife travel-writing team, called "America's premier cruise specialists" by the *Chicago Sun Times.*

Loads of charts and tables and helpful hints, plus 74 maps and 50 b/w photos.

$18.95

Fielding's
Rome Agenda

The sophisticated insider's guide to the glories of the Eternal City!

Authors Lynn and Lawrence Foster have traveled extensively in Italy and lived in Rome. In this highly authoritative and readable handbook, they share their vast knowledge of Roman history and art and deliver a wealth of insider information. Page after page, readers are treated to collections of art, monumental historic sites, as well as not-to-be-missed excursions, and an array of marvelous regional cuisines.

With b/w photos, maps and 3-D tour guides.

$14.95